The Canterbury and York Society

GENERAL EDITOR: DR P. HOSKIN

ISSN 0262-995X

CANTERBURY AND YORK SOCIETY VOL. CIII

Supplications
from England and Wales
in the Registers of the
Apostolic Penitentiary
1410–1503

VOLUME I: 1410–1464

EDITED BY

PETER D. CLARKE & PATRICK N. R. ZUTSHI

The Canterbury and York Society

The Boydell Press
2012

© CANTERBURY AND YORK SOCIETY 2013

All Rights Reserved. Except as permitted under current legislation
no part of this work may be photocopied, stored in a retrieval system,
published, performed in public, adapted, broadcast,
transmitted, recorded or reproduced in any form or by any means,
without the prior permission of the copyright owner

First published 2013

A Canterbury and York Society publication
published by The Boydell Press
an imprint of Boydell & Brewer Ltd
PO Box 9, Woodbridge, Suffolk IP12 3DF, UK
and of Boydell & Brewer Inc.
668 Mt Hope Avenue, Rochester, NY 14620-2731, USA

website: www.boydellandbrewer.com

ISBN 978-0-907239-75-8

A CIP catalogue record for this book is available
from the British Library

Details of previous volumes are available from Boydell & Brewer Ltd

The publisher has no responsibility for the continued existence
or accuracy of URLs for external or third-party internet websites
referred to in this book, and does not guarantee that any content
on such websites is, or will remain, accurate or appropriate

Papers used by Boydell & Brewer Ltd are natural, recyclable products
made from wood grown in sustainable forests

Typeset in Monotype Baskerville by Word and Page, Chester, UK

Printed and bound in Great Britain by
CPI Group (UK) Ltd, Croydon, CR0 4YY

CONTENTS

Preface	vii
Abbreviations	viii
Introduction	xiii
The history and organisation of the papal penitentiary	xiii
The treatment of supplications in the papal penitentiary	xv
The sources for the papal penitentiary	xx
The subject-matter of the supplications	xxvi
The historical value of the supplications	xlvi
Editorial method	lix
Symbols	lxi
Alexander V (1409–10)	1
Super defectu natalium in forma ampliori	3
De sancto sepulcro et sancto Iacobo et commutatione votorum	5
John XXIII (1410–15)	7
De officio procuratoris	9
Super defectu natalium in ampliori forma	9
De matrimonialibus	14
De sancto sepulcro et sancto Iacobo et commutatione votorum	20
In diversis formis	23
Eugenius IV (1431–47)	37
De diversis formis	39
De matrimonialibus	46
De declaratoriis	47
De perpetuis confessionalibus, etc.	50
De diversis formis	73
Super diversis formis	81
Super homicidiis et iniectionibus	86
De diversis formis	88
Nicholas V (1447–55)	133
De diversis formis	135
De defectu natalium et de uberiori	166

Calixtus III (1455–58)   179
    De diversis formis   181
    De confessionalibus in forma 'Cupientes'   188
    De confessionalibus perpetuis   188
    De defectu natalium   192
    De matrimonialibus   198
    De defectu etatis   203
    De promotis et promovendis   205
    Super defectu etatis et de promotis et promovendis   206
    De promotis et promovendis   207
    De uberioribus   210

Pius II (1458–64)   213
    De matrimonialibus   215
    De diversis formis   219
    De declaratoriis   229
    De defectu natalium   230
    De uberiori   237
    De promotis et promovendis   238
    De confessionalibus perpetuis   240
    De sententiis generalibus   243
    De confessionalibus in forma 'Cupientes'   243

PREFACE

This edition has been almost ten years in the making. During that time we have accumulated many debts of gratitude that we wish to acknowledge here. Firstly we thank the Leverhulme Trust for generously funding our project in its initial stages in 2002–5. This supported Peter Clarke's employment as a full-time researcher for three years and financed his and Patrick Zutshi's essential travel to Rome in order to complete the basic research for the edition. It also paid for Dr Kirsi Salonen's work in checking for relevant entries that we had missed in our trawl through the penitentiary registers to 1503. We are grateful to her for this crucial help and for freely sharing with us her expertise on archival sources concerning the penitentiary. The British Academy provided additional funding to employ Dr Kelcey Wilson-Lee to compile the index of personal and place-names and the chronological index to the edition, and we are grateful to the Academy for this generous support and to Dr Wilson-Lee for her meticulous and substantial work. We also thank the Council of the Canterbury and York Society for agreeing to publish our edition, and in particular the Society's General Editor Dr Philippa Hoskin for her guidance and seeing our edition through the press. We received helpful advice from Professor Jeffrey Denton, then chairman of the Society's Council, on identifying place-names with the aid of his *Taxatio* database, but he sadly died in 2009 before our edition appeared. We are also grateful to Dr Oliver Padel for his invaluable advice on Welsh personal names. Furthermore we are grateful to S. E. Mons. Sergio Pagano, the Prefect of the Archivio Segreto Vaticano, and his staff for assisting our research on the penitentiary registers in their care. We thank the Penitenzieria Apostolica, in particular S. E. Mons. Luigi de Magistris, the former regent of that tribunal, for permission to consult the registers and have copies made from selected pages therein, and S. E. Mons. Gianfranco Girotti, the current regent, for permission to publish our edition. Finally, we wish to thank Ludwig Schmugge, the doyen of historians of the penitentiary, for his generous encouragement, advice and assistance. As a small return, we dedicate these volumes to him.

Peter D. Clarke, University of Southampton
Patrick N. R. Zutshi, University of Cambridge

ABBREVIATIONS

General

BCL	Bachelor of Civil Law
BCnL	Bachelor of Canon Law
BCn & CL	Bachelor of Canon and Civil Law
Berks.	Berkshire
BTh	Bachelor of Theology
Bucks.	Buckinghamshire
BVM	Blessed Virgin Mary
Cambs.	Cambridgeshire
Cornw.	Cornwall
dau.	daughter
DCL	Doctor of Civil Law
DCnL	Doctor of Canon Law
DCn & CL	Doctor of Canon and Civil Law
Derbys.	Derbyshire
dioc.	diocese
DTh	Doctor of Theology
fol./fols.	folio/folios
Fr	Frater, Brother
Glamorgs.	Glamorganshire
Glos.	Gloucestershire
Herts.	Hertfordshire
Hunts.	Huntingdonshire
Leics.	Leicestershire
LicCL	Licenciate in Civil Law
LicCnL	Licenciate in Canon Law
Lancs.	Lancashire
Lincs.	Lincolnshire
Montgom.	Montgomeryshire
MTh	Master of Theology
Norf.	Norfolk
Northants.	Northamptonshire
Notts.	Nottinghamshire
OCarm	Order of Carmelite Friars
OESA	Order of Austin Friars
OFM	Order of Friars Minor (Franciscans)
OP	Order of Preachers (Dominicans)

OSA	Order of St Augustine
OSB	Order of St Benedict
Oxon.	Oxfordshire
Reg.	Archivio Segreto Vaticano, Penitenzieria Apostolica, Reg. Matrim. et Div.
Staffs.	Staffordshire
STP	Sacrae Theologiae Professor
Suff.	Suffolk
Warwicks.	Warwickshire
Wilts.	Wiltshire
Worcs.	Worcestershire
Yorks.	Yorkshire

BIBLIOGRAPHICAL

BRUC	A. B. Emden, *A Biographical Register of the University of Cambridge to 1500* (Cambridge, 1963).
BRUO	A. B. Emden, *A Biographical Register of the University of Oxford to A.D. 1500*, 3 vols. (Oxford, 1957–9).
Clarke, 'Central authority and local powers'	P. D. Clarke, 'Central authority and local powers: the apostolic penitentiary and the English church in the fifteenth century', *Historical Research*, 84 (2011), 416–42.
Clarke, 'New evidence'	P. D. Clarke, 'New evidence of noble and gentry piety in fifteenth-century England and Wales', *Journal of Medieval History*, 34 (2008), 23–35.
Clementinae	*Clementinae*, printed in *Corpus iuris canonici*, ed. E. Friedberg (Leipzig, 1879), ii. 1128–1200.
Complete Peerage	*The Complete Peerage*, ed. G. E. Cockayne *et al.*, 12 vols. (London, 1910–59).
CPL	*Calendar of Entries in the Papal Registers Relating to Great Britain and Ireland: Papal Letters*, ed. W. H. Bliss *et al.*, 20 vols. to date (London, 1893–1960, Dublin 1978–).
CPR	*Calendar of the Patent Rolls Preserved in the Public Record Office* (London, 1891–1986).
Dugdale	W. Dugdale *et al.*, *Monasticon Anglicanum: A History of the Abbies and other Monasteries, Hospitals, Frieries, and Cathedral and Collegiate Churches, with their Dependencies, in England and Wales*, 6 vols in 8 (London, 1817–30).
Eubel	K. Eubel, *Hierarchia catholica medii et recentioris aevi*, 6 vols (Münster, 1913–67).
Göller	E. Göller, *Die päpstliche Pönitentiarie von ihrem Ursprung bis zu ihrer Umgestaltung unter Pius V*, 2 vols in 4 pts, Bibliothek des Königlich-Preussischen Historischen Instituts in Rom, 3, 4, 7, 8 (Rome, 1907–11).

Greatrex	J. Greatrex, *Biographical Register of the English Cathedral Priories of the Province of Canterbury, c. 1066–1540* (Oxford, 1997).
Harvey, *Obedientiaries*	B. Harvey, *The Obedientiaries of Westminster Abbey and their Financial Records, c. 1275–1540* (Woodbridge, 2002).
Kempe Visitations	'Documents relating to Diocesan and Provincial visitations from the registers of . . . John Kempe' [archbishop of York, 1426–52], ed. A. Hamilton Thompson in *Miscellanea*, ii, Surtees Society, 127 (1916), 201–90.
Knowles and Hadcock	D. Knowles and R. N. Hadcock, *Medieval Religious Houses in England and Wales* (2nd edn, London, 1971).
Le Neve, *Fasti 1300–1541*, xi: *Welsh Dioceses*	John Le Neve, *Fasti Ecclesiae Anglicanae 1300–1541*, xi: *The Welsh Dioceses*, comp. B. Jones (London, 1965).
Le Neve, *Fasti 1300–1541*, i: *Lincoln*	John Le Neve, *Fasti Ecclesiae Anglicanae 1300–1541*, i: *Lincoln Diocese*, comp. H. P. F. King (London, 1962).
Liber extra	*Liber extra* (or *Decretales Gregorii IX*) printed in *Corpus iuris canonici*, ed. E. Friedberg (Leipzig, 1879), ii. 2–928.
Liber sextus	*Liber sextus*, printed in *Corpus iuris canonici*, ed. E. Friedberg (Leipzig, 1879), ii. 933–1124.
Logan	F. D. Logan, *Runaway Religious in Medieval England c. 1240–1540* (Cambridge, 1996).
Lunt	W. E. Lunt, *Financial Relations of the Papacy with England*, i: *to 1327*; ii: *1327–1534* (Cambridge, MA, 1939–62).
ODNB	*Oxford Dictionary of National Biography*, ed. H. G. C. Matthew and B. Harrison, 60 vols (Oxford, 2004).
Penitenzieria Apostolica, ed. Ostinelli	*Penitenzieria Apostolica: le suppliche alla Sacra Penitenzieria Apostolica provenienti dalla diocesi di Como (1438–1484)*, ed. P. Ostinelli, Materiali di storia ecclesiastica lombarda (secoli XIV–XVI), 5 (2003).
Reg. Bekynton	*The Register of Thomas Bekynton, Bishop of Bath and Wells, 1443–1465*, ed. H. C. Maxwell-Lyte and M. C. B. Mawes, 2 vols, Somerset Record Society, 49–50 (1934–5).
Reg. Boulers	*Registrum Reginaldi Boulers, episcopi Herefordensis, A.D. MCCCCL–MCCCCLIII*, ed. A. T. Bannister, Canterbury and York Society, 25 (1919).
Reg. Bourgchier	*Registrum Thome Bourgchier, Cantuariensis archiepiscopi, A.D. 1454–1486*, ed. F. R. H. Du Boulay, Canterbury and York Society, 54 (1957).
Reg. Bubwith	*The Register of Nicholas Bubwith, Bishop of Bath and Wells, 1407–1424*, ed. T. S. Holmes, 2 vols, Somerset Record Society, 29–30 (1914).

Reg. Chichele	*The Register of Henry Chichele, Archbishop of Canterbury, 1414–1443*, ed. E. F. Jacob (vol. ii with H. C. Johnson), 4 vols, Canterbury and York Society, 42, 45–7 (1938–47).
Reg. Hallum	*The Register of Robert Hallum, Bishop of Salisbury, 1407–17*, ed. J. M. Horn, Canterbury and York Society, 72 (1982).
Reg. Lacy, ed. Hingeston-Randolph	*The Register of Edmund Lacy, Bishop of Exeter (A.D. 1420–1455)*, i: *The Register of Institutions, with some Account of the Episcopate of John Catrik (A.D. 1419)*, ed. F. C. Hingeston-Randolph (London and Exeter, 1909).
Reg. Lacy, ed. Dunstan	*The Register of Edmund Lacy, Bishop of Exeter (A.D. 1420–1455): Registrum Commune*, ed. G. R. Dunstan, 5 vols., Canterbury and York Society, 60–3, 66 (1963–72).
Reg. Mascall	*Registrum Roberti Mascall, episcopi Herefordensis, A.D. MCCCCIV–MCCCCXVI*, ed. J. H. Parry, Canterbury and York Society, 21 (1917).
Reg. Rede	*The Episcopal Register of Robert Rede, Ordinis Predicatorum, Lord Bishop of Chichester, 1397–1415*, ed. C. Deedes, 2 vols., Sussex Record Society, 8, 10 (1908–10).
Reg. Roffense	*Registrum Roffense*, ed. J. Thorpe (London, 1769).
Reg. St David's	*The Episcopal Registers of the Diocese of St David's, 1397 to 1518*, ed. R. F. Isaacson, 3 vols, Cymmrodorion Record Series, 6 (1917–20).
Reg. Spofford	*Registrum Thome Spofford, episcopi Herefordensis, A.D. MCCCCXXII–MCCCCXLVIII*, ed. A. T. Bannister, Canterbury and York Society, 23 (1919).
Reg. Stafford (Exeter)	*The Register of Edmund Stafford* [bishop of Exeter] *(A.D. 1395–1419): An Index and Abstract of its Contents*, ed. F. C. Hingeston-Randolph (London and Exeter, 1886).
Reg. Stafford (Bath and Wells)	*The Register of John Stafford, Bishop of Bath and Wells, 1425–1443*, ed. T. S. Holmes, 2 vols, Somerset Record Society, 31–2 (1915–16).
Reg. Stanbury	*Registrum Iohannis Stanbury, episcopi Herefordensis, A.D. MCCCCLIII–MCCCCLXXIV*, ed. J. H. Parry and A. T. Bannister, Canterbury and York Society, 25 (1919).
RPG	*Repertorium Poenitentiariae Germanicum: Verzeichnis der in den Supplikenregistern der Pönitentiarie vorkommenden Personen, Kirchen und Orte des Deutschen Reiches*, 8 vols to date: *RPG*, i: *Eugen IV., 1431–47*, ed. L. Schmugge, P. Ostinelli and H. Braun (Tübingen, 1998); *RPG*, ii: *Nikolaus V., 1447–55*, ed. L. Schmugge, K. Bukowska,

	and A. Mosciatti (Tübingen, 1999); *RPG*, iii: *Calixt III., 1455–58*, ed. L. Schmugge and W. Müller (Tübingen, 2001); *RPG*, iv: *Pius II., 1458–64*, ed. L. Schmugge, P. Hersperger and B. Wiggenhauser (Tübingen, 1996); *RPG*, v: *Paul II., 1464–71*, ed. L. Schmugge, P. Clarke, A. Mosciatti, and W. Müller (Tübingen, 2002); *RPG*, vi: *Sixtus IV., 1471–84*, ed. L. Schmugge, M. Marsch, and A. Mosciatti (Tübingen, 2005); *RPG*, vii: *Innozenz' VIII., 1484–92*, ed. L. Schmugge, A. Mosciatti and W. Müller (Tübingen, 2008); *RPG*, viii: *Alexander VI., 1492–1503* (Berlin, 2012).
Salonen, *Penitentiary*	K. Salonen, *The Penitentiary as a Well of Grace in the Late Middle Ages: The Example of the Province of Uppsala 1448–1527*, Annales Academiae Scientiarum Fennicae, 313 (2001).
Schmugge *et al.*, *Supplikenregister*	L. Schmugge, P. Hersperger and B. Wiggenhauser, *Die Supplikenregister der päpstlichen Pönitentiarie aus der Zeit Pius' II. (1458–1464)*, Bibliothek des Deutschen Historischen Instituts in Rom, 84 (Tübingen, 1996).
Smith, *Heads of Religious Houses*, iii	D. M. Smith, *The Heads of Religious Houses: England and Wales*, vol. iii: *1377–1540* (Cambridge, 2008).
Thompson, *Visitations*	*Visitations of Religious Houses in the Diocese of Lincoln: Injunctions and other Documents from the Registers of Richard Flemyng and William Gray, Bishops of Lincoln, A.D. MCCCCXX–MCCCCXXXVI*, ed. A. Hamilton Thomson, 3 vols, Lincoln Record Society, 7, 14, 21 (1914–29); Canterbury and York Society, 17, 24, 33 (1915–27).
VCH (Cambs.)	*Victoria County History: Cambridgeshire*, ed. L. F. Salzman *et al.*, 10 vols (London, 1938–2002).
VCH (Essex)	*Victoria County History: Essex*, ed. H. A. Doubleday *et al.*, 10 vols to date (London, 1903–).
VCH (Lancs.)	*Victoria County History: Lancashire*, ed. W. Farrer and J. Brownbill, 8 vols (London 1906–14).
VCH (Kent)	*Victoria County History: Kent*, ed. W. Page, 3 vols. (London, 1908–32).
VCH (Middlesex)	*Victoria County History: Middlesex*, ed. W. Page *et al.*, 13 vols to date (London, 1911–).
VCH (Oxon.)	*Victoria County History: Oxfordshire*, ed. W. Page *et al.*, 15 vols to date (London, 1907–).
VCH (Yorks.)	*Victoria County History: Yorkshire*, ed. W. Page, 3 vols. (London, 1907–25).
Weiss, *Humanism*	R. Weiss, *Humanism in England during the Fifteenth Century* (3rd edn, Oxford, 1967).

INTRODUCTION

THE HISTORY AND ORGANISATION OF THE PAPAL PENITENTIARY

The papal penitentiary[1] was the department of the Roman Curia which dealt with the sins reserved to papal absolution and which produced documents relating to this process as well as certain other dispensations and graces. It thus had a double function. On the one hand, it was responsible for hearing confessions, including those of men and women guilty of sins whose absolution was reserved to the apostolic see, and for imposing penance upon them. On the other, it issued letters which dealt with the legal consequences of such transgressions. In addition, it issued letters which conferred an increasingly wide variety of dispensations and graces on their beneficiaries. The former area of activity of the papal penitentiary, known as the *officium minus*, concerned the *forum internum*, the latter, known as the *officium maius*, the *forum externum*.[2]

The origins of the papal penitentiary are no doubt to be found in the growth during the twelfth century of the practice of reserving the absolution of certain categories of sins to the pope.[3] The latter, presumably because he was unable to deal with all these cases in person, delegated them to cardinals and others. The first known occurrence of this is under Alexander III (1159–81), when a 'magnus pontifex' appears, to whom the pope 'confessionum curam iniunxerat'. During the pontificate of Innocent III (1198–1216), several cardinals appear who heard confessions in the Curia, for instance, in 1200, John of St Paul, 'qui confessiones pro papa tunc recipiebat'. Whether or not John of St Paul held the office which later became known as that of cardinal penitentiary, it seems clear that such an office came into being in the course of the first half of the thirteenth century. The cardinal penitentiary issued letters in his own name, and this activity was sufficiently frequent to require the appointment of special scribes to engross the letters. They first appear under Innocent IV (1243–54). From this time onwards, one of the main functions of the papal penitentiary was as a writing office, comparable to, but more modest in scale than, the papal chancery. By the early fourteenth century, the scribes of the penitentiary, like those of the chancery, were organised as a college.[4]

---

[1] The English terminology is somewhat ambiguous, since 'penitentiary' is used to describe both the institution and its staff. In the Introduction we use 'papal penitentiary', 'apostolic penitentiary' or 'penitentiary' alone to denote the institution and 'cardinal penitentiary' or 'minor penitentiaries' to denote its staff. The modern institution is known as the (*Sacra*) *Penitenzieria Apostolica*. We have not found the term (*sacra*) *penitentiaria apostolica* in the fifteenth-century sources.

[2] See F. Tamburini, 'Il primo registro di suppliche dell'Archivio della Sacra Peniteniziera Apostolica', *Rivista di storia della chiesa in Italia*, 23 (1969), 384–427, at 389.

[3] For what follows, see P. Zutshi, 'Petitioners, proctors, popes: the development of curial institutions, c. 1150–1250', in *Pensiero e sperimentazioni istituzionali nella 'Societas Christiana' (1046–1250)*, ed. G. Andenna (Milan, 2007), 265–93, at 275–7 (with references to the sources and earlier literature).

[4] B. Schwarz, *Die Organisation kurialer Schreiberkollegien von ihrer Entstehung bis zur Mitte des 15. Jahrhunderts* (Tübingen, 1972), 22–4.

In 1311 Clement V had restricted their number to twelve, but under Boniface IX (1389–1404) the limit had risen to twenty-four. This remained the theoretical limit in the fifteenth century.[5] By the time of Alexander IV (1254–61), the penitentiary had been accommodated in its own building near the Lateran.[6]

During the pontificates of Innocent III and Honorius III (1216–27), men who were not cardinals appear acting as penitentiaries in the Curia. It is unclear whether they were subordinates of the cardinal penitentiary and precursors of the minor penitentiaries. The main duty of the minor penitentiaries was to hear confessions, and for this reason they represented the principal languages of Latin Christendom. Their numbers fluctuated considerably, but Eugenius IV in 1435 specified that there should be no more than eleven minor penitentiaries, consisting of two Italians, two Frenchmen, two Spaniards, one Englishman (who would also hear the confessions of the Scots and Irish), one Hungarian, one for Poland, Bohemia, Slavonia and Russia, one for 'upper Germany' and one for 'lower'.[7] The minor penitentiaries issued their own letters, known as *littere ecclesie*, which recorded the penitents' absolution.[8]

The cardinal penitentiaries and minor penitentiaries exercised authority delegated to them by the pope through a series of faculties (or *concessiones*). This is reflected in the phraseology of the cardinal penitentiary's own letters, which refer to the bureau over which he presided as the penitentiary *of the pope*. The faculties specified with which cases the cardinal penitentiary and minor penitentiaries respectively were empowered to deal; and they were collected together in the so-called *Summa* of Nicholas IV of 1291. This pope's successors added faculties for the cardinal penitentiary as the need arose. Eugenius IV sought to re-organise and codify them in his constitution 'In apostolice dignitatis' of 1438.[9] There was no comparable expansion in the faculties for the minor penitentiaries.

In addition to the cardinal penitentiary, minor penitentiaries and scribes, another group of curialists played a prominent role in the production of documents issued by the cardinal penitentiary: the proctors of the penitentiary.[10] Whether or not they were present in person in the papal Curia, the supplicants needed to employ a proctor, who would formulate the petition in the correct way (that is, according to the *stilus curie Romane*), arrange for it to be approved by the cardinal penitentiary or the acting head of the papal penitentiary (normally called the *regens*), and ensure that the various stages necessary for the issue of a letter of

---

[5] L. Schmugge, *Kirche, Kinder, Karrieren: päpstliche Dispense von der unehelichen Geburt im Spätmittelalter* (Zürich, 1995), 97–100; Schmugge et al., *Supplikenregister*, 16–17.
[6] A. Paravicini Bagliani, *La vita quotidiana alla corte dei papi nel Duecento* (Rome and Bari, 1996), 59.
[7] Göller, i/2. 123. See also T. Majic, 'Die apostolische Pönitentiarie im 14. Jahrhundert', *Römische Quartalschrift*, 50 (1955), 129–77, at 160–73.
[8] See Salonen, *Penitentiary*, 56–7; K. Salonen and L. Schmugge, *A Sip from the 'Well of Grace': Medieval Texts from the Apostolic Penitentiary* (Washington, 2009), 86–8.
[9] See C. H. Haskins, 'The sources for the history of the papal penitentiary', *American Journal of Theology*, 9 (1905), 421–50, at 426–8; A. Lang, 'Beiträge zur Geschichte der apostolischen Pönitentiarie im 13. und 14. Jahrhundert', *Mitteilungen des Instituts für österreichische Geschichtsforschung*, 7. Ergänzungsband (1907), 20–43; Göller, i/1. 100–25; Schmugge, *Kirche, Kinder, Karrieren*, 86–9; Salonen, *Penitentiary*, 58–64.
[10] On the proctors, see Schmugge, *Kirche, Kinder, Karrieren*, 100–3; Schmugge et al., *Supplikenregister*, 19–21.

the cardinal penitentiary in response to the supplication were completed. The proctors thus had a vital role as intermediaries between the supplicants and the staff of the penitentiary.[11]

THE TREATMENT OF SUPPLICATIONS IN THE PAPAL PENITENTIARY

The proctors no doubt made use of formularies in drawing up supplications. The earliest formulary of supplications apparently dates from the pontificate of Boniface IX (1389–1404).[12] Few original supplications survive.[13] Nonetheless we are well informed about the treatment of the supplications in the papal penitentiary, since they were copied in large numbers – over 3,000 *per annum* in the second half of the fifteenth century – into the penitentiary's registers of supplications.[14] It is these registers which form the basis of the present publication. The supplications were addressed to the pope, although they were normally approved and signed by the cardinal penitentiary or *regens*. The copies of the supplications in the registers include this response.[15] Since it invariably approved the supplication, it is clear that, if a supplication was rejected, it was not registered. The response *Fiat in forma* is thought to mean that approval of the request fell within the authority of the ordinary (an authority which could also be exercised by the cardinal penitentiary, *regens* and minor penitentiaries). The most common response was *Fiat de speciali*, while requests for more extensive favours received the response *Fiat de speciali et expresso*. Thus, a request for permission to receive priest's orders below the canonical age of twenty-five years was granted with the words *Fiat de speciali* for ordination at the age of twenty-four and with *Fiat de speciali et expresso* for ordination at the age of twenty-three or younger. It is very difficult to establish the significance in procedural terms of the expressions *Fiat de speciali* and *Fiat de speciali et expresso*. It may be that *Fiat de speciali* means that the cardinal penitentiary was acting on the basis of the faculties that he received from the pope at the beginning of each pontificate, and that *Fiat de speciali et expresso* means that, at least in theory, he was acting on the basis of an *ad hoc* oral command from the pope.[16] Another expression that occurs is *Fiat de speciali*

---

[11] See also below at nn. 82–5.
[12] See Haskins, 'The sources for the history of the papal penitentiary', 440–1; Göller, i/1. 55–7, i/2, 147–71.
[13] See below at n. 56.
[14] See *Penitenzieria Apostolica*, ed. Ostinelli, 76.
[15] The individuals involved are listed in the Index of Curial Personnel under 'Signatories'. Biographical details of many of them will be found in *Penitenzieria Apostolica*, ed. Ostinelli, 61–8.
[16] Cf. Schmugge *et al.*, *Supplikenregister*, 13–14; W. Müller, 'Die Gebühren der päpstlichen Pönitentiarie (1338–1569)', *Quellen und Forschungen aus italienischen Archiven und Bibliotheken*, 78 (1998), 189–261, at 215–16; Salonen, *Penitentiary*, 77–9; P. Zutshi, '*Inextricabilis curie labyrinthus*: the presentation of petitions to the pope in the chancery and the penitentiary during the fourteenth and first half of the fifteenth century', in *Päpste, Pilger, Pönitentiarie: Festschrift für Ludwig Schmugge*, ed. A. Meyer, C. Rendtel and M. Wittmer-Busch (Tübingen, 2004), 393–410, at 404–5; Salonen and Schmugge, *A Sip from the 'Well of Grace'*, 74–6. For evidence of the cardinal penitentiary consulting the pope in the early months of the pontificate of Urban VI, see P. Zutshi, 'Jean de Cros and the papal penitentiary on the eve of the Great Schism', *Francia*, 37 (2010), 335–51, at 340. Occasionally under Eugenius IV, *Concessum* was used in place of *Fiat* (e.g., **101–7**); for the significance of this, see Zutshi, '*Inextricabilis curie labyrinthus*', 405.

ut petitur. When a clerk of illegitimate birth, having already been dispensed to hold a benefice with cure of souls, requested a dispensation to hold a further compatible benefice, the signature *Fiat de speciali* was insufficient to grant the request, and the signature *Fiat de speciali ut petitur* was needed.[17] Such supplications appear in the registers under the heading *De uberiori*.

Sometimes the *Fiat*-clause approved the request subject to some condition or limitation. Thus, when the Franciscan Thomas Roding requested a dispensation allowing him to eat meat, eggs and dairy produce on Lenten and other fasting days, the response was 'Fiat de speciali extra tamen reffectionem . . .' (**3555**), meaning presumably that he was not permitted to partake of these foods in the refectory.[18] The *Fiat*-clause might also impose a penalty on the supplicant. The most common penalty occurs under the heading *De promotis et promovendis* and concerns those who had had themselves promoted to holy orders, whether knowingly or in ignorance of the law, below the canonical age. They were suspended from ministering at the altar for a period of one or two months.

Most types of supplications in the registers of the penitentiary resulted in the issue of a letter addressed to an executor (known as a *commissarius*). He was responsible for checking the veracity of the supplicant's claims and, if they were found to be correct, for implementing the terms of the letter. The *commissarius* was normally the ordinary, that is, the supplicant's diocesan bishop or one of the officials who assisted the bishop in administrative and judicial business, notably the vicar general. In responses to certain supplications, in particular to those registered under the heading *De declaratoriis*, it is often specifically mentioned that the matter should be committed to the ordinary.[19] With other categories of business, reference to the ordinary can be inferred, even when it is not explicitly stated. This applies, for instance, to marriage dispensations, as can be seen from the many entries published below in which episcopal registers record the receipt of letters of the cardinal penitentiary and the proceedings that followed from them.[20]

The supplications sometimes request an executor other than the ordinary and, in order to justify this, explain that it would be difficult or unsafe to approach the ordinary.[21] Another ground for the supplicant to avoid his ordinary was that he doubted his impartiality.[22] A more unusual reason given for avoiding the ordinary

---

[17] See *Penitenzieria Apostolica*, ed. Ostinelli, 73.
[18] Cf. **3610**: 'extra refectorium et dormitorium'.
[19] *De declaratoriis* supplications were referred to the auditor, whose response was normally along the lines *Committatur ordinario et, si vocatis vocandis premissa vera esse invenerit, declaret ut petitur*, or gave more detailed instructions. The penitentiary's own rules specified which categories of letters were addressed to executors and which to the beneficiaries: Göller, i/2. 70–7.
[20] See Clarke, 'Central authority and local powers'.
[21] E.g., **719**: Henry Everton, abbot of Stoneleigh, seeks a licence to eat meat on fast days and to wear linen clothing; he requests 'quod committatur priori eiusdem monasterii attento quod ab ordinario suo longe distat et propter infirmitatem eunden ordinarium adire non potest'.
[22] E.g., **1378**: Richard de Aircourt, who had his wife and his *familiaris* William killed on suspicion of adultery, seeks absolution and a dispensation to remarry; he asks that the case be committed to the abbot of Osney in his own diocese of Lincoln 'cum ordinarium suum habeat suspectum'.

was the latter's excessive severity.[23] If the supplicant was present in the Curia, he could request an executor resident there.[24] Thomas Sollay, priest of the diocese of Lincoln, conducted a wedding in the English hospice of St Edmund in Trastevere without the banns having been published and in a chapel that may have been unconsecrated. He requested absolution from excommunication and from suspension from celebrating the divine office and a dispensation from irregularity. Sollay further requested that the case be committed to the bishop of Penne; this was Iohannes de Polena, an auditor of the Rota.[25] One potential problem with appointing an executor in the Curia was that the executor might need to interrogate witnesses. On occasion it was therefore specifically mentioned that witnesses were present in the Curia.[26]

The canon 'Si quis suadente' (C. 17 q. 4 c. 29) required those guilty of presbytericide to undertake penitential pilgrimage to Rome and seek papal absolution there. Some of those who admitted perpetrating such a crime explicitly requested that they might perform public penance in the Curia rather than in the place where the deed had taken place. Henry Dabilis, a layman of the diocese of Canterbury, successfully made such a request in 1439.[27] The desire of Walter de Vulley and John Joynor, laymen of the diocese of Coventry and Lichfield, to perform their public penance in Bologna, where the Curia was then resident, met with the cardinal penitentiary's response to the effect that the penance should take place nearer the scene of the crime. But the matter was referred to the auditor (the papal penitentiary's legal expert and a doctor of canon law). He was more flexible on this question: if the supplicants could not perform penance locally, they were to perform it where the executor specified, either in the Curia or nearer their own diocese (**57**).

Some supplications requested that the matter be left to the consciences of the beneficiaries. This applies particularly to dispensations permitting them to eat certain foods on Lenten and other fasting days.[28] The effect of this provision was that no executor was appointed, and it seems to have been granted to supplicants

---

[23] In **851** William Drapo and his wife Agnes complain that the archibishop of York has imposed on them 'nonnullas penitencias atrocissimas' as a result of the death of their three-year old son. They request that the case be committed to a neighbouring bishop 'attento quod loci ordinarius est minus [*recte* nimis] in huiusmodi casu austerus'.
[24] The formulary of Walter of Strasbourg specifically allows this: Göller, i/2. 75.
[25] **732**: 'Et quod committatur episcopo Pennensi attento, pater sancte, quod huiusmodi delictum in Urbe perpetratum fuit'.
[26] E.g., a request from John Whelpdale for a declaration of innocence of homicide (**2221**): 'Et committatur [in] Romana curia cum orator sit hic presens et habet probationes necessarias'. The supplicant submitted a similar request which was committed to his ordinary (**2222**). Whelpdale presumably thus had a choice of where the process of execution should take place.
[27] **454**: '... sibique [ut?] publicam penitentiam, quam in loco delicti peragere tenetur, in Roman[a curia?] in tribus ver quatuor locis seu ecclesiis maioribus peragere possit, cum suum ordinarium in hac parte habet suspectum [concedere dignemini]'. For public penance in the Curia, see P. D. Clarke, 'Between Avignon and Rome: minor penitentiaries at the papal Curia in the thirteenth and fourteenth centuries', *Rivista di storia della chiesa in Italia*, 64 (2009), 455–510, at 467–8, 498–9.
[28] E.g., **3550**: 'Et relinquatur eorum conscientie'. For such licences see below at nn. 173–81.

of high rank or to those who were viewed favourably by the Curia.[29] Richard de Beauchamp, bishop of Salisbury, in 1466 requested a dispensation to eat meat, eggs and dairy produce on fasting days, justifying it by reference to his old age and frail state (**1368**). He made the additional request 'quod relinquatur conscientie sue'. Both requests were approved, and evidently the bishop's diet was beneficial to him, for he lived for another fifteen years.

When they were submitted to the papal penitentiary, the supplications were undated. After they had been approved, they received a date. The formulary of Walter Murner of Strasbourg, from the beginning of Urban VI's pontificate, says of the scribes of the penitentiary: 'datam in supplicatione registrata notatam ponant in litteris iuxta stilum officii'.[30] The earliest extant supplication signed by the cardinal penitentiary (from the same pontificate) displays a date written on the dorse by the *registrator*.[31] This may suggest that the date was the date of registration, rather than the date when the supplication was approved.[32] However, by the mid-fifteenth century, a change in the procedure had occurred, for the dating clause was now written on the face of the supplication by a named official. Three men are known who acted in this capacity: A. de Aquila,[33] who appears elsewhere as a *corrector* of the penitentiary registers;[34] P. de Albingana, also a *corrector*;[35] and Coradinus de Regio, auditor of the penitentiary.[36] Another addition made to the original supplication was a brief summary of its contents written in the upper left corner.[37] This was sometimes copied in the margin of the supplication's entry in the registers.

The next stage involved the registration of the supplication. It is apparent already from the formulary of Walter Murner of Strasbourg that not all the supplications approved by the cardinal penitentiary or the *regens* were registered.[38] This is also evident in Reg. 1, where a supplication for absolution from a vow of chastity and its commutation into other works of piety (**29**) is cancelled with the words: 'Cassata . . . quia est in forma . . . et restitui pecunias registri'. This implies that supplications approved *in forma* were not normally registered.[39] There are indeed few such supplications among those published in these volumes.[40] Where they do occur, this may result from an oversight, as in the case just mentioned (where the signature 'Fiat de speciali' may well be a mistake for 'Fiat in forma'), or it may result from

---

[29] See *Penitenzieria Apostolica*, ed. Ostinelli, 71.
[30] Göller, i/1. 187.
[31] See F. Tamburini, 'Note diplomatiche intorno a suppliche e lettere di penitenzieria', *Archivum Historiae Pontificiae*, 11 (1973), 149–208, at 158, 165.
[32] For a different view, see Salonen and Schmugge, *A Sip from the 'Well of Grace'*, 93.
[33] Tamburini, 'Note diplomatiche', 172.
[34] See **865** n., **918**.
[35] Tamburini, 'Note diplomatiche', 175–7.
[36] Auctoritate Papae, *The Church Province of Uppsala and the Apostolic Penitentiary 1410–1526*, Diplomatarium Suecanum Appendix, Acta Pontificum Suecica, ii: Acta Poenitentiariae (Stockholm, 2008), ed. S. Risberg and K. Salonen, 88. Cf. Salonen and Schmugge, *A Sip from the 'Well of Grace'*, 91–2.
[37] Salonen and Schmugge, *A Sip from the 'Well of Grace'*, 71, 92.
[38] Göller, i/1. 187–8. See also Schmugge *et al.*, *Supplikenregister*, 38–9. On the formulary, see below at n. 67.
[39] On the meaning of *in forma*, see above at nn. 15–16.
[40] Admittedly the supplications registered under the heading *De declaratoriis* normally requested a declaration *ut in forma*, but the meaning of *in forma* here appears to be different.

the special request of the supplicant. The passage quoted above also shows that a fee was charged for registration, which in this particular instance was paid back. It seems that prior to the pontificate of Sixtus IV the entries in the registers do not normally reproduce the full text of the supplications. Standard phrases were often represented by *etc.* or simply omitted. It is frequently necessary to refer back to an earlier entry in order to reconstruct the text. On the rare occasions when it is possible to compare the original supplication with its register entry, the latter is briefer.[41]

The letters of the cardinal penitentiary in response to the approved supplications were composed on the basis of formularies.[42] The letters survive scattered across the archives of Latin Christendom.[43] Such letters have a number of conspicuous features, including the signature of the scribe who engrossed the letter, which appears on the *plica* to the right, and the tax mark, which appears under the *plica* to the left. The latter represents the fee payable by the supplicant for the engrossment of the letter. The basis of the fee was a schedule promulgated by Benedict XII.[44] The original letters also display the proctor's signature on the dorse.

The fee for the engrossment was not the only one payable by the supplicant, for there were separate charges for sealing, for registration and for the proctor's services. In the fifteenth century, there was a sharp increase in the fees.[45] This was no doubt partly the result of the tendency for curial offices, including those of the papal penitentiary, to become saleable.[46] This occurred mainly during the second half of the century,[47] although the sale of the office of scribe of the penitentiary goes back to the pontificate of Boniface IX (1389–1404).[48] The normal procedure was for someone to acquire an office for a lump sum, which tended to be calculated at around ten times its annual income. He was then able to enjoy the revenues of the office and appoint a substitute to perform its duties. The income from the sale of office was boosted by the creation of new colleges of different categories of office-holders, enabling a large number of positions to be sold in one go. This occurred, for instance, with the office of proctor of the penitentiary.[49]

---

[41] See Salonen, *Penitentiary*, 429–30; *Penitenzieria Apostolica*, ed. Ostinelli, 59–60.
[42] See below at nn. 64–8.
[43] They can now most conveniently be studied in Salonen and Schmugge, *A Sip from the 'Well of Grace'*, plates 4, 8, 10, 11, 13, 15–16, 20a–b. For these letters and the process by which they were produced see ibid., 84–105; Göller, i/1. 190–202; Schwarz, *Schreiberkollegien*, 149–51; Tamburini, 'Note diplomatiche'. We hope to publish the penitentiary letters that we have found in English archives elsewhere.
[44] See H. Denifle, 'Die älteste Taxrolle der apostolischen Pönitentiarie', *Archiv für Literatur- und Kirchengeschichte des Mittelalters*, 4 (1888), 201–38.
[45] See Müller, 'Gebühren'; idem, 'The price of papal pardon: new fifteenth-century evidence', in *Päpste, Pilger, Pönitentiarie*, ed. Meyer, Rendtel and Wittmer-Busch, 457–81.
[46] For the background, see B. Schwarz, 'Ämterkäuflichkeit, eine Institution des Absolutismus und ihre mittelalterliche Wurzeln', in *Staat und Gesellschaft in Mittelalter und früher Neuzeit: Gedenkschrift für Joachim Leuschner* (Göttingen, 1983), 176–96; idem, 'Die Entstehung der Ämterkäuflichkeit an der römischen Kurie', in *Ämterhandel im Spätmittelalter und im 16. Jahrhundert*, ed. I. Mieck (Berlin, 1984), 61–5.
[47] See B. Schimmelpfennig, 'Der Ämterhandel an der römischen Kurie von Pius II. bis zum Sacco di Roma (1458–1527)', in *Ämterhandel im Spätmittelalter*, ed. Mieck, 3–41.
[48] See Schwarz, *Schreiberkollegien*, esp. 181–5.
[49] See A. Sohn, *Deutsche Prokuratoren an der römischen Kurie in der Frührenaissance (1431–1474)* (Cologne, Weimar and Vienna, 1997), 78–80.

Another element in the increase in costs borne by the supplicants was the payment of compositions for the benefit of the apostolic chamber.[50] The earliest references to compositions in the present volumes are from the pontificate of Nicholas V and concern cases of simony. Compositions were much more common under his successors Pius II and Calixtus III, when the payments were made to the datary (*datarius*). The development of the practice has been particularly associated with Calixtus III's datary, who was the pope's confessor, Cosmas de Monteserrato.[51] Compositions were most frequently paid by those who had contracted and consummated marriage knowing that a canonical impediment existed between them.

Despite the various tendencies which meant a rise in supplicants' expenses in the fifteenth century, it remained cheaper and simpler to acquire a grace in the penitentiary than in the chancery.[52] This is reflected in a reform proposal of 1497 which complained that the penitentiary was imitating the procedure of the chancery 'que longior est et lucrosior'.[53] It is understandable that a petitioner might request the issue of a letter through the penitentiary on the grounds of poverty.[54] The discrepancy in costs is of especial significance because there were many graces which could be obtained in both the penitentiary and the chancery; the supplicants thus had some choice over which department they approached.[55]

THE SOURCES FOR THE PAPAL PENITENTIARY

The sources published here comprise supplications regarding England and Wales recorded in the registers of the papal penitentiary to 1503 housed in the Archivio Segreto Vaticano. Before describing these registers, other sources concerning the penitentiary need to be briefly discussed. Firstly original supplications directed to this curial office survive in some archives, but they are very rare for the fifteenth century and only one is known to survive before this period;[56] none are known concerning England and Wales. Examples may survive because the papal graces that they requested were granted *sola signatura*; this means that the original supplication signed by a penitentiary official was the only proof which the supplicant had to show that their request had been approved. But this form of approval was rare; more commonly the penitentiary issued a letter in response to a supplication approved by its officials. If supplicants obtained this more formal proof of approval, their original supplications became redundant and so were not normally preserved.

---

[50] On compositions see Schmugge, *Kirche, Kinder, Karrieren*, 115–18; Schmugge *et al.*, *Supplikenregister*, 48–51; Salonen, *Penitentiary*, 86; *Penitenzieria Apostolica*, ed. Ostinelli, 69–70
[51] See Schimmelpfennig, 'Ämterhandel', 19–20; Müller, 'Gebühren', 201.
[52] See Schmugge, *Kirche, Kinder, Karrieren*, 118; Salonen, *Penitentiary*, 85–6; Salonen and Schmugge, *A Sip from the 'Well of Grace'*, 79–80.
[53] Göller, ii/2. 130–1: 'imitati sunt magis ordinationem et consuetudinem cancellarie apostolice, que longior est et lucrosior, in magnum gravamen et retardationem pauperum penitentium . . .'.
[54] E.g., **3081**: 'quod littere expediantur per penitentiariam attenta paupertate oratoris'.
[55] See B. Schwarz, 'Dispense der Kanzlei Eugens IV. (1431–1447)', in *Illegitimität im Spätmittelalter*, ed. L. Schmugge and B. Wiggenhauser (Munich, 1994), 133–47; Schmugge *et al.*, *Supplikenregister*, esp. ch. 11; Zutshi, '*Inextricabilis curie labyrinthus*'.
[56] F. Tamburini, 'Note diplomatiche', 149–52; four examples are edited and discussed at 157–77. Another example is edited by Risberg and Salonen in *The Church Province of Uppsala*, 201–2 (discussed at 86–9); reproduced with an English translation by Salonen and Schmugge, *A Sip from the 'Well of Grace'*, 89–94, 114–17, 166 (photograph).

Consequently there are many more original letters of the penitentiary than original supplications, and some of the former concern England and Wales.⁵⁷ But archival inventories frequently fail to identify them correctly, above all because the cardinal who issued the letter is not specifically identified as the cardinal penitentiary in the *intitulatio*. It is a phrase in the text – 'auctoritate domini pape, cuius penitentiarie curam gerimus' – which reveals that the letter was issued by the cardinal penitentiary. They do not survive in large numbers; in most cases there was little practical reason to preserve them beyond the life-time of the impetrants since they usually benefited these individuals alone.⁵⁸ We have not searched systematically for original letters of the penitentiary corresponding to supplications edited here from the office's registers.⁵⁹ Letters of the penitentiary obtained by English and Welsh supplicants also survive as copies in episcopal registers from England and Wales, and these copies are numerous. Where editions of these registers have been published, we have checked them for letters responding to the supplications edited below; any such letters identified are cited in the annotation to the supplications concerned. A bishop's register normally recorded penitentiary letters when the latter were addressed to the bishop in question or his vicars-in-spiritual. Some penitentiary letters were addressed to the supplicants who impetrated them, but most were addressed to a commissary, usually the bishop of the supplicant concerned, and supplicants therefore had to present such letters to him. Such a letter normally recounted the details of a supplicant's request and instructed the commissary to verify these; if he found them to be correct, the letter authorised him to confer the grace requested, but if not, he might refuse it. This procedure was known as execution,⁶⁰ and often episcopal letters of execution were copied into English or Welsh bishops' registers along with the penitentiary letters which they executed. Any evidence of execution is also cited from editions of episcopal registers in the annotation to related supplications published below.

The penitentiary enregistered its own letters, although there is little evidence to support Tamburini's assumption that it was doing so by the early fifteenth century.⁶¹ No registers are known to survive before 1570, and those preserved in the Archivio Segreto Vaticano (557 registers for the period 1570–1890) are not currently available for consultation.⁶² Nevertheless a few penitentiary letters were copied into the office's registers of supplications before 1503.⁶³ It is not clear why this happened,

---

⁵⁷ Examples of the latter include: London, British Library, Additional Charters 73914, 73878; Bangor University Archives, Penrhyn MS 12 (all three are discussed by Clarke, 'Central authority and local powers', 421, 422, 423–4, 427–8). On the form of such letters see Tamburini, 'Note diplomatiche', 178–82, 189–201.
⁵⁸ Letters for marriage dispensations are an exception because these had implications for the legitimacy and thus inheritance rights of children born of the marriage dispensed, hence these were preserved in family archives and are the most common kind of penitentiary letter to survive.
⁵⁹ Indeed we have matched only one supplication in our edition (**2033**) with an original letter.
⁶⁰ Further discussed by Clarke, 'Central authority and local powers', in relation to English and Welsh sources; cf. *Penitenzieria Apostolica*, ed. Ostinelli, 79–126, for an excellent analysis of similar Italian evidence, but preserved in notarial rather than episcopal registers.
⁶¹ Tamburini, 'Il primo registro', esp. pp. 384–8.
⁶² The archives of the Penitentiary in the ASV are presently consultable only up to 1564.
⁶³ Notably in Reg. 28, fols. 287v–288r; 30, fols. 216v–217r; 31, fol. 197r. Incidentally these

but generally they are contemporary with the registers where they occur, although they appear in isolation from supplications copied there. None of them concern England or Wales. The principal types of letters issued by the penitentiary will be found in formularies compiled for the use of the office's staff, notably the scribes, who used the letters contained in them as models for drafting similar ones.[64] The earliest of the formularies has been ascribed to Cardinal Thomas of Capua; it contain letters which, when they can be dated, are from the years 1234–43.[65] The most significant of the later formularies was compiled at the behest of Pope Benedict XII in 1334. It was one of the largest, running to over a hundred folios in most copies, and it survives in many more manuscripts than any other formulary of the penitentiary, unsurprisingly since by the late fourteenth century the office's own rules required every penitentiary scribe to acquire a copy of this formulary within six months of his appointment.[66] During the Great Schism, in the obedience of Urban VI, Walter Murner of Strasbourg prepared a greatly expanded version of the formulary of Benedict XII.[67] No new formulary on a comparable scale is known to have been prepared in the fifteenth century, but Walter of Strasbourg's formulary was kept up to date with additions from the time of the Great Schism (1378–1417) and later.[68] Formularies are useful for indicating the range and nature of the penitentiary's business in the thirteenth and fourteenth centuries for which no penitentiary registers survive, but, like most formularies, they usually omit names of persons and places specified in letters, which were irrelevant to their purpose but are of obvious interest to historians. We have used formularies to help make sense of some abbreviated supplications edited below.

The penitentiary's registers of supplications to 1503 survive for 1410–11, 1438–43, and in a near continuous series from 1448 onwards. A recent explanation of this pattern of survival suggests that the earliest extant registers arose from 'special circumstances', namely the Great Schism and the conciliar movement, but that regular registration only began in the mid-fifteenth century when the papacy moved back to Rome following these crises.[69] However, there is evidence that the penitentiary was already enregistering supplications by the late fourteenth century,[70] so it seems more likely that gaps in the registration before 1448 represent losses. These may have occurred during the Sack of Rome (1527) and following Napoleon's conquest of the papal state in 1809, when he had the papal archive

---

examples are all from Sixtus IV's pontificate (1471–84). A letter of Sixtus IV to the cardinal penitentiary also oddly appears in the register for 1488–9 (Reg. 38, fol. 2r) from his successor Innocent VIII's pontificate.

[64] Göller, i/1. 20–5, 28–57, 65–74, describes the formularies and lists manuscripts of them.
[65] Edited by H. C. Lea, *A Formulary of the Papal Penitentiary in the Thirteenth Century* (Philadelphia, 1892). Its date and compiler were established by Haskins, 'The sources for the history of the papal penitentiary', 431–3
[66] Göller, i/2. 64. A much-needed edition of Benedict XII's formulary is planned by Dr Arnaud Fossier (Sorbonne).
[67] *Die Pönitentiarie-Formularsammlung des Walter Murner von Strassburg*, ed. M. Meyer (Freiburg im Breisgau, 1979).
[68] Göller, i/1. 46–7.
[69] Salonen and Schmugge, *A Sip from the 'Well of Grace'*, 6–7.
[70] The earliest known original penitentiary supplication (1384) displays a registration mark (Tamburini, 'Note diplomatiche', 158; idem, 'Il primo registro', 387).

moved to Paris; it was returned to Rome after his defeat but not in its entirety.[71]

The penitentiary registers to 1503 that survived these events consist of fifty bound volumes written on paper and ranging in size from 109 to 989 folios;[72] most contain between *c.* 200 and 500 folios. They are more voluminous from the mid-1480s, reflecting both the growth of the office's business and changing methods of registration. On average the penitentiary was enregistering more supplications per month by Innocent VIII's papacy (1484–92) than under Calixtus III (1455–8). Nevertheless the registers do not show a steady year-by-year rise in supplications during the second half of the fifteenth century.[73] Peaks and troughs occurred throughout this period, notably the dramatic increases in business during the Jubilee years of 1450, 1475 and 1500, when escalations in pilgrim traffic to Rome must have brought many more supplications than usual to the penitentiary. Such anomalies especially account for the two biggest registers before 1503, those for 1499–1500 and 1500–1, containing 989 and 828 folios respectively.[74]

Entries also tended to be longer in the later registers, especially from Sixtus IV's pontificate (1471–84), further contributing to the bulk of these volumes. Not only does the handwriting become larger as time goes on, but the supplications also seem to be copied into the registers increasingly in full. Those recording entries in earlier registers abbreviated the supplications much more, especially the more formulaic and less complex requests, from which standard phrases were often omitted and sometimes represented by 'etc.' An extreme case are the two registers from Nicholas V's pontificate (1447–55), where supplications were copied in such a truncated form and often in such hasty scrawl that the resulting entries are virtually incomprehensible in some instances.[75] The overwhelming number of supplications associated with the Jubilee of 1450 helps to explain such unusually defective registration, but other factors account for the increasing length of later register entries. One is apparently financial; Salonen and Schmugge have observed that those enregistering supplications by the late fifteenth century 'were paid according to the number of pages they produced', though they cite no evidence in support of this intriguing claim.[76] Another element is papal reform of the curial administration, notably the improvement in the Latinity of its personnel, in particular under the humanist pope Sixtus IV; it is surely no coincidence that during his pontificate penitentiary supplications began to be enregistered *in extenso*. A related change in registration is that before Pius II's time each penitentiary register tended to cover several years,[77] even an entire pontificate in the case of Calixtus III (1455–8), but from Pius II's time a register normally covered no more than twelve months, at first usually running from January to December and by Sixtus IV's pontificate corresponding to a pontifical year.

---

[71] Schmugge *et al.*, *Supplikenregister*, 4–5. On the Sack's effect on the penitentiary's activity, see also P. D. Clarke, 'Canterbury as the new Rome: Dispensations and Henry VIII's Reformation', forthcoming in the *Journal of Ecclesiastical History*.
[72] The lower figure relates to Reg. 1 (1410–11); the higher to Reg. 48 (1499–1500). The present binding of the volumes, consisting of 'boards covered with red velvet', is not original but from the seventeenth century (Salonen and Schmugge, *A Sip from the 'Well of Grace'*, 5).
[73] Salonen and Schmugge, *A Sip from the 'Well of Grace'*, 19.
[74] Reg. 48–9 (covering the eighth and ninth years of Alexander VI's pontificate).
[75] Reg. 3–4.
[76] Salonen and Schmugge, *A Sip from the 'Well of Grace'*, 5.
[77] Reg. 2–2bis (1438–43), 3 (1448–53), 4 (1448–54), 5–6 (1455–8).

Entries in these registers are usually arranged under subject-headings. The latter occur in the earliest extant registers, but a fixed set of headings only begins to appear from Pius II's time (1458–64), which comprises the following and normally in this order: *De matrimonialibus*; *De diversis formis*; *De declaratoriis*; *De defectu natalium*; *De uberiori*; *De promotis et promovendis*; *De sententiis generalibus*; *De confessionalibus perpetuis*; *De confessionalibus in forma 'Cupientes'*. The latter three headings were often merged into one, notably from Sixtus IV's time. During his pontificate supplications seeking licences for portable altars first occur in the penitentiary registers, appearing under this tripartite heading, hence it was extended to refer to them by 1479, usually in the form *De perpetuis, 'Cupientes', sententiis generalibus ac altaribus portatilibus*. The meanings of these standard headings are explained in the next section of the introduction, where the typical content of entries appearing under them is also described. It is not necessary to list here which folios in each of our fifty registers contain the headed sections above, since detailed descriptions of the registers have already appeared in other editions of entries drawn from them.[78]

These divisions of the registers were written on different quires (typically quinternions, i.e., gatherings of five folios). The quires were filled with entries apparently before being bound to form registers. The quires were often marked as numbered parts of these headed sections, presumably as a guide to the registers' binders.[79] Blank folios often occur at the end of headed sections, which further suggests that they were compiled separately before binding. Within each section, however, entries were usually recorded continuously one after the other, by a single hand and in rough chronological order.[80] A date appears beside almost every entry in the left margin of each page, and it records when the supplication concerned was approved or registered.[81] The relevant pontifical year normally appears as a running heading in the upper margin, usually accompanied by the *data topographica* referring to where the pope then resided, although in practice this was normally also where the penitentiary was. The *data topographica* also appears with the dates beside individual entries by Pius II's time. They suggest that the penitentiary moved around with the Curia. For example, the first extant register recorded supplications at Bologna since they were approved by the penitentiary of the Pisan popes who were based there. Similarly, entries in the next two surviving registers from 1438–43 were dated initially at Ferrara then at Florence, since Pope Eugenius IV (1431–47) was then presiding over a council which moved from Ferrara to Florence in 1439. By the mid-fifteenth century when the papacy had returned to Rome, entries were normally dated at St Peter's, but occasionally elsewhere. For example, under Pope Paul II (1464–71) entries were often dated at S. Marco instead, since that Roman basilica stood next to his preferred residence, Palazzo Venezia. Some late-fifteenth-century entries are dated outside Rome, at other places in the papal state or further north in Italy, notably in the summer months when the Curia habitually moved out of Rome. Under Pius II, for example, many

---

[78] See *RPG*, i–viii for Reg. 2–50. Cf. *Penitenzieria Apostolica*, ed. Ostinelli, 44–57, for Reg. 2–33. For Reg. 1 see Tamburini, 'Il primo registro', 390–5.

[79] E.g., 'Quinternus septimus de diversis. Anno 3. Pontificatus domini Nicholai pape quinti Rome 1449' (Reg. 3, fols. 69r–82v).

[80] In this edition entries are in strict chronological order and so do not always follow the sequence in which they appear in the registers.

[81] See above at n. 30.

entries were dated at his home town of Siena. In addition, by Pius II's time, beside each enregistered supplication the diocese from which it came was noted in the right margin. This has facilitated the identification of entries concerning English and Welsh dioceses for these volumes, although occasionally the diocese indicated beside an entry does not correspond to that in the entry itself; therefore the one always needs checking against the other.

Other details occasionally accompany entries, notably the names of proctors who drew up the supplications. The two earliest extant penitentiary registers comprise sections headed *De officio procuratoris* (or *procuratorum*), which record the appointment of proctors, including one Englishman.[82] Later registers do not include such material; but the work of proctors is especially well documented under Pius II, for the registers of supplications from 1458–60 (Reg. 7 and 8) regularly give the name of the proctor by the entry.[83] In subsequent registers, however, the proctor is named only when there is an error or omission in the supplication, which therefore had to be referred back to the proctor who had submitted it. In most cases he had omitted the supplicants' diocese or, less often, their surname.[84] Some lacunae related to the substance of a request, notably where proctors had not specified whether a marriage dispensation was sought from an impediment of consanguinity or affinity, or whether the marriage was consummated or not.[85] Such details were vital, for penitentiary letters which took over incorrect details from the supplications might be invalid. Indeed penitentiary letters normally instructed a commissary to verify their content, and only if he found it to be correct, would he grant the grace requested. Thus proctors needed to take care over the information provided in the supplications. Doubtless they were also expected to pay on their clients' behalf the penitentiary's fees for issuing letters; these taxes are shown beside a few entries,[86] but do not appear regularly in penitentiary registers before the early sixteenth century.

Finally the registers contain annotations reflecting how the personnel of the penitentiary compiled them. In registers from Sixtus IV's and Innocent VIII's pontificates (1471–92), thematic headings appear beside some entries briefly describing the kinds of grace that they requested, for example, 'Licencia visitandi sepulcrum dominicum pro religioso'.[87] Such headings are particularly numerous in registers from the years 1483–6,[88] and they also occur on original supplications, which suggests that they were copied from there into the registers. Other notes added to the penitentiary registers indicate a growing professionalism in the

---

[82] Reg. 1, fols. 2r–4r; Reg. 2, fols. 83r–85r. For the Englishman see **6**.
[83] See Schmugge *et al.*, *Supplikenregister*, 41–3; *Penitenzieria Apostolica*, ed. Ostinelli, 74; and below **1008-1088** passim.
[84] E.g., Reg. 29, fols. 57r, 228v, 232v; Reg. 30, fols. 51r, 73v, 76r, 79v, 96v, 99v, 104v, 114v, 131r, 215r, 216r; etc.
[85] E.g., Reg. 29, fol. 68v; Reg. 30, fol. 56v, 63r, 83r, 97r; Reg. 31, fol. 68v; etc. Other missing details of this kind included the status of the parents of supplicants seeking dispensations from illegitimacy (e.g., Reg. 33, fols. 230v, 253r; etc.).
[86] Notably in Reg. 2; see, e.g., **101**.
[87] Reg. 23, fol. 102v. Similar headings occur in Reg. 24, fol. 117r; 25, fol. 149v; Reg. 33, fols. 93v, 94r, 95r, 102r, 104r, 105r, 105v, 106v; etc.
[88] Reg. 33–5, corresponding to the final (thirteenth) pontifical year of Sixtus IV and first two of Innocent VIII; over eighty such headings occur in Reg. 34 and ten in Reg. 35, too many to cite at length here.

office's record-keeping. The registers were probably not compiled by penitentiary scribes, as is sometimes assumed, but by other clerks, who are sometimes named in them.[89] Their work was checked by a corrector, and correctors' interventions in the registers appear from 1467, often signed with their names.[90] The correctors compared enregistered supplications with the originals for accuracy, particularly from Sixtus IV's pontificate, when their interventions in the registers become more frequent. It was undoubtedly they who noted significant defects in original supplications and referred these to the proctors responsible. They probably also added the cross-references in the registers, usually referring to entries which belonged to one section but were wrongly recorded in another.[91] From 1480 they further noted beside enregistered supplications lacking dates of approval that letters were expedited in response to them, giving the date of expedition, presumably in case their approval was in doubt.[92] By the late 1480s they also crossed through some enregistered supplications, noting that letters were not expedited.[93] They sometimes cancelled entries because the same supplication had been mistakenly enregistered twice.[94] Such quality control seems to have become the responsibility of the penitentiary's *sigillator* by Alexander VI's pontificate (1492–1503), since those signing corrections to the registers in this period often identified themselves as such.[95] Possibly at this time one official united the functions of correcting and sealing the office's documentation.[96]

THE SUBJECT-MATTER OF THE SUPPLICATIONS

As indicated in the previous section, supplications copied in the penitentiary registers were arranged systematically under subject-headings by Pius II's pontificate (1458–64), and this scheme of headings will be used below to explain the main categories of business which the office handled. It will also be necessary to sketch the canon law background to each of these categories, since it is difficult to make sense of any supplication to the penitentiary without understanding the canon law that gave rise to it. Firstly a supplication to the penitentiary might seek absolution from a violation of canon law and any penalty incurred as a consequence, notably excommunication, in most cases where canon law reserved this absolution to the pope. Secondly it might seek a dispensation, which usually released the supplicants from observing canon law in particular circumstances. Thirdly it might solicit a

---

[89] Notably 'Ia(cobus) de Parma' in Reg. 1 (1410–11), fols. 21r, 64r, 70r, 73v; 'Io(hannes) Vendesa' in Reg. 15 (1467), fol. 198r; and 'Nicolaus Clever' in Reg. 50 (1501–3), fol. 527v, who noted there that he began to register on 20 July [1502].
[90] E.g., 'Io(hannes) Antonius' in Reg. 15 (1467), fols. 18r, 248v; Reg. 18 (1470), fol. 13r; and Reg. 23 (1474–5), fol. 263r.
[91] E.g., Reg. 29 (1479–80), fol. 80r; Reg. 42 (1492–3), fols. 180r ('Quere inter declaratoriis quia ibidem registrata existit per errorem registrantis'), 301v; Reg. 43 (1493–4), fol. 239r.
[92] E.g., Reg. 30 (1480–1), fols. 83v, 144r, 178r; Reg. 31 (1481–2), fols. 12r, 97v; etc.
[93] E.g., Reg. 37 (1487–8), fol. 275v; Reg. 44 (1494–5), fol. 172v; Reg. 46 (1497–8), fol. 492r; Reg. 47 (1498–9), fol. 270r; etc.
[94] E.g., Reg. 41 (1491–2), fols. 400v, 403r; Reg. 42, fol. 306r; Reg. 45 (1495–6), fol. 36v; Reg. 46, fol. 26v; Reg. 49 (1500–1), fols. 32r, 650v.
[95] E.g., Reg. 34 (1484–5), fol. 9v (correction dated 26 January 150[–]!); Reg. 41 (1491–2), fols. 349r, 356v; Reg. 45, fol. 36v (*sigillator* named 'Io(hannes) f. de Beka' here and in subsequent examples); Reg. 46, fol. 26v; Reg. 47, fols. 77r, 270r; Reg. 49, fols. 522v, 532v, 650v.
[96] On the relationship between these two functions, see Göller, i/1. 181–2.

licence that permitted the supplicants to do things usually forbidden by canon law. Finally, and much less commonly, it might request a *littera declaratoria* which 'declared' invalid any allegations that the supplicants were somehow in breach of canon law. These four kinds of papal grace issued by the penitentiary regarded a wide range of canonical issues, which will be surveyed briefly below.

Arguably the most important category of business was marriage dispensations, and this was reflected by the fact that normally it was the subject of the first section in the penitentiary registers, headed *De matrimonialibus*. It was certainly one of the largest single categories of business handled by the office. Statistical analysis of the registers shows that marriage accounted for 27 per cent of supplications enregistered under Calixtus III and Pius II (1455–64), a figure almost doubling to 47 per cent under Innocent VIII (1484–92).[97] Marital supplications from England and Wales display a comparable trend, rising from 47 in the penitentiary registers for 1455–64 to 211 in those for 1484–92.[98] This evidence counters the view that papal favours concerning marriage, specifically dispensations, were not widely available in the later Middle Ages and largely sought by couples of high social status.[99] In fact few English and Welsh supplicants requesting such favours were classed as *nobiles*[100] in the penitentiary registers, and the penitentiary was not the only source of these favours: many others sought them from the papal chancery and from legates and other ecclesiastical officials who obtained papal faculties to grant such favours. Several such officials resided in England and Wales, albeit temporarily, hence they represented the most convenient and so potentially most widely solicited source of papal graces, including those concerning marriage, but their activity in issuing these is sparsely documented and requires further investigation.[101]

In any case the penitentiary registers provide important new evidence concerning medieval marriage. They largely contain requests for dispensations from marital impediments. The two most cited impediments were consanguinity (kinship through blood) and affinity (relationship through marriage). Since 1215 canon law had prohibited matrimony between those related within four degrees of affinity or consanguinity.[102] In terms of consanguinity this meant that relatives were not permitted to marry if they were separated from a common ancestor by four generations or fewer in a direct line of descent (those who were great-grandchildren of the same forebear were related in the fourth degree of consanguinity). Theoretically affinity was created only by marriage, usually the former marriage of one spouse to a relative of the other, but in practice it could arise from an illicit

---

[97] Salonen, *Penitentiary*, 112.
[98] This suggests a four-fold increase in real terms but the rate of growth is less dramatic when these supplications are considered as a proportion of all English and Welsh supplications enregistered, the proportion rising from 13 per cent (47 out of 362) in 1455–64 to 33 per cent (211 out of 637) in 1484–92.
[99] See, notably, R. H. Helmholz, *Marriage Litigation in Medieval England* (Cambridge, 1974), 85–7.
[100] Penitentiary supplications used this term to cover a broad social spectrum ranging from royalty to gentry: see Clarke, 'New evidence'.
[101] Some of their letters granting papal graces survive as originals (e.g., Lambeth Palace Library, Papal Documents 129b–135) or as copies in episcopal registers (e.g., that for Coventry and Lichfield diocese, 1490–1502, Lichfield Record Office, B/A/1/13, fols 124v, 161v, 164, 249v).
[102] Fourth Lateran Council (1215), canon 52 (*Liber extra* 4.14.8).

sexual union between the spouse and relative, even though Pope Alexander III (1159–81) had ruled that this union was not a marital impediment.[103] The degree of affinity was generally calculated to be the same as the degree of consanguinity within which one spouse was related to the other's former marital or sexual partner; for example, a man who married his dead brother's widow was related to her in the first degree of affinity, for siblings were related in the first degree of consanguinity.[104]

By the fifteenth century the cardinal penitentiary enjoyed papal faculties to grant marriage dispensations for the third and the fourth degrees of consanguinity and/or affinity.[105] Indeed in the registers most supplications from England and Wales for marriage dispensations concerned permutations of these degrees, and the cardinal or his deputies generally approved them with the formula *Fiat de speciali*, i.e., by a special papal faculty. Occasionally requests for dispensations from the second degree of affinity, or less often consanguinity, appear in the registers, but those from England and Wales are rare and almost always refer to the second degree combined with the third or fourth,[106] although unusually one concerns the first and second degrees (**2779**). It is unclear whether the cardinal penitentiary had a faculty to grant these more unusual requests, for some were approved in the registers *Fiat de speciali* as if he did,[107] but others (including the request regarding the first and second degrees) *Fiat de speciali et expresso* as if he did not.[108] The latter formula apparently means that the cardinal or his deputies had to ask the pope for express authority to approve such requests since these lay outside their competence.

The penitentiary normally issued a letter of dispensation in response to all the above requests if approved, usually with the same date as that of the supplication. But supplications for dispensations from the third and fourth degrees combined, or from the second degree combined with others, normally also requested a *littera declaratoria*. This 'declared' that the dispensation was valid for both degrees, and extant examples are dated a few days after the letter of dispensation. Usually they claim that the couple in question had sought a dispensation for the more remote degree but then realised that they were also related in the closer degree and thus requested a *littera declaratoria* confirming that their dispensation also covered the latter as if they had originally mentioned it.[109] This was probably a procedural fiction since in the penitentiary registers one supplication usually sought a dispensation for both degrees from the outset and the *Fiat*-clause approving this conceded the *littera declaratoria*; only rarely did a separate supplication request the declaration.[110]

---

[103] *Liber extra* 4.14.1; Schmugge et al., *Supplikenregister*, 72–3; Salonen, *Penitentiary*, 106–7.
[104] Henry VIII was, of course, in precisely this situation when he sought to marry Catherine of Aragon, widow of his brother Arthur, Prince of Wales.
[105] Göller, i/1. 113–14; Salonen, *Penitentiary*, 110.
[106] **1924, 1939**, 2003, 2034, 2071, **2772, 2776, 2780, 2798, 2867, 2912, 2917, 2928, 3465, 3498–9, 3511, 3513–14, 3544**. Apparently only one concerns the second degree alone: **2078**.
[107] **1924, 1939, 2078, 2776, 2780, 2798, 2867, 2917, 3544**. Göller does not refer to any such faculty.
[108] 2003, 2034, 2071, 2772, 2779, 2912, 2928, 3465, 3498, 3511, 3513.
[109] See Clarke, 'Central authority and local powers', 424, 426, on such letters in English episcopal registers; cf. also *Penitenzieria Apostolica*, ed. Ostinelli, 102–3.
[110] E.g., **3498–9, 3513–14**. Penitentiary officials generally approved these requests with

Both the dispensation and the *littera* were required because Pope Clement VI (1342–52) had stipulated this in cases where the third and fourth degrees were combined, and Pope Gregory XI (1370–8) in cases of the second degree combined with others.[111] The reason for these papal rulings is unclear, but their requirement for extra documents generated more income for the curial administration.

Two other marriage impediments cited in the penitentiary registers were 'public honesty' and *cognatio spiritualis*, but far fewer English and Welsh supplicants sought dispensations from these than from consanguinity or affinity. The impediment of public honesty arose where one spouse was formerly betrothed to a relative of the other, often a sibling and certainly someone related in the prohibited degrees, but where the betrothal had ended without consummation.[112] Medieval canonists defined betrothal (*sponsalia*) as future consent (to marry) and agreed that this did not create a binding marriage unless followed by consummation, but it might create a dispensable impediment to a future marriage. Meanwhile *cognatio spiritualis* meant spiritual kinship and arose where a relation of one spouse had acted either as a godparent at the other's baptism or, less commonly, as a sponsor at his or her confirmation. In most English or Welsh supplications seeking dispensations from the impediment, this relative was a spouse's mother or father.[113] Normally penitentiary officials approved supplications concerning public honesty by *Fiat de speciali* but those concerning *cognatio spiritualis* by *Fiat de speciali et expresso*, for the cardinal penitentiary had a special faculty to dispense from the former impediment but not the latter (for which express papal consent was apparently required).[114]

Besides the impediment, supplications for marriage dispensations in the penitentiary registers specified other details. Normally they named both spouses as supplicants, and even if couples were already married, they usually gave the woman's surname as her family name rather than her husband's surname: an illuminating detail for women's history. As already implied, supplications also distinguished whether a couple sought a dispensation for a future marriage or an existing one. In the latter case it was often added that they had contracted marriage *per verba de presenti* (as opposed to *per verba de futuro*), since most medieval canonists agreed that present consent (consent to marry in the present, not the future) made a marriage binding. However a minority canonistic opinion held that consummation was needed to make present consent truly binding, and doubtless because of this, supplications also specified whether the marriage had been consummated (and

Fiat in forma.
[111] Clement VI's ruling was printed by E. Baluze, *Miscellanea*, iii: *Monumenta diplomatica et epistolaria* (Lucca, 1762), 118. It applied to consanguinity, but Gregory XI extended it to affinity and added the stipulation concerning the second degree: see *Regulae cancellariae apostolicae: Die päpstlichen Kanzleiregeln von Johannes XXII. bis Nikolaus V.*, ed. E. von Ottenthal (Innsbruck, 1888), 40, § 74. Clement's ruling is cited very frequently below; **3465** and **3511** cite Gregory's ruling.
[112] E.g., **1216, 1837, 3444** (out of a mere 13 entries on the impediment of public honesty in the subject index).
[113] E.g., **1231, 1244, 1802, 1817** (out of 89 entries for *cognatio spiritualis* in the subject index).
[114] From 1374 the cardinal enjoyed a faculty to dispense from public honesty those who married unaware of this impediment. In 1438 Pope Eugenius IV extended his faculties to include dispensations for couples who married knowing of any impediment (Göller, i/1. 113; i/2. 23, 43).

whether it had resulted in offspring).

In addition supplications concerning existing marriages normally specified whether or not the couple already knew of the impediment before marrying. The distinction was important, since couples who married knowing that they were related in the prohibited degrees violated canon law and incurred excommunication.[115] Although canon law did not expressly reserve absolution in this case to the pope or extend this sanction to other impediments,[116] supplicants who married knowing of any impediment usually requested both absolution and dispensation (couples ignorant of the impediment until after their marriage required only the dispensation). Such impediments were expected to be known as a result of reading the banns; since 1215 canon law had required every priest to announce marriages in his parish so that impediments to them could be reported before they took place.[117] Canon law condemned marriages held 'in secret' as clandestine, and such marriages were apparently common in England. Some couples knew of an impediment and doubtless married secretly to prevent objectors from using it to stop their marriage. English and Welsh couples contracting clandestine marriages despite an impediment, whether they knew of it or not, required a dispensation and absolution from the penitentiary, since they incurred excommunication for this breach of canon law.[118] In addition couples who consciously married in the prohibited degrees faced a financial penalty, initially payable to the papal chamber but by Pius II's pontificate to the datary.[119] Couples who sought dispensations from the third degree were also liable to such a 'composition' with the datary even if they had married unaware of this impediment.[120]

Supplicants seeking marriage dispensations normally also asked the penitentiary to recognise their offspring as legitimate. They requested this for future issue and, if their marriage already existed, for any existing issue. This was necessary because their marriage was technically invalid without the dispensation and therefore its existing offspring might be considered illegitimate. According to canon law the papacy did not normally legitimise children in regard to temporal matters, but it was prepared to declare children legitimate when it validated the parents' marriage by dispensation.[121] Legitimacy in temporal matters usually implied the right to inherit property and titles; secular law, especially in England and Wales, denied this right to illegitimate children. Hence supplicants for marriage dispensations were motivated at least partly by a desire to safeguard their offspring's inheritance rights.

The second section in the penitentiary registers was usually headed *De diversis formis*, which, as its title implies, comprised miscellaneous requests. These are so

---

[115] *Clementinae* 4.un.un.
[116] As noted by the canonist Johannes Andreae (d. 1348), *Glossa ordinaria* on *Clementinae* 4.un.un. v. *eos*, v. *obtinere*; *Constitutiones Clementis Quinti* . . . (Venice, 1567), 132a, 133a.
[117] Fourth Lateran Council (1215), canon 51 (*Liber extra* 4.3.3).
[118] E.g., **1917, 2773, 2832, 2863**, etc. This excommunication was apparently imposed by local ecclesiastical legislation not canon law (see **2773**).
[119] See above at n. 51. Cf. **24**, where the couple had to make a donation to their parish church and fast weekly as penance.
[120] E.g., **1795, 1833** (future marriage), etc.
[121] Especially clandestine marriages (*Liber extra* 4.17.9); the Fourth Lateran Council (see above n. 117) declared children of such marriages illegitimate. Innocent III's decretal 'Per venerabilem' stated that temporal rulers, not the pope, usually legitimated children in temporal affairs (*Liber extra* 4.17.13).

varied that it is impossible to characterise them all, but the main kinds will be described here.[122] Some of the most recurrent requests among English and Welsh supplications under this heading concern study at university.[123] This contrasts curiously with the German evidence, where such requests formed one of the smallest categories of *De diversis formis* business.[124] This peculiarity of the English and Welsh sources is even more anomalous given that it comprises some requests which did not need to be referred to the Curia but might be granted by local ordinaries. These consist of supplications from parish clergy seeking licences to study at university, normally for a period of seven years.[125] These licences released clergy from an obligation to reside in any benefices they held;[126] beneficed clergy normally also asked the penitentiary that they might still receive the fruits of their benefices while absent at university. In 1298 Pope Boniface VIII had issued the constitution 'Cum ex eo' which allowed bishops to grant precisely these favours to clergy beneficed in their dioceses.[127] In England this constitution was not applied to perpetual vicars, hence they had to turn to the Curia for such favours, but it is unclear why some rectors requested study licences from the penitentiary when they might have sought these from their ordinary; possibly the latter had denied these. 'Cum ex eo' provided a legal framework for the penitentiary's grants of study licences. It required that fitting substitutes should be appointed to replace clergy absent for study, and requests to the penitentiary for study licences often recognised this obligation.[128] It also provided that beneficed clergy might not be obliged to take holy orders while on study leave,[129] except for the subdiaconate, to which they had to be promoted within a year. Few English or Welsh supplicants for study licences explicitly sought immunity from ordination beyond the subdiaconate,[130] but the penitentiary sometimes granted study licences on condition that supplicants were ordained as subdeacons within a year.[131] The purpose of 'Cum ex eo' was to improve the education of the parish clergy, and the approved subjects for their studies included canon law and theology, which were clearly useful for their pastoral responsibilities. Consequently many English and Welsh clergy petitioned the penitentiary for licences to study these subjects specifically.[132] However, Honorius III's constitution 'Super speculam' banned beneficed clergy as well as religious from studying civil

[122] For fuller surveys see Schmugge *et al.*, *Supplikenregister*, ch. 5; Salonen, *Penitentiary*, 119–78. What follows largely adopts Schmugge's categorisation of the subject-matter.
[123] In the subject index some 160 entries are listed under 'university' and a further 102 under (licences to study) 'canon law' (36), 'civil law' (46) and 'theology' (20). See also below at nn. 268–72.
[124] Schmugge *et al.*, *Supplikenregister*, 161–2; Salonen, *Penitentiary*, 122–3.
[125] But sometimes only five: e.g., **1383**.
[126] Imposed by the Council of Lyons II (1274), canon 13 (*Liber sextus* 1.6.14), and local ecclesiastical legislation (see **2112, 2114**, etc.).
[127] *Liber sextus* 1.6.34. See L. E. Boyle, 'The constitution "Cum ex eo" of Boniface VIII: education of parochial clergy', *Mediaeval Studies*, 24 (1962), 263–302; R. M. Haines, *Ecclesia Anglicana: Studies in the English Church of the Later Middle Ages* (Toronto, 1989), pp. 138–55.
[128] Sometimes explicitly (as **3002**) but more often implicitly by such clauses as 'dummodo dictus vicariatus debitis non fraudetur obsequiis' (in, e.g., **1399**).
[129] Otherwise required by *Liber sextus* 1.6.14 (see n. 126).
[130] E.g., **2191**.
[131] E.g., **2186, 2200**, etc.
[132] See above at n. 123.

law or medicine on pain of excommunication.[133] Clergy might be exempted from this ban and penalty on papal authority; thus it is understandable that they should have petitioned the penitentiary for licences to study these subjects;[134] almost fifty English and Welsh clergy did so in order to study civil law. These clergy included regulars as well as seculars since the ban applied to both, but religious also petitioned the penitentiary for permission to study approved subjects, and some of their supplications explicitly claimed that they did so since their superiors had refused them such permission.[135] It apparently lay outside the penitentiary's special faculties to grant requests to study civil law or for religious to study without a superior's consent, for these were approved by *Fiat de speciali et expresso*, but it might freely grant other study licences, including to religious studying with a superior's consent,[136] since it normally authorised them by *Fiat de speciali*.

Another large group of English and Welsh supplications under the heading *De diversis formis* concern issues specific to the religious life, notably apostasy.[137] Professed religious committed apostasy when they left their religious house without their superior's consent, thus breaching their vows of obedience and in the case of monks and nuns stability.[138] Since 1298 canon law had stated that apostates incurred automatic excommunication, especially if they appeared to return to the secular life by abandoning their religious habit.[139] Apostates thus normally asked the penitentiary for absolution from this sentence and their apostasy.[140] If they were men, they usually also sought a dispensation from irregularity, a canonical impediment which prevented them from receiving holy orders or exercising existing ones. In the penitentiary registers such apostates were usually already in holy orders and irregular because they had celebrated divine offices while excommunicated for apostasy (or any other reason).[141] Therefore they required a dispensation to resume exercising their orders licitly. But not all apostates wished to continue their ecclesiastical careers as religious; some petitioned the papal chancery for a dispensation to hold a benefice with cure of souls as secular priests. The penitentiary was not competent to bestow this favour, but apostates often sought it from the chancery at the same time as they asked the penitentiary for absolution.[142]

---

[133] *Liber extra* 3.50.10 (issued by Pope Honorius III in 1219).
[134] 'Cum ex eo' did not authorise bishops to grant such licences; see above at n. 123 for what follows.
[135] E.g., **2176, 2201**, etc.
[136] E.g., **526**.
[137] For fuller discussion of this material and related English and Welsh supplications under other headings, see P. D. Clarke, 'New sources for the history of the religious life: the registers of the Apostolic Penitentiary', *Monastic Research Bulletin*, 11 (2005), 1–21.
[138] See Logan.
[139] *Liber sextus* 3.2.24.
[140] See the 92 entries for 'apostasy' in the subject index.
[141] In addition religious promoted to holy orders while apostate needed a papal dispensation for their orders to be considered valid (*Liber extra* 5.9.6).
[142] Such parallel approaches to both curial offices are evident from comparing their registers: the same apostates noted in the chancery registers by Logan (56, 63–5, 134, 195, 240), for example, also occur below in **423, 626, 633, 1048, 2139**. Monks, however, might ask the penitentiary for licences to serve parish churches as chaplains with their superiors' consent and while remaining affiliated to their houses, usually on the grounds that the latter were too poor to support them: see **521, 576–7, 583, 585**.

Certainly the many apostates who visited the Curia in person must have had some other reason for doing so beyond petitioning the penitentiary for absolution, since they would not have needed this if they had not come to the Curia in the first place.¹⁴³ Thus one apostate stated that his purpose at the Curia was to accuse his abbot of various crimes (**426**).¹⁴⁴ Such grievances doubtless prompted many apostates to abandon their houses, and even to escape the religious life by becoming secular clergy. However, apostates petitioning the penitentiary rarely specified what their motives were. Regardless of these reasons, many still wished to return to the religious life and sought absolution for this purpose. Presumably some of them sought re-admission to their own houses, although few specifically said so in their supplications.¹⁴⁵ Pope Benedict XII's constitution 'Pastor bonus' (1335) provided for the reconciliation of apostates to their former houses. Others, however, preferred not to return to their original house, probably for the reasons which had driven them away. Instead they asked the penitentiary that they might change house.¹⁴⁶ Pope Innocent III's decretal 'Licet quibusdam' (1206) had provided that religious might request a papal licence to transfer to another house or order 'of equal or stricter observance'.¹⁴⁷ Even religious who were not apostates requested such licences from the penitentiary, often for reasons that might otherwise have driven them to commit apostasy.¹⁴⁸ Normally the vow of stability required monks and nuns to stay in the house where they had been professed, but this was not the only area in which the penitentiary permitted deviations from monastic regulations. It also authorised requests from religious for licences to wear linen as opposed to rough woollen habits, to be released from their daily round of offices, and to eat meat despite Benedictine restrictions on this.¹⁴⁹ These concessions were usually sought on grounds of ill health or old age.¹⁵⁰ Other more serious deviations from monastic norms also occasionally appear in penitentiary supplications, notably violations of the chastity vow.¹⁵¹ Penitentiary officials approved most of these supplications concerning the religious life, notably requests for licences to

---

¹⁴³ Admittedly Pope Benedict XII (1334–42) had authorised the cardinal penitentiary to absolve apostates if they appeared at the Curia within three months of leaving their houses (Göller, i/1. 116), but apparently not all requested absolution there in person by the fifteenth century.
¹⁴⁴ Cf. **617** and **2202**, where the supplicants reached the Curia after escaping imprisonment by their abbots. The apostate in **2137** also claimed to have left his house because of *molestias* inflicted on him there.
¹⁴⁵ **563, 634, 701, 996, 2091**. In at least one supplication the apostate had already been re-admitted and done penance for his apostasy (**422**).
¹⁴⁶ A few supplicants seeking to return to their former houses also sought transfers as an alternative, presumably in case those houses declined to re-admit them: e.g., **617, 625**, etc.
¹⁴⁷ *Liber extra* 3.31.18.
¹⁴⁸ **444, 479, 618, 2103, 2122**. Three of these supplicants explained that they no longer felt able to remain in their present houses.
¹⁴⁹ Linen: **490–1, 637, 708–9, 719, 1031**. Offices: **729, 1363, 2141**. Meat: **719, 2165** (faculty sought by abbot to dispense his monks to eat meat). Two religious also sought licences to read offices by candle-light: **637, 708**.
¹⁵⁰ Cf. **581, 852** (concerning two religious who 'retired' on health grounds).
¹⁵¹ **528** (supplicant as a cleric, before becoming a Premonstratensian, fornicated with a pregnant woman causing her to miscarry), **563** (apostate who married but then abandoned his wife), **584, 626, 857**.

deviate from monastic norms, by *Fiat de speciali*,[152] but they authorised others by *Fiat in forma*, notably requests to transfer to other houses.[153] Both kinds of approval were granted in apostasy cases without apparent distinction.

A major category of English and Welsh supplications registered under *De diversis formis* that was more directly concerned with human frailty comprised dispensations from *defectus corporis*.[154] Canon law required that candidates for ordination be physically perfect. In other words they should not have a physical defect that could impede them from celebrating mass, notably poor eyesight (which made it hard to read the mass) or deformed hands (which made holding the chalice and host difficult). Such defects gave rise to irregularity, which prohibited promotion to higher orders and ministry in existing ones. Men with physical defects accordingly needed a papal dispensation to receive and exercise orders legitimately. The penitentiary granted such dispensations largely to men with defective eyesight or hands, normally on condition that their defect was not so great that it would impede their celebrating mass or give rise to scandal. Bishops were supposed to inspect ordinands for physical defects and reject those exhibiting them, but some men with these defects were still ordained despite this requirement and sought a retrospective dispensation for their existing orders.[155] The penitentiary usually committed a request for dispensation from *defectus corporis* to the supplicant's ordinary, who was thereby authorised to grant the dispensation subject to the condition above;[156] in other words he had to examine the supplicant's defect and decide how serious it was. Penitentiary officials usually authorised such dispensations by *Fiat de speciali*, except those concerning defects of the right eye,[157] which they approved by *Fiat de speciali et expresso*, since these presumably lay outside the office's special faculties.

Supplicants usually explained physical defects as the result of natural deformity or accidental injury, often insisting in the latter case that this came about through no fault of their own; but sometimes clergy suffered deliberate physical violence, ending in their wounding, mutilation, or even death.[158] The canon 'Si quis suadente' (1139) sought to protect ecclesiastics from such assaults, imposing automatic excommunication on anyone who laid 'violent hands' on them and requiring such assailants to seek absolution in person from the Holy See.[159] Such cases feature frequently in the *De diversis formis* material and form the largest category there among supplications from Scandinavia and the German Empire, at least under

---

[152] E.g., **141, 490–1, 536, 617–18, 621, 624, 633, 637**, etc. On these faculties see Göller, i/1. 115–16.

[153] E.g., **415, 418–19, 421–2, 424–7, 429, 431, 444, 479**, etc. But transfers to another order were approved by *Fiat de speciali et expresso*, i.e., by express papal mandate, since they lay outside the office's faculties: **2122**.

[154] The subject index lists 39 examples from England and Wales under 'defect, physical'. Cf. Schmugge *et al.*, *Supplikenregister*, 143–7; Salonen, *Penitentiary*, 156.

[155] E.g., **534, 839**. But some supplicants seeking dispensations for existing orders apparently suffered the physical defect through injury after their ordination, e.g., **850, 3012**.

[156] E.g., **995**. See also Clarke 'Central authority and local powers', 436–7.

[157] E.g., **1371, 2096–7, 2105**; etc. This is hard to explain, for Schmugge *et al.*, *Supplikenregister*, 143, 144–5, argue that the left eye (the so-called *oculus canonis*) was of greater significance, as it was used to read mass.

[158] E.g., **2983** (priest mutilated losing left eye, thus left unfit to celebrate divine offices), **3090** (dispensation for defect of left hand caused by assailant).

[159] Second Lateran Council, canon 15 (C.17 q.4 c.29).

Pope Pius II.[160] But violence against clergy is a less dominant theme among English and Welsh supplications. One explanation is that in England those attacking clergy were often absolved by their bishop without reference to the Curia;[161] canon law provided that bishops might grant such absolution in cases of moderate injury.[162] Cases of serious assault were still to be referred to the Curia, and indeed these predominate among English and Welsh supplications regarding anti-clerical violence; the latter mainly concern presbytericide, or at least severe injury.[163] Some of the assailants sought absolution in person at the Curia, as 'Si quis suadente' required, and had to perform a public penance there, usually assigned by one of the minor penitentiaries.[164] Most assailants, however, did not specify in these supplications that they were present at the Curia, which suggests that they were not; in such cases the penitentiary authorised their ordinary to absolve them and require them to do penance locally, notably in those places where they had committed the offence.[165] Supplicants rarely explained what had motivated these assaults in the first place. Many claimed to have acted 'at the instigation of the devil', but this was a formulaic excuse taken from the text of 'Si quis suadente' and simply suggested in mitigation that they were not in their right mind during the attack.[166] Doubtless some had attacked in the heat of the moment, perhaps as a result of quarrels which had degenerated into brawls,[167] but others had acted with accomplices, sometimes on a superior's order, in what seem like premeditated attacks, in at least one case to exact revenge on a clerk.[168] Most English and Welsh supplicants seeking absolution from violence were laymen,[169] and their victims were clergy (except in two unusual cases).[170] This is what 'Si quis suadente' presupposed. Some

---

[160] Schmugge *et al.*, *Supplikenregister*, 98–116; Salonen, *Penitentiary*, 122, 128–38.

[161] R. H. Helmholz, '"Si quis suadente" (C.17 q.4 c.29): theory and practice', in *Proceedings of the Seventh International Congress of Medieval Canon Law*, ed. P. Linehan, Monumenta Iuris Canonici, Series C, 8 (Vatican City, 1988), 425–38, esp. 429–30. Most supplications regarding anti-clerical violence edited below were from Welsh assailants: **645, 651, 687, 698, 713, 1389, 2129–30, 2132, 2149, 2187, 2996, 3033–4, 3055, 3631, 3637**.

[162] *Liber extra* 5.39.17: the decretal 'Pervenit ad nos' of Pope Clement III (1187–91).

[163] See the 22 entries under presbytericide in the subject index; cf. also **645, 654, 2129**. Wounding of clergy features in **1385** (in a gang assault), **2130** (by a sword), **2149**; and their mutilation in **1375** (castration) and **2983** (loss of left eye).

[164] **57, 454, 2187**. See above at n. 27, and P. D. Clarke, 'Between Avignon and Rome: minor penitentiaries at the papal Curia in the thirteenth and fourteenth centuries', *Rivista di storia della chiesa in Italia*, 63 (2009), 455–510, which notes that the minor penitentiaries employed boys to guide such penitents around the Roman churches where they had to do penance.

[165] E.g., **3034** and n. Also implied in **713** and **2187**.

[166] **698, 1389, 2129, 2132, 2996, 3576, 3583, 3631, 3657**.

[167] As suggested by similar cases in the English church courts (Helmholz, '"Si quis suadente"') and by other supplications to be discussed at nn. 214–22.

[168] **687** (priest crucified by agents of a temporal lord), **698** (supplicant and *familiares*), **1375** (priest castrated by three men who found him with a woman).

[169] **1042** is an exception in the *De diversis formis* entries; the supplicant was a regular canon who had killed another cleric.

[170] **1029, 1378**. The first is perhaps erroneous since it is unclear why a lay killer required absolution unless his victim was a clerk (likewise the victim's status in **2129** is unstated but he was presumably a clerk). The second is a case of uxoricide, a grave sin that might require penitential pilgrimage to Rome; the supplicant, who ordered the murder of his wife and her suspected lover, also sought a dispensation to remarry (see n. 22 above).

English and Welsh supplicants involved in violence were clergy, and sometimes their victims were other clergy.[171] Generally their supplications belong to the category *De declaratoriis*; hence they will be treated in the discussion of that section of the penitentiary registers below. As to petitions concerning violence in the *De diversis formis* category, penitentiary officials usually approved these by either *Fiat de speciali* or *Fiat in forma*;[172] the distinction here is unclear, but both kinds of approval indicate that such cases lay within the office's normal faculties.

While absolution from anti-clerical violence had long been reserved to the papacy, other papal graces issued by the penitentiary were of more recent origin, notably the relaxation of fasting rules. Adult Christians up to the age of 60 in the medieval West were required to abstain from eating meat, eggs and dairy produce (notably butter and cheese) during Lent and other fasting periods. The papacy only began issuing licences to eat foods forbidden at such times in the fifteenth century.[173] Certainly English and Welsh supplications requesting such licences do not occur in the penitentiary registers until the 1460s. From then the penitentiary usually approved such requests by *Fiat de speciali*, which suggests that it had acquired a faculty to grant them around that time.[174] These licences were only meant to be conceded in specific circumstances, which English and Welsh supplications carefully cited in order to obtain them, especially physical infirmity,[175] old age (i.e., turning 60),[176] lack of oil or fish (foods permitted by the church authorities in fasting periods as substitutes for butter and meat respectively),[177] and poverty and hard manual work.[178] All licences allowed consumption of dairy produce on fasting days; some supplicants requested permission to eat eggs too, and others, meat, eggs and dairy produce.[179] Such licences were mostly solicited by individuals for their personal use, but some were sought by married couples, and a few for groups, including communities.[180] When the penitentiary registered such requests, it was often recorded after the *fiat*-clause approving them that the matter was left to the

---

[171] See above n. 169; cf. **696** (a priest seeking absolution and dispensation for his illicit participation in warfare).

[172] *Fiat de speciali*: **57, 629, 713, 1042, 1375, 1385, 2177**, etc. *Fiat in forma*: **645, 654, 651, 1389, 2129–30, 2132, 2149**, etc. **654** was approved by *Fiat de expresso*, probably an anomaly, and **687** by a mere *Fiat* and *sola signatura*, implying that no letter of absolution was issued but the supplication signed by a penitentiary official was proof of absolution. See Salonen, *Penitentiary*, 130–1, on the office's faculties regarding violence.

[173] Schmugge *et al.*, *Supplikenregister*, 151–7; Salonen, *Penitentiary*, 160–1. These were the so-called *Butterbriefe* later condemned by Luther.

[174] E.g., **1032** (the only one under Pius II), **1361–2, 1368, 1372**, etc.

[175] E.g., **1361, 1368, 1372**, etc. This claim was sometimes allegedly supported by medical opinion (see, e.g., **3087**).

[176] E.g., **1032, 1394–6, 2089, 3000**, etc.

[177] E.g., **1380, 2128, 2999, 3031**, etc. Often accompanied by claims that supplicants found oil 'noxious' or that it was too cold to grow oil-producing plants in regions where they lived.

[178] E.g., **3031**.

[179] In the subject index see the 13 entries under 'dairy produce' for licences permitting this alone, the 22 under 'eggs' for licences permitting both of these, and 28 under 'meat' for those permitting all three.

[180] Individuals: **1031, 1361–2, 1368–9, 1372, 1380, 1394–6**, etc. Couples: **1405, 2124, 2179–80, 2985**, etc. Groups: **2128** (deposed queen, her household and guests at her table), **2999** (priest and community), **3031** (two parishes), etc.

supplicant's conscience. This meant that penitentiary letters in response to these supplications were addressed to the supplicants, not to a commissary charged with verifying their claims and authorising their request. This seems to have been true of requests from individuals or households, but not communities, in which case the matter was apparently committed to their ordinary.[181]

Another group of supplications under the heading *De diversis formis* also sought relaxation of obligations, enshrined in oaths or vows.[182] An oath was a religious undertaking, since it was sworn in God's name or on the Bible, and those who broke oaths were considered perjurers according to canon law and thus might be tried and punished by the church courts.[183] Despite this religious aspect, perjury cases in English church courts often concerned failure to keep promises of a worldly nature, notably repayment of debts; this is also true of the English and Welsh supplications seeking absolution from oaths and perjury, though none specifically regard debt. Most of the supplicants were clergy, who might otherwise have faced perpetual suspension from their offices and benefices for perjury. Some supplicants explained why they could not fulfil their oaths.[184] While a few claimed to have sworn these at the suggestion of others,[185] none alleged that they had done so under duress, even though oaths sworn as a result of coercion or fear were invalid under canon law, and absolution from them was reserved to the papacy.[186]

By contrast a vow was a less serious form of promise than an oath, and its non-fulfilment did not technically entail perjury and associated sanctions. Vows featured in the penitentiary registers were generally promises to carry out some kind of religious devotion, notably pilgrimage, lay chastity and entry to the religious life or holy orders.[187] Those swearing them were bound by conscience to fulfil them and might fear for their salvation if they did not. The papacy reserved the absolution of vows of perpetual chastity, for entry to a religious house and pilgrimages to Rome, Compostella and Jerusalem.[188] Such absolution might be conceded in cases where some legitimate impediment prevented completion of these vows, and the penitentiary released supplicants from vows on this basis. English and Welsh supplicants cited such impediments as poverty and old age.[189] Some women asked the penitentiary for absolution from chastity vows on the grounds that they had already broken them by marrying and wished to remain married.[190]

---

[181] **3031** and n.; Clarke, 'Central authority and local powers', 421, 437.
[182] Schmugge *et al.*, *Supplikenregister*, 140–2, 157–60; Salonen, *Penitentiary*, 152–6.
[183] See the 17 entries under 'oaths' in the subject index; their promises on oath are too miscellaneous to describe here. Incidentally the supplicant in **3100** had sworn her oath on a missal.
[184] E.g., **486, 693, 3100**.
[185] E.g., **844, 2157, 3100**.
[186] *Liber extra* 2.24.8. This contrasts with German supplications regarding oaths that often cite force and fear (Schmugge *et al.*, *Supplikenregister*, 140–1). Some English supplicants were released from vows on grounds of force and fear, however, in *de declaratoriis* entries, discussed below at nn. 211–13.
[187] See the 29 entries under 'vows' in the subject index.
[188] Schmugge *et al.*, *Supplikenregister*, 157–8.
[189] E.g., **30, 855**. **1376** and **2101** refer to unspecified permanent impediments. One female supplicant had vowed as a widow to visit Rome on pilgrimage but then remarried, claiming that she was no longer free to fulfil this vow being subject to her husband's will (**35**).
[190] **29, 838, 1377**, etc. Cf. **3089** (man who vowed to become a priest but then married).

In addition or as an alternative to absolution supplicants might request commutation of their vows. This meant that the intention of the vow was changed into some other religious obligation (*in alia opera pietatis*); supplicants also cited impediments in this case to explain why they could not fulfil their original intention.[191] Some who vowed long-distance pilgrimages claimed that they lacked sufficient funds to complete the journey; therefore their vow was commuted to a shorter pilgrimage.[192] Others were impeded from fulfilling their pilgrimage vow in person but might pay a substitute to do so on their behalf.[193] Thus commutation might make use of money that supplicants would otherwise have spent in fulfilling their vows; the funds might also be converted into offerings to shrines which a would-be pilgrim had vowed to visit, and by the late fifteenth century into payments to the papal datary.[194] Even when those who vowed to go on pilgrimage to the Holy Land still intended to do so, they faced a legal impediment to fulfilling their vow: canon law restricted contacts between Christians and Muslims; Christian pilgrims visiting Jerusalem and other holy places in Muslim lands thus needed a papal licence to do so without incurring excommunication.[195] Several English and Welsh supplicants gained such licences from the penitentiary enabling them to observe pilgrimage vows to visit the Holy Land, often with a specified number of companions.[196] The supplicants comprised laity and clergy, and religious in particular requested licences for long-distance pilgrimages.[197] The penitentiary usually approved these various supplications regarding oaths, vows, and pilgrimage licences by *Fiat de speciali*, since it lay within the office's faculties to do so.[198]

Various other kinds of English and Welsh supplications also appear under *De diversis formis*, but these are less recurrent than those noted above and will not be described exhaustively here. Several concern simony.[199] In penitentiary supplications it usually involved payments to obtain benefices. Clergy implicated in simony incurred excommunication under papal rulings;[200] the latter reserved absolution to the papacy, hence clergy requested this from the penitentiary. They usually also sought dispensations either to keep benefices simoniacally acquired or from irregularity contracted by celebrating divine offices while excommunicate, or

---

[191] E.g., **29, 30, 38, 462, 855, 1376, 2101, 2095, 2196**, etc.
[192] **30, 2095**.
[193] **36, 462**.
[194] **2095, 2101, 2196**; Clarke, 'Central authority and local powers', 438. The latter case was committed to the supplicant's ordinary; another (**855**), to the minor penitentiaries since the supplicant was present in the Curia and they also had faculties to commute vows (Salonen, *Penitentiary*, 154–5).
[195] Salonen, *Penitentiary*, 167–8.
[196] **5, 31–4, 37, 476, 509, 600, 692, 695, 733, 849, 854, 856, 858, 1414, 2107, 2111, 2113, 2120, 3564–6**. Cf. **841** and **2199** (for visiting Compostella).
[197] Monks: **644, 841, 1414, 2120**; cf. **476** (friar), **600** (anchorite), **695** (regular canon). Their superiors had perhaps refused such permission and they feared incurring apostasy without it: see **625**. Secular clergy who had sworn oaths to reside in their benefices also required it: see **37**.
[198] Salonen, *Penitentiary*, 152, 154–5, 167 (on related faculties).
[199] See the 20 entries under 'simony' in the subject index; Schmugge *et al.*, *Supplikenregister*, 134–7; Salonen, *Penitentiary*, 147–8.
[200] Notably the constitutions 'Multi quidem' of Martin V (1417–31) and 'Cum detestabile scelus' of Eugenius IV (1431–47) cited in **487–8, 492**, etc.

both. Some supplicants appeared less culpable, claiming that an intermediary had helped secure their benefice and that they only suspected that simony was involved. Their requests were usually authorised by *Fiat de speciali*.[201] However, others admitted to obtaining benefices deliberately through simony or at least holding them for some time knowing of the simony.[202] The penitentiary usually approved their supplications by *Fiat de speciali et expresso* since absolution from their conscious fault presumably needed express papal approval. Their graver sin also resulted in a fine, payable initially to the vicar of St Peter's and later to the datary, since they had profited financially from their simony by receiving income from benefices acquired thus.[203]

Other clerical crimes that resulted in canonical penalties absolved by the penitentiary involved abuse of clerical office, notably celebrating mass and administering sacraments such as confession or baptism without holding priest's orders,[204] or blessing clandestine marriages (i.e., those without three readings of the banns).[205] Penitentiary officials also absolved from sentences of excommunication incurred for crimes committed mostly by laymen, notably sacrilege.[206] This meant violating sacred places, and it was a particular problem in Wales, especially in St David's diocese. Several Welsh supplicants requested absolution for sacrilege which arose from their theft of livestock from sacred places, i.e., church lands.[207] Other Welshmen sought absolution since the ordinary, primarily the bishop of St David's, had excommunicated them for non-sacrilegious theft of livestock, a felony normally punished by secular justice; this suggests co-operation between ecclesiastical and lay authorities in dealing with a local crime problem.[208]

The third section in the registers was usually headed *De declaratoriis*. It comprised, unsurprisingly, requests for *littere declaratorie*, normally to clear supplicants of potential or actual allegations that they had somehow breached canon law.[209] These supplications are the longest in the registers since they usually contain a detailed narrative. Generally it described the supplicants' involvement in situations which might occasion such allegations, but where they claimed to be innocent of wrongdoing. Much of the content is non-formulaic and appears to be in the supplicants' own words (rather than their proctors'). Each supplication, therefore, tells a different story, and they seem as miscellaneous as those under *De diversis formis*, though they are far less numerous. They usually concern one of three

---

[201] E.g., **1408, 3046, 3049, 3661**.
[202] E.g., **837, 3010, 3588**.
[203] **642, 671, 700, 711, 3010**.
[204] Subdeacons: **3054, 3080, 3669**. Deacons: **702, 2193**. Layman(!): **3066**. As in the case of simony, penitentiary officials approved requests by *Fiat de speciali* where supplicants claimed to have erred unwittingly (**702, 3066, 3669**), but by *Fiat de speciali et expresso* where they did not (**2193, 3054, 3080**). See also Salonen, *Penitentiary*, 169–70.
[205] **61, 423, 732** (also in an unconsecrated chapel; see above, n. 24). One priest had read the banns but still blessed the marriage despite an alleged impediment (**1050**).
[206] Schmugge *et al.*, *Supplikenregister*, 132–3; Salonen, *Penitentiary*, 148–50.
[207] **1068–70, 1357–60** (all St David's dioc.), **1366–7** (Welshmen in Hereford dioc.), **1373** (St David's and Bangor dioceses). Penitentiary officials approved these requests by *fiat in forma* and those in n. 208 by *Fiat de speciali* (i.e. both through the office's normal faculties).
[208] **1039** (Hereford dioc.), **1040, 1043–6** (all St David's dioc.).
[209] Schmugge *et al.*, *Supplikenregister*, 175–85. It is uncertain whether such letters were ever used to block proceedings in the church courts.

themes: runaway novices seeking freedom from the religious life; clergy involved in violence; and complicated marriage cases.

English and Welsh supplications from runaway novices, all men, generally claimed that they had been admitted to religious houses while under age.[210] The legal age for boys to begin the noviciate was 14, but these runaways mostly alleged that they had become novices under the age of 14, sometimes specifying their age on admission, in one case as young as six (**707**). Some said that they had professed below the minimum age, which was after a year's probation, thus 15 at the earliest; two alleged having done so aged 10.[211] Profession was invalid if made under age or through duress; hence many supplicants added that they had professed owing to coercion. Some held their parents responsible for their premature entry to religious houses and a few of them cited actual parental pressure. Most of those alleging forced profession blamed it on brethren of the house concerned. A few purportedly suffered beatings at the latter's hands; one even alleged that brethren had imprisoned him until he professed (**635**). Monks and friars in England were notorious for inducing under-age boys to enter their houses. A few supplicants referred to such persuasion, though not subsequent coercion; and two of them added that their parents did not know of their entry to the religious life, one even alleging that the Franciscans had moved him from their Nottingham convent to Reading to stop his parents finding out (**621**). The supplicant admitted to the religious life at six likewise alleged that he had been abducted from his parents at that age, taken to an Augustinian house, and beaten by its canons until he made profession. Emotive as such stories are, these supplications were drawn up by proctors who deliberately shaped such accounts in order to get what their clients wanted. They supplied legal devices to this end, notably the recurrent claim that the coercion of a supplicant was enough to move a 'constant man', the canonical standard which invalidated vows sworn through force and fear.[212] The aim of these supplications was to show that these runaways were not legally professed religious (their profession being under-age or coerced) and so not technically apostates. They did not request absolution from apostasy but declarations that they were not bound to the religious life and free to remain in the world, though some wished to stay there as secular priests. Two related supplications from runaway nuns did not allege profession below the minimum age (12 for girls), but one supplicant had married and sought a dispensation to remain married, while the other aspired to marry, pleading forced profession as grounds to be declared free from her religious vows.[213]

Clerical involvement in violence is an even more common theme among English and Welsh supplications under *De declaratoriis*.[214] Clergy accused of homicide and other violent crimes were meant to be tried by the church courts, and if found guilty there, the canonical penalties usually comprised deposition from ecclesiastical offices and suspension from altar service for life; in England clerks

---

[210] 621, 635, 660, 664, 669, 682, 685–6, 688–9, 703–4, 707, 716–17, 1075, 2220, 2225, 3106, 3967. On under-age profession, see Logan, 10–25.
[211] 3106, 3967.
[212] Derived from *Liber extra* 1.40.4.
[213] 3101, 3114.
[214] 53, 59, 77, 87, 118, 453, 455–6, 463, 569, 636, 643, 655, 665, 694, 696, 710, 715, 722, 1076, 1402, 1415, 1418, 1421, 1426–7, 1429, 2205, 2210, 2212–13, 2217, 2221–2, 3020, 3108–9, 3111–13, 3548, 3632, 3671, 3678, 3681–2, 3687, 3968–70.

convicted of such crimes normally also faced life-imprisonment in a bishop's gaol.[215] Clergy usually sought acquittal from criminal charges in the church courts through purgation, and their chances of success were normally high. However, since the thirteenth century clergy in England were increasingly tried first in the royal courts, which then sought to have convictions enforced in the church courts. A means for clergy involved in violence to avoid judgement and punishment was to petition the penitentiary. In some cases they sought absolution from homicide and dispensation from irregularity, usually when they admitted their guilt, though they might remain suspended from altar service.[216] But more often they asked the penitentiary for a *littera declaratoria* clearing them of homicide charges and any consequent irregularity or other canonical penalties. This favour might be granted in mitigating circumstances, notably self-defence.[217] Therefore supplications seeking this favour gave a detailed narrative in order to demonstrate these circumstances. In such cases the supplicant normally blamed the 'victim' (often a layman) for initiating the violence and stated that he had fought back 'repelling force with force' (*vim vi repellendo*). This formula was derived from Roman law, and proctors drawing up such supplications used this and other recurrent devices to show that their clients had lawfully exercised their right of self-defence. For instance, supplicants were often said to have resorted to it since they could not otherwise avoid death,[218] and to have used moderate force, by striking a single, small blow. Canon law forbade clergy to bear weapons, but they might carry a small knife, which some supplicants claimed to have used in self-defence.[219] Such violence often allegedly arose from private quarrels, sometimes between university students and local people,[220] but other supplicants were involved in more public forms of violence, notably warfare. Canon law had long banned clerical participation in warfare on pain of excommunication and other sanctions.[221] Clergy who had been in war zones therefore asked the penitentiary for absolution and dispensation or a *littera declaratoria*, even if they had allegedly not participated in fighting or killed anyone.[222] Some of them claimed in mitigation that they had been present at battles on the orders of a lay superior (i.e., not of their free will), and others, that they had only fought defensively, occasionally under siege conditions. Likewise clergy might be held responsible for judicial killings if they co-operated with secular court procedures which resulted in death sentences. Canon law forbade clergy to impose

---

[215] *Liber extra* 5.12.24, 5.25.1; L. C. Gabel, *Benefit of Clergy in England in the Later Middle Ages* (Northampton, Mass., 1929; repr. New York, 1969).

[216] E.g., **78, 87, 453, 455–6, 463, 569, 696, 715, 722, 1402**, etc. Salonen, *Penitentiary*, 129.

[217] E.g., **665, 715, 1076, 1415, 1418**, etc. Accidental killing was another, less common excuse: e.g., **463, 1426**.

[218] The constitution 'Si furiosus' of Pope Clement V (1305–14) had declared that any clerk who killed in self-defence, not being able to escape death otherwise, did not incur irregularity (*Clementinae* 5.4.un.).

[219] E.g., **1418**. *Liber extra* 3.1.2 (on bearing weapons).

[220] E.g., **665, 1415, 1421, 2221**, etc.

[221] F. Poggiaspalla, 'La chiesa e la partecipazione dei chierici alla guerra nella legislazione conciliare fino alla Decretali di Gregorio IX', *Ephemerides iuris canonici*, 15 (1959), 140–53.

[222] E.g., **77, 132, 453, 455–6, 569, 696, 710, 1429, 2212–13** (many were present at conflicts in the Hundred Years War and Wars of the Roses). Canonistic teachings on guilt implied that non-combatants might even be held responsible for killings which they aided, supported or otherwise consented to.

'sentences of blood' on pain of deposition. Clergy therefore requested absolution and dispensation or a *littera declaratoria* from the penitentiary where their actions had led to the execution of criminals or might be construed as such; in mitigation their supplications usually claimed that they had not intended this outcome.[223]

Finally, complex marriage cases feature prominently among English and Welsh supplications under *De declaratoriis*.[224] Most supplicants sought a *littera declaratoria* affirming the validity of their intended or existing marriage.[225] Their supplications usually described circumstances casting doubt on this, which often amounted to a suspected impediment, notably spiritual kinship (*cognatio spiritualis*).[226] Normally these circumstances involved convoluted familial and sexual relationships; and it is unsurprising that supplicants feared allegations of impediments arising from these.[227] Rather than seeking dispensation from possible impediments, they asked the penitentiary to declare that no such impediments existed, in order to block any attempt to prevent or dissolve their marriage on these grounds.[228] Conversely, other supplicants sought a *littera declaratoria* stating that their marriage was invalid because of such impediments, in effect annulling it without recourse to the church courts.[229] This left them free to remarry or even to return to a pre-existing marriage.[230] Some supplicants also requested absolution, notably couples who had committed adultery or even married when one or the other's spouse was still living. Confessors usually forbade such couples to marry or have further sexual relations after that spouse's death; hence they also required a dispensation if they wished to do so.[231] Advice from confessors doubtless often prompted complex marriage supplications, but the latter also suggest that widespread knowledge of canon law led couples to think that they were living in sin. Penitentiary officials usually authorised the various requests for *littere declaratorie* by *Fiat ut infra*. This normally referred to two conditions for approval, first that the request had to be checked by the auditor, an expert in canon law who advised the office on such complex cases, and second that it had to be committed, usually to the supplicants' ordinary; the latter had to verify supplicants' claims largely on the basis of witness evidence (*vocatis vocandis*) before executing their decision.[232]

The fourth and fifth sections of penitentiary registers were usually titled *De defectu natalium* and *De uberiori*, both of which concerned illegitimacy. The latter had long been an impediment to ordination. But since the late eleventh century the papacy had dispensed from the irregularity arising from defect of birth, and by the late twelfth century it increasingly conceded to bishops faculties to grant

---

[223] *Liber extra* 3.50.4, 5, 9. E.g., **78, 597, 643, 2205**.
[224] **152, 154, 517, 1416, 1420, 1422–5, 2203–4, 2206, 2208–9, 2211, 2214–16, 2219, 2224** etc. However, they barely feature among German and Scandinavian *De declaratoriis* supplications: Salonen, *Penitentiary*, 123, 287.
[225] E.g., **1416, 1422–5, 2203–4, 2208, 2209**, etc.
[226] E.g., **1416, 1425, 2204, 2208, 2209**, etc.
[227] E.g., **2208**, where a man had fornicated with his fiancée's daughter, his mother was his fiancée's godmother and his fiancée was his brother's godmother.
[228] Or, in the case of **1425**, to allow the marriage's solemnisation and consummation.
[229] E.g., **152, 154, 1420, 2206**, etc.
[230] Or, in the case of **1420**, for the man to continue a clerical career.
[231] E.g., **152, 517**, etc.
[232] See Clarke, 'Central authority and local powers', for how this worked in practice.

such dispensations.²³³ In 1298 Boniface VIII limited episcopal dispensations to allowing men of illegitimate birth to receive minor orders and a benefice without cure of souls; anything more required a papal dispensation.²³⁴ Since the thirteenth century the papacy had authorised the cardinal penitentiary to grant two main kinds of dispensation concerning illegitimacy; and the penitentiary became the chief source of these during the later Middle Ages. The first was a dispensation *in prima forma* which normally allowed men of illegitimate birth to receive holy orders and a benefice with cure of souls. The section *De defectu natalium* largely comprises requests for this favour. The second kind was *De uberiori* (or *In ampliori forma*), an extra dispensation for recipients of the first, allowing them to hold an additional benefice or benefices. English and Welsh supplications regarding illegitimacy mostly requested dispensations *in prima forma*; the few under *De uberiori* were largely from Wales, probably owing to the widespread practice there of dividing a benefice (and its revenues) between several portioners.²³⁵

Not all supplications under *De defectu natalium* requested dispensations *in prima forma* as described above. Some supplicants had already been ordained or obtained a benefice without dispensation *in prima forma*, hence they sought this retrospectively. Bishops were meant to examine those seeking ordination or admission to benefices in their dioceses for defects such as illegitimacy, but most of these supplicants had not disclosed their *defectus natalium* when examined.²³⁶ Given this conscious violation of canon law, they usually asked the penitentiary for absolution as well as dispensation. But supplicants did not require absolution if, as some alleged,²³⁷ they were ignorant of their illegitimacy when presented for ordination or benefices. The section *De defectu natalium* includes requests not only from secular clerks but also from religious. Illegitimate birth was not an impediment to entering the religious life but it was for male religious seeking ordination and for religious of both sexes seeking promotion to offices in their house or order. Thus religious petitioned the penitentiary for dispensation from illegitimacy enabling them to achieve one or other of these ambitions, notably nuns aspiring to be abbesses or prioresses.²³⁸ The various supplications regarding illegitimacy are largely formulaic but one variable detail is worth noting: the status of the supplicant's parents. In many cases both were unmarried and in some others one was single but the other married; this adds to the evidence of church court records concerning the extent of pre-marital sex and adultery in medieval society. Even more strikingly some supplications describe a parent as a member of the clergy, usually the father. Clergy in minor orders might marry and father legitimate children, but clergy in subdeacon's or higher orders might not and had to be celibate. Many supplicants explicity identify their fathers as holding one of these holy orders, notably the

---

²³³ Schmugge, *Kirche, Kinder, Karrieren*, esp. ch. 2; Salonen, *Penitentiary*, 192–203.
²³⁴ *Liber sextus* 1.11.1. For what follows see the numerous entries under 'birth, defect of' in the subject index.
²³⁵ E.g., **1141–2, 1613–14, 1616–17, 1620–6**, etc. A general preponderance of Welsh supplications regarding illegitimacy might also suggest the persistence of some native customs, notably marriages within the prohibited degrees (allegedly common in thirteenth-century Wales), which were invalid and their issue illegitimate without dispensation: see H. Pryce, *Native Law and the Church in Medieval Wales* (Oxford, 1993).
²³⁶ E.g., **727, 742, 835**, etc.
²³⁷ E.g., **475**.
²³⁸ **1100, 1470, 1496, 1503, 1594, 2234–5, 2306, 2383, 2406, 2438, 2440, 2444**, etc.

priesthood, which provides evidence of clerical violations of celibacy. Others even claimed to be children of avowedly chaste religious, including an abbess, who bore a son by a priest, and two abbots, one of whom fathered three sons who petitioned the penitentiary together.[239] Even in such extreme cases the penitentiary normally approved the supplications by *Fiat de speciali* (or *Fiat de speciali ut petitur* in the case of those under the heading *De uberiori*) since these lay within the office's 'special' faculties.

The sixth section in the penitentiary registers was usually called *De promotis et promovendis*, and it also concerned ordination.[240] Most English and Welsh supplications under this heading regarded defect of age (*defectus etatis*). Canon law required men to be 25 years old before they might receive priest's orders;[241] those ordained as priests below this age without a papal dispensation were irregular. Hence many English and Welsh men aged below 25 asked the penitentiary for a dispensation before taking priest's orders, so that they might receive these under the legal age without incurring irregularity.[242] Most were said to be aged 24,[243] and some 23.[244] Men ordained under the canonical age without having first obtained this dispensation required papal absolution as well as a dispensation permitting them to minister in their illicitly acquired orders on reaching the canonical age.[245] Absolution was required since they had incurred excommunication and other penalties by violating canon law. Pius II's constitution 'Cum ex sacrorum' (17 November 1461) notably reinforced canon law on this point, declaring that men receiving orders illicitly under age were suspended from these and incurred irregularity if they ministered in them during this suspension.[246] After this ruling appeared, supplications from men illicitly ordained under age increased, which implies that it was enforced, and indeed they normally stated whether the supplicants had been ordained before or after its promulgation.[247] Its sanctions still applied regardless of this distinction, and when the penitentiary absolved men ordained under age, it normally ordered that they should remain suspended from altar service for one or two months whether their ordination occurred before or after 'Cum ex sacrorum'.[248] English and Welsh supplications for such dispensations and absolutions were not evenly spread geographically. Under Paul II (1464–71), for instance, three quarters came from just three dioceses (York, Norwich and Lincoln).[249] The large size of these dioceses partly accounts for this, but it is an inadequate explana-

---

[239] **1518, 1545–7, 2332**.
[240] See the entries under 'age, defect of' in the subject index; Schmugge et al., *Supplikenregister*, 196–206; Salonen, *Penitentiary*, 178–92.
[241] *Clementinae* 1.6.3.
[242] Almost all asked that they might receive all holy orders below the age of 25 even though they might legally be ordained subdeacons at 18 and deacons at 20. Heads of religious houses also requested faculties to dispense specified numbers of brethren in their houses for under-age ordination as priests (e.g., **592, 1159**).
[243] E.g., **99, 101, 103, 111, 122, 124–5, 130**, etc.
[244] E.g., **304, 511, 530–1, 533, 566, 574, 579**, etc.
[245] E.g., **413–14, 461, 508**, etc.
[246] Schmugge et al., *Supplikenregister*, 202.
[247] E.g., **1162–3, 1628–31, 1634–5, 1638–41**, etc.
[248] E.g., **1153, 1162, 1628, 1630–1, 1634, 1638–9, 1641, 1643–4**, etc.
[249] Over one third of the total came from Norwich diocese and a fifth and a sixth from Lincoln and York dioceses respectively.

tion because few such requests came from the likewise extensive Coventry and Lichfield diocese under Paul II. Rather this pattern may reflect local shortages of priests. The number of clergy available for parish ministry in Lincolnshire, for example, had shrunk by the end of the fifteenth century to the extent that some churches were not served by chaplains. Absenteeism and pluralism were largely to blame for this, so under-age ordinations remedied the resulting lack of pastoral care by enabling junior clerks to benefit from the employment opportunities as parish chaplains.[250] Various other requests under *De promotis et promovendis* also sought to allow supplicants to progress in their clerical careers, notably letters dimissory permitting their ordination by any bishop even at the Curia;[251] absolutions and dispensations for those violating ordination rules, especially being promoted to holy orders without having first taken minor ones; and so on.[252] Penitentiary officials normally approved supplications under this heading by *Fiat de speciali*. But by Pius II's pontificate supplications for ordination to the priesthood at the age of 23 had to be approved by *Fiat de speciali et expresso* in line with his stricter prohibition of under-age ordination.[253]

The remaining sections of the penitentiary registers were increasingly merged under a single composite heading,[254] where supplications principally regarded confession. These predominantly requested *littere confessionales*,[255] licences to appoint a personal confessor. Since 1215 canon law had required all adult Catholics to confess their sins at least once a year at Easter to 'their own priest' (*proprio sacerdoti*).[256] The latter phrase was generally understood to mean their parish priest, but the subsequent popularity of the friars, especially as spiritual counsellors in aristocratic households, doubtless encouraged the papacy to permit the laity to choose them and other suitable priests as confessors. Indeed the letter of canon law could be interpreted more broadly such that one's 'own priest' could signify one's private chaplain. From the thirteenth century popes authorised the penitentiary to issue licences to appoint personal confessors, freeing their recipients from the obligation of confessing to their parish priest. By the mid-fifteenth century the office registered successful requests for these under the heading *De perpetuis confessionalibus*, since these licences were usually granted for life, although some were valid for shorter periods, normally five years. The penitentiary registers reflect initial high demand for these from England and Wales; the office registered over 260 English and Welsh requests for them in 1439–43.[257] However, far fewer such requests were recorded thereafter, with only 28 from England and Wales under Pius II (1458–64). It is more likely that Catholics were seeking such licences from a different source by the late fifteenth century, notably curial agents or local bishops with papal faculties to grant these in England and Wales, than that demand for

---

[250] D. M. Owen, *Church and Society in Medieval Lincolnshire* (repr. Lincoln, 1981), 134.
[251] E.g., **1143, 1146–7, 2605, 2640**, etc. Otherwise clergy normally had to be ordained by their local ordinary.
[252] E.g., **1640, 1679, 2620**, etc; cf., e.g., **2603, 2639**.
[253] E.g., **978, 1144, 1681, 1686, 1696**, etc. Salonen, *Penitentiary*, 184–5.
[254] See above at n. 78.
[255] See entries under this phrase in the subject index; Schmugge *et al.*, *Supplikenregister*, 207–13; Salonen, *Penitentiary*, 203–10.
[256] Fourth Lateran Council (1215), canon 21 (*Liber extra* 5.38.12).
[257] Clarke, 'New evidence', 29–30.

them had declined. Indeed by Innocent VIII's pontificate (1484–92) English and Welsh supplicants mostly asked the penitentiary for particular kinds of *littere confessionales*, which were presumably harder to obtain outside the Curia, especially those *in forma 'Provenit'* or *in forma 'Fervens'*. Under Alexander VI (1492–1503) almost all English and Welsh requests for *littere confessionales* sought the latter kind, which gave personal confessors special powers to absolve supplicants once in their lives from sins reserved to papal or episcopal absolution and to give them plenary remission (in other words an indulgence), at the point of death (*in mortis articulo*). Another kind of *littere confessionales*, qualified as *in forma 'Cupientes'*, was requested from the penitentiary by confessors rather than penitents.[258] These supplicants were usually parish priests, who sought faculties to absolve their parishioners from certain grave sins for a limited period, normally five years. A related group of supplications came from clergy who requested letters allowing them to grant absolution from general sentences,[259] meaning excommunication or other penalties incurred by violators of canon law, notably clerks illicitly keeping concubines. Finally English and Welsh supplications for licences for portable altars appear in the penitentiary registers from Sixtus IV's ninth pontifical year (1479–80) onwards.[260] The composite heading in the registers began referring to *altaribus portatilibus* in that year, suggesting that the pope empowered the penitentiary to grant such licences around then. Thereafter English and Welsh requests for them in the penitentiary registers rose steadily from six under Sixtus IV to 153 under Alexander VI.[261] Supplicants sought these licences to celebrate divine offices (if clergy) or have them celebrated at portable altars in suitable places, often, by Alexander VI's time, with their household present.[262] Moreover, under Alexander VI some English and Welsh supplicants even requested that offices might be held at their portable altars in circumstances which canon law did not normally allow, especially before day-break or in interdicted places. Penitentiary officials normally approved requests for ordinary *littere confessionales* and those *in forma 'Cupientes'*, *littere de sententiis generalibus* and standard licences for portable altars by *Fiat de speciali*, since these grants lay within the office's normal faculties. Other special kinds did not, notably *littere confessionales in forma 'Provenit'* and licences to celebrate before daybreak at portable altars, since requests for these favours were usually approved by *Fiat de speciali et expresso*.

THE HISTORICAL VALUE OF THE SUPPLICATIONS

This section of the Introduction is intended to provide some examples of the interest of the supplications published below to historians of the fifteenth century. We have not attempted a comprehensive discussion, but we have concentrated on four areas: clerical careers, the English universities, political marriages and aristocratic piety.

Clerical careers. The supplications published in these volumes provide new information on the careers of thousands of members of the English and Welsh clergy. One reason for this is that men of illegitimate birth who wished to pursue a clerical

---

[258] See relevant entries under 'absolution' in the subject index; Schmugge *et al.*, *Supplikenregister*, 214–17.
[259] See relevant entries under 'absolution' in the subject index.
[260] See the entries under 'portable altars' in the subject index.
[261] Clarke, 'New evidence', 27.
[262] E.g., **3775–84**, **3787–802**, etc.

career and to hold a benefice with cure of souls needed a papal dispensation. The same applied to those who wished to be ordained below the canonical age. These two categories of men, whose supplications were registered under the headings *De defectu natalium* and *De promotis et promovendis* respectively, constitute the greater proportion of the clerical supplicants in the registers. Also registered under *De defectu natalium* were supplications from those who had acquired benefices without obtaining the necessary dispensation beforehand. These supplicants sought absolution and permission to retain their benefices. Similarly under *De promotis et promovendis* were included supplications from those who had been ordained below the canonical age without the necessary dispensation. They requested absolution and permission to minister in their existing orders. The historical interest of the supplications in the sections *De defectu natalium* and *De promotis et promovendis* is enhanced by the fact that the former specified the parents' status (without, however, naming them), while the latter often gave the age of the supplicants.[263]

Many of the *De defectu* supplicants remain shadowy figures, but in some cases it seems that the approval of their supplication was the commencement of a successful ecclesiastical or academic career. Thomas Metcalf of the diocese of York in 1486 requested a dispensation to be promoted to all orders and to retain a benefice with cure of souls (**3242**). He can be identified with a fellow of Peterhouse, Cambridge, who was ordained deacon and priest two years later, became rector of Peldon in Essex, and held other benefices. In 1502 he was at the university of Ferrara and became DTh, probably of Ferrara.

One of the men who requested a dispensation to be ordained to the priesthood at the age of 23 was John Fisher, acolyte of the diocese of Lincoln, in 1490 (**3176**). This is very likely to be the future bishop of Rochester and cardinal, who was executed for his opposition to Henry VIII's divorce and later canonised. The year after supplicating in the papal penitentiary, Fisher, when aged 22 or thereabouts and a fellow of Michaelhouse, Cambridge, obtained from the papal chancery a dispensation to be promoted to the priesthood, even outside the legally appointed times, by any Catholic bishop.[264] This extension to the terms of his previous dispensation was necessary because he was obliged as a fellow of Michaelhouse to be ordained to the priesthood within a year of his election.

Illegitimate birth and being under the canonical age for promotion to orders were not the only bars to a clerical career. A physical defect was another impediment which required a papal dispensation. Supplications concerning this, which were most commonly registered in the section *De diversis formis*, invariably specify the nature of the defect and normally explain how it arose. In 1455, for instance, Edmund Woddis, acolyte of the diocese of York, requested a dispensation to be ordained to holy orders, notwithstanding the deformity in one of his eyes occasioned by an accident during his youth (**997**).

Both clergy and laity frequently applied to the papal penitentiary to obtain what can be described as spiritual favours, for example, licences to choose a private confessor or to have a portable altar. The papal penitentiary issued the latter

---

[263] We see no reason to follow the view put forward in *Humanism, Reform and the Reformation: The Career of Bishop John Fisher*, ed. B. Bradshaw and E. Duffy (Cambridge, 1989), 235, that the age specified was a 'bureaucratic convention'.
[264] *CPL*, xv, no. 739 (14 June 1491).

licence only from the pontificate of Sixtus IV onwards.²⁶⁵ One of the beneficiaries was William Smith, who requested this grace as dean of St Stephen's chapel, Westminster (**3390**). He later became bishop of Coventry and Lichfield, and he was co-founder of Brasenose College, Oxford. Another beneficiary was Pietro Carmeliano in 1491 (**3398**). He described himself as secretary of Henry VII (and he held the same office under Henry VIII). He had arrived in England in 1481–2 and was employed by the printers Theoderic Rood and William Caxton. The most prominent ecclesiastic in these volumes to have obtained the licence was Christopher Bainbridge (**3936**). He supplicated as archdeacon of Surrey, one of the many offices and benefices that he held prior to his provision to the see of Durham in 1507. He was translated to York the following year and created a cardinal in 1511. He was Henry VIII's orator at the Roman Curia from 1509 until his death in 1514.

The registers of the papal penitentiary must be used in conjunction with the registers of papal letters in the Vatican Archives (the Lateran and Vatican Registers). These are available for the fifteenth and early sixteenth centuries in the *Calendar of Papal Letters*. Countless footnotes to the entries published below illustrate this point. However, the different series of registers are not always in harmony. John Southam, archdeacon of Oxford, in 1440 petitioned the penitentiary for absolution from excommunication and dispensation from irregularity (**417**). He feared that he had incurred these penalties as a result of visiting his archdeaconry through a deputy and exacting dues from it. Yet he also stated his belief that he had an apostolic dispensation permitting him to do these things, having sent an envoy to the Curia to obtain one. He was indeed the beneficiary of such a dispensation, granted three years previously.²⁶⁶ It is therefore unclear why he feared that he had incurred excommunication and irregularity. Possibly the dispensation never reached Southam, or it was found for some reason to be defective.

Doctrinal questions rarely feature in the supplications, but a notable exception is a supplication from John Jekyn, vicar of Send in Surrey. He had formed the heretical opinion that it was better to observe the Old Testament than the New and wished to go to a place 'ut secundum ritum Iudeorum viveret' (**1384**). Having seen the error of his ways, he requested absolution and a dispensation from irregularity.²⁶⁷

The English universities. Many of the clergy who appear as supplicants in these volumes had a university career. Honorius III's constitution 'Super speculam' of 1219 (*Liber extra* 3.50.10) extended Alexander III's prohibition on religious studying civil law to certain categories of the secular clergy and to all those in priest's orders.²⁶⁸ Accordingly any priest wishing to study civil law at a university needed a papal dispensation, and requests for such dispensations occur frequently in the penitentiary registers. One supplicant was Ieuan Manavon, priest of the diocese of St Asaph, in 1442. He requested a dispensation to study civil law in any univer-

---

²⁶⁵ The earliest licence below is **2764**. See Clarke, 'New evidence', 26–7. The supplications concerning portable altars from the pontificate of Paul II in *RPG*, v (e.g., no. 1179), are different in character

²⁶⁶ *CPL*, viii. 636.

²⁶⁷ There is no trace of this case in *The Apostolic See and the Jews: Documents 1464–1521*, ed. S. Simonsohn (Toronto, 1990).

²⁶⁸ See S. Kuttner, 'Papst Honorius III. und das Studium des Zivilrechts', in his *Gratian and the Schools of Law* (London, 1983), ch. 10 (with addenda on pp. 43–7).

sity for up to seven years and to receive the doctorate of civil law there (**564**). Three days later, he obtained in the chancery the conferment of the office of notary public by apostolic authority. Here too his status as a priest was problematic, since as a rule the office was only bestowed upon those in minor orders. For this reason no doubt he was permitted to exercise the office only 'in pious and ecclesiastical causes'.[269] Thomas Langton, priest of the diocese of Durham and a future bishop, requested a licence to study canon and civil law (**1379**). He seems to have undertaken these studies in Italy, first at Padua and then at Bologna, where he became a doctor of canon law in 1473. Another priest who wished to study civil law, Hugh Tapton, vicar of Greasley (Notts.), is already known as a Cambridge *alumnus* from A. B. Emden's *Biographical Register*, but without any mention there of his interest in civil law.[270]

A different type of supplication concerning university careers comes from perpetual vicars who wished to study at a university while receiving the fruits of their benefices. Boniface VIII's constitution 'Cum ex eo' of 1298 (*Liber Sextus* 1.6.34) modified the requirement that anyone appointed to a parish church had to be ordained to the priesthood within a year and to reside in that church. It permitted bishops to licence holders of churches to receive their fruits for up to seven years while studying; nor were they obliged to be ordained beyond the subdiaconate.[271] However, in England this constitution was not applied to perpetual vicars, who needed a papal dispensation in order to do the same. Thomas Goodwyn, perpetual vicar of Elmdon (Essex), for instance, requested a dispensation to study canon law or theology for seven years (**2092**). Sometimes rectors also requested such licences, even though under the terms of 'Cum ex eo' they could presumably have obtained them from the ordinary.[272]

Supplications requesting permission to study civil law or to receive the fruits of ecclesiastical benefices while studying provide additional information for the entries in Emden's invaluable *Biographical Register*, although one cannot assume that every supplicant who expressed the wish to study at university actually did so. Other supplications provide details of university clerks who do not appear in Emden at all. Robert Pecok, subdeacon of the diocese of London, for instance, was involved in a fight while studying at the university of Cambridge, as a result of which one of the participants died. He requested a declaration that he had not thereby incurred irregularity and could be ordained to deacon's and priest's orders (**516**). Richard Pennert and Morgan ap Iolyn, clerks of the diocese of Bangor, requested comparable declarations as a result of incidents when they were studying at Oxford (**665, 1421**).

There are some supplications which throw light on the institutional history of the English universities, although they are much less common than those which concern the careers of individuals. A series of supplications from the pontificate

---

[269] *CPL*, ix. 323.
[270] See **570**; *BRUC*, 576.
[271] See L. E. Boyle, 'The constitution "Cum ex eo"'; P. N. R. Zutshi, 'Some inedited papal documents relating to the university of Cambridge in the fourteenth century', *Archivum Historiae Pontificiae*, 26 (1988), 393–409; L. Schmugge, 'Boyle and Boniface: *Cum ex eo*-dispensations in the fifteenth century', in *Omnia disce: Medieval Studies in Memory of Leonard Boyle, O.P.*, ed. A. J. Duggan, J. Greatrex and B. Bolton (Aldershot, 2005), 61–9.
[272] E.g., **2093, 2109**.

of Alexander VI concerning Gonville Hall, Cambridge, may serve as an example. In 1501 the warden and fellows were finding the college statutes issued by William Bateman, bishop of Norwich, burdensome. They requested dispensation from the requirement to say the 'Ave Maria' while genuflecting, a reduction in the number of disputations in which they had to engage, that the warden should have to observe only the original statutes of the foundation, that they might alienate the less useful books and replace them with more suitable ones, and absent themselves from the college in time of plague. When there was no plague, only a half or a third should be required to reside in college as long as their number did not exceed twelve. Among their other requests, they wished to be able to lease the fruits of benefices appropriated to the college and of their own benefices (**3675**). This last request was repeated later in the year in a supplication in which the warden and scholars also desired to depute each year two graduates who would preach to the clergy and people throughout England (**3679**). There was also a requirement in Bateman's statutes that no fellow of the college should ever be involved in legal proceedings against the bishop, church or chapter of Norwich. Walter Stubbe, as a fellow of the college, had sworn an oath to this effect and requested a relaxation of his oath (**3685**).

Political marriages. Although the penitentiary registers suggest that many couples of lower social status requested marriage dispensations from the bureau,[273] they also record such requests from some aristocratic supplicants concerning marriages of major political significance.[274] The registers thus comprise sources valuable not only for religious, social and cultural history, as several studies indicate, but also for political and diplomatic history. Indeed this edition contains evidence for the dispensation of four English royal marriages. Three were so politically sensitive that the supplications did not explicitly identify the high-profile couples involved, doubtless in order to avoid attracting too much attention at the Curia, for there were powerful opponents to these unions.

The earliest of the four marriages is a case in point. In November 1467 the cardinal penitentiary Filippo Calandrini approved a supplication from Charles of Burgundy, Cambrai diocese, and Margaret, daughter of the late Richard, York diocese, intending to marry in the third and fourth degrees of consanguinity (**1250**).[275] These supplicants can be identified as Charles the Bold, duke of Burgundy, and Margaret, daughter of Richard, duke of York, and sister of the English king Edward IV. Their enregistered supplication hardly makes this explicit, not even styling them *nobiles*, as those of higher status, including gentry, were routinely designated in the penitentiary registers. Doubtless, this reflected the wording of their original supplication, and the couple had good reasons for wanting to conceal their identity. Their planned marriage was highly controversial at both an international and domestic political level. In late 1465 or early 1466 Charles, then count of Charolais, had first proposed the marriage when he sent an agent Guillaume de Cluny to Edward IV for this purpose. He doubt-

---

[273] See above at nn. 99–100.
[274] For a fuller treatment of this subject, see P. D. Clarke, 'English royal marriages and the papal penitentiary in the fifteenth century', *English Historical Review*, 120 (2005), 1014–29.
[275] Given this combination of degrees they required a dispensation and *littera declaratoria* so that their marriage might be deemed valid and its future issue legitimate; see above at nn. 109–11.

less intended it to cement a diplomatic alliance with England in order to protect Burgundy against likely French attack.[276] On 22 March 1466 Edward responded by sending an embassy, including the earl of Warwick, to treat concerning the marriage. No agreement was then reached, and it has been argued that Warwick conceived a dislike for Charles, preferring an alliance with France; Edward charged the same embassy with discussing a truce or peace treaty with the king of France, Louis XI. And by February 1467 Louis, fearing an alliance between England and Burgundy, was offering French suitors for Margaret's hand. Edward played a double game, continuing his diplomatic contacts with Charles while allowing Warwick to carry on negotiations with Louis XI. Louis apparently sought through Warwick an alliance with Edward IV in order to invade Burgundy and divide its territory between them.[277] But by May 1467 he learned that Charles and Edward were negotiating the Anglo-Burgundian marriage alliance in secret, and Charles's succession as duke of Burgundy on his father's death (15 June 1467) lent fresh impetus to these dealings. Edward then moved quickly towards an alliance with Burgundy: on 20 September he sent an embassy to finalise the marriage details; his sister's public consent to the union was obtained on 1 October; and later that month Charles despatched a messenger to Rome for the marriage dispensation, clearly that approved by the cardinal penitentiary and dated 24 November 1467. French opposition to his marriage plans doubtless explains why Charles and his fiancée were so prosaically identified in their supplication; apparently they did not want it to stand out from the many similar requests handled in that busy curial office. Louis XI was not resigned to the marriage despite the marriage treaty finally being agreed between England and Burgundy on 16 February 1468 and ratified by Edward on 14 March. The treaty required Charles to obtain a further dispensation, apparently in response to doubts raised by the papal legate in England about the existing one; the latter did not cover all impediments to the marriage. By April Louis XI had sent an agent Olivier le Roux to the Curia to plead against the dispensation.[278] These French machinations and Edward's difficulties in raising the generous dowry stipulated by the treaty delayed the wedding, due to take place on 4 May, but not for long. The required dispensation was issued on 17 May.[279] It covered the third and fourth degrees of consanguinity *and* affinity (the previous dispensation had omitted to refer to affinity). It was granted at Westminster by Stefano di Trenti, papal *orator* in England, under faculties that Trenti had received from Pope Paul II on being appointed the latter's envoy to the English court in 1466. Doubtless Charles and Edward considered it safer and more convenient to approach Trenti for the dispensation than the Curia, where French influence worked against them. Charles's wedding to Margaret of York went ahead on 3 July 1468 at Damme near Bruges.

---

[276] On the marriage negotiations and political context see J. Calmette, 'Le mariage de Charles le Téméraire et de Marguerite d'Yorck', *Annales de Bourgogne*, 1 (1929), 194–214; R. Vaughan, *Charles the Bold. The Last Valois Duke of Burgundy* (London, 1973), 45–53; C. D. Ross, *Edward IV* (Berkeley, 1974), 107–12.
[277] *CSP Milan*, i. 119.
[278] *CSP Milan*, i. 122–3. Louis also solicited Neapolitan and Milanese support for this strategem.
[279] It survives as an original letter in the Burgundian ducal archive at Lille and is edited by Clarke, 'English Royal Marriages', 1027–9.

The second royal marriage was in some sense a political consequence of the first. Edward IV had duped and alienated the French king and earl of Warwick in his underhand pursuit of the Burgundian alliance. Warwick was so disaffected by 1470 that he led a revolt against Edward and on its failure fled to France. This gave Louis XI the chance to realise a plan which he had apparently considered as early as May 1467, that Warwick should back Henry VI's restoration to the English throne. Warwick's support had been decisive to Edward's seizure of power from Henry in 1461. Louis's plan therefore implied for Warwick an extraordinary reversal of allegiance and a difficult reconciliation with Henry's court in exile. Our second marriage was meant to seal this improbable alliance and facilitate the court's restoration: the union of Anne Neville, Warwick's younger daughter, and Henry's heir, Prince Edward of Wales.[280] Following tense negotiations encouraged by Louis XI, Warwick and the exiled court agreed to the union on 22 June 1470 at Angers. The prince's mother Margaret of Anjou consented to his marriage on 15 July but reluctantly, perhaps because of Warwick's former betrayal of her husband and her consequent distrust of the earl.[281] Prince Edward and Anne were betrothed on 25 July at Angers Cathedral but apparently not married, since a dispensation was needed; they were related in the fourth degree of consanguinity through their common great-grandfather, John of Gaunt, duke of Lancaster. Louis XI initially tried to obtain the required dispensation within France, but it was eventually granted by the penitentiary with the date 17 August 1470 in response to as many as three different supplications (**1336–7**). These describe the couple as *nobiles* (and Anne as *domicella*) but do not specify their exact status, rather like Charles the Bold's supplication, and again doubtless because of the political sensitivity of the marriage alliance. Confusingly, the first of our three supplications refers to a proposed marriage, the other two to an existing one which the couple had contracted knowing of their impediment of consanguinity.[282] The second supplication also sought legitimation of the marriage's future *and* existing issue, but the third of its future issue alone. In fact the couple probably did not marry until 13 December 1470, at Amboise. Hence it seems that those who initiated these supplications, possibly agents of Louis XI at the Curia, sought several dispensations in order to cover a range of eventualities, including the unlikely existence of offspring.[283] Doubtless they knew of Louis XI's pressure for a swift marriage and that any dispensation which did not exactly fit the couple's circumstances was invalid. In any case the penitentiary apparently approved all three supplications with the same date.[284] However, the eventual marriage was to be as short-lived as the political ambitions it served. Warwick's overthrow of Edward IV in October 1470 was reversed in six months; Edward returned from exile in March 1471 with Burgundian support,

[280] See *ODNB*, ii. 180, xvii. 804; Ross, *Edward IV*, 147.
[281] Margaret was acting head of the exiled court since Henry VI remained in Edward IV's custody in England.
[282] The second and third supplications seek absolution as well as a dispensation since the couple had consciously violated canon law, therefore the *Fiat*-clause approving the second (but oddly not the third) also required them to make a composition with the datary; see above at nn. 50–1, 119–20.
[283] The late chairman of the Society's Council, Prof. Jeff Denton, indeed observed that they seem to have entered a 'fantasy world'.
[284] **1336** lacks a *fiat*-clause but probably through scribal omission since it is dated, which suggests that it was approved.

guaranteed by the marriage that had caused Warwick to change sides, and in his conclusive victory at Tewkesbury on 4 May 1471 Prince Edward was killed.

This left Anne Neville a widow, and she was captured after the battle. Edward IV's forces had slain her father too, which also made her a potentially wealthy heiress and thus an attractive catch for a suitor on the winning side. She passed into the custody of her brother-in-law and Edward IV's brother George, duke of Clarence. He tried to prevent her re-marriage since he did not wish to share the extensive Warwick inheritance, to which he had a claim through his wife, Anne's elder sister Isabel.[285] When he learned that his brother Richard, duke of Gloucester, wished to marry Anne, he apparently concealed her as a kitchen-maid in London, but Richard discovered her and placed her in sanctuary at St Martin-le-Grand.[286] The subsequent quarrel between the royal dukes required the king's intervention, and Edward IV persuaded Clarence to agree to their brother's marriage to Anne by February 1472. This was the occasion for our third marriage dispensation. On 22 April 1472 the cardinal penitentiary Filippo Calandrini authorised a dispensation for Richard and Anne to marry in the third and fourth degrees of affinity (**1824**).[287] Their supplication requesting this explicitly identifies Richard as duke of Gloucester but prosaically describes his fiancée as Anne Neville of York diocese;[288] he evidently saw no need to conceal his identity since political controversy over the marriage had largely ceased by this time, unlike in the previous two cases. The dispensation from the penitentiary did not, however, cover all impediments to their marriage, which also included the second and third degrees of consanguinity and first degree of affinity (because of their siblings' marriage). Dispensations were certainly available from these impediments, but no evidence has yet been found that they secured a further dispensation.[289] The couple married in any case, perhaps soon after receiving the penitentiary's decision; older historians give 12 July 1472 as the date of their marriage but on uncertain authority. They had certainly married by May 1474, when

---

[285] See M. Hicks, 'Descent, Partition and Extinction: the Warwick inheritance', *Historical Research*, 52 (1979), 116–28; C. D. Ross, *Richard III* (London, 1981), 28–9; *Glamorgan County History*, iii, ed. T. B. Pugh (Cardiff, 1971), 200, 687.

[286] *The Crowland Chronicle Continuations: 1459–1486*, ed. N. Pronay and J. Cox ([Stroud], 1986), 130–3.

[287] He also approved the *littera declaratoria* required for marriage in this combination of degrees; see above at nn. 109–11.

[288] Supplications usually give a supplicant's diocese of origin; Richard was said to be of Lincoln diocese since he was born there at Fotheringay, but Anne was born in Worcester diocese at Warwick. She was said to be of York diocese here probably since the Neville estates assigned to Richard by 25 March 1472 mainly lay in Yorkshire; her father's earldom of Salisbury had passed to Clarence by then, which is probably why she was no longer said to be of Salisbury diocese as in **1336–7**.

[289] The penitentiary might dispense from the second and third degrees (see above at nn. 105–8), and fifteenth-century popes, notably Martin V, were prepared to allow dispensations from the first degree of affinity; J. J. Scarisbrick, *Henry VIII* (London, 1968), 177. Possibly the further dispensation required by Richard and Anne was issued by a local papal agent, as for Charles the Bold; such dispensations are notoriously hard to locate. Hicks and Ross (see n. 285) went too far in assuming the marriage was not dispensed at all (cf. C. S. L. Davies, 'Bishop John Morton, the Holy See, and the accession of Henry VII', *English Historical Review*, 102 (1987), 2–30, at p. 20) though Hicks recently amended this view: *Anne Neville: Queen to Richard III* (repr. Stroud, 2007), 133–4.

a parliamentary act arranged the division of the Warwick estates between the dukes of Clarence and Gloucester.[290]

Gloucester was to make even greater gains when he seized power as Richard III shortly after his brother Edward IV died in 1483. He declared Edward's marriage to Elizabeth Woodville invalid and thus its issue illegitimate and debarred from inheriting the throne. He took into his custody Elizabeth Woodville, her two sons and eldest daughter Elizabeth. Plots to overturn Richard's usurpation gathered pace after news spread in August 1483 that his nephews had died as his prisoners, allegedly murdered on his orders. A focus for these conspiracies was a rival claimant to the throne, Henry, son of Edmund Tudor, earl of Richmond; his cause was promoted by his mother Margaret Beaufort. She secured Elizabeth Woodville's support for Henry by promising that he would marry one of her daughters when he deposed Richard and became king. On Christmas Day 1483 Henry, then in exile in Brittany, swore in the presence of other English refugees to marry the dowager queen's daughter Elizabeth.[291] This oath gave rise to our final case, for Henry and Elizabeth required a dispensation. On 27 March 1484 the penitentiary granted one so that they might marry in the double fourth degree of consanguinity (**2080**).[292] In their enregistered request for this, they are described in the same opaque fashion as the first two couples, being called Henry Richmond (so called after his father's title) and Elizabeth Plantagenet. Admittedly hers was a name long associated with the English royal family, but it is questionable that it would have attracted much attention in an office mainly employing Italians. The couple were not identified more explicitly doubtless owing to the need to maintain secrecy about their marriage plan, for Richard III would have opposed it and Elizabeth was his prisoner. After Henry invaded England in 1485 and Richard was killed by his forces at Bosworth, he was proclaimed king as Henry VII on 31 October but he did not immediately marry Elizabeth and came under pressure at his first parliament to fulfil his oath. Although the lack of a dispensation was apparently not the problem, the one authorised by the penitentiary was possibly defective, as the couple secured another from the papal legate James of Imola on 16 January 1486 and married two days later. The second dispensation released them from the same impediment as the first, but a third dispensation granted by Pope Innocent VIII on 2 March 1486 also referred to a possible impediment of the fourth degree of affinity.[293]

For all four of these English royal marriages the dispensations obtained from the penitentiary were legally and politically important. Without them the marriages would have been invalid, and their validity was essential to the political and dynastic alliances which they were designed to reinforce. These unions also faced political opponents who might exploit the lack of an appropriate dispensation, as Louis XI did in the case of Charles the Bold's marriage. In addition, the supplicants sought these dispensations to ensure that the issue of their marriages were recognised as legitimate, crucial for their offspring's inheritance rights and for dynastic continuity, especially during the Wars of the Roses, when the throne

---

[290] *Rotuli Parliamentorum* (London, 1783), vi. 100–1.
[291] See R. L. Storey, *The Reign of Henry VII* (London, 1968), 54–62; S. B. Chrimes, *Henry VII* (London, 1972), 19–49, 330–1; Davies, 'Bishop John Morton'.
[292] This apparently removes ground for speculation that Morton solicited their dispensation on his visit to Rome in early 1485; Davies, 'Bishop John Morton', 14.
[293] *CPL*, xiv. 1–2, 14–27.

changed hands several times between rival dynasties; Richard III indeed displaced his nephews as heirs to the throne on the basis of their parents' allegedly invalid marriage. These supplicants may also have had pious motives for seeking these dispensations, but they solicited them largely because canon law required this and out of political expediency.

Aristocratic piety. Recent research on the late-medieval English Church has focused increasingly on lay, notably noble and gentry, piety. One reason for this is a preoccupation in the historiography with the origins of the English Reformation. Older 'Protestant' historians traced these to the allegedly corrupt state of the pre-Reformation Church, concluding that its reform was inevitable. But revisionist historians have challenged this view by examining lay attitudes to late-medieval religion and finding much evidence to show that the pre-Reformation Church was popular with most of the laity. This makes the English Reformation much harder to explain, for, even if we conclude that it was largely imposed from above, it is hard to reconcile the fact that nobles and gentry voted for it in the parliaments of the 1530s with their apparent commitment to 'traditional' religion, which they continued to demonstrate, notably by founding chantry chapels, until the eve of the English Reformation. Colin Richmond tried to resolve this conundrum by arguing that a split between 'elite' and 'popular' religion emerged in late-medieval England and this led the way to the Reformation. He described the religion of the social elite as 'privatised'; late-medieval gentry were retreating from the parish church into their private chapels and 'redefining' their religion, which they imposed on others at the Reformation.[294] Most historians have found this unconvincing. Christine Carpenter considered it 'political suicide' for English gentry to have withdrawn from communal religion as they reaffirmed their authority over local communities through their presence at church.[295] Eamon Duffy has emphasised the gentry's involvement in communal religion, expressed through their gifts to parish churches and leadership of projects to rebuild and beautify these, and he has rejected a distinction between 'elite' and 'popular' religion.[296] Most of the evidence underlying this historiographical debate has been drawn from local records. But papal sources are relevant too, not least because they illustrate lay attitudes to papal authority on the eve of Henry VIII's break with Rome. In the fifteenth century, Thomson argued, Englishmen largely regarded the Curia as 'the well of grace', a source of dispensations and other papal graces. Thomson's evidence for this mainly came from the papal chancery's registers of letters, which, as he admitted, supply an incomplete picture of English contacts with Rome.[297]

---

[294] C. Richmond, 'Religion and the fifteenth-century English gentleman', in *The Church, Politics and Patronage in the Fifteenth Century*, ed. R. B. Dobson (Gloucester, 1984), 193–208, esp. 197–9. For more references to related historiography and fuller discussion of what follows see Clarke, 'New evidence'.

[295] C. Carpenter, 'The religion of the gentry of fifteenth-century England', in *England in the Fifteenth Century: Proceedings of the 1986 Harlaxton Symposium*, ed. D. Williams (Woodbridge, 1987), 53–74, esp. 63–6.

[296] E. Duffy, *The Stripping of the Altars: Traditional Religion in England 1400–1580* (New Haven and London, 1992), esp. 121–3; 'Elite and popular religion: the Book of Hours and lay piety in the later Middle Ages', in *Elite and Popular Religion*, ed. K. Cooper and J. Gregory, Studies in Church History, 42 (2006), 140–61, esp. 151–7.

[297] J. A. F. Thomson, '"The well of grace": Englishmen and Rome in the fifteenth century', in *The Church*, ed. Dobson, 99–114.

The penitentiary registers significantly supplement this evidence, particularly as regards lay piety. In the fifteenth century the chancery was petitioned principally by the clergy, especially for graces that the penitentiary was not competent to grant, such as dispensations for plurality. For certain favours available from both offices it seems that the laity increasingly turned to the penitentiary, perhaps since it charged lower fees than the chancery. Thomson noted a decline in English petitioners, for example, asking the chancery for licences for portable altars in the fifteenth century; in fact they were able to obtain these from the penitentiary by the late 1470s.[298] Indeed requests for these licences together with other supplications in the penitentiary registers provide important new evidence for lay, especially noble and gentry, piety in late medieval England and Wales.

The licences allowed their recipients to hear divine offices celebrated at their portable altar almost anywhere. Under Pope Innocent VIII (1484–92) the penitentiary registered 30 supplications from England and Wales seeking this favour, of which 11 came from laity identified as *nobiles* and 17 from clergy. This aristocratic dominance among the lay petitioners might appear to confirm the Richmond thesis of the fifteenth-century gentry 'privatising' their religion, but in fact aristocratic petitioners had been soliciting such licences from the papal chancery since at least the thirteenth century. Moreover, by Alexander VI's time (1492–1503) many of those seeking such licences from the penitentiary did not intend to be lone participants in services at their portable altar but wished to include their household in these, since they asked that such services might be held for them *and* their domestic familiars. Such rituals were not necessarily an alternative to collective worship in parish churches but rather supplementary to it; under Alexander VI some petitions from England and Wales asked for rites to be held at portable altars in specific circumstances where this was not allowed in parish churches, notably before daybreak or under an interdict. Finally, nobles and gentry formed a smaller proportion of the English and Welsh petitioners requesting licences for portable altars under Alexander VI: of 153 such requests approved by the penitentiary under Alexander VI, 38 came from *nobiles*, 33 from other laity and 82 from clergy.[299]

A related group of petitions registered under the heading *De diversis formis* sought licences to hold divine offices in chapels. Such licences were usually available from the ordinary, and requests for them are indeed rare in the penitentiary registers. Perhaps the petitioners' bishops had refused them, so that the petitioners turned to the penitentiary instead, or more likely they sought a special licence reserved to papal authority; some indeed asked for chapels to be licensed with a portable altar. Six of the English and Welsh petitions were from *nobiles* seeking licences for chapels on their estates (all but one with a portable altar), but a further four came from local communities, most justifying their need for chapels by their remoteness from the parish church.[300] Again this evidence is not cogent support for Richmond's thesis. Admittedly, whether petitioners sought licences for portable altars, private

---

[298] See above at nn. 260–2; Thomson, 'Englishmen and Rome', 109–10.
[299] The *nobiles* comprise some historically significant figures at **3826** (Richard, duke of York, or more likely the imposter Perkin Warbeck who claimed to be him), **3833** (Edward Courtenay, earl of Devon, his son William and their wives), and **3951** (Edward Stafford, duke of Buckingham).
[300] Communities: **1392, 3578, 3659, 3684**. *Nobiles*: **2126, 2994, 3591, 3633, 3646, 3688**. Two petitions also came from non-noble couples: **1392, 3642**.

chapels or both, they normally requested that offices might be celebrated there by their own or another priest; and noble and gentry households often had private chaplains by the fifteenth century. But while Richmond saw this as another sign of 'privatised' religion, Carpenter pointed out that episcopal licences for private chapels still required minimum attendance at the parish church,[301] and the penitentiary indeed licensed chapels on condition that this did not prejudice the parish church.

Nevertheless private chaplains might be an alternative to parish priests in one respect: as confessors. The penitentiary registers comprise many requests for *littere confessionales* allowing petitioners to appoint a personal confessor other than their parish priest.[302] Such requests were especially numerous from England and Wales in the registers for 1439–43, totalling over 260, but barely a quarter of these came from *nobiles*, comprising 37 couples and 30 individuals; of the remaining petitioners over 100 were other laity and the rest clergy. *Nobiles* counted for an even smaller share of subsequent requests for *littere confessionales* from England and Wales, although these also declined as a whole: a mere four out of 37 under Calixtus III (1455–8) and three out of 28 in Pius II's pontificate (1458–64).[303] This contrasts with requests to have a portable altar where nobles and gentry usually outnumber other lay petitioners, and it confirms that a desire to observe religious devotions outside the parish church, notably confession, was far from exclusive to the aristocracy.

There are other petitions in the penitentiary registers that are indicative of aristocratic piety but by no means unique to nobles and gentry. They mostly comprise requests for relaxation of vows or other religious obligations so that these might be left unfulfilled with a clear conscience. In at least one case a noblewoman had undertaken and broken such an obligation publicly and her petition was doubtless motivated by a desire to avoid scandal,[304] but others might have approached the penitentiary out of more personal feelings of guilt, especially if their obligation was not public knowledge. For example, when the penitentiary issued licences relaxing the Church's fasting rules, its registers often recorded that the matter was left to the petitioner's conscience, thus stressing personal responsibility.[305] Fifteen English and Welsh requests to the penitentiary for these licences came from *nobiles* (five couples and eleven individuals). The latter even include Margaret of Anjou, 'formerly queen of England but now held captive in the hands of her enemies' (**2128**),[306] who sought

---

[301] C. Carpenter, 'Religion', in *Gentry Culture in Late Medieval England*, ed. R. Radulescu and A. Truelove (Manchester, 2005), 134–50, at 143.

[302] See above at nn. 255–6.

[303] See statistics in Clarke, 'New evidence', 35. The *nobiles* again include prominent figures at **891** (Eleanor, duchess of Norfolk), **1173** (Anne, countess of Warwick), **1190** (William Herbert and his wife Joan), **1738** (Anne, duchess of Buckingham, and her husband Walter Blount, lord Mountjoy), **1753** (George, duke of Clarence; Richard Neville, earl of Warwick, and his wife Anne), **3821** (Jasper Tudor, duke of Bedford, and his wife Catherine Woodville), and **3826** (see n. 299 above).

[304] Public vow: **3100**. Private vow (albeit non-aristocratic): **1428**.

[305] See above at nn. 28–9.

[306] Similar requests by prominent *nobiles* also occur at **1361–2** (Margaret, widowed countess of Salisbury; William Herbert), **1372** (Eleanor, widowed duchess of Somerset), **2124** (John de Mowbray, duke of Norfolk, and his wife Elizabeth), **2985** (John Blount, lord Mountjoy, and his wife), **3001** (William Stanley, lord chamberlain), **3567** (Sir John Dinham, lord Dinham, and his wife), and **3656** (Elizabeth, wife of Viscount Beaumont, and her mother Eleanor Wyndham).

this favour for herself, her household, and others eating at her table. But these grants were not limited to the aristocracy, and other laity obtained them.[307] Likewise lay women who had sworn chastity vows asked the penitentiary to release them from these so that they might marry or remain married in good conscience. Only one is identified as noble, the one noted above who had made her vow publicly; she did so at her dying husband's request, and the penitentiary perhaps considered it to have been sworn under pressure and so invalid. Pious motives did not entirely influence women seeking absolution from such vows, or even swearing them in the first place. The noble widow in this case remarried largely out of financial necessity since her husband left her with considerable debts (and absolution from her vow was crucial for the legitimacy of her second marriage and its issue), while another widow made her vow in order to avoid such pressure to remarry from noble suitors; the penitentiary declared it invalid because it was allegedly sworn out of fear (**3115**).[308] Two English nobles likewise petitioned the penitentiary for commutation of pilgrimage vows from mixed motives.[309] A noblewoman claimed that she had married since making her vow to visit Rome and her husband now forbade her to go. Lord Dinham was probably also impeded from visiting Compostella by worldly reasons, his duties as Richard III's lieutenant at Calais, doubtless heightened by Henry Tudor's flight to Brittany and the threat of French support for his claim to Richard's throne. Dinham's vow nonetheless weighed so much on his conscience that he petitioned the penitentiary at least twice about it, perhaps because the office's original commutation did not reach him. Five other English noblemen supplicated the penitentiary out of still purer spiritual motives, seeking licences to visit the Holy Land. All but one sought this both for themselves and several travelling companions. One of these noblemen was John Tiptoft, earl of Worcester, who in 1457 obtained the penitentiary's licence to go on pilgrimage with six others; he certainly used it, sailing to the Holy Land from Venice in 1458.[310]

As this example shows, nobles and other petitioners would hardly have expended money and effort to secure such favours from the penitentiary if they did not intend to use them. Though we may question their motives, they clearly valued the Curia as a 'well of grace', as Thomson has argued. Many of these favours admittedly allowed them to practise a more private kind of religion, notably *littere confessionales*. But, while the Curia issued these in response to the supplications submitted, it would hardly have licensed behaviour likely to result in religious deviancy. Rather it wished to encourage more personal piety, not less. Many supplicants soliciting such favours were clergy, and the Curia in extending these favours to the laity was in a sense encouraging them to be more like the clergy. A desire to pursue this more personal kind of religious devotion was expressed also at the lower levels of lay society, as non-noble petitioners show, subverting any distinction between elite and popular piety. And such piety could manifest itself in collective forms too. Indeed 'private' and communal forms of devotion were not opposed or completely distinct but part of the spectrum of religious experience in fifteenth-century England and Wales.

---

[307] See above at nn. 173–81.
[308] See above at nn. 187–98 on vows and pilgrimage licences (below).
[309] **35**, **2196–7**, **2984**.
[310] **31**, **692** (no companions specified), **854**, **858** (Tiptoft), **2107**. That all were men is hardly surprising given the social restrictions on married women making long-distance pilgrimages.

EDITORIAL METHOD

The purpose of these volumes is to publish all the supplications from England and Wales (in other words, from the ecclesiastical provinces of Canterbury and York) in the registers of the penitentiary, beginning with the earliest register and covering all the extant registers until the death of Alexander VI (1503). Where we have noticed supplicants with English names residing outside England and Wales, we have included their supplications, but we cannot claim to have searched systematically or thoroughly for such supplications. In a few cases, largely as a result of errors in spelling place-names or of omissions, there is some doubt about whether the supplicants were from England or Wales: such entries are normally also included, with an explanatory footnote. In most of the registers, the supplications are grouped together by subjects and appear in roughly chronological order. We have retained the original arrangement by subjects, but within these we have placed the supplications in strict chronological order. For the earlier registers (Alexander V to Calixtus III) we have treated each register separately. From Pius II (when a more systematic division of the supplications by subject is apparent) we have grouped together all the registers of each pope under the subject heading.

The large number of supplications contained in these volumes has made it impracticable to print them all *in extenso*. We have adopted the practice of printing the longer and more complex supplications and calendaring the shorter, more formulaic ones. Since these methods differ significantly, they are described separately below.

Supplications printed in full. After the entry number, we provide, in English and in italics, the *data topographica*, the date according to the modern calendar, and a summary of the contents of the supplication (the summaries have been compiled according to similar conventions to those of the calendared entries, for which see below). This is followed by the register number and folio number. The text of the supplication is printed in Roman type, beginning with the dating clause as it appears in the margin. The transcription of the supplications' text preserves the spelling of the manuscript, while punctuation and capitalisation are editorial. The response of the papal penitentiary which approved the supplication (beginning with *Fiat*) is given on a new line. This was copied from the original supplication, where the response is in the hand of the cardinal penitentiary, the *regens* of the papal penitentiary or, more rarely, another official.[1] Supplications registered under the heading *De declaratoriis* were normally referred by the signatory to the auditor of the papal penitentiary (beginning with the words *Videat eam*). This too is recorded on a new line. The line following this gives the auditor's decision, which was almost invariably to commit the matter to the supplicant's ordinary for investigation (*Committatur ordinario...*).

Calendared supplications. The entry number is followed by the date according to the modern calendar, which derives from the date given in the margin of the register. The summary of the supplication seeks not only to convey its contents but also to follow its wording as closely as possible. However, in order to shorten the

---

[1] All these figures are listed in the Index of Curial Personnel under 'Signatories'.

entries, cross-references are given to supplications with identical or almost identical wording. Latin Christian names and patronymics are given in their English equivalents, but unusual or doubtful Christian names are retained and printed in italics. Surnames and place-names are given as they appear in the registers, but with place-names the modern form (where it has been established) is given first. Personal names in supplications from the Welsh dioceses (Bangor, Llandaff, St Davids, St Asaph) are treated in the same way *mutatis mutandis* as the English. The standard Welsh forms of Christian names and patronymics are used (thus, Ieuan, not Iohannes or John);[2] but rare, eccentric or possibly incorrect forms are preserved and printed in italics. The surnames of Welshmen are left as they appear in the registers, even though they often take the form of Christian names. For those unfamiliar with Welsh names, it may be useful to bear in mind that *ap* means son and *verch* daughter (something the register scribes often seem to have failed to grasp). After the summary, we give the response of the papal penitentiary, in italics and in Latin. This seeks to reproduce the exact wording of the registers. The calendar entries end with the register and folio numbers.

Groups of supplications. Supplications are often grouped together in the registers in such a way that two or more supplications received a single signature, in the form *Fiat de speciali pro utrisque* or *Fiat de speciali pro omnibus* or a similar expression. The purpose was doubtless merely to save the registers' scribes the trouble of having to copy out the signatory's approval for all the supplications, and it is likely that each original supplication received a signature. Nonetheless, the grouping may also reflect the fact that supplications deriving from the same individual, family, place or diocese were submitted together. If a supplication in the present volumes forms part of a group of supplications, this is indicated in the form 'approved with **1610**' or by a similar expression. It may be that some of the supplications in the group do not concern England or Wales and therefore do not appear in this publication. In these cases, the form of words used is 'approved with **1611** and other supplications not from England or Wales' or something similar.

Additional matter. It is clear that the entries in the registers of supplications of the papal penitentiary are more or less abbreviated versions of the original supplications. The scribes frequently omitted standard words or phrases or referred back to earlier entries for fuller wording, the omissions sometimes being indicated by *etc.* or *ut supra*, but sometimes not being indicated at all. We have sought to reconstruct the missing sections of these supplications, supplying additional matter from common form or from other register entries and placing it within square brackets. This applies to both the edited and the calendared entries.

Annotation. The footnotes provide identifications of the people mentioned in the supplications and (mainly brief) biographical notes about them. Where this seemed necessary and possible, places, institutions and events are identified. We also refer to documentation in episcopal registers concerning the execution of letters of the papal penitentiary issued in response to the supplications.

---

[2] We have used the 'approved names' contained in A. D. M. Barrell, *The Dyffryn Clwyd Court Roll Database: a Manual for Users* (Aberystwyth, [1996]), 31–53, except that we have preferred Dafydd to Dd.

SYMBOLS

[ ]		*In entries printed in full:*
		Text supplied by the editors *or* foliation (Roman)
		Editorial comments on text *or* headings supplied by the editors (italics)
		In calendared entries:
		Text supplied by the editors in English (Roman)
		Latin text supplied by the editors (italics)
[. . .]		Missing text
( )		*After the main text in entries printed in full*:
		General editorial comments (italics)
		In calendared entries:
		Original wording (italics) *or* editorial comments (Roman)
\ /		Text added above the writing line
/ \		Text added on the line
\\ //		Text added in the margin

ALEXANDER V
(1409–1410)

Super defectu natalium in forma ampliori

Supplicationes signate per dominum meum cardinalem Aniciensem maiorem penitentiarium de mense Aprilis pontificatus domini Alexandri pape V anno primo

1. [*Bologna*],[1] *8 April 1410. Thomas Cullurdonse, priest, perpetual vicar of Diseworth, Lincoln dioc.,[2] was granted a papal dispensation from defect of birth to be promoted to all orders and obtain a benefice even with cure of souls. He seeks a further dispensation to hold an additional benefice.* Reg. 1, fol. 8r.

[Bononie], vi idus Aprilis. Supplicatur sanctitati vestre pro parte devoti vestri Thome Cullurdonse, presbiteri, perpetui vicarii parrochialis ecclesie de Diseworch', Lincolniensis diocesis, cum quo alias ut non obstante defectu natalium quem patitur de soluto[3] genitus et soluta et ad omnes ordines promoveri et beneficium ecclesiasticum etiam si curam habeat animarum [obtinere posset] auctoritate apostolica fuit dispensatum, cuius vigore dispensationis se fecit ad omnes ordines promoveri et dictam parrochialem ecclesiam est assecutus, quatinus sibi uberiorem gratiam facientes ut unum aliud ecclesiasticum beneficium una cum dicta vicaria posset licite retinere, ex causa permutationis vel alias simul vel successive totiens quotiens sibi videbitur dimittere et loco dimissi vel dimissorum aliud vel alia similia [*sic*] simile vel dissimile aut similia vel dissimilia beneficium seu beneficia, unum vel duo dumtaxat alia beneficia ecclesiastica, etiam si eorum alterum curatum, libere recipere et licite retinere valeat dignemini misericorditer dispensare, Pictavensi consilio non obstante et aliis constitutionibus et statutis etc. in contrarium editis non obstantibus quibuscumque de gratia speciali.

Fiat de speciali ad unum et quod semel.

2. [*Bologna*], *8 April 1410. William Wyreton, priest and rector of Crosby upon Eden, Carlisle dioc., was granted a papal dispensation from defect of birth to be promoted to the priesthood and obtain a benefice. He seeks a further dispensation to hold an additional benefice.* Reg. 1, fol. 8r.

[Bononie], vi idus Aprilis. Exponitur sanctitati vestre pro parte Wilhelmi Wyreton, presbiteri et rectoris parrochialis ecclesie de Crosby, Karlyolensis diocesis, de soluto geniti et soluta, cum quo alias per sedem apostolicam erat dispensatum quod dicto defectu non obstante ad sacerdotium promoveri posset et beneficium ecclesiasticum obtinere etc. ut in forma. Quare humiliter supplicari fecit eidem sanctitati vestre quatinus cum dicto beneficio et [*sic*] unum aliud beneficium simile vel dissimile etiam si sit canonicatus

---

[1] The pope's location at this time is indicated in C. Eubel, 'Das Itinerar der Päpste zur Zeit des grossen Schismas', *Historisches Jahrbuch*, 16 (1895), 545–64, at 563.

[2] Thomas 'Cullurdoufe' was granted a further dispensation on 27 November 1413 to hold as many as six compatible benefices (*CPL*, vi. 416). He had by then exchanged Diseworth (Leics.) for the rectory of Church Lawton (Cheshire), Coventry and Lichfield dioc.

[3] He was granted a similar dispensation at **3**, but there he is said to be the son of a priest and not simply of an unmarried man. It was also said in 1413 that he was the son of a priest.

et prebenda in ecclesia collegiata obtinere illudque licite permutare valeat de gratia vestra uberiori gratiose concedere dignemini.

Fiat de speciali et quod semel.

3. [*Bologna*], *22 April 1410. Thomas Cullurdonse, priest, perpetual vicar of Diseworth, Lincoln dioc., was granted a papal dispensation from defect of birth to be promoted to all orders and obtain a benefice even with cure of souls. He seeks a further dispensation to hold an additional compatible benefice.*[4] Reg. 1, fol. 10v.

[Bononie], x kal. Maii. Supplicatur sanctitati vestre pro parte devoti vestri oratoris Thome Cullurdonse, presbiteri, perpetui vicarii parochialis ecclesie de Diseworth', Lincolniensis diocesis, cum quo alias super defectu natalium quem patitur de presbitero genitus et soluta ut ipso non obstante defectu ad omnes ordines possit promoveri et beneficium ecclesiasticum etiam si curam habeat animarum [obtinere] auctoritate apostolica fuit dispensatum, cuius vigore dispensationis se fecit ad omnes ordines promoveri et dictam parrochialem ecclesiam est assecutus, quatinus sibi uberiorem gratiam facientes ut unum aliud beneficium ecclesiasticum compatabile recipere et una cum dicta parrochiali ecclesia licite retinere valeat ipsaque beneficia obtenta et obtinenda ex causa permutationis vel alias simul vel successive totiens quotiens sibi placuerit dimittere et loco dimissi vel dimissorum aliud vel alia beneficium seu beneficia ecclesiasticum seu ecclesiastica similia vel dissimilia invicem compatibilia etiam si alterum ipsorum curatum fuerit libere recipere et licite retinere valeat cum eodem T. dignemini misericorditer dispensare, dicto defectu, constitutionibus etc. [in contrarium editis] non obstantibus quibuscumque, de gratia speciali.

Fiat de speciali et quod semel.

4. [*Bologna*], *26 April 1410. John Clerk, priest and perpetual vicar of Hunston, Chichester dioc.,*[5] *was granted a dispensation from defect of birth to be promoted to all holy orders and obtain a benefice even with cure of souls. He seeks a further dispensation to hold an additional compatible benefice.* Reg. 1, fol. 11r.

[Bononie], vi kal. Maii. Exponitur sanctitati vestre pro parte devoti vestri Iohannis Clerk, presbiteri ac perpetui vicarii de Hunston, ~~Cis~~ Cicestrensis diocesis, quod olim ut non obstante defectu natalium quem patitur de soluto genitus et soluta secum erat dispensatum ad omnes sacros ordines promoveri et [quod] beneficium ecclesiasticum etiam si curam habeat animarum obtinere possit, vigore cuius dispensationis dictam vicariam canonice est assecutus. Quare humiliter supplicatur eidem sanctitati vestre pro parte ipsius exponentis quatinus secum ut unacum dicta parrochiali ecclesia unum aliud beneficium ecclesiasticum compatibile etiam in ecclesia cathedrali

---

[4] Cf. **1**.
[5] He obtained a further dispensation, in which he was described as the son of a priest, not simply an unmarried man, on 8 June 1411 to hold three compatible benefices (*CPL*, vi. 300). The register of the then bishop of Chichester contains several references to someone of this name: *Reg. Rede*, 91, 246, 252, 262.

citra canonicatum et prebendam etc. ipsamque parrochialem ecclesiam et beneficium obtinendum ex causa permutationis vel alias simul vel successive dimittere seu permutare etc. ut in forma concedere [*recte* dispensare] dignemini de gratia speciali.

Fiat de speciali et quod semel.

De sancto sepulcro et sancto Iacobo /et commutatione votorum\

Supplicationes signate per dominum cardinalem Aniciensem maiorem penitentiarium de mense Maii [recte *Aprilis*] *pontificatus domini Alexandri pape V anno primo.*

5. [*Bologna*], *1 April 1410. Thomas Corpp, chaplain, seeks a licence to go on pilgrimage to the Holy Sepulchre and other holy places with six companions.* Reg. 1, fol. 61r.

[Bononie], kal. Aprilis. Supplicatur sanctitati vestre pro parte devoti vestri Thome Corpp, capellani, quatinus licentiam ad peregrinandum et visitandum sacrum sepulcrum et alia loca sacra inter [in]fideles situata unacum vi personis, quas duxerit nominandas, eidem concedere dignemini de gratia speciali.

Fiat de speciali.

JOHN XXIII*
(1410–1415)

*John XXIII (Baldassare Cossa) is today generally regarded as an anti-pope.

De officio procuratoris

Procuratores per dominos cardinales Aquilegensem et Aniciensem. Supplicationes signate per reverendum in Christo patrem et dominum A. episcopum Portuensem, cardinalem Aquilegensem, in Bononia. Registrate per me Ia. de Parma prout infra pontificatus d. Io. pape xxiii anno primo.

6. [*Bologna*], *11 June 1410. Major Parys, priest, Exeter dioc., requests appointment as a proctor of the penitentiary.*[1] Reg. 1, fol. 2r.

> iii id. Iunii. Supplicat sanctitati vestre devotus vester orator Maior Parys, presbiter Exoniensis diocesis, qui aliquandiu Bononie et Oxonie in iure canonico studuit, quatinus eundem in procuratorem sacre penitentiarie eiusdem sanctitatis vestre litterarum cum omnibus honoribus, oneribus et emolimentis [*sic*] consuetis recipere ac aliorum procuratorum dicte sacre penitentiarie consortio favorabiliter aggregare dignemini, ita quod idem M. omnibus privilegiis, libertatitbus, et immunitatibus uti et gaudere possit et debeat quibus dicti procuratores hactenus usi sunt et quomodolibet gaudebunt in futurum, cum non obstantibus et clausulis opportunis.

> Fiat de speciali iii id. Iunii pontificatus sanctissimi domini nostri domini Iohannis divina providentia pape xxiii A.

> Examinetur per correctores A.

> Videtur michi quod in litteratura est satis sufficiens et audivit iura canonica et bene intelligit et scribit, in practica autem nichil. P. Textoris.

> Videtur michi B. de Monticulo idem quod dictus magister P. Textoris, practica autem addiscet per usum.

Super defectu natalium in ampliori forma

De uberiori per dominum Aquilegensem. Supplicationes signate per reverendum in Christo patrem et dominum d. A. episcopum Portuensem cardinalem Aquilegensem maiorem penitentiarium. Registrate per me Ia. de Parma in Bononia pontificatus domini Iohannis xxiii pape anno primo.

7. [*Bologna*], *5 June 1410. John Henton, priest, rector of a moiety of Okeford Shilling (or Shillingstone) parish church, Salisbury dioc.,*[2] *was granted a papal dispensation from defect of*

---

[1] This entry is also printed in Sohn, *Deutsche Prokuratoren*, 308. Parys was granted a licence to have a portable altar on 8 April 1413 (*CPL*, vi. 346). He may be the Paris charged for rent of a room in University College, Oxford, in 1410–11 and 1413–14 (*BRUO*, iii. 1424). He exchanged his benefice of Pillaton (Cornwall) with Reginald Lange, rector of Portlemouth (Devon), on 9 February 1425 (*Reg. Lacy*, ed. Hingeston-Randolph, i. 31). He had been bequeathed 20s. by his friend John de Lydeford, archdeacon of Totnes (ibid., 389). He was dead by July 1438 (ibid., i. 235).

[2] He exchanged this moiety for the vicarage of Downton (Wilts.), Salisbury dioc., on 15 July 1416 (*Reg. Hallum*, no. 627). See also ibid., nos. 815, 1033.

birth to be promoted to all orders and obtain a benefice even with cure of souls. He seeks a further dispensation to hold an additional compatible benefice. Reg. 1, fol. 21v.

[Bononie], nonas Iunii. Exponitur sanctitati vestre ex parte Iohannis Henton', presbiteri, rectoris medietatis parrochialis ecclesie Ocfordshyllyng' Saresbirensis diocesis, quod olim secum ut non obstante defectu natalium quem patitur de presbitero genitus et soluta ad omnes ordines promoveri et beneficium ecclesiasticum etiam si curam habeat animarum obtinere posset auctoritate apostolica fuit misericorditer dispensatum, cuius dispensationis vigore ad omnes ordines rite promotus dictam parrochialem ecclesiam canonice est assecutus, de cuius fructibus commode sustentari non potest. Supplicatur igitur eidem sanctitati vestre pro parte dicti exponentis quatinus ut unum aliud beneficium compatibile unacum dicta ecclesia, si sibi alias canonice conferatur, libere recipere et licite retinere valeat, illaque simul vel successive ex causa permutationis vel alias semel tantum dimittere et loco sic dimissi vel dimissorum aliud vel alia duo tantum beneficia ecclesiastica similia vel dissimilia, etiam si alterum eorum curatum fuerit, libere recipere et insimul retinere valeat dicto defectu non obstante [et] constitutionibus apostolicis in contrarium editis quibuscumque [non obstantibus] cum eodem dignemini misericorditer dispensare de uberiori dono de gratia speciali.

Fiat de speciali ut petitur A.

8. [*Bologna*], *19 June 1410. William Hyde, priest, vicar of Sandon, Coventry and Lichfield dioc., was granted a papal dispensation from defect of birth to be promoted to all orders and obtain a benefice even with cure of souls. He seeks a further dispensation to hold an additional compatible benefice.* Reg. 1, fol. 23v.

[Bononie], xiii kal. Iulii. Supplicatur ex parte Willelmi Hyde, presbiteri Conventrensis et Lichefeldensis diocesis, cum quo alias ut non obstante defectu natalium quem patitur de soluto genitus et soluta ad omnes posset ordines promoveri et beneficium ecclesiasticum etiam si curatum fuerit libere recipere et licite retinere possit [*sic*] extitit auctoritate apostolica misericorditer dispensatum, [cuius dispensationis] vigore se fecit alias tamen rite ad omnes ordines promoveri et vicariam ecclesie de Sondon' dicte diocesis extitit canonice assecutus que beneficium existit, et quia de fructibus eiusdem commode sustentari non vale[a]t, quare supplicatur quatinus secum ut unum aliud beneficium ecclesiasticum dicto beneficio compatibile libere recipere et licite retinere [valeat], illaque beneficia ex causa permutationis vel alias simul vel successive semel tantum dimittere et loco dimissi vel dimissorum aliud vel alia simile vel dissimile aut similia vel dissimilia duo tantum beneficia ecclesiastica invicem compatibilia libere recipere et licite retinere valeat dignemini misericorditer dispensare de gratia vestra speciali.

Fiat de speciali ut petitur semel A.

John XXIII (1410–1415)

Supplicationes de ampliori signate per dominum cardinalem Aniciensem de mense Octobris

9. [*Bologna*], *11 October 1410. John Spenser, MA, priest, vicar of Tilney, Norwich dioc.*,[3] *was granted a papal dispensation from defect of birth to be promoted to all holy orders and obtain a benefice even with cure of souls. He seeks a further dispensation to hold an additional compatible benefice.* Reg. 1, fol. 45r.

[Bononie], v id. Octobris. Supplicatur sanctitati vestre pro parte devoti vestri Iohannis Spenser, presbiteri, \magistri in artibus/, vicarii parrochialis ecclesie de Tilney Norwicensis diocesis, cum quo alias ut non obstante defectu natalium quem patitur de soluto genitus et soluta ad omnes sacros ordines promoveri et beneficium ecclesiasticum etiam si curam haberet animarum obtinere posset apostolica fuit auctoritate dispensatum, cuius dispensationis vigore ad omnes ordines rite promotus dictam perpetuam vicariam pacifice assecutus [extitit], ~~cumque dictus exponens de fructibus ipsius vicarie comode sustentari non potest~~ \\cuius fructus etc. [redditus et proventus] lx marcas sterlingorum annuatim non excedunt//, quatinus secum ut ~~non~~ unum aliud beneficium ecclesiasticum compatibile unacum dicta perpetua vicaria, si sibi alias canonice conferatur, recipere illaque simul vel successive ex causa permutationis vel alias semel tantum dimittere et loco dimissi vel dimissorum aliud vel alia simile vel dissimile similia vel dissimilia duo dumtaxat beneficia ecclesiastica retinere libere et licite valeat de uberiori dono gratie dignemini misericorditer dispensare dicto defectu etc. [non obstante] de gratia speciali.

Fiat de speciali ad unum aliud et quod semel.

10. [*Bologna*], *13 November 1410. John Treyngoeff, priest, perpetual vicar of St Michael's Mount in Cornwall, Exeter dioc., was granted a papal dispensation from defect of birth to be promoted to all orders and obtain a benefice even with cure of souls. He seeks a further dispensation to hold an additional compatible benefice.* Reg. 1, fol. 47v.

[Bononie], id. Novembris. Exponitur sanctitati vestre pro parte Iohannis Treyngoeff, presbiteri, perpetui vicarii parrochialis ecclesie Sancti Montis in Cornubia Exoniensis diocesis, quod olim secum ut non obstante defectu natalium quem patitur de presbitero genitus et soluta ad omnes posset ordines promoveri et beneficium ecclesiasticum obtinere etiam si curam habeat animarum auctoritate apostolica fuit dispensatum, cuius dispensationis vigore se fecit ad dictos ordines promoveri et dictam vicariam, cuius fructus, redditus et proventus viginti marcharum sterlingorum secundum communem extimationem valorem annuum non excedunt, fuit assecutus. Supplicatur eidem sanctitati vestre quatinus sibi gratiam uberiorem facientes et [*recte* ut] unum aliud beneficium ecclesiasticum cum dicta vicaria recipere et retinere, huiusmodique vicariam et beneficium ecclesiasticum sic

---

[3] A fellow of Pembroke College, Cambridge, probably in 1390, by when he was BA, he was MA by 1409. He was in priest's orders by 1390, when he was included in a university roll for papal graces as petitioner for a benefice. He was presented by his college as vicar of Tilney All Saints (Norf.) on 6 November 1409, which he retained until his death in 1424 (*BRUC*, i. 544).

obtinendum vel [ex causa] permutationis vel alias simul vel successive semel tantum dimittere et loco sic dimissi vel dimissorum aliud vel alia duo tantum beneficia ecclesiastica invicem compatibilia recipere et retinere valeat dignemini misericorditer dispensare, dicto deffectu, constitutionibus apostolicis ac statutis et consuetudinibus ecclesiarum ac aliis in contrarium editis non obstantibus, de gratia speciali.

[Fiat de speciali] ad unum aliud et quod semel B.

11. [*Bologna*], *16 November 1410. Nicholas Wythe, priest, perpetual vicar of Bishop's Nympton, Exeter dioc., kept silent about his defect of birth when promoted to minor orders and then obtained a papal dispensation to minister in those orders, be promoted to all, even holy orders, and obtain a benefice even with cure of souls. He seeks a further dispensation to hold an additional compatible benefice.* Reg. 1, fol. 47v.

[Bononie], xvi kal. Decembris. Beatissime pater, alias cum devoto vestro Nicolao Wythe, presbitero, perpetuo vicario parrochialis ecclesie de Byschopis Nymyt alias Nymytton Episcopi Exoniensis diocesis, super deffectu natalium quem patitur de presbitero genitus et soluta ac quod tacito de dicto deffectu alias tamen rite promoveri se fecit ad omnes minores ordines ut in ipsis susceptis ordinibus ministrare et ad omnes etiam sacros ordines promoveri et beneficium ecclesiasticum etiam si curam haberet animarum obtinere posset extitit auctoritate apostolica dispensatum, cuius dispensationis vigore ad omnes sacros ordines rite promotus perpetuam vicariam ecclesie de Byschopis Nymyt alias Nymytton Episcopi dicte diocesis sibi collatam fuit assecutus, quare supplicat humiliter eidem sanctitati Nicholaus predictus quatinus secum ut unum aliud beneficium ecclesiasticum cum eadem vicaria compatibile recipere necnon vicariam et beneficium huiusmodi permutare valeat de gratia uberiori misericorditer dispensare dignemini, deffectu predicto, constitutionibus apostolicis ac aliis in contrarium facientibus non obstantibus quibuscumque, cum clausulis oportunis, de [gratia] speciali.

Fiat de speciali et quod semel B.

12. [*Bologna*], *24 November 1410. William Tregodok, priest, perpetual vicar of Walkhampton, Exeter dioc.,*[4] *was granted a papal dispensation from defect of birth to be promoted to all orders and obtain a benefice even with cure of souls. He seeks a further dispensation to hold an additional compatible benefice.* Reg. 1, fol. 49r.

[Bononie], viii kal. Decembris. Exponitur sanctitati vestre pro parte oratoris vestri Wilhelmi Tregodok', presbiteri, perpetui vicarii ecclesie parrochialis de Walkampton' Exoniensis diocesis, quod dudum cum eo ut non obstante defectu natalium quem patitur de soluto genitus et soluta ad omnes posset ordines promoveri et beneficium ecclesiasticum etiam si curam haberet animarum obtinere extitit auctoritate apostolica misericorditer dispensatum,

---

[4] For William Tregodok's institution to Walkhampton (Devon), see *Reg. Stafford (Exeter)*, ii. 88. Presumably the William Tregodek ordained by the bishop of Exeter as a subdeacon on 22 December 1397 (ibid., 450).

cuius dispensationis vigore se fecit rite ad omnes etiam sacros ordines promoveri et dictam perpetuam vicariam parrochialis ecclesie de Walkampton' dicte diocesis, cuius fructus etc. [redditus et proventus] xx marcharum sterlingorum valorem annuum secundum communem extimationem non excedunt, sibi collatam fuit assecutus etc. Quare humiliter supplicatur eidem sanctitati pro parte dicti Willelmi ut una cum dicta vicaria unum aliud beneficium ecclesiasticum eidem vicarie compatibile, etiam si canonicatus et prebenda in collegiata ecclesia fuerit, obtinere ipsamque vicariam ac beneficium obtinendum simul aut aut [sic] successive permutare valeat secum dispensari de gratia ampliori misericorditer concedere dignemini, constitutionibus apostolicis etc. [ac statutis et consuetudinibus ecclesiarum ac aliis in contrarium editis] non obstantibus quibuscumque.

Fiat de speciali ad unum aliud et quod semel.

De mense Decembris per dominum Aniciensem

13. [*Bologna*], *4 December 1410. William Benyngworth, priest, Lincoln dioc., was granted a papal dispensation from defect of birth to be promoted to all, even holy orders and obtain a benefice even with cure of souls. He seeks a further dispensation to hold an additional compatible benefice.* Reg. 1, fol. 50r.

[Bononie], ii nonas Decembris. Exponitur sanctitati vestre pro parte devoti vestri Willemi Benyngworth', presbiteri Lincolniensis diocesis, cum quo alias ut non obstante defectu natalium quem patitur de presbitero genitus et soluta ad omnes etiam sacros ordines promoveri ac beneficium ecclesiasticum etiam si curam haberet animarum obtinere posset apostolica fuit auctoritate dispensatum, cuius dispensationis vigore ad omnes ordines rite promotus parrochialem ecclesiam de Bramiswell[5] dicte diocesis, cuius fructus etc. [redditus et proventus] xxv marcharum sterlingorum communis extimationis valorem annuum non excedunt, pacifice est assecutus. Supplicatur igitur pro parte dicti exponentis quatinus secum ut unum aliud beneficium ecclesiasticum compatibile una cum dicta parrochiali ecclesia recipere si alias sibi canonice conferatur, illaque simul vel successive ex causa permutationis vel alias semel tantum dimittere et loco dimissi vel dimissorum aliud vel alia simile vel dissimile similia vel dissimilia, duo dumtaxat beneficia ecclesiastica invicem compatibilia retinere libere et licite valeat de uberiori dono gratie dignemini misericorditer dispensare, dicto defectu et [constitutionibus apostolicis ac] aliis in contrarium facientibus non obstantibus quibuscumque de gratia vestra speciali.

Fiat de speciali ad unum aliud et quod semel.

14. [*Bologna*], *27 January 1411. Ieuan ap Rhys, BCnL, priest, rector of Whitechurch-in-Kemes, St David's dioc.,[6] was granted a papal dispensation from defect of birth to be promoted*

---

[5] Perhaps Bradwell (Bucks.).

[6] As a subdeacon and rector of this church he was granted an episcopal licence on 3 June 1400 to study for a year at Oxford (*Reg. St David's*, i. 172). The above entry shows that he was BCnL by 1411; he was DCL by 1432. Besides the said rectory, he held varous ecclesiastical

to all orders and obtain a benefice even with cure of souls. He seeks a further dispensation to hold an additional benefice with or without cure of souls. Reg. 1, fol. 54r.

[Bononie], vi kal. Febr'. Supplicatur sanctitati vestre pro parte devoti vestri Iohannis de\ap/ Rys, presbiteri, rectoris parrochialis [ecclesie] de Alba Ecclesia et bacallarii in decretis Menevensis diocesis, cum quo alias super defectu natalium quem patitur de presbitero genitus et soluta coniugata ut ad omnes sacros ordines posset promoveri et beneficium ecclesiasticum etiam si curam haberet animarum obtinere auctoritate apostolica fuit dispensatum, cuius vigore dispensationis se fecit ad omnes ordines promoveri et dictam rectoriam est assecutus, cuius fructus etc. [redditus et proventus] quatuor marcharum sterlingorum [valorem annuum secundum communem extimationem non excedunt], quatinus sibi ampliorem gratiam facientes ut unum aliud beneficium ecclesiasticum curatum et [*recte* vel] non curatum etiam si canonicatus et prebenda in cathedralibus seu metro nec metropolitanis etiam in collegiatis ecclesiis existat, si sibi alias canonice conferantur [*sic*], libere recipere et licite retinere illaque simul vel alias successive ex causa permutationis semel tantum dimittere et loco dimissi vel dimissorum aliud simile vel dissimile libere recipere et licite retinere valeat cum eodem Io. dicto defectu non obstante dignemini misericorditer dispensare de gratia speciali.

Fiat de speciali et quod semel.

[*De matrimonialibus*]

15. [*Bologna*], *31 May 1410. John Hynton, layman, and Matilda Gregory, Lincoln dioc., are related in the third and fourth degrees of consanguinity; they seek a dispensation to marry with legitimation of future issue.* Reg. 1, fol. 20r.[7]

[Bononie], ii kal. Iunii. Exponitur sanctitati vestre pro parte devotorum vestrorum Iohannis Hynton' [filii] Iacobi Hynton' laici et Matilde Gregorii filie Iohannis Gregorii de Acleston',[8] mulieris Lincolniensis diocesis, quod ipsi ex certis causis cupiunt matrimonialiter invicem copulari, ipsorum tamen desiderium in hac parte absque dispensatione sedis apostolice, prout libenter vellent, adimplere non possunt, eo quod tercio et quarto gradibus consanguinitatis a communi sp stipide computandis se invicem attingunt.

---

offices and benefices in St David's dioc., including the archdeaconry of Cardigan (*BRUO*, ii. 1018–19). He obtained a papal dispensation to hold any number of compatible benefices on 30 November 1429 (*CPL*, viii. 166). Here he is described as the son of an unmarried nobleman and a married woman and is said to have had a papal dispensation to receive all, even holy orders; the dispensation in the entry above is also mentioned, whereafter he apparently exchanged the rectory of Whitechurch-in-Kemes for that of Bridell. He obtained another dispensation on 6 December 1429 to hold an additional incompatible benefice as well as a licence on 13 December to celebrate mass before dawn (*CPL*, viii. 166, 185).

[7] Actually entered under 'Super defectu natalium in forma ampliori' rather than its proper heading here.

[8] Hackleton (Northants.).

Quare supplicatur eidem sanctitati vestre pro parte dictorum exponentium quatinus cum ipsis ut dicto impedimento ac aliis non obstantibus matrimonium inter se publice in facie ecclesie contrahere et in ipso sic contracto licite remanere valeant prolesque suscipiendas legitimas discernere gratiose dispensare dignemini de gratia speciali.

Fiat de speciali cum declaratoria B.

Supplicationes signate aut signande per reverendum in Christo patrem et dominum dominum Antonium presbiterum cardinalem tituli sancti Marci vulgariter Tudertin. nuncupatum in absentia reverendorum in Christo patrum et dominorum dominorum Antonii Portuensis et Petri Tusculan. episcoporum, maiorum domini nostri penitentiariorum, videlicet die xvi mensis Aprilis pontificatus domini Iohannis pape xxiii anno primo Rome.

16. [*Rome*], *22 April 1411. Giles Daubeney, nobleman, Lincoln dioc.,*[9] *and Elizabeth le Scrope, noblewoman, York dioc., seek a dispensation to marry, notwithstanding an impediment of public honesty, with legitimation of future issue. Reg. 1, fol. 55r.*

[Rome], x kal. Maii. Beatissime pater, exponitur sanctitati vestre pro parte devotorum vestrorum nobilis viri Egidii Daubeney Lincolniensis diocesis et nobilis mulieris Elizabeth le Scrop' Eboracensis diocesis quod ipsi de consensu parentum suorum utriusque partis desiderant invicem matrimonialiter copulari, sed quia quondam Iohannes Daubeney, ipsius Egidii frater carnalis dum viveret in humanis, et dicta Elizabeth, ipso Iohanne in xiiii° et Elizabeth in xvi° etatis sue anno constitutis,[10] nupciali federe fuerunt invicem copulati, eorum desiderium adimplere non possunt, sedis apostolice dispensatione super hoc non obtenta. Verum pater sancte infra tres menses post huiusmodi matrimonii solempnizationem ~~cognoscere attemptavit~~ prefatus Iohannes, sicut deo placuit, diem suum clausit extremum et dictam Elizabeth carnaliter non cognovit nec cognoscere attemptavit. Supplicatur igitur vestre(?) sanctitati quatinus huiusmodi publice honestatis impedimento non obstante matrimonium inter se libere contrahere et in ipso postquam contractum fuerit licite remanere valeant cum eisdem Egidio et Elizabeth dignemini misericorditer dispensare, prolem exinde suscipiendam legitimam decernentes, de gratia speciali.

Fiat de speciali A.

17. [*Rome*], *7 May 1411. Dafydd Vechan ap Dafydd Gerchyn and Gwladus verch Dafydd, Llandaff dioc., married, unaware that they were related in the fourth degree of affinity; they seek a dispensation to remain married with legitimation of any issue. Reg. 1, fol. 56r.*

---

[9] Sir Giles Daubeney of South Ingleby (Lincs.), born in 1395, did not marry Elizabeth le Scrope but firstly Joan Darcy, then Mary Leke before May 1436, and after her death in February 1443, Alice. He died on 11 January 1446, aged 50 (*Complete Peerage*, iv. 100–1).

[10] John Daubeney, born *c.* 1394, married Elizabeth, dau. of Sir Roger le Scrope of Bolton (Yorks.), in 1409, but died on 24 September 1409. She subsequently married not his brother Giles but Thomas Goldington; a pardon for her remarrying without licence was issued on 29 May 1411, only five weeks after the above dispensation. She died childless on 17 February 1421 (*Complete Peerage*, iv. 99).

[Rome], non. Maii. Exponitur sanctitati vestre ex parte devotorum vestrorum David Vechan ap David Gerchyn et Groladus verch David mulieris, coniugum Landovensis [*sic*] diocesis, quod ipsi olim ignorantes aliquod impedimentum inter eos existere quominus possint invicem matrimonialiter copulari matrimonium inter se per verba legitime de presenti secundum morem patrie bannis editis nemine contradicente in facie ecclesie publice contraxerunt. Postea vero ad eorum noticiam pervenit quod quidem David ap Ieuan Moyl laicus dicte diocesis, qui prefato David Vechan quarto consanguinitatis gradu attingebat, ipsam Groladus [*sic*] actu fornicario carnaliter precognovit. Verum pater sancte si divortium etc. [fieret inter eos, possent inter amicos et parentes discordie verisimiliter exoriri.] Supplicatur igitur pro parte dictorum coniugum quatinus huiusmodi quarto affinitatis gradu qui ex consanguinitate provenit non obstante in dicto sic contracto matrimonio licite valeant remanere cum eisdem dignemini misericorditer dispensare, prolemque susceptam exinde si qua sit et suscipiendam legitimam decernentes, de gratia speciali.

Fiat de speciali pro omnibus A.

18. [Rome], 7 May 1411. Meurig (*Meurit*) ap Ieuan ap Llywarch (*Llwarch*) and Lleucu verch Philip, a married couple from Llandaff (*Landovensis*) dioc., unaware that they were related in the fourth degree of consanguinity, contracted marriage publicly [before the church *per verba legitime de presenti*, after the banns were read according to local custom, with nobody objecting]; they seek a dispensation [so that they may remain married with legitimation of any existing and future issue]. *Fiat de speciali A*. Reg. 1, fol. 56r.

19. [Rome], 7 May 1411. Same dispensation as **18** sought by Philip Pant and Hester (*Hest*) verch Dafydd, a married couple from Llandaff (*Landovensis*) dioc. *Fiat de speciali A*. Reg. 1, fol. 56r.

20. [Rome], 7 May 1411. Same dispensation as **18** sought by Hywel (*Howel*) ap Dafydd ap Ieuan Hwych and Gwenllian verch Hywel (*Howel*), a married couple from Llandaff dioc. *Fiat de speciali A*. Reg. 1, fol. 56r.

21. *[Rome], 7 May 1411. Gruffydd ap Dafydd Vachan Laut(?) and Gwenllian verch Ieuan ap Madog, Llandaff dioc., married and had issue, unaware that they were related in the fourth degree of consanguinity; they seek a dispensation to remain married with legitimation of any issue.* Reg. 1, fol. 56v.

[Rome], nonas Maii. Exponitur sanctitati vestre pro parte devotorum vestrorum Gr' ap Dafydd Vachan Laut(?) et Wellin verch Ieu' ap Ma' mulieris, Landavensis diocesis, quod ipsi olim ignorantes aliquod impedimentum inter eos existere quominus possent matrimonialiter copulari matrimonium inter se per verba legitime de presenti bannis editis in facie ecclesie et aliis solempnitatibus iuxta morem patrie publice contraxerunt, illudque carnali copula subsecuta consumarunt et proles procrearunt. Deinde ad eorum noticiam pervenit eos in quarto gradu consanguinitatis sunt coniuncti [*recte* fore coniunctos], et si divortium etc. [fieret inter eos, possent inter amicos et parentes discordie verisimiliter exoriri.] Supplicatur igitur eidem sanctitati vestre pro parte dictorum coniugum quatinus impedimento huiusmodi non obstante in matrimonio sic contracto licite possent invicem remanere cum eisdem coniugibus dignemini misericorditer dispensare, prolemque susceptam si qua sit [et] suscipiendam legitimam decernentes, de gratia speciali.

Fiat de speciali A.

Supplicationes signate per reverendum in Christo patrem et dominum d. P. episcopum Tuscullanum, maiorem penitentiarium, in Roma. Registrate per me Ia. de Parma prout infra.

22. [*Rome*], *10 May 1411. Hywel ap Rhys, layman, and Angharad verch Dafydd ap Owain, Llandaff dioc., are related in the third and fourth degrees of affinity; they seek a dispensation to marry with legitimation of future issue.* Reg. 1, fol. 58r.

[Rome], vi idus Maii. Exponitur sanctitati vestre pro parte devotorum vestrorum Howel ap Rys, laici, et Angharat verch David ap Oweyn, mulieris, Landavensis diocesis, quod ipsi certis et rationabilibus causis desiderant invicem matrimonialiter copulari, sed quia quondam Howel ap Gruffuth ap Rys, laicus dicte diocesis, qui prefato Howel ap Rys quarto consanguinitatis gradu dum viveret attinebat, prefatam Angharat habuit in uxorem, necnon et quia prefatus Howel ap Rys quandam Lleucu verch Owyllum [*recte* Gwyllum] Lloyt mulierem que dicte Angharat tercio et quarto consanguinitatis gradibus attinebat actu fornicario carnaliter cognovit, eorum desiderium adimplere non possunt, sedis apostolice dispensatione super hoc non obtenta. Supplicatur igitur eidem sanctitati vestre pro parte ipsorum H. et A. quatinus premissis non obstantibus matrimonium inter se libere contrahere et in eodem postquam contractum fuerit licite valeant remanere cum eisdem dignemini misericorditer dispensare, prolemque suscipiendam exinde legitimam decernentes, de gratia speciali.

Fiat de speciali cum declaratoria B.

23. [*Rome*], *10 May 1411. Ieuan Theire, layman, and Joan, daughter of Ieuan Robert, Llandaff dioc., married, knowing that they were related in the fourth degree of affinity and consanguinity; they seek absolution from excommunication and a dispensation to remain married with legitimation of any issue.* Reg. 1, fol. 58r.

[Rome], vi idus Maii. Exponitur sanctitati vestre ex parte devotorum vestrorum Iohannis Theire, laici, et Iohanne filie Iohannis Robert, mulieris, coniugum Landavensis diocesis, quod ipsi olim scientes se in quarto consanguinitatis gradu ex utroque latere fore coniunctos, necnon quod prefatus Iohannes quandam Iohannam Nerbere mulierem que quarto consanguinitatis gradu predicte Iohanne filie Iohannis Robert attinebat actu fornicario carnaliter precognovit, matrimonium inter se per verba legitime de presenti candestine [*recte* clandestine] contraxerunt carnali copula subsecuta. Verum pater sancte si divortium etc. [fieret inter eos, possent inter amicos et parentes discordie verisimiliter exoriri.] Supplicatur igitur eidem sanctitati vestre pro parte ipsorum coniugum quatinus ipsos a sententiis excommunicationis quas propter premissa incurrerunt absolvi mandare necnon cum eis ut in matrimonio sic contracto huiusmodi quarto consanguinitatis et affinitatis gradu non obstante licite valeant remanere dignemini misericorditer dispensare, prolemque susceptam exinde si qua sit [et] suscipiendam legitimam decernentes, de gratia speciali.

Fiat de speciali et dent unum calicem duarum marcharum f argenti f ecclesie parrochiali eorum et ieiunent vi feria per annum B.

24. [*Rome*], *10 May 1411. Thomas Levy, layman, and Joan Taylour, Llandaff dioc., married, knowing that they were related in the third and fourth degrees of affinity; they seek a dispensation to remain married with legitimation of any issue.* Reg. 1, fol. 58r.

[Rome], vi id. Maii. Item similem dispensationis gratiam facientes devotis vestris Thome Levy, laico, et Iohanne Taylour, mulieri, coniugum [*recte* coniugibus] Landavensis diocesis, qui, scientes quondam Iohannem Clerk iuniorem, laicum dicte diocesis, qui tercio et quarto consanguinitatis gradibus eidem Thome attingebat, prefatam Iohannam per nonnulla tempora habuisse in uxorem, matrimonium inter se per verba legitime de presenti bannis editis nemine contradicente in facie ecclesie publice contraxerunt. Verum pater sancte si divortium etc. [fieret inter eos, possent inter amicos et parentes discordie verisimiliter exoriri.] Supplicatur eidem sanctitati vestre [quatinus cum eisdem] ut in matrimonio sic contracto premissis non obstantibus licite valeant remanere dignemini etc. [misericorditer dispensare], prolemque susceptam et suscipiendam etc. [legitimam decernentes, de gratia speciali].

Fiat de speciali et dent unum calicem duarum marcharum f argenti f eorum ecclesie parrochiali et ieiunent vi feria per annum B.

25. [*Rome*], *13 May 1411. William Amys of Barrowby, layman, and Alice, daughter of Alexander Philip, Lincoln dioc., married, unaware that they were related in the third and fourth degrees of consanguinity; they seek a dispensation to remain married with legitimation of future issue.* Reg. 1, fol. 58v.

[Rome], iii id. Maii. Exponitur sanctitati vestre pro parte devotorum vestrorum Willelmi Amys de Borughby, laici, et Alicie Philip filie Alexandri Philip, mulieris, coniugum Lincolniensis diocesis, quod ipsi olim ignorantes aliquod impedimentum inter eos existere quominus possent matrimonialiter copulari matrimonium inter se legitime per verba de presenti bannis editis in facie ecclesie iuxta morem patrie publice contraxerunt, illudque carnali copula consumarunt. Deinde ad eorum noticiam pervenit quod in tercio et quarto consanguinitatis [gradibus] fuerunt coniuncti, et si divortium etc. [fieret inter eos, possent inter amicos et parentes discordie verisimiliter exoriri]. Supplicatur igitur pro parte dictorum coniugum quatinus cum ipsis ut non obstantibus impedimentis predictis possunt [*sic*] in dicto matrimonio sic contracto remanere dispensare dignemini de gratia vestra speciali, prolem suscipiendam legitimam decernentes.

Fiat de speciali B.

26. [*Rome*], *13 May 1411. Ieuan ap Gronw, layman, and Nesta verch Philip, Llandaff dioc., married and had issue, unaware that they were related in the fourth degree of consanguinity; they seek a dispensation to remain married with legitimation of any issue.* Reg. 1, fol. 58v.

[Rome], iii id. Maii. Exponitur sanctitati vestre pro parte devotorum vestrorum Ier' ap Grone, laici, et Neste verch Ph', mulieris, Landavensis diocesis, quod olim ipsi ignorantes aliquod impedimentum inter eos existere quominus possent invicem matrimonialiter copulari matrimonium inter se per verba legitime de presenti bannis editis in facie ecclesie ut [*recte* et] aliis solempnitatibus iuxta morem patrie fieri consuetis observatis publice contraxerunt, illudque carnali copula consumarunt et prolem exinde procrearunt. Postea vero ad eorum pervenit noticiam quod in quarto consanguinitatis gradu sunt coniuncti, et si divortium etc. [fieret inter eos, possent inter amicos et parentes discordie verisimiliter exoriri.] Quare supplicatur igitur eidem sanctitati vestre pro parte dictorum coniugum quatinus impedimento consanguinitatis huiusmodi non obstante in eorum sic contracto matrimonio licite remanere [valeant] dignemini misericorditer dispensare, prolem susceptam si qua sit et suscipiendam legitimam decernentes, de gratia speciali.

Fiat de speciali B.

27. [*Rome*], *14 May 1411. John Helay junior, layman, and Margaret, daughter of Adam Dowgel, York dioc., married, unaware that they were related in the third and fourth degrees of consanguinity; they seek a dispensation to solemnise their marriage and remain in it with legitimation of any issue and a declaratory letter.* Reg. 1, fol. 58v.

[Rome], ii id. Maii. Exponitur sanctitati vestre pro parte devotorum vestrorum Iohannis Helay iunioris, laici, et Margarete filie Ade Dowgel, Eboracensis diocesis, quod ipsi olim ignorantes aliquod impedimentum inter eos existere quominus possent matrimonialiter copulari matrimonium invicem contraxerunt per verba de presenti, illudque carnali copula consumarunt, ad ipsius tamen solempnizationem in facie ecclesie nondum processerunt. Demum ad eorum pervenit noticiam quod se invicem attingebant in tercio et quarto gradibus consanguinitatis, quare ipsorum desiderium, apostolice sedis dispensatione super hoc non obtenta, prout libenter vellent adimplere non possunt. Quare humiliter supplicatur eidem sanctitati vestre pro parte dictorum exponentium quatinus [sibi ut] ad ipsius matrimonii solempnizationem ad in facie ecclesie procedere et in ipso sic contracto et consumato licite remanere valeant, prolem si qua sit atque suscipiendam legitimam decernentes, concedere dignemini de gratia speciali cum declaratoria ut in forma.

Fiat de speciali et cum declaratoria B.

28. [*Rome*], *20 May 1411. Same dispensation as* **16** *sought by Giles Daubeney, nobleman,* domicellus, *Lincoln dioc., and Elizabeth le Scrope, noblewoman,* domicella, *York dioc.* Reg. 1, fol. 59v.

[Rome], xiii kal. Iunii. Beatissime pater, exponitur pro parte devotorum vestrorum nobilis viri Egidii Daubeney, Lincolniensis diocesis domicelli, et nobilis mulieris Elizabeth le Scrop', domicelle Eboracensis diocesis, quod ipsi de consensu parentum suorum utriusque partis desiderant invicem matrimonialiter copulari, sed quia quondam Iohannes Daubeney, ipsius Egidii frater carnalis, dum viveret in humanis, et dicta Elizabeth, ipso Iohanne in xiiii^{mo} et Elizabeth in xvi^{mo} etatis sue anno constitutis, nupciali federi fuerint invicem copulati, eorum desiderium adimplere non possunt, sedis apostolice dispensatione super hoc non obtenta. Verum pater sancte infra tres menses post huiusmodi matrimonii solempnizationem prefatus Iohannes, sicut deo placuit, diem suum clausit extremum et dictam Elizabeth non cognovit nec cognoscere attemptavit. Supplicatur igitur sanctitati vestre pro parte [ipsorum] quatinus huiusmodi [publice] honestatis impedimento non obstante matrimonium inter se libere contrahere et in ipso postquam contractum fuerit licite remanere valeant cum eisdem dignemini misericorditer dispensare, proles [sic] exinde suscipiendam legitimam decernentes, de gratia speciali.

Fiat de speciali B.

De sancto sepulcro et sancto Iacobo et commutatione votorum

De mense Septembris per eundem dominum Cardinalem Aniciensem maiorem penitentiarium

29. [*Bologna*], *29 September 1410. Joan Sanut of York took a vow of chastity but then married; she seeks absolution and commutation of her vow.* Reg. 1, fol. 66v.

[Bononie], iii kal. Octobris. Exponitur sanctitati vestre pro parte devote vestre Iohanne Sanut mulieris Eboracensis quod ipsa olim fervore vovit votum deo et omnibus sanctis quod nunquam caperet hominem nec maritum sed caste vivere promisit et postea quod cum quodam viro accedit quod matrimonium contraxit et sine homine vivere non potuit. Quare supplicatur igitur eidem sanctitati vestre pro parte exponentis quatinus ipsam a premisso voto mandare absolvere [*recte* absolvi] et in alia opera pietatis commutare dignemini misericorditer dispensari de gratia speciali.

Fiat de speciali.

[*Whole entry crossed through with marginal note:*] Cassata per me quia est in forma. Charen(?) et restitui pecunias regestri.

30. [*Bologna*], *10 October 1410. Morgan, abbot of St Mary's monastery, Talley, Premonstratensian order, St David's dioc.*,[11] *vowed to go on pilgrimage to Rome but could only go as far as Bologna; he seeks commutation of his vow.* Reg. 1, fol. 67r.

[Bononie], vi id. Octobris. Exponit sanctitati vestre devotus vester Morcanus, abbas monasterii beate Marie de Callun, ordinis Premonstraten-

---

[11] He is recorded as abbot in 1409–16 (Smith, *Heads of Religious Houses*, iii. 585). Talley Abbey was dedicated to BVM and St John the Baptist.

sis, Menevensis diocesis, quod ipse olim fervore devotionis accensus vovit absque tamen certi termini prefixione limina beatorum Petri et Pauli apostolorum de Urbe peregre personaliter visitare. Verum pater sancte quod dictus exponens cupiens complere votum predictum de prefato suo monasterio de partibus ad civitatem Bononiensem peregre pervenit personaliter et ulterius propter paupertatem usque ad limina predicta commode ire non valeat. Supplicat eidem sanctitati vestre dictus exponens quatinus huiusmodi votum nondum completum ut prefertur infra civitatem Bononiensem sibi in alia opera pietatis dignemini misericorditer commutare de gratia speciali.

Fiat de speciali.

31. [Bologna], 25 October 1410. The pope is requested to grant a licence for William Banastre, esquire, Coventry and Lichfield dioc., to visit the Holy Sepulchre etc. with six people of his choice. *Fiat de speciali.* Reg. 1, fol. 67r.

32. [Bologna], 6 November 1410. The pope is requested to grant a licence for Roger Grene, layman, Lincoln dioc., to go on pilgrimage to the Holy Sepulchre and certain other holy places overseas with three companions of his choice. *Fiat de speciali B.* Reg. 1, fol. 67r.

33. [Bologna], 8 November 1410. The pope is requested to grant a licence *cum clausulis opportunis* for John Schillyng, Winchester dioc., not present at the Roman Curia, to visit the Holy Sepulchre and certain other holy places overseas with eight people of his choice. *Fiat de speciali.* Reg. 1, fol. 67v.

34. [Bologna], 24 November 1410. The pope is requested to grant a licence for Thomas Taylour, layman, Salisbury dioc., to visit the Holy Sepulchre and certain other holy places overseas with five people of his choice. *Fiat de speciali.* Reg. 1, fol. 67v.

De mense Decembris per dominum Aniciensem maiorem penitentiarium

35. *[Bologna], 8 December 1410. Alice Fynderne, noblewoman, London dioc., vowed to visit Rome, but now that she has married William Fynderne, she cannot fulfil her vow; she seeks absolution and commutation of that vow.* Reg. 1, fol. 68r.

[Bononie], vi id. Decembris. Exponitur sanctitati vestre pro parte nobilis mulieris Alicie Fynderne Londoniensis diocesis quod ipsa olim in sua pura viduitate existens vovit absque termini prefixione visitare limina apostolorum Petri et Pauli de Urbe, deinde dicto voto nondum adimpleto cuidam nobili viro Guillelmo Fynderne eius marito matrimonialiter est coniuncta, sic tamen non sit compos sue voluntatis, obstante ei sui mariti precepto, dictum suum votum prout libenter vellet adimplere non potest. Quare humiliter supplicatur eidem sanctitati vestre quatinus ipsam propter serenitatem sue conscientie absolvere ac ipsum votum in alia opera pietatis commutare gratiose dignemini de gratia speciali.

Fiat de speciali.

36. [*Bologna*], *12 December 1410. Thomas Crook, layman, Winchester dioc., vowed to visit Rome, but since he could no longer fulfil his vow, he paid for a priest to do so; he seeks absolution from his vow.* Reg. 1, fol. 68r.

[Bononie], ii id. Decembris. Exponitur sanctitati vestre pro parte devoti vestri Thome Crook, laici Wyntoniensis diocesis, quod ipse olim fervore devotionis accensus vovit visitare limina apostolorum Petri et Pauli absque termini prefixione, iamque deo faciente perpetuo impedimento laborans dictum suum votum prout libenter vellet adimplere non valet, quemdam tamen presbiterum propriis expensis ad dicta limina visitanda misit cum effectu. Quare supplicatur eidem sanctitati vestre pro parte dicti exponentis quatinus ipsum propter serenitatem sue conscientie ab huiusmodi voto gratiose absolvere dignemini de gratia speciali.

Fiat de speciali et quod plus esse expensurus exponat.

37. [*Bologna*], *3 January 1411. Thomas Yafford, priest, perpetual vicar of Monk Hesledon, Durham dioc., seeks a licence to visit Rome, the Holy Sepulchre, and certain other holy places overseas, and lease the fruits of his vicarage for a year, regardless of his oath to reside continuously in his benefice.* Reg. 1, fol. 69r.

[Bononie], iii nonas Ianuarii. Exponit sanctitati vestre devotus vester Thomas Yafford, presbiter, perpetuus vicarius de Heselden Dunelmensis diocesis, quod in regno Anglie quedam existat constitutio legitime approbata quod omnes perpetui vicarii ecclesiarum parrochialium in eorum admissione corporale prestabunt iuramentum quod continuam servabunt residenciam in eorum vicariis. Idem tamen exponens fervore devotionis accensus intendit visitare limina apostolorum Petri et Paul in Urbe, ac etiam sepulcrum dominicum et quedam alia loca transmarina. Quare humiliter supplicat eidem sanctitati vestre propter serenitatem sue conscientie quatinus [sibi ut] huiusmodi iuramento ac aliis in contrarium editis non obstantibus supradicta loca sancta visitare, ac interim fructus, redditus et proventus ~~seu~~ sue vicarie locare seu arrendare quibusvis personis, et quibus condicionem suam et dicte sue vicarie facere valeat meliorem, hinc ad annum gratiose concedere dignemini de gratia speciali.

Fiat de speciali proviso quod dicta vicaria interim servitiis debitis non fraudetur.

MCCCCXI de mense Februarii. Supplicationes signate de sepulcro dominico, sancto Iacobo ac commutatione votorum per reverendum in Christo patrem et dominum dominum A. episcopum Portuensem ac maiorem penitentiarium. Registrate per me Ia. de Parma prout ut infra.

38. [*Bologna*], *30 March 1411. William Freton, priest, [Norwich] dioc., swore a simple vow and an oath to join St Giles' Hospital, Norwich, for life, but for certain legitimate reasons he cannot consummate them without danger to body and soul; he seeks commutation of his vow, absolution from his oath, and a dispensation or declaration that he may leave that hospital.*[12] Reg. 1, fol. 72r.

---

[12] For the hospital at this time, see C. Rawcliffe, *Medicine for the Soul: The Life, Death and Resurrection of an English Medieval Hospital* (Stroud, 1999), 254–5. Freton was granted a licence to have a portable altar on 26 April 1413 (*CPL*, vi. 346).

[Bononie], iii kal. Aprilis. Exponitur sanctitati vestre ex parte devoti vestri Wilhelmi Freton, presbiteri [Norwicensis] diocesis, quod ipse iam dudum vovit et iuravit fidelitatem, stabilitatem et perpetuam fraternitatem in hospitali sancti Egidii de Norwico et obedientiam tunc magistro domus sive hospitalis huiusmodi et suis in huiusmodi hospitali canonice successoribus ad terminum vite sue. Verum pater sancte cum dictus presbiter et alii in dicto hospitali colligialiter [sic] viventes sint penitus seculares, ipseque exponens votum simplex et non solempne necnon iuramentum predicta hactenus per eundem secundum posse observata propter certas et legitimas causas, videlicet discordias, contentiones regularum antiquarum suis adhuc temporibus observatarum, eversiones, merentes(?), angustias et perturbationes, non sine gravi corporis et anime suorum periculo et detrimento valeat consummare, supplicatur igitur humiliter eidem sanctitati vestre quatinus sibi huiusmodi votum, attento quod nemo ad simplicis voti sive iuramenti in corporis periculum et anime dampnationem vergentis observantiam coneatur, commutari, ipsumque ab huiusmodi iuramento absolvi, secumque ut hospitale et congregationem predictas exire valeat declarari vel dispensari mandare dignemini, si dispensetur, de gratia speciali.

Fiat de speciali si vera sunt cause narrate quod votum commutet in alia opera pietatis et absolvat a iuramento A.

[*In diversis formis*]

Supplicationes signate aut signande per reverendum in Christo patrem et dominum dominum Antonium tituli sancti Marci presbiterum cardinalem, Tudertinum vulgariter nuncupatum, in absentia reverendorum dominorum Antonii Portuensis et Petri Tusculani episcoporum ac domini nostri pape maiorum penitentiariorum, die Iovis xvi mensis Maii pontificatus domini Iohannis pape xxiii anno primo. Rome.

39. [Bologna], 6 March [*1411*]. *Philip ap Rhys, priest, perpetual vicar of Penbryn, St David's dioc.,*[13] *seeks a dispensation to study canon law for three years.* Reg. 1, fol. 76v.

[Bononie], ii nonas Martii. Supplicat sanctitati vestre devotus orator vester Philipus ap Rys, presbiter, perpetuus vicarius ecclesie parrochialis de Pembeyn Menevensis diocesis, qui per quadrigennium [sic] continue in iure civili studuit inclusive, quatinus secum ut per triennium ibidem in iure canonico vel alibi in studio ubi illud videat [recte vigeat] generale insistendo licite valleat residere dignemini misericorditer dispenssare [sic], Octonis et Octoboni sedis apostolice legatorum olim in regno Anglie et aliis constitutionibus apostolicis contrariis non obstantibus quibuscumque necnon quod prefatus P. ad personalem residentiam faciendam in dicta vicaria iuramento sit astrictus de gratia vestra speciali.

Fiat de speciali A.

---

[13] Presumably the man of this name who was ordained by the bishop of St David's as an acolyte on 17 December 1401 and as a subdeacon on 18 February 1402 (*Reg. St David's*, i. 228, 255). He was a *magister* by 1404 and official of the archdeacon of Cardigan in 1406 (ibid., 316, 348). For his benefices see *CPL*, vi. 215–16; *Reg. St David's*, ii. 542. For someone of the same name see *CPL*, viii. 167.

40. [Bologna], 10 March [1411]. The pope is requested to grant *littere confessionales* for life or in perpetuity to John Theldewelle and his wife Katherine, London dioc. *Fiat de speciali A*. Reg. 1, fol. 77v.

41. [*Bologna*], *11 March [1411]. Ralph, rector of Copdock, Norwich dioc., requests that he may absolve all his parishoners* in forma 'Cupientes' *for two years*. Reg. 1, fol. 78r.

> [Bononie], v id. Martii. Supplicat sanctitati vestre devotus vester Radulphus, rector ecclesie parrochialis de Coppedook Norwicensis diocesis, quatinus sibi ut omnium et singulorum utriusque sexus suorum parrochianorum sibi peccata sua pro tempore confitentium, quotiens fuerit oportunum, huiusmodi eorum confessionibus eorum confe diligenter auditis, pro commissis per eos etiam in casibus episcopalibus debitam absolutionem impendere et penitentiam salutarem iniungere libere et licite valeat in forma 'Cupientes' hinc ad biennium dignemini misericorditer impartiri de gratia vestra speciali ut in forma.
>
> Fiat de speciali ad quinquennium A.

42. [Bologna], 13 March [1411]. Same grant as **40** sought by Henry Libune(?) and Peter Shelton,[14] priests, Norwich dioc., and Ralph Medilton, citizen of London, and his wife Margery. *Fiat de speciali A*. Reg. 1, fol. 79r.

43. [Bologna], 17 March [1411]. The pope is requested to grant *littere confessionales* for life to Ralph Chaunberleyn and his wife Joan, Canterbury dioc., John Gryge and his wife Cecily, and Thomas Brydlyngton, citizen of London. *Fiat de speciali I*. Reg. 1, fol. 81v.

44. [Bologna], 17 March [1411]. Same grant as **43** sought by Ieuan Gody, citizen of Brecon (*civi Breconie*), and his wife Margaret, St David's dioc. Approved with **45**? Reg. 1, fol. 81v.

45. [Bologna], 17 March [1411]. Same grant as **43** sought by Joan, widow of the late Walter Laghull', St David's dioc. *Fiat de speciali I*. Reg. 1, fol. 81v.

46. [Bologna], 18 March [1411]. Same grant as **43** sought by Nicholas Walter, priest, perpetual vicar of Shottisham (*Shotisham*) parish church, Norwich dioc. *Fiat de speciali I*. Reg. 1, fol. 83r.

47. [Bologna], 18 March [1411]. Same grant as **43** sought by Gilbert Brydde, priest, perpetual vicar of Docking (*Dockyng*) parish church, Norwich dioc. *Fiat de speciali I*. Reg. 1, fol. 83r.

48. [Bologna], 18 March [1411]. Same grant as **43** sought by Richard Wyntere, priest, Norwich dioc. *Fiat de speciali I*. Reg. 1, fol. 83r.

---

[14] Presumably Peter Shelton, fellow of Trinity Hall, Cambridge, in 1399 and still in 1401, and Junior Proctor of Cambridge University in 1391–2. He was MA and, by 1399, BCL. He was ordained a priest to the title of his fellowship in 1401 and included in a university roll for papal graces as a petitioner for a benefice in 1399 (*BRUC*, 522). For his benefices see ibid. and *CPL*, vi. 216; vii. 361; viii.17.

49. [Bologna], 18 March [1411]. Same grant as **43** sought by William Dockyng, rector of Cockley Cley (*Kocchcleye*) parish church, Norwich dioc. *Fiat de speciali I.* Reg. 1, fol. 83r.

50. [Bologna], 19 March [1411]. Same grant as **43** sought by Roger of Wood Rising (*de Woderysyng*), priest, Norwich dioc. *Fiat de speciali I.* Reg. 1, fol. 83r.

51. [Bologna], 19 March [1411]. Same grant as **43** sought by Robert Norwyche, priest, Norwich dioc. *Fiat de speciali I.* Reg. 1, fol. 83r.

52. [Bologna], 19 March [1411]. Same grant as **43** sought by Alice Pye, Norwich dioc. *Fiat de speciali I.* Reg. 1, fol. 83r.

53. *[Bologna], 20 March [1411]. Richard ap Gwilym alias Caunton,*[15] *priest, St David's dioc., tried to separate some of his associates who were fighting in a town with some local men, but one of the latter struck him with a sword, so he drew his own sword to defend himself, and his attacker lost two fingers in the fight though it was not clear by whose blow. The supplicant then had himself promoted to all orders and now seeks a declaration that he did not thereby contract irregularity, or at least absolution* ad cautelam *and a dispensation from irregularity.* Reg. 1, fol. 83v.

[Bononie], xiii kal. Aprilis. Exponit sanctitati vestre devotus vester Ricardus ap Gwillyn alias Caunton', presbiter Menevensis diocesis, quod olim ipse in quadam villa cum sociis suis exeunte [*recte* exeuns] accidit quod aliqui de dictis sociis contra unum de dicta villa ex antiqua inimitia [*recte* inimicitia] exosum habentes et gladiis extractis ex utraque insultum fecerunt. Exponens vero volens ipsos separare et defendere ne damnum invicem sibi inferrent, et illa [*recte* illi] de villa dictum exponentem cum gladiis evaginatis aggressi fuerunt, et unus de villa, ex eo quod ipse exponens eum impedebat ne alios percuteret et vulneraret, ipsum exponentem cum gladio tetigit et vulneravit. Dictus vero exponens ipsum evadere non valens propter pressuram gentium extraxit gladium suum non animo mutilandi vel occidendi sed solummodo se ipsum defendendi, et percussiens ipsum aggredientem, prout alii plures percussiebant, duo digiti de manu dicti eum aggredientis fuerunt abscisi et nescitur bene ex quo ictu fuerunt abscisi, ac ex ictu exponentis vel ex ictu dictorum sociorum. Deinde ipse exponens non formatus sibi conscientiam super premissis tamquam simplex et iuris ignarus se fecit alias tamen rite ad omnes ordines promoveri. Verum pater sancte cum dictus exponens premissa bona fide fecerit volens eos separare ut tenebatur et alias in premissis culpabilis non fuerit, cum alias ipsum evadere non posset, supplicat igitur eidem sanctitati vestre dictus exponens quatinus ipsum nullam occasione

---

[15] Presumably the Richard ap Gwillim, rector of Bridell, St David's dioc., by 11 March 1399, when his bishop granted him a licence to be ordained by any Catholic bishop; he was ordained by his bishop as a deacon on 24 May 1399 (*Reg. St David's*, i. 94, 114). His bishop granted him a licence to study for a year on 1 June 1399, and again, to study in Oxford, on 3 June 1400, and again in March 1404; by December 1404 he was a *magister* (ibid. 118, 172, 308, 320). He was BCn & CL of Oxford by 11 February 1413 (*CPL* vi. 377). Probably not the same as the Richard Caunton who incepted as DCL of Oxford in 1433, and was DCnL & CL by 1450, whom Emden notes to have been ordained as a priest in 1430 (*BRUO*, i. 373-4).

premissorum irregularitatis maculam contraxisse declarare dignemini vel saltim in quantum indiget ad cautelam absolvere et super irregularitate si quam inde contraxit misericorditer dispensare de gratia speciali.

Fiat de speciali secundum iudicium auditoris A.

Si vera sunt narrata, videtur dispensandus: iudicium auditoris A.

54. [Bologna], 20 March [1411]. Same grant as **43** sought by Ralph Gronehurst, DCL, Salisbury (*Sarisburgensis*) dioc.;[16] Henry Trendon, priest, Exeter dioc.; Joan de Deham, nun of the monastery of Wix (*Wykys*), OSB, London dioc.; Anne Reydon and Emma Barre, sisters of that monastery and order. *Fiat de speciali A.* Reg. 1, fol. 83v.

55. [Bologna], 20 March [1411]. Same grant as **40** sought by John Wintham, priest, Norwich dioc. *Fiat de speciali A.* Reg. 1, fol. 83v.

56. [Bologna], 20 March [1411]. Same grant as **43** sought by William Levyot, priest, Hereford dioc.[17] *Fiat de speciali A.* Reg. 1, fol. 84r.

57. [*Bologna*], *24 March [1411]. Walter de Vulley and John Joynor, laymen, Coventry and Lichfield dioc., together killed John Halbys* alias *Soyeromi, priest, perpetual vicar of Wirksworth of the same dioc. They seek absolution from the general sentence of excommunication thereby incurred, the commission of the matter to the abbot of Sta. Giustina, Padua, at the Curia, and a dispensation to do public penance in Bologna Cathedral and before the penitentiaries at S. Petronio, Bologna.* Reg. 1, fol. 85v.

[Bononie], viiii kal. Aprilis. Exponunt sanctitati vestre humiles vestri Gualterus de Vulley et Iohannes Joynor, laici Conventrensis et Lichefeldensis diocesis, quod olim ipsi instigante dyabulo quendam Iohannem Halbys alias Soyeromi presbiterum, perpetuum [vicarium] parrochialis ecclesie de Wynkesworth dicte diocesis, simul interfecerunt, qui quidem presbiter curatus proprius dicti Iohannis existebat, propter quod excommunicationis incurrerrunt sententiam in tales generaliter promulgatam, in quam sententiam fuerunt per ordinarium eorum in certis parrochialibus ecclesiis diocesis predicte incidisse declarari et ut tales publice nunciari. Verum pater sancte cum ipsi exponentes propter huiusmodi delictum dioceseim suam nec regnum Anglie intrare non sunt ausi, supplicat [*recte* supplicant] igitur eidem sanctitati vestre dicti exponentes quatinus ipsos a dicta sententia et huiusmodi presbitericidii reatu ac excessu quam propter hoc incurrerrunt absolventur ipsosque sic absolutos fu \ubi/ et quando expediens fuerit publice facere nunciari et huiusmodi negotium abbatem [*recte* abbati] sancte Iustine in presenti curia residenti committere

---

[16] Ralph Greenhurst was admitted to New College, Oxford, as a scholar in 1389 and as a fellow in 1391 until 1401. He was DCL by 1410 and a notary public. He was granted the first tonsure to all orders in 1402 but was married. He served on diplomatic missions to Brittany in 1411–1413. He died in 1413 (*BRUO*, ii. 816).

[17] He was appointed commissary of the bishop of Hereford in 1404 (*Reg. Mascall*, 2–3, 42). He was also BCnL and rector of Kinnersley (Herefordshire) in 1404. He was granted a year's licence by his bishop on 18 September 1410 to visit Rome (ibid., 189).

dignemini, cum ad ~~locum~~ locum dilicti [*sic*] nec ad dictum regnum ut premittitur accedere non sint ausi, ac penitentias publicas quas ad locum dilicti propter huiusmodi homicidium agere debebant hic in ecclesia cathedrali presentis civitatis et coram penitentiariis sanctitatis vestre in sancto Patronio cedentibus [*scilicet* sedentibus] facere valeant ac possint cum ipsis dignemini misericorditer dispensare hac [vice et] litteras super hoc opportunas patentes et apertas concedere de gratia speciali.

Fiat de speciali secundum iudicium auditoris, locus autem penitentie sit in partibus propinquioribus loco dilicti A.

Iudicium auditoris: viderentur absolvendi in forma, et si penitentiam in loco adimplere non possunt, in loco qui commissario videatur ydoneus illam adimpleatur vel loco propinquiori delicto vel in curia A. I.

58. [Bologna], 26 March [1411]. William Lavam, clerk, Lincoln dioc., requests that he may be promoted to all, even holy orders by any bishop having the grace and communion of the apostolic see, and thereafter minister in them, notwithstanding apostolic constitutions etc. *Fiat de speciali A.* Reg. 1, fol. 86v.

59. *[Bologna], 28 March [1411]. John Dudley alias Philippes, subdeacon, Hereford dioc.,*[18] *had part of a finger cut off with a sword by John Turner, priest, Hereford dioc., during an argument, and struck back at Turner's fingers with his own sword; hence Dudley seeks a declaration that he did not thereby contract irregularity, or at least a dispensation from irregularity.* Reg. 1, fol. 88r.

[Bononie], v kal. Aprilis. Exponitur [*sic*] sanctitati vestre Iohannes Dudley alias dictus Philippes, subdyaconus Herefordensis diocesis, quod olim orta briga inter quendam Iohannem Turnour pro presbitero Herefordensis diocesis pro tempore se gerentem et ipsum exponentem, verbose prorumpentes, amicitia continua et societate semper inter ipsos prehabitis non obstantibus, idem Iohannes presbiter spiritu dyabolico instigante ipsum Iohannem Dudley gladio evaginato taliter est aggressus quod sibi mediam partem digiti mutilati manus dextre amputavit, vidensque exponens sibi digitum sic abscisum quendam gladium quem tunc penes se habebat evaginavit et prefatum presbiterum ipsum invadentem cum dicto gladio in tribus digitis sinistre sue manus vim vi repellens repercussit, ita quod quorumdam opinione dictus presbiter fuit exinde mutulatus [*sic*]. Pater sancte, cum dictus exponens fuit hinc inde concordes [*recte* concors] et alter alteri satisfecerit competenter, supplicatur igitur eidem sanctitati vestre pro parte exponentis quatinus ipsum premissorum occasione nullam irregularitatis maculam incurrisse declarari mandare vel saltim secum super irregularitate ex premissis contractis [*sic*] dignemini misericorditer dispensare de gratia speciali.

Fiat de speciali secundum iudicium auditoris A.

Non diceretur vim vi repellere sed vindicare nisi forte ad repercutiendum paratus fuisset adversarius, sed propter iustum dolorem, licet numerum

---

[18] Perhaps the John Phelipes or Phelip of the city of Hereford who was ordained by the bishop of Hereford as an acolyte on 14 April 1408 and as a subdeacon on 22 March 1409 (*Reg. Mascall*, 137, 141).

excesserat quia digitos pro digito, et considerata concordia, videtur dispensandus: iudicium auditoris A.

60. [Bologna], 30 March 1411. The pope is requested to grant Robert Stok(?), deacon, Lincoln dioc., a licence to receive the holy order of the priesthood from any Catholic bishop *in forma dimissoria*. Fiat de speciali A. Reg. 1, fol. 90v.

Supplicationes signate per reverendum in Christo patrem et dominum dominum Antonium presbiterum cardinalem tituli sancti Marci, vulgariter Tudertinum nuncupatum, in absentia reverendorum in Christo patrum et dominorum dominorum Antonii Portuensis et Petri Tusculani episcoporum, maiorum domini nostri pape penitentiariorum, Rome, die xvi mensis Aprilis pontificatus domini Iohannis pape xxiii anno primo.

61. [Rome], *15 April 1411. Richard(?) Hankin, priest, [Coventry and] Lichfield dioc., solemnised a marriage although the banns were read only once; he seeks absolution from excommunication and infamy and a dispensation from irregularity.* Reg. 1, fol. 92r.

[Rome] xvii kal. Maii. Exponitur sanctitati vestre ex parte Cicardi [*recte* Ricardi?] Hankin, presbiteri Lichefeldensis diocesis, quod ipse olim, bannis semel tantum editis, inter quosdam virum et mulierem matrimonium in facie ecclesie alias tamen rite publice solempnizavit, propter quod incurrit sentenciam excommunicationis generaliter per constitutiones provinciales in tales promulgatas [*sic*] ac sic ligatus inmiscuit se divinis, missas et alia divina sacramenta ministrando, propter quod timet se maculam irregularitatis incurrisse. Quare humiliter supplicatur pro parte dicti exponentis quatinus ipsum ab omni huiusmodi sentencia excommunicationis absolvere ac secum super omni irregularitate quam premissorum occasione forsan incurrit ipsumque suo statui integre restituere, omnem infamie notam abolendam, graciose dispensare dignemini de gratia vestra speciali.

Fiat de speciali A.

[*Whole entry crossed out with marginal note*:] Canzelata quia expedita fuit in forma.

62. [Rome], 15 April 1411. Same grant as **43** sought by Fr John Bleye(?), OESA, Cambridge (*Cantabriggie*) convent, Ely dioc. *Fiat de speciali A.* Reg. 1, fol. 92r.

63. [Rome], 15 April 1411. Same grant as **43** sought by John Layceby, priest, Lincoln dioc. Approved with **71**. Reg. 1, fol. 92r.

64. [Rome], 15 April 1411. Same grant as **43** sought by Robert Welmade, priest, Lincoln dioc. Approved with **71**. Reg. 1, fol. 92r.

65. [Rome], 15 April 1411. Same grant as **43** sought by Elizabeth Patenere, Lincoln dioc. Approved with **71**. Reg. 1, fol. 92r.

66. [Rome], 15 April 1411. Same grant as **43** sought by John Yonge, priest, Chichester dioc.[19] Approved with **71**. Reg. 1, fol. 92r.

[19] Probably the John Yonge presented to the vicarage of Westbourne (Sussex), Chichester

67. [Rome], 15 April 1411. Same grant as **43** sought by Mary Scake, Winchester dioc. Approved with **71**. Reg. 1, fol. 92r.

68. [Rome], 15 April 1411. Same grant as **43** sought by Nicholas Cleyere, priest, Lincoln dioc. Approved with **71**. Reg. 1, fol. 92r.

69. [Rome], 15 April 1411. Same grant as **43** sought by Semeine Laxfeld and his wife Agnes, citizens of Lincoln. Approved with **71**. Reg. 1, fol. 92r.

70. [Rome], 15 April 1411. Same grant as **43** sought by Richard Tymberland, priest, Lincoln dioc. Approved with **71**. Reg. 1, fol. 92r.

71. [Rome], 15 April 1411. Same grant as **43** sought by Stephen Bay, priest, Lincoln dioc. *Fiat de speciali A.* (Approved with **63–70**.) Reg. 1, fol. 92r.

72. [Rome, 16 April 1411]. The pope is requested to grant that Nicholas Cleyere, priest, perpetual vicar of Beeby(?)[20] (*Bibere*), Lincoln dioc., may absolve all parishoners of both sexes *in forma 'Cupientes'* for five years. *Fiat de speciali ad quinquennium A.* Reg. 1, fol. 92r.

73. [Rome], 17 April 1411. Same grant as **43** sought by John Perleman, priest, Norwich dioc. *Fiat de speciali A.* Reg. 1, fol. 92v.

74. [Rome], 17 April 1411. Same grant as **43** sought by Edmund Perk, priest, Norwich dioc. *Fiat de speciali A.* Reg. 1, fol. 92v.

75. [Rome], 18 April 1411. Same grant as **43** sought by Thomas Claymondi and his wife Isabel, Lincoln dioc. *Fiat de speciali G(?).* Reg. 1, fol. 92v.

76. [Rome], 20 April 1411. Thomas Maning, deacon, Canterbury dioc., requests of the pope that he may be promoted to priest's orders by any Catholic bishop having the grace and communion of the apostolic see and willing to lay sacred hands on him and thereafter licitly minister in those orders, notwithstanding any papal constitutions and customs to the contrary. *Fiat de speciali A.* Reg. 1, fol. 92v.

77. *[Rome], 21 April 1411. John Belgrene, clerk, Coventry and Lichfield dioc., with the inhabitants of his town followed a temporal lord who promised to show them that Richard II was still alive, but instead he led them into a battle against his enemies, in which Belgrene was forced to take part.*[21] *Belgrene subsequently had himself promoted to all holy orders and now seeks a dispensation from irregularity.* Reg. 1, fol. 93r.

dioc., on 20 February 1399 and to Holy Trinity chantry in Hungerford parish church (Wilts.), Salisbury dioc., on 30 November 1413 (*Reg. Rede*, ii. 252, 326).

[20] Alternatively it may be Bamber (Lincs.).

[21] After Richard II's death in early 1400, several uprisings in his name and claims that he was still alive overshadowed the reign of Henry IV (d. 1413). This entry probably refers to the most significant revolt, that led by Hotspur, son of Henry Percy, earl of Northumberland. At Chester in early July 1403 he 'had issued proclamations to the effect that Richard was alive and would join an army of his supporters, first at Sandiway in Delamere Forest in

[Rome], xi kal. Maii. Exponitur sanctitati vestre pro parte Iohannis Belgrene, Conventrensis et Lichefeldensis diocesis tunc clerici, quod cum olim quidam potens dominus temporalis in villa ubi ipse exponens tunc inhabitaverat populo eiusdem opidi illic convocato et insimul congregato proclamasset publice seu proclamari procurasset quod eisdem, si per modicum spatium secum tendere vellent, regem Ricardum totius Anglie et presertim ville antedicte, dum vel si viveret, dominum temporalem dilectissimum, qui ab aliquibus mortuus et ab aliquibus vivus asserabatur, vivum ostenderet, ipse exponens una cum dicte ville villanis dicti domini temporalis verbis fidem adhibens eundem dominum causa videndi dictum regem vivere dumtaxat et propter nullum aliud associavit. Qui quidem exponens postquam per modicum spatium cum dicto domino temporali tetendisset et dictum regem nondum videre potuisset, timens se deceptum libenter versus dictam villam reversus fuisset, sed prout timuit accidit, et procedere usque in hostes dicti domini temporalis vi compellebatur, necnon coactus et invitus non in hostes sed sursum ne aliquem lederet sagittavit et isto modo homicidiis, mutilacionibus et sanguinis effusionibus interfuit defraudatus. Post hec dictus exponens se fecit ad omnes sacros ordines tamquam simplex et iuris ignarus promoveri propter quod idem exponens se irregularitatis maculam timet incurrisse. Verum pater sancte cum sepedictus ad dictum bellum fraudulenter et non ex proposito deceptus pervenerit, eidemque coactus et invitus interfuit neminemque leserit nec causa ledendi illic venerit sed potius anima et corpores si potuisset impedivisset, supplicatur igitur eidem sanctitati vestre ex parte eiusdem exponentis quatinus secum super irregularitate si quam per premissa contraxit dispensari sed in suis susceptis ordinibus licite valeat ministrare mandare dignemini de gratia speciali.

Fiat de speciali et commitatur ordinario A.

78. [*Rome*], *22 April 1411. Lewis Coychinche, priest, Llandaff dioc., studying at Oxford, had himself ordained as an acolyte and subdeacon on the same day without a dispensation. He later read a document for a lay seneschal, in which the bishop of Llandaff agreed to hand over to Lord Despenser[22] any men captured in his lordship who had committed crimes in the lord's lordship, and the seneschal then handed over two thieves to be hanged by the lord's men. Coychinche seeks absolution from his excesses and a dispensation from irregularity,* inhabilitas *and infamy.* Reg. 1, fol. 93r.

[Rome], x kal. Maii. Exponitur sanctitati vestre pro parte Lodowici Coychinche, presbiteri Landavensis diocesis in universitate Oxoniensi studens, quod ipse olim antequam clericali caractere insignitus existeret,

---

Cheshire and later at Prees in north Shropshire' – all of which places are in Coventry and Lichfield dioc. – 'in order to overthrow the usuper Henry of Lancaster' (P. Morgan, 'Henry IV and the shadow of Richard II', in *Crown, Government and People in the Fifteenth Century*, ed. R. E. Archer (Stroud, 1995), 1–31, esp. pp. 23–4). Hotspur raised an army which fought in Richard's name against the 'usurper' outside Shrewsbury on 21 July 1403.

[22] The barony of Despenser was attainted following the rebellion of Thomas, Lord Despenser (d. 1400), against Henry IV. This document may refer to Thomas's son and heir, Richard (d. 1414), a minor in royal wardship in 1411 (*ODNB*, xv. 918–19; *Complete Peerage*, iv. 278–82).

habitu subdyaconali indutus epistolas infra missarum solempnia pluries publice legit et deinde clericali el caractere insignitus se fecit ad acolitatus et subdyaconatus ordines uno et eodem die absque dispensatione aliqua alias tamen rite et statuto a iure tempore promoveri. Subsequenter quoque [per] officialem laicum senescallum nuncupatum pro tunc in illis partibus curiis secularibus presidentem cordialiter rogatus ut quandam cartam quam ipse officialis tunc penes se habebat legeret et sibi vulgariter exponeret, illam statim perlegit et idem exposuit nesciens tamen malum seu preiudicium alicui exinde posse evenire. Cum autem in huiusmodi scriptura contineretur quedam compositio seu ordinatio facta inter venerabilem in Christo patrem tunc episcopum Landovensem ex una et quendam dominum de Spenser parte ex altera quod si aliqui furta, latrocinia seu alia malicia infra dictam dominium domini de Spenser perpetrassent et in dominio episcopi predicti capti essent per ipsius episcopi ministros, [ministris] domini de Spenser predicti tradirentur et in loco dilicti [*sic*] de eis fieret iusticia, accidit quod post modicum temporis duo latrones qui ut dicebatur erant capti in dominio dicti episcopi Landovensis et in quodam suo castro detenti per officialem prefatum ministris dicti domini de Spenser traditi et assignati ac per ipsos ad ultimum supplicium damnati iudicialiter fuerunt et suspensi. Verum pater sancte cum in morte predictorum alias quam ut premittitur culpabilis non existat, supplicatur igitur eidem sanctitati vestre pro parte dicti exponentis quatinus ipsum ab excessibus huiusmodi ac peccatis suis aliis mandare dignemini absolvi, secum super irregularitate et inhabilitate ac infamia ex premissis contracta misericorditer dispensare, ipsumque ad statum pristinum restituere et [quod] dictis ordinibus sic susceptis uti possit, non obstantibus constitutionibus apostolicis seu aliis in contrarium editis non obst quibuscumque.

Fiat de speciali A.

79. [Rome], 24 April 1411. Same grant as **43** sought by Roger Buxton, priest, York dioc. *Fiat de speciali A.* Reg. 1, fol. 94r.

80. [Rome], 6 May 1411. Same grant as **43** sought by Roger Lovote, rector of Buildwas (*Boulewas*) parish church, [Coventry and] Lichfield dioc. *Fiat de speciali A.* Reg. 1, fol. 96r.

81. [Rome], 6 May 1411. Same grant as **43** sought by Fr Roger Tyshurst, prior of Combwell Priory, OSA, Canterbury dioc.[23] *Fiat de speciali A.* Reg. 1, fol. 97v.

---

[23] Roger de Tycehurst was prior by 1387. When his priory received a visitation from William Courtenay, archbishop of Canterbury, on 16 September 1387, Tyshurst had been absent since 6 August 1387; he was accused of 'dilapidating' the priory's goods, adultery, and apostasy, and removed as prior, but re-admitted as a canon. One of the charges against him was cutting down trees, and at a later visitation on behalf of Courtenay's successor he had to swear not to do this without the archbishop's permission (see **82**). He was replaced as prior by Simon Madiston, but after prolonged litigation at the Curia Roger secured a definitive sentence condemning Simon and reinstating himself (*CPL*, iv. 522–3). Roger was succeeded before 1421 by William Bourgeys (Smith, *Heads of Religious Houses*, iii. 418).

82. [*Rome*], *6 May 1411. Fr Roger Tyshurst, prior of Combwell Priory, OSA, Canterbury dioc., was compelled by Philip Morgan,*[24] *a commisary of the archbishop of Canterbury*[25] *sent to conduct a visitation of the priory, to swear not to cut down or sell woods or large oaks without the archbishop's express permission. Tyshurst seeks a dispensation from this oath.* Reg. 1, fol. 98r.

[Rome], nonas Maii. Exponitur sanctitati vestre ex parte fratris Rogeri Tyshurst, prioris prioratus de Combwell ordinis sancti Augustini Cantuariensis diocesis, quod dudum Philippus Morgan, utriusque iuris doctor, ex parte reverende [*sic*] patris Thome archiepiscopi Cantuariensis ad visitandum dictum prioratum tam in capite quam in membris commissarius specialiter deputatus, quoddam illicitum iuramentum contra conscientiam et ordinationem dicti prioratus necnon et consuetudines inviolabiliter in eodem hactenus observatas ab ipso priore exegit et realiter prestare compellebat, videlicet quod idem prior nullo modo nemora vel quercus grandes sine concilio et expressa licentia ipsius reverendi patris sub litteris auctenticis sub sigillo sigillatis obtenta etiam si ad commodum et utilitatem sui prioratus abscindere, vendere seu alienare presumeret, in dicti prioris preiudicium non modicum et gravamen. Verum pater sancte nullum illicitum iuramentum a canone est observatum [*recte* observandum], et sine gravi dispendio prioris et conventus dicti prioratus ipse prior huiusmodi iuramentum observare non potest. Supplicat[ur] igitur pro parte exponentis quatinus secum huiusmodi non obstante iuramento arbores, nemora, quercus grandes et parvas abscindere et alia ligna quecumque vendere et, ut pre[de]cessores sui prioris in utilitatem dicti prioratus facere consueverunt, alienare libere et licite valeat dignemini misericorditer dispensare, constitutionibus apostolicis in contrarium editis non obstantibus quibuscumque, de gratia speciali.

Fiat de speciali A.

Supplicationes signate per reverendum in Cristo patrem et dominum d. P. episcopum Tuscullanum, maiorem penitentiarium, in Roma. Registrate per me Ia. de Parma prout infra.

83. [Rome], 9 May 1411. The pope is requested to grant Richard Maryn, priest, rector of Hampstead Marshall (*Hamsted Marchell*) parish church, Salisbury dioc.,[26] a faculty to absolve all his parishoners of both sexes *in forma 'Cupientes'* for five years. *Fiat de speciali ad quinquennium B.* Reg. 1, fol. 99r.

84. [Rome], 10 May 1411. Same faculty as **83** sought by Richard FitzJohn, rector of Ampton (*Amton*), Norwich dioc. *Fiat de speciali B.* Reg. 1, fol. 99r.

85. [Rome], 10 May 1411. Same grant as **43** sought by John Strangman, priest, Lincoln (*Linconiensis*) dioc. *Fiat de speciali B.* Reg. 1, fol. 99r.

---

[24] Philip Morgan was DCL by 1397, DCn & CL by 1404, auditor of causes in the court of Canterbury 1410–13, bishop of Worcester 1419–26, bishop of Ely from 1426 until his death in 1435. For his career, benefices and diplomatic activities, see *BRUO*, ii. 1312–13; *ODNB*, xxxix. 136–7.

[25] Thomas Arundel, archbishop of Canterbury, 1396–7, 1399–1414.

[26] Richard Moryn exchanged this benefice for the vicarage of East Garston (Berks.), Salisbury dioc., on 4 February 1417 (*Reg. Hallum*, no. 658).

John XXIII (1410–1415) 33

86. [Rome], 10 May 1411. Same grant as **43** sought by Ralph Maysand, priest.[27] *Fiat de speciali B.* Reg. 1, fol. 99r.

87. [*Rome*], *12 May 1411. Gwilym Gwyn, priest, St David's dioc.,*[28] *found a penny that he had dropped, but Robert, parish priest of Olveston, Worcester dioc., claimed that it was his, and disbelieved Gwilym's protests to the contrary, asserting that he and all his nation were liars. Robert and then Gwilym drew knives and Robert was fatally wounded, dying two days later. Gwilym seeks absolution from this excess, and a dispensation from irregularity or a declaration that he may minister in his orders and hold a benefice.* Reg. 1, fol. 99r–v.

[Rome], iiii id. Maii. Exponit sanctitati vestre devotus vester Willelmus Gwyn, presbiter Menevensis diocesis, quod ipse olim et unus alius nomine Robertus, presbiter parrochialis ecclesie de Oldeston' Wygoniensis diocesis, simul existentes in quadam domo ubi solebant commedere et bibere, accedit casualiter ut unus denarius Anglicanus ad terram in ipsa domo de manibus dicti exponentis cecidit, quem diligenter perquirens sed tamen cum denarium propter obscuritatem noctis tunc temporis instanter invenire non potuit, lumen petiit quo portato statim in presentia dicti Roberti et cuiusdam familiaris ipsius Roberti denarium huiusmodi predictum invenit. Quo denario viso [fol. 99v] ipsius Roberti familiaris asseruit ipsum denarium esse et pertinere debere ad dictum Robertum magistrum suum, dictusque exponens e converso asseruit prefatum denarium suum esse, ipseque Robertus incontinenti [*recte* incontinenter] dixit animo furibundo et iniuriandi causa dictum exponentem mentire ut falsus ribaldus. Cui pacificare volens exponens prefatus et ut malam suspicionem fraudibus diabolibus [*sic*] suscitatus penitus tolleret iuravit super crucem quod huiusmodi denarium erat suus. Quo iuramento emisso, prefatus Robertus animo protervo e converso dixit: 'Non maiorem fidem dictis tuis adhibeam quam si super stramen aut aliam rem iurasses, cum tu et omnes de natione tua sunt falsi et proditores.' Cui Roberto dictus exponens prefatus voce placida et non animo litem aut discordiam suscitandi respondit quod erat et sui de natione fuerunt ita fideles sicut ipse Robertus umquam fuit. Qui quidem Robertus absque intervallo et sine mora cultellum extraxit, volens exponentem predictum interficere. Quo viso dictus exponens cum inclusus fuit in domo predicta ubi ut premissum est commedere et bibere solebant ipse et dictus Robertus, et fugere non potuit, dictus exponens suum cultellum e converso extraxit quod videns dictus Robertus in exponentem antedictum irruit et casualiter a cultello dicti exponentis erat lesus, de qua lesione post duos dies, primitus perceptis sacramentis ecclesiasticis, diem suum clausit extremum. Verum pater sancte lite fuerit licet [*recte* licet fuerit licite] vim vi repellere et precipue cum dictus exponens fugere non potuit, tamen exponens prefatus numquam se inmiscuit divinis, quare supplicat eidem sanctitati vestre quatinus ipsum ab huiusmodi excessu et peccatis suis aliis mandare absolvi et super irregularitatis maculam si quam propter premissa incurrisset dispensare, aut declarare

---

[27] The gap left for the diocese has not been filled in.
[28] Presumably the William Gwyn, choral vicar of the collegiate church of Abergwili, St David's dioc., who was ordained by the bishop of St David's as a deacon on 18 February 1402, and as priest on 25 March 1402 (*Reg. St David's*, i. 256, 260).

quod in susceptis ordinibus ministrare et beneficium ecclesiasticum obtinere et obtinendum retinere et recipere libere et licite valeat dignemini misericorditer dispensare de gratia speciali.

Fiat de speciali B.

88. [Rome], 12 May 1411. Same grant as **43** sought by John Bowland, rector of Hickling (*Hyklyng*), York dioc. *Fiat de speciali B.* Reg. 1, fol. 100r.

89. [*Rome*], *13 May 1411. Fr John Gloucestre, priest, professed monk of Glastonbury Abbey, OSB, Bath and Wells dioc.,*[29] *was convicted by his brethren of numerous crimes at a visitation of the archbishop of Canterbury, and he was moved to another monastery, but later sent back to his abbey by the archbishop. He seeks a dispensation from his infamy and* inhabilitas. Reg. 1, fol. 100r.

[Rome], iii id. Maii. Exponitur sanctitati vestre \pro parte/ devoti vestri fratris Iohannis Gloucestre, presbiteri, monachi professi monasterii Glastonie ordinis sancti Benedicti Vellensis diocesis, quod dudum in quadam visitatione reverendi patris archiepiscopi Cantuariensis in capite quam in membris dicti monasterii ordinarie facta ipse per confratres suos criminibus quamplurimis accusatus et de ipsis iudicialiter convictus per sententiam diffinitivam ad aliud monasterium eiusdem ordinem translatus fuit, ibidem commoraturus donec idem archiepiscopus aliud de eo duxisset ordinandum. Prefatus exponens in monasterio ad quod sic translatus fuit aliquamdiu conversatus ad proprium monasterium de G. in quo professus fuerat per prefatum archiepiscopum remissus extitit. Verum pater sancte tales de criminibus convicti per constitutionem et statuta dicti ordinis et alias a iure efficiunt[ur] infames et ad dignitates, administrationes et officia obtinenda redantur inhabiles. Supplicatur igitur quatinus ipsum ad statum pristinum restitui mandare secumque super inhabilitatis ac infamie maculis ex premissis contractis et ut ad omnes dignitates, administrationes et officia dicti ordinis licite eligi, prefici et assumi valeat dignemini misericorditer dispensare de gratia speciali.

Fiat de speciali et commitatur ordinario qui dispenset cum eo si sibi videatur quod sit bene conversatus dum tamen non sit scandalum in ordine B.

90. [Rome], 14 May 1411. Same grant as **43** sought by John Mauri, priest of Winchester. *Fiat de speciali B.* Reg. 1, fol. 101v.

91. [Rome], 19 May 1411. Same grant as **43** sought by Alan Hocost, priest, expressly professed canon, OSA, of Thornton [Abbey], Lincoln dioc. *Fiat de speciali B.* Reg. 1, fol. 104v.

92. [Rome], 19 May 1411. The pope is requested to grant William Schefeld,[30] priest, rector of Sall (*Salle*) parish church, Norwich dioc., a licence to absolve all his parishoners of both sexes of all their sins for five years. *Fiat de speciali [B].* Reg. 1, fol. 104v.

---

[29] As proctor for the abbey's prior and convent he sought episcopal confirmation of their abbot-elect on 10 September 1420 (*Reg. Bubwith*, 481).

[30] He was granted *littere confessionales* on 10 April 1405, when he is described as rector of 'Gulle' (*recte* Salle), Norwich dioc. (*CPL*, vi. 21).

93. [Rome], 19 May 1411. Same grant as **43** sought by Thomas Penkrith, chaplain, London dioc. *Fiat de speciali* [*B*]. Reg. 1, fol. 104v.

94. [*Rome, c. 20–1 May 1411*].[31] *Walter Tewkysbury, friar of Ludlow convent, OCarm, Hereford dioc., had celebrated divine offices as one promoted to all orders and exercised offices conferred on him in his order, when his mother told him on her deathbed that his father was not the man whom he thought but another, married man. Walter had then continued to exercise his offices and hear confessions but he now requests absolution from this excess and a dispensation.* Reg. 1, fol. 106r.

Beatissime pater, exponitur sanctitati vestre pro parte devoti vestri Walteri Tewkysbury, fratris domus sive conventus de Ludlowe, ordinis fratrum Carmelitarum, Herfordensis diocesis, quod ipse olim ad omnes tam minores quam etiam sacros ordines rite promotus divina celebravit officia et alias se inmiscuit eisdem quodque ad officia et dignitates dicti ordinis preelectus et assumptus in hiis que ad ministrationem huiusmodi officiorum sive dignitatum pertinebant ad dei laudem et sue ordinis utilitatem prout sibi commissum fuerat administravit. Postmodum vero ipsius Walteri mater languens in extremis eundem exalterum [*sic*] filium suum ad presentiam suam venire fecit, cui in huiusmodi presentia constituto prefata mater dicti Walteri exposuit eidem dicendo inter cetera quod ille quem dictus Walterus habebat pro patre et reputabatur patrem suum esse eius pater genitive non fuerat sed quod quidam alius vir coniugatus ipsius Walteri pater erat, ut asseruit in extremis sic constituta, quibus relatis, sicut deo placuit, diem suum clausit extremum. Verum pater sancte licet dictus Walterus credentiam matris sue relatibus pro tunc dederat, in eisdem ordinibus, officiis et dignitatibus susceptis administrare non cessavit, necnon comporalium [*recte* corporalium] et spiritualium sive laicorum et clericorum personarum ex admissione locorum ordinariorum et prelatorum audivit pro tempore confessiones. Nunc autem ipse Walterus quasi in septuagesimo sue etatis anno constitutus ac aliis variis infirmitatibus laborans, conscientia motus, suum reatum confitetur. Quare pro parte ipsius Walteri eidem sanctitati vestre supplicatur quatinus ipsum a predicta excessu et a peccatis suis aliis absolvi mandare et ut in susceptis ordinibus ministrare ac ad officia et dignitates dicti ordinis eligi et assumi valeat cum eodem W. misericorditer dispensare [dignemini] de gratia speciali.

Fiat de speciali B.

---

[31] The entry is undated, but the last entry on fol. 105v is dated 20 May and an entry on fol. 106r 21 May.

EUGENIUS IV
(1431–1447)

De diversis formis

95. [Ferrara, 1 July 1438]. The pope is requested to grant *littere confessionales* in perpetuity to Anne Cowhin, noblewoman, Lincoln dioc., and Sybil de la Bere,[1] noblewoman, Hereford dioc. *Fiat de speciali Io.* Reg. 2, fol. 91r.

96. [Ferrara], 1 July 1438. The pope is requested on the part of William Wortham, priest, rector of Bassingham (*Basinglam*),[2] Lincoln dioc., BCL and CnL, to grant him a licence to attend lectures (*audire*), study, and read for five years in a faculty of civil law (*in facultate iuris civilis bachalarii*) and receive a licence and a doctorate there, notwithstanding any apostolic or other constitututions to the contrary. *Fiat de speciali Io.* Reg. 2, fols. 92v–93r.

97. [Ferrara], 29 August 1438. [The pope is requested to grant *littere confessionales*] for life to Geoffrey Chittok, citizen of London, and his wife Margery.[3] Approved with **98**. Reg. 2, fol. 95v.

98. [Ferrara], 29 August 1438. Same grant as **97** sought by Robert Gode, BCnL, rector of Ashprington (*Aysshpryngton*), Exeter dioc.[4] *Fiat de speciali Io.* (Approved with **97**.) Reg. 2, fol. 95v.

99. [Ferrara], 31 August 1438. The pope is requested on the part of Richard Norman, clerk, Norwich dioc., aged 21, to grant him a dispensation so that on reaching the age of 24 he may be promoted to priest's orders and thereafter minister in them. *Fiat de speciali in vicesimoquarto Io.* Reg. 2, fol. 101v.

100. [Ferrara], 13 September 1438. Same grant as **97** sought by Thomas Richeford, esquire, and his wife Margaret, nobles, Norwich dioc. *Fiat de speciali Io.* Reg. 2, fol. 99v.

101. Ferrara, 29 December 1438. The pope is requested on the part of William Bayly, clerk of the vill of Teigh (*Tey*), Lincoln dioc., to grant him a dispensation

---

[1] She was granted a licence to have a portable altar on 24 June 1438, when she was also described as a *domicella* (*CPL*, viii. 393).

[2] He held this rectory by 5 October 1437 when he was granted a dispensation to hold two incompatible benefices; he was described then as simply BCL, of noble birth, and having the surname Witham (*CPL*, viii. 659).

[3] Geoffrey Chyttok (or Chittok), lord of Lampetts in Fyfield parish, London dioc., and his wife were also granted a plenary indulgence *in mortis articulo* and a licence to have a portable altar on 30 August 1438 (*CPL*, viii. 393–4).

[4] He was admitted as rector of Ashprington (Somerset) on 9 April 1424 and secured a licence to celebrate in three chapels of that parish on 5 June 1424 (*Reg. Lacy*, ed. Hingeston-Randolph, i. 78; *Reg. Lacy*, ed. Dunstan, i. 103). He obtained a licence of non-residence for a year in 1425, again in 1426, 1427 (for two years), and 1429, during which years he was probably studying canon law, maybe at Oxford (*Reg. Lacy*, ed. Hingeston-Randolph, i. 26; *Reg. Lacy*, ed. Dunstan, i. 134–5, 190, 223). He was still alive in April 1441 (ibid., ii. 231). See also *Reg. Lacy*, ed. Hingeston-Randolph, i. 19; *Reg. Lacy*, ed. Dunstan, ii. 207–9.

so that on reaching the age of 24 he may be promoted to priest's orders and minister in them, notwithstanding his defect of age and any constitutions of the Lateran and Lyons councils and any other constitutions to the contrary. *Concessum de speciali in presentia domini Cardinalis Pe. de Noxeto.* In left margin: *gross' VI.* Reg. 2, fol. 5v.

102. Ferrara, 30 December 1438. Richard Prowdfot, clerk, Lincoln dioc, requests that the pope grant him a licence so that, notwithstanding any apostolic consitutions and customs to the contrary, he may be promoted to all orders successively by any Catholic bishop having the grace and communion of the apostolic see, and that after he has been promoted he may minister in the same, since he cannot approach his ordinary to receive the same orders because of the distance of the place. *Concessum de speciali in presentia domini Cardinalis Pe. de Noxeto.* Reg. 2, fol. 24r.

103. Ferrara, 4 January 1439. The pope is requested on the part of John Dolman, clerk, Norwich dioc., to grant him a dispensation so that on reaching the age of 24 he may be promoted to all even holy orders and minister in them, notwithstanding his defect of age and any constitutions of the Lateran and Lyons councils and any other constitutions to the contrary. Approved with **105**. Reg. 2, fol. 12r.

104. Ferrara, 4 January 1439. Same dispensation as **103** sought by Thomas Rutlond, clerk, Norwich dioc. Approved with **105**. Reg. 2, fol. 12r.

105. Ferrara, 4 January 1439. The pope is requested to grant *littere confessionales* in perpetuity to Roger Harsyk, knight, and his wife Alice, nobles, Norwich dioc. *Concessum de speciali pro omnibus supradictis in presentia domini cardinalis Pe.* (Approved with **103–4**.) Reg. 2, fol. 12r.

106. Ferrara, 10 January 1439. Richard Rowe, acolyte, Norwich dioc., requests that the pope grant him a licence so that, notwithstanding any apostolic constitutions and customs to the contrary, he may be promoted to all holy orders by any Catholic bishop having the grace and communion of the apostolic see, and after he has been promoted that he may minister in the same, since he cannot approach his ordinary to receive the same orders because of the distance of the place. *Concessum de speciali in presentia domini Cardinalis Pe.* Reg. 2, fol. 16v.

107. Ferrara, 13 January 1439. The pope is requested to grant *littere confessionales* for life to John Cok and his wife Agnes, Canterbury dioc. *Concessum de speciali in presentia domini Cardinalis Pe.* Reg. 2, fol. 18v.

108. Florence, 3 February 1439. The pope is requested to order that Fr John Kyllyng, priest, professed monk of St Mary's monastery, Croxden (*Crokesden*), Cistercian order, Coventry and Lichfield dioc., be absolved of all general sentences *in forma assertiva cum clausula concubinatus. Fiat in forma Io.* Reg. 2, fol. 21r.

109. [Florence], 13 February 1439. Same licence as **106** sought by Robert Sanych, acolyte, Norwich dioc., notwithstanding constitutions and anything else to the contrary. Approved with **110**. Reg. 2, fol. 28r.

110. [Florence], 13 February 1439. Same letters dimissory as in **106** sought by Richard Wegener, acolyte, Norwich dioc. *Fiat de speciali N.* (Approved with **109**.) Reg. 2, fol. 28r.

111. [Florence, *c.* 19 February 1439].⁵ Same dispensation as **101** sought by John Smyth, clerk, Norwich dioc.⁶ *Fiat de speciali N.* Reg. 2, fol. 32v.

112. [Florence, *c.* 19 February 1439]. Same grant as **107** sought by Robert Barellis and Margaret, his wife, of Halesworth (*Hallesworth*), Norwich dioc. Approved with **113**. Reg. 2, fol. 32v.

113. [Florence, *c.* 19 February 1439]. Same grant as **107** sought by John Hopton and his wife Margaret, Norwich dioc.⁷ *Fiat de speciali N.* (Approved with **112**.) Reg. 2, fol. 32v.

114. [Florence, *c.* 19 February 1439]. Same grant as **107** sought by John Smyth and his wife Joan, Norwich dioc. Approved with **115**. Reg. 2, fol. 32v.

115. [Florence, *c.* 19 February 1439]. Same grant as **107** sought by John Scharpe, priest of Halesworth (*Hallesworth*), Norwich dioc. *Fiat de speciali N.* (Approved with **114**.) Reg. 2, fol. 32v.

116. Florence, 1 March 1439. Same grant as **107** sought by John Hervy and his wife Agnes (*Agneli*), Norwich (*Narwicensis*) dioc. Approved with **117**. Reg. 2, fol. 36r.

117. Florence, 1 March 1439. Same grant as **107** sought by Robert Wode, priest, Norwich dioc.⁸ *Fiat de speciali N.* (Approved with **116**.) Reg. 2, fol. 36r.

118. [*Florence*], *11 March 1439. Fr John Kylling, priest, professed monk of Croxden Abbey, Cistercian order, Coventry and Lichfield dioc., had been ejected from his monastery without just cause and with letters of doubtful authority. He accompanied an army overseas for five weeks and supported but did not commit looting, killing and arson. He seeks absolution from excommunication and his excesses and the said wrongs and a dispensation from irregularity.* Reg. 2, fols. 61v–62r.

> [Florentie], v id. Martii. Beatissime pater, exponit sanctitati vestre devotus vester frater Iohannes Kylling, presbiter, monachus professus monasterii beate Marie de Croskeden, ordinis Cisterciensis, Lichclfeldensis [*sic*] diocesis, quod cum ipse olim sine causa rationabili et iusta precedente de monasterio in quo

---

⁵ The entry is undated; the only dated entry on fol. 32v, which follows it, has the date 'xi kal. Martii'.
⁶ Unlikely to be the man of this name who was rector of Bawdeswell (Norf.), 1436–55, and a Cambridge graduate (see *BRUC*, 534; *CPL*, ix. 8, 517).
⁷ Perhaps the John Hopton, nobleman, lord of Swillington, York dioc., who with his wife Margaret was granted a licence to have a portable altar on 2 April 1435 (*CPL*, viii. 570).
⁸ Presumably the man of this name who was rector of Thorington (Suff.) by 16 May 1439 when he was granted a dispensation to hold an additional incompatible benefice (*CPL*, ix. 60).

professus erat eiectus extiterat et, ut verisimile erat, per invidiam cuiusdam persone regularis ipsius monasterii, et littere licentie sibi date erant sub [fol. 62r] sigillo illius qui pro tunc non prefuit regimini monasterii tamquam abbas sed per prius cesserat abbaciali dignitati, pretextu cuius parvi vel nullius valoris huiusmodi littere erant. Tamquam desperatus, habitu et ordine derelictis, illicentiatus cum quodam exercitu mare ad alienas partes transfretavit et in eodem exercitu per quinque septimanas, ubi spolia, rapine, homicidia laicalia et incendia in locis sacris et non sacris perpetrata fuerunt, interfuit et ad ea consilium, auxilium prestitit et favorem, nec tamen aliqua earum manu propria perpetravit, propter quod excommunicationis incurrit sententias in tales etc. [generaliter promulgatas] et sic ligatus divina celebravit officia ac alias inmiscuit se in eisdem. Nunc vero ad cor reversus [est] cupitque ad ovile redire et inibi altissimo perpetuum prebere famulatum in omnibus suis ordinibus prout tenetur. Supplicat igitur sanctitati vestre dictus exponens quatinus ipsum a sententiis excommunicationum excessibusque ac reatibus rapinarum, spoliorum, homicidiorum, et incendiorum huiusmodi absolvi mandare secumque super irregularitate ex premissis contracta quodque in favorem religionis in omnibus suis ordinibus libere et licite ministrare valeat dignemini misericorditer dispensare de gratia speciali.

Concessum de speciali in presencia d. Cardinalis Pe.

119. [Florence], 22 March 1439. Peter Cantelen, acolyte, Norwich dioc., requests that the pope grant him a licence so that, notwithstanding any apostolic, provincial, synodal and other constitutions to the contrary, he may be promoted to all holy orders by any Catholic bishop having the grace and communion of the apostolic see, and after he has been promoted, that he may minister in the same, since he cannot approach his ordinary to receive the same orders because of the distance of the place. *Fiat de speciali N.* Reg. 2, fol. 55r.

120. [Florence], 26 March 1439. Same grant as **107** sought by John Spark, priest, Norwich dioc. *Fiat de speciali N.* Reg. 2, fol. 52r.

121. [Florence], 26 March 1439. Same grant as **107** sought by Robert Ston, notary, and his wife Margaret, Norwich dioc. *Fiat de speciali N.* Reg. 2, fol. 52v.

122. [Florence], 27 March 1439. Same dispensation as **101** sought by John Rugg, clerk, Norwich dioc. [*Fiat de speciali N.*] Reg. 2, fol. 50v.

123. [Florence], 27 March 1439. The pope is requested on the part of John Estweycht, scholar, [Norwich?] dioc., born of an unmarried man and an unmarried woman, to grant him a dispensation from his defect of birth so that he may be promoted to all holy orders and obtain a benefice even with cure of souls. *Fiat de speciali N.* Reg. 2, fol. 51r.

124. [Florence], 27 March 1439. Same dispensation as **101** sought by Robert Hamond, clerk, Norwich dioc. Approved with **125**. Reg. 2, fol. 51v.

125. [Florence], 27 March 1439. Same dispensation as **101** sought by Thomas Bonett, clerk, Norwich dióc. *Fiat de speciali* [*N*]. (Approved with **124**.) Reg. 2, fol. 51v.

126. [Florence], 30 March 1439. Robert Eschton, acolyte, Lincoln dioc., requests that the pope grant him a licence so that, notwithstanding any apostolic, provincial, and synodal constitutions to the contrary, he may be promoted to all holy orders by any Catholic bishop having the grace and communion of the apostolic see, and after he has been promoted, that he may minister in the same, since he cannot approach his ordinary to receive the same orders because of the distance of the place. *Fiat de speciali N.* Reg. 2, fol. 49v.

127. [Florence], 30 March 1439. Same grant as **107** sought by John Teye, esquire, and his wife Mary, nobles, London dioc. Approved with **129**. Reg. 2, fol. 49v.

128. [Florence], 30 March 1439. Same grant as **107** sought by Thomas Sent and his wife Marion, London dioc. Approved with **129**. Reg. 2, fol. 49v.

129. [Florence], 30 March 1439. Same grant as **107** sought by Robert Priore and his wife Elizabeth, London dioc. *Fiat de speciali N.* (Approved with **127–8**.) Reg. 2, fol. 49v.

130. [Florence], 30 March 1439. The pope is requested on the part of Richard Brothere, clerk, Norwich dioc., to grant him a dispensation so that on reaching the first day of his twenty-fourth year he may be promoted to all orders and minister in them, [notwithstanding any] constitutions to the contrary. *Fiat de speciali N.* Reg. 2, fol. 61v.

131. [Florence], 3 [April] 1439. Same grant as **107** sought by Robert Walweyn, priest, Winchester dioc. *Fiat de speciali N.* Reg. 2, fol. 64r.

132. *[Florence], 7 April 1439. Thomas Cok, priest, Coventry and Lichfield dioc., was in a nobleman's retinue when it was attacked by a knight and his men; he wounded one of these men, who quickly recovered. Later Cok took part in the defence of Calais against the king's enemies, and then he celebrated divine offices. He requests absolution from excommunication and infamy and a dispensation from irregularity.* Reg. 2, fol. 75r–v.

> [Florentie], vii idus Aprilis. Exponit sanctitati vestre devotus vester Thomas Cok, presbiter Lichefeldensis diocesis, quod cum ipse olim in comitiva cuiusdam nobilis qui cum uno milite lites ex certis causis habebat existeret, et quia nobilis ille, una die ecclesiam suam parrochialem ad divina audienda ire volens, securius ad eandem accedere poterat, quosdam suos vicinos et amicos pro sui tuitione et securitate in eius societate convocari fecit, et dum ad dictam ecclesiam accedere vellet, quosdam ex familiaribus suis premisit ad videndum si dictus miles ibidem in ecclesia predicta esset, quos familiares cum dictus miles vidisset spiritu diabolico motus eosdem graviter insultavit, in quo insultu dictus nobilis supervenit, dictorum familiarium dominus, qui pro dictis suis familiaribus secum aliis suis vicinis et amicis defencioni dedit, in qua defencione duo laici /de\ ~~pra~~ parte dicti militis interfecti fuerunt, necnon ipse exponens in eius defencione, qui cum prefato nobili erat, unum alium laicum de parte [fol. 75v] dicti militis in capite v[u]lneravit, de quo vulnere idem laicus cito sanitatem recuperavit. Postmodum vero per nonnulla temporum intervalla, ipso exponente in villa Calesie Morinensis

diocesis moram trahente, dum dictam villam inimici capitales circumvallabant et eam obcessam habebant, illos quos dictus exponens armis invasivis et defensivis [. . .]⁹ cum aliis sacerdotibus et laicis pro defencione dicte ville et patrie adiacentis aliquotiens invadebant, domorum inimicorum huiusmodi incendiis et rapinis ex premissa causa per homines in quorum societate tunc erat perpetratis interessendo et participando, cum eisdem illisque inimicis dicte ville insultum dantibus vi et armis cum aliis armatis viris ecclesiasticis et secularibus pro ville et patrie predictarum ac iuris sui regis defencione in quantum poterat resistebat; in quibus conflictibus, resistencia et insultu multi interfecti erant, prout dictum fuerat, sed nullum sciebat ad mortem vel alias per ipsum vulneratum fuisse, et nullis super premissis absolutione et dispensatione per eum obtentis, pluries celebravit divina officia et alias inmiscuit se eisdem. Cum autem ipse in morte ipsorum laicorum alias quam premittitur culpabilis non fuerit et ex magno devotionis fervore cupiat in omnibus suis ordinibus perpetuo domino famulari, supplicat igitur sanctitati vestre dictus exponens quatinus ipsum ab excommunicationis sententia qua forsan propter premissa ligatus est [absolvere], necnon secum super irregularitate per ipsum premissorum occasione contracta dispensare, ac omnem infamie maculam sive notam quibus ipsum ex premissis innodatum esse asseritur abolere dignemini de gratia speciali, premissis et aliis in contrarium facientibus non obstantibus quibuscumque.

Fiat ut infra N. Signanda per fiat de speciali sed de spoliis, incendiis et rapinis fiat littera de per se ut in forma.

133. [Florence], 5 [April] 1439. Same grant as **107** sought by John Acham, priest, rector of Barnham(?) (*Bernaham*),¹⁰ Norwich dioc. Approved with **134**. Reg. 2, fol. 70v.

134. [Florence], 5 [April] 1439. Same grant as **107** sought by Semeine Burton, merchant, Norwich dioc. *Fiat de speciali N.* (Approved with **133**.) Reg. 2, fol. 70v.

135. [Florence], 9 [April] 1439. The pope is requested on the part of Thomas Kebows, clerk, Norwich dioc., to grant him a dispensation so that on reaching the age of 24 he may be promoted to priest's orders and minister in them, notwithstanding his defect of age and any constitutions of the Lateran and Lyons councils and any other apostolic constitutions to the contrary. *Fiat de speciali N.* Reg. 2, fol. 68r.

136. [Florence], 9 [April] 1439. Same grant as **107** sought by John Odam and his wife Margaret, Norwich dioc. *Fiat de speciali N.* Reg. 2, fol. 70r.

137. [Florence], 13 [April] 1439. The pope is requested to grant John Saxmundham, priest, rector of St Peter's parish church, Dunwich (*de Donwico*), Norwich dioc., a licence to absolve all his parishoners of either sex for five years. *Fiat de speciali N.* Reg. 2, fol. 71r.

⁹ Illegible word.
¹⁰ Alternatively it may be Barnham Broom or Barningham in Norfolk or Barningham in Suffolk.

138. [Florence], 13 [April] 1439. Same grant as **107** sought by Richard Ventre, nobleman, knight, Norwich dioc. *Fiat de speciali N.* Reg. 2, fol. 71r.

139. [Florence], 20 [April] 1439. Same dispensation as **101** sought by Fr William Smyth, deacon, professed of the monastery of Whitby (*Whiteby*), OSB, York dioc. *Fiat de speciali N.* Reg. 2, fol. 80r.

140. [Florence], 23 April 1439. The pope is requested on the part of John Nugate, clerk, Norwich dioc., to grant him a dispensation so that on reaching the age of 20[11] he may be promoted to priest's orders and minister in them, notwithstanding his defect of age and any constitutions of the Lateran and Lyons councils and any other constitutions to the contrary. *Fiat de speciali N.* Reg. 2, fol. 78r–v.

141. *[Florence], 23 April 1439. Fr William Dalton, priest, professed monk of Whitby Abbey, OSB, York dioc., incurred excommunication for apostasy when he was 17 by making an unauthorised visit to his mother, who had sought contact with him, and then had himself promoted to all holy orders; he seeks absolution and a dispensation.* Reg. 2, fol. 78v.

> [Florentie], viiii kal. Maii. Exponitur sanctitati vestre pro parte devoti vestri fratris Willelmi Dalton, presbiteri, monachi professi monasterii beate Marie de Whitbi ordinis sancti Benedicti Eboracensis diocesis, quod olim, ipso in decimoseptimo sue etatis anno et in minoribus ordinibus constituto, mater carnalis eiusdem exponentis ad villam seu locum ubi dictum monasterium situatum est, ut exponentem ipsum eius filium videre et visitare posset, accessit et ibidem cum eodem exponente filio suo per modicum temporis spatium colloquium habuit. Tamen exponens predictus, quia cum eadem matre sua tunc prout affectabat diu colloquium habere non potuit, nocte sequenti etiam ut dicitur ad instigationem aliquorum amicorum suorum dictum monasterium, habitu suo tamen retento, illicentiatus exivit et ad domum seu locum ubi dicta mater sua erat et hospitabatur accessit, et inibi cum matre sua licet per modicum temporis spatium locutus et eam consolatus fuit. Quo facto exponens ipse statim ad dictum suum monasterium reversus fuit, propter quod exponens ipse excommunicationis incurrit sententiam in tales per constitutiones et statuta dicti ordinis generaliter promulgatam, et sic ligatus, nullis super premissis absolutione et dispensatione obtentis, licet de premissis ut asseritur abbati suo confessus fuit et ei propter hoc penitentiam iniunxerit illamque peregerit, tamquam simplex et iuris ignarus et non in contemptum se fecit alias tamen rite ad omnes sacros ordines promoveri et in ipsis ministravit. Quare supplicatur eidem sanctitati pro parte dicti exponentis quatinus ipsum a dicta excommunicationis sententia et excessibus huiusmodi et peccatis suis aliis etc. absolvi secumque super irregularitate ex premissis contracta et ipsorum sic susceptorum ordinum execucione dispensare [*recte* dispensari] misericorditer mandare dignemini de vestra gratia speciali.
>
> Fiat de speciali N.

---

[11] Presumably the age of 23 or 24 is meant, which is the norm in entries of this kind. A supplication for a twenty-year-old to become a priest (five years below the canonical age of 25) would have to be signed *de speciali et expresso*, i.e., with the pope's personal approval, since it fell outside the penitentiary's normal competence.

142. [Florence], 26 April 1439. Same grant as **107** sought by William Harre and his wife Katherine, Norwich dioc. *Fiat de speciali N.* Reg. 2, fol. 78r.

143. [Florence], 26 April 1439. Same grant as **107** sought by John Bukke and his wife Beatrice, Norwich dioc. *Fiat de speciali N.* (Approved with **145**.) Reg. 2, fol. 79r.

144. [Florence, 28 April 1439].[12] Same dispensation as **101** sought by John Nugate, clerk, Norwich dioc. *Fiat de speciali N.* Reg. 2, fol. 78r–v.

145. [Florence], 30 April 1439. Same grant as **107** sought by John Bulmer alias Smeth, priest, London dioc. Approved with **143**. Reg. 2, fol. 79r.

De matrimonialibus

146. [Ferrara, 20 April 1439]. Ralph Swiftor, layman, and Alice (*Licia*) Bisscop, Lincoln dioc., wish to marry, but since they are related twice in the fourth degree of affinity, they may not do so [without a dispensation, hence they request one]. [*Fiat de speciali N.*] Reg. 2, fol. 108r.

147. [Ferrara, 15 May 1439]. Iankin (*Iakyn*) ap Mered, layman, and Margaret, daughter of Dafydd ap Rhys (*Ree*), St David's dioc., wish to marry, but since they are related in the fourth degree of consanguinity, they may not do so [without a dispensation, hence] they request one and *littere declaratorie* regarding the third degree of consanguinity.[13] *Fiat de speciali Io.* Reg. 2, fol. 108v.

148. [*Ferrara, 16 May 1439*]. *Dafydd ap Thomas ap Ieuan ap Dawkin, layman, and Joan, daughter of Gronw ap Ieuan ap Leyson, St David's dioc., married knowing that they were related in the fourth degree of affinity; they seek a dispensation to stay married or remarry with legitimation of issue and declaratory letters.*[14] Reg. 2, fol. 108v.

> [Ferrarie], xvii kal. Iunii. Exponitur pro parte David ap Thome ap Ieuan ap Dawkin, laici, et Iohanne filie Ogrono ap Ieuan ap Leyson, mulieris, coniugum Menevensis diocesis, quod ipsi, scientes quod quondam Thomas Thlode ap Iankin, primus dicte Iohanne maritus dum viveret, et prefatus David iiii° consanguinitatis gradu simul erant coniuncti, matrimonium inter se per verba de presenti [fol. 109r] publice de facto contraxerunt, illudque carnali copula consumarunt. Cum autem in huiusmodi matrimonio remanere non possunt [*sic*], et si divorcium etc. [fieret inter eos, possent inter amicos et parentes discordie verisimiliter exoriri], supplicatur quatinus absolutione previa quodque impedimento affinitatis etc. [non obstante] in contracto remanere vel de novo inter se contrahere etc. [valeant dignemini misericorditer dispensare], prolem susceptam si qua sit et suscipiendam etc. [legitimam decernentes]. Item declaratorias super iii° affinitatis [gradu].
>
> Fiat de speciali Io.

[12] Date supplied from the previous entry.
[13] Evidently they were related not only in the fourth but also in the third degree of consanguinity.
[14] That such letters were required indicates that they were actually related in both the third *and* fourth degrees of affinity.

Eugenius IV (1431–1447) 47

[*De declaratoriis*]

149. [*Florence, c. 21 February 1439*].[15] *John Killing, priest, professed monk of Croxden Abbey, Cistercian order, [Coventry and] Lichfield dioc., having obtained from the penitentiary absolution from excommunication and a dispensation from irregularity and* inhabilitas,[16] *seeks a declaration that he may be appointed to and exercise all* administrationes, *dignities and offices of his order.* Reg. 2, fol. 120r–v.

Beatissime pater, alias devotus sanctitati vestre Iohannes Killing, presbiter, monachus professus monasterii beate Marie de Crohesdor' ordinis Cisterciensis Lichfeldensis diocesis, obtinuit a sede apostolica et sub officio penitentiarie sanctitatis vestre absolvi a sententia excommunicationis, quam incurrerat ex eo quia, habitu et ordine suis derelictis, ad seculum fuit reversus et, malis associatus hominibus, rapinis, spoliis, homicidiis laicalibus, et incendiis in locis sacris et non sacris presens fuerat, et licet aliqua manu propria non perpetravit, tamen ad ea auxilium, consilium prestiterat et favorem, et excessibus huiusmodi, et penitentiam sibi propter premissa iniungendam peragere sit paratus, ac etiam super irregularitate exinde contracta, ex eo quia sic ligatus tamquam simplex et iuris ignarus in suis, non tamen in contemptum [fol. 120v] clavium, ordinibus ministraverat et alias inmiscuerat se divinis, et inhabilitate etiam exinde proveniente secum dispensare [*recte* dispensari] obtinuit. Cum autem ad ovile proprium reverti et in eadem vitam monachalem ducere cupiat, tamen ab aliquibus simplicibus et iuris ignaris ac ipsius exponentis forsan emulis asseritur ipsum exponentem propter premissa inhabilem effectum fore ad quascumque et quecumque administrationes, dignitates et officia dicti ordinis. Ad obstruenda igitur ora talium et aliorum sibi super hoc in futurum loqui volencium emulorum, supplicat humiliter eidem sanctiati vestre dictus exponens quatinus sibi compatientes dignemini declarare ipsum premissis non obstantibus posse eligi, prefici et admitti ad omnes administrationes, dignitates, et officia omnia, etiam si prioratus, conventuales, abbatiales, curate et elective fuerint, [et] uti proprius potuisset de benignitate vestra et clementia.

Fiat si est ita N. Signanda per fiat si est ita.

150. [*Florence, c. 21 February 1439*].[17] *John Dunsford, layman, York dioc., contracted and consummated marriage but then had himself promoted to all holy orders. At his wife's request, the local ordinary's official instructed him to return to her. He seeks absolution and a dispensation to remain married.* Reg. 2, fol. 138r.

Exponitur sanctitati vestre pro parte devoti vestri Iohannis Dunsford, laici Eboracensis diocesis, quod ipse olim matrimonium cum quadam muliere publice per verba de presenti contraxit illudque carnali copula consumavit, deinde ex quadam animi levitate et instabilitate se fecit alias tamen rite ad

---

[15] The entry is undated; the nearest preceding dated entry is on fol. 118r and bears this date: 'Datum Florentie viiii kalendas Martii pontificatus etc. anno octavo.'
[16] Above **118** (and cf. **108**).
[17] The entry is undated; the nearest preceding dated entry is on fol. 136v and is dated: 'Datum Florentie viiii kalendas Martii pontificatus etc. anno octavo etc.'

omnes sacros ordines promoveri et in ipsis ministravit. Demum audiens hec prefata mulier eundem exponentem coram officiali ordinarii loci traxit in causam. Qui quidem officialis, debita rei cognicione prehabita et iuris ordine servato, diffinitivam pro ipsa muliere et contra ipsum exponentem tulit sententiam, ac pronuntiavit et declaravit predictum exponentem ad matrimonium cum dicta muliere contractum astrictum et obligatum fore et in eo licite remanere etc. Supplicatur igitur sanctitati vestre pro parte dicti exponentis quatinus ipsum ab excessibus et prophanationibus huiusmodi absolvi mandare, quodque libere et licite in matrimonio cum ipsa muliere contracto remanere valeat, quodque ratione ordinum sic per eum susceptorum ad horas canonicas dicendas minime teneatur dispensare dignemini de gratia speciali.

Fiat ut infra N. Signanda per fiat si est ita.

151. [*Florence, c. 21 February 1439*]. *Thomas Clyff, priest, York dioc., suffers from mild epilepsy once a year at most; as he knows when to expect an attack, he requests that, abstaining from celebration for six to eight days both before and after it, he may celebrate at other times.* Reg. 2, fol. 141v.

Supplicatur sanctitati vestre pro parte devoti vestri Thome Clyff, presbiteri Eboracensis diocesis, quod cum ipse non sui culpa sed causa infirmitatis sibi superveniente aliquando patiatur morbum caducum, videlicet ad plus semel in anno et non multum aspere, et postmodum toto residuo temporis sit bone disposicionis et bene sanus, velletque ex devocionis causa aliquando missam [fol. 142r] celebrare, et ab aliquibus sibi dicatur quod non debet missas celebrare nec sacramentum corporis Christi et sanguinis domini nostri Iesu Christi conficere nec tractare obstante morbo predicto, quatinus [concedere] dignemini [ut] post eventum dicti morbi et ante, quia communiter sit tempus quando sibi talis casus evenire debet, abstinendo per vi vel octo [dies] ante et totidem post, in residuo temporis missas et alia officia divina celebrare [valeat], prout faciunt et facere debent fideles et devoti presbiteri, predictis et aliis in contrarium facientibus non obstantibus quibuscumque de gratia vestra speciali.

Fiat ut infra N. Signanda per fiat si est ita, si sit tempus quando casus dicti morbi evenire debeat et abstineat a celebracione per dies octo ante et totidem post.

152. [*Florence, c. 21 February 1439*]. *William Andrew of Beckford, Worcester dioc., married Margaret Lediis of Corringham parish, Lincoln dioc. After ten years of marriage, he had sexual relations with and married Isabel Draper, Lincoln dioc. He then divorced Margaret, who later died from grief. He and Isabel then separated at the instruction of their confessor. William seeks absolution for himself and Isabel and a declaration that their marriage was never lawful.* Reg. 2, fol. 147r–v.

Supplicatur pro parte Willelmi Andrew de villa de Bekford, Wigorniensis diocesis, quod ipse olim per verba legitime de presenti publice cum quadam Margareta [fol. 147v] Lediis, muliere de parrochia Coryngham Lincolniensis diocesis, ~~quod ipse olim~~ matrimonium contraxit illudque carnali copula consumavit. Et cum ipsi simul per decem annos vel circiter ut maritus et uxor cohabitarunt, deinde quandam Ysabellam Draper Lincolniensis diocesis actu fornicario carnaliter cognovit, et postmodum vivente dicta Margareta cum dicta Ysabella de facto per verba de presenti matrimonium contraxit, et cum ea per aliquod tempus cohabitavit. Et dum in iudicio coram iudice competenti dictus ~~W~~ Willelmus et Margareta super premissis vocati fuissent, et mediantibus certis falsis testimoniis sententia divortii inter ipsum exponentem et dictam Margaretam lata fuit, et sic a dicta Margareta de facto divorciatus extitit. Et cum dicta Ysabella et Willelmus simul inhabitabant per plures annos, videns dicta Margareta pre dolore, nullo tamen dictorum ~~W~~ Willelmi et Ysabelle in morte ipsius Margarete machinantibus [*sic*], postmodum ut asseritur diem suum clausit extremum. Et dum postmodum dicti Willelmus et Ysabella certo eorum confessori confiterentur eorum peccata, idem confessor eis mandavit ut insimul ulterius non cohabitarent, qui volentes parere monicionibus et mandatis dicti confessoris ulterius insimul non cohabitaverunt, sed per octo annos et ultra se ab invicem abstinuerunt. Supplicavit humiliter eidem sanctitati [vestre] sibi et dicte Ysabelle de debite absolucionis beneficio provideri ac declarari inter dictos G. et Ysabellam matrimonium non fuisse nec esse de iure validum.

Fiat ut infra N. Signanda per fiat si est ita. Et committatur ordynario, absolucione previa ab adulterio et excessibus cum impositione gravis penitentie.

153. [*Florence, c. 4 March 1439*].[18] *Dafydd Goch* alias *ap Ieuan ap Madog, priest, Bangor dioc., entered Penmon Priory, OSA, Bangor dioc., and wore the habit for half a year but did not make profession; he then left the priory without permission. He seeks a declaration that he may remain a secular clerk.* Reg. 2, fol. 131v.

Exponit sanctitati vestre devotus vester David Goch' alias ap Ieuan ap Madoc, presbiter Bangorensis diocesis, quod ipse olim simplex clericus existens prioratum conventualem de Penmon ordinis sancti Augustini dicte diocesis ingressus fuit, et habitum ipsius ordinis ibidem assumpsit illumque per dimidium annum dumtaxat protavit [*recte* portavit], nullam tamen professionem tantam [*recte* tacitam] seu expressam in dictis prioratu et ordine emisit regularem. Sed tamen infra tempus predictum se fecit alias tamen rite ad omnes ordines promoveri et in ipsis ministravit. Tandem vero prioratum ipsum, habitu et ordine penitus derelictis, illicentiatus exivit et ad seculum fuit reversus, quo de cetero remanere intendit. Cum autem nonnulli simplices et iuris ignari ac ipsius exponentis forsan emuli asserunt eundem exponentem ob premissis dicto ordine astrictum et obligatum fore, ad ora talium obstruenda, supplicat eidem sanctitati dictus exponens quatinus ipsum non obstantibus premissis ad dicti seu alterius ordinis observanciam minime teneri sed ipsum in dicto seculo remanere posse declarare misericorditer dignemini.

Fiat N. Signanda per fiat si est ita, si professionem tacitam vel expressam non fecit.

---

[18] The entry is undated; the nearest preceding dated entry is on fol. 130r and is dated: 'Datum Florentie sub sigillo officii penitentiarie iiii[to] nonas Martii pontificatus domini Eugenii pape quarti anno octavo.'

154. [*Florence, c. 25 March 1439*].[19] *William Park, layman, York dioc., married but did not consummate the marriage. Believing himself free to remarry, he married Elizabeth Boterwile. He seeks a declaration that this second marriage was invalid and that he may return to his original wife and consummate their marriage.* Reg. 2, fol. 124r–v.

Exponitur sanctitati vestre pro parte devoti vestri Wilhelmi Park, laici Eboracensis diocesis, quod ipse olim cum quadam muliere dicte diocesis in aliquo gradu prohibito sibi non coniuncta vel attinente matrimonium per verba legitime de presenti contraxit, carnali tamen copula minime subsecuta. Et deinde dictus exponens, simplicitate ductus et credens ex quo matrimonium predictum carnali copula non fuerit consummatum matrimonium cum quacumque alia muliere, non tamen in gradu prohibito sibi coniuncta seu attinente, licite contrahere posse, matrimonium seu pocius contubernium cum quadam Elizabella Boterwile muliere per similia verba de presenti contraxit illudque carnali copula consummavit. Cum autem dictus exponens et Elizabella predicta in huiusmodi matrimonio seu potius contubernio ut premissum est sic inter eos de facto contracto remanere non possint, cupiatque propterea idem exponens ad dictam priorem mulierem suam legitimam coniugem redire et cum ea ut tenetur in matrimonio libere remanere, et ne aliqui simplices et iuris ignari seu ipsius exponentis emuli in eum labia detractionis aprire possint asserentes sibi hoc minime licere etc., ad obstruendum ora talium etc. [et aliorum sibi super hoc in futurum obloqui volentium emulorum] supplicatur sanctitati vestre pro parte dicti exponentis quatinus matrimonium seu [fol. 124v] potius contubernium cum predicta Elizabella contractum invalidum fore, quodque libere in matrimonio cum prima muliere contracto remanere, illudque licite carnali copula consummare valeat dignemini misericorditer declarare.

Fiat ut infra N. Signanda est per fiat si est ita.

De perpetuis confessionalibus, [etc.]

155. [*Rome, St. Peter's*], 15 May 1432. *The pope is requested to grant* littere confessionales *for life to Walter Perceval and his wife, London dioc.* Fiat de speciali Io. Reg. 2, fol. 149v.

156. [*Florence*], 29 December 1439. *Same grant as* **155** *sought by Richard Storthwayt, priest, York dioc.* Fiat de speciali N. Reg. 2, fol. 155v.

157. [*Florence*], 31 January 1440. *The pope is requested to grant* littere confessionales *in perpetuity to William Gladeum, notary, Augustine Mawnger, layman, John Clerk and his wife Joan, Norwich dioc. Approved with* **158**. Reg. 2, fol. 155v.

---

[19] The entry is undated; that preceding it bears the date: 'Datum Florentie etc. sub anno etc. viii kalendas Aprilis pontificatus etc. anno nono.'

158. [Florence], 31 January 1440. Same grant as **157** sought by Thomas de Herrington, nobleman, and his wife Elizabeth, York dioc.[20] *Fiat de speciali N.* (Approved with **157**.) Reg. 2, fol. 155v.

159. [Florence], 6(?) February 1440.[21] Same grant as **155** sought by Thomas Crosse, *domicellus*, and his wife Margaret, nobles, Ely dioc. Approved with **161**. Reg. 2, fol. 155v.

160. [Florence], 7 February 1440. Same grant as **155** sought by [. . .] Chambur[22] and his wife Margaret, Salisbury dioc.; Roger Gyldeford and his wife Isabel, Lincoln dioc.; John Potter, priest, [Coventry and] Lichfield dioc. *Fiat de speciali N.* Reg. 2, fol. 155v.

161. [Florence], 7 February 1440. Same grant as **155** sought by \William Horncastell and his wife Alice of Lincoln dioc./.[23] *Fiat de speciali N.* (Approved with **159**.) Reg. 2, fol. 155v.

162. [Florence], 8 February 1440. Same grant as **155** sought by Henry Newman, clerk, London dioc. *Fiat de speciali N.* Reg. 2, fol. 155v.

163. [Florence], 19 February 1440. Same grant as **155** sought by Elizabeth Tenderyng, noble\woman/, Norwich dioc. *Fiat de speciali N.* Reg. 2, fol. 156r.

164. [Florence], 19 February 1440. Same grant as **155** sought by William Baldok, nobleman, Norwich dioc. *Fiat de speciali N.* Reg. 2, fol. 156r.

165. [Florence], 19 February 1440. Same grant as **155** sought by William Hall and his wife Isabel, London dioc. *Fiat de speciali N.* Reg. 2, fol. 156r.

166. [Florence], 19 February 1440. Same grant as **155** sought by John Flowr', priest, BCL and CnL, canon of the church of St David's.[24] *Fiat de speciali N.* Reg. 2, fol. 156r.

167. [Florence], 26 February 1440. Same grant as **155** sought by Walter Marys, priest, Worcester dioc. *Fiat de speciali.* Reg. 2, fol. 156r.

168. [Florence], 26 February 1440. Same grant as **157** sought by Robert Rows and his wife Margaret; Henry Rows and his wife Joan, Norwich dioc. Approved with **169**. Reg. 2, fol. 156r.

---

[20] Thomas Haryngton, knight, nobleman, lord of Hornby Castle and the manor of Brierley, and his wife Elizabeth, noblewoman, York dioc., were also granted licences for a portable altar and to have mass celebrated before daybreak, respectively on 9 and 21 April 1446 (*CPL*, ix. 584–5).
[21] The date in the margin appears to be '[v?]iii id. Februarii'.
[22] Christian name omitted.
[23] Addition signed by corrector 'Pe.'
[24] For John Flour see Le Neve, *Fasti 1300–1541*, xi: *Welsh dioceses*, 85 n. 2; *CPL*, ix. 233.

169. [Florence], 26 February 1440. Thomas Rowlond, priest, rector of Chilmark (*Schylmarg*) parish church, Salisbury dioc., requests that the pope grant him a licence for five years to absolve all his parishoners of either sex from all their sins except [those whose absolution is reserved to the apostolic] see. *Fiat de speciali N.* (Approved with **168**.) Reg. 2, fol. 156r.

170. [Florence], 27 February 1440. Same grant as **155** sought by William Kychynner, priest, perpetual vicar of Asthall parish church, Lincoln dioc. *Fiat de speciali N.* Reg. 2, fol. 156r.

171. [Florence], 1 March 1440. Same grant as **157** sought by William Newmanis, layman, Salisbury dioc. *Fiat de speciali N.* Reg. 2, fol. 156r.

172. [Florence], 1 March 1440. Same grant as **155** sought by Richard Cosyn, priest, rector of Felmingham (*Felmygham*) parish church, Norwich dioc. Approved with **173**. Reg. 2, fol. 156r.

173. [Florence], 1 March 1440. Same grant as **155** sought by Margaret Irmyglondi, noblewoman, Norwich dioc. *Fiat de speciali N.* (Approved with **172**.) Reg. 2, fol. 156r.

174. [Florence], 4 March 1440. Same grant as **157** sought by Thomas Swything, regular priest, York dioc. *Fiat de speciali N.* (Approved with another supplication not from England or Wales.) Reg. 2, fol. 157r.

175. [Florence], 5 March 1440. Same grant as **157** sought by Thomas Crakchyld, professed canon of St Mary's monastery, Walsingham, OSA, Norwich dioc.[25] *Fiat de speciali N.* Reg. 2, fol. 157r.

176. [Florence], 7 March 1440. Same grant as **155** sought by Thomas Halcok, layman, Norwich dioc. Approved with **177**. Reg. 2, fol. 157r.

177 [Florence], 7 March 1440. The pope is requested to grant Henry,[26] priest, perpetual vicar of Sporle with Palgrave (*Sporlee*) parish church, Norwich dioc., a licence for five years to absolve all his parishoners. *Fiat de speciali N.* (Approved with **176**.) Reg. 2, fol. 157r.

178. [Florence], 8 March 1440. Same grant as **155** sought by Nicholas Mannyng and his wife Joan, Norwich dioc. Approved with **181**. Reg. 2, fol. 156v.

179. [Florence], 8 March 1440. Same grant as **155** sought by Edmund Tyler and his wife, Norwich dioc. Approved with **181**. Reg. 2, fol. 156v.

180. [Florence], 8 March 1440. Same grant as **155** sought by William Hylle and his wife, Norwich dioc. Approved with **181**. Reg. 2, fol. 156v.

---

[25] He was also granted a dispensation to hold a benefice with cure of souls for life on 16 September 1441 (*CPL*, ix. 206); his surname is given there as 'Crakschillde'.

[26] The absence of his surname is signalled by a *gemipunctus* in the register.

181. [Florence], 8 March 1440. Same grant as **155** sought by William Knight (*Villelmus Knght*) and his wife Alice, Norwich dioc. *Fiat de speciali N.* (Approved with **178–80**.) Reg. 2, fol. 156v.

182. [Florence], 8 March 1440. Same licence as **177** sought by Geoffrey Goli, priest, perpetual vicar of Holkham parish church, Norwich dioc. Approved with **184**. Reg. 2, fol. 156r–v.

183. [Florence], 8 March 1440. Same grant as **155** sought by Richard Palmer, priest, rector of Smallburgh (*Smalberowe*) parish church, Norwich dioc. Approved with **184**. Reg. 2, fol. 156v.

184. [Florence], 8 March 1440. Same grant as **155** sought by Richard Barker, priest, Norwich dioc. *Fiat de speciali N.* (Approved with **182–3**.) Reg. 2, fol. 156v.

185. [Florence], 10 March 1440. Same grant as **157** sought by John Severyton, layman, Salisbury dioc. *Fiat de speciali N.* Reg. 2, fol. 156v.

186. [Florence], 10 March 1440. Same grant as **155** sought by John Marowe and his present wife, of Norwich. Approved with **188**. Reg. 2, fol. 156v.

187. [Florence], 10 March 1440. Same grant as **155** sought by William Grey, citizen of Norwich. Approved with **188**. Reg. 2, fol. 156v.

188. [Florence], 10 March 1440. Same grant as **155** sought by William Gode and his wife, of Norwich. *Fiat de speciali N.* (Approved with **186–7**.) Reg. 2, fol. 156v.

189. [Florence], 15 March 1440. Same grant as **155** sought by Richard Brigge of Huntingdon (*Huntyndon*), Lincoln dioc. Approved with **193**. Reg. 2, fol. 156v.

190. [Florence], 15 March 1440. Same grant as **155** sought by Richard Wright and his wife, Ely dioc. Approved with **193**. Reg. 2, fol. 156v.

191. [Florence], 15 March 1440. Same grant as **155** sought by John Gere of Cambridge (*Cantebrigia*) and his wife, Ely dioc. Approved with **193**. Reg. 2, fol. 156v.

192. [Florence], 15 March 1440. Same grant as **155** sought by Robert Komis and his wife Margaret, Norwich dioc. Approved with **193**. Reg. 2, fol. 156v.

193. [Florence], 15 March 1440. The pope is requested to grant Robert Brigge, scholar of Huntingdon (*Huntyndon*), Lincoln dioc., letters dimissory since he cannot approach his ordinary because of the distance of the place. *Fiat de speciali N.* (Approved with **189–92**.) Reg. 2, fol. 156v.

194. [Florence], 23 March 1440. Same grant as **155** sought by Elizabeth, widow, Norwich dioc. *Fiat de speciali N.* Reg. 2, fol. 157r.

195. [Florence], 29 March 1440. Same grant as **155** sought by John Smyth, priest, Norwich dioc. Approved with **197**. Reg. 2, fol. 157v.

196. [Florence], 29 March 1440. Same grant as **155** sought by Thomas Toppefeld, priest, London dioc. Approved with **197**. Reg. 2, fol. 157v.

197. [Florence], 29 March 1440. Same grant as **155** sought by Thomas Lambe, priest, London dioc. *Fiat de speciali N.* (Approved with **195–6**.) Reg. 2, fol. 157v.

198. [Florence], 3 April 1440. Same grant as **155** sought by Nicholas Lawutenale and his wife Alice, Salisbury dioc. Approved with **202**. Reg. 2, fol. 157v.

199. [Florence], 3 April 1440. Same grant as **157** sought by Richard Page and his wife Margaret, Salisbury dioc. Approved with **202**. Reg. 2, fol. 157v.

200. [Florence], 3 April 1440. Same grant as **157** sought by John Basket, squire, and his wife Alice, nobles, Salisbury dioc. Approved with **202**. Reg. 2, fol. 157v.

201. [Florence], 3 April 1440. Same grant as **157** sought by John Thurlow, priest, Norwich dioc. Approved with **202**. Reg. 2, fol. 157v.

202. [Florence], 3 April 1440. Same grant as **157** sought by Robert Chatysle, priest, Norwich dioc. *Fiat de speciali N.* (Approved with **198–201**.) Reg. 2, fol. 157v.

203. [Florence], 3 April 1440. Same grant as **157** sought by Henry Crosson and his wife Elizabeth, Norwich dioc. *Fiat de speciali N.* Reg. 2, fol. 157v.

204. [Florence], 3 April 1440. Same grant as **155** sought by Fr William Anderby, priest, professed monk of the monastery of Humberston (*Humberstan'*), OSB, Lincoln dioc., with the licence of his superior. Approved with **209**. Reg. 2, fol. 157v.

205. [Florence], 3 April 1440. Same grant as **155** sought by Sister Joan Frabuces, professed nun of the conventual priory of Legbourne (*Legeburne vidi*?), Cistercian order, Lincoln dioc. Approved with **209**. Reg. 2, fol. 157v.

206. [Florence], 3 April 1440. Same grant as **157** sought by Joan Batley, widow, Lincoln dioc. Approved with **209**. Reg. 2, fol. 158r.

207. [Florence], 3 April 1440. Same grant as **157** sought by Robert Myte, priest, Lincoln dioc. Approved with **209**. Reg. 2, fol. 158r.

208. [Florence], 3 April 1440. Same grant as **157** sought by Walter Parke, squire and lord of the vill of Upton, nobleman, Salisbury dioc.[27] Approved with **209**. Reg. 2, fol. 158r.

209. [Florence], 3 April 1440. Same grant as **157** sought by Alice Obsburn, widow and lady of Warminster (*Wermester*), noblewoman, Salisbury dioc. *Fiat de speciali N.* (Approved with **204–8**.) Reg. 2, fol. 158r.

---

[27] Presumably the Walter Parke, nobleman, Salisbury, who was granted a licence for a portable altar on 6 June 1442 (*CPL*, ix. 316).

210. [Florence], 4 April 1440. Same grant as **157** sought by Simon Thornham, priest, Norwich dioc. *Fiat de speciali N.* Reg. 2, fol. 158r.

211. [Florence], 4 April 1440. Same grant as **157** sought by John Cellisson, priest, Norwich dioc.; Elizabeth Clere, widow, noblewoman, Norwich dioc.; Thomas Het, priest, Lincoln dioc.; Robert (*Rubertus*) Child and his wife Alice, Norwich dioc. *Fiat de speciali N.* Reg. 2, fol. 158r.

212. [Florence], 4 April 1440. Same grant as **155** sought by Ralph Lampet, squire, and his wife Margery, nobles, Norwich dioc. *Fiat de speciali N.* Reg. 2, fol. 158r.

213. [Florence], 5(?) April 1440.[28] Same grant as **157** sought by William Wynam, priest, Chichester dioc. *Fiat de speciali N.* Reg. 2, fol. 158r.

214. [Florence], 7 April 1440. Same grant as **155** sought by Richard Toppefeld, priest, London dioc. *Fiat de speciali N.* Reg. 2, fol. 158r.

215. [Florence], 26 April 1440. Same grant as **157** sought by Ieuan ap Ieuan, priest, Hereford (*Herfordidn'*) dioc.[29] *Fiat de speciali N.* Reg. 2, fol. 159r.

216. [Florence], 29 April 1440. Same grant as **157** sought by Michael Cruller, York dioc. *Fiat de speciali N.* Reg. 2, fol. 159r.

217. [Florence], 6 May 1440. Same grant as **155** sought by Robert Darsy, clerk, [Coventry and] Lichfield dioc. *Fiat de speciali N.* Reg. 2, fol. 159r.

218. [Florence], 3 June 1440. Same grant as **155** sought by Sybil Boys, noblewoman, Norwich dioc. Approved with **224**. Reg. 2, fol. 159v.

219. [Florence], 3 June 1440. Same grant as **155** sought by Erddylad verch Hywel (*Erdudinyl verche Howell*), noblewoman.[30] Approved with **224**. Reg. 2, fol. 159v.

220. [Florence], 3 June 1440. Same grant as **155** sought by Isabel Beynam, widow, noblewoman, Hereford dioc. Approved with **224**. Reg. 2, fol. 159v.

221. [Florence], 3 June 1440. Same grant as **155** sought by Richard Carpynter and his wife Gwendolin(?) (*Wentlyane*), Hereford dioc. Approved with **224**. Reg. 2, fol. 159v.

---

[28] 'non. Aprilis' is the date written in the margin, but it is unclear whether a number was given before 'non.'

[29] Perhaps John ap Jevan Gwyn, priest, rector of Llanfihangel Cilfargen, St David's dioc., who was granted a dispensation on 11 May 1430 to hold another benefice incompatible with that church for two years (*CPL*, viii.162); but more likely John ap Jevan ap David, rector of Corwen, St Asaph dioc., who was granted a plenary indulgence *in mortis articulo* and a licence for a portable altar on 30 March 1431 (*CPL*, viii. 359–60). For clerks with the same or similar names, see *Reg. Spofford*, 294, 304–7.

[30] The diocese is not named but, given her Welsh name, it is most likely to be Bangor, Llandaff, St Asaph, or St David's.

222. [Florence], 3 June 1440. Same grant as **155** sought by Robert Boys, squire, nobleman, Norwich dioc. Approved with **224**. Reg. 2, fol. 159v.

223. [Florence], 3 June 1440. Same grant as **155** sought by William Hunt and his wife, Worcester dioc. Approved with **224**. Reg. 2, fol. 159v.

224. [Florence], 3 June 1440. Same grant as **155** sought by Martin Karon, *litteratus*, Worcester dioc. *Concessum de speciali in presentia d. Card. Pe.* (Approved with **218–23**.) Reg. 2, fol. 159v.

225. [Florence], 6 June 1440. Same grant as **155** sought by John Brown, deacon, professed of OCarm., Norwich convent. *Concessum de speciali in presentia d. Card. Pe.* Reg. 2, fol. 159v.

226. [Florence], 10 June 1440. Same grant as **155** sought by John Cawse, clerk, Lincoln dioc. Approved with **227**. Reg. 2, fol. 159v.

227. [Florence], 10 June 1440. Same grant as **155** sought by Joan Barley, [Coventry and] Lichfield dioc. *Fiat de speciali N.* (Approved with **226**.) Reg. 2, fol. 159v.

228. [Florence], 14 June 1440. Same grant as **157** sought by John Ansty senior, Ely dioc., and his wife Joan.[31] *Fiat de speciali N.* Reg. 2, fol. 160v.

229. [Florence], 14 June 1440. Same grant as **157** sought by William Eryngton, layman, dwelling at Evreux.[32] Approved with **231**. Reg. 2, fol. 160r.

230. [Florence], 14 June 1440. The pope is requested to grant the same as **157** to William Herbotel, layman, dwelling at Evreux. Approved with **231**. Reg. 2, fol. 160r.

231. [Florence], 14 June 1440. The pope is requested to grant the same as **157** to William Holemen, layman, and his wife Agnes, citizens of Evreux. *Fiat de speciali N.* (Approved with **229–30**.) Reg. 2, fol. 160r.

232. [Florence], 30(?) June 1440.[33] Same grant as **157** sought by Robert Bertyn, citizen of London (*Londen'*).[34] Approved with **233**. Reg. 2, fol. 160r.

---

[31] John Ansty, *domicellus*, Ely dioc., and his wife Joan, noblewoman, were also granted a licence for a portable altar on 26 January 1429 (*CPL*, viii. 125).

[32] Perhaps the William Haryngton, nobleman, baron, York dioc., who with his wife was granted a plenary indulgence *in mortis articulo* on 13 April 1441 (*CPL*, ix. 240). Therefore 'Evreux' (*Ebroicensis*) may be an error for 'York' (*Eboracensis*) in the entry above, though it is found with others regarding supplicants of Evreux dioc. with English or French names. This William, Lord Harington, fought in the Anglo-French wars. He died on 3 March 1457 (*Complete Peerage*, vi. 318–19). A William Haryngton, knight, Exeter dioc., was granted with his wife Margaret, noblewoman, a licence on 20 December 1428 to choose a confessor, who might absolve them of their sins except where reserved to the pope (*CPL*, viii. 127–8).

[33] The date of **232–3** appears to be '[ii?] kal. Iulii'.

[34] Presumably the Robert Bertyn, citizen of London, who with his wife Catherine was granted a plenary indulgence *in mortis articulo* on 14 July 1441 (*CPL*, ix. 312).

Eugenius IV (1431–1447)

233. [Florence], 30(?) June 1440. Same grant as **157** sought by Stephen Marchant, citizen of London (*Londen'*). *Fiat de speciali N.* (Approved with **232**.) Reg. 2, fol. 160r.

234. [Florence], 1 July 1440. Same grant as **155** sought by John Shirlei, squire, and his wife Margaret, nobles dwelling in London. Approved with **235**. Reg. 2, fol. 160r.

235. [Florence], 1 July 1440. Same grant as **155** sought by Richard Hoogh, *litteratus*.[35] *Fiat de speciali N.* (Approved with **234**.) Reg. 2, fol. 160r.

236. [Florence], 13 July 1440. Same grant as **157** sought by John Scos, perpetual vicar of Bampton parish church, Lincoln dioc.[36] Approved with **237**. Reg. 2, fol. 160v.

237. [Florence], 13 July 1440. Same grant as **157** sought by John Grene, priest, Lincoln dioc. *Fiat de speciali N.* (Approved with **236**.) Reg. 2, fol. 160v.

238. [Florence], 22 July 1440. Same grant as **155** sought by Thomas David, nobleman, and his present wife, London dioc. *Fiat de speciali N.* Reg. 2, fol. 160v.

239. [Florence], 22 July 1440. Same grant as **155** sought by James Penuaris, priest, Exeter dioc. Approved with **240**. Reg. 2, fol. 161r.

240. [Florence], 4 August 1440. Same grant as **155** sought by Alice Walkyn, Chichester dioc. *Fiat de speciali N.* (Approved with **239**.) Reg. 2, fol. 161r.

241. [Florence], 28 September. Same grant as **155** sought by William Bell [and] his wife.[37] *Fiat de speciali N.* Reg. 2, fol. 162r.

242. [Florence], 2 November 1440. Same grant as **155** sought by Hugh Rodeley, priest, [Coventry and] Lichfield dioc. Approved with **243**. Reg. 2, fol. 162r.

243. [Florence], 2 November 1440. Same grant as **155** sought by Thomas Wryghtt, priest, Norwich dioc. *Fiat de speciali N.* (Approved with **242**.) Reg. 2, fol. 162r.

244. [Florence], 9 December 1440. The pope is requested to grant the same as **157** to Nicholas Dreyton, citizen of London(?) (*Lindoniensi*), and his wife Agnes. *Fiat de speciali N.* Reg. 2, fol. 162v.

245. [Florence], 7 January 1441. Same grant as **157** sought by *Philosophus* Steryngham and John Staffort, laymen staying in Seéz dioc. *Fiat de speciali N.* Reg. 2, fol. 163r.

---

[35] No diocese indicated.
[36] He probably vacated this benefice by 3 October 1442 when another is named as vicar (*CPL*, ix. 247).
[37] No diocese is indicated. The previous entry, dated 27 October, concerned Moray diocese in Scotland, and Bell is certainly a common Scottish surname. The next entry in the register is **242**.

246. [Florence], 24 January 1441. Same grant as **157** sought by John Mikelbarcg, priest, rector of Barkby(?) (*Bekeby*) parish church,[38] Lincoln dioc. *Fiat de speciali N.* Reg. 2, fol. 163v.

247. [Florence], 27 January 1441. Same grant as **155** sought by Richard Coll, priest, Exeter dioc.[39] *Fiat de speciali N.* Reg. 2, fol. 163v.

248. [Florence], 29 January 1441. Same grant as **157** sought by Walter Roberdes, priest, rector of Matson(?) (*Mattisdon*) parish church, Worcester dioc. *Fiat de speciali N.* Reg. 2, fol. 163v.

249. [Florence], 3 February 1441. Same grant as **155** sought by Robert Gill and his wife Helen, Worcester dioc. *Fiat de speciali N.* Reg. 2, fol. 164r.

250. [Florence], 5 February 1441. Same grant as **155** sought by John Sturmy, priest, rector of Swindon parish church, Worcester dioc. *Fiat de speciali N.* Reg. 2, fol. 163v.

251. [Florence], 14 February 1441. Same grant as **157** sought by Henry Rossell, priest, Norwich dioc. *Fiat de speciali N.* Reg. 2, fol. 164r.

252. [Florence], 14 February 1441. The pope is requested to grant *littere confessionales* for five years to Robert Trust, priest; William Reyner and his wife Alice, Norwich dioc. *Fiat N.* Reg. 2, fol. 164r.

253. [Florence], 17 February 1441. The pope is requested on the part of John Philipp, scholar, Norwich dioc., to grant that on reaching the age of 24 he may be promoted to priest's orders and minister in them. Approved with **261**. Reg. 2, fol. 164r.

254. [Florence], 17 February 1441. Same dispensation as **253** sought by John Wylkeschere, scholar, Norwich dioc. Approved with **261**. Reg. 2, fol. 164r.

255. [Florence], 17 February 1441. Same dispensation as **253** sought by William Brook, scholar, Norwich dioc. Approved with **261**. Reg. 2, fol. 164r.

256. [Florence], 17 February 1441. Same grant as **155** sought by John Redegrave, priest, Norwich dioc. Approved with **261**. Reg. 2, fol. 164r.

257. [Florence], 17 February 1441. Same grant as **155** sought by John Wilkeschere, scholar, Norwich dioc. Approved with **261**. Reg. 2, fol. 164r.

---

[38] Alternatively it may be Beckley (Oxon.).
[39] Presumably Richard Cole, perpetual vicar of St David's, Davidstow (Devon), Exeter dioc., who was given a licence on 6 November 1429 to farm out his benefice for five years (*CPL*, viii. 117). A DCnL of Padua (1450), he was dead by February 1455. For his clerical and university career see *Reg. Lacy*, ed. Hingeston-Randolph, i. 66, 234–5, 393; *Reg. Lacy*, ed. Dunstan, ii. 132, 181, 252, 277, 324, iii. 139, 164, 193, iv. 84; *BRUO*, i. 481.

258. [Florence], 17 February 1441. Same grant as **155** sought by Richard Cranke, priest, Norwich dioc.[40] Approved with **261**. Reg. 2, fol. 164v.

259. [Florence], 17 February 1441. Same grant as **155** sought by William Toyt, priest, Norwich dioc. Approved with **261**. Reg. 2, fol. 164v.

260. [Florence], 17 February 1441. Same grant as **155** sought by Richard Cook, layman, Norwich dioc. Approved with **261**. Reg. 2, fol. 164v.

261. [Florence], 17 February 1441. The pope is requested to grant that John Sturmyng, acolyte, Norwich dioc., may be promoted to all holy orders by any Catholic bishop having the grace and communion of the apostolic see and minister in them since [he cannot approach his ordinary to receive these orders] because of the distance of the place. *Fiat de speciali N.* (Approved with **253–60**.) Reg. 2, fol. 164v.

262. [Florence], 20 February 1441. Same grant as **157** sought by William Passynger, priest, Salisbury dioc.[41] Approved with **263**. Reg. 2, fol. 164v.

263. [Florence], 20 February 1441. Same grant as **157** sought by Thomas Stokton, canon of the collegiate church of Llanddewi Brefi (*Llandewybrevy*), St David's dioc. *Fiat de speciali N.* (Approved with **262**.) Reg. 2, fol. 164v.

264. [Florence], 22 February 1441. Same grant as **155** sought by Denise Swanland, noblewoman and lady of Harefield (*Herfeld*), London dioc. Approved with **266**. Reg. 2, fol. 164v.

265. [Florence], 22 February 1441. Same grant as **155** sought by Richard Ketyll and his wife Margaret, London dioc. Approved with **266**. Reg. 2, fol. 164v.

266. [Florence], 22 February 1441. Same grant as **155** sought by John Lincoln, priest, Norwich dioc. *Fiat de speciali N.* (Approved with **264–5**.) Reg. 2, fol. 164v.

267. [Florence], 5 March 1441. Same grant as **155** sought by William Craller, priest, Chichester dioc. Approved with **268**. Reg 2, fol. 165r.

268. [Florence], 5 March 1441. Same grant as **155** sought by John Drapier, layman, Chichester dioc. *Fiat de speciali N.* (Approved with **267**.) Reg 2, fol. 165r.

269. [Florence], 7 March 1441. Same grant as **155** sought by Richard Bastard of Bedford, squire, nobleman and lord of the castle of La Haye-du-Puits (*Haydepuche*),

---

[40] Presumably Richard Cranke, priest, nobleman, lord of Crankard, Norwich dioc., who was granted a licence for a portable altar on 4 May 1443 (*CPL*, ix. 366).

[41] Perhaps the William Passinger, canon of Abergwilly, St David's dioc., granted a dispensation on 13 May 1437 to hold four additional compatible benefices; he had been previously dispensed as the son of unmarried parents to be promoted to all, even holy orders and hold a benefice even with a cure of souls, and hence he had obtained this canonry (*CPL*, viii. 645).

Coutances dioc.[42] *Fiat de speciali N.* Reg 2, fol. 165r.

270. [Florence], 7 March 1441. Same grant as **155** sought by John Dalle, priest, Norwich dioc. *Fiat de speciali N.* Reg 2, fol. 165r.

271. [Florence], 10 March 1441. Same grant as **157** sought by Faukys Eyton, layman, nobleman, [Coventry and] Lichfield dioc.[43] *Fiat de speciali N.* Reg 2, fol. 165r.

272. [Florence], 16 March 1441. Same grant as **157** sought by John Prille, layman, and his wife Alice, Norwich dioc.[44] *Fiat de speciali N.* Reg. 2, fol. 165v.

273. [Florence], 28 March 1441. Same grant as **155** sought by Thomas Straherne, layman, Evreux dioc. *Fiat de speciali N.* (Approved with another supplication from a French married couple of Evreux dioc.) Reg. 2, fol. 165r.

274. [Florence], 28 March 1441. Same grant as **155** sought by Elizabeth Berdwell, noblewoman, Norwich dioc. *Fiat de speciali N.* Reg. 2, fol. 165v.

275. [Florence], 22 April 1441. Same dispensation as **253** sought by William Sly, clerk, Norwich dioc. Approved with **282**. Reg. 2, fol. 166r.

276. [Florence], 22 April 1441. Same dispensation as **253** sought by William Dense, clerk, Norwich dioc. Approved with **282**. Reg. 2, fol. 166r.

277. [Florence], 22 April 1441. Same dispensation as **253** sought by John Brown, clerk, Norwich dioc. Approved with **282**. Reg. 2, fol. 166r.

278. [Florence], 22 April 1441. Same dispensation as **253** sought by John Wrytht [*recte* Wryght], clerk, Norwich dioc. Approved with **282**. Reg. 2, fol. 166r.

279. [Florence], 22 April 1441. Same grant as **155** sought by Thomas Pekke, priest, Norwich dioc. Approved with **282**. Reg. 2, fol. 166r.

280. [Florence], 22 April 1441. Same grant as **155** sought by Joan Topyas, Norwich dioc. Approved with **282**. Reg. 2, fol. 166r.

281. [Florence], 22 April 1441. Same grant as **155** sought by Cecily Pape, Norwich dioc. Approved with **282**. Reg. 2, fol. 166r.

---

[42] Perhaps an illegitimate son of John, duke of Bedford, third son of Henry IV of England, who was regent of France from 1422 until his death in 1435 (*Complete Peerage*, ii. 70–2; *ODNB*, xxx.183–90).

[43] Fulk Eyton, *domicellus*, lord of Hetland (or Eteland), Coventry and Lichfield dioc. or Rouen dioc., a possessor of lands in both England and France, and born of noble parents, was also granted on 23 March 1441 a plenary indulgence *in mortis articulo* and on 26 March 1441 a licence for a portable altar on which he might have mass celebrated before daybreak (*CPL*, ix. 237, 239).

[44] They also received a plenary indulgence *in mortis articulo* on 12 February 1441 (*CPL*, ix. 237).

282. [Florence], 22 April 1441. Same grant as **155** sought by William Cryowr and his wife Alice, Norwich dioc. *Fiat de speciali N.* (Approved with **275–81**.) Reg. 2, fol. 166r.

283. [Florence], 28 April 1441. Same grant as **157** sought by John Tredyngton and his wife, Winchester dioc. *Fiat de speciali N.* Reg. 2, fol. 166r.

284. [Florence], 23 May 1441. Same grant as **155** sought by Robert Gowsill, priest, rector of Cromwell (*Crumwell*) parish church, York dioc. Approved with **291**. Reg. 2, fol. 167r.

285. [Florence], 23 May 1441. Same grant as **155** sought by Thomas Haiwod, priest, canon of the church of Lichfield.[45] Approved with **291**. Reg. 2, fol. 167r.

286. [Florence], 23 May 1441. Same grant as **155** sought by William Lagao, squire, and his wife Margaret, nobles, Lincoln dioc. Approved with **291**. Reg. 2, fol. 167r.

287. [Florence], 23 May 1441. Same grant as **155** sought by John Lychebarwe, priest, rector of Litchborough (*Lychebarwe*) and Ashwell (*Asche*) parish churches, BCnL, Lincoln dioc.[46] Approved with **291**. Reg. 2, fol. 167r.

288. [Florence], 23 May 1441. Same grant as **155** sought by Reginald Newton, priest, rector of Blisworth (*Blyseworth*) parish church, Lincoln dioc. Approved with **291**. Reg. 2, fol. 167r.

289. [Florence], 23 May 1441. Same grant as **155** sought by Richard Wemines *alias* Weming, nobleman, merchant, Lincoln dioc. Approved with **291**. Reg. 2, fol. 167r.

290. [Florence], 23 May 1441. Same grant as **155** sought by Lawrence Barry, priest, rector of St Mary's parish church, Maidwell (*Maidewell*), and BCnL, Lincoln dioc. Approved with **291**. Reg. 2, fol. 167r.

291. [Florence], 23 May 1441. Same grant as **155** sought by Richard Hert, priest, Lincoln dioc. *Concessum de speciali in presentia domini Card. Pe.* (Approved with **284–90**.) Reg. 2, fol. 167r.

292. [Florence], 23 May 1441. Same grant as **252** sought by William Ode, priest, perpetual vicar of Nottingham (*Notyngham*) parish church, York dioc. *Concessum Pe.* Reg. 2, fol. 167r.

---

[45] Thomas Haywood, born of a noble family, was BCL of Oxford University by 1430, BCn & CL by 1452, and later DCnL. He died on 25 October 1492. For his ecclesiastical and university career and benefices, see *BRUO*, ii. 897–8; *CPL*, ix. 579–80, 584, x.115, xi. 88.

[46] John Lychbarow as rector of Litchborough (Northants.), Lincoln dioc., BCnL, had been granted a dispensation on 14 May 1436 to hold another benefice incompatible with that church (*CPL*, viii. 618); he was presumably appointed as rector of Ashwell by virtue of this grant. For his university career (BCL of Oxford University by 1431 and BCnL by 1444, and incepted as DCnL in 1452), see *BRUO*, ii.1183.

293. [Florence], 5 June 1441. Same grant as **157** sought by Thomas Kyriell, knight, and his wife Cecily, nobles, Canterbury dioc.⁴⁷ Approved with **295**. Reg. 2, fol. 167v.

294. [Florence], 5 June 1441. Same grant as **157** sought by Thomas Chedder and his wife Isabel, nobles, Bath [and Wells] dioc.⁴⁸ Approved with **295**. Reg. 2, fol. 167v.

295. [Florence], 5 June 1441. Same grant as **157** sought by John Pollard and his wife Isabel, nobles, Exeter dioc.⁴⁹ *Concessum de speciali in presentia d. Card. Pe.* (Approved with **293–4**.) Reg. 2, fol. 167v.

296. [Florence], 7 June 1441. Same grant as **157** sought by John Ryall and his wife Joan, citizens of Winchester. Approved with **297**. Reg. 2, fol. 167r.

297. [Florence], 7 June 1441. Same grant as **157** sought by John Troys and his wife Joan, Bath [and Wells] dioc. *Concessum de speciali in presentia d. Card. Pe.* (Approved with **296**.) Reg. 2, fol. 167r.

298. [Florence], 7 June 1441. Same grant as **252** sought by Sister Joan Bamfild, professed nun of the priory of nuns of Buckland (*Bokelond*), Order of St John of Jerusalem, Bath [and Wells] dioc. *Concessum de generali Pe.* Reg. 2, fol. 167r.

299. [Florence], 7 June 1441. Same grant as **155** sought by John Chamburleyn, priest, Lincoln dioc. *Concessum de speciali in presentia d. Card. Pe.* Reg. 2, fol. 167r.

300. [Florence], 12 June 1441. Same grant as **155** sought by Robert Warre and his present wife, nobles, Bath [and Wells] dioc. Approved with **301**. Reg. 2, fol. 167v.

301. [Florence], 12 June 1441. Same grant as **155** sought by John Glayser, clerk, Bath [and Wells] dioc. *Concessum de speciali in presentia d. Card. Pe.* (Approved with **300**.) Reg. 2, fol. 167v.

302. [Florence], 12 June 1441. Same grant as **252** sought by Nicholas Hoper and his wife, London dioc. *Concessum Pe.* Reg. 2, fol. 167v.

303. [Florence], 27 June 1441. Same grant as **155** sought by John Cawte, nobleman, Exeter dioc.; John Torike, nobleman, Salisbury dioc.; Robert Coruw and

---

⁴⁷ They were also granted a plenary indulgence *in articulo mortis* on 28 June 1441 (*CPL*, ix. 242); the surname is given there as 'Kyryell'.

⁴⁸ They were granted a plenary indulgence *in articulo mortis* on 9 June 1441 and a licence for a portable altar on 27 June 1441 (*CPL*, ix. 238, 242) and already on 20 December 1428 (*CPL*, viii. 127). Thomas Cheddre esq. made presentations to parish churches, namely to Uphill on 17 February 1441 and Thorn Falcon on 3 June 1443, both in Bath and Wells dioc. (*Reg. Stafford (Bath and Wells)*, 823, 927). Presumably after her husband's death, Isabel Chedder, Lady of Thorn Falcon, made presentations to its parish church on 7 June 1453 and 1 March 1458 (*Reg. Bekynton*, 754, 1117).

⁴⁹ They were also granted a plenary indulgence *in articulo mortis* on 9 June 1441 and a licence for a portable altar on 27 June 1441 (*CPL*, ix. 239, 242); he is identified as lord of Putford in the latter grant.

his wife Isabel, nobles, Exeter dioc.; John Basset and his wife Joan, nobles, Exeter dioc.;⁵⁰ Robert Wylsford, nobleman, Exeter dioc. *Concessum de speciali in presentia d. Card. Pe.* Reg. 2, fol. 168r.

304. [Florence], 28 June 1441. John Holme, deacon, York dioc., requests that the pope grant him a dispensation so that on reaching the age of 23 he may be promoted to priest's orders and minister in them. Approved with **308**. Reg. 2, fol. 168r.

305. [Florence], 28 June 1441. The pope is requested to grant William Bedale, priest, rector of Biddenden (*Byddyngden*) parish church, Canterbury dioc.,⁵¹ a licence for five years to absolve all his parishoners of either sex. Approved with **308**. Reg. 2, fol. 168r.

306. [Florence], 28 June 1441. Same licence as **305** sought by John Lasby, priest, perpetual vicar of Welton parish church, Lincoln dioc. Approved with **308**. Reg. 2, fol. 168r.

307. [Florence], 28 June 1441. Same grant as **155** sought by John Saxany and his present wife, London dioc. Approved with **308**. Reg. 2, fol. 168r.

308. [Florence], 28 June 1441. Same grant as **155** sought by William Cogeyn, priest, rector of Northmoor (*More*) parish church, Lincoln dioc.⁵² *Concessum de speciali in presentia d. Card. Pe.* (Approved with **304–7**.) Reg. 2, fol. 168r.

309. [Florence], 28 June 1441. Same grant as **157** sought by Elizabeth Purcoll, noblewoman, Lincoln dioc. *Concessum de speciali in presentia d. Card. Pe.* Reg. 2, fol. 168r.

310. [Florence], 31 July 1441. Same grant as **155** sought by Thomas Darsy, priest, [Coventry and] Lichfield dioc.⁵³ *Concessum de speciali in presentia domini Card. Pe.* Reg. 2, fol. 169r.

311. [Florence], 15 August 1441. Same grant as **155** sought by John Waget and his wife Agnes, nobles, Lincoln dioc. *Fiat de speciali N.* Reg. 2, fol. 169r.

---

⁵⁰ They were also granted a plenary indulgence *in articulo mortis* on 27 June 1441 (*CPL*, ix. 242). For churches in Basset's patronage, see *Reg. Lacy*, ed. Hingeston-Randolph, i. 87, 92–4, 132, 216, 335, 342; *Reg. Lacy*, ed. Dunstan, i. 316; ii. 25, iii. 44–7, 63, 66, 337, 353. He was sworn in as sheriff of Cornwall on 5 January 1450 (ibid., iii. 55). For a case concerning the counterfeiting of his seal bearing his coat-of-arms, see ibid., iii. 125–9.
⁵¹ Perhaps the William Bedale, rector of Akenham, Norwich dioc., who exchanged with William Root, rector of St John the Evangelist's, London, on 1 April 1432 (*Reg. Chichele*, i. 276).
⁵² He was also granted a dispensation on 18 April 1439 to hold another benefice incompatible with that of Northmoor (Oxon.); he is said in this grant to be of noble parentage and chaplain of Richard Neville, earl of Warwick (*CPL*, ix. 64).
⁵³ As rector of Bucknell (Oxon.) he was granted a licence on 12 August 1441 to farm his benefice for seven years while he studied letters at university and was non-resident. He was also given a dispensation on 26 January 1443 to hold for life another benefice with Bucknell, or any two benefices; in this grant he was said to have studied canon and civil law long enough to have taken a bachelor's degree in one or other of them (*CPL*, ix. 185, 280).

312. [Florence], 15 August 1441. Same grant as **252** sought by William Estby, layman, [Lincoln dioc.?]. *Fiat N.* Reg. 2, fol. 169r.

313. [Florence], 21 August 1441. Same grant as **155** sought by John Stanley, esquire, and his wife Katherine, nobles, [Coventry and] Lichfield dioc.[54] *Fiat de speciali N.* Reg. 2, fol. 169r.

314. [Florence], 1 September 1441. Same grant as **155** sought by Matthew Trompe, clerk, and his wife Joan, Meaux dioc. and Lincoln dioc. *Fiat de speciali N.* Reg. 2, fol. 169v.

315. [Florence], 18 October 1441. Same grant as **155** sought by John Well, citizen and fishmonger (*Fyschmonger*) of London, and his wife Joan. *Fiat de speciali N.* Reg. 2, fol. 171r.

316. [Florence], 2 January 1442. Same grant as **155** sought by Robert Osbern and his wife Margery, Lincoln dioc. *Fiat de speciali N.* Reg. 2, fol. 172r.

317. [*Florence*], *22 January 1442. John Lydyard*, domicellus, *nobleman, and his present wife, Lincoln dioc., seek* littere confessionales *in perpetuity.* Reg. 2, fol. 172v.

> [Florentie], xi kal. Februarii. Supplicatur sanctitati vestre pro parte nobilis Iohannis Lydyard, domicelli, et eius uxoris in presenciarum Lincolniensis diocesis quatinus ipsis litteras confessionales, ut quilibet presbiter ydoneus secularis vel religiosus ipsos ab omnibus peccatis nisi talia sint etc. [propter que merito sit sedes apostolica consulenda] perpetuis temporibus duraturas absolvere valeat, dignemini misericorditer concedere etc. [de gratia vestra speciali].
>
> Fiat de speciali N.

318. [Florence], 24 January 1442. Same grant as **157** sought by Eliot Blantourp and his wife Joan, Evreux dioc. *Fiat de speciali N.* Reg. 2, fol. 172v.

319. [Florence], 3 February 1442. Same grant as **155** sought by John Wodeward, priest, Norwich dioc. Approved with **321**. Reg. 2, fol. 173r.

320. [Florence], 3 February 1442. Same grant as **155** sought by William Thweyt, clerk, Norwich dioc. Approved with **321**. Reg. 2, fol. 173r.

321. [Florence], 3 February 1442. Same grant as **155** sought by John Mooth and his wife Agnes, Norwich dioc. *Fiat de speciali N.* (Approved with **319–20**.) Reg. 2, fol. 173r.

322. [Florence], 6 February 1442. Same grant as **155** sought by Thomas William

---

[54] John Stanley, nobleman, lord of 'Hoean', [Coventry and] Lichfield dioc., and his wife Catherine, noblewoman, were granted a licence for a portable altar on 9 September 1442 (*CPL*, ix. 244).

alias del Wardrope and his wife Agnes, Worcester dioc.[55] Approved with **323**. Reg. 2, fol. 173r.

323. [Florence], 6 February 1442. Same grant as **155** sought by Brian Pomlyon and his wife Elizabeth, London dioc. *Fiat de speciali N.* (Approved with **322**.) Reg. 2, fol. 173r.

324. [Florence], 16 February 1442. Same grant as **155** sought by George Ascheby and his wife Margaret, London dioc. *Fiat de speciali N.* Reg. 2, fol. 173r.

325. [Florence], 19 February 1442. Same grant as **155** sought by John Heton, esquire, and his wife Isabel, nobles, Lincoln dioc. Approved with **327**. Reg. 2, fol. 173r.

326. [Florence], 19 February 1442. Same grant as **155** sought by John Sey, priest, rector of Brockhall (*Brokhole*) parish church, Lincoln dioc.[56] Approved with **327**. Reg. 2, fol. 173r.

327. [Florence], 19 February 1442. Same grant as **155** sought by John Chylton, priest, perpetual vicar of Norton (*Norton iuxta Daventre*) parish church,[57] Lincoln dioc. *Fiat de speciali N.* (Approved with **325–6**.) Reg. 2, fol. 173v.

328. [Florence], 19 February 1442. Same grant as **155** sought by Henry Drury and his present wife, Norwich dioc. Approved with **330**. Reg. 2, fol. 173v.

329. [Florence], 19 February 1442. Same grant as **155** sought by Philip Chetwyn, nobleman, knight, [Coventry and] Lichfield dioc.[58] Approved with **330**. Reg. 2, fol. 173v.

330. [Florence], 19 February 1442. Same grant as **155** sought by William Bretun, priest, perpetual vicar of All Saints' parish church, Northampton, Lincoln dioc. *Fiat de speciali N.* (Approved with **328–9**). Reg. 2, fol. 173v.

331. [Florence], 27 February 1442. Same grant as **155** sought by William Catton, prior of the conventual priory of Arbury (*Erbury*), OSA, [Coventry and] Lichfield dioc.[59] Approved with **334**. Reg. 2, fol. 173v.

332. [Florence], 27 February 1442. Same grant as **155** sought by James Romayn, London dioc. Approved with **334**. Reg. 2, fol. 173v.

---

[55] Thomas William *alias* de Wardrope, nobleman, lord of places in Cardiff, Llandaff dioc., and his wife Agnes, noblewoman, both dwelling in Worcester dioc., were also granted a licence for a portable altar on 1 March 1442 (*CPL*, ix. 238).
[56] He was also granted a dispensation to hold for life another benefice incompatible with this church, or any two benefices, on 28 February 1442 (*CPL*, ix. 156).
[57] Norton parish is indeed next to that of Daventry (Northants.).
[58] He was also granted a licence for a portable altar on 17 March 1442, when he was said to be lord of a number of places and lands in that diocese (*CPL*, ix. 311).
[59] He was also granted a licence for a portable altar on 17 March 1442 (*CPL*, ix. 311; see also **566**).

333. [Florence], 27 February 1442. Same grant as **155** sought by Robert Gray, nobleman, esquire, [London dioc.?].⁶⁰ Approved with **334**. Reg. 2, fol. 173v.

334. [Florence], 27 February 1442. Same grant as **155** sought by Thomas Boughton and his wife Elizabeth, [London dioc.?]. *Fiat de speciali N.* (Approved with **331–3**.) Reg. 2, fol. 173v.

335. [Florence], 10 March 1442. Same grant as **155** sought by John Wyksworth and his wife Matilda, [Coventry and] Lichfield dioc. Approved with **338**. Reg. 2, fol. 174r.

336. [Florence], 10 March 1442. Same grant as **155** sought by William Edy and his wife Katherine, London dioc. Approved with **338**. Reg. 2, fol. 174r.

337. [Florence], 10 March 1442. Same grant as **155** sought by John Say and his wife Joan, Lincoln dioc. Approved with **338**. Reg. 2, fol. 174r.

338. [Florence], 10 March 1442. Same grant as **155** sought by Ellen Besseford, noblewoman, Lincoln dioc. *Fiat de speciali N.* (Approved with **335–7**.) Reg. 2, fol. 174r.

339. [Florence], 15 March 1442. Same grant as **155** sought by Fr John Worxham, priest, professed of the Norwich convent, OESA;⁶¹ Thomas Fullar, priest, Norwich dioc.; John Ivy and his wife Alice, London dioc.; William Collys and his wife Alice, Norwich dioc. *Fiat de speciali N.* Reg. 2, fol. 174v.

340. [Florence], 15 March 1442. Same grant as **157** sought by William Stub and his wife Margaret, Norwich dioc.; William Caley and his wife Margaret, Norwich dioc.; Fr Nicholas Coutissale, prior of St Faith's monastery, wont to be governed by a prior, OS[B],⁶² Norwich dioc. *Fiat de speciali N.* Reg. 2, fol. 174v.

341. [Florence], 18 March 1442. Same grant as **155** sought by Humphrey Stafford, knight and lord of Grafton (*Graffton*), and his present wife, nobles, Worcester dioc.⁶³ *Fiat de speciali N.* Reg. 2, fol. 175r.

342. [Florence], 18 March 1442. Same grant as **252** sought by Richard Stormer, priest, and his father, mother, brothers and sisters, [Worcester dioc.?]. *Fiat N.* Reg. 2, fol. 175r.

---

⁶⁰ Robert Grey, nobleman, esquire, lord of a number of places and lands in Lincoln dioc., was granted a licence for a portable altar on 17 March 1442 (*CPL*, ix. 311).

⁶¹ John Wroxham, Austin friar of the Norwich house, was granted a licence on 18 March 1442 to choose a personal confessor who might absolve him except in cases reserved to the pope (*CPL*, ix. 310).

⁶² A gap is left after 'ordinis Sancti'. The house is Horsham St Faith Priory (Norf.). Nicholas Conteshale occurs as its prior 1452–62 (Smith, *Heads of Religious Houses*, iii. 183).

⁶³ Humphrey Stafford and his then wife, noblewoman, Worcester dioc., were granted a licence for a portable altar on 9 August 1443 (*CPL*, ix. 370). Probably not Humphrey Stafford, earl of Stafford by 1403, count of Perche by 1431, and duke of Buckingham by 1444, slain at the battle of Northampton in 1460 (*Complete Peerage*, ii. 388–9; *ODNB*, lii. 52–4; see also *CPL*, ix. 238, 310, 364).

343. [Florence], 21 March 1442. Same grant as **155** sought by Gilbert Sprot, priest, Lincoln dioc.; Thomas Flowter, priest, [Lincoln dioc.]; Thomas Edmund and his wife Joan, [Lincoln dioc.]; William Beveth, priest, [Lincoln dioc.];[64] William Flerth, priest, [Lincoln dioc.]; William Sprot and his wife Margaret, [Lincoln dioc.]; William Blougyn and his wife Margery, Lincoln dioc. *Fiat de speciali N.* Reg. 2, fol. 175r.

344. [Florence], 21 March 1442. Same grant as **252** sought by John Beveth and his wife Agnes, [Lincoln dioc.?], and Agnes de la Laund, [Lincoln dioc.?]. *Fiat N.* Reg. 2, fol. 175r.

345. [Florence], 23 March 1442. Same grant as **155** sought by Simon Broun and his wife Catherine, Lincoln dioc. *Fiat de speciali N.* Reg. 2, fol. 175r.

346. [Florence], 28 March 1442. Same grant as **155** sought by Thomas Goos and his wife Matilda, London dioc. *Fiat de speciali N.* Reg. 2, fol. 174v.

347. [Florence], 8 April 1442. Same grant as **155** sought by Adam Pittecock and his wife Katherine, Norwich dioc. *Fiat de speciali N.* Reg. 2, fol. 175v.

348. [Florence], 8 April 1442. Same grant as **155** sought by Robert Wedereld and his present wife, Norwich dioc. *Fiat de speciali N.* Reg. 2, fol. 175v.

349. *[Florence], 9 April 1442. John Scherewynd, rector of Thorpe Morieux, Norwich dioc., seeks a licence to appoint a substitute to his cure of souls.* Reg. 2, fol. 175v.

[Florentie], v id. Aprilis. Supplicat sanctitati vestre Iohannes Scherewynd, rector parrochialis ecclesie de Morunga Norwicensis diocesis, quatinus sibi licentiam et facultatem ut aliquem presbiterum ydoneum curam animarum regere sufficientem loco eius in sua parrochiali ecclesia ponere valeat concedere dignemini de vestra gratia speciali etc.

Fiat de speciali N.

350. [Florence], 9 April 1442. Same grant as **155** sought by William Lance, priest, Norwich dioc. Approved with **351**. Reg. 2, fol. 175v.

351. [Florence], 9 April 1442. Same grant as **155** sought by Henry Wr'th, priest, Lincoln dioc. *Fiat de speciali N.* (Approved with **350**.) Reg. 2, fol. 175v.

352. [Florence], 9 April 1442. Same grant as **252** sought by John Tylly, priest, Norwich dioc.; Edmund att Welle, priest, Norwich dioc.; Thomas Caley and his wife Elizabeth, Norwich dioc.; Robert Fawk and his wife Christine, Norwich dioc.; John Farman and his wife Joan, Norwich dioc. *Fiat N.* Reg. 2, fol. 175v.

353. [Florence], 10 April 1442. Same grant as **155** sought by Robert Langwade, priest, Norwich dioc. *Fiat de speciali N.* Reg. 2, fol. 175v.

---

[64] Perhaps the William Bennett who resigned the vicarage of Theddlethorpe, Lincoln dioc., by May 1443 (*CPL*, ix. 410).

354. [Florence], 10 April 1442. Same grant as **252** sought by Catherine Albone, Norwich dioc. *Fiat N.* Reg. 2, fol. 175v.

355. [Florence], 13 April 1442. Same grant as **157** sought by John Haeyngton [*recte* Haryngton] and his wife Isabel, nobles, York dioc.[65] *Fiat de speciali N.* Reg. 2, fol. 176r.

356. [Florence], 15 April 1442. The pope is requested to grant Fr Thomas Medeley, priest, professed canon of St Oswald's conventual priory, Nostell, OSA, [York] dioc., *littere confessionales cum clausula* for life with the licence of his superior. Approved with **357**. Reg. 2, fol. 176r.

357. [Florence], 15 April 1442. Same grant as **155** sought by Richard Beet, priest, rector of Great Smeaton (*Smeton*) parish church, [York?] dioc. *Fiat de speciali N.* (Approved with **356**.) Reg. 2, fol. 176r.

358. [Florence], 30 April 1442. The pope is requested to grant three *littere confessionales* for life under the seal of the penitentiary to Hugh Cokesey, knight, nobleman, and his wife Alice, Worcester dioc.;[66] Walter Skull, esquire, nobleman, and his wife Margaret, Worcester dioc.;[67] William Catesby, esquire, nobleman, and his wife Philippa, Lincoln dioc.[68] *Fiat de speciali N.* Reg. 2, fol. 177r.

359. [Florence], 3 May 1442. Same grant as **155** sought by Richard ap Tudur ap Iorwerth (*Ior'*) Seys, priest, Bangor dioc.[69] *Fiat de speciali N.* Reg. 2, fol. 177r.

360. [Florence], 19 May 1442. Same grant as **155** sought by Thomas Fetherstone and his wife Katherine, citizens of London;[70] Joan Bachiler *alias* Rinkin of London;[71] John Howell, priest, Bath and Wells dioc.;[72] John Upton, citizen of London.[73] *Fiat de speciali N.* Reg. 2, fol. 178r.

[65] John Haryngton, nobleman, lord of a place in Doncaster (Yorks.), York dioc., and his wife Isabel were also granted a licence for a portable altar on 20 April 1442 (*CPL*, ix. 306).
[66] He and his wife Alice, noblewoman, were also granted a licence on 2 May 1442 to have mass celebrated before daybreak (*CPL*, ix. 313).
[67] Walter Skulle, lord of Holt manor (Worcs.), Worcester dioc., and his wife Margaret, noblewoman, were granted a licence for a portable altar on 5 May 1442 (*CPL*, ix. 312).
[68] William Catesby, lord of Ashby St Ledgers manor (Northants.), Lincoln dioc., and his wife Philippa, noblewoman, were granted a licence for a portable altar on 5 May 1442 (*CPL*, ix. 312).
[69] Probably the Richard ap Tudur ap Jer(worth), BCL, priest, Bangor dioc., to whom the parish church of Llanrhaidr-in-Kinmerch, Bangor dioc., was to be collated under a papal mandate of 29 March 1441 (*CPL*, ix. 191).
[70] They were also granted a licence for a portable altar on 5 June 1442, and on the day after a plenary indulgence subject to their fasting every Friday for a year, during which they were to give seven gold florins of the papal chamber to the poor (*CPL*, ix. 309, 316).
[71] Joan Bachiler *alias* Remkyn of London was granted on 6 June 1442 a plenary indulgence subject to her fasting every Friday for a year, during which she was to give five gold florins of the papal chamber to the poor (*CPL*, ix. 309).
[72] The same indulgence as that received by Joan Bachiler (see **360** n.) was issued to him on 6 June 1442; he was also granted a licence for a portable altar on 14 July 1442 (*CPL*, ix. 303, 309). For his benefices see *Reg. Bekynton*, 320, 546, 812, 850.
[73] The same indulgence as that received by Joan Bachiler (see **360** n.) was issued to him on 6 June 1442 (*CPL*, ix. 309).

361. [Florence], 29 May 1442. Same grant as **155** sought by Thomas Mayre, nobleman, Exeter dioc.[74] Approved with **362**. Reg. 2, fol. 178r.

362. [Florence], 29 May 1442. Same grant as **155** sought by John Schehyers(?) and his wife Sybil, nobles, Salisbury dioc. *Concessum de speciali in presentia d. Card. Pe.* (Approved with **361**.) Reg. 2, fol. 178r.

363. [Florence], 29 May 1442. Same grant as **157** sought by John More and his wife Audrey (*Etheldreda*), citizens of London. Approved with **372**. Reg. 2, fol. 178r.

364. [Florence], 29 May 1442. Same grant[75] as **157** sought by Walter Gorfen and his wife Margaret, nobles, Exeter dioc.[76] Approved with **372**. Reg. 2, fol. 178r.

365. [Florence], 29 May 1442. Same grant as **157** sought by John Aps and his present wife, a noblewoman, Exeter dioc. Approved with **372**. Reg. 2, fol. 178r.

366. [Florence], 29 May 1442. Same grant as **157** sought by Simon Halle and his wife Christine, nobles, Exeter dioc.[77] Approved with **372**. Reg. 2, fol. 178r.

367. [Florence], 29 May 1442. Same grant as **157** sought by William Clenche and his wife Joan, citizens of London.[78] Approved with **372**. Reg. 2, fol. 178r.

368. [Florence], 29 May 1442. Same grant as **157** sought by John Custe and his wife Christine, Rochester dioc.[79] Approved with **372**. Reg. 2, fol. 178r.

369. [Florence], 29 May 1442. Same grant as **157** sought by Robert Styk and his wife Alice, citizens of London. Approved with **372**. Reg. 2, fol. 178r.

370. [Florence], 29 May 1442. Same grant as **157** sought by Katherine Lamplowh, noblewoman, Canterbury dioc.[80] Approved with **372**. Reg. 2, fol. 178r.

---

[74] Perhaps the Thomas Mayer who sued John Burgh for rent arrears before justices at Westminster on 6 March 1455 (*Reg. Lacy*, ed. Dunstan, iii. 208).

[75] Opposite this entry is noted 'regularem et secularem', presumably meaning that they could appoint a secular or regular priest as their personal confessor (see **317**). The same is noted against **371–2**.

[76] They were also granted a licence for a portable altar on 30 June 1442; he is identified there as lord of Gorhuish in Inwardleigh (Devon). As Walter Gorfyn, layman, London dioc., he was also granted with his wife on 10 April 1445 a licence to choose a confessor, who might absolve them except in cases reserved to the pope (*CPL*, ix. 315, 516).

[77] They were also granted a licence for a portable altar on 30 May 1442 (*CPL*, ix. 316).

[78] They were also granted a licence for a portable altar on 30 May 1442 and an indulgence *in mortis articulo* on 3 June 1442; the latter allowed them to receive plenary remission of sins from the confessor of their choice once in their lifetime and at death, even in cases reserved to the pope, and required them to distribute seven gold florins of the papal chamber to the poor (*CPL*, ix. 316–17).

[79] John Cust, *domicellus*, nobleman, Rochester dioc., and his wife Christine, noblewoman, were also granted a licence for a portable altar on 2 April 1435 (*CPL*, viii. 570).

[80] She was also granted the same indulgence as that received by William Clenche and his wife Joan (see **367** n.) on 3 June 1442 except that she was to distribute five gold florins (*CPL*, ix. 317).

70   *Supplications from England and Wales*

371. [Florence], 29 May 1442. Same grant as **157** sought by Thomas Knolles, noble-man, citizen of London.⁸¹ Approved with **372**. Reg. 2, fol. 178r.

372. [Florence], 29 May 1442. Same grant as **157** sought by Thomas Bodulgate and his present wife, noblewoman, Exeter dioc.⁸² *Concessum de speciali in presentia domini Card. Pe.* (Approved with **363–71**.) Reg. 2, fol. 178r.

373. [Florence], 1(?) June 1442. Same grant as **155** sought by William Geffray, priest, Exeter dioc.⁸³ [*Concessum de speciali in presentia domini Card. Pe.*]. Reg. 2, fol. 178r.

374. [Florence], 2 June 1442. Same grant as **155** sought by William Lacy, esquire, nobleman. *Concessum de speciali in presentia domini Cardinalis. Pe.* Reg. 2, fol. 178v.

375. [Florence], 8 June 1442. Same grant as **155** sought by Edmund Tyler and his wife Agnes, Norwich dioc. *Concessum de speciali in presentia domini Cardinalis. Pe.* Reg. 2, fol. 178v.

376. [Florence], 10 June 1442. Same grant as **155** sought by Thomas Bery and his wife Elizabeth, nobles, Exeter (*Oxomensis*)⁸⁴ dioc. *Concessum de speciali in presentia domini Cardinalis Pe.* Reg. 2, fol. 178v.

377. [Florence], 22 June 1442. Same grant as **155** sought by William Pyrton and his present wife, nobles.⁸⁵ *Concessum de speciali in presentia domini Cardinalis. Pe.* Reg. 2, fol. 179r.

378. [Florence], 6 July 1442. Same grant as **155** sought by Thomas Peunde of the town of Hull, York dioc., inhabitant of the city of London.⁸⁶ Approved with **379**. Reg. 2, fol. 181r.

---

[81] Thomas Knolles, citizen of London and lord of North Mimms (Herts.), was also granted a licence for a portable altar on 30 May 1442 (*CPL*, ix. 315). See **364** n. on this entry.

[82] Thomas Bodulgath, nobleman, lord of Bodulgate (Cornw.), Exeter dioc., and his then wife were also granted a licence for a portable altar on 29 May 1442 (*CPL* ix. 315). Thomas Bodulgat or Bodulgate, esq., held the advowson of Lanreath parish church (Cornw.). He was appointed by Bishop Lacy of Exeter on 1 February 1450 as an agent to recover goods stolen from a ship in Plymouth harbour (*Reg. Lacy*, ed. Hingeston-Randolph, i. 121; *Reg. Lacy*, ed. Dunstan, ii. 239; iii. 57). See **364** n. on this entry.

[83] He was also granted a licence for a portable altar on 6 June 1442 and the same indulgence as that received by William Clenche and his wife Joan (see **367** n.) on 10 June 1442 (*CPL*, ix. 307, 317). For ordinations of men of this name by the bishop of Exeter see *Reg. Lacy*, ed. Dunstan, iv. 71b, 82–4, 96, 126, 131–2, 134, 177b, 178c.

[84] *Oxomensis* refers to Osma in Spain, but the supplicants' names are not Spanish.

[85] William Pirton, *domicellus*, Térouanne dioc., was also granted a plenary indulgence *in mortis articulo* on 22 November 1429 (*CPL*, viii. 183).

[86] Presumably the Thomas Pounde of the town of Hull, nobleman, *domicellus*, York dioc., inhabitant of the city of London, who was granted a licence for a portable altar and the same indulgence as that received by William Clenche and his wife Joan (see **367** n.) on 16 July 1442 (*CPL*, ix. 316–17).

379. [Florence], 6 July 1442. Same grant as **155** sought by John Pontrell of Lincoln. *Concessum de speciali in presentia d. Card. Pe.* (Approved with **378** and **380**.) Reg. 2, fol. 181r.

380. [Florence], 7 July 1442. Same grant as **155** sought by Thomas Yonge, nobleman, *domicellus*, Canterbury dioc., and his wife Margaret, inhabitants of the city of London.[87] Approved with **379**. Reg. 2, fol. 180v.

381. [Florence], 9 July 1442. Same licence as **305** sought by Thomas Codlyng, priest, rector of Hingham (*Hengham*) parish church, Norwich dioc.[88] Approved with **385**. Reg. 2, fol. 181r.

382. [Florence], 9 July 1442. Same grant as **155** sought by Simon Honchyns, clerk, Salisbury dioc. Approved with **385**. Reg. 2, fol. 181r.

383. [Florence], 9 July 1442. Same grant as **155** sought by John Wise, layman, Salisbury dioc. Approved with **385**. Reg. 2, fol. 181r.

384. [Florence], 9 July 1442. Same grant as **155** sought by Thomas Hatfeld and his wife Isabel (*Izabella*), London dioc. Approved with **385**. Reg. 2, fol. 181r.

385. [Florence], 9 July 1442. Same grant as **155** sought by John Clerck, citizen of London, and his present wife. *Concessum de speciali in presentia d. Card. Pe.* (Approved with **381–4**.) Reg. 2, fol. 181r.

386. [Florence], 10 July 1442. Same grant as **155** sought by John Beaufitz and his wife Juliana, Exeter dioc. Approved with **388**. Reg. 2, fol. 181r.

387. [Florence], 10 July 1442. Same grant as **155** sought by John Clerke, nobleman, Exeter dioc.[89] Approved with **388**. Reg. 2, fol. 181r.

388. [Florence], 10 July 1442. Same grant as **155** sought by Roger Harper, priest, rector of Box parish church, Salisbury dioc.[90] *Concessum de speciali in presentia d. Card. Pe.* (Approved with **386–7**.) Reg. 2, fol. 181r.

389. [Florence], 11 July 1442. Same grant as **155** sought by Walter Wylmyn, *litteratus*, Salisbury dioc. *Concessum de speciali in presentia d. Card. Pe.* Reg. 2, fol. 181r.

---

[87] They were also granted a licence for a portable altar on 16 July 1442; Margaret is identified there as a noblewoman (*CPL*, ix. 316).

[88] He was also granted a dispensation on 27 September 1442 to hold for life this church with another benefice, or two other benefices (*CPL*, ix. 284–5).

[89] He was granted a licence for a portable altar on 14 July 1442 (*CPL*, ix. 303). Perhaps the John Clerke who as patron made presentations to Gidleigh parish church (Devon) on 24 and 31 July 1434 (*Reg. Lacy*, ed. Hingeston-Randolph, i. 172; see also *Reg. Lacy*, ed. Dunstan, i. 272; ii. 202; iv. 63).

[90] He was also granted a licence for a portable altar on 14 July 1442 and, four days later, a licence to hear confessions of parishioners of Box and any other churches held by him and absolve them even in cases reserved to ordinaries. He was further granted a dispensation on 25 July 1442 to hold for life any benefice incompatible with his church of Box, or two other benefices; he was said in this grant to be of noble parentage (*CPL*, ix. 250, 288, 309).

390. [Florence], 11 July 1442. Same grant as **155** sought by Thomas Sudden, squire, and his present wife, nobles, Salisbury dioc. *Concessum de speciali in presentia d. Card. Pe.* Reg. 2, fol. 181r.

391. [Florence], 19 July 1442. Same grant as **155** sought by Thomas Scindis and his wife Sybil, nobles, Salisbury dioc. *Fiat de speciali N.* Reg. 2, fol. 181v.

392. [Florence], 22 July 1442. Same grant as **155** sought by Geoffrey Ghriggelei, monk of the house or hospital of Burton, order of St Lazarus of Jerusalem living under the rule of St Augustine, Lincoln dioc. *Fiat de speciali N.* Reg. 2, fol. 181v.

393. [Florence], 22 July 1442. Same grant as **155** sought by Robert Monter, priest, rector of Olney parish church, Lincoln dioc. *Fiat de speciali N.* Reg. 2, fol. 181v.

394. [Florence], 16 August 1442. Same grace as **155** sought by William Wardy and his wife in the town of Bristol(?) (*Briscalie*). *Fiat de speciali N.* Reg. 2, fol. 180v.

395. [Florence], 21 August 1442. Same grant as **252** sought by Robert Stanschaw and his wife Isabel (*Izabella*), nobles, and their children. *Fiat N.* Reg. 2, fol. 180v.

396. [Florence], 21 August 1442. Same grant as **155** sought by William York, layman, Salisbury dioc. *Fiat de speciali N.* Reg. 2, fol. 180v.

397. [Florence], 12 September 1442. Same grant as **157** sought by Robert Lyker, canon of the church of Exeter, and John, priest, rector of N. parish church, Exeter dioc. *Fiat de speciali N.* Reg. 2, fol. 179v.

398. [Florence], 13 September 1442. Same grant as **157** sought by Thomas Franck and his wife Elizabeth, staying at London.[91] *Fiat de speciali N.* Reg. 2, fol. 179v.

399. [Florence], 2 October 1442. Same grant as **155** sought by Henry Ovegan, knight, and his wife Margaret, nobles, St David's dioc. *Fiat de speciali N.* Reg. 2, fol. 182r.

400. [Florence], 4 November 1442. Same grant as **155** sought by Fr Robert Botyll miar(?), nobleman, prior of the order of brothers of the hospital of St John of Jerusalem of the house of St John of Jerusalem, London.[92] *Fiat de speciali N.* Reg. 2, fol. 183r.

401. [Florence], 19 December 1442. Same grant as **155** sought by William Port, clerk, Winchester dioc.[93] *Fiat de speciali N.* Reg. 2, fol. 184r.

---

[91] They were also granted plenary remission *in mortis articulo* on 16 September 1442, when their name was given as 'Frank'. As Thomas Franck, *domicellus*, citizen of London, and his wife Elizabeth, noblewoman, they were granted a licence on 16 October 1436 to have mass celebrated before daybreak (*CPL*, viii. 616; ix. 313).

[92] St John's, Clerkenwell, the principal house of the Hospitallers in England. Robert Botyll was prior in 1439, still in 1444 and 1467; he vacated the office in 1468 (Dugdale, vi/2. 799; *VCH (Middlesex)*, i. 200).

[93] He was also granted a licence for a portable altar on 10 May 1441 (*CPL*, ix. 304).

402. [Florence], 12 February 1443.[94] Same grant as **157** sought by John Ferot and his wife Alice; John Here, priest; Joan Lawude; Thomas Karker, priest; John Gyir, priest, rector of Stibbard (*Stebryd*) parish church, Norwich dioc. *Fiat de speciali N.* Reg. 2, fol. 185v.

403. [Florence], 15 February 1443. Same grant as **157** sought by Nicholas Wennford and his wife Isabel, [Norwich dioc.]. *Fiat N.* Reg. 2, fol. 185v.

404. [Florence], 15 February 1443. Same grant as **155** sought by Margaret Suffin; John Rabet and his wife; Thomas Hungier and his wife; John Hunger, priest; Constantine Dalby, clerk; Edmund Wrichet and his wife, Norwich dioc. *Fiat de speciali N.* Reg. 2, fol. 185v.

405. [Florence], 21 February 1443. Same grant as **157** sought by William Welton of Apley (*Appully*), priest, Lincoln dioc. *Fiat de speciali N.* Reg. 2, fol. 185v.

406. [Florence], 3 March 1443. Same grant as **155** sought by John Spryng, priest, Norwich dioc.[95] Approved with **408**. Reg. 2, fol. 185v.

407. [Florence], 3 March 1443. Same grant as **155** sought by Agnes Spryng, Norwich dioc. Approved with **408**. Reg. 2, fol. 186r.

408. [Florence], 3 March 1443. Same grant as **252** sought by Margaret Dyer, widow, Norwich dioc. *Fiat de speciali N.* (Approved with **406–7**.) Reg. 2, fol. 186r.

409. [Florence], 3 March 1443. Same grant as **155** sought by Bartholomea Pady, Norwich dioc. *Fiat de speciali N.* Reg. 2, fol. 186r.

410. [Florence], 4 March 1443. Same grant as **155** sought by Joan W^{r}ytd, Norwich dioc. *Fiat de speciali N.* Reg. 2, fol. 186r.

411. [Florence], 6 April 1443. Same grant as **157** sought by John Brigeham, priest, Norwich dioc.; Adam Pyttecok and his wife Katherine, Norwich dioc.; Robert Fyllesson and his wife Christine, Norwich dioc. *Fiat de speciali N.* Reg. 2, fol. 184v.

[*De diversis formis*]

412. [Florence, 11 March 1439 x 10 March 1440].[96] Henry Mare, priest, York dioc., seeks absolution [from excommunication] since he had himself promoted to all holy orders outside his diocese and without his ordinary's licence and administered divine offices in these orders several times. *Fiat in forma N.* Reg. 2, fol. 196v.

---

[94] The date is given as 'xviii kal. Martii' rather than the more correct 'ii id. Februarii'.
[95] He was also granted a licence on 4 May 1443 to have a portable altar and celebrate mass or have it celebrated before daybreak (*CPL*, ix. 366).
[96] **412–15** are undated but appear to fall within Eugenius's seventh pontifical year.

413. [Florence, 11 March 1439 x 10 February 1440]. Henry Mare, priest, [Coventry and] Lichfield dioc., guilelessly (*simplicitate ductus*) formerly had himself promoted to all holy orders while under age but otherwise legally and participated thus in divine offices; [he requests] absolution from sentence of excommunication and that he may minister in his existing orders now that he has reached the legitimate age. *Fiat in forma N.* Reg. 2, fol. 197r.

414. [Florence, 11 March 1439 x 10 February 1440]. Robert Filt, priest, [Coventry and] Lichfield dioc., had himself promoted to the priesthood while under age but otherwise legally [and participated thus in divine offices; he requests] a letter of absolution [from sentence of excommunication and that he may minister in his existing orders now that he has reached the legitimate age]. *Fiat in forma N.* Reg. 2, fol. 197r.

415. [Florence, 11 March 1439 x 10 February 1440]. John Affordly, priest, York dioc., [when he was formerly a prior, as a result of certain injuries done to him, left his monastery with permission, but having abandoned his habit returned to the secular life for some time, and celebrated divine offices; he seeks] a letter of absolution. *Fiat in forma N.* Reg. 2, fol. 197r.

416. [Florence], 8 February [1440]. Walter Marys, priest, Worcester dioc., guilelessly (*tamquam simplex*) formerly had himself promoted to all, even holy orders while under age but otherwise legally and ministered in them several times and otherwise participated in divine offices. Now that he has reached the legitimate age, the pope is requested to order his absolution from such excesses. *Fiat de speciali N.* Reg. 2, fol. 206v.

417. [*Florence*], *4 July* [*1440*]. *John Southam, priest, archdeacon of Oxford, Lincoln dioc., had his archdeaconry visited by another and received its dues several times without a proper papal dispensation; he seeks absolution from excommunication and dispensation from irregularity.*[97] Reg. 2, fol. 213r.

> [Florentie], iiii nonas Iulii. Exponitur sanctitati vestre pro parte Iohannis Southam, presbiteri ac archidiaconi Ox[o]nie in ecclesia Lincolniensi, quod ipse olim per interpositam personam archidiaconatum predictum visitari fecit, cole[c]tas, visitationes et alia tributa ipsius archidiaconatus pluries recepit, credendo quod per apostolicam sedem secum esse dispensatum cum per nuntium ad dictam sedem pro dispensatione alias misisset, propter quod dubitat ne in aliqua excommunicationis sententia etc. [incidisset]. Et sic ligatus tamquam simplex ~~in et~~ missas et alia divina officia pluries celebravit. Quare pro parte dicti exponentis supplicatur quatinus ipsum a dicta excommunicationis [sententia] excessibusque huiusmodi etc. [ac peccatis suis aliis] absolvi mandare necnon super irregularitate si quam etc. [ex premissis contraxit] secum dispensare dignemini.
>
> Fiat in forma N.

[97] He had been granted a dispensation for life on 22 February 1438 to visit his archdeaconry through a deputy and receive procurations, even in money, as he was then almost 70 and impeded by an incurable disease (*CPL*, viii. 636). For his benefices and university and clerical career, see *BRUO*, iii.1732–3; *CPL*, viii. 497.

418. [*Florence*], *1 August* [*1440*]. *Fr Henry Penson, priest, professed canon of Fordham Priory, Gilbertine order, Norwich dioc., incurred excommunication for apostasy; he seeks absolution from this sentence, a licence to transfer to another monastery of his order, and dispensation from irregularity.* Reg. 2, fol. 213v.

[Florentie], kal. Augusti. Exponitur sanctitati vestre pro parte fratris Henrici Penson, presbiteri, canonici professi prioratus conventualis de Fordham ordinis fratrum sancti Gilberti sub regula sancti Augustini degentium Norwicensis diocesis, quod ipse olim, habitu et ordine derelictis, ipsum prioratum in quo se voto professionis astrinxerat illicentiatus exivit et ad seculum est reversus, in quo aliquamdiu dampnabiliter evagando sic ligatus tamquam simplex etc. divina celebravit officia et alias inmiscuit se eisdem. Cum autem dictus exponens non valeat animum suum ad reditum dicti prioratus aliqualiter inclinare etc., supplicat quatinus ipsum a generali excommunicationis sententia excessibusque huiusmodi absolvi mandare, quodque ad aliud prioratum sive monasterium eiusdem ordinis professionis et habitus parum vel artioris observantie regularis se transferre valeat licentiam eidem concedere dignemini, necnon ~~suus~~ super irregularitate dicto modo contracta dispensari.

Fiat in forma N.

419. [*Florence*], *12 September* [*1440*]. *Fr Richard Wyrdyn, priest, professed monk of Sheen Priory without the walls of London, Carthusian order, incurred excommunication for apostasy; he seeks absolution from this sentence and a licence to transfer to another monastery of his order.* Reg. 2, fol. 216r.

[Florentie], ii id. Septembris. Exponit sanctitati vestre frater Richardus Wyrdyn, presbiter, monachus professus prioratus conventualis salutacionis beate Marie virginis extra muros Londonienses ordinis Cartusiensis, quod ipse olim carceres prioratus in quibus detinebatur fregit et ipsos ac prioratum in quo se voto professionis astrinxerat illicentiatus exivit et ad seculum est reversus, in quo aliquamdiu dampnabiliter evagando extiterat. Cum autem, patre sancte, non valeat animum suum ad reditum dicti prioratus aliqualiter inclinare, cupiat tamen etc. [sub regulari habitu domino perpetuo famulari], supplicat eidem sanctitati vestre quatinus ipsum a generali excommunicationis sententia si quam etc. [incurrit] et excessibus huiusmodi absolvi mandare, quodque ad aliquod aliud prioratum sive monasterium eiusdem ordinis professionis et habitus paris vel artioris observantie regularis se transferre valeat licentiam [eidem] concedere dignemini.

Fiat in forma N.

420. [*Florence*], *29 March* [*1441*]. *Thomas Wolle^{mi}, priest, rector of St Peter-le-Bailey, Oxford, Lincoln dioc., read and imposed certain sentences as an official as a result of which he fears having incurred excommunication; he seeks absolution from that sentence and a dispensation from irregularity.*[98] Reg. 2, fol. 223r.

---

[98] Thomas Woller was principal of St James Hall, Oxford, 1438–52, a *magister* by 1444, and rector of St Peter-le-Bailey, Oxford, by 1435 and until death; he died by June 1454 (*BRUO*, iii. 2077).

[Florentie], iiii kal. Aprilis. Exponitur sanctitati vestre pro parte Thome Wolle[mi], presbiteri, rectoris parrochialis ecclesie in Trybali ville Oxoniensis Lincolniensis diocesis, quod cum ipse olim in diversis locis et diversis temporibus officialis, vicarius seu locumtenens constitutus esset, prefatus exponens nonnullas sententias, non tamen in crimine sanguinis vel ubi mors subsecuta esset, legit et tulit, propter quod timet excommunicationis sententias incurrisse et sic forte ligatus divina celebravit [officia] etc. [Supplicatur eidem sanctitati vestre] quatinus ipsum a dictis sententiis excessibusque huiusmodi etc. [ac peccatis suis aliis absolvi necnon super irregularitate dispensari mandare dignemini].

Fiat in forma N.

421. [*Florence*], *22 August* [*1441*]. *Fr Hugh Grobham, priest, professed canon of Bridgwater Hospital, OSA,*[99] *Bath* [*and Wells*] *dioc., incurred excommunication for apostasy; he seeks absolution from this sentence and dispensation from irregularity.*[100] Reg. 2, fol. 229r.

[Florentie], xi kal. Septembris. Exponitur sanctitati vestre pro parte fratris Hugonis Grobham, presbiteri, canonici professi domus seu hospitalis sancti Iohannis evangeliste ordinis sancti Augustini Batoniensis diocesis, quod ipse domum ipsam in qua etc. [se voto professionis] astrinxerat, habitu et ordine penitus derelictis, illicentiatus exivit et in seculo per plures annos vagando remansit etc. [Cum autem sit] ad cor reversus cupiatque redire etc. [sub regulari habitu domino perpetuo famulari, supplicatur eidem sanctitati vestre] quatinus ipsum a sententia et apostasie reatu huiusmodi ac peccatis etc. [suis aliis] absolvere secum[que] super irregularitate quam missam etc. [et alia divina officia] celebrando sic ligatus non tamen in contemptum clavium contraxit dispensare seu absolvi et dispensari mandare dignemini.

Fiat in forma N.

422. [*Florence*], *30 August* [*1441*]. *Fr Robert de Sailby, professed canon of Sixhills Priory, Gilbertine order,* [*Lincoln dioc.*], *incurred excommunication for apostasy; he seeks absolution from this sentence and a dispensation from irregularity.* Reg. 2, fol. 228v.

[Florentie], iii kal. Septembris. Exponitur sanctitati vestre pro parte fratris Roberti de Sailby, canonici professi prioratus conventualis de Syxhull' ordinis sancti Gilberti sub regula sancti Benedicti degentium [Lincolniensis diocesis], quod ipse dictum prioratum in quo se voto professionis astrinxerat, habitu et ordine derelictis, illicentiatus exivit et in mundo per plures annos extitit evagatus, et sic ligatus non in contemptum clavium divina

---

[99] Conventual hospital dedicated to SS. John the Baptist and Giles (Hadcock and Knowles, 315). St John the Evangelist is also named as its dedicatee in this entry and *CPL*, ix. 203.

[100] Bishop Stafford of Bath and Wells had granted him a licence on 10 November 1429 to receive Stogursey Priory (Somerset) at farm and administer its property (*Reg. Stafford (Bath and Wells)*, 253). Grobham was also granted a dispensation on 26 August 1441 to hold any benefice with cure of souls (*CPL*, ix. 203). By virtue of this grant he was admitted as vicar of Halse (Somerset) on 22 December 1457; he resigned this benefice by January 1464 (*Reg. Bekynton*, 1100, 1551).

officia celebravit etc. Cum autem ad ovile reversus sit penitentiamque pro delicto apostasie peregerit etc. [supplicatur eidem sanctitati vestre] quatinus ipsum a generali excommunicationis sententia et excessibus huiusmodi etc. [ac peccatis suis aliis] absolvi mandare secumque super irregularitate dispensare dignemini.

Fiat in forma N. Et committatur magistro dicti ordinis. Fiat N.

423. [*Florence*], *1 January* [*1442*]. *John Northeron, priest, Salisbury dioc., incurred excommunication for marrying Racius Estbero and his wife Joan without banns; he seeks absolution from this sentence and a dispensation from irregularity.* Reg. 2, fol. 233v.

[Florentie], kal. Ianuarii. Exponitur sanctitati vestre pro parte Iohannis Northeron', presbiteri Saresbiriensis diocesis, quod ipse quemdam Racium Estbero laicum et Iohannam eius coniugem clandestine, bannis non edictis ut moris est patrie, matrimonialiter copulavit, propter quod excommunicationis sententiam etc. [incurrit] et sic forte ligatus divina celebravit etc. [officia. Supplicat] quatinus ipsum a dicta sententia si quam etc. [incurrit] et excessibus huiusmodi ac peccatis etc. [suis aliis] absolvi mandare secumque super irregularitate dispensare dignemini.

Fiat in forma N. etc.

424. [*Florence*], *3 January* [*1442*]. *Fr John Elkyngton, priest, professed canon of Grimsby Abbey, OSA*,[101] *Lincoln dioc., incurred excommunication for apostasy; he seeks absolution from this sentence, dispensation from irregularity, and a licence to transfer to another monastery of his order.*[102] Reg. 2, fol. 233v.

[Florentie], iii nonas Ianuarii. Exponit sanctitati vestre frater Iohannes Elkyngton', presbiter, canonicus professus monasterii sanctorum Augustini et Olavi Grimmisbodio' [ordinis] eiusdem sancti Augustini Lincolniensis diocesis, quod ipse monasterium ipsum in quo astrictus fuit illicentiatus exivit et ad seculum est reversus etc., propter quod etc. [excommunicationis sententiam incurrit] et sic ligatus divina celebravit officia non in contemptum etc. [clavium]. Cum autem ad reditum dicti monasterii animum suum nequaquam inclinare potest, cupiat tamen sub regulari habitu domino perpetuo famulari, supplicat etc. [eidem sanctitati vestre] quatinus ipsum a dicta sententia excessibusque huiusmodi et peccatis suis aliis absolvi mandare, secumque super irregularitate dispensare, quodque ad aliquod aliud monasterium eiusdem ordinis paris vel arcioris observancie regularis se transferre valeat licenciam dignemini impartiri.

Fiat de absolutione tantum in forma N.

---

[101] Also known as Wellow Abbey.
[102] A William Elkyngton, Augustinian canon of Wellow (*alias* Grimsby), Lincoln dioc., was granted a dispensation on 31 January 1442 to hold for life any benefice with cure of souls (*CPL*, ix. 218). He was a recidivist apostate, and Bishop Alnwick of Lincoln had enjoined the abbot of Wellow on a visitation of 7 July 1440 to seek this William out and bring him back. The first time that he was said to have left his abbey was to go to the Roman Curia albeit with the abbot's licence (Thomson, *Visitations*, iii. 391, 393–4; Logan, 134, 227).

425. [*Florence*], *9 January* [*1442*]. *John* [*Gisborne*] *alias Nyghtegalle, priest, professed monk of Whitby Abbey, OSB, York dioc., incurred excommunication for apostasy; he seeks absolution from this sentence and a dispensation from irregularity.*[103] Reg. 2, fol. 242v.

[Florentie], v idus Ianuarii. Item similem absolutionem a sentencia excommunicationis petit Iohannes [Gisborne] alias Nyghtegalle, presbiter, monachus professus monasterii de Whytteby ordinis sancti Benedicti Eboracensis diocesis, quod ipse olim monasterium ipsum in quo se voto professionis astrinxerat, habitu et ordine derelictis, illicentiatus exivit et ad seculum est reversus, in quo aliquamdiu extitit dampnabiliter evagatus etc. [propter quod excommunicationis sententiam incurrit] et sic ligatus tamquam simplex et iuris ignarus et non tamen contemptu clavium divina celebravit officia, aliquibus etiam ministravit sacramenta ac alias inmiscuit se eisdem. Cum autem ad cor etc. [nunc domino favente reversus sit], supplicat sanctitati vestre idem exponens etc. [quatinus ipsum a sentencia excommunicationis, excessibusque huiusmodi et peccatis suis aliis absolvi mandare secumque super irregularitate dispensare dignemini] ut in forma.

Fiat in forma N.

426. [*Florence, c. 7 February 1442*].[104] *John Gisborne alias Nyghtegalle, priest, professed monk of Whitby Abbey, OSB, York dioc., went to the Curia to prosecute a case against his abbot, but the latter then died. The new abbot refused to re-admit him, and he incurred excommunication for apostasy. He seeks* [*absolution from this sentence and*] *dispensation* [*from irregularity*]. Reg. 2, fol. 243r.

Exponit sanctitati vestre devotus vester Iohannes Gisborne alias Nyghtegalle, presbiter, monachus professus monasterii sancti Petri et Hylde de Whytteby ordinis sancti Benedicti Eboracensis diocesis, quod ipse olim monasterium ipsum in quo se voto professionis astrinxerat, licet de consensu aliquorum fratrum sine tamen licentia sui abbatis, habitu retento, exivit et ad curiam Romanam ut abbatem dicti monasterii de diversis criminibus accusaret pervenit, causamque contra dictum suum abbatem reverendissimo domino cardinali Placentino[105] committi et citationem decerni obtinuit. Nichilominus antequam dicta citatio executa fuerat sepe dictus abbas sicut domino placuit diem suum clausit extremum et alter loco ipsius in dicto monasterio effectus est abbas, qui dictum exponentem ad monasterium suum revertentem omnino recipere et admittere omnino recusavit. Videns hoc dictus exponens, habitu et ordine derelictis, ad seculum est reversus, in quo dampnabiliter aliquamdiu extitit evagatus etc. propter quod sententiam excommunicationis incurrit in tales generaliter promulgatam, et sic ligatus tamquam simplex et iuris ignarus etc. [divina celebravit officia, aliquibus

---

[103] This John Gysborne *alias* Nyghtengalle was also granted a dispensation on 24 January 1442 to hold for life any benefice with cure of souls (*CPL*, ix. 214). Perhaps the John Gisburne, *magister*, named as a monk of Durham Cathedral Priory on 14 January 1438 (*Kempe Visitations*, 223).

[104] The preceding entry on fol. 242v bears this date.

[105] Branda da Castiglione, created cardinal priest of S. Clemente 1411, cardinal bishop of Porto 1431, cardinal bishop of Sabina 1440, died 1444 (Eubel, ii. 4).

etiam ministravit sacramenta ac alias inmiscuit se eisdem]. Cum autem ad cor nunc domino favente etc. [reversus sit], supplicat etc. [sanctitati vestre idem exponens quatinus ipsum a sententia excommunicationis, excessibusque huiusmodi et peccatis suis aliis absolvi mandare secumque super irregularitate] dispensare dignemini ut in forma.

Fiat in forma N.

427. [*Florence*], *30 March* [*1442*]. *Fr Bartholomew Leyd, priest, professed monk of Boxley Abbey, Cistercian order, Canterbury dioc., incurred excommunication for apostasy; he seeks absolution from this sentence and dispensation from irregularity.* Reg. 2, fol. 241r.

[Florentie], iii kal. Aprilis. Item similem absolutionem a sententia excommunicationis petit frater Bartholomeus Leyd, presbiter, monachus professus monasterii de Bonsle ordinis Cisterciensis Cantuariensis diocesis, qui alias ex quadam animi levitate monasterium ipsum in quo se vinculo professionis astrinxerat, habitu et ordine derelictis, minime anima apostandi illicentiatus exivit et ad seculum est reversus, in quo dampnabiliter evagatus extitit et sic ligatus divina celebravit officia et alias inmiscuit se eisdem. Supplicatur [*sic*] igitur sanctitati vestre dictus exponens etc. [quatinus ipsum a sententia excommunicationis, excessibusque huiusmodi et peccatis suis aliis absolvi mandare secumque super irregularitate dispensare dignemini] ut in forma.

Fiat in forma N.

428. [*Florence*], 4 *April* [*1442*]. Richard Symich, priest, Lincoln(?) (*Lincopensis*) dioc.,[106] formerly had himself promoted to all holy orders while under age but otherwise legally and ministered in them; he seeks absolution from sentence of excommunication. [*Fiat in forma N.*] Reg. 2, fol. 239v.

429. [*Florence, 16 May 1442*]. *Fr John Burten, priest, professed canon of Penmon Priory, OSA, Bangor dioc., incurred excommunication for apostasy; he seeks absolution.* Reg. 2, fol. 238v.

[Florentie, xvii kal. Iunii]. Exponit sanctitati vestre devotus vester frater Iohannes Burten, presbiter, canonicus professus prioratus de Penmon' ordinis sancti Augustini Bangorensis diocesis, quod ipse olim ex quadam causa [*recte* animi] levitate sui prioratum ipsum in quo se vinculo professionis astrinxerat, habitu tamen semper retento, illicenciatus exivit et ad quodam [*recte* quoddam] studium se transtulit in quo aliquamdiu remansit, propter quod excommunicationis etc. [sententiam incurrit]. Quare supplicatur sanctitati vestre quatinus ipsum a dicta sententia etc. [ac excessibus huiusmodi et peccatis suis aliis] mandare dignemini absolvi ut in forma.

Fiat in forma N.

430. [*Florence*], *18 May* [*1442*]. *Fr John Wratinge, priest, professed canon of Anglesey Priory, OSA, Ely dioc., incurred excommunication for disguising his habit on a journey to the Curia; he*

---

[106] *Lincopensis* refers to Linköping in Sweden, but the supplicant's name is not Swedish.

seeks absolution from this sentence and dispensation from irregularity.[107] Reg. 2, fol. 239r.

[Florentie], xv kal. Iunii. Item similem absolutionem a sententia excommunicationis petit frater Iohannes \Wratinge/, presbiter, canonicus professus monasterii de Angeleseye ordinis sancti Augustini Eliensis diocesis, qui alias de sui superioris licentia veniendo ad curiam Romanam per viam aliquando habitum suum portavit in abscondito, propter quod timet etc. [excommunicationis sententiam incurrisse]. Supplicat igitur sanctitati vestre dictus N. [*sic*] etc. quatinus ipsum a sententia excommunicationis huiusmodi etc. [secumque super irregularitate] dignemini dispensare ut etc. [in forma].

Fiat in forma N.

431. [*Florence, 23 May 1442*]. *Robert Fyviam, priest, professed canon of St Osyth's Abbey, OSA, London dioc., remained at his* studium *for some time beyond the term set by his superior; he seeks absolution from excommunication and dispensation from irregularity.* Reg. 2, fol. 238r.

[Florentie, x kal. Iunii]. Exponitur sanctitati vestre pro parte devoti vestri Roberti Fyviam, presbiteri, canonici professi monasterii sancte Osythe ordinis sancti Augustini Londoniensis diocesis, quod ipse olim ultra terminum a suo superiori sibi concessum et prefixum per a [*sic*] in studio per aliquod spatium temporis stetit et in studio permansit, propter quod excommunicationis sententiam timet ex illa inobedientia incurrisse etc. et sic forte ligatus divinis inmiscuit se officiis. Supplicatur igitur sanctitati vestre pro parte dicti exponentis quatinus ipsum a dicta sententia si quam propter premissa incurrit excessibusque huiusmodi et peccatis suis etc. [aliis absolvi mandare secumque super irregularitate] misericorditer dispensare dignemini ut in forma.

Fiat in forma N.

Et committatur si placet priori monasterii sancte Trinitatis Londoniensis ordinis eiusdem.[108] Fiat N.

432. [*Florence, 22 July 1442*]. *Fr Thomas Hankeysberi, priest, professed monk of Kingswood Abbey, Cistercian order, Worcester dioc., incurred excommunication for apostasy; he seeks absolution from this sentence and dispensation from irregularity.*[109] Reg. 2, fol. 235v.

[Florentie, xi kal. Augusti]. Exponit sanctitati vestre devotus vester frater Thomas Hankeysberi, presbiteri [*sic*], monachus professus monasterii de Kyngeswore ordinis Cysterciensis Wygorniensis diocesis, quod ipse olim licentia a suo superiore petita et non amicabiliter vel legittime obtenta monasterium ipsum in quo se vinculo professionis astrinxerat, habitu retento, non animo apostotandi [*sic*] exivit et ad seculum est reversus in quod [*recte* quo]

---

[107] John Wrattyng was also granted a dispensation on 23 May 1442 to hold for life any benefice with cure of souls (*CPL*, ix. 266).
[108] At this time the prior of the priory of Holy Trinity, Aldgate, was John Sevenoke (Smith, *Heads of Religious Houses*, iii. 471).
[109] Thomas Haukesbury was granted a dispensation as a priest on 4 August 1442 to hold for life any benefice with cure of souls usually held by secular clerks (*CPL*, ix. 271).

aliquamdiu habitum suum absconditum sub habitu seculari dampnabiliter evagatus extitit, propter quod excommunicationis incurrit sententiam in tales etc. [generaliter promulgatam] et sic ligatus divina celebravit officia ac alias inmiscuit se eisdem, necnon ecclesiastica ministravit sacramenta, quare notam irregularitatis dinoscitur incurrisse. Supplicatur igitur sanctitati vestre pro parte dicti exponentis quatinus ipsum a dicta sententia excessibusque huiusmodi et peccatis suis aliis misericorditer absolvi mandare secumque super irregularitate et [sic] ex premissis contracta dispensare dignemini ut in forma.

Fiat N.

Super diversis formis

433. [Florence], 15 April 1439. Supplication on the part of Robert Alcok, scholar, Lincoln dioc., that on reaching the age of 24 he may be promoted to the order of the priesthood and minister in it, and that the pope may grant him a dispensation notwithstanding that defect of age and constitutions of the Lyons and Lateran councils and any others to the contrary. *Fiat de speciali N.* Reg. 2bis, fol. 9v.

434. [Florence], 17 April 1439. The pope is requested to grant *Padulf* [son of?] William Fun, clerk, Lincoln dioc., a licence with *clause opportune* that on reaching the age of 24 he may be promoted to priest's orders, notwithstanding any constitutions. *Fiat de speciali N.* Reg. 2bis, fol. 10v.

435. [Florence], 2 May 1439. Supplication on the part of William Brito, MA,[110] for the pope to grant him a faculty to study civil law in a *studium generale*, perform all scholastic acts and receive degrees in the same, for five years. *Fiat de speciali N.* Reg. 2bis, fol. 4v.

436. [Florence], 19 May 1439. The pope is requested to grant John Banaster, acolyte, [Coventry and] Lichfield dioc., a licence so that he may be promoted to all holy orders by any bishop having the grace and communion of the apostolic see, he being unable to approach his ordinary for certain reasons. *Fiat de speciali N.* Reg. 2bis, fol. 11r.

437. [Florence], 23 May 1439. The pope is requested to grant *littere confessionales* in perpetuity to Thomas Towe, Master of St Mary's hospital of the New Work, Strood (*novi operis de Strode*), Rochester dioc.[111] [*Fiat de speciali N.*]. Reg. 2bis, fol. 29r.

---

[110] No diocese given. Perhaps the William Breton, MA, DTh by 1449, who was vicar of All Saints', Northampton, admitted 31 July 1434, till death; he was still alive in 1460 (*BRUO*, i. 261).

[111] Thomas Thowe was master of this hospital by 1444 and resigned in 1465 (*VCH (Kent)*, ii. 229). As rector of Adstock (Bucks.), Lincoln dioc., he was granted a dispensation on 17 August 1423 to hold another incompatible benefice for five years. This dispensation was extended for life on 7 December 1427, when he was said to be of noble race (*CPL*, vii. 273, viii. 17). By then he had obtained the rectory of St Mary Magdalen's, Canterbury, and exchanged Adstock for Horsemonden (Kent), Rochester dioc.

438. [Florence], 30 May 1439. Supplication on the part of Robert Hasgardby, clerk, Lincoln dioc., for the pope to grant him a dispensation so that, notwithstanding constitutions of the Lyons and Lateran councils and any others to the contrary, on reaching the age of 24 he may be promoted to all holy orders and retain a benefice with cure of souls. *Fiat de speciali N.* Reg. 2bis, fol. 17v.

439. [Florence], 30 May 1439. Supplication on the part of Robert Hasgarby, clerk, Lyons (*Lugdunensis*) dioc.,[112] for the pope to grant him a dispensation so that on reaching the age of 24 he may be promoted to all holy orders and retain a benefice with cure of souls. *Fiat de speciali N.* Reg. 2bis, fol. 26r.

440. [Florence], 1 June 1439. The same grant as **437** for Stephen Howys and his wife Matilda, Norwich dioc. *Fiat de speciali N.* Reg. 2bis, fol. 29r.

441. [Florence], 22 June 1439. Same grant as **437** for John Knyght of Crewkerne, anchorite(?) (*Crukerne Anathorite*), Bath [and Wells] dioc. Approved with **442**. Reg. 2bis, fol. 29v.

442. [Florence], 22 June 1439. Same grant as **437** for Sister Joan Willus, professed nun of the monastery of Swine (*Swyn*), Order of St Bernard [i.e. Cistercian], York dioc. *Fiat N.* (Approved with **441**.) Reg. 2bis, fol. 29v.

443. [Florence], 6 July 1439. Same grant as **437** for Lancelot and his wife Janet.[113] *Fiat N.* Reg. 2bis, fol. 29v.

444. [Florence, *c.* June-July 1439].[114] Supplication on the part of Sister Margaret Broirer, professed nun of the monastery of Kilburn (*Kilbourne*), OSA,[115] London dioc., for the pope to grant her a licence to transfer to another monastery of the same order, profession, and habit, of equal or stricter regular observance, since she cannot remain in the said monastery with a calm spirit and clear conscience (*cum sue anime quiete et sana conscientia*). *Fiat in forma N.* Reg. 2bis, fol. 32v.

445. [Florence], 19 July 1439. Supplication on the part of Thomas Oxford, subdeacon, York dioc., for the pope to grant him a dispensation so that on reaching the age of 24 he may be promoted to deacon's and priest's orders and minister in them, notwithstanding that defect of age and constitutions of the Lyons and Lateran councils and any others to the contrary. *Fiat de speciali N.* Reg. 2bis, fols. 37v–38r.

446. [Florence, *c.* July-August 1439].[116] Supplication on the part of William Coo *alias* Combe, priest, rector of Ibstone (*Ibestan*) parish church, Lincoln dioc., for the

---

[112] Given that the surname is English, perhaps *Lugdunensis* is an error for *Lincolniensis*.
[113] No diocese is specified.
[114] This entry is undated but that preceding it is dated 19 June 1439 and that following it, 15 July 1439.
[115] Knowles and Hadcock, 281, note that this house 'apparently began and ended as Benedictine' though it was 'sometimes referred to as Augustinian', as here.
[116] This entry is undated but preceded by **447** in the register; the entry following it is dated 30 July 1439.

pope to grant him a licence and faculty to read and study in any *studium generale* in a faculty of civil law for five years, notwithstanding the constitution ['Super speculam'] of Pope Honorius IV [*recte* III] and any others to the contrary. *Fiat N.* Reg. 2bis, fol. 36v.

447. [Florence], 6 August 1439. Supplication on the part of Thomas Sollay, priest, perpetual vicar of All Saints parish church, Theddlethorpe (*Thetiltorpe*), Lincoln dioc.,[117] for the pope to grant him *littere confessionales in forma 'Cupientes'*. *Fiat de speciali N.* Reg. 2bis, fol. 36v.

448. [Florence], 1 September 1439. Supplication on the part of Gwilym Conwey, subdeacon, Bangor (*Bangaren.*) dioc.,[118] for the pope to grant him a licence so that he may hear, read, and study civil law (*leges*) in any university, *studium generale vel privatum alias studium* for five years, while in his existing and future orders. *Fiat de speciali N.* Reg. 2bis, fol. 46v.

449. [Florence], 5 September 1439. The pope is requested to grant William Speke, priest, rector of Marsh Baldon (*Mershbaldyngten*) parish church, Lincoln dioc., MA, a licence to absolve all and each of his parishoners of either sex for five years. *Fiat N.* Reg. 2bis, fol. 46v–47r.

450. [*Florence*], *17 September 1439. John Steppe, priest, rector of Landulph, Exeter dioc.,*[119] *was presented to that church by his father; he has now learned that his father obtained the advowson of that church with that intention and since he was too young to receive that church at first, his father presented it to another on the understanding that the latter resigned it when he came of age, and thus he came to hold it. He seeks absolution from simony and dispensation from irregularity.* Reg. 2bis, fol. 49r–v.

[Florentie], xv kal. Octobris. Beatissime pater, exponitur sanctitati vestre pro parte devoti oratoris vestri Iohannis Steppe, presbiteri, rectoris parrochialis ecclesie de Landilpe Exoniensis diocesis, quod olim ipsius exponentis pater, dominum [*recte* dominium] eiusdem loci de Landylpe ad firmam a vero ipsius temporali domino cum advocacione dicte ecclesie ea intencione, ut creditur et ut ipse [fol. 49v] exponens postmodum intellexit, ad ecclesiam ipsam, que de iure patronatus ipsius domini temporalis existit, dum vacaret, ut ipsum exponentem suum filium presentare et illam sibi conferre facere posset, ipso tamen exponente hoc ignorante, recepit. Et deinde, dicta ecclesia isto modo vacante, quia ipse exponens nondum erat in etate sufficiente ad illam ecclesiam obtinendum, dictus suus pater quemdam Petrum presbiterum ad ecclesiam sic vacantem tali adiecta condicione presentavit, quod ipse presbiter eandem ecclesiam quousque dictus exponens ad etatem

---

[117] He was granted a dispensation on 30 March 1443 to hold this vicarage with another incompatible benefice for life (*CPL*, ix. 334).
[118] Perhaps the William Conwhay in priest's orders by 1444 and recorded as an Oxford alumnus. Emden suggests that he was the same as magister William Conway, BCnL, rector of Chetton (Salop), 1466–80 (*BRUO*, i. 479).
[119] For his clerical career and benefices, see *Reg. Lacy*, ed. Hingeston-Randolph, i. 153, 209; ed. Dunstan, i. 332; ii. 47, 191, 193; iii. 151; iv. 114a, 143b, 151; *CPL*, viii. 530).

legitimam perveniret retineret et eidem deserviret et propterea xi libras sterlingorum annuatim ex fructibus illius ecclesie solum perciperet, et postquam exponens ipse in legitima esset etate constitutus, eandem ecclesiam pure et simpliciter resignare et sibi dimittere teneretur, prout etiam sic factum extitit, ipseque exponens ad eandem ecclesiam tandem per liberam eiusdem Petri resignationem vacantem per dictum suum patrem episcopo Exoniensi loci ordinario presentatus et per ipsum episcopum admissus fuit, illamque iam per plures annos tenuit et possedit prout tenet et possidet de presenti pacifice et pure, fructus percipiens ex eadem. Cum, pater sancte, dictus exponens, qui premissa per symoniam sic facta fuisse diucius ignoravit et adhuc nuper ignorabat, conscientia ductus dubitet ecclesiam predictam posse retinere nisi per eandem sanctitatem sibi super hoc de remedio opportuno provideretur. Supplicatur igitur eidem sanctitati pro parte dicti exponentis, qui etiam quam primum de ipso tractatu symoniaco noticiam habuit ad obtinendum eiusdem sanctitatis remedium transmisit, quatinus ipsum a reatu symonie huiusmodi si quam ob premissa incurrit ac peccatis suis aliis nisi sint etc. [talia propter que sit sedes apostolica consulenda] absolvere, secumque super irregularitate premissorum occasione qualitercumque contracta, quodque in suis ordinibus ministrare, et dictam ecclesiam, quam sic symoniace ignoranter tamen assecutus est, et quecumque alia [fol. 50r] ecclesiastica beneficia, si sibi quavis auctoritate canonice conferantur, recipere et retinere possit et valeat cum rehabilitatione opportuna dispensare misericorditer dignemini de gratia speciali, iuribus, constitutionibus, et ordinationibus apostolicis ac aliis in contrarium facientibus non obstantibus quibuscumque, cum clausis opportunis.

Fiat N.

451. [Florence, *c.* 23–5 September 1439].[120] Supplication on the part of Meurig ap Einion (*Eynon*), priest, professed monk of St Mary's monastery, Whitland (*Albalanda*), Cistercian order, St David's dioc., for the pope to grant him a licence that with his superior's permission he may hear, study, and read canon law and graduate in a faculty of canon law, notwithstanding any constitutions, ordinances, distinctions, rules and privileges of that order and any others to the contrary. *Fiat de speciali N.* Reg. 2bis, fol. 50r.

452. [*Florence*], *23 November 1439. Thomas, duke of Gloucester,*[121] *founded a college of priests at Pleshey, London dioc., and gave it statutes, confirmed by apostolic authority, which its members swore an oath to observe and which specified the number of members; but because he left the college inadequately endowed, its members cannot observe its statutes, especially concerning the number of members. Hence John Stangryff, master of the college,*[122] *and other members request absolution from breaking their oath and a declaration that they are not bound by these statutes in*

---

[120] It is undated, but the entries immediately following and preceding it in the register are dated 23 and 25 September 1439 respectively.

[121] Thomas of Woodstock (b. 1355), seventh and youngest son of Edward III, was created Constable of England in 1376, earl of Buckingham in 1377, and duke of Gloucester in 1385; he also became earl of Essex in 1380 by right of his wife. He was condemned as a traitor and put to death in 1397 (*Complete Peerage*, v. 719–29; *ODNB*, liv. 277–84).

[122] John Stangryffe was presented as master in 1433 and died in 1477 (*VCH (Essex)*, ii. 195).

regard to numbers and other matters beyond the college's resources until the latter are increased.[123]
Reg. 2bis, fol. 53r.

[Florentie], viiii kalendas Decembris. Beatissime pater, licet dudum Thomas dux Gloucestrie dum viveret in humanis, qui Edwardi regis Anglie filius extiterat, de bonis sibi a deo collatis unum collegium presbiterorum et clericorum apud villam de Plecy Londoniensis diocesis fundaverit, et certa ordinationes et statuta, que magister et persone que in dicto collegio pro tempore fuerint servare tenerentur per iuramentum per ipsos magistrum et personas in eorum assumptione prestandum, et inter alia de certo numero personarum huiusmodi ibidem pro tempore ponendarum et assumendarum continue, et ut statuta et ordinationes predicta robur firmitatis obtinerent, ea obtinuit auctoritate apostolica confirmari. Proposueritque dictus fundator ipsum collegium adeo habunde de bonis suis predictis dotare quod persone ordinate secundum statuta et ordinationes predicta ut premittitur confirmata possent commode sustentari, et preventus morte non fecerit ut proposuerat et propterea magister et persone que in dicto collegio hactenus fuerunt [fol. 53v] dicta statuta et ordinationes iuramento confirmata ut predicitur servare non potuerunt nec possent ob defectum dicte dotis. Idcirco dubitent dicti magister et persone que inpresentiarum sunt in dicto collegio reatum periurii incurrisse, nec possent in futurum illa servare, nec personas in tanto numero iuxta tenorem earundem statutorum et ordinationum in dicto collegio recipere et manu tenere ob defectum facultatum predictarum. Supplicatur igitur sanctitati vestra [*recte* vestre] pro parte devoti vestri Iohannis Stangryff prefati collegii magistri moderni et aliarum personarum ibidem degentium quatinus ipsos ab huiusmodi iuramenti trangressione absolvere, ipsosque ad illa ordinationes et statuta imposterum in parte qua cavetur de personarum numero recipiendarum et alia quecumque in statutis et ordinationibus predictis comprehensa sic servanda ultra quam facultates suppetant, donec et quousque de facultatibus vel alias dotatum fuerit quod persone ipse secundum statuta et ordinationes predicta sustentari et alia onera illis incumbentia huiusmodi supportari possint, non teneri declarare dignemini de gratia speciali, statutis et ordinationibus prefatis ceterisque in contrarium editis non obstantibus quibuscumque et cum clausis opportunis.

Fiat ut infra N. Signanda per fiat de speciali quo ad absolutionem. Quo ad reliqua vero signanda per fiat si est ita, videlicet quod magister et persone que inpresentiarum sunt in dicto collegio non teneantur recipere personas

---

[123] Richard II granted his uncle, Thomas, duke of Gloucester, a licence on 25 January 1394 to found a college at Pleshey for nine chaplains, including a master, two clerks and two choristers. The founder issued statutes for the college on 20 February 1395. He and his wife obtained a further royal licence on 6 July 1396 to increase the number of chaplains. The college subsequently complained to Martin V about the inadequacy of its revenues and severity of its statutes. After a further petition an episcopal inquiry was conducted by authority of Eugenius IV on 6 July 1441. It found that the founder had never increased the college's endowment as he had intended, and its revenues were not sufficient to support a master and eight fellows. Bishop Gilbert of London declared that the master was not bound to the first foundation and reserved the right to himself and his successors to interpret and alter the statutes as necessary (*VCH (Essex)*, ii. 193–4).

nec alia facere quam suspetant [*recte* suppetant] facultates sed illis excrescentibus teneantur prout super excreverint facultates. Et committatur ordinario.

Super homicidiis et iniectionibus

453. [*Florence*], *25 May 1439. Robert Westrin, priest, Durham dioc., around the age of 20 travelled with his lord to Hainault and was present when men were killed in fighting there; he later had himself promoted to all orders and ministered in them. He requests absolution from these killings and dispensation from irregularity.* Reg. 2bis, fol. 62r.

[Florentie], viiii kal. Iunii. Beatissime pater, exponit sanctitati vestre devotus vester Robertus Westrin, presbiter Dunelmensis diocesis, quod ipse olim existens in xx sue etatis anno vel circa de partibus Anglie ad Hannoniam cum quodam nobili viro cuius familiaris erat se transtulit, et arma sui domini portasset, nulla alia; in aliquibus conflictibus ubi certa homicidia perpetrata erant presens armatus fuit, nullum tamen dictus exponens percussit seu volneravit [*sic*] aut interfecit. Et deinde nullis super premissis absolutionibus obtentis se fecit alias tamen rite ad omnes ordines promoveri et in ipsis ministravit. Cum autem exponens ipse in premissis alias quam ut premittitur culpabilis non fuerit cupiatque in omnibus suis sic susceptis ordinibus perpetuo domino famulare, supplicat igitur eidem sanctitati quatinus ipsum ab huiusmodi homicidiorum reatibus absolvi et secum super iregularitate dispensari mandare dignemini de gratia vestra speciali.

Fiat ut infra N. Signanda per fiat de speciali.

454. [*Florence*], *27 September 1439. Henry Dabilis, layman, Canterbury dioc., incurred excommunication for killing a priest; he requests absolution from this sentence and a public penance to be performed in Rome.* Reg. 2bis, fol. 81v.

[Florentie], v kal. Octobris. Exponit sanctitati vestre devotus vester Henricus Dabilis, laicus Cantuariensis diocesis, quod ipse olim diabolo instigante necnon ex certis racionabilibus causis ipsum ad hoc urgentibus quendam presbiterum interfecit propter quod excommunicationis incurrit sententiam in tales etc. [generaliter promulgatam]. Supplicat igitur sanctitati vestre humiliter dictus exponens quatinus ipsum a sententia excommunicationis huiusmodi et peccatis suis etc. [aliis] nisi sit [*recte* sint] etc. [talia propter que sit sedes apostolica consulenda] misericorditer absolvi mandare sibique [ut?] publicam penitentiam, quam in loco delicti peragere tenetur, in Roman[a curia?] in tribus vel quatuor locis seu ecclesiis maioribus peragere possit, cum suum ordinarium in hac parte habet suspectum, [iniungere dignemini?] de gratia speciali.

Fiat de expresso N.

455. [*Florence*], *11 October 1439. Fr John Kylling, priest, professed monk of Croxden Abbey, Cistercian order, [Coventry and] Lichfield dioc., had been ejected from his monastery without just cause and with letters of doubtful authority. He accompanied an army overseas for five weeks and* *encouraged but did not commit looting, arson, and killing. He seeks absolution from excommunication and these wrongs and a dispensation from irregularity.*[124] Reg. 2bis, fol. 85r.

[Florentie], v id. Octobris. Beatissime pater, exponit sanctitati vestre devotus vester frater Iohannes Kylling, presbiter, monachus professus monasterii beate Marie [de] Cyoskeden [*sic*] ordinis Cisterciensis Lichelfeldensis [*sic*] diocesis, quod cum ipse olim sine causa rationabili et iusta precedente de monasterio in quo professus erat eiectus extiterat et, ut verisimile erat, per invidiam cuiusdam persone regularis ipsius monasterii, et littere licentie sibi date fuissent sub sigillo illius qui pro tunc non prefuit regimini monasterii tamquam abbas sed per prius cesserant [*sic*] abbatiali dignitati, pretextu cuius parvi vel nullius valoris huiusmodi littere erant. Tamquam desperatus, habitu et ordine derelictis, illicentiatus cum quodam exercitu mare ad alienas partes transfretavit et in eodem exercitu per quinque septimanas, ubi spolia, rapine, homicidia laicalia, [et] incendia in locis sacris et non sacris perpetrata fuerunt, interfuit et ad ea auxilium, consilium prestitit et favorem, nec tamen aliqua earum manu propria perpetravit, propter quod excommunicationis sententiam incurrit in tales etc. [generaliter promulgatam] et sic ligatus divina celebravit officia ac alias inmiscuit se eisdem. Nunc vero ad cor reversus [est] cupiatque [ad] ovile suum redire et inibi altissimo perpetuum prebere famulatum in omnibus suis ordinibus prout tenetur. Supplicat igitur sanctitati vestre dictus exponens quatinus ipsum a sententiis excommunicationis excessibusque huiusmodi et reatibus rapinarum, spoliorum, homicidiorum, et incendiorum huiusmodi absolvi mandare secumque super irregularitate ex premissis contracta quodque in favorem religionis et [*recte* in] omnibus suis ordinibus libere et licite ministrare valeat dignemini misericorditer dispensare de gratia speciali.

Concessum de speciali in presencia domini Cardinalis Pe.

456. [*Florence*], *18 October 1439. Gwilym Heroll of Wales, clerk, St David's dioc., was sent with a scholar to ask a layman to return some boots, and consequently a quarrel broke out between the scholar and layman, in which the scholar wounded the layman's head with a knife, as a result of which the layman later died. Subsequently he was ordered by his brother to join him in the army against the king of England's enemies and did so. He seeks [dispensation from irregularity?] or, if he should be guilty of homicide, absolution ad cautelam.* Reg. 2bis, fol. 86v.

[Florentie], xv kal. Novembris. Exponit sanctitati vestre devotus vester Wilhelmus Heroll' de Valia, clericus Men[e]vensis diocesis, quod ipse olim cum quodam scolare socio suo fuit rogatus ut cum eodem scolare iret ad quandam villam pro quibusdam caligis quas penes quendam laicum habuisset, et postquam dictus scolaris dictas caligas ab illo laico repetiisset, laicus dicto scolari socio suo respondit quod dictas caligas per unum familiarem suum sibi direxisset. Dictus laicus et scolaris iste propterea ad rixas devenerunt ita quod cum cultellis mutuo inter se dimicarunt et inter alia dictus scolaris dictum laicum cum cultello ad capud volneravit [*sic*], cum quo volnere seu percussione dictus laicus aliquamdiu labores suos manuales seu mechanicos

---

[124] A virtually identical supplication dated 11 March 1439 is recorded at **118**.

exercuit et laboravit, de quo volnere dicitur postmodum vita functus; verum, pater sancte, quod dictus ~~scolaris~~ exponens scolari socio suo quoad hoc in nullo auxilium neque favorem dedit. Deinde accidit quod inimici capitales regni Anglie invaserunt; preceptum fuit a rege certis capitaneis ut gentem ut gentem [*sic*] contra dictos inimicos ordinarent. Tandem fratri exponentis preceptum fuit ut cum dictis capitaneis ad exercitum iret, et frater dicti exponentis precepit exponenti ut secum iret, et sic exponens ad exercitum iverat, in quo exercitu nullus homo fuit mortuus etc. Verum, pater sancte, quod dictus exponens non alias quam ut premittitur culpabilis existat. Supplicatur igitur quatinus secum [super irregularitate contracta?] occasione premissorum declarari [*recte* dispensare?] dignemini vel ipsum absolvi mandare si reatum homicidii incurrisset absolvi [*sic*] ad cautelam etc.

Fiat de speciali N.

[*De diversis formis*]

457. [*Florence*], *4 November 1439. Richard Hangkoc and Agnes Bauw of St David's, unaware that they were related in the fourth degree of consanguinity, married and had issue. They seek a dispensation to remain married with legitimation of issue.* Reg. 2bis, fol. 89r.

[Florentie], ii non. Novembris. Exponitur sanctitati vestre pro parte devotorum vestrorum Ricardi Hangkoc et Angnete [*sic*] Bauw(?) mulieris Menevensis metu [*sic*] ignorantes quod fuerunt in quarto gradu consanguinitatis invicem coniuncti matrimonium contraxerunt solempniter per verba de presenti, ut est moris patrie, carnali copula subsecuta, et prolem procrearunt. Verum si divortium esset inter eos, forte exinde gravia scandala evenire possint; desiderium eorum in hac parte adimplere non possunt etc.[125] ut supra. [dispensatione super hoc non obtenta. Supplicatur igitur sanctitati vestre pro parte dictorum exponentum quatinus cum eis ut in matrimonio sic contracto licite et libere remanere possint et valeant dispensare misericorditer dignemini, prolem exinde susceptam et suscipiendam legitimam decernentes etc.]

Fiat de speciali N.

458. [Florence], 4 November 1439. Thomas Pollard, acolyte, Durham dioc., requests [that the pope grants a licence so that he may receive the other holy orders from any Catholic bishop having the grace and communion of the apostolic see and that the same bishop may confer these orders on him, as he cannot approach his ordinary for certain legitimate reasons]. *Fiat de speciali N.* Reg. 2bis, fol. 91v.

459. [Florence], 5 December 1439. William Bayly, acolyte, Lincoln dioc., [requests a licence] so that [he may receive all holy orders] from any Catholic bishop [having the grace and communion of the apostolic see] since he cannot approach his ordinary to receive these orders because of the distance of the place. Approved with **460**. Reg. 2bis, fol. 92v.

---

[125] This phrase beginning with 'desiderium' has no place here since the supplicants had already married.

460. [Florence], 5 December 1439. Same licence as **459** for William Hardye, clerk, Lincoln dioc. *Fiat de speciali N.* (Approved with **459**.) Reg. 2bis, fol. 92v.

461. [*Florence*], *5 January 1440. Thomas Moore, priest, Hereford dioc.*,[126] *had himself promoted to all, even holy orders when aged 23; he seeks a dispensation to celebrate mass and other offices on reaching the age of 24.* Reg. 2bis, fol. 114r–v.

[Florentie], tercio non. Ianuarii. Exponitur sanctitati vestre pro parte devoti vestri [Thome] Moore, presbiteri Herfordensis diocesis, quod ipse olim tamquam simplex et iuris ignarus se fecit alias tamen rite in xxiii° sue etatis anno constitutus ad omnes etiam sacros [fol. 114v] ordines promoveri, sed non adhuc missam celebravit. Sed cum ipse exponens ex magno devotionis fervore cupit [ut] cum xxiiii sue etatis annum attigerit in sic susceptis ordinibus ministrare ac missas et alia divina officia celebrare valeat, supplicatur eidem sanctitati vestre pro parte dicti exponentis quatinus, defectu etatis predicto ac Lugdunensis et Lateranensis conciliorum et quibusvis aliis constitutionibus contrariis non obstantibus quibuscumque, cum eodem Thome dignemini misericorditer dispensare de gratia vestra speciali.

Fiat de speciali N.

462. [*Florence*], *10 January 1440. Alnua(?) Skipwith, widow, and her late husband John Skipwith, Lincoln dioc., had vowed to go on pilgrimage to the Holy Sepulchre but did not complete the journey, sending a religious there on their behalf, who, however, lacked his superior's licence. Now that she is aged 80, she seeks commutation of that vow.* Reg. 2bis, fol. 115r.

[Florentie], iiii^{to} ydus Ianuarii. Supplicatur humiliter pro parte devote vestre Alnue(?) Skipwith, vidue, uxoris quondam Iohannis Skipwith, Lincolniensis diocesis, quod cum olim dictus Iohannes et exponens zelo devotionis accensi vovissent sacrum sepulchrum dominicum personaliter peregre visitare, et cum iter arripuissent et usque ad insulam Rodis se transtulissent, nec ulterius propter nonnullas causas ire valentes, quendam religiosum ad dictum sepulchrum pro eis, nullius tamen superioris licentia accedente, transmiserunt; deinde dictus Iohannes viam universe carnis ingressus fuit, dubitat tamen dicta Alnua eius conscientiam propter dictum votum gravari et cum ammodo sit octuagenaria nec valeat dictum votum propter senectutem commode sicut vellet adimplere, quatinus dignemini sibi, facta sibi quod ipsa exponens fuisset in residuo dicti itineris expensura si illuc personaliter accessisset compensationem et remissionem in eo quod expendidit in mittendo dictum religiosum vice sui, dictum votum sibi [*sic*] in alia opera pietatis commutari mandare de vestra gratia speciali.

Fiat ut infra N. Signanda per fiat de speciali et illud plus quod expendisset si personaliter accessisset solvat ut in forma consueta.

463. [*Florence*], *23 January 1440. Stephen Malsonby, acolyte, professed canon of St Oswald's*

---

[126] Presumably the Thomas More, Hereford dioc., who was ordained as an acolyte on 20 December 1438, as a subdeacon on 17 February, and as a priest on 4 April 1439 (*Reg. Spofford*, 329–30, 332).

Priory, Nostell, OSA, York dioc., once as a youth accidentally shot a little girl with an arrow as a result of which she later died. He obtained a dispensation to minister in minor orders; he seeks absolution from that homicide and a further dispensation to be promoted to and minister in all holy orders. Reg. 2bis, fol. 117v.

> [Florentie], x kal. Februarii. Exponitur sanctitati vestre pro parte devoti vestri Stephani Malsonby, acoliti, canonici professi monasterii sancti Oswaldi de Wistollis [*recte* Nostellis] ordinis sancti Augustini Ebroicensis [*recte* Eboracensis] diocesis, quod ipse olim tempore sue iuventutis necdum capax maturi consilii aut deliberationis ymmo ex mera simplicitate et inadvertencia nulla precogitata malicia quandam sagittam sursum recte in aerem traxit, que quidem sagitta inde sensu et reversione ex casu fortuito quandam puellam parvam pertranseuntem in capite percussit et vulneravit, de quo quidem vulnere dicta puella deinde post aliquos dies debitum mortis persolvit. Cum autem, pater sancte, licet cum ipsa exponente nuper ut in suis susceptis videlicet in minoribus ordinibus dumtaxat ministrare valeat dispensatum extitit, tamen ex huiusmodi dispensationis gratia parum vel nullum commodum reportare possit nisi per eandem sanctitatem vestram uberius provideatur, et cum etiam in morte ipsius puelle alias quam ut premittitur culpabilis non existit cupiatque ex magno devotionis fervore de ad omnes sacros ordines libere promoveri et in ipsis domino perpetuo famulari, ad obstruendum ora suorum emulorum et aliorum sibi in futuro obloqui volentium etc. supplicatur sanctitati [vestre] pro parte dicti exponentis quatinus ipsum a reatu homicidii huiusmodi absolvi mandare secumque quatinus premissis non obstantibus ad dictos ordines libere promoveri et in ipsis omnibus licite ministrare valeat dignemini misericorditer dispensare de gratia vestra speciali.
>
> Fiat ut infra N. Signanda per fiat de speciali favore religionis suspenso ad tempus a ministerio altaris. Et committatur ordinario.

464. [Florence], 26 January 1440. Same dispensation as **433** sought by Adam Bulman, acolyte, Norwich dioc. *Fiat de speciali N.* Reg. 2bis, fol. 118r.

465. [Florence], 9 February 1440. The pope is requested to grant John Jonsen, clerk, Lincoln dioc., letters dimissory so that he may [be promoted to all holy orders] by any Catholic bishop having the power, since he cannot easily go to his ordinary, notwithstanding any constitutions to the contrary etc. Approved with **466**. Reg. 2bis, fol. 121v.

466. [Florence], 9 February 1440. Same grant as **465** sought by Thomas Wenslai, clerk, Lincoln dioc. *Fiat de speciali N.* (Approved with **465**.) Reg. 2bis, fol. 121v.

467. [Florence], 10 February 1440. Same grant as **465** sought by Thomas Cotys, acolyte, Lincoln dioc. *Fiat de speciali N.* Reg. 2bis, fol. 121v.

468. [Florence], 10 February 1440. John Pani, scholar, Norwich dioc., requests that the pope grant him a licence so that he may be promoted to all, even holy orders [by any Catholic bishop having the power] and thereafter minister in them, since he cannot approach his ordinary to receive these orders because of the distance of the place, notwithstanding any apostolic, provincial, synodal and other constitutions to the contrary. *Fiat de speciali N.* Reg. 2bis, fol. 121v.

469. [*Florence*], *18 February 1440. The abbot of Malmesbury Abbey, OSB, Salisbury dioc.*,[127] *requests that he may not be bound to observe statutes of that abbey contrary to* iura communia, *morals and the rule of his order, even under oath.* Reg. 2bis, fol. 122v.

[Florentie], xii kal. Martii. Supplicat sanctitati vestre devotus vester abbas monasterii beate Marie de Malmsbuy ordinis sancti Benedicti Sarisburiensis diocesis quatinus sibi ut ipse ad observationem statutorum ipsius monasterii et contra iura communia et bonos mores et contra regulam ordinis sancti Benedicti ac illius regularia editorum [*recte* regularium edictorum] necnon ~~consuetudinum~~ constitutionum rationi non conformium eiusdem monasterii etiam iuramento roboratorum minime teneatur, nec ad prestandum ad observationem illicitam a quoquam invitus valeat coartari, concedere et indulgere sibique iuramentum huiusmodi relaxare, premissis ac aliis contrariis non obstantibus quibuscumque, cum clausis oportunis dignemini concedere de gratia vestra speciali.

Fiat ut infra. Signanda per fiat de speciali quo ad relaxationem iuramenti, et demum per fiat si est ita in futurum si predicte constitutiones et statuta non sint auctoritate apostolica confirmate.

470. [Florence], 27 February 1440. Thomas Swytyng, rector of Bentham parish church, York dioc., requests that the pope grant him a licence and faculty for five years so that he may absolve all his parishoners of either sex from all their sins except those on which the [apostolic] see [is to be consulted], and enjoin a fitting penance on them.[128] *Fiat de speciali N.* Reg. 2bis, fol. 125r.

471. [Florence], 29 February 1440. The pope is requested to grant Thomas Sweting, priest, rector of Bentham parish church, York dioc., a licence to absolve all his parishoners of either sex for five years.[129] *Fiat de speciali N.* Reg. 2bis, fol. 125v.

472. [Florence], 1 March 1440. John Aunse(?), acolyte, Lincoln dioc., requests that the pope grant him [a licence] so that he [may] be promoted to all holy orders by any [Catholic bishop having the power], as he cannot conveniently approach his ordinary because of the distance of the place. *Fiat de speciali N.* Reg. 2bis, fol. 125r.

473. [Florence], 7 March 1440. Richard Kasyn, priest, rector of Felmingham (*Felmyngham*) parish church, Norwich dioc., requests that the pope grant him a licence *in forma 'Cupiente*[*s*]*'* so that for five years he may absolve all his parishoners of either sex from all their sins except [those on which the apostolic see is to be consulted]. *Fiat de speciali N.* Reg. 2bis, fol. 126r.

---

[127] Thomas Bristow had been elected as abbot in 1434. He died on 2 December 1456 (Smith, *Heads of Religious Houses*, iii. 50).
[128] An almost identical supplication to the next one.
[129] An almost identical supplication to the previous one.

474. [*Florence*], *19 March 1440. Roger Brese, priest, Lincoln dioc., was presented to the parish church of Arovilla, Trier dioc., by his friend John Runelung, clerk, Trier dioc.,*[130] *in order that he might be promoted to all orders in the Roman Curia; he was so ordained by the archbishop of Corinth*[131] *to the false title of that church and outside the times appointed by law. John then made a supplication to the cardinal penitentiary on his behalf requesting absolution and dispensation, and following its approval the archbishop granted these to him. He now requests them again since he doubts the validity of the archbishop's grant.* Reg. 2bis, fols. 130v–131r.

[Florentie] xiiii kal. Aprilis. Exponitur [*sic*] sanctitati vestre devotus vester Rogerus Brese, presbiter Lincolniensis diocesis, quod cum ipse olim adhuc simplex clericus et in Romana curia pro tunc residens desideraret ad omnes ordines promoveri et sufficientem titulum non haberet, quida[m] Iohannes Runelung, clericus Treverensis diocesis, eiusdem exponentis amicus, asserens se tunc esse procuratorem fratrum cuiusdam prioratus de Sanceo ordinis etc. dicte Treverensis diocesis, occasione cuius procurationis collationem seu presentationem omnimodam cuiusdam parrochialis ecclesie in Arovilla dicte diocesis per resignationem cuiusdam Nicholai de Brugg' ultimi posessoris eiusdem idem Iohannes ut asseruit habebat, ecclesiam predictam idem Iohannes prefato exponenti ut ad huiusmodi ordines promoveri [posset] contulit, cuius quidem collationis sic de dicta ecclesia prefato exponenti facte confirmationem seu novam provisionem a felicis recordationis domino Martino papa V obtinuit, et sic supplicatione super huiusmodi nova provisione signata et nulla commissione a sede apostolica ut ad huiusmodi ordines promoveri posset prehabita, idem exponens ad titulum huiusmodi parrochialis ecclesie et extra tempora a iure statuta asserens se tunc ad hoc fore artatum occasione dicte parrochialis ecclesie, et constitutionis felicis recordationis domini Clementis pape IIII de non ordinandis ab episcopis Ytalie clericis ultramontanis prorsus ignarus,[132] se fecit per simplicitatem et iuris ignorantiam sui diocesani licentia non obtenta et absque vitio symonie primo in die sancti Andree[133] ad omnes minores et subdiaconatus, et demum in die sequente in festo S. Eligii[134] a[d] dyaconatus, in die vero dominica post festum sancti Eligii predictum ad presbiteratus ordinem per archiepiscopum Corinthiensem in dicta Romana curia et in camera ipsius archiepiscopi secrete promoveri, ignorans quod in tales esset excommunicationis etc. [sententia generaliter promulgata]; [fol. 131r] in quibus quidem sic susceptis ministrare postmodum noluit donec dictus Iohannes felicis recordationis reverendo in Christo patri domino Iordano episcopo Sabinensi tunc maiori penitentiario[135] exposuisset et supplicationem ei porrexisset continentem qualiter exponens ipse extra tempora a iure statuta et sub ficto titulo, nulla commissione a sede apostolica prehabita, se fecerat per archiepiscopum

---

[130] See *RPG*, i, no. 498.
[131] Not identifiable from Eubel, ii. 136, or from G. Fedalto, *La Chiesa latina in Oriente*, ii: *Hierarchia latina orientis* (2nd edn, Verona, 2006), 110.
[132] *Liber sextus* 1.9.1 ('Saepe contingit').
[133] 30 November.
[134] 1 December.
[135] Giordano Orsini was cardinal penitentiary from 1415 until his death in 1438 (see Göller, i/1. 96).

supradictum promoveri, virtute cuius supplicationis sic prefato quondam domino maiori penitentiario porrecte et demum per ipsam [*recte* ipsum] signate, nullis tamen litteris super huiusmodi supplicatione confectis, idem archiepiscopus eundem exponentem a dictis sententiis quas ob premissa incurrerat absolvit et cum eo super irregularitate de facto dispensavit, super quibus omnibus idem ~~epi~~ archiepiscopus litteras testimoniales suas sigillo suo sigillatas exponenti predicto dedit et concessit, et sic exponens ipse postmodum in sic susceptis ordinibus suis pluries ministravit. Cum autem exponens ipse dubitet absolutionem et dispensationem huiusmodi sic sibi per prefatum archiepiscopum factas viribus non subsistere, supplicat sanctitati vestre dictus exponens quatinus ipsum a dictis sententiis et excessibus huiusmodi ~~sic sibi per prefatum archiepiscopum factas~~ absolvi secumque super irregularitate dicto modo et ex premissis contracta dignemini dispensare.

Fiat ut infra N. Signanda per fiat de speciali interdicto sibi ministerio altaris ad tempus.

475. [*Florence*], *24 March 1440. Richard Coppefeld, priest, vicar of Tillingham, London dioc., had himself promoted to all orders by his ordinary and obtained this vicarage, unaware that he was of illegitimate birth; his mother later told him that he was the son of a priest. He seeks a dispensation from this impediment.* Reg. 2bis, fol. 131r–v.

[Florentie], ix kal. Aprilis. Exponitur sanctitati vestre pro parte Richardi Coppefeld, presbiteri Londoniensis diocesis, perpetui vicarii parrochialis ecclesie de Tyllyngham dicte diocesis, quod ipse olim, nullum credens illegittimitatis impedimentum sibi obstare quominus posset ad ad [*sic*] omnes ordines promoveri et in eis postmodum ministrare et beneficium ecclesiasticum obtinere, se fecit alias tamen rite ad huiusmodi ordines per suum ordinarium promoveri et in ipsis ministravit, et demum dictam perpetuam vicariam alias canonice assecutus fuit. Cum autem mater carnalis ipsius exponentis [fol. 131v] postmodum in agone mortis laborans dictum exponentem filium suum ad se vocaverit eique dixerit: 'Fili mi, tu non es filius mariti mei sed talis presbiteri.' Et hiis dictis eadem mater exponentis ab hac luce migraverit et huiusmodi revelatio dicte matris, ut id exponens asserit, penitus sit occulta. Supplicatur igitur pro parte dicti exponentis quatinus defectu predicto non obstante cum eodem dispensare in sic susceptis ordinibus ministrare et dictam perpetuam vicariam licite retinere possit [*sic*] dispensari mandare dignemini ~~de gratia~~[136] speciali.

Fiat de speciali. In foro conscientie.

476. [*Florence*], *3 April 1440. The pope is requested to grant Fr John Osburn, priest, professed of OFM, Salisbury convent, a licence to visit the Holy Sepulchre and some other places overseas. Fiat de generali N.* Reg. 2bis, fol. 139v.

477. [*Florence*], *6 April 1440. John Vallis, priest, rector of Melsonby, York dioc., requests that a servant Agnes may look after him in his old age.* Reg. 2bis, fol. 135r.

---

[136] Incorrectly crossed out.

[Florentie], viii id. Aprilis. Exponit sanctitati vestre Iohannes Vallis, presbiter, rector parrochialis ecclesie de Melshambi Eboracensis diocesis, qui adeo senio vectus [*sic*] quatinus sibi ut qua[m]dam Agnetam mylyerem [*recte* mulierem] famulam senem amodo sexagenariam vel quasi que ipsum exponentem et eius domum sine aliqua suspitione aut infamia carnali, non obstantibus constitutionibus apostolicis etc. [et aliis editis in contrarium quibuscumque], procuret et, ut moris est patrie, gubernat dignemini misericorditer impartiri.

Fiat de speciali N.

478. [Florence], 7 April 1440. William Coupland, acolyte, York dioc., relates that guilelessly (*tamquam simplex*) and in ignorance of the law he previously had himself promoted to all orders while keeping silent [about his defect of birth] but in all other respects legally; hence he requests that the pope may grant him a dispensation that, notwithstanding this defect, he may be promoted to all holy orders[137] and obtain and retain a benefice even with cure of souls. *Fiat de speciali N.* Reg. 2bis, fol. 135r.

479. [Florence], 7 April 1440. Fr John Peyton, priest, professed monk of St Alban's monastery, St Albans (*monasterii sancti Albini de sancto Albino*), OSB, Lincoln dioc., requests that, as he cannot stay in that monastery by any means, the pope grant him a licence to transfer to another monastery of that order with the same or a stricter habit and regular observance.[138] *Fiat in forma N.* Reg. 2bis, fol. 139v.

480. [Florence], 10 April 1440. John Gardener, clerk, Lincoln dioc., requests that, as he cannot approach his ordinary conveniently, the pope may grant that he may be promoted to all orders by any [Catholic bishop] and minister in them. Approved with **481**. Reg. 2bis, fol. 140r.

481. [Florence], 10 April 1440. Same grant as **480** sought by Robert Assyke [clerk, Lincoln dioc.?]. *Fiat de speciali N.* (Approved with **480**.) Reg. 2bis, fol. 140r.

482. [Florence], 10 April 1440. William Couplandi, acolyte, York dioc., wishes [to be promoted] to holy orders but he cannot approach his ordinary at all; hence he requests that the pope grant him a licence so that he may be promoted to the said orders by any [Catholic bishop] and minister in them. *Fiat de speciali N.* Reg. 2bis, fol. 140v.

---

[137] Strictly speaking, he should have requested a dispensation to minister in his existing orders.

[138] He apparently remained, and was cellarer of St Alban's Abbey in 1445. He was prior of Wallingford (Berks.), a dependency of the abbey, in 1452, but resigned in 1453. He was appointed prior of Binham (Norf.), another dependency, on 23 April 1464, until 1465. He was described as infirm, 1480. He was MA by 1444 and DCnL by 1465, both degrees probably of Oxford (*BRUO*, iii. 1475; Smith, *Heads of Religious Houses*, iii. 98, 154). He had been granted a dispensation on 17 October 1444 to hold for life a benefice with cure of souls in the city or diocese of Lincoln; it was stated that he had often preached in public (*CPL*, ix. 459).

483. [Florence], 11 April 1440. The pope is requested [to grant] John Bedford, acolyte, Lincoln dioc., letters dimissory so that he may be promoted to all orders by any Catholic [bishop], since he cannot easily [approach] his ordinary, notwithstanding constitutions to the contrary. *Fiat de speciali N.* Reg. 2bis, fol. 136r.

484. [Florence], 1 May 1440. The pope is informed on the part of Fr Ralph Seyton, priest, professed canon of the monastery of St Mary de Pré, Leicester, OSA, Lincoln dioc.,[139] that he wishes to hear, study and read civil law (*leges civiles*) publicly, but because of the prohibition of canon law [he may not]. Therefore the pope is requested [to grant] him [a licence] so that he may read, hear, and study this law *cum clausa* with the licence of his superior, notwithstanding anything to the contrary. *Fiat de speciali N.* Reg. 2bis, fol. 143v.

485. *[Florence], 15(?) May 1440. Thomas Dycun, priest, Coventry and Lichfield dioc., had himself promoted successively to all orders outside the legally appointed times and to a false title by a bishop in the Curia, as the latter claimed to have power to this effect from the papal chamberlain. He now suspects the validity of his promotion and that he has incurred excommunication; hence he seeks absolution* ad cautelam *from that sentence and dispensation* ad cautelam *from irregularity.* Reg. 2bis, fol. 144r–v.

[Florentie], id. Maii. Supplicat sanctitati vestre devotus vester Thomas Dycun', presbiter Conventrensis et Lichfeldensis diocesis, quod ipse olim constitutionis felicis recordationis domini Clementis pape quarti de non ~~d~~ ordinandis etc. [ab episcopis Italie clericis ultramontanis][140] prorsus ignarus tamquam simplex clericus tantum existens, confisus de verbis cuiusdam episcopi in curia Romana existentis asserentis se habere licentiam a reverendo patre domino tunc camerario ~~a sede predicta specialiter facta ordinandi ad omnes ordines quoscumque~~ sedis apostolice ex commissione eidem domino camerario a sede predicta specialiter facta ordinandi ad omnes ordines quoscumque et etiam extra tempora a iure facta [*recte* statuta] intra dictam curiam existentes, [fol. 144v] se fecit per dictum episcopum infra dictam curiam, sui ordinarii licentia non obtenta, absque vitio symonie, extra tempora a iure statuta, et ad fictum titulum, excedere non credens, ignorans quod in tales etc. [excommunicationis sententia generaliter promulgata fuisset?], ad omnes ordines successive promoveri, et in ipsis ministravit, etiam missas celebrando, super qua promotione et attestatione dicte facultatis et promotionis idem episcopus ordinans eidem exponenti certas litteras sub nomine dicti domini camerarii sigillatas sigillo officii camerariatus dedit. Tandem cum prospectis dictis litteris per ipsum exponentem littere ipse non apparerent sibi secundum stillum camere apostolice confecte, suspicans [*recte* suspiciens] ipsas litteras et sigillum fore surreptas [*recte* surreptitias] et falsificatas, dubitetque [*recte* dubitet] ipsum episcopum ad sic dictum exponentem ordinandum potestatem non habuisse, et sic excommunicationis incurrisse sententiam, quatinus dignemini ipsum ad cautelam a dicta sententia si quam incurrit et excessibus huiusmodi absolvere et cum ipso super irregularitate

---

[139] He was a scholar at Oxford in 1440 and preached at the Augustinian General Chapter in 1443 (*BRUO*, iii. 1676).
[140] *Liber sextus* 1.9.1 ('Saepe contingit').

etc. [ex premissis contracta] cautela simili dispensari et quod in sic susceptis ordinibus libere et licite ministrare possit etc. [mandare].

Fiat de speciali ad cautelam N.

486. [*Florence*], *17 May 1440. Fr Stephen Lundon, STP, priest, professed monk of St Alban's Abbey, Lincoln dioc., swore that he would preach a sermon in the University of Oxford after graduating as MTh, but he cannot fulfil the oath as his abbot ordered him to return to his abbey. He seeks absolution from that oath.*[141] Reg. 2bis, fol. 146r–v.

[Florentie], xvi kal. Iunii. Exponitur sanctitati vestre pro parte fratris Stephani Lundon', presbiteri, monachi professi monasterii sancti Albani de sancto Albano Lincolniensis diocesis et in sacra theologia professoris, [fol. 146v] quod cum ipse olim in studio generali universitatis Oxoniensis existeret et in eadem universitate insignia et gradum magisterii sacre theologie recipere desiderasset, prefatus exponens non ex consuetudine introducta nec ex privilegio aut statuto aliquo ipsius universitatis sed ad instanciam et requisitionem dicte universitatis promisit et iuravit quod postquam insignia et gradum magisterii huiusmodi reciperet, unum sermonem in universitate predicta facere vellet. Quem quidem sermonem exponens ipse antequam illum facere poterat post promotionem eandem, abbas dicti monasterii sui per certas litteras suas dicto exponenti stricte precipiendo mandavit ut visis presentibus ipso facto ad monasterium ipsum sub excommunicationis et inobedientie aliisque penis rediret, prout pre timore mandati sui superioris, sermone minime facto, ad dictum suum monasterium rediit, quare timet reatum periurii incurrisse. Cum autem pater sancte idem exponens propter distanciam loci et obedientiam sui superioris etc. observantiam iuramenti huiusmodi commode adimplere non potest, supplicatur igitur sanctitati vestre quatinus ipsum exponentem a temeritate iurandi absolvi mandare ipsumque ab observantia iuramenti predicti penitus relaxare misericorditer dignemini.

Fiat ut infra N. Signanda per fiat de speciali.

487. [*Florence*], *30 May 1440. Thomas Caylart, priest, rector of Barrowby,* [*Coventry and*] *Lichfield dioc., paid the lay patron of that church to present him to it and thus incurred excommunication; then he celebrated divine offices. He seeks absolution from that sentence on his resigning the benefice and dispensation from irregularity.*[142] Reg. 2bis, fol. 149r.

[Florentie], iii kal. Iunii. Exponitur sanctitati vestre pro parte Thome Caylart, presbiteri, rectoris parrochialis ecclesie de Seroblghby [*sic*] Lichefeldensis diocesis, quod ipse olim, post constitutiones felicis recordationis domini Martini pape V^{ti} que incipit 'Multi quidem etc.' necnon domini Eugenii

---

[141] London was DTh by 1444, when he was again prevented by his monastic duties from fulfilling the requirement of the grace that he preach a Latin sermon; he was again granted a dispensation. He resigned as archdeacon of St Albans in 1447, when he was confirmed as prior of Wymondham (Norf.) on 5 March. He was provided as the first abbot of Wymondham on 16 September 1449. He resigned in 1465 and returned to St Albans (*BRUO*, ii. 1158; Smith, *Heads of Religious Houses*, iii. 88–9).

[142] Cf. **488**.

pape IIII^ti moderni que incipit 'Cum detestabile scelus etc.',[143] ad hoc ut quidem nobilis vir, patronus dicte parrochialis [ecclesie], que de iure patronatus laicorum existit et ad quem parrochialem [*recte* nobilem] ius conferendi eandem ecclesiam et presentandi spectare dinoscitur, ipsam ecclesiam eidem exponenti conferrit [*recte* conferret] prout contulit de facto eumque presentavit [*recte* presentaret] ad eandem, certam summam pecuniarum persolvit, propter quod excommunicationis etc. [sententias in tales generaliter promulgatas incurrit] et sic ligatus tamquam simplex et iuris ignarus divina celebravit officia et aliis alias inmiscuit se eisdem. Supplicat igitur sanctitati vestre dictus exponens quatinus ipsum a sententiis excommunicationum etc., dimisso prius beneficio predicto, absolvi mandare secumque super irregularitate misericorditer dispensare [dignemini].

Concessum de speciali in presentia d. Cardinalis Pe. Signanda per fiat de speciali dimisso dicto beneficio per prius.

488. [*Florence*], *4 June 1440. Thomas Tylart, priest, rector of Barrowby, Lincoln dioc., paid the lay patron of that church to present him to it and thus incurred excommunication; then he celebrated divine offices. He obtained letters to be absolved and dispensed and to hold another benefice instead;*[144] *he now seeks a dispensation to hold the above church, should it be conferred on him again after he has resigned it.* Reg. 2bis, fols. 149v–150r.

[Florentie], ii non. Iunii. Exponitur sanctitati vestre pro parte Thome Tylart, presbiteri, rectoris parrochialis ecclesie de Borrwghby' Lincolniensis diocesis, quod ipse olim, post constitutiones felicis recordationis domini Martini pape V^ti que incipit 'Multi quidem etc.' necnon domini Eugenii pape IIII^ti moderni que incipit 'Cum detestabile scelus etc.',[145] ad hoc ut quidem nobilis vir, patronus dicte ecclesie, que de iure patronatus laicorum existit, [eandem ecclesiam] ipsi exponenti conferret eumque presentaret ad eandem, prout sibi contulit de facto, certam summam pecuniarum dicto patrono persolvit per mediam personam, propter quod excommunicationis etc. [sententias in tales generaliter promulgatas incurrit] et sic ligatus divina celebravit officia ac alias inmiscuit se eisdem. Verum, pater sancte, licet dictus exponens alias litteras absolutionis et [fol. 150r] et [*sic*] dispensationis super premissis obtinuit ut quoddam aliud beneficium preter dictam parrochialem ecclesiam libere recipere et licite retinere possit, tamen per hec non datur sibi quod dictam ecclesiam dimissam si de novo sibi conferatur obtinere valeat. Supplicatur igitur sanctitati vestre pro parte dicti exponentis quatinus sibi dictam iam libere dimissam si de novo sibi con et de ea [*recte* qua] paucos fructus etc. percepit, quod si sine fraude et dolo seu illicito pacto de novo conferatur, licite retinere valeat dignemini misericorditer dispensare.

Concessum de speciali in presentia d. Cardinalis Pe.

---

[143] Martin V's constitution of 21 March 1418 was issued at session 43 of the Council of Constance. It is printed in *Conciliorum oecumenicorum decreta*, ed. J. Alberigo et al. (Bologna, 1973), 448. Eugenius IV's constitution (18 May 1434) is printed in *Bullarium diplomatum et privilegiorum sanctorum Romanorum pontificum*, ed. A. Tomasetti, v (Turin, 1860), 16–17.
[144] Granted in response to **487**.
[145] For these constitutions see **487** n.

489. [*Florence*], *15 July 1440. Thomas Coper, priest, vicar of St Mary the Virgin's, Wiggenhall, Norwich dioc., had a lay intermediary pay his predecessor in that church to resign it in order that he might obtain it and thus incurred excommunication; then he celebrated divine offices. He seeks absolution from that sentence and dispensation from irregularity.*[146] Reg. 2bis, fol. 158r–v.

[Florentie], idus Iulii. Exponitur sanctitati vestre pro parte Thome Coper, presbiteri, perpetui vicarii parrochialis ecclesie sancte Marie de Wygenale Norwicensis diocesis, quod ipse olim, post constitutiones felicis recordationis domini Martini pape V^{ti} que incipit 'Multe contra symoniacam pravitatem' necnon domini Eugenii pape IV^{ti} que incipit 'Cum detestabile scelus',[147] ad hoc ut quidem presbiter, dum viveret, ipsius exponentis predecessor, dictam parrochialem ecclesiam sibi et ad eius utilitatem et petitionem in manibus cuiuscumque ad hoc potestatem habentis resignaret, prout in manibus sui ordinarii resignavit et resignationem eandem per ipsum ordinarium admissam, certam pecunie quantitatem ex quodam illicito pacto precedente dicto presbitero predecessori suo per manus eiusdem [*recte* cuiusdam] laici in eadem conventione mediatore et interposita persona [*sic*] persolvit, ita quod idem exponens casu dicto laico mediatori quandam mansionem valoris viginti sex marcharum monete illius patrie ex pacto supradicto det et assignet, cuius resignationis et admissionis pretextu prefatus exponens possessionem dicte ecclesie assecutus fuit realem et actu actualem, propter quod excommunicationis etc. [sententias in tales generaliter promulgatas incurrit] et sic ligatus tamquam simplex et iuris ignarus, non in contemptum clavium, divina celebravit officia et alias imiscuit se eisdem etc. Supplicatur igitur sanctitati vestre pro parte dicti exponentis quatinus ipsum a dictis sententiis excessibusque huiusmodi [fol. 158v] absolvi mandare secumque super irregularitate ex premissis contracta misericorditer dispensare dignemini.

Fiat de speciali N. Signanda per fiat de speciali dimissa ecclesia per prius et restitutis fructibus perceptis.

490. [*Florence*], *28 July 1440. William Walsche, priest, professed monk of Westminster Abbey, OSB, London dioc., seeks a licence to wear linen clothing.*[148] Reg. 2bis, fol. 164v.

[Florentie], v kal. Augusti. Exponitur sanctitati vestre pro parte fratris Willermi Walsche, presbiteri monachi professi [monasterii] sancti Petri de Westmonasteri [*sic*] ordinis sancti Benedicti Lundoniensis diocesis, qui propter immuundiciam [*sic*] et nimium fastidium vermium gravem mentis et corporis sui patitur anxietatem et inquietatem quatinus sibi ut pannos lineos uti et portare valeat licentiam dignemini inpartiri.

Fiat de speciali N.

---

[146] Cf. **492**.
[147] For these constitutions see **487** n.
[148] At Westminster he held various offices and was elected prior late in 1441, serving until 1456 (Harvey, *Obedientiaries*, II. 6–7, 20–2; IV. 66; VI. 81; VII. 66–79; X. 184–5, 189; XII. 41; XIII. 18–19; XIX.ii.30–3; XIX.iii.1–3, 111–12; XXII. 13–28; XXIII. 52–60; XXIV. 108–10, 207–11).

491. [*Florence*], *4 August 1440. John Henten, priest, professed monk of Westminster Abbey, OSB, London dioc., seeks a licence to wear linen clothing.*[149] Reg. 2bis, fol. 162r.

[Florentie], ii non. Augusti. Beatissime pater, Iohannes Henten, presbiter, monachus professus monasterii sancti Petri Westmonasterii ordinis sancti Benedicti Lundoniensis diocesis, supplicat sanctitati vestre quatinus sibi specialem gratiam facientes ut, non obstantibus sui ordinis constitutionibus, pro sue vite sustentatione, quia absque intrinsiccis pannis lineis commode sustentare non potest propter immundiciam et nimium fastidium vermium que corpori suo gravem inferunt anxietatem, quatinus ut pannos huiusmodi lineos libere et licite portare possit et illis uti valeat secum licentiam impartiri dignemini.

Fiat de speciali N.

492. [*Florence*], *9 August 1440. Thomas Coper, priest, vicar of St Mary the Virgin's, Wiggenhall, Norwich dioc., had a lay intermediary pay his predecessor in that church to resign it in order that he might obtain it and thus incurred excommunication; then he celebrated divine offices. He obtained letters to be absolved of that sentence, dispensed from irregularity, and to hold another benefice instead; he now seeks a dispensation to hold this vicarage, should it be conferred on him again after he has resigned it.*[150] Reg. 2bis, fols. 162v–163r.

[Florentie], v id. Augusti. Exponitur sanctitati vestre pro parte Thome Coper, presbiteri, perpetui vicarii parrochialis ecclesie sancte Marie de Wygenalle Norwicensis diocesis, quod ipse olim, post constitutiones felicis recordationis domini Martini pape V^{ti} que incipit 'Multi quidem contra symoniacam pravitatem etc.' necnon domini Eugenii pape IV^{ti} que incipit 'Cum detestabile scelus etc.',[151] ad hoc ut quidem presbiter, predecessor ipsius exponentis, dum viveret, dictam perpetuam vicariam sibi et ad eius utilitatem et petitionem in manibus cuiuscumque ad hoc potestatem habentis resignaret, prout in manibus sui ordinarii resignavit et resignationem ipsam per ipsum ordinarium admissam, certam pecunie quantitatem illicito pacto precedente dicto presbitero predecessori suo per manus cuiusdem laici in eadem conventione mediatoris et interposite persone persolvit, ita tamen quod idem exponens etiam dicto laico mediatori quandam mansionem valoris xxvi marcharum monete illius patrie ex pacto supradicto daret et assignaret, cuius resignationis et admissionis pretextu prefatus exponens possessionem dicte vicarie realem et actualem assecutus fuit, propter quod excommunicationis etc. [sententias in tales generaliter promulgatas incurrit] et sic ligatus tamquam simplex et iuris ignarus et non in contemptum clavium divina celebravit officia et alias inmiscuit se eisdem. Deinde \vero/ exponens ipse, sicut asseritur, a sede apostolica et ab officio penitentiarie litteras in forma debita et consueta certo commissario super hoc in ipsis litteris deputato super facultate ipsum, postquam dictam vicariam de facto

---

[149] John Henton, monk of Westminster, was kitchener there *c.* 1436–7 and treasurer, 17 December 1435–29 September 1437 (Harvey, *Obedientiaries*, XIII. 101, XXIV. 105–6).
[150] Cf. **489**.
[151] For these constitutions see **487** n.

libere dimiserit et de fructibus ex ea perceptis convertendis in utilitatem dicte vicarie satisfecerit, absolvendi a sententiis et excessibus huiusmodi, et secum dispensandi super irregularitate et inhabilitate ex premissis contractis, quodque quodcumque aliud beneficium ecclesiasticum preter dictam ecclesiam si sibi canonice conferatur libere recipiendi et licite retinendi obtinuit, que littere propter temporis brevitatem suum nondum sunt sortite effectum. Cum autem idem exponens dictam vicariam libere dimittere sit paratus, supplicatur sanctitati vestre pro parte dicti exponentis [fol. 163r] quatinus secum ut dictam perpetuam vicariam quam sic dimittere et relaxare se offert, postquam ipsam si non dimisit dimiserit, quodque dicte littere totalem fuerunt consecute effectum, ut, premissis non obstantibus, si dicta perpetua vicaria sibi de novo cano[n]ice conferatur, libere recipere et licite retinere possit dignemini dispensare, constitutionibus apostolicis et aliis in contrarium editis non obstantibus quibuscumque, de gratia speciali.

Fiat ut infra N. Signanda per fiat de speciali, restitutis primo fructibus perceptis et libere et cum effectu, libere dimisso dicto beneficio.

493. [Florence], 1 September 1440. The pope is requested to grant Thomas Wentlay, rector of South Wheatley (*Sowthe Bekwetelay*) parish church, York dioc., the power to absolve all his parishoners of either sex for five years *in forma 'Cupientes'*. *Fiat de speciali N.* Reg. 2bis, fol. 132v.

494. [Florence], 18 October 1440. Supplication on the part of Henry Lavyn, scholar, Lincoln dioc., for the pope to grant him a dispensation so that he may be made a clerk (*clericali maluerit caractere insigniri*) and promoted to all, even holy, orders by any [Catholic bishop]. *Fiat de speciali N.* Reg. 2bis, fol. 175v.

495. [Florence], 2 November 1440. The pope is informed on the part of John Freschdyke, priest, perpetual vicar of Gedney (*Gednai*) parish church, Lincoln (*Lyconinensis*) dioc., MA, that he wishes to hear, read and study civil law (*leges civiles*) publicly in the schools, take part in other scholastic acts and take a doctoral degree etc. The pope is requested to grant him a licence so that he may read, hear and study this law, take a doctoral degree in it, and take part in other scholastic acts for five years [notwithstanding any] constitutions [to the contrary]. (Unsigned.) Reg. 2bis, fol. 180v.

496. [Florence], 16 November 1440. William Ainsley, acolyte, Durham dioc., requests that the pope grant him a licence so that he may be promoted to all orders by any [Catholic bishop]. *Fiat de speciali N.* Reg. 2bis, fol. 180r.

497. [Florence], 30 December 1440. Roger (*Rugerus*) Asby, clerk, Lincoln dioc., requests that the pope grant him letters dimissory so that he may be promoted to all orders in succession by any Catholic bishop [having the grace and communion of the apostolic see], since for certain reasons he cannot approach his ordinary to receive these orders. Approved with **498**. Reg. 2bis, fol. 189r.

498. [Florence], 30 December 1440. Same grant as **497** sought by William Scot, Lincoln dioc. *Fiat de speciali N.* (Approved with **497**.) Reg. 2bis, fol. 189r.

499. [Florence], 25 January 1441. Supplication on the part of Thomas Swan, priest, Norwich dioc., for the pope to grant him a licence so that he can hear, study and read civil law (*leges seu iura civilia*) in any university (*universitate generali*) and receive the insignia of the doctorate.[152] Approved with **500**. Reg. 2bis, fol. 191v.

500. [Florence], 25 January 1441. The same grant as **499** requested on the part of John Olyne, priest, Norwich dioc. *Fiat N.* (Approved with **499**.) Reg. 2bis, fol. 191v.

501. [*Florence*], *13 February 1441. John Payrsan, priest, rector of Stanbridge, Lincoln dioc., promised a layman that if the latter procured the said church for him, he would grant him that church in return for an annual pension, which he did, and thus he fears that he has incurred excommunication. He seeks absolution from that sentence and from simony.* Reg. 2bis, fol. 198r.

[Florentie], id. Februarii. Exponitur sanctitati vestre pro parte Iohannis Payrsan', presbiteri, rectoris parrochialis ecclesie de Stahnbruch Lincalniemsis [*sic*] diocesis, quod ipse olim, post [constitutiones] felicis recordationis domini Martini pape V^{ti} que incipit 'Multo quidem contra simianatam [*recte* simoniacam] pravitatem' necnon domini Eugenii pape IV^{ti} moderni que incipit 'Cum detestabile scelus etc.',[153] cuidam laico promisit quod si ordinaret et procuraret quod ipse exponens dictam parrochialem ecclesiam in possessione haberet prout habuit, exponens ipse dicto laico eandem ecclesiam ad summam pensionem [*sic*] singulis annis pro undecim marchas [*recte* marchis] monete illius patrie que valet et ascendit in viginti marchas annuatim dare et concedere vellet, prout dedit et concessit, propter quod timet ex pacto predicto excommunicationum sententias in tales etc. [generaliter promulgatas incurrisse]. Supplicatur sanctitati vestre pro parte dicti exponentis quatinus ipsum a dictis sententiis et labe symoniace pravitatis huiusmodi absolvi mandare etc.

Fiat de speciali N.

502. [Florence], 14 February 1441. Nicholas Cran, scholar, Norwich (*Norvicen.*) dioc., requests that the pope grant that [he may be promoted] to all [orders] by any bishop having the grace and communion of the apostolic see, as on certain reasonable grounds he cannot conveniently approach his ordinary to receive orders. *Fiat de speciali N.* Reg. 2bis, fol. 198r.

503. [Florence], 20 February 1441. Supplication on the part of Thomas Cranewys, priest, curate of the parish church in Burgh (*Bur*), Norwich dioc.,[154] for the pope [to grant] that he may absolve all his parishoners of either sex from all sins, except those on which the apostolic see is rightly to be consulted, for five years *in forma* '*Cupientes*' and [enjoin fitting penances] regarding these. Approved with **504**. Reg. 2bis, fol. 199r.

---

[152] Probably not the Thomas Swan recorded in *BRUO*, iii.1829.
[153] For these constitutions see **487** n.
[154] BCL by 1442, perhaps of Cambridge, he was granted plenary remission *in mortis articulo* on 6 November 1442 (*CPL*, ix. 304).

504. [Florence, 20 February 1441].[155] Supplication on the part of the following clerks for the pope to grant them a dispensation so that, notwithstanding their defect of age, after they have been promoted to the order of acolyte and the holy orders of subdeacon and deacon and provided that they have reached the age of 24, they may be promoted to the holy order of the priesthood and minister in these orders: Fr John Donham, clerk, professed monk of [Bury] St Edmund's monastery, [Norwich dioc.]; Fr John Ratyllysiden, clerk, professed of the same monastery; William Browine, clerk, Norwich dioc.; John Boner, clerk, Norwich; Thomas Tran, clerk, Norwich dioc.; John Carneweys, clerk of the same dioc.; Richard Lesse, clerk, Norwich dioc. *Fiat de speciali N.* (Approved with **503**.) Reg. 2bis, fol. 199r–v.

505. [Florence], 13 March 1441. The pope is requested to grant Robert Semen, priest, Chichester dioc., *littere confessionales* in perpetuity. Approved with **506**. Reg. 2bis, fol. 203v.

506. [Florence], 13 March 1441. Supplication on the part of John Atwold, clerk, Norwich dioc., for the pope to grant him a dispensation so that, notwithstanding his defect of age, after he has been promoted to minor orders and the orders of subdeacon and deacon and provided that he has reached the age of 24, he [may] be promoted to the holy order of the priesthood and [minister] in them. *Fiat de speciali N.* (Approved with **505**.) Reg. 2bis, fol. 203v.

507. [Florence] 21 March 1441. The pope is requested to grant Geoffrey ap Ednyfed (*Edn'*), clerk, St Asaph dioc., that he may be promoted to all orders by any Catholic bishop having the grace and communion of the apostolic see and minister in them, since he cannot approach his ordinary to receive them because of the distance of the place, notwithstanding the constitution of Clement IV[156] and provincial, synodal or other constitutions to the contrary. *Fiat de speciali N.* Reg. 2bis, fol. 206r.

508. [Florence] 5 April 1441. It is explained on the part of Richard Wym[o]ndham, priest, Norwich dioc., that guilelessly (*tamquam simplex*) and in ignorance of the law he formerly had himself promoted to all holy orders by his ordinary (*ordinarie*) while under age but otherwise legally, ministered in them several times, and otherwise participated in divine offices. Now that he has reached the legitimate age, the pope is requested to order his absolution from these excesses, etc. *Fiat in forma N.* Reg. 2bis, fol. 213v.

509. [Florence, early April 1441]. The pope is requested to grant Hywel (*Howell*) ap Ieuan ap Madog (*Madoc*) and his brother Dafydd, laymen, St Asaph dioc., a licence to visit the Holy Sepulchre etc. *Fiat de speciali N.* Reg. 2bis, fol. 214r.

510. [Florence], 17 April 1441. William Gorald, priest, rector of Marlingford (*Merlyford*) parish church,[157] Norwich (*Norvicen.*) dioc., requests that he may absolve

---

[155] Undated but it immediately follows **503** dated thus in the register.
[156] *Liber sextus* 1.9.1 ('Saepe contingit').
[157] Alternatively it may be Marlesford (Suff.). William Gorald, priest, Norwich dioc., who

each and every one of his parishoners of either sex from all their sins, except those on which the apostolic see is to be consulted, for five years [*in forma*] 'Cupientes'. *Fiat de speciali N.* Reg. 2bis, fol. 198v.

511. [Florence], 17 April 1441. Supplication on the part of Fr Robert Westgate, deacon, professed monk of the church of Winchester, OSB,[158] for [the pope to grant him a dispensation] so that, notwithstanding his defect of age, provided that he has reached the age of 23, he may be promoted to the holy order of the priesthood and [minister] in his existing and future orders. *Fiat de speciali N. Et si placet committatur priori dicti monasterii. Fiat N.* Reg. 2bis, fol. 215r.

512. [*Florence*], *24 April 1441*. Hugh Cromyng,[159] *priest, rector of Kington Magna, Salisbury dioc., seeks a licence to study and take a doctorate in civil law.* Reg. 2bis, fol. 216r–v.

[Florentie], viii kal. Maii. Exponitur sanctitati vestre pro parte Hugonis Cromyng, presbiteri, rectoris parrochialis ecclesie de Kyngton magna Saresburensis [*sic*] diocesis, qui, propter maiorem informacionem et intelligentiam iuris canonici habendam, cupit leges civiles in scolis publice audire, studere et legere, aliisque actibus scolasticis uti, ac gradum doctoratus in eo recipere, sed propter inhibitionem iuris canonice hoc facere non licet. Supplicatur igitur sanctitati vestre pro parte dicti exponentis quatinus sibi leges predictas sic ut premittitur legere, audire, et studere, ac gradum doctoratus in eo recipere, aliisque actibus [fol. 216v] scolasticis uti valeat ad quinquennium licentiam concedere etc. [dignemini].

Fiat de speciali.

513. [Florence], 24 April 1441. The pope is requested to grant *littere confessionales* for five years to Ralph Robyns, his wife, and their children, to Henry Hostini, layman, and his brother and sisters.[160] *Fiat N.* Reg. 2bis, fol. 216v.

514. [Florence, *c.* 1–2 May 1441].[161] The pope is requested to grant William Fen, priest, Norwich dioc., *littere confessionales* in perpetuity. (Unsigned.) Reg. 2bis, fol. 196r.

---

was to be appointed a notary public by papal authority under a faculty of 27 April 1441 (*CPL*, ix. 228).
[158] He was ordained as a priest on 15 April 1447 and licensed as a penitentiary in Winchester diocese on 28 March 1457. He had been a scholar at Oxford, probably Canterbury College, in December 1450. He was elected prior of Winchester Cathedral on 15 May 1457 and died or resigned by March 1470 (Greatrex, 747; *BRUO*, iii. 2022).
[159] Hugh Crownyng *alias* Laurens was born *c.* 1409 in Utrecht dioc. He was granted a licence to study at an English university for four years on 4 July 1434, and admitted as BCnL of Oxford in June 1449. He died by February 1477. For his university career and benefices see *BRUO*, i. 521. As an unmarried clerk, aged about 20, he was to be appointed a notary public by the bishop of Worcester under a papal faculty of 5 May 1429 (*CPL*, viii. 145, 197).
[160] No diocese is indicated, but the first name appears to be English.
[161] Undated, but the entry preceding it in the register is dated 1 May and that following it 2 May.

515. [*Florence*], *13 May 1441. Fr John le Gonz, priest, expressly professed monk of St Martin's Abbey, Séez, OSB, was presented by his abbot and convent as prior of St Mary's Priory, Lancaster, York dioc., but he was prevented from taking possession by the nuns of Syon Abbey, London dioc. He began litigation at the Roman Curia, Rouen, and elsewhere but ran out of money, so he seized goods of his abbey from St Martin's church, Tours, selling them to fund his case and for other uses. He was kidnapped by brigands who then took his father hostage in his place but when he could not borrow a ransom from his abbot or anybody else, he tried taking goods of his abbey by force, attacking St Martin's monastery with troops, one of whom wounded the abbot, but his father died. He requests absolution and a dispensation. Reg. 2bis, fols. 228v–9r.*

[Florentie], iii idus Maii. Beatissime pater, pro parte humilis et devoti oratoris vestri fratris Iohannis le Gonz, presbiteri, monachi expresse professi monasterii sancti Martini Sagiensis ordinis sancti Benedicti, sanctitati vestre lacrimabiliter exponitur quod dudum videlicet de anno etc. [pontificatus] eiusdem sanctitatis septimo[162] vacante prioratu beate Marie de Lancastria dicti ordinis Eboracensis diocesis a prefato monasterio dependente per obitum quo[n]dam fratris Egidii Lowel extra Romanam curiam defuncti[163] item [*recte* idem] frater Iohannes ad eundem prioratum sic vacantem per abbatem et conventum dicti monasterii fuit presentatus cuius possessionem numquam habere [*recte* habuit?] impedientibus monialibus monasterii de Chesme [*sic*] dicte Leod. [*recte* Londoniensis] diocesis,[164] quamvis super eodem tam in Romana curia quam in partibus et in civitate Rothomagensi et alibi diu litigaverit quod omnia bona de Chestre [*sic*] dicte Londoniensis diocesis quamvis super eodem tam in Romana curia quam in partibus ac in civitate Rothomagensi et alibi diu litigaverit quod omnia bona[165] mobilia que habet et habuit seu eciam habere mutuo ab amicis suis et aliis potuit, in cuius prosecutione disposuit, quare ipse frater Iohannes videns quod non habebat unde causam huiusmodi amplius prosequi posset pecuniis defecientibus et quod de bonis dicti monasterii cuius professus existit sustineri debet et quod dicti prioratus presentacio etc. ad abbatem eiusdem monasterii pro tempore existentem pertinet et quod ipsius presentacio sibi reddebatur inutilis, sciens quod in inicio guerrarum pro deh(?) dolor in regno Francie nunc vigencium aliqua bona dicti monasterii sancti Martini Sagiensis per bone memorie quondam Andream abbatem eiusdem monasterii et de eius mandato in ecclesia sancti Martini Turonensis in custodia reposita fuerant, minus sano consilio usus ad valorem ii^c. lxx^ta saluciorum(?) auri ad eandem ecclesiam sancti Martini Turonensis cum quodam falso procuratorii instrumenti [*recte* instrumento] accessit et inscientibus abbate et conventu dicti monasterii de bonis huiusmodi usque ad valorem ii^c. lxx^ta saluciorum(?) auri[166] vel eo circa inter que erant baculus

---

[162] 1437–8.
[163] Giles Lovel, prior of Lancaster, admitted on 15 December 1399, died by September 1428 (Smith, *Heads of Religious Houses*, iii. 185–6).
[164] The English crown took possession of Lancaster and the other alien priories in 1414, and after Prior Lovel's death the priory was granted to Syon Abbey (*VCH* (*Lancs.*), ii. 171; Smith, *Heads of Religious Houses*, iii. 186; *CPL*, ix. 267–9).
[165] The words 'de Chestre ... quod omnia bona' are superfluous.
[166] The currency appears to be the *saluto* (or *carlino*) *d'oro*, but this was in use in Sicily and Naples rather than in France (see P. Spufford, *Handbook of medieval exchange* (London, 1986), 59, 62).

pastoralis dicti abbatis et unus calix argenteus deauratus falso suscepit et secum portavit, vendidit, alienavit ac pecunias inde habitas in prosecucione huiusmodi prioratus et aliis quamplurim[i]s(?) et malis usibus per tabernas et loca inhonesta eciam prodigaliter seu unius(?) parte exposuit. Et deinde cum postmodum a casu idem frater Iohannes per brigandos et latrones currentes per paturam(?) huiusmodi in dormitorio dicti monasterio captus et in nemoribus et silvis ductus et in compedibus ferreis per mensem positus fuisset et coactus per torturam rantionari ad summam clx saluciorum auri et non habens aliquem qui pro ipso iuberet, ipsi latrones eundem fratrem Iohannem cogerunt ut patri suo qui iam annosus [fol. 229r] et senio confractus erat sua super deliberatione et fideiussione rescriberet et mandaret, qui quidem pater ad rescriptionem dicti filii sui ibidem inter latrones veniat et pro eo fideiuberetssit. Quiquidem frater Iohannes sic liberatus nu[n]c ad abbatem et conventum suum ut ipsum adiuvare[n]t pro redempcione patris sui et ibidem per novem ebdomidas [*sic*] vel circa tam in dicto monasterio quam inter alios suos st amicos stetit et ab ipsis nec ab aliquo ipsorum dictam sententiam summam quamvis relaxata esset ad lx saluc' auri etc. recuperare non potuit. Quinymo cum ipse frater Iohannes venisset ad monasterium sancti Martini prefatum cum quibusdam armatis et guerram excercentibus sub spe capiendi et rapiendi et ra vi et violentia de bonis dicti monasterii usque ad redempcionem patris sui eo quod abbas nullo modo ipsum liberare volebat, non tantum intendens in abbatem per se aut alios manus inicere. Quidem de sociis illis armatis non pretermittens [*recte* permittens?] dictum abbatem ianuam dicti monasterii exire ipsum abbatem cum quodam baculo leviter tamen in digito vel manu ut asseritur vulneravit usque ad sanguinis effusionem. Quibus sic fract stantibus pater dicti exponentis adhuc existens in manibus dictorum brigandorum et latronum, ut deo placuit et creditur quod mortem naturali quia annosus erat, ut prefertur, diem suum clausit extremum. Cum autem, pater sancte, idem exponens, qui a sentencia excommunicacionis huiusmodi per ordinarium necnon eciam a quadam excommunicacionis sententia per suum abbatem in eum lata, que ad tempus aliquando eciam relaxata fuit, absolutus fuerit et quia eciam ipse postea multociens se divinis inmiscuit, non tantum propterea habitum suum dimisit cupiatque ex magno devocionis affectu super huiusmodi oportuno remedio misericorditer provideri et ab intimis de premissis doleat, supplicat eidem sanctitati vestre idem frater Iohannes quatinus sibi pro compaciente affectu ipsum ab quibuscumque censuris, penis et malis quas propterea et occasione premissorum incurrit absolvere et cum eo super apostasia et qualibet per eum contracta irregularitate et sacrilegio quodque ut ipse in sacris ordinibus per eum susceptis ministrari [*sic*] et quodcumque beneficium ecclesiasticum dicti ordinis recipere et obtinere libere et licite possit et valeat misericorditer dispensare dignemini omnem dig^{tur} etc.

Fiat ut infra N. Signetur per fiat de speciali satisfacto dicto monasterio de bonis per exponentem ablatis et si non habet prestita cautione de restituendo cum pervenerit ad pigniorem fortunam.

516. [*Florence*], *18 May 1441. Robert Pecok, subdeacon, London dioc., while studying at Cambridge University, once refused to pay the salary of his* familiaris, *and when the latter complained to his brother, the brother and another layman sought out Pecok and attacked him; during the struggle the brother was fatally wounded though it was not known how. Pecok seeks a declaration that he did not thereby incur irregularity and that he may be promoted to deacon's and priest's orders.* Reg. 2bis, fol. 230r–v.

[Florentie], xv kal. Iunii. Exponitur sanctitati vestre pro parte devoti vestri Roberti Pecok, subdiaconi Lindoniensis [*sic*] diocesis, quod cum ipse olim in studio Cantebrigensi cum quodam familiare studuisset, prefatus familiaris, lapsis duobus annis vel circa, solarium [*recte* salarium] ab ipso exponente petiit, cui exponens respondit quod non promisit sibi solarium et quod bene sufficeret sibi victum et amictum(?) dedisse ac inde secum in scolis causa discendi tenuisse. Tunc predictus familiaris de hiis minime contentus se ad quendam fratrem suum carnalem laicum accessit sibique premissa lamentabiliter narravit. Ad cuius instanciam idem frater familiaris una cum quodam alio laico manu armato ipsum exponentem hincinde querentem in quodam hospitio civitatis Lundoniensis invenit, sibique petendo solarium fratris sui cum ipso exponente de verba ad verbera venerunt, et statim pretactus frater ipsius familiaris quendam baculum super caput ipsius exponentis in pluries pecias fregit. Tunc exponens videns se non posse fugam dare et grave periculum mortis sibi imminere quandam dagam de latere socii ipsius fratris extraxit et quantum potuit se defendit, et sic invicem luctantes ambo ad terram ceciderunt et sic iacendo insimul prenominatus laicus socius ipsius fratris dagam ipsam de manibus ipsius exponentis extraxit; eandem antedictis [*recte* idem antedictus] frater dicti familiaris sentiens se vulneratum de terra surrexit, et quis vel quomodo aliqualiter vulneratus fuit neuter eorum contendentium scire potuit. Demum lapsis tribus septimanis idem laicus frater dicti familiaris ac peperteus [*sic*] exponentis diem suum clausit extremum. Cum autem, pater sancte, dictus exponens in morte ipsius laici alias quam ut premittitur culpabilis non existit, nec umquam in veritate scire potuit an ipse laicus se ipsum vulneravit aut per ipsum exponentem vulneratus fuit, et bonorum mentium est ibi tumere culpam [ubi] minime reperitur, cupiatque ex magno devotionis fervore ad sacros dyaconatus et presbiteratus ordines libere promoveri et ipsi [*recte* in ipsis] domino perpetuo famulari, et ne aliqui simplices et iuris ignari sibi alloqui [fol. 230v] possint asserentes ipsum notam irregularitatis et inhabilitatis incurrisse, ad obstruendum ora talium etc. supplicatur humiliter sanctitati vestre pro parte dicti exponentis quatinus ipsum occasione premissorum nullam irregularitatis maculam incurrisse quodque ad dictos diaconatus etc. [et presbiteratus ordines promoveri possit declarare misericorditer dignemini].

Fiat ut infra N. Signanda per fiat de speciali.

517. [*Florence*], *10 June 1441. Joan Radeclif of London at the age of 12 was persuaded to marry one John Lichtfot* alias *Dissyngton, London dioc., who mistreated her so much that she left him and sought refuge in a nunnery in Bath and Wells dioc. for six years, before settling in Winchester, where she married John Ryall of that city. They had four children together before she told him about her first husband, but then they continued to cohabit and had two more children. After* *her first husband died, she confessed her story to a priest who enjoined her to cease sexual relations with Ryall, which she has done. She and Ryall request absolution from fornication and adultery, a dispensation to marry, and the legitimation of their children.* Reg. 2bis, fols. 238r–239r.

[Florentie], iiii id. Iunii. Exponitur sanctitati vestre pro parte devote vestre Iohanne Radeclif, mulieris Lundoniensis ~~diocesis~~, quod cum ipsa in duodecimo sue etatis anno vel circa constituta persuasionibus cuiusdam viri et eius uxoris Londoniensis diocesis quibus tunc serviebat inducta esset ad contrahendum matrimonium per verba legitime de presenti cum quodam Iohanne Lichtfot alias Dissyngton, laico dicte diocesis, etatis tunc quinquaginta annorum et ultra, prefatus Iohannes, post contractum huiusmodi, bannis more patrie precedentibus, in facie ecclesie celebratum et carnali copula consumatum, infra quinque menses vel circa, ob malam quam verisimiliter habuit licet sine causa rationabili de uxore suspicionem, ita austere et crudeliter [in]cepit eam tractare et cum verbis inhonestis quam verberibus quasi per triennium frequenter afficere, quod eadem [fol. 238v] tantam mariti sui sevitiam patienter tollerare nequiens ab ipsius consortio se subtraxit per tres septimanas vel circa. Quibus lapsis, per mediationem certorum amicorum dicte Iohanne ipsa reducta fuit ad domum prefati mariti sui promitentis tunc eam in posterum honestius quam antea fecerat tractare. Qui quidem maritus contra promissum suum huiusmodi postea veniens dictam Iohannam per quindenam ligatam tenuit cum cathena ferrea per unam tibiam in quadam camera sua, et tandem cum ipsa Iohanna ope et auxilio certorum vicinorum suorum sibi compatientium ab huiusmodi cathena liberata esset, infra tres septimanas vel circa a tempore dicte reductionis sue ad maritum iterum recessit ab eodem, transferrens se successu temporis in honesta comitiva ad quoddam monasterium monialium in comitatu Somersetie, Bathoniensis et Vellensis diocesis, ubi per sex annos vel circa obsequiis abbatisse dicti monasterii insistebat. Et deinde ad Londoniensem ac consequenter ad Wintoniensem civitates se divertit. Postquam vero ibi per annum vel quasi continuo permansisset, contraxit de novo publice in ecclesia, bannis prius editis, matrimonium seu verius contubernium cum quodam Iohanne Ryall', laico dicte civitatis Wintoniensis, ignorante tunc ipsam Iohannam habuisse alium virum tunc superstitem. Qui Iohannes Ryall et Iohanna sub tali pretensa copula coniugali per quadriennium vel circa insimul habitarunt, quatuor filios et filias invicem procurando. Tandem prefata Iohanna, timens ne relatu alterius persone venisset in noticiam secundi mariti ipsam alium maritum prius habuisse tunc viventem, narravit sola quadam die eidem secundo marito qualiter alium maritum habuit tunc superstitem, exponendo sibi causam ob quam se ab ipsius consortio separavit. Post huiusmodi tamen illius mulieris narrationem ipsa et secundus maritus cohabitantes sicut ante ut vir et uxor carnalem invicem postea copulam per annum vel circa sepius ac unum filium et unam filiam habuerunt. Demum prefato Iohanne primo marito viam universe carnis ingresso, dicta Iohanna reversa ad cor de excessibus suis huiusmodi confessa fuit in partibus cuidam religioso presbitero, qui eidem Iohanne iniunxerit in foro penitentie quod abstineret postea a carnali copula secundi mariti, prout abstinuit semper hucusque et abstinere intendit donec apostolice sedis gratiam valeat desuper sibi(?) obtinere. Cum autem, pater sancte, dictus secundus maritus tempore quo contraxit cum prefata Iohanna et per quatuor quasi annos proximo tunc sequentes ignoravit eam alium tunc viventem habuisse maritum, cupiatque eidem Iohanne, de qua ut premissum est plures liberos suscitavit quorum tres adhuc vivere putantur, ut sue uxori legitime quamdiu ambo vixerint adherere, cum etiam nec ipse secundus maritus nec Iohanna in mortem primi mariti aliquid machinati fuerint, supplicatur sanctitati vestre pro parte Iohannis Riall' et Iohanne prefatorum quatinus ipsos et eorum quemlibet a reatu fornicationis et adulterii huiusmodi absolvi mandare [fol. 239r] quodque premissis non obstantibus ipsi Iohannes et Iohanna matrimonium in presentia duorum vel trium testium absque aliis solempnitatibus inter eos susceptam iterandis de novo contrahere et in eo postquam contractum fuerit libere et licite remanere valeant, prolem inter eos susceptam ante notificatam secundo viro primi vitam legitimam declarari et post notificationem huiusmodi gen[i]tam quoad omnia legitimam mandando, dispensare misericorditer dignemini etc., presertim ad conservandam dictorum exponentium famam, quorum excessus prefati omnibus quasi in partibus eorum, exceptis eorum confessoribus, sunt occulti, in contrarium facientibus non obstantibus.

Concessum de premissis expresso in presentia domini Cardinalis.

518. [*Florence*], *20 June 1441*. *Richard Michill* alias *Multum, priest, professed monk of Crowland Abbey, OSB, Lincoln dioc.,*[167] *once bought some goods from John Fayrihaed, layman of Térouanne, but they argued over the bill and John threatened him with a knife, so he defended himself with a stick, striking John; later John took ill and had to be put to bed, where he died that night. Richard requests absolution and a dispensation from irregularity.* Reg. 2bis, fols. 240r–v.

[Florentie], xii kal. Iulii. Supplicat sanctitati vestre frater Ricardus Michill' alias dictus Multum, presbiter, monachus professus monasterii de Croylande ordinis sancti Benedicti Lincolniensis diocesis, quod cum ipse olim deputatus esset ad emendum certa necessaria pro monachis dicti monasterii, pro vestiariis et aliis incumbentibus, et plura mercimonia diversis vicibus emisset a quo[dam] Iohan[n]e Fayrihaed, laico Morinensi, et de receptis ab ipso laico et datis(?) devenisset ad ponendum et firmandum calculum adinvicem, dictusque laicus pluries res vendidisse dicto exponenti, que in veritate non vendiderat, assignaretur et asseraret, ipseque exponens assereret non fuisse sic sicut ipse laicus asserebat; dictus laicus animo irato contra dictum exponentem ad verba iniuriosa prorupit, appellando ipsum exponentem pluries et pluries ribaldum et falsarium, et cum ipse exponens eidem laico humiliter diceret quod non deberet dicere talia, laicus ipse multo magis prorumpens ad verba iniuriosa contra ipsum exponentem manum ad cultellum quem apud se habebat apposuit, annuens [*recte* annuntians] velle ipsum exponentem cum dicto cultello percutere, cui cum dictus opponens domestice diceret, 'Amice, cogita melius et vade pro factis [fol. 240v] tuis. Non debes pro me contra me ad talia sic prorumpere', dictus laicus magis calescens contra ipsum exponentem, ponendo manum ad dictum cultellum ut ipsum exponentem percuteret, irruit; quod videns dictus exponens dubitans quod

---

[167] The same Richard Michel *alias* Multum, monk of Crowland, who was granted a dispensation to hold for life a benefice with cure of souls on 30 December 1441 (*CPL*, ix. 221).

si dictus laicus ipsum cum dicto cultello percuteret leviter, periculum mortis sibi imminere possit, non videns modum sine periculo mortis recedendi, et cum dictus laicus semper magis in ipsum irruebat, quemdam parvum baculum pro sui defensione in manu accepit, et dum dictus laicus magis appropinquasset ad exponentem, ut ipsum a se expelleret amenando [*sic*] cum dicto baculo, contigit quod aliquantulum super capud ipsius laici ipsum laicum tetigit et percussit absque aliquali fractura vel sanguinis effusione et sine aliqua inflatione; quibus sic peractis mediantibus viris astantibus dictus exponens et laicus ab invicem divisi, laicus ipse ac si nullatenus fuisset percussus ad negotia sua peragenda recessit et per totam diem in nundinis que ibidem celebrabantur, bibendo, comedendo et negotia sua peragendo cum aliis qui in dictis nundinis erant stetit et fuit. Adveniente vero sero dictus laicus ut ad certum hospitium in quo de nocte se reducebat accedere posset quandam navem et flumen transfretare posset[168] ascendit, et cum in dicta navi esset, supervenit ut asseritur eidem laico aliqualis infrigiditatem [*recte* infrigiditas], quare naute et alii qui in dicta navi erant ipsum laicum ad hospitium quoddam conduxerunt et ipsum supra quendam lectum posuerunt, et ut asseritur de nocte eidem laico supervenit certus vomitus ex quo per os suum plura emisit adeo quod ab astantibus asserabatur aliquod apostema debuisse fuisse sibi ab intra ruptum et apertum, ac finaliter idem laicus eadem nocte diem suum clausit extremum. Cum autem ipse exponens in morte dicti laici alias quam ut premittitur culpabilis non fuerat cupiatque in suis ordinibus perpetuo domino famulari ad omnem scrupulum conscientie sue purgandum [supplicat] quatinus dignemini ad cautelam ipsum a premissis absolvere et, si quam irregularitatis etc. [maculam ex premissis contraxisset, secum dispensare].

Concessum ut infra in presentia domini Cardinalis.

519. [Florence], 13 August 1441. Supplication on the part of Richard Radhale, priest, rector of New Radnor (*Radnor nova*), Hereford dioc., BCn and CnL,[169] for the pope [to grant] him [a licence] so that he may hear, study and read civil law (*leges*) and receive the insignia of the doctorate in a faculty of civil law in any university (*universitate studii generalis*). *Fiat de speciali N*. Reg. 2bis, fol. 257v.

520. [Florence], 22 August 1441. Supplication on the part of John Patengham, deacon, Winchester (*Wynteniensis*) dioc., for the pope to grant that, after he has been promoted to priest's orders, he may hear, study and read civil law (*leges sive iura civilia*) in any university (*studio generalis universitatis*) for seven years and receive the insignia of the doctorate. Approved with **521**. Reg. 2bis, fol. 277r.

521. [*Florence, 22 August 1441*]. *Thomas Bolragw, priest, professed of Halesowen Abbey, Premonstratensian order, Worcester dioc., seeks to minister with a parish rector or curate.* Reg. 2bis, fol. 277r.

---

[168] This word is redundant.
[169] Richard Rudhale was BCn & CL of Oxford by 1435 and incepted as DCnL of Padua in 1442. For his clerical and university career, benefices and offices see *BRUO*, iii.1603; see also *CPL*, x. 22, 39, 141, xi. 367, 681–2; *Reg. Spofford*, 317, 365, 366, 370).

[Florentie, xi kal. Sept.]. Supplicatur sanctitati vestre pro parte devoti vestri fratris Thome Bolragw, presbiteri, professi monasterii de Haliswan ordinis Premonstratensis Wygorniensis diocesis, quatinus sibi ut de sui superioris licentia et scientia cum parrochialis ecclesie rectore seu curato stare sibique in divinis officiis servire et celebrare ac ecclesiastica sacramenta ministrare dummodo tamen ad id voluntarius ipsius rectoris accedat consensus ita tamen quod pro moneta(?) exinde recipi [possit concedere dignemini?].

Fiat de speciali N. (*Approved with* **520**.)

522. [Florence], 28 August 1441. Same dispensation as **511** sought by Richard Cotyng, deacon, London dioc. *Fiat de speciali N*. Reg. 2bis, fol. 260v.

523. [*Florence*], *29 August 1441. John del Kirke, priest, Coventry and Lichfield dioc., had himself promoted to all holy orders while under age. Now that he is 24, he seeks absolution from these excesses and a dispensation from his former defect of age and irregularity*. Reg. 2bis, fol. 260v.

[Florentie], iiii kal. Septembris. Exponitur sanctitati vestre pro parte Iohannis del Kirke, presbiteri Lichefeldensis diocesis, quod ipse olim minor annis existens tamquam simplex et iuris ignarus se fecit alias tamen rite ad omnes sacros ordines promoveri et in ipsis ministravit. Cum autem vicesimumquartum etatis sue annum attingit de presenti et ex magno devotionis fervore cupiat in ipsis ministrare, supplicatur humiliter sanctitati vestre pro parte ipsius exponentis quatinus ipsum ab excessibus huiusmodi et peccatis suis aliis, nisi talia fuerint propter que merito sit sedes apostolica consulenda, absolvi misericorditer mandare ac super defectu etatis sue predicto ut erat(?), Lugdunensis et Lateranensis conciliorum et quibusvis aliis constitutionibus contrariis non obstantibus, super irregularitate ex premissis forte contracta et ipsorum sic susceptorum ordinum executione dispensare etc. [misericorditer dignemini].

Fiat de speciali N.

524. [Florence], 5 September 1441. [Request] on the part of Thomas Saynigeo,[170] acolyte, Exeter dioc., that the pope may grant him a dispensation that on reaching the age of 23, he may be promoted to the order of the priesthood and minister in the same, notwithstanding his defect of age and [constitutions] of the Lyon and Lateran councils and any other constitutions to the contrary, etc. Approved with **525**. Reg. 2bis, fol. 266v.

525. [Florence], 5 September 1441. The pope is requested to grant letters dimissory for the same T.[171] that he may be promoted to all holy orders by any Catholic bishop having the grace and communion of the apostolic see and minister (*imministrare*) in them. *Fiat* [*N*.] (Approved with **524**.) Reg. 2bis, fol. 266v.

---

[170] Doubtless the Thomas Saynger (Sayngeor, Sangeour) ordained as acolyte on 20 February 1440, subdeacon on 24 February 1442, deacon on 26 May and priest on 22 September 1442; he was chaplain at Harberton parish church (Devon) by February 1450 (*Reg. Lacy*, ed. Dunstan, iii. 63, iv.175c, 185, 186, 189).
[171] Thomas Saynigeo as in **524**.

526. [Florence, 16 November 1441].[172] Supplication on the part of Fr Robert Fynon, priest, professed canon of the monastery of St Osyth, OSA, London [dioc.], for the pope [to grant] that, with his superior's permission, he may study in any university (*universitate studii generalis*) and in any faculty etc. *Fiat de speciali N.* Reg. 2bis, fol. 297r.

527. [Florence], 1 December 1441. The pope is requested [to grant] Thomas Marchal, clerk, Lincoln dioc., letters dimissory so that he may be promoted to all, even holy, orders by any Catholic bishop having the grace and communion of the apostolic see and, after he has been promoted, minister in them, since he cannot approach his ordinary to receive them because of the distance of the place. *Fiat de speciali [N].* Reg. 2bis, fol. 295v.

528. [*Florence*], *17 January 1442. Fr Robert Heth, professed canon of Wendling Abbey, Premonstratensian order, Norwich dioc., as a young clerk fornicated with a pregnant woman, who then gave birth prematurely, and the child died after five days. He then had himself promoted to all holy orders, ministered in them, and obtained a benefice, without a dispensation, before becoming a monk. He has ceased to celebrate and now, aged about 80, seeks a dispensation to minister in his orders.* Reg. 2bis, fol. 351v.

> [Florentie], xvi kal. Februarii. Exponitur pro parte fratris Roberti Heth, canonici professi monasterii de Nendelyng ordinis Premonstratensis Norwicensis diocesis, quod ipse olim tempore iuventutis sue cum adhuc in seculo et clericali caractere insignatus esset quamdam mulierem fetum in utero vivificatum habentem actu fornicario de ipsius bona voluntate carnaliter cognovit, que quidem mulier, ut exponens ipse timet, ex aliqua lesione ipsius coytus seu ex aliqua alia alteratione sui corporis ante tempus debitum quendam infantulum vivum peperit, qui baptizatus infra quinque dies, ut deo placuit, diem suum clausit extremum. Deinde exponens ipse ex simplicitate, nulla super hoc a sede apostolica dispensatione obtenta, se fecit alias tamen rite ad omnes sacros ordines promoveri et in ipsis divina ac alia sacramenta ecclesiastica ministravit et inmiscuit se eisdem, necnon quoddam beneficium ecclesiasticum quod aliquamdiu in possessione tenuit [obtinuit]. Tandem vero exponens prefatus, seculo ac beneficio dimissis, monasterium et ordinem predictos ingressus, habitum assumpsit et professionem emisit regularem. Cum etc. [autem] exponens in morte ipsius infantuli alias quam ut premittitur culpabilis non fuerit et in morte ipsius etc.[173] etiam ex remorsione sui(?) ipsius conscientie iam diu a ministratione et celebratione divinorum cessavit, prout cessat de presenti, cupiat nunc tamen, cum sit octuagenarius vel quasi, in suis ordinibus libere ministrare etc.
>
> Fiat de speciali N.

529. [Florence], 26 January 1442. The pope is requested to grant Thomas Faubys, priest, rector of St Bride's parish church, London, that [he may absolve] each and every one of his parishoners of either sex as often as they wish to confess. *Fiat de speciali N.* Reg. 2bis, fol. 352r.

---

[172] The entry is undated, but this date appears beside the entry preceding it in the register.
[173] The words 'in morte ipsius etc.' are redundant.

530. [Florence], 3 February 1442. Supplication on the part of Fr John de Norham, clerk, professed regular canon, Ixworth Priory, OSA, Norwich dioc., for the pope to grant him [a dispensation] so that notwithstanding his defect of age, provided that he has reached the age of 23, he may be promoted to all holy orders, even the priesthood, and minister in them. Approved with **531**. Reg. 2bis, fol. 356r.

531. [Florence], 3 February 1442. Same dispensation as **530** sought by Fr John Newe, clerk, professed regular canon, Ixworth Priory, OSA, Norwich dioc. *Fiat N.* (Approved with **530**.) Reg. 2bis, fol. 356r.

532. [Florence], 3 February 1442. The pope is requested to grant John Nicoll, priest, Norwich dioc.,[174] a licence to attend lectures on civil law (*audiendi leges*) in any *studium* for seven years, notwithstanding constitutions and ordinances [to the contrary]. *Fiat de speciali N.* Reg. 2bis, fol. 356r.

533. [Florence], 4 March 1442. The pope is informed on the part of Peter Toubeck, acolyte, Norwich dioc., that he wishes to be promoted to all, even holy, orders, but on account of his defect of age, he being aged 23, [he cannot be promoted] without a papal dispensation; hence [the pope is requested to grant] him one, notwithstanding that defect, so that he [may be promoted] to all holy orders [and minister in them]. *Fiat de speciali N.* Reg. 2bis, fol. 322v.

534. *[Florence], 7 March 1442. John Edward, priest, Norwich dioc., had himself promoted to all holy orders, including the priesthood, and ministered in them, despite a physical defect in his right hand; he seeks a dispensation to minister.* Reg. 2bis, fol. 322v.

[Florentie], non. Martii. Exponitur [sanctitati vestre] pro parte Iohannis Edward, presbiteri Norwicensis diocesis, qui alias ad omnes ordines sacros usque ad presbiteratus ordinem inclusive inclusive [*sic*], non obstante quod unam petiam prioris articuli primi digiti dextre manus, videlicet tantam quantam unguis cooperuit, amisit, se fecit promoveri et in illis ministravit. Quare etc. [supplicatur sanctitati eidem pro parte dicti exponentis] quatinus secum ut in omnibus suis ordinibus susceptis, macula predicta non obstante quo magnum scandalum etc. [populo non possit generari, ministrare possit dispensare misericorditer dignemini].

Fiat de speciali N.

535. [Florence], 8 March 1442. The pope is requested [to grant] that Richard Garnon, clerk, Lincoln dioc., may be promoted to all holy orders by any Catholic bishop having the grace and communion of the apostolic see and minister in them, since he cannot approach his ordinary to receive them because of the distance of the place, notwithstanding the constitution of Clement [IV][175] etc. *Fiat de speciali* [N]. Reg. 2bis, fol. 316r.

---

[174] He was also granted a licence on 11 April 1442 to have a portable altar and celebrate mass before daybreak. He was appointed a notary public in the Roman Curia on 14 April 1442 (*CPL*, ix. 311, 322).

[175] *Liber sextus* 1.9.1 ('Saepe contingit').

536. [*Florence*], *16 March 1442. Fr William Hotost, priest, professed canon of the Order of St Gilbert of Sempringham, of Bullington Priory, Lincoln dioc., incurred excommunication for apostasy; he has been absolved from that sentence and now seeks [a dispensation from irregularity and a licence to transfer to another monastery of his order]*. Reg. 2bis, fol. 318v.

[Florentie], xvii kal. Aprilis. Exponitur [*recte* exponit] sanctitati vestre frater Wilhellmus Hotost, presbiter, canonicus professus ordinis fratrum sancti Gilberti in Sympyinghamen' sub regula sancti Augustini degentium domus de Bolargotan' Lincolniensis diocesis, quod ipse olim ex quadam animi levitate domum ipsam in quo [*recte* qua] se voto professionis astrinxerat, habitu et ordine derelictis, illicentiatus exivit et ad seculum est reversus, in quo aliquamdiu evagatus extitit, propter quod excommunicationis incurrit sententiam in tales etc. [generaliter promulgatam], et sic forte ligatus divina celebravit officia et alias inmiscuit se eisdem. Cum etc. [autem sit] nunc ad cor reversus cupiatque ad suum ovile reverti et in eo domino perpetuo etc. [famulari], supplicat igitur etc. [sanctitati eidem dictus exponens], qui iam de dicta excommunicationis sententia et excessibus absolutus etc. [fuit], quatinus secum ut, non obstantibus constitutionibus etc. [in contrarium editis quibuscumque, super irregularitate dispensare] quodque etc. [ad aliquod aliud monasterium eiusdem ordinis paris vel artiori observantie regularis se transferre valeat licentiam concedere dignemini?].

Fiat ut infra N. Signanda per fiat de speciali, et scandalum ex hoc non generetur in loco.

537. [Florence], 22 March 1442. Supplication on the part of Gilbert Sprot, priest, Lincoln dioc., for the pope to grant that when he should hold some parish church *in titulum aut in commendam* or otherwise under his rule, he may absolve all parishoners of that church of either sex *in forma 'Cupientes'*. Approved with **540**. Reg. 2bis, fol. 320r.

538. [Florence], 22 March 1442. Same grant as **537** sought by John Bordun, priest, Lincoln dioc. Approved with **540**. Reg. 2bis, fol. 320r.

539. [Florence], 22 March 1442. Same grant as **537** sought by Thomas Flowter, priest, Lincoln dioc. Approved with **540**. Reg. 2bis, fol. 320r.

540. [*Florence*], *22 March 1442. Gilbert Sprot and Thomas Flowter, priests, Lincoln dioc., seek exemption from a diocesan custom requiring the ordained to accept a cure of souls*. Reg. 2bis, fol. 320r.

[Florentie, xi kal. Aprilis]. Supplicant sanctitati vestre Gilbertus et Thomas predicti quod cum in partibus certa consuetudo per ordinarium dicti loci servetur que dicenda est potius corruptula [*recte* corruptela], videlicet ad dictos ordinarios recursum habent, qui ordinarii dictos capellanos invitos ad dictam curam suscipiendam astringunt. Supplicant igitur quatinus ipsos a tali onere eximere, cum nullus invitus, dummodo non sit astrictus ratione sue ecclesie, ad tale onus astringi debet, non obstantibus constitutionibus, ordinationibus seu consuetudinibus aliquibus etc.

Fiat de speciali [N]. (*Approved with* **537–9**.)

541. [*Florence, 5 April 1442*]. *Robert, priest, Norwich dioc., had himself ordained in Italy and thereby incurred excommunication; he seeks absolution from that sentence and a dispensation from irregularity.* Reg. 2bis, fol. 325r.

[Florentie, non. Aprilis]. Exponit sanctitati vestre devotus vester Robertus, presbiter Norwicensis diocesis, quod ipse olim, contra constitutionem felicis recordationis domini Clementis iiii^{ti} de non ordinandis ab episcopis Italie clericis ultramontanis, prorsus ignarus, tamquam simplex et iuris ignarus se fecit, sui diocesani licentia non obtenta, per quendam episcopum ~~Ytalie~~ catholicum gratiam et communionem sedis apostolice habentem successive alias tamen rite in partibus Italie promoveri, ignorans etc. [quod in tales esset excommunicationis sententia generaliter promulgata]. Supplicat quatinus ipsum a dicta sententia excommunicationis huiusmodi absolvi etc. [et secum super irregularitate dispensari mandare dignemini].

Fiat de speciali N.

542. [Florence], 7 April 1442. Same dispensation as **511** sought by Fr William Gerneys, clerk, professed canon of St Mary's monastery, Butley (*Buttele*), wont to be governed by a prior, OSA, Norwich dioc. Approved with **545**. Reg. 2bis, fol. 326r.

543. [Florence], 7 April 1442. Same dispensation as **511** for John Gerneys, clerk, professed canon of the same monastery. Approved with **545**. Reg. 2bis, fol. 326r.

544. [Florence], 7 April 1442. Same dispensation as **511** for Robert Bury, professed canon of the same monastery. Approved with **545**. Reg. 2bis, fol. 326r.

545. [Florence], 7 April 1442. Same dispensation as **511** for Robert Chenyngton, clerk, professed canon of the same monastery. *Fiat de speciali N.* (Approved with **542–4**.) Reg. 2bis, fol. 326r.

546. [Florence], 9 April 1442. The pope is requested to grant John Medw, priest, rector of Alburgh (*Albwrgh*) parish church,[176] Norwich dioc., licence and authority to absolve all his parishoners of either sex *in forma 'Cupientes'*. Approved with **547**. Reg. 2bis, fol. 326r.

547. [Florence], 9 April 1442. Same grant as **546** for Robert Langwade, priest, rector of Bicham Welles (*Bych'm*) parish church,[177] Norwich dioc. *Fiat de speciali N.* (Approved with **546**.) Reg. 2bis, fol. 326r.

548. [Florence], 9 April 1442. Supplication on the part of William Cabyl, deacon, Norwich dioc., for the pope to grant him [a dispensation] so that when he has reached the age of 23, he may be promoted to the order of the priesthood and minister in it [notwithstanding] that defect of age and [constitutions] of the Lyons [and Lateran councils and any others to the contrary]. (Unsigned.) Reg. 2bis, fol. 326r.

---

[176] Alternatively it may be Aldborough (Norf.) or Aldeburgh (Suff.).
[177] Or possibly Bircham Newton, Bircham Tofts, or Great Bircham, all in Norf.

549. [*Florence*], *9 April 1442. John Edward, priest, Norwich dioc., seeks a licence not to be compelled by his ordinary to serve churches in his diocese.* Reg. 2bis, fol. 326v.

[Florentie], v idus Aprilis. Beatissime pater, cum ordinarii in regno Anglie presbiteros officia annualia sive stipendiaria obtinentes de ipsorum officiis annualibus stipendiariis expellunt et ad deserviendum parrochialibus ecclesiis in eorum diocesibus mittunt et compellunt, hinc est quare supplicat devotus vester Iohannes Edward, presbiter Norwicensis diocesis, quatinus sibi licentiam et facultatem ut officiis deservire [possit] et ad serviendum ecclesiis compelli non posse [*recte* possit] etc. [concedere misericorditer dignemini].

Fiat de speciali N.

550. [Florence, 13 April 1442].[178] Robert Brech, priest, Norwich dioc., informs the pope that formerly guilelessly (*tamquam simplex*) and out of ignorance of the law he had himself promoted to all holy orders while under age but otherwise legally and ministered in them. He requests that the pope orders his absolution from such excesses and grants him [a dispensation] so that, notwithstanding his defect of age, provided that he has reached the age of 23, he may minister in all his existing orders. *Fiat de speciali N.* Reg. 2bis, fol. 329r.

551. [Florence], 14 April 1442. Same dispensation as **511** sought by Thomas Kempe, clerk, Lincoln dioc. *Fiat de speciali N.* Reg. 2bis, fol. 328v.

552. [Florence], 14 April 1442. Same dispensation as **548** sought by Robert Aclerk, acolyte, York dioc. *Fiat de speciali N.* Reg. 2bis, fol. 328v.

553. [*Florence*], *20 April 1442. William Schort, priest, Norwich dioc., had himself promoted to all holy orders in Italy and thereby incurred excommunication; he seeks absolution from that sentence and a dispensation from irregularity.* Reg. 2bis, fol. 331r.

[Florentie], xii kal. Maii. Exponitur sanctitati vestre pro parte vestri Willelmi Schort presbiteri Norwicensis diocesis quod ipse olim constitutionem felicis recordationis domini Clementis pape iiii de non ordinandis ab episcopis Ytalie clericis ultramontanis prorsus ignorans se fecit per simplicitatem et iuris ignorantiam sui diocesani licentia non obtenta statutis a iure temporibus ad omnes sacros ordines successive alias tamen rite [in partibus Italie promoveri] ignorans quod in talibus esset sicut erat excommunicationis etc. [sententia generaliter promulgata]. Supplicatur quatinus ipsum a sententia huiusmodi et excessibus etc. [absolvi et secum super irregularitate dispensari mandare dignemini].

Fiat de speciali N.

554. [Florence], 26 April 1442. The pope is informed on the part of Robert Cole, priest, dwelling in Lincoln diocese, that in order to have greater knowledge and understanding of canon law he wishes to study, read [and attend lectures on] civil

[178] The entry is undated, but that preceding it bears the date 'xviiii kal. [*recte* id.] Maii.'.

law publicly in the schools, take part in other scholastic acts and receive a doctoral degree in it, but because of a prohibition in canon law he may not do so. The pope is requested [to grant him a licence] so that he may read, study and attend lectures on civil law, receive a doctoral degree in it, and take part in other scholastic acts, notwithstanding [papal] and other [constitutions to the contrary]. Approved with **555**. Reg. 2bis, fol. 333r.

555. [Florence], 26 April 1442. Same licence as **554** for John Rourne, priest, dwelling in Lincoln dioc. *Fiat de speciali N. ad septennium.* (Approved with **554**.) Reg. 2bis, fol. 333r.

556. [*Florence*], *30 April 1442. Robert Smythson and Isabel Watten of Amotherby, Appleton-le-Street parish in Ryedale, York dioc., married and had issue, unaware that they were related in the fourth degree of consanguinity, but when they wished to solemnise their marriage, their vicar refused because of this impediment. They seek a dispensation to solemnise their marriage and the legitimation of any issue.* Reg. 2bis, fol. 336r–v.

> [Florentie], ii kal. Maii. Exponitur pro parte devotorum vestrorum Roberti Smythson de willa de Aymindole parrochie de Appllton' in R[i]dale, laici Eboracensis diocesis, et Ysabelle Watten, mulieris parrochie et diocesis predictarum, quod ipsi olim ignorantes aliquod impedimentum inter se [existere matrimonium] per verba de presenti contraxerunt illudque carnali copula consumaverunt ac prolem exinde procreaverunt. Et deinde tribus bannis in facie ecclesie iuxta morem patrie proclamatis cum iidem exponen[te]s ad solempnizationem matrimonii huiusmodi, ut moris [est], procedere vellent, vicarius parrochialis ecclesie sub qua ipsi exponentes moriantur, solus excipiendo, asseruit eosdem exponentes quarto consanguinitatis gradu invicem fore coniunctos ac ipsos sine canonica dispensatione ad solempnizationem dicti matrimonii ~~matrimonii~~ dicti matrimonii [*sic*] procedere et in eo remanere non posse, ipsumque matrimonium propterea ulterius solempnizare recusavit. Verum, pater sancte, si divortium [fol. 336v] fieret inter eos, gravia scandala et dissentiones inter eorum parentes et amicos verisimiliter exoriri possent, dictaque Ysabella perpetuo diffamata remaneret et proles illegitime censeretur. Supplicatur quatinus cum ipsis ut, impedimento non obstante predicto, in matrimonio predicto remanere et ad illius solempnizationem procedere iuxta morem patrie valeant dispensare prolemque susceptam huiusmodi et suscipiendam ex eo legitimam decernere dignemini etc. (*Approved with* **557**).

557. [*Florence*], *30 April 1442. John Smyth of Langton and Catherine Willman, York dioc., married and had issue after his unconsummated marriage to and the death of her sister Alice, but when they wished to solemnise the marriage, their curate refused because of this impediment of public honesty. They seek a dispensation to solemnise the marriage and the legitimation of any issue.* Reg. 2bis, fol. 336v.

> [Florentie, ii kal. Maii]. Exponitur sanctitati vestre pro parte Iohannis Smyth de villa de Langton', laici, et Chatherine Willman, mulieris, Eboracensis diocesis, quod postquam idem Iohannes olim cum quondam Alisia

Wilman, sorore carnali dicte Catherine, matrimonium per verba de presenti legitime contraxerat, tandem eadem A[l]isia ab ipso Iohanne incognita et intacta remanente, sicut domino placuit, viam universe carnis ingressa [est]. Iidem exponentes matrimonium inter se per verba de presenti similia de presenti contraxerunt, illudque carnali copula consumaverunt ac prolem procrearunt. Et cum ipsis [*recte* ipsi] exponentes, bannis propterea iuxta morem patrie editis, ad ipsius matrimonii solempnizationem in facie ecclesie, ut est moris, procedere vellent, curatus parrochialis ecclesie sub qua exponentes ipsi moriantur hoc permittere noluit, asserens ipsos propter impedimentum publice honestatis iusticie expresse [*recte* ex premissis] proveniens hoc facere non posse. Supplicatur pro parte dictorum exponentium quatinus ad evitandum scandala et dissentiones que inter eorum parentes, consanguineos et amicos verisimiliter exoriri possent si divortium fieret inter eos, quatinus [*sic*] cum ipsis [ut], impedimento publice honestatis iusticie huiusmodi non obstante, ad solempnizationem dicti matrimonii procedere etc. [iuxta morem patrie valeant dispensare prolemque susceptam huiusmodi et suscipiendam ex eo legitimam decernere dignemini].

Fiat de speciali N. (*Approved with* **556**.)

558. [Florence], 7 May 1442. Same dispensation as **511** on the part of Henry Dier, deacon, Winchester dioc. Approved with **559**. Reg. 2bis, fol. 340v.

559. [Florence], 7 May 1442. The pope is requested to grant John Steven, acolyte, Lincoln dioc., that [he may be promoted to all holy orders] by any Catholic bishop having the grace and communion of the apostolic see [and minister in them], as on certain reasonable grounds he cannot conveniently approach his ordinary to receive them. *Fiat de speciali N.* (Approved with **558**.) Reg. 2bis, fol. 340v.

560. [Florence], 7 May 1442. The pope is requested [to grant] John Ruyt, clerk, York dioc., that, since he wishes out of great fervour of devotion to serve the Lord but he has not yet reached the age of 24, [notwithstanding that defect of age, he may be promoted to all holy orders and minister in them]. *Fiat de speciali N.* Reg. 2bis, fol. 340v.

561. [Florence], 10 May 1442. Same dispensation as **548** sought by William Oldeton, deacon, [Coventry and] Lichfield dioc. *Fiat de speciali N.* Reg. 2bis, fol. 342r.

562. [Florence], 15 May 1442. Supplication on the part of Adam Coppandale, priest, York dioc., BCL,[179] for the pope to grant that he may hear, read and study in a faculty of civil law in any *studium generale* for up to seven years and take the degree and insignia of the doctorate, [notwithstanding] the constitution ['Super speculam'] of Pope Honorius III and any others to the contrary. *Fiat de speciali N.* Reg. 2bis, fol. 343r.

---

[179] Adam Coppendale was a fellow of King's Hall, Cambridge, 1431–9, and was charged as a commoner there from 1441/2 to 1452/3. He was *magister* by 1438/9 and a DCL of Cambridge by 1448/9. He was rector of Kirklington (Yorks.) from 1439, and a canon of Salisbury from 1466 and of Beverley (Yorks.) from 1479 (*BRUC*, 159).

563. [*Florence*], *27 May 1442. Richard Malton, clerk, professed monk of Garendon Abbey, Lincoln dioc., Cistercian order, incurred excommunication for apostasy, then married a certain Jonelle, but later left her; he seeks absolution, readmission to his abbey, and promotion to all orders.* Reg. 2bis, fol. 346v.

[Florentie], vi kal. Iunii. Exponitur pro parte devoti vestri Ricardi Malton, clerici, monachi professi monasterii de Gardon Lincolniensis diocesis ordinis Cisterciensis, quod ipse olim ex quadam animi sui levitate monasterium ipsum in quo se vinculo professionis astrinxerat, habitum [*recte* habito] et ordine derelictis, illicentiatus exivit et ad seculum est reversus, in quo dampnabiliter aliquamdiu evagatus exstitit, propter quod excommunicationis incurrit sententiam in tales etc. [generaliter promulgatam]. Et demum cum quadam Ionella unica virgine matrimonium potius contubernium per verba de presenti de facto contraxit illudque carnali copula consumavit, et per aliquod tempus cum ea habitavit, et tandem dum exponens ipse quadam gravi infirmitate teneretur, timens ne infirmitas illa ex iniquitate et peccato suo pervenisse[t], dictam mulierem dimisit. Cum autem exponens ipse pro nunc ad cor reversus dolet intime de commissis cupiatque ad suum ovile reverti ibique domino, ut tenetur, sub habitu regulari perpetuo domino [*sic*] famulari et ad omnes ordines promoveri et ne aliqui simplices et iuris ignari etc. supplicatur quatinus ipsum absolvi etc.

Fiat in foro consciencie.

564. [Florence], 2 June 1442. Same grant as **562** sought by Ieuan Manavon, priest, St Asaph dioc.[180] *Concessum de speciali.* Reg. 2bis, fol. 362v.

565. [Florence], 2 June 1442. The pope is requested [to grant] Robert Gudal, priest, rector of St Thomas the Apostle's parish church, London,[181] a licence to absolve his parishoners of either sex for five years. *Concessum de speciali.* Reg. 2bis, fol. 362v.

566. [Florence], 2 June 1442. [Request that] the pope grant William Forstere, [professed canon] of Kirby Bellers (*Kyrkely super Vrechok*) [conventual priory, OSA], deacon, Lincoln dioc., [that on reaching the age of 23 he may be promoted to the order of the priesthood etc.]. *Fiat de speciali N.* (Approved with **574**.) Reg. 2bis, fol. 371r.

567. [*Florence*], *14 June 1442. John Lytster alias Chapman, priest, York dioc., heard that his brother was being killed by another priest, and when he intervened, the priest attacked him with a knife, so he defended himself with a dagger, whereby the priest was fatally wounded; but the priest excused him of blame before dying. He seeks [a declaration of innocence and a dispensation from irregularity].* Reg. 2bis, fols. 367v–368r.

[180] Probably the John Manavon, rector of Garthbeibio (Montgom.), St Asaph dioc., who was granted a licence for a portable altar on 2 June 1442. On the same date he was also granted a dispensation to hold Garthbeibio and the rectory of Llanwrin (Montgom.), St Asaph dioc., for five years. He was appointed a notary public 'in pious and ecclesiastical causes only' in the Roman Curia on 5 June 1442 (*CPL*, ix. 312, 320–1, 323).
[181] Robert Goodall, nobleman, rector of St Thomas the Apostle's, London, was granted a licence to have a portable altar, on 10 May 1441 (*CPL*, ix. 315).

[Florentie], xviii kal. Iulii. Exponitur sanctitati vestre pro parte Iohannis Lytster alias Chapman, presbiteri Eboracensis diocesis, quod cum olim ei ut quidem presbiter, ipsius exponentis valde amicus, cum fratre suo carnali dicti exponentis pugnasset et sese mutuo invicem percussissent ac graviterque [*sic*] unus alterum ac alter alterum vulnerasset ac idemque [*sic*] presbiter dictum fratrem suum interfecisset nunctiatum esset, prefatus exponens ad ipsos pugnantes accessit dictoque presbitero dictus tamquam amico satis moderate dixit hec verba vel eorum in effectu similia, attenensque illum per brachium dixit [*sic*]: 'Cur, vir, fratrem meum interficere?' [fol. 368r] Qui quidem presbiter versus ipsum exponentem se revolvit, illumque cum quodam cultello furore repletus invasit, eumque percussit et vulneravit. Tunc exponens ipse videns se et fratrem suum crudeliter vulneratos et propter locum strictum in quo erat commode fugam dare non poterat, timensque etiam sibi gravius periculum imminere quemdam basilardum quem ibi invenit arripuit et evaginavit ac pro defensione illum ante se tenuit, sed predictus presbiter quasi furiosus et insensatus iterum in exponentem ipsum cum dicto cultello suo irruit et se ipsum in dicto basilardo se [*sic*] vulneravit, qui vero presbiter post paucos dies expiravit. Et tandem dictus presbiter ante obitum suum dictum exponentem et fratrem eius coram se venire fecit, illisque pepertit et publice dixit quod ipsemet causa sue mortis fuit exponentemque inculpabilem reddidit. Cum autem, pater sancte, ipse in morte ipsius presbiteri alias quam ut premittitur culpabilis non existit et de morte ipsius valde doluit, prout dolet de presenti, et vim vi repellere etc., cupiat in suis ordinibus etc. [libere ministrare]. Supplicat quatinus ipsum etc. [reatum nullum homicidii incurrisse, nullamque irregularitatis sive inhabilitatis notam contraxisse, sed libere in suis susceptis ordinibus ministrare posse declarari mandare dignemini].

Signanda per fiat de speciali N.

568. [Florence], 15 June 1442. *Supplication on the part of William Hunte, priest, Lincoln dioc., [for the pope to grant] that he may attend lectures, read and study in a faculty of civil law in any* studium generale *for up to seven years.* Concessum de speciali N. Reg. 2bis, fol. 368r.

569. [*Florence*], *21 June 1442. Thomas Aleyn, priest, Lincoln dioc., hurled stones from the walls of the castle where he was chaplain to defend it against those laying siege to it; some of them were killed, but he does not know whether his action was to blame. He seeks absolution from homicide and a dispensation from irregularity.* Reg. 2bis, fol. 370r.

[Florentie], xi kal. Iulii. Exponitur sanctitati vestre pro parte devoti Thome Aleyn, presbiteri Lincolniensis diocesis, quod cum olim quoddam castrum in quod [*recte* quo] dictus exponens cappellanus erat per inimicos obsessum esset illudque hostiliter pugnassent, prefatus exponens pro defensione et metu persone quod in constantem virum cadere possit una cum illis muros ascendit et lapides adversus dictos inimicos volentes per muros dicti castri intrare ac illos ad terram proicere proiecit, et quamvis aliqui intrarent extra castrum, cum bombardis, pixidis [*recte* pixidibus?], sagitta [*recte* sagittis?] et lapidibus interfecti fuissent, tamen exponens ipse numquam scire potuit si quem cum dictis lapidibus percussit, vulneravit seu interfecit. Cum autem, pater sancte, dictus exponens in dictorum laicorum morte alias quam ut premittitur culpabilis non fuerit, et ea que fecit pre metu mortis fecit quia fama erat quod nisi se defenderent omnes et singuli homines in eo castro existentes gladio pererent, cupiatque in omnibus suis ordinibus etc. [libere ministrare], supplicat quatinus ipsum a reatibus homicidiorum etc. [absolvi et secum super iregularitate dispensari mandare dignemini].

Concessum ut infra etc. Fiat de speciali.

570. [*Florence*], *29 June 1442. Hugh Tapton, priest, perpetual vicar of Greasley, York dioc.*,[182] *seeks a licence to study and receive a doctorate in civil law.* Reg. 2bis, fol. 371v.

[Florentie], iii kal. Iulii. Item similem absolutionem a sententia excommunicationis[183] petit Hugonis [*recte* Hugo] Tapton', presbiter, perpetui vicarii [*recte* perpetuus vicarius] parrochialis ecclesie de Gresley Eboracensis diocesis, qui propter maiorem informationem et intelligentiam iuris canonici habendam cupit leges civiles in scolis publice audire, studere, legere aliisque actibus scolasticis uti ac gradum doctoratus in eo recipere. [Sine dispensatione] sedis apostolice [propter] inhabilitatem iuris canonici hoc facere non licet. Supplicat igitur etc. [quatinus sibi ut leges predictas sicut premittitur legere, audire et studere, ac gradum doctorale in eo recipere, aliisque actibus scolasticis uti licentiam concedere dignemini] ut in forma de gratia vestra speciali. (*Approved with* **573**.)

571. [Florence], 29 June 1442. Same licence as **570** for seven years for Roger Kyrkeby, priest, perpetual vicar of Great Dalby parish church, Lincoln dioc.[184] Approved with **573**. Reg. 2bis, fol. 371v.

572. [Florence], 29 June 1442. Same licence as **570** for seven years for Thomas Puson, priest, perpetual vicar of Hungerton (*Hungarton*), Lincoln dioc. Approved with **573**. Reg. 2bis, fol. 371v.

573. [Florence] 29 June 1442. The pope is requested to grant the same licence as **471** to Roger Kyrkeby, priest, perpetual vicar of Great Dalby, Lincoln dioc. *Concessum de speciali in presentia d. Cardinalis Pe.* (Approved with **570–2**.) Reg. 2bis, fol. 371v.

574. [Florence], 1(?) July 1442. Same grace as **566** sought on the part of Fr Richard Sensterne, deacon, professed canon of Kirby Bellers (*Kyrkby super Wrechek*) conventual priory, OSA, Lincoln dioc. Approved with **566**. Reg. 2bis, fol. 371r.

575. [Florence], 7 August 1442. [Supplication] on the part of Walter Penmarth, priest, Bangor dioc.,[185] for the pope to grant him a licence so that he may attend

---

[182] He was a fellow of Godshouse, Cambridge, before 1442. He was MA and BTh by 1451, later LicTh. He was admitted as vicar of Greasley (Notts.) on 5 March 1442 and resigned by July 1445. He died on 15 July 1481. For his university career and benefices, see *BRUC*, 576; *CPL*, ix. 245, x. 91.

[183] These opening words are irrelevant to the rest of the entry.

[184] He was granted a licence on 11 July 1442 to farm out his benefice and not reside there for seven years while studying at university (*CPL*, ix. 245).

[185] Perhaps the Walter Pennarth who was at Oxford in April 1443 (*BRUO*, iii.1457).

576. [*Florence*], *21 August 1442. Fr John Merburi, priest, professed of OESA, Warrington convent, Coventry and Lichfield dioc., seeks a licence to act as a chaplain and serve at divine offices with a curate or rector in a parish church.* Reg. 2bis, fol. 381r.

[Florentie], xii kal. Septembris. Item [supplicatur sanctitati vestre] pro parte [devoti] vestri fratris Iohannis Merburi, presbiteri professi ordinis fratrum heremitarum sancti Augustini conventus Werrington Lichfeldensis diocesis, quatinus sibi ut de sui superioris licentia ex causa necessitatis ad acquirendum victum et vestitum cum quocumque curato vel rectore parrochialis ecclesie a quo benivole receptus fuerit tamquam pro cappellano in ecclesia ipsi [*recte* ipsa] stare valeat et servire in divinis officiis, dummodo tamen ad id voluntarius [assensus] ipsius curati vel rectoris licentiam accedat [*recte* accedat, licentiam] dignemini etc. [misericorditer impartiri] de gratia speciali.

Fiat de speciali N.

577. [*Florence*], *22 August 1442. Fr Thomas Belgrave, priest, professed canon of Halesowen Abbey, Premonstratensian order, Worcester dioc., seeks a licence to act as a chaplain, serve at divine offices, and administer sacraments with a curate or rector in a parish church.* Reg. 2bis, fol. 381v.

[Florentie], xi kal. Septembris. Item [supplicatur sanctitati vestre] pro parte devoti vestri fratris Thome Belgrave, presbiteri, canonici professi monasterii de Haleswan ordinis Premonstratensis Wygorniensis diocesis, quatinus sibi ut de sui superioris licentia ex causa necessitatis ad acquirendum victum et vestitum, que propter inopiam ipsius monasterii ab ipso monasterio commode habere non potest, cum quocumque curato vel rectore parrochialis ecclesie seu vice rectore, a quo benivole receptus fuerit et ad id voluntarius eorum accedat assensus, tamquam pro cappellano seu vice rectore libere stare et in divinis officiis licite servire ac ecclesiastica sacramenta ministrare valeat licentiam dignemini misericorditer impartiri de gratia speciali.

Fiat de speciali N.

578. [Florence], 13 September 1442. [Same absolution and dispensation] as **553** sought on the part of Thomas Aytroppe, priest, Lincoln dioc. *Fiat de speciali N.* Reg. 2bis, fol. 384v.

579. [Florence], 19 September 1442. [Supplication] on the part of John Fyscher of Marston Trussel (*Merston Trissell*), priest, deacon,[186] Lincoln dioc., [for the pope to grant] him [a dispensation] so that, notwithstanding his defect of age, provided that he has reached the age of 23 and been promoted to the holy order of the diaconate, he may be promoted to the order of the priesthood, minister in these orders and [obtain] a benefice. Approved with **580**. Reg. 2bis, fol. 385r.

---

[186] His request implies that he was not yet either a priest or a deacon.

580. [Florence], 19 September 1442. [The pope is requested] to grant John Fischer of [Marston Trussell, deacon, Lincoln dioc.,][187] a licence so that he may attend lectures on, study and read civil law (*leges iura civilia*) in any university (*universitate studii generalis*) for seven years and receive the doctoral insignia of that faculty after he has been promoted to the order of the priesthood. *Fiat de speciali N.* (Approved with **579**.) Reg. 2bis, fol. 385r.

581. [*Florence*], *25 September 1442. John Digon, BCL & CnL, priest, recluse of Sheen Priory, Winchester dioc.,*[188] *requests that when he is afflicted by infirmities and frailties he may leave his cell to convalesce in nearby London.* Reg. 2bis, fol. 387r.

[Florentie], vii kal. Octobris. Beatissime pater, cum plerumque devotum vestrum Iohannem Digon', presbiterum Wintoniensis diocesis, in utroque iure baccallarium, reclusum in reclusorio regio loci de Bethelem alias de Shene nuncupati dicte diocesis,[189] qui etiam senio gravatus est, infirmitatum et langworum [*sic*] obrui deffendiis [*sic*] et necessariis pro cupanda [*recte* recuperanda] sanitate in eodem reclusorio careat, supplicat etc. [sanctitati vestre igitur] quatinus sibi ut ipse quotiens infirmitatibus et languoribus quibusvis quomodolibet gravatus seu detentus fuerit ad civitatem Londoniensem, que per modicum spatium videlicet vii miliarum vel circiter partium illarum a dicto reclusorio distat, et ad quam navigio commode accedere potest pro recuperatione sanitatis se transferre et ibidem ad perfectam convalescentiam in loco honesto et congruo remanere ac postea ad dictum reclusorium redire valeat concedere et indulgere dignemini, non obstantibus quibusvis per eum de non exeundo dicto suo reclusorio et aliis in specie vel in genere qualitercumque factis promissionibus etc. ceterisque contrariis quibuscumque clausis oportunis.

Fiat de speciali N.

582. [*Florence*], *17 October 1442. William Symondi, MA, BCnL, priest, rector of Standlake, Lincoln dioc., and domestic chamberlain of the pope,*[190] *enjoyed such fame as a scholar of theology that the archbishop of Canterbury allowed him to preach throughout his province; he requests a licence for five years to enjoin penance on any who wish to confess to him and absolve them from all their sins except those reserved to the apostolic see.* Reg. 2bis, fol. 391r–v.

---

[187] Perhaps the John Fysher, *magister*, resident in the parish of St Mary-the-Less, Cambridge, who paid personal tithes to Peterhouse in respect of his lectures in 1445–6 and 1447–8 (*BRUC*, 249).

[188] John Dygon was BCL in 1406 and BCn & CL by 1435, both of Oxford. He was ordained as a deacon on 27 March 1406 and held various parochial benefices between *c.* 1406 and 1435. He was admitted as a recluse to a cell in Sheen Priory in the summer of 1435, and still alive in 1445 (*BRUO*, i. 615–16).

[189] The Carthusian priory of Jesus of Bethlehem, Sheen (Surrey). The petitioner should have been given in the nominative, not the accusative.

[190] He was a fellow of Oriel College, Oxford, in 1410–11, and still in 1414–15. He was MA, BCnL, and by 1444 LicCnL. He was junior proctor of Oxford University in 1412–14 and chaplain to Humphrey, duke of Gloucester, in 1427. He acted as a proctor at the Roman Curia in 1440 and 1443, was a papal chaplain by 1444, and was appointed as a papal minor penitentiary on 16 June 1444. For his university career and ecclesiastical benefices and offices, see *BRUO*, iii.1841; *CPL*, vii. 280, 501, viii. 319, ix. 43, 68–9; *Reg. Chichele*, i. 272, 336.

[Florentie], xvi kal. Novembris. Supplicat sanctitati vestre devotus vester Wylhelmus Symondi, presbiter, rector parrochialis ecclesie de Stanlak, Lincolniensis diocesis, magister artium et baccallarius in decretis ac domini nostri pape cubicularius, qui adeo sexagenarius et ultra existit et per multa tempora in sacra theologia studuit ita quod ex bona fama sua dominus Cantuariensis metropolitanus eius provincie proprio motu sine requisitione ut ubique per totam provinciam Cantuariensem verbum dei in corda fidelium seminare et predicare possit licentiam concessit, prout per viros fidedignos ac litteris et sigillis dicti domini archiepiscopi Cantuariensis testimonium reddere potest, quatinus sibi ut si qui [fol. 391v] Christi fideles causa devotionis et non alias sine aliqua spe pretii seu muneris quia exponens ipse satis habundat sibi confiteri voluerint, ad hoc cum instanter requisitus fuerit tamen dum tamen accedet consensus curatorum et sine preiudicio ipsorum curatorum illos audire et ab omnibus peccatis, nisi talia sint propter que merito sedes apostolica sit consulenda, absolvere ipsisque penitentiam debitam iniungere valeat licentiam et facultatem ad quinquennium dignemini misericorditer impartiri de gratia speciali.

Fiat de speciali ad quinquennium N.

583. [*Florence*], *26 October 1442. Fr William Ipswich alias Red, priest, professed canon of Holy Trinity Priory, Ipswich, OSA, Norwich dioc., seeks a licence to serve with a rector or deputy rector of a parish church.* Reg. 2bis, fol. 392v.

[Florentie], vii kal. Novembris. Supplicatur sanctitati vestre pro parte devoti vestri fratris Willelmi Zypswich [*sic*] alias dicti Red, presbiteri, canonici professi monasterii sancte Trinitatis in villa Zypswich ordinis sancti Augustini Norwicensis diocesis, quatinus sibi ut de sui superioris licentia cum quocumque rectore vel vicerectore parrochialis ecclesie causa acquirendi victum et vestitum, cum monasterium ipsum taliter desolatum extitit ut facultates illius non suppetant ipsum retinere et de victu et vestitu providere, valeant [*recte* valeat] libere stare et in divinis servire, dummodo tamen rectoris seu vicerectoris voluntarius accedat consensus, licentiam dignemini misericorditer impartiri de gratia speciali.

Fiat de speciali N.

584. [Florence], 26 October 1442. [Supplication on the part of] Fr William Ipswich *alias* Red, priest, professed canon of the monastery of the Holy Trinity, Ipswich, OSA, [Norwich dioc.], that the pope order his absolution from all general sentences *in forma assertiva cum clausula de concubinatu*. *Fiat in forma N*. Reg. 2bis, fol. 392v.

585. [*Florence*], *30 October 1442. Fr Richard Michell alias Moltan, priest, professed monk of Crowland Abbey, OSB, Lincoln dioc., seeks a licence to serve with a curate or his deputy.* Reg. 2bis, fol. 393v.

[Florentie], iii kal. Novembris. Supplicatur sanctitati vestre pro parte devoti vestri fratris Ricardi Michell' alias dicti Moltan', presbiteri, monachus professus [*sic*] monasterii de Croyland ordinis sancti Benedicti Lincolniensis diocesis, quatinus sibi ut de sui superioris licentia ad acquirendum victum et vestitum cum quocumque curato vel eius locum tenenti [valeat] libere stare et in divinis servire officiis in locis debitis et congruis, cum facultatibus [*recte* facultates] illius monasterii non suppetant, licentiam dignemini misericorditer impartiri de gratia speciali.

Fiat de speciali N.

586. [Florence], 1 November 1442. Same licence as **554** sought by John Benet, priest, Lincoln dioc.[191] *Fiat de speciali N.* Reg. 2bis, fol. 393v.

587. [Florence], 1 November 1442. Supplication on the part of Robert Dyktvy, clerk, Lincoln dioc., for the pope to grant him a dispensation so that, notwithstanding his defect of age, provided that he has reached the age of 23, he may be promoted to all holy orders and minister in them. *Fiat de speciali N.* Reg. 2bis, fol. 393v.

588. [Florence], 6 November 1442. Same licence as **554** sought by Richard Langstrothir, priest, Carlisle dioc.[192] *Fiat de speciali N.* Reg. 2bis, fol. 394v.

589. [*Florence*], *15 November 1442. Robert Hylle, notary by apostolic authority and married clerk, Bath [and Wells] dioc., seeks a dispensation to act as a scribe or registrar in any ecclesiastical court in Canterbury province.* Reg. 2bis, fol. 395r.

[Florentie], xvii kal. Decembris. Supplicatur humiliter vestre sanctitati ex parte devoti vestri Roberti Hylle, apostolica auctoritate notarii et clerici coniugati Battoniensis diocesis, quod cum ipse pro sua sustentatione officii notariatus in aliqua curiarum provincie Cantuariensis et in causis spiritualibus, etiam ubi ad correctionem anime, etiam si ex iudicis officio, proceditur, coram iudice quocumque ecclesiastico seu notionem et iurisdictionem ecclesiasticum [*recte* ecclesiasticam] habente etiam inferiore episcopo, ut scriba exercere ac registrationis seu registri custos existere desideret, et obstantibus certis constitutionibus synodalibus seu provincialibus a sede apostolica tamen non confirmatis impune non possit, quatinus sedes apostolica super premissis ut non obstantibus constitutionibus predictis exponens ipse dictum officium exercere ac iudex, vicarius et officialis quibuscumque [*recte* quicumque], etiam, ut prefertur, [coram] episcopo inferiore, eum ad dictum notoriatus et custodis officium admittere recipereque impune libere ac licite valeat et possit [*recte* valeant et possint] secum necnon cum huiusmodi iudicibus, officialibus et vicariis misericorditer dispensare dignemini de gratia speciali.

Fiat ut infra N.

---

[191] He was granted an indult of plenary remission *in mortis articulo* on 13 December 1442 (*CPL*, ix. 301).
[192] Presumably the Richard Langstrother, said to be of noble birth, who supplicated for BCnL at Oxford in 1448, having studied for five years at Cambridge and three at Oxford; he was admitted thus in 1449. He was dead by September 1467. For his university career and benefices, see *BRUC*, 351; *BRUO*, ii.1098–9; *CPL*, x. 24, 161.

590. [Florence], 23 December 1442. Same licence as **519**(?) sought by Robert Barnebus [*recte* Barneby?], priest, York dioc.[193] *Fiat de speciali N.* Reg. 2bis, fol. 404r.

591. [*Florence*], *4 January 1443*. *William Petri, a married clerk, Rochester dioc., notary public by apostolic authority, requests a dispensation to exercise his office of notary in any spiritual courts of Canterbury province in spiritual cases as a scribe or registrar.*[194] Reg. 2 bis, fol. 407v.

> [Florentie], ii non. Ianuarii. Exponitur sanctitati vestre pro parte devoti vestri Wilhelmi Petri, clerici coniugati Rossensis [*recte* Roffensis] diocesis, publici apostolica auctoritate notarii, qui officium notar' in quibuscumque spiritualibus curi[i]s provincie Cantuariensis et in causis spiritualibus eciam ubi ad correctionem animarum et ex iudicis solum officio procedatur coram iudice ecclesiastico quocumque seu alio notionem ac iurisdictionem ecclesiasticam habente eciam episcopo inferiore ut scriba seu alias registrarius exercere ac registracionis seu registri custos existere desiderat et obstantibus ut asseritur quibusdam constitutionibus synodalibus seu provincialibus in contrarium editis id facere impune non possit nec aliquis iudex ordinarius presertim episcopus inferior ad dictum officium absque certarum penarum incursu acceptare valeat. Supplicatur igitur sanctitati vestre pro parte dicti exponentis quatinus secum et cum ipsis iudicibus aliisve huiusmodi curiis presidentibus vel alias huiusmodi iurisdictionem sive nocionem qualitercumque habentibus super hiis ut non obstantibus constitutionibus predictis officium ipsum modo premisso libere et licite exercere ac iudex archidiaconusque vicarius et officialis seu alias iurisdictionem habens, quicumque[195] sit, eciam si ut prefertur episcopus inferior existat, ipsum ad dictum notarii et registratoris ac custodis officium admittere, recipere et acceptare etc. [possit misericorditer dispensare dignemini].

> Fiat ut infra N.

592. [*Florence*], *11 January 1443.* *The abbot of Reading Abbey, OSB, Salisbury dioc.,*[196] *seeks a faculty and licence to dispense six monks of his abbey from the defect of age.* Reg. 2bis, fol. 403r.

---

[193] The entry is too abbreviated to be absolutely certain but most closely resembles **519**: 'Supplicatur sanctitati vestre ... quatinus sibi ut in quacumque universitate studii generalis iur' etc. audire etc.' The supplicant may be the Robert Barneby, York dioc., *magister* and priest by 1459, recorded at Oxford as a witness in 1442 and 1459 (*BRUO*, i.111).

[194] Doubtless the William Petir, clerk, Rochester dioc., married once only, to a virgin, and notary public by papal authority, who obtained a similar papal grant on 14 February 1443 to exercise his office of notary in any spiritual courts of the city, diocese and province of Canterbury in spiritual cases and act as a scribe or registrary etc. (*CPL*, ix. 287). See also *Reg. Roffense*, 510, 571, 577, 588.

[195] Corrected from 'quibusque'.

[196] Thomas Henley was abbot from 1431 until his death on 11 November 1445 (Smith, *Heads of Religious Houses*, iii. 61). As abbot he obtained an indult on 4 September 1443 for himself and his successors to give any of the abbey's monks their first tonsure and bless its vestments and ornaments of divine worship (*CPL*, ix. 352).

[Florentie], iii id' Ianuarii. Supplicatur sanctitati vestre pro parte devoti vestri A., abbatis monasterii de Radyng' ordinis sancti Benedicti Saresburiensis diocesis, quatinus sibi, ut divinus cultus in eodem monasterio augmentetur, cum sex monachis suis dicti monasterii qui defectum etatis patiuntur ut, dicto defectu non obstante, postquam vicesimum tercium etatis annum compleverint et ad minores, subdyaconatus et dyaconatus ordines promoti fuerint, ut [sic] ad sacros presbiteratus ordines promoveri possint, cum ipsis libere etc. [facultatem et licentiam dispensandi impartiri misericorditer dignemini]. (*Approved with* **593**.)

593. [Florence], 11 January 1443. Same faculty and licence as **592** sought on the part of A., abbot of the monastery of Osney, OSA, Lincoln dioc.[197] *Concessum de speciali in presentia d. Cardinalis Pe.* (Approved with **592**.) Reg. 2bis, fol. 403r.

594. [Florence], 25 January 1443. William Lyndesey, clerk, Lincoln dioc.,[198] requests that [the pope grant] him [a dispensation] so that, notwithstanding his defect of age, provided that he has reached the age of 23, he may be promoted to holy orders and minister in them. *Fiat de speciali N.* Reg. 2bis, fol. 409v.

595. [Florence], 25 January 1443. William Lyndesey, clerk, Lincoln dioc., requests [that the pope grant that he may be promoted to holy orders by any Catholic bishop having the grace and communion of the apostolic see and minister in them], as on certain reasonable grounds he cannot conveniently approach his ordinary to receive them. *Fiat N.* Reg. 2bis, fol. 409v.

596. [*Florence*], *29 January 1443. Robert Darsy, clerk, Coventry and Lichfield dioc., incurred a penalty for erasing what he thought was an error in a friend's papal letter; he seeks absolution from this sentence.* Reg. 2bis, fol. 414r.

[Florentie], iiii kal. Februarii. Exponitur sanctitati vestre pro parte devoti vestri Roberti Darsy, clerici Lichefeldensis et Coventrensis diocesis, quod cum olim ipse certas litteras apostolicas pro quodam amico suo sibi de Romana curia missas legisset et in data ipsarum litterarum propter annum bisextum 'primo secundo kalendas Martii' scriptum invenisset, prefatus exponens, credens scriptorem in hoc errasse et amicum suum illius littere detrimentum propterea sustinuisse, ex mera et pura simplicitate sine malicia aliqua, ac penitus ignorans ex hoc aliquam penam seu sententiam incurrisse, unam illarum dictionum, putans illam superfluam fore et unum [sic?] ingenerare, abrasit. Demum idem exponens per quendam doctorem postmodum informatus penam etc. incurrisse. Supplicatur humiliter etc. [eidem

---

[197] Thomas Hooknorton was elected as abbot in 1430 and died in office in 1452 (Smith, *Heads of Religious Houses*, iii. 498). As abbot he obtained an indult on 11 May 1446 for himself and his successors to have a portable altar and celebrate mass or have it celebrated in the presence of household servants (*CPL*, ix. 587).

[198] Probably the same as William Lyndesey, deacon, Lincoln dioc., who was to be appointed a notary public by the abbot of Bourn under a papal faculty of 1 June 1443 (*CPL*, ix. 344).

Eugenius IV (1431–1447)

sanctitati] quatinus ipsum a dicta sententia si quam incurrit etc. [absolvi mandare dignemini].

Fiat de speciali N.

597. [*Florence*], *1 February 1443. William Lydesey, clerk, Lincoln dioc., was ordered to record as a notary public accusations and proceedings at the trial of some laymen, who were not executed or mutilated; he seeks a declaration that he incurred no* inhabilitas *or infamy and may be promoted to all orders.* Reg. 2bis, fol. 414v.

[Florentie], kal. Februarii. Exponitur sanctitati vestre pro parte devoti vestri Wilhelmi Lydesey, clerici Lincolniensis diocesis, quod cum olim certi laici de quibusdam criminibus suspecti et iuxta statuta et ordinationes illius patrie coram duodecim viris legalibus, qui ad hoc ut inquisitiones ad huiusmodi terminibus [*sic*] facerent deputati [fuerunt], per eorum inimicos accusati essent, prefatus exponens post inquisitiones de terminibus predictis dictata et accusationes dictorum duodecim virorum in forma processus tamquam publicus notarius in presentia iudicum maleficiorum de mandato sui domini successive alternatis vicibus iuris ignorantia emanualiter [*recte* manualiter] scripsit. Cum autem de processibus et accusationibus per eum sic scriptis mors de dictis laicis ~~excu~~ accusatis minime subsecuta fuerit aut membrorum mutilatio, cupiatque ex magno devotionis fervore ad omnes ordines etiam sacros promoveri et in ipsis licite ministrare, et ne aliqui simplices et iuris ignari seu ipsius exponentis emuli in eum labia detractionis aperire possunt, asserentes ipsum inhabilitatis et infamie maculam propter premissa incurrisse, et [ad] obstruendum ora dictorum emulorum in futurum sibi ut [*recte* forsan] obloquentium et ad servandum eius conscientiam, supplicatur sanctitati vestre pro parte dicti exponentis quatinus ipsum premissorum occasione nullam inhabilitatis seu infamie maculam incurrisse quodque libere ad omnes ordines promoveri et [in] ipsis licite ministrare valeat dignemini misericorditer declarare.

Fiat ut infra N. Signanda per fiat de speciali quod promoveri possit.

598. [Florence], 6 February 1443. The pope is informed on the part of Robert Asyl, priest, Lincoln dioc., that guilelessly (*tamquam simplex*) and in ignorance of the law he formerly had himself promoted to all holy orders while under age but otherwise legally and ministered and celebrated in them. The pope is requested to [order his absolution from such excesses and grant him a dispensation from irregularity]. *Fiat de speciali N.* Reg. 2bis, fol. 414v.

599. [Florence, 12 February 1443]. William Bartzam, acolyte, professed canon of St Mary's monastery, 'Lukelen',[199] OSA, Norwich dioc., requests that the pope [grant] him [a dispensation] so that, notwithstanding his defect of age [. . .].[200] Reg. 2bis, fol. 416r.

600. [Florence], 12 February 1443. Supplication on the part of Thomas Bindloy, anchorite recluse (*anacorita reclusus*), Norwich dioc., for the pope [to grant] him [a

---

[199] Perhaps Letheringham Priory (Suff.), dedicated to BVM.
[200] This entry was left incomplete and marked 'va-cat'.

licence] so that he may visit in person as a pilgrim the Holy Sepulchre and other places overseas, including the *limina* of the apostles SS. Peter and Paul, notwithstanding provincial and synodal constitutions and ordinances and those of any order. *Fiat de speciali N.* Reg. 2bis, fol. 416r.

601. [*Florence*], *12 February 1443. Leonard Crosby, priest, Norwich dioc., seeks a licence so that he may not be compelled by rectors to serve in their parish churches at divine offices.* Reg. 2bis, fol. 416v.

[Florentie], xviii kal. Martii. Exponit sanctitati vestri devotus vester Leonardus Crosby, presbiter Norwicensis diocesis, quod cum consuetudo sive constitutio provincialis vel synodalis in illis partibus habeatur ut quilibet curatus seu rector parrochialis ecclesie quemlibet presbiterum secularem non habentem curam animarum cum litteris et mandato ordinarii sub pena excommunicationis ut ecclesie curate cum magna provisione deserviat illamque gubernat in divinis, ipso presbitero invito, coartari et compelli [*recte* coartare et compellere] potest in maximum ipsius presbiteri preiudicium et gravamen. Supplicat igitur eidem sanctitati dictus exponens quatinus sibi ut, constitutionibus et ordinationibus provincialibus et synodalibus ac consuetudinibus si que sint non obstantibus, per dictos rectores parrochialium ecclesiarum ipsis et eorum ecclesiis serviendum in divinis aut per aliquem alium a quoquomodo compelli nec coartari possit licentiam dignemini misericorditer impartiri de gratia speciali.

Fiat de speciali N.

602. [Florence], 13 February 1443. John Zatys, priest, Norwich dioc., requests the same licence as **601**. *Fiat de speciali N.* Reg. 2bis, fol. 416v.

603. [Florence], 13 February 1443. John Rolegrave, priest, Norwich dioc., requests the same licence as **601**. *Fiat de speciali N.* Reg. 2bis, fol. 416v.

604. [*Florence*], *14 February 1443. John Kilborne, acolyte, Norwich dioc., who has chosen to become a hermit, seeks letters dimissory.* Reg. 2bis, fol. 416v.

[Florentie], xvi kal. Martii. Dignetur sanctitas vestra devoto vestro Iohanni Kilborne, acolito Norwicensis diocesis, quatinus, sibi gratiam specialem facientes, cum ipse ex magno devotione cupit deo famulari et ipse vitam heremiticam elegit et renunciavit mundo, sed propter magnam distantiam ad suum ordinarium de facili transire non potest, quapropter petit ut possit recipere omnes ordines a quocumque catholico episcopo habenti executionem sive potestatem.

Fiat de speciali N.

605. [Florence], 18 February 1443. The pope is informed on the part of John Royke, scholar, Norwich dioc., that he wishes to be promoted to all holy orders, but because of his defect of age, he being 23 years of age, he cannot be promoted without a papal dispensation; hence he requests that [the pope grant] him a licence to be promoted after he reaches the age of 24, and that he may minister in these orders after his promotion. *Fiat de speciali N.* Reg. 2bis, fol. 417r.

606. [Florence], 18 February 1443. The pope is informed on the part of John Harald, scholar, Norwich dioc., that he wishes out of great fervour of devotion to be promoted to all orders, but because of his defect of age he cannot obtain them; hence he requests that [the pope grant] him a licence [to be promoted] after he reaches the age of 24, [and that he may minister in these orders after his promotion]. *Fiat de speciali N.* Reg. 2bis, fol. 417r.

607. [Florence], 18 February 1443. Supplication on the part of William Bunche, clerk, Norwich dioc., for the pope to grant him [a dispensation] so that, notwithstanding his defect of age, provided that he has reached the age of 23, he may be promoted successively to all holy orders. *Fiat de speciali N.* Reg. 2bis, fol. 417r.

608. [Florence], 18 February 1443. John Stanford, scholar, Lincoln dioc.,[201] requests that [the pope grant] that he [may be promoted to all orders] by any Catholic bishop having the grace and communion of the apostolic see [and minister in them], as on certain reasonable grounds he cannot conveniently approach his ordinary to receive them. *Fiat de speciali N.* Reg. 2bis, fol. 417r.

609. *[Florence], 22 February 1443. John Salli, priest, perpetual vicar of Happisburgh parish church, Norwich dioc.,[202] seeks a licence to live elsewhere in that parish since his vicarage is so inadequate.* Reg. 2bis, fol. 418v.

> [Florentie], viii kal. Martii. Exponitur sanctitati vestre pro parte devoti vestri Iohannis Salli, presbiteri, perpetui vicarii in ecclesia parrochiali de Hapesburch Norwicensis diocesis, quod cum habitatio ipsius vicarie in eadem parrochia existente [*sic*] tanta exigua et structa existit quod exponens ipse commode et decenter cum sua familia stare non potest, et ne \ab/ aliquo in eadem domo seu habitatione ipsius vicarie invitus residentiam facere coartari aut compelli potest, supplicatur sanctitati vestre pro parte dicti exponentis quatinus sibi ut in domo patriemi [*recte* paterna *or* patrini?] sui in eadem parrochia ex\cons/istente vel iuxta illam in aliquo alio loco honesto secundum status sui decentiam, dummodo tamen ipsa vicaria in divinis congrue deserviatur et in ipsis non defraudetur ac ipsa habitatio in omne conservatur, licentiam dignemini misericorditer impartiri, constitutionibus etc. [in contrarium editis non obstantibus]. (*Unsigned.*)

610. [Florence], 3 March 1443. Supplication on the part of John Bond, clerk, Norwich dioc., for the pope to grant him a dispensation so that, notwithstanding his defect of age, provided that he has reached the age of 23, he may be promoted to all, even holy, orders and minister [in them]. *Fiat de speciali N.* Reg. 2bis, fol. 420r.

---

[201] Perhaps the same as John Steyle *alias* Stanford, perpetual vicar of Aldenham (Herts.), Lincoln dioc., who was granted a licence to farm out his benefice for seven years while studying at a university on 8 May 1445 (*CPL*, ix. 488). He was possibly the *magister* John Staunford recorded at Oxford in 1447 (*BRUO*, iii.1768).

[202] Perhaps the John Salle, DCnL, who was a fellow of Trinity Hall, Cambridge, in 1455–6, and rector of Burnham Westgate (Norf.) till death; he died by 1498 (*BRUC*, 503).

611. [Florence], 5 March 1443. John Pyke, clerk, Norwich dioc., requests the pope to grant that he may be promoted to priest's orders [and minister in them] after he reaches the age of 24, as he is now aged 23 and wishes to serve the Lord forever. *Fiat de speciali N.* Reg. 2bis, fol. 420r.

612. [Florence], 5 March 1443. Same grant as **611** sought by John Lavemam, acolyte, Norwich dioc., aged 23. *Fiat de speciali N.* Reg. 2bis, fol. 420r.

613. *[Florence], 6 March 1443. Stephen Ywys, deacon, Norwich dioc., seeks letters dimissory with a dispensation to be promoted to the priesthood after reaching the age of 23.* Reg. 2bis, fol. 420v.

> [Florentie], ii non. Martii. Exponit sanctitati vestre devotus vester Stephanus Ywys, diaconus Norwicensis diocesis, quatinus cum eo ut, non obstante defectu etatis quem patitur, dummodo vicesimum tercium sue etatis annum compleverit, ad sacrum presbiteratus ordinem etiam a quocumque antistite catholico gratiam et communionem sedis apostolice habente, cum ordinarium suum pro receptione ordinum commode adire non potest aliisque rationabilibus causis, ad dictum presbiteratum ordinem libere recipere [*sic*] et licite ~~retinere~~ promoveri et in ipsis [*recte* ipso] ministrare valeat dignemini misericorditer dispensare necnon licentiam impartiri etc.
>
> Fiat de speciali N.

614. [Florence, 6 March 1443]. Supplication on the part of William Berker, clerk, Norwich dioc., for the pope to grant him [a dispensation] so that, notwithstanding his defect of age, provided that he has reached the age of 23, he may be promoted to all orders and minister in them. *Fiat de speciali N.* Reg. 2bis, fol. 420v.

615. *[Florence], 6 March 1443. William Clerck, priest, Lincoln dioc., fears that he has incurred excommunication for not serving in parish churches when required to do so by his local ordinary; he seeks absolution from that sentence and a licence so that he may not be compelled to do so.* Reg. 2bis, fol. 420v.

> [Florentie], pridie non. Martii. Exponit sanctitati vestre devotus vester Wilhelmus Clerck, presbiter Lincolniensis diocesis, quod cum quedam consuetudo seu constitutio provincialis alias synodalis in partibus illis existat in qua cavetur quod quilibet presbiter non habens curam animarum ad serviendum in ecclesiis parrochialibus et ad curam animarum ad instanciam vestrorum [*recte* rectorum] parrochialium invitus per ordinarium loci sub pena excommunicationis lata sententia, cum certa pensione pro dicto servitio deputata, etc. [coartari et compelli possit], hic dubitet forte vigore consuetudinis seu constitutionis etc. [dictam sententiam incurrisse]. Supplicatur etc. quatinus, non obstante consuetudine etc. [huiusmodi, ipsum a dicta sententia si quam incurrit absolvi mandare et sibi, ut ipse ad serviendum in ecclesiis parrochialibus per ordinarium loci compelli et coartari non possit, licentiam dignemini misericorditer impartiri de gratia speciali].
>
> Fiat de speciali N.

616. [Florence], 6 March 1443. Same grant as **608**[203] sought by William Jonson, acolyte, Lincoln dioc. *Fiat de speciali N.* Reg. 2bis, fol. 420v.

[203] Like **608** this entry does not specify which kind of orders the supplicant wished to receive.

NICHOLAS V
(1447–1455)

De diversis formis

617. [*Rome*], *26 February 1448. Fr Thomas Elkyngton, monk, priest, professed of the monastery of SS. Peter, Paul and Oswald, [Bardney], OSB, Lincoln dioc., was imprisoned by his abbot but escaped and came to the Roman Curia; he requests absolution and a licence to return to his monastery or transfer to another of the same order.*[1] Reg. 3, fol. 8r.

[Rome], 4 kal. Marcii. Beatissime pater, supplicat humiliter sanctitati vestre devotus orator eiusdem frater Thomas Elkyngton, monachus, presbiter, professus monasterii apostolorum Petri et Pauli ac sancti Oswaldi regis et martiris ordinis sancti Benedicti Lincolniensis diocesis, quod cum olim abbas suus dicti monasterii nullis precedentibus iustis causis concepit rancorem et inimiciciam [*sic*] contra ipsum et ipsum exponentem in carceribus retrudi fecisset et ipse exponens pluries ipsum abbatem rogari fecisset ut sibi iusticiam ministraret et sicut iniuste captivum de non deberet et ipse abbas ipsum audire nollet, ipse tediatus dictis carceribus cum iniuste detineretur diruttis [*recte* diruptis] dictis carceribus sine licencia auffugit et de dicto monasterio recessit et ad Romanam curiam venit, habitu suo tamen semper retento, propter quod timet excommunicationis incurrisse sentenciam in tales adhuc per constituciones et statuta dicti ordinis generaliter promulgatam; cum autem tamen propter premissa et alias rationabiles causas animum suum ad reditum dicti monasterii inclinare non possit, ne in opprobrium dicti ordinis et detrimentum anime sue cogatur per mundum evagare, quatinus dignemini ipsum a dicta sentencia, si quam incurrit, et excessibus huiusmodi ac peccatis suis aliis etc. absolvi mandare et ut ad dictum monasterium suum vel ad aliquod aliud monasterium eiusdem ordinis professionis et habitus paris vel [artioris] observancie regularis se transferre valeat licenciam concedere misericorditer de gratia speciali.

Fiat de speciali D. s. †. Datum Rome quarto kal. Marcii anno 2° Ant'.

618. [*Rome*], *1 March 1448. William Wysbech, priest, professed of St Alban's Abbey, OSB, Lincoln dioc., seeks a dispensation and licence to transfer to Wymondham Priory, Norwich dioc.*[2] Reg. 3, fol. 8v.

[Rome], kal. Martii. Exponitur sanctitati vestre pro parte devoti vestri Willelmi Wysbech', presbiteri professi monasterii sancti Albani ordinis sancti

---

[1] The same Thomas Elkyngton, monk of Bardney Abbey (Lincs.), petitioned the papal chancery that as the serf of a certain nobleman in the realm of England he might not receive holy orders or be appointed to dignities without that noble's consent according to certain constitutions of that realm; he obtained a papal grant on 1 April 1444 that he might receive all holy orders and be appointed to any dignities of that monastery where he made profession (*CPL*, ix. 423).

[2] Presumably the William Wubeche who with three other monks of St Albans, all in priest's orders, was granted a papal licence on 12 December 1448 to transfer to Wymondham without their abbot's consent (*CPL*, x. 46). Wymondham was a dependency of St Albans until it became an independent abbey in 1449.

Benedicti Lincolniensis diocesis sedi apostolice subiecti, quod ipse sana conscientia et \ad/ quietem animi sui et ex certis aliis rationabilibus causis animum suum ad hoc moventibus in dicto monasterio remanere non potest. Supplicatur eidem sanctitati vestre pro parte dicti exponentis quatinus secum ut ad monasterium de Faymundham dicti ordinis Norwicensis diocesis hac vice se transferre et in eo altissimo gratum reddere famulatum possit et valeat dispensare ac licentiam impartiri dignemini de gratia speciali, constitutionibus et ordinationibus dictorum monasterii et ordinis ac aliis contrariis non obstantibus quibuscumque cum clausis opportunis.

Fiat de speciali ad monasterium eiusdem ordinis, professionis et habitus, vel artioris. D. s. †.

619. [Rome], 1 March 1448. Supplication on the part of Robert Kemp, deacon, Norwich dioc., for the pope to grant him a dispensation so that on reaching the age of 24 he may be promoted to priest's orders and minister in them. *Fiat de speciali D. s. †.* Reg. 3, fol. 8v.

620. [Rome], 6 March 1448. Supplication on the part of Richard Wynyene of Ixworth, deacon, Norwich dioc., who wishes out of great fervour of devotion to be promoted to priest's orders, for the pope to grant him a dispensation so that, notwithstanding his defect of age, on reaching the age of 24 he may be promoted to priest's orders and minister in them. *Fiat de speciali quem* [recte *quam*] *primum xxiiii annum attigerit D. s. †.* Reg. 3, fol. 14v.

621. *[Rome], 20 March 1448. Fr Robert Burg, priest, Lincoln dioc., was persuaded to enter Nottingham convent, OFM, York dioc., by certain friars at the age of about 10 and then transferred to Reading convent, Salisbury dioc., where he made profession. He ran away several times before the age of 19 when the friars had him promoted to all holy orders. He then left the order without permission and acted as a secular priest. He seeks absolution from excommunication, apostasy and these excesses and a dispensation from irregularity.* Reg. 3, fol. 25r.

[Rome], xiii kal. Aprilis. Exponit sanctitati vestre devotus vester frater Robertus Burg, presbiter Lincolniensis diocesis, quod ipse olim in decimo vel circa sue etatis anno constitutus existens conventum Notinghan' ordinis fratrum minorum Eboracensis diocesis ex indictione [recte inductione] et allectione quorumdam fratrum dicti ordinis intravit, et ne parrentes [sic] ipsius perciperent inductionem predictam, custos et fratres dicti conventus ipsum exponentem eodem anno ad conventum de Redyng dicti ordinis Sacresbriensis [sic] diocesis transtulerunt, in quo postquam complevit annum, computato tempore quo fuit in priori conventu, exponens professionem regularem emisit ibidem. Deinde vero antequam xii dicti etatis sue annum complevisset ac professionem emisisset, dictum conventum illicentiatus exivit, credens professionem predictam nullam et invalidam fuisse. Postmodum vero iterum in duobus dicti ordinis conventibus variis vicibus reversus extitit et aliquando de eisdem absque licentia exivit, habitu tamen suo retento. Postquam vero ad decimumnovum dicte etatis annum pervenit, fratres dicti ordinis fecerunt eum ad omnes sacros ordines promoveri et in ipsis ministrare, et ex post in diversis dicti ordinis conventibus cum dicto habitu permansit. Demum ex

Nicholas V (1447–1455)

quadam animi levitate, habitu et ordinis [*sic*] penitus derelictis, illenciatus [*recte* illicenciatus] exivit et ad seculum est reversus, in quo dampnabiliter et evagando parrochiales ecclesias rexit, et parrochionorum [*sic*] confessiones audivit, ac ipsos in casibus anime forte sibi non permissis absolvit, [et] ecclesiastica sacramenta ministravit. Nunc autem ad cor domino faciente reversus, ad aliquem dicti ordinis conventum redire cupiens, supplicat igitur sanctitati vestre quatinus ipsum a generali propter premissa excommunicationis sententia, apostasie reatu, excessibus huiusmodi ac peccatis suis aliis absolvi mandare et super irregularitate ex premissis dicto modo contracta quodque in suis ordinibus omnibus ministrare et ad aliquem conventum dicti ordinis in quo benivolos inveniat receptores transferri valeat misericorditer dispensari dignemini de gratia speciali.

Fiat de speciali D. sancte crucis.

622. [*Rome*], *20 March 1448. John Donnyng, priest, rector of Aston parish church, York dioc., seeks absolution from perjury, incest, misappropriating the property of his church, excommunication, and other excesses.* Reg. 3, fol. 25r.

[Rome], xiii kal. Aprilis. Exponit sanctitati vestre devotus vester Iohannes Donnyng, presbiter, rector parrocialis ecclesie de Aston' Eboracensis diocesis, quod ipse olim quoddam periurium precomisit, videlicet quia contra iuramentum a se prestitum aliquociens reversus fuit ad locum habitacionis cuiusdam mulieris de qua quidam sui emuli eum iniuste de incontinencia diffamaverant. Preterea idem exponens quandam mulierem in cognacione spirituali sibi attinentem actu fornicario carnaliter cognovit, ac eciam inciscit quasdam arbores dicte ecclesie parrochialis, quas in restauracione domus dicte ecclesie poni fecit, propter quod obiectum est sibi quod bona dicte ecclesie dilapidaverunt [*sic*], necnon ad redimendum quandum [*sic*] uxoracionem suam assignavit quasdam decimas garborum ex arbitramento quorumdam clerici et laici, postquam extitit in possessionem dicte ecclesie sue, cuidam Thome \Tylney/, a quo eandem ecclesiam habuit permutacionis causa, super quibus supplicat humiliter sanctitati vestre dictus exponens quatinus ipsum a reatibus periurii, incestus, delapidacionis bonorum (si que fuerit propter dictas arborum incisiones, solucionem decimarum garbarum pro redimendo uxacionem [*sic*] suam predictam), excommunicationis sententia (si quam per constitutiones provinciales et synodales aut alias propter premissa incurrit), excessibus huiusmodi aut peccatis suis aliis absolvere seu absolvi mandare dignemini ut in forma.

Fiat de speciali D. sancte crucis.

623. [Rome], 15 April 1448. The pope is informed on the part of Fr John Bokenham, subdeacon, professed of Norwich convent, OP, that previously he guilessly (*tamquam simplex*) and in ignorance of the law had himself promoted to subdeacon's orders without a clerical tonsure but otherwise legally, and subsequently received the tonsure (*se misit clericali caractere insigniri*). The pope is therefore requested to grant him absolution from the aforesaid excesses and a dispensation so that he may exercise his existing orders and be promoted to all others. *Fiat de speciali D. sancte crucis.* Reg. 3, fol. 31v.

624. [*Rome*], *15 April 1448. John Pakyngnton, priest, professed canon of Kirby Bellers Priory, OSA, Lincoln dioc., left the priory with his superior's permission, put aside his habit and celebrated divine offices as a secular priest. He seeks absolution from excommunication, other censures and the aforesaid excesses and a dispensation from irregularity or* inhabilitas. *Reg. 3, fol. 32r.*

[Rome], 17 kal. Maii. Beatissime pater, exponit sanctitati vestre devotus vester orator Iohannes Pakyngton', presbiter, canonicus professus prioratus de Kirkby ordinis sancti Augustini Lincolniensis diocesis, quod cum ipse olim de licentia sui superioris dictum prioratum exivisset et suum habitum non causa apostatandi deposuisset, demum non in contemptum clavium divina officia ut secularis presbiter celebravit et alias inmiscuit se eisdem, propter quod sententiam excommunicationis et alias censuras ecclesiasticas per constitutiones dicti ordinis timet incurrisse. Supplicat igitur sanctitati vestre quatinus ipsum ab huiusmodi sententiis et censuris ecclesiasticis ac excessibus huiusmodi ac peccatis suis aliis misericorditer absolvi mandare [dignemini] secumque super irregularitate vel inhabilitatis macula ex premissis forsam [*sic*] contracta dispensare de gratia speciali.

Fiat de speciali D. s. † I.

625. [*Rome*], *15 April 1448. Fr John Baret, priest, professed canon of Shouldham Priory, Gilbertine order, Norwich dioc., asked his superior's permission to visit Rome and was refused, but he left his priory, put aside his habit and ministered as a secular priest. He seeks absolution from excommunication and these excesses, a dispensation from irregularity, and permission to stay and minister in Rome then return to his priory or transfer to another of that order. Reg. 3, fol. 32r.*

[Rome], 17 kal. Maii. Beatissime pater, exponit sanctitati vestre devotus vester orator frater Iohannes Baret, presbiter, canonicus professus prioratus de Schuldham ordinis sancti Gilberti de Simpurghen' sub regula sancti Augustini degentium [*sic*] Norwicensis diocesis, quod cum ipse olim licenciam a suo superiori pecusset [*recte* petisset] ut limina beatorum Petri et Pauli de Urbe pro salute anime sue visitare posset, qua licentia petita licet non obtenta, ipsum prioratum exivit et habitum suum non animo apostatandi dimisit et in habitu secularis aliquandiu vagavit, et in suis ordinibus divina officia celebravit ac alia sacramenta certis Christi fidelibus ministravit; qui nunc de premissis sibi facit scrupulum conscientie et timet propter premissa sententiam excommunicationis incurrisse et desiderat de huiusmodi sententia et excessibus absolvi, et aliquemdiu [*sic*] postmodum in curia et Urbe Romana permanere et pro salute anime sue in suis ordinibus ministrare, et demum ad suum monasterium vel aliud monasterium huiusmodi ordinis paris vel artioris observantie redire. Supplicat igitur sanctitati vestre quatinus ipsum a sententia excommunicationis et excessibus huiusmodi misericorditer absolvi mandare, secum super irregularitate ex premissis contracta dispensare et quod libere in Urbe in suis ordinibus possit ministrare et demum ad dictum suum vel aliud monasterium paris vel artioris observantie transire et se transferre valeat licentiam misericorditer impartiri dignemini de gratia speciali.

Fiat de speciali D. sancte crucis.

626. [*Rome*], *16 June 1448. Fr William Stirte, priest, professed monk of Glastonbury Abbey, OSB, Bath and Wells dioc., accused before his superior of various charges of incontinence, was granted a licence by his superior to transfer to another monastery of his order, but he was refused admission and then went to the Roman Curia without permission. He seeks absolution from excommunication, fornication and other crimes of incontinence, a dispensation from irregularity and* inhabilitas, *and rehabilitation so that he may be appointed to any offices of his order.*[3] Reg. 3, fol. 36v.

[Rome], xvi kal. Iulii. Exponit sanctitati vestre devotus vester frater Wilhelmus Stirte, presbiter, monachus professus monasterii beate Marie de Glastonie ordinis sancti Benedicti Barthoniensis [*sic*] diocesis, quod cum ipse olim de concubinatu et quibusdam aliis criminibus incontinencie apud suum superiorem fuisset accusatus, superior suus prefatus scandalis que inde possent exoriri cupiens obviare licencia[m] transferendi se ad quoddam aliud monasterium eiusdem ordinis, professus [*recte* professionis], habitus [et] paris abservancie [*sic*] regularis concessit, et cum exponens ipse tanquam filius obediencie ad huiusmodi monasterium se transtulisset et recipi in eodem recusaretur, malecontentus intercessit et nulla alia super hoc licentia obtenta habitu suo tamen semper retento ad Romanam curiam venit, propter quod excommunicationis incurrit sententiam in tales generaliter promulgatam, et sic ligatus tamquam simplex et iuris ignarus et non [in] contemptum clavium divina celebravit officia et alias inmiscuit se eisdem. Supplicat igitur sanctitati vestre quatinus ipsum a dicta sententia et fornicationis huiusmodi reatibus ac aliis criminibus incontinencie et excessibus huiusmodi atque peccatis suis aliis absolvi mandare et super irregularitate et inhabilitate dicto modo contracta dispensare eumque ad pristinum statum prout antequam prefata fierunt erat [*sic*] restituere misericorditer dignemini, sic et taliter ut ad dignitates, beneficia et officia atque alia quecumque sui ordinis privilegia elegi et assumi posset ex [*sic*] premissis et aliis in contrarium facientibus non obstantibus quibuscumque concedere et indulgere dignemini de gratia speciali.

Fiat de speciali D. s. †.

---

[3] William Strete, monk of Glastonbury, was signified for arrest by a royal writ of 1 November probably 1448 or 1449 (Logan, 195). He was granted a royal pardon on 24 February 1449 for obtaining a papal bull to transfer to another house or order (*CPR 1446–52*, 218). In accordance with this bull, the bishop of Bath and Wells granted him a licence on 14 March 1449 to transfer to Thetford Priory (Norf.) at his own request and apparently with his abbot's consent (*Reg. Bekynton* 409). He was still, however, styled a monk of Glastonbury on 7 August 1450 when he was granted a papal dispensation to hold a benefice with or without cure of souls for life (*CPL*, x. 170). He subsequently petitioned the pope that he had gone to Rome for the Jubilee (1450) with his abbot's consent, when the abbot of Bury St Edmunds, the king of England's proctor at the Curia, had him imprisoned at the instance of John Lax, clerk, Bath and Wells dioc. After three months he escaped when the other prisoners broke out, but when he returned to Glastonbury, he was excluded by the abbot. A papal mandate of 10 April 1451 ordered his absolution and readmission (*CPL*, x. 530–2).

627. [*Rome*], *28 August 1448. Fr Robert,*[4] *priest, professed of Marton Priory, OSA, York dioc., obtained a licence from his superior to leave that monastery for two years but thereafter he failed to return. He seeks absolution from excommunication and these excesses, dispensation from irregularity, and a licence to transfer to another monastery of the order.* Reg. 3, fol. 46r.

[Rome], v kal. Septembris. Exponitur sanctitati vestre pro parte devoti vestri fratris Roberti, presbiteri, professi monasterii de Marton ordinis sancti Augustini diocesis Eboracensis, quod ipse olim postquam licentiam a suo superiore extra ipsum standi per duos annos obtinuerat, lapsis dictis duobus annis ad ipsum monasterium redire neglexit, propter quod excommunicationis sententiam incurrit in tales generaliter promulgatam et sic ligatus tanquam simplex et iuris ignarus non tamen in contemptum clavium divina celebravit officia et alias inmiscuit se eisdem. Cum autem dictus exponens cor ad redditum dicti monasterii inclinare non possit cupiatque tamen sub regulari habitu ut tenetur perpetuo famulari, supplicatur igitur eidem sanctitati vestre pro parte dicti exponentis quatinus ipsum a dicta sententia et excessibus huiusmodi ac peccatis suis aliis misericorditer etc. absolvi secumque super irregularitate dicto modo contracta dispensari misericorditer mandare dignemini quodque ut ad unum aliud monasterium dicti ordinis paris vel artioris observantie regularis se transferre possit eidem concedere licenciam ut in forma.

Fiat in forma B. Vasaten.

628. [*Rome*], *31 January* [*1449*]. *Edmund Freman of Kersey, priest in Suffolk, Norwich dioc., seeks a licence and faculty so that he is not obliged under English provincial and synodal constitutions to serve the benefice of another priest as long as he lacks a benefice with cure of souls.* Reg. 3, fol. 62v.

[Rome], pridie kal. Februarii. Edmundo [*sic*] Freman de Kersey, presbitero in Sulfochia Norwicensis diocesis, [exponit] quod in regno Anglie quedam constitutiones provinciales et synodales existunt quibus caveri dicitur quod presbiteri non habentes beneficia curata ad serviendum aliis beneficiis etiam curatis aliorum presbiterorum eis etiam invitis compelli possunt, sed quia dictus exponens huiusmodi beneficium curatum non habet neque alicui beneficio curato aut alio servire vult aut potest sana conscientia, quare sibi ut quamdiu huiusmodi beneficium curatum non habuerit alicui beneficio curato servire non teneatur licentiam et facultatem petit impartiri.

Fiat de speciali D. s. †. I.

629. *Rome, 14 February 1449. John Salvage senior of Pottesgrove and his brother John Salvage junior, laymen, Lincoln dioc., fatally struck and wounded John Brigge, vicar of Pottesgrove parish church, priest, Lincoln dioc. They seek absolution from excommunication.* Reg. 3, fol. 49v.

Rome, xvi kal. Martii a° 2. Exponitur sanctitati vestre pro parte devotorum vestrorum Iohannis Salvage senioris de Pottesgrave et Iohannis iunioris Salvage fratrum carnalium, laicorum Lincolniensis [diocesis], quod ipsi olim quendam Iohannem Brigge, vicarium olim parrochialis ecclesie de

---

[4] Surname omitted.

Pottesgrave, presbiterum dicte diocesis, percusserunt et vulneraverunt, de quibus percussionibus et vulneracionibus diem suum clausit extremum, propter quod ipsi exponentes sententiam excommunicationis incurrerunt. Quare supplicatur eidem sanctitati vestre humiliter pro parte dictorum exponencium quatinus ipsos et eorum quemlibet a dicta sentencia excommunicationis quam propter hoc incurrerunt necnon ex [*sic*] aliis suis peccatis absolvere seu absolvi mandare dignemini de gratia speciali.

Fiat de speciali D. s. crucis.

630. [*Rome*], *5 December 1449. John Pakyngton, married clerk, Lincoln dioc., seeks to be absolved from excommunication and to be able to write letters of condemnation.* Reg. 3, fol. 69r.

[Rome], nonas Decembris. Supplicatur pro parte Iohannis Pakyngton, clerici coniugati Lincolniensis diocesis, absolutionem a quadam excommunicatione lata ab ordinario Cantuariensi [et] quod quando fuerit requisitus libere et licite scribere possit litteras condempnationis etc.

Fiat de speciali D. s. †.

631. [Rome], 16 December 1449. William (*Villelmus*) Onclade, priest, professed canon of the monastery of Notley (*Notthele*), OSA, Lincoln dioc., [left that monastery without permission where he had bound himself by vow of profession and wandered in the world, as a result of which he incurred the sentence of excommunication generally promulgated on such persons,] and thus bound he ministered. He requests [absolution and dispensation and that he may transfer to another monastery of the same order and] minister. *Fiat de speciali D. s. †. Committatur uni ex minoribus penitentiariis. Fiat D. s. †.* Reg. 3, fol. 71v.

632. [Rome], 16 December 1449. William (*Vilgelmus*) Onclade, priest, professed canon of the monastery of Notley (*Notele*), OSA, Lincoln dioc., [was ordained without the permission of his bishop and ministered. He requests absolution from excommunication and other excesses thereby contracted and a dispensation]. *Fiat de speciali D. s. †.* Reg. 3, fol. 71v.

633. [Rome, December] 1449. Fr William (*Villermus*) Pomis, priest, professed of the monastery of Christ, OSB, Canterbury dioc.,[5] who left the said monastery, administered the sacraments and celebrated other divine offices. He requests that the pope order his absolution from excommunication and excesses thereby contracted. *Fiat de speciali D. s. †.* Reg. 3, fol. 72r.

---

[5] William Pouns made his profession at Canterbury Cathedral Priory (Christchurch) on 30 November 1422. He was previously a monk of St Albans and had secured this transfer against his abbot's wishes through the intervention of Archbishop Chichele of Canterbury. On 3 February 1439 he was licensed with other monks to leave 'pro recreacione'. He was granted a papal dispensation on 2 August 1441 to hold a benefice with a cure of souls for life, but when he went to London to obtain a benefice without leave, he was declared an apostate (2 November 1441) and forced to return. He was subsequently expelled from Christchurch, and on 25 April 1443 the abbot of Boxley (Kent), Cistercian order, authorised his admission to that house and order (Logan, 63–5; Greatrex, 258; *CPL*, ix. 206).

634. [Rome], 2 January 1450. Thomas Imry, priest, professed canon in the priory of Bullington (*Blincthon*), order of St Gilbert, Lincoln dioc., informs [the pope] that he left the priory without his superior's permission but still wearing his habit and proceeded to Rome, as a result of which he incurred the sentence of excommunication generally promulgated on such persons and thus bound he ministered. He wishes to go back and requests that the pope absolve him and grant him a dispensation from irregularity *ut in forma. Fiat in forma D. s. †. Committatur fratri Io. penitentiario.*[6] *Fiat D. s. †.* Reg. 3, fol. 77v.

635. *[Rome], 16 January 1450. John Chisithon, priest, Coventry and Lichfield dioc., was persuaded by friends to enter a certain monastery of Holy Trinity, OSA,*[7] *at the age of 10; when at the age of 13 he decided that he did not want to stay, the monks imprisoned him and induced him to make profession, but when they released him from prison he returned to the world. He seeks a declaration that he is not bound to that monastery and may remain in his orders as a secular priest.* Reg. 3, fol. 86r.

[Rome], xvii kal. Februarii. Exponit Iohannes Chisithon, presbiter Conventrensis et Lichefeldensis diocesis, quod cum esset annorum x et a quibusdam amicis ad quodam [*sic*] monasterium sancte Trinitatis ordinis sancti Augustini ductus et presentatus esset ut inibi frater fieri et proficere debet [*sic*], et cum exponens aliquamdiu inibi permansisset, ante xiii annum etatis sue deliberasset ut nullo modo in monasterio manere vellet, et cum fratres exponentis voluntatem intellississent [*recte* intellexissent], in finem ut ipsum in fratrem habere possent captivaverunt et per metum contra voluntatem exponentis ipsum induxerunt ut professionem dicti conventus et ordinis liberare[t]. Non animo retirendi sed quam primum posset recedere de monasterio, professionem emisit, et quam cito post relaxationem \de/ [*sic?*] ca[r]ceris habere poterat, ante dictum x annum etatis recessit ad seculum et presbiter manere desiderat. [Ad] abstruendum [*sic*] ergo exponentis emulorum ora dicentium ipsum ordini et conventui fore obligatum, supplicat ut ad monasterium istum etc. non sit obligatus sed quod libere in suis ordinibus tamquam secularis presbiter permanere [possit] declarare dignemini.

Fiat si ita est et si factus maior huiusmodi professionem tacite vel expresse ratam non habuit D. s. †.

636. *[Rome], 22 January 1450. William, priest of Woking(?), Winchester dioc., was struck with a sword by John Berthon, whom he wounded in self-defence. Berthon later died through poor care of this wound. William seeks absolution from excommunication, his excesses and sins, and a dispensation to minister in his orders.* Reg. 3, fol. 88v.

[Rome], xi kal. Februarii. Exponit Wilgelmus, presbiter de Wokkling Wintoniensis diocesis, quod quidam Iohannes Berthon verbis iniuriosis ipsum molestasset et cum evaginato gladio percussisset; exponens animo defendendi

---

[6] There were two minor penitentiaries called Iohannes under Nichoals V, Iohannes Sagun and Iohannes Goldner: *RPG*, ii, p. xviii.

[7] Perhaps Repton Priory (Derbys.) or less likely Breadsall Priory (Derbys.), a small house. Both had this dedication and were in Coventry and Lichfield dioc.

vulneravit ipsum. Accidit quod propter malam curam dicti vulneris ut asseritur a medicis in xxiii^a die est mortuus. Cum exponens alias quam ut premittitur culpabilis non fuerit, confessus fuit non esse in culpa si mor[s] ipsum contigit. Desiderat in suis ordinibus ministrare. Timens non posse absque dispensatione, supplicat ipsum ab excommunicatione, excessibus et peccatis absolvere et quod ministrare possit de gratia speciali.

Fiat de speciali ad cautelam si iudicio medicorum vulnera illata mortalia non fuerint, de malo regimine mortuus fuit et de his constet D. s. †. Et committatur episcopo Vasatensi.⁸ Fiat D. s. †.

637. [*Rome*], *22 January 1450. Fr John Sthickfort, monk of* [*Revesby*]⁹ *Abbey, Cistercian order, Lincoln dioc., seeks a dispensation to read by candlelight and wear linen.* Reg. 3, fol. 88v.

[Rome], xi kal. Februarii. Exponitur pro parte fratris Iohannis Sthickfort, monachi monasterii beate Marie ordinis Cisterciensis Limconiensis [*recte* Lincolniensis] diocesis, quod ad tantam senectutem devenerit quod horas canonicas quod [*sic*] absque candela legere neque corpus absque pannis lineis possit substentare, quare supplicat ut possit legere omnes cum candelis ubique et uti pannis lineis dispensari de gratia speciali.

Fiat de speciali de lumine et de pannis lineis consilio medici D. s. †.

638. [*Rome*], *23 January 1450. Geoffrey Blasan, priest, St David's dioc., had himself promoted to the diaconate and priesthood by someone other than his ordinary, [as a result of which he incurred a sentence of excommunication] and thus bound he ministered. He seeks absolution from the sentence of excommunication and his other sins etc. [and dispensation from irregularity].* Fiat de speciali D. s. †. Reg. 3, fol. 87v.

639. [*Rome*], *2 February 1450. The pope is requested to grant letters* in forma '*Cupientes*' *to John Bordon, priest, Lincoln* [*Bincolniensis*] *dioc.,* locum tenenti sive beneficiato personatu *in the parish church of Swineshead(?)* (*Sunmischd*), *Lincoln dioc., for the parishoners of that church with the consent of its principal rector.* Fiat de speciali D. s. †. Reg. 3, fol. 84v.

640. [*Rome*], *3 February 1450. Fr Robert* (*Rubertus*) *alias Conventre, Coventry* (*Conventin'*) [*and Lichfield*] *dioc., explains that he left his monastery, having abandoned his habit and tonsure, returned to the world, and then had himself made a clerk* (se fecit clericali karactere insigniri). *He requests that [the pope declare him] innocent of apostasy, order his absolution from [excommunication, these excesses] and his sins, and [grant him a licence] to return to another monastery or order [of the same or stricter regular observance]* ut in forma. Fiat in forma D. s. †. Reg. 3, fol. 90v

---

⁸ The bishop of Bazas at this time was Raymond de Tulle, presumably resident in the Curia (Eubel, ii. 288).
⁹ Indicated in **91** below.

641. [Rome], 10 February 1450. John Damis(?), priest, Norwich (*Norvicensis*) dioc., requests that the pope grant him a licence so that he may celebrate divine offices in any place. *Fiat de speciali D. s. †.* Reg. 3, fol. 94r.

642. [*Rome*], *12 February 1450. John Valkener, priest, rector of All Saints' parish church, Maltby-le-Marsh, Lincoln dioc., incurred excommunication for simony; he requests absolution from that sentence and a dispensation from irregularity.* Reg. 3, fol. 129r.

[Rome], pridie idus Februarii a. 3º. Similem absolutionem Iohanni Valkener', presbitero, rectori parrochialis ecclesie omnium sanctorum de Maltbe in Muresco Lincolniensis diocesis, quod cuidam suo compermutanti secum beneficium cum beneficio suo summam de x[. . .](?) nobilium vel circa donavit, [propter quod sententiam excommunicationis in tales generaliter promulgatam incurrit], et sic ligatus ministravit etc. Supplicat ut supra [absolvi secumque dispensari ecclesiamque valeat retinere].

Fiat ut supra de verbo ad verbum [de speciali et expresso et quod absque dimissione beneficii illud canonice retineat et componat cum Lu. vicario sancti Petri] D. s. †.

643. [*Rome*], *13 February 1450. Henry de Herspympoynt* [scil. *Hurstpierpont*], *priest, Chichester dioc., promised a reward if anyone identified the thief who stole some of his goods, and a certain* familiaris *of his was accused and hanged; he requests that he may minister in his orders.* Reg. 3, fol. 91r.

[Rome], idibus Februarii [anno 3º]. Supplicat presbiter Henricus de Herspympoynt Cistestrernsis [*recte* Cicestrensis] diocesis quod cum ab aliquibus quidam suus familiaris accusatus esset de furto videlicet quod quedam sua bona subtraxerat, de qua se fecit presbiter prefatus nuntiari omnibus ut si quis reperiat promisit se dare duos duc[atos], repertus est, fuit in ultimo suplicio traditus subsecuta morte, tamen cum in morte sua non fuerit presens et absque consilio, favore, supplicat nullum reatum homicidii etc. ac etiam irregularitatem, in suis ordinibus ministrare [posse] ut in forma.

Fiat ut infra D. s. †.

Signetur per fiat si ita [est], si non captatus ut mors inde sequeretur vel alias laicum capi voluit sed pro reparanda bona.

644. [Rome], 21 February 1450. Fr John Briti, professed monk of St Cuthbert's monastery, OSB, Durham dioc.,[10] requests a licence to come to the current Jubilee. *Fiat de speciali D. s. †.* Reg. 3, fol. 94r.

645. [Rome], 25 February 1450. Absolution for Adam Seegom, layman, St David's dioc., because he killed a certain clerk. *Fiat in forma D. s. †.* Reg. 3, fol. 90r.

646. [Rome], 27 February 1450. The priest Thomas de Vonton, York dioc., who had himself promoted to all orders while under age [but otherwise] legally and

---

[10] Probably Durham Cathedral Priory. Less likely to be Lindisfarne Priory (Northumberland).

thus ministered, requests absolution from these and his other sins. *Fiat in forma D. s.* †. Reg. 3, fol. 92r.

647. [Rome], 18 March 1450. Same grant as **648** sought by John Knot, priest, Norwich dioc. *Fiat de speciali D. s.* †. Reg. 3, fol. 135v.

648. [*Rome*], *19 March 1450. Thomas Bokenham, priest, Norwich dioc., requests that he may not be compelled to serve in parish churches but may serve wherever he pleases.* Reg. 3, fol. 135v.

> [Rome], xiiii kal. Aprilis. Exponit Thomas Bokenham, presbiter Norvicensis diocesis, quod cum in civitate et diocese constitutio synodalis sit quibus [*recte* qua] cavetur quod presbiteri non habentes curam animarum ad serviendum in ecclesiis parrochialibus ad instanciam rectoris ipsarum ecclesiarum compelli possint per ordinarium loci sub excommunicationis pena sine [*sic*] certa modica mercede pro huiusmodi servitio deputata. Supplicat ut propter hoc ad [id] cogi non possit dispensare dignemini et ubicumque placuerit sibi valeat deservire.
>
> Fiat de speciali D. s. †.

649. [Rome], 19 March 1450. Same grant as **648** sought by Ralph Bokenham, priest of the same place and diocese. *Fiat* [*de speciali*] *D. s.* †. Reg. 3, fol. 135v.

650. [Rome], 20 March 1450. Same grant as **648** sought by Walter Vitsinon', priest, Lincoln dioc. *Fiat de speciali D. s.* †. Reg. 3, fol. 135v.

651. [Rome], 22 March 1450. Richard Grono, layman, St David's dioc., who killed a priest, [requests absolution from the sentence of excommunication, that excess and his sins *ut in forma*]. (Approved with **654**.) Reg. 3, fol. 102v.

652. [Rome], 22 March 1450. Same grant as **648** for William (*Wilgelmus*) Jonson of Saltfleetby (*Salfletby*), priest, [Lincoln dioc. *Fiat de speciali D. s.* †.] Reg. 3, fol. 135v

653. [Rome], 22 March 1450. Same grant as **648** sought by John de W'son of Wigtoft (*Wygtoft*), priest, [Lincoln dioc. *Fiat de speciali D. s.* †.] Reg. 3, fol. 135v.

654. [Rome], 27 March 1450. [Request] for Peter Vamy (*recte* Varny?), layman, Norwich dioc., who killed a clerk in a certain valley, [to be absolved from sentence of excommunication, such excesses and his other sins *ut in forma*]. *Fiat in forma D. s.* † (Approved with **651**.) Reg. 3, fol. 102v.

655. [*Rome*], *27 March 1450. Geoffrey Glase, priest, Hereford dioc.,*[11] *was attacked by some enemies in his home and severely wounded; he fought back, fatally wounding Roger Bruge, layman, with a knife. He seeks a declaration that he is not guilty of murder and did not incur irregularity or* inhabilitas. Reg. 3, fol. 101v.

---

[11] David Glace (Glaas, Glaace) was ordained in Hereford diocese as an acolyte on 17 December 1446, as a subdeacon on 4 March, and as a deacon on 8 April 1447 (*Reg. Spofford*, 346–8).

[Rome], vi kal. Aprilis. Exponit Galfredus Glase, presbiter Herfordensis diocesis, quod in quadam sua domo constitutus certi adversarii sui causa ipsum interficiendi, ut presumi poterat, manu armata ipsum invaserunt et graviter vulneraverunt; exponens videns [se] in periculo mortis constitutum vim vi repellendo quemdam laicum Rugerium Bruge cum cultello pro sui defensione vulneravit quare post 3 dies decessit. Ne [iuris] ignari et simplices etc. [asserunt ipsum exponentem premissorum occasione reatum homicidii incurrisse et inhabilitatis seu irregularitatis maculam contraxisse, ad ora talium obstruenda] supplicat [quatinus] declarare dignemini [ipsum] nullum reatum homicidii incurrisse premissorum occasione seu inhabilitatis seu super [*sic*] irregularitatis [maculam] contrassisse [*recte* contraxisse] [et quod] libere in suis ordinibus ministrare [possit] declarare dignemini [*sic*] ut in forma.

Fiat in ut infra D. s. †. Signetur per fiat si ita est et si morte alias evadere non poterat.

656. [Rome], 27 March 1450. Same grant as **661** for Robert (*Roberthus*) Chyr, Lincoln dioc. [*Fiat de de speciali D. s. †*]. Reg. 3, fol. 137r.

657. [Rome], 27 March 1450. Same grant as **661** for William (*Villgelmus*) Rowd', [Lincoln dioc. *Fiat de speciali D. s. †*.] Reg. 3, fol. 137r.

658. [Rome], 27 March 1450. Luke [son] of Philip, rector of the church of the vill of St Austell (*Austoli*), Exeter dioc.,[12] requests the pope that he may study canon law. *Fiat de speciali D. s. †.* Reg. 3, fol. 142r.

659. [Rome], 29 March 1450. The pope is requested to grant a licence to Richard Togin(?), vicar of Wrexham (*Vrixim*), St Asaph dioc., so that he may attend a *studium universale*. [*Fiat D. s. †*.] Reg. 3, fol. 138v.

660. [*Rome*], *31 March 1450. Richard Victone, priest, Lincoln dioc., left Tupholme Abbey, Premonstratensian order, Lincoln dioc., which his parents had forced him to enter as a boy; he seeks absolution and a declaration that he may stay in the world.* Reg. 3, fol. 80r.

[Rome], ii kal. Aprilis a. 4. Similem gratiam Richardo Victone, presbitero Linculniensis diocesis, habitu derelicto monasterium \Tuphan dicte diocesis ordinis Premonstratensis/, quod per vim et per metum parentum suorum intravit \ante xiiii annum/, exivit \post professionem dicti/ monasterii emitti solitam vi et metu cessantibus ad seculum reversus. Supplicat declarare dignemini dicto monasterio ipsum in nullo obligari et in seculo posse remanere.

Fiat ut infra D. s. †. Signetur per fiat si ita est.

---

[12] Luke Philip was ordained in Exeter diocese as an acolyte on 8 March 1438, and as such was granted letters dimissory for all holy orders on 26 September 1440 (*Reg. Lacy*, ed. Dunstan, ii. 206; iv. 165b). As a chaplain he was admitted as vicar of St Austell (Cornw.) on 1 January 1449 (ibid., i. 336). By February 1449 he petitioned his bishop concerning the dilapidation of the vicarage left by the neglect of the last vicar (ibid., iii. 28, 30). He subsequently made use of the above licence to study, since he supplicated for BCnL at Oxford University on 30 January and was admitted as BCnL on 15 December 1455 (*BRUO*, iii.1476).

661. [*Rome*], *2 April 1450. William,*[13] *priest, Norwich dioc., requests that he may not be compelled to serve in parish churches but may celebrate wherever he pleases.* Reg. 3, fol. 137r.

[Rome], iiii non' Aprilis. Exponit Vilgermus, presbiter Norvicensis diocesis, quod in diocese predicta constitutio est synodalis sive provincialis quibus [*recte* qua] cavetur quod presbiteri non habentes curam animarum ad serviendum in parrochialibus ecclesiis possunt compelli per ipsorum rectores sub excommunicationis pena sin[e] [*sic*] certa modica mercede ad hoc deputata. Quare supplicat ut ad hoc compelli non possit et celebrare valeat quocumque sibi placuerit.

Fiat de speciali D. s. †.

662. [Rome], 2 April 1450. Same grant as **661** for Robert Grene, priest, Norwich dioc. *Fiat de de speciali D. s. †.* Reg. 3, fol. 137r.

663. [Rome], 3 April 1450. Same grant as **661** for Thomas Trindal, priest, BA, Lincoln dioc. *Fiat de speciali D. s. †.* Reg. 3, fol. 137r.

664. [Rome], 7 April 1450. Same absolution and declaration as **660** sought by Thomas Domet, priest, London dioc., with regard to St Mary's monastery, Coggeshall (*Cogigeshale*), Cistercian order. *Fiat ut supra D. s. †. Signetur per fiat si ita est.* Reg. 3, fol. 80r.

665. [*Rome*], *9 April 1450. Richard Pennert', clerk, Bangor dioc., scholar of Oxford University, was once out walking when he met a layman who seized him, threatening him with a knife; he struck the layman in self-defence, as a result of which the layman died. He seeks a declaration of innocence from murder and irregularity so that he may be promoted* [*to all holy orders*]. Reg. 3, fol. 82v.

[Rome], v idus Aprilis. Exponitur pro [parte] Ricardi Pennert' clerici Bangariensis diocesis scholaris universitatis Exoniensis [*recte* Oxoniensis] quod olim iuxta consuetudinem scolarium universitatis predicte in campo dicto vulgariter Bemond'[14] iuxta fratres Augustinenses pro solatiis acedens intra sabbath[um] more solito studium [*recte* studii?] ambulavit. Quidam laicus robustus potens dicto R. obviavit quem ipse non novit nec secum loquitur. Laicus dixit: 'Quare super me respicit [*recte* respicis]?' Respondit: 'Neque in bono neque in malum [*sic*] respicio.' Laicus obbrebriosa verba dixit et dictum exponentem fortiter tenuit arrepto cultello, subiugensque manus suas que numquam unus evadet. Ergo timens mortem non posse evadere vim vi repellendo dictum laicum cum cultello percussit, de quo ipse laicus decessit. Cum autem ut supra [animo] defendendi [hoc] fecerit [nec alias culpabilis fuerit, ad ora simplicium obstruenda] supplicatur nullam etc. [maculam irregularitatis nec reatum homicidii contraxisse] declarare et quod possit promoveri etc. [ad omnes sacros ordines].

Fiat ut infra D. s. †. Signetur per fiat si ita est et si mortem alias evadere non potuit de his constet B. Spol.

---

[13] Surname omitted.
[14] Probably Beaumont, North Oxford (see H. E. Salter, *Medieval Oxford*, Oxford Historical Society, 100 (Oxford, 1936), p. 75).

666. [Rome], 9 April 1450. A licence for Edward (*Aduardo*) Alburbar, vicar of Llangollen (*Lagugollen*), priest, St Asaph dioc., so that he may study canon law and theology. *Fiat D. s. †*. Reg. 3, fol. 140v.

667. [Rome], 10 April 1450. Request for Dafydd Methoi, priest, St David's dioc., [to study] civil law. [*Fiat de speciali D. s. †*.] Reg. 3, fol. 142r.

668. [Rome], 10 April 1450. John Fabri, priest, Lincoln dioc., requests that he may not be bound nor compelled by virtue of a certain synodal or provincial constitution to celebrate in a parish church, according to the usage (*mos*) for those not having cure of souls. *Fiat de speciali D. s. †*. Reg. 3, fol. 142r.

669. [Rome], 11 April 1450. Same absolution and declaration as **660** for Robert Marcham, priest, Lincoln (*Bicolniensis*) dioc., with regard to Nottingham (*Notingam*) convent, OFM, York dioc. *Fiat si ita est D. s. †. Signetur per fiat si ita est. B. Spol'*. Reg. 3, fol. 80r.

670. [Rome], 11 April 1450. [The pope is requested to grant a licence] to Ieuan ap Hywel (*Oel*), rector of St Peter's church, [Bryngwyn], Llandaff (*Landunensis*) dioc., so that he may study civil law.[15] [*Fiat D. s. †*.] Reg. 3, fol. 141r.

671. [Rome], 11 April 1450. Absolution from simony for Henry [son] of Simeon, priest, Lincoln dioc., who paid William (*Wilgelmus*) Pergi', priest of Lincoln, to have a benefice with cure of souls, he now having resigned the benefice. *Fiat de speciali et expresso et componat cum [vicario de] sancto Petro D. s. †*. Reg. 3, fol. 144v.

672. [Rome], 13 April 1450. Same grant as **658** for Ieuan ap Hywel (*Choel*), priest of St Peter's parish church, Bryngwyn (*Brimgwan*), [Llandaff dioc. *Fiat de speciali D. s. †*.] Reg. 3, fol. 142r.

673. [Rome], 13 April 1450. Same grant as **658** for Thomas (*Thomassus*) Rose, priest, Llandaff (*Landunensis*) dioc.[16] [*Fiat de speciali D. s. †*.] Reg. 3, fol. 142r.

674. [Rome], 13 April 1450. Fr Thomas Mani, professed of OP, Bangor (*Bugorensis*) convent, [requests that he may study] theology. [*Fiat de speciali D. s. †*.] Reg. 3, fol. 142r.

675. [Rome], 17 April 1450. Same grant as **667** for Adam ap Dafydd (*Dd'*), rector of [. . .] parish church,[17] St David's (*Mencensis*) dioc. [*Fiat de speciali D. s. †*.] Reg. 3, fol. 142r.

---

[15] Probably the John Hoell, priest, Llandaff dioc., who was appointed in the Curia as a notary public on 27 April 1450 (*CPL*, x. 483). Possibly the John Howell who was at Oxford University by 1444 and supplicated there for BCnL on 14 March 1449; he was in priest's orders by 1449 (*BRUO*, ii. 976–7).

[16] Perhaps the Thomas Roos bound over before the chancellor of Oxford University to keep the peace in August 1448, by when he was in priest's orders; he was banished from the university on 5 December 1450 (*BRUO*, iii.1590).

[17] Parish name omitted.

676. [Rome], 17 April 1450. Same grant as **658** for Philip Loblis, priest of North Ormsby (*Nortorcszboy*) parish church, Lincoln dioc. [*Fiat de speciali D. s. †.*] Reg. 3, fol. 142r.

677. [Rome], 17 April 1450. Same grant as **658** for Philip ap Ieuan ap Dafydd, priest, Llandaff (*Landonensis*) dioc. [*Fiat de speciali D. s. †.*] Reg. 3, fol. 142r.

678. *[Rome], 18 April 1450. George Norweche, monk of Bromholm Priory(?),*[18] *OSB, Norwich dioc., incurred excommunication for apostasy; he seeks absolution from that sentence and a dispensation from irregularity.* Reg. 3, fol. 108v.

[Rome], xiiii kal. Maii. Exponit[ur] pro presbitero Georgio Norweche, monacho monasterii Brinol ordinis sancti Benedicti Narwocensis diocesis, quia ut supra exivit [monasterium, habitu dimisso per annos viii vagabando, propter quod sententiam excommunicationis incurrit in tales generaliter promulgatam] et sic [ligatus] ministravit \non in contemptu clavium/ propter quod etc. [irregularitatis maculam contraxit]. Supplicat absolvi secumque super irregularitate dispensari.

Committatur priori monasterii in Galgano ordinis sancti Trinitatis.[19] Fiat D. s. †.

679. [Rome], 20 April 1450. William Dankster, priest of the order of Holy Trinity,[20] requests that he may celebrate in any diocese, he having requested a licence to do so from his superior and not obtained it. *Fiat de speciali D. s. †.* Reg. 3, fol. 142v.

680. [Rome], 20 April 1450. Thomas Vinfray, priest, Norwich (*Nowliconensis*) dioc., requests that he may not be obliged to celebrate in any parish church by virtue of any statute or custom. [*Fiat de speciali D. s. †*]. Reg. 3, fol. 146v.

681. [Rome], 20 April 1450. Same grant as **680** for John Vistard, priest, Norwich dioc. *Fiat de speciali D. s. †.* Reg. 3, fol. 146v.

682. *[Rome], 21 April 1450. William Coplin, Norwich dioc., as a boy was persuaded by friends to enter St Mary's Priory, Modney(?), Norwich dioc., OSB. The monks forced him to make profession at Castle Acre Priory, but he later escaped from the first monastery before the age of 14. He seeks a declaration that he is not bound to that monastery and may remain in the world.* Reg. 3, fol. 109r.

[Rome], xi kal. Maii. Exponit Guilgelmus Coplin Norwicensis diocesis quod infra annos suos personaliter(?) existens, cum quorumdam amicorum suorum persuasionibus et blandis verbis ductus, monasterium de beata virgine de Mordan dicte diocesis ordinis sancti Benedicti intrasset et infra annum

---

[18] Or perhaps Binham Priory (Norf.).
[19] This monastery has not been identified; it can hardly be the Benedictine priory of Monte Gargano.
[20] Diocese omitted, but the name is English. For Trinitarian houses in England and Wales see Hadcock and Knowles, 205–7.

probationis stetisset. Monachi videntes ipsum non habentem animum inclinatum ad dictam religionem de facto contra eius voluntatem ad monasterium de Castelachor duxerunt; in eodem profiteri fecerunt. Sub arta custodia remissus ad primum monasterium, postea captata oportunitate, habitu dimisso et ordine, exivit, ad seculum rediens, ante annum ipsius xiiii completum. Supplicat [quatinus] declarare dignemini ut dicto monasterio et religioni obligatum non fore sed in seculo remanere possit ut in forma.

Fiat ut infra D. s. †. Signetur per fiat si ita est et si metu professus etiam ante annum 14 extitit. B. Spol.

683. [Rome], 29 April 1450. John [son] of Philip, professed monk of St Mary's monastery, Cistercian order, Llandaff (*Landunensis*) dioc.,[21] [requests that he may celebrate anywhere. *Fiat de speciali D. s. †.*] Reg. 3, fol. 141v.

684. [*Rome*], *2 May 1450. Richard Row, priest, Hereford dioc., requests that he may preach(?) anywhere without anyone's permission.* Reg. 3, fol. 145r.

[Rome], vi non' [Maii]. Supplicat Riccardus Row, presbiter Her[e]fordensis diocesis, ut sine licentia alicuius possit ubi[que] locorum fuerit sive in dicta diocese verbum exornandum(?) ad populum facere.

Fiat D. s. †.

685. [*Rome, c. 8–9 May 1450*].[22] *John Pomine, priest, Bath and Wells dioc., was persuaded by friends as a child to enter Athelney Abbey, OSB. The brethren forced him to make profession, but before the end of his noviciate he escaped. He requests a declaration that he is not bound to that monastery.* Reg. 3, fol. 122r.

Exponit Iohannes Pomine, presbiter Bathoniensis et Wellensis diocesis, quod minor annis existens persuasionibus aliquorum amicorum ad monasterium sancti Salvatoris et Petri et Pauli apostolorum ordinis sancti Benedicti intrasset. Infra annum probationis per vim et metum a fratribus illatum professionem per dictos fratres emicti solitam contra ipsius voluntatem emisit, animo [tamen] et intentione religioni non obligari. Capt[at]o tempore ante annum probationis [completum], habitu dimisso, exivit et ad seculum reversus [est] in quo morari concupiscit. Supplicat declarari non obligatum fore dicto monasterio.

Fiat ut infra D. s. †. Signetur per fiat si ita est et fuerit metus talis et vis qui cadat in constantem virum et de his constet B. Spol.

686. [*Rome*], *10 May 1450. Roger Vermyham, priest, Coventry and Lichfield dioc., was persuaded by friends as a child to enter Warrington convent, OESA. The brethren forced him to make profession, but before the end of his noviciate he escaped. He requests a declaration that he is not bound to that convent and order.* Reg. 3, fol. 121v.

---

[21] Cistercian abbies in this diocese comprised Grace Dieu, Llantarnam, Margam, Neath, and Tintern. All were dedicated to BVM, like most houses of the order.
[22] Undated; the previous entry is dated 8 May and the next 9 May.

[Rome], vi idus Maii. Exponit Rogerius Vermyham, presbiter Conventrensis et Bichfedensis [*sic*] diocesis, quod minor annis existens per persuasionibus [*sic*] amicorum suorum conventum de Vergyneton' ordinis [fratrum heremitarum] sancti Augustini intrasset. Infra annum probationis per vim et metum a fratribus sibi illatum compulsus professionem per fratres dicti conventus emicti solitam contra ipsius voluntatem emisit, animo tamen et intentione quod nulli propterea vellet religioni obligari. Captato tempore ante annum probationis completum secundum institutionem ipsius monasterii, monasterium exivit, habitu dimisso, reversus est ad seculum in quo morari concupiscit. Supplicat, ne simplices etc. [et iuris ignari asserunt ipsum dicto conventui et ordini obligari], declarari in illo dicto conventui et ordini [non] obligari.

Fiat ut in forma si ita rite vel expresse professionem \metum habuerit/ [*sic*] non fecerit D. s. †. Signetur per fiat si ita est et metus fuit talis quod cadat in constantem virum et de his constet B. Spol.

687. [*Rome*], *17 May 1450. Morys* [*and*] *R'odo(?), sons of Yceaneala, laymen, Hereford dioc., were involved with others in the crucifixion of a priest.* Reg. 3, fol. 124v.

[Rome], xvi kal. Iunii. Exponunt Mauricius [et] R'odo(?), filii Yceaneala, laici Hefertonsis [*recte* Herefordensis] diocesis, quia quemdam presbiterum per laicum dominum temporalem una cum aliis consiliariis crucifixerunt et interfecerunt. Et si placet quod sola [signatura?] sufficiat.

Fiat D. s. †.

688. [*Rome*], *18 May 1450. Roger Paker, priest of Canterbury,* [*was persuaded and compelled*] *as a child* [*to enter*] *St Mary's Hospital, Dover, OSA,* [*and forced by its brethren to make profession, but he later escaped. He seeks a declaration that he is not bound to that hospital*]. Reg. 3, fol. 124r.

[Rome], xv kal. Iunii. Similem declarationem et gratiam de verbo ad verbum in omnibus[23] Rogero Paker, presbitero Cantuariensi, [quod] cum ipse esset minor annis, [quorundam persuasionibus et per vim et metum qui cadere poterunt in constantem virum] \hospitalem beate Marie de Dovia sub regula sancti Augustini degentium/ [intravit, et suscepto habitu fratrum dicti hospitalis, vi et metu ducentibus predictorum, professionem emisit regularem per fratres dicti hospitalis emicti solitam, nullatenus tamen corde gerens quod alicui propterea vellet religioni obligari. Istis vi et metu cessantibus, quam primum poterit, ad seculum est reversus. Supplicat quatinus dignemini declarare dicto hospitali in nullo obligatum fore].

Fiat ut infra D. s. †. Signetur per fiat si ita est et si vi et metu professionem emisit nec expresse vel tacite lapsu temporis eam approbaverit et de his constet.

689. [*Rome*], *30 May 1450. John Poule, priest, Bath and Wells dioc., was persuaded and compelled at the age of 13 to enter Bruton Priory, OSA, Bath and Wells dioc.,*[24] *and forced by its*

---

[23] This refers to **689**.
[24] Presumably the John Pawle who had no voice in the election of a prior at Bruton on

brethren to make profession, but he later escaped. He seeks a declaration that he is not bound to that convent. Reg. 3, fol. 124r.

[Rome], iii kal. Iunii. Exponitur pro Iohanne Poule, presbitero Bathonensis et Vellensis diocesis, quod constitutus in xiii° anno quorumdam persuasionibus et per vim et metum qui cadere poterunt etc. [in constantem virum] conventum beate Marie de Bruten ordinis sancti Augustini dicte diocesis intravit, et suscepto habitu fratrum dicti conventus, vi et metu ducentibus predictorum, professionem emisit regularem per fratres dicti conventus emicti solitam, nullatenus tamen corde gerens quod alicui propterea vellet religioni obligari. Istis vi et metu cessantibus, quam primum poterit, ad seculum est reversus. Supplicat [quatinus] dignemini declarare dicto conventui in nullo obligatum fore.

Fiat ut infra D. s. †. Signetur per fiat si ita est et si nec expresse ne[c] tacite per declarationem huiusmodi(?) et metu cessante aut alias professionem ratam habuerit B. Spol.

690. *Rome at St Peter's, 8 June 1450. Robert Whyte, priest, Bath and Wells dioc.,*[25] *seeks a licence so that he may not be compelled to preside over parish churches in accordance with a custom of that diocese.* Reg. 3, fol. 217r

Dat. Rome apud sanctum Petrum sexto idus Iunii anno quarto. Exponitur sanctitati vestre pro parte devotus vester Robertus Whyte, presbiter Batoniensis et Wellensis diocesis, quod licet in civitate et diocese Batoniensi et Wellensi consuetudo est quod presbiteri quibus cura animarum non est commissa ad instanciam rectorum seol parrochialium ecclesiarum ipsarum civitatis et diocesis possint ipsis invitis per ordinarium loci cogi et compelli ad regendum parrochiales ecclesias certo modo, salarium [*recte* salario] pro ipsis dictis presbiteris deputatum [*recte* deputato], et quia, pater beatissime, ipse exponens ad gubernandum et regendum ipsas ecclesias animum suum inclinare non potest, quare supplicat [*recte* supplicatur] pro parte dicti exponentis quatinus sibi invito [ad] huiusmodi parrochiales ecclesias regendum per quemcumque etiam ordinarium loci minime cogi et compelli possit licenciam concedere dignemini de gratia speciali. (*Not signed.*)

691. [Rome], 10 June 1450. William Lawson (*Lauuson*), priest, Lincoln dioc.,[26] requests that he may not be compelled to celebrate divine offices in any parish church by virtue of any statute or custom. *Fiat de speciali D. s.* †. Reg. 3, fol. 151v.

692. [Rome], 10 June 1450. [Request] for Baldwin Fulfor, Exeter dioc., for a licence to visit the [Holy] Sepulchre.[27] *Fiat I. o* [recte *Io.*] *P. et A. episcopus.* Reg. 3, fol. 151v.

---

4 October 1440 because he had 'long ago left the priory' (Logan, 227; *Reg. Beckynton*, 1640).
[25] Perhaps the Robert White, chaplain, admitted as rector of Pylle (Somerset), Bath and Wells dioc., on 25 September 1462 (*Reg. Bekynton*, 1457).
[26] Presumably the William Lawson, priest, Lincoln dioc., who was appointed in the Curia as a notary public on 17 June 1450 (*CPL*, x. 482).
[27] Baldwin Fulford, esq., Exeter dioc., son and heir of Henry Fulford and 'Willelma'

693. *Rome at St Peter's, [12.?] June 1450. Fr Stephen Lundini, abbot of Wymondham Abbey, OSB, Norwich dioc., STP, had sworn an oath at his graduation as an MTh of Oxford University that he would preach a public sermon there but did not do so. He seeks absolution from that oath and dispensation from irregularity.* Reg. 3, fol. 217v.

Dat. Rome apud sanctum Petrum pridie [idibus?] Iunii anno quarto. Exponitur sanctitati vestre pro parte fratris Stephani Lundini, abbatis monasterii de Vimumdam' ordinis sancti Benedicti Norvicensis diocesis, sacre theologie professor, quod cum ipse alias, antequam huiusmodi abbacie preficeretur et ad eandem assumetur, in universitate Oxoniensi, dum gradum magesterii [*sic*] in dicta facultate sacre theologie reciperet, iuravit tunc infra certum tempus unum sermonem publice in dicta universitate facere, sed propter viarum discrimina et vero alia impedimenta et pericula huiusmodi non fecit neque facere potuit. Supplicat igitur sanctitati vestre quatinus ipsum ab huiusmodi iuramento absolvere et super irregularitate si quam incurrerit dispensare misericorditer dignemini. (*Not signed.*)

694. [*Rome*], *21 June 1450. John Crosby, priest, Lincoln dioc.,*[28] *wounded a layman with the latter's sword during a quarrel over an alleged theft; the layman initially recovered but died a few months later. He seeks absolution and a dispensation* ad cautelam. Reg. 3, fol. 198v

[Rome], xi kal. Iulii anno 4[to]. [Exponit] Iohannes Crosbi, presbiter diocesis Lincolniensis, quod olim facta collatione cum quodam Henrico Isteis(?) in hospitio, intellexit quod quedam mappa quam habuerant in mensa fuisse furta. Habitis verbis propter istam mappam cum quodam laico, arepit gladium ipsius laici [et] vulneravit ipsum taliter quod stetit per aliquos dies in lecto, deinde sanatus equitavit hinc inde per aliquos menses et deinde post aliquos dies decessit. Quare supplicat ad cautelam absolutionem impartiri [si] indigeat ac dispensari.

Fiat de speciali ad cautelam Io. P. episcopus.

Morton (see *Reg. Lacy*, ed. Hingeston Randolph, i. 343; *Reg. Lacy*, ed. Dunstan, i. 276, 278, 317; iii. 54). Doubtless the Baldwin Fulforde, nobleman, who obtained a papal safe-conduct for one year on 30 April 1451 for himself and a retinue of up to four persons to visit various parts of the world (*CPL*, x. 216).

[28] As a clerk of Carlisle diocese he fatally wounded a lay glover during a row over the latter's failure to make him a pair of gloves by an agreed date; he was granted a dispensation from irregularity on 8 March 1430 so that he might be promoted to all holy orders and hold a benefice with or without cure of souls (*CPL*, viii. 173, cf. x. 214–17). He claimed to be the son of John Soulby, priest, rector of Britwell Salome (Oxon.), Lincoln dioc., and an unmarried woman, and had obtained a dispensation from this impediment by April 1432 so that he might be promoted to all, even holy, orders and hold a benefice even with cure of souls. He was in minor orders and had succeeded his father, but not directly, as rector of Britwell Salome, when he was granted a dispensation on 13 April 1432 to hold three other compatible benefices with or without cure of souls (*CPL*, viii. 443–4, cf. 601). He was BA and had been studying canon and civil law for five or six years at Oxford University by 1432; he was BCn & CL by 1448 and DCL. In 1441–9 he was charged rent for rooms in University College, Oxford. He was judicial commissary of the bishop of Lincoln in 1448. He was also collated to a canonry and the treasurership at Lincoln on 19 December 1448; he vacated the former by August 1471 but retained the latter till death. He died in 1477 (*BRUO*, i. 517).

695. [Rome], 28 July 1450. For Robert Bruntun, canon regular, OSA, Bath and Wells dioc.,[29] a licence to go to the [Lord's] sepulchre. [*Fiat Io. P. et A. episcopus*]. Reg. 3, fol. 152r.

696. [*Rome*], *3 October(?) 1450*.[30] *Geoffrey Malaortia, priest, York dioc., took part in wars and defending a castle but did not kill or wound anyone; he requests absolution and a dispensation.* Reg. 3, fol. 159r.

[Rome], v non. [Novembris]. Absolutio et dispensatio pro Gefroy Malaortia, presbitero Eboracensis diocesis, quia in guerris publicis interfuit armatus ubi homicidia et mutilationes fuerunt et in quodam castro extitit ubi lapides contra inimicos proiecit, tamen neminem interfecit nec alicui mutilavit membrum.

Fiat ut infra si de his legitime constiterit D. s. †. Fiat de speciali in foro conscientie si ad homicidia et mutilationes consilium aut favorem non dederit.

697. [*Rome*], *3 October 1450*. *Lewis ap Dafydd, priest, perpetual vicar of Meifod, St Asaph dioc., requests a dispensation to study canon law or any other subject except civil law at university for seven years.* Reg. 3, fol. 163v.

[Rome], v nonas Octobris. Exponit etc. [sanctitati vestre devotus vester] Lodovicus ap David, presbiter, perpetuus vicarius de Meynot Assavensis diocesis, cui cura animarum adheret, quia ipse propter scientiarum amenitatem cupiat scientiis acquirendis adherere, quare supplicat etc. [eidem sanctitati vestre] quatinus secum ut in studiis universalibus ius canonicum aut alias scientias, legibus exceptis, studere, legere, et audire valeat ad septennium, constitutionibus et ordinationibus apostolicis in contrarium facientibus quibuscumque non obstantibus, dispensare dignemini. (*Not signed*.)

698. [*Rome*], *14 October 1450*. *Gwilym son of Matthew, layman, Llandaff dioc., seeks absolution for himself and his* familiares *for having killed a priest.* Reg. 3, fol. 167r.

[Rome], ii id. Octobris. Exponitur etc. [sanctitati vestre] pro parte Villermi Mathei, laici Landavensis diocesis, quod ipse olim una cum etc. suis familiaribus laicis dyabolo instigante quemdam presbiterum interfecerunt, propter quod sententiam excommunicationis incurrerunt etc. Quare supplicatur pro parte dictorum exponentium quatinus ipsos ab huiusmodi sententiis ac peccatis eorum aliis absolvi etc. (*Not signed*.)

699. [Rome], 12 November 1450. Absolution for the priest Ieuan Mogan, Llandaff (*Landunensis*) dioc., since he celebrated after having been promoted [to holy orders] while under age. *Fiat de speciali D. s.* †. Reg. 3, fol. 158r.

---

[29] Augustinian houses in Bath and Wells diocese comprised Barlinch Priory, Bruton Priory, Keynsham Abbey, Stavordale Priory, Taunton Priory, and Woodspring Priory.

[30] There is no such date as 'v non. Novembris', unless 1 November was meant; 'v nonas Octobris', i.e. 3 October, thus seems more likely.

700. [Rome], 23 November 1450. John Brampton, who obtained North Lynn(?) (*No'telin*) parish church, Norwich dioc., by authority of his ordinary (*ordinarie*), fears that he has incurred simony but since he did not incur it, he requests absolution *ad cautelam*. *Fiat de expresso et componat cum vicario sancti Petri D. s. †.* Reg. 3, fol. 173r.

701. [Rome], 18 December 1450. Fr Henry Goffris, priest, professed of the Cistercian order, Hereford dioc.,[31] committed apostasy, presided over (*regebat*) churches with cure of souls as a secular [priest] in the world, [as a result of which he incurred the sentence of excommunication generally promulgated on such persons], and bound thus celebrated. Since he wishes to return to his monastery, he seeks absolution and a dispensation. *Fiat de speciali D. s. †.* Reg. 3, fol. 175r.

702. [Rome], 19 December 1450. Ieuan ap Dafydd ap Ieuan, Worcester (*Wigarniensis*) dioc., guilelessly (*tamquam simplex*) celebrated divine offices while in deacon's orders, [as a result of which he incurred a sentence of suspension?], and thus bound, he had himself promoted to the priesthood. *Fiat de speciali et quod in susceptis valeat tamen ministrare D. s. †.* Reg. 3, fol. 188v.

703. *[Rome], 20 December 1450. William London, priest professed of Abbey Dore, Cistercian order, Hereford dioc.,*[32] *was persuaded to enter that monastery at the age of 11 and forced to make profession while under age; he later escaped. He seeks a declaration that he is not bound to that order.* Reg. 3, fol. 203v.

> [Rome], xiii kal. Ianuarii. Willelmus London, professus presbiter sancte Marie de Duror(?) ordinis Cisterciensis Herefordensis diocesis, dum esset annorum xi, animi levitate ex allicionibus [*recte* allectionibus] quorumdam fratrum dictis [*sic*] ordinis [dictum monasterium] intravit et ante legitimam etatem cohartus fecit professionem, quam non ratificavit nec ratificat, sed dictum monasterium exivit, habitu et ordine derelictis. Supplicat declarari dicto ordini non teneri et in seculo legitime posse stare et celebrare tamquam presbiter secularis.
>
> Fiat si ita est et si huiusmodi professionem factus maior tacite vel expresse non habuit ratam D. s. †.

704. *[Rome], 20 December 1450. Ieuan ap Dafydd, priest professed of Conwy Abbey, Cistercian order, Bangor dioc., was persuaded to enter that monastery at the age of 12 and made profession but left after three months. He seeks a declaration that he is not bound to that monastery and order.* Reg. 3, fol. 204v.

> [Rome], xiii kal. [Ianuarii]. Iohannes ap David, presbiter professus monasterii de Conven(?) ordinis Cisterciensis Bangoriensis diocesis, in xii° anno

---

[31] Presumably the Henry Geffus, monk of Flaxley Abbey (Glos.), Cistercian order, Hereford dioc., said to be of noble birth, who obtained a dispensation on 8 February 1451 to hold a benefice with or without cure of souls for life (*CPL*, x. 170).

[32] As a monk of Abbey Dore he was ordained in Hereford diocese as a priest on 23 December 1424 (*Reg. Spofford*, 297). Perhaps the William London who vacated the Childeshalle portion of Pontesbury, Hereford dioc., by 24 July 1451 (*Reg. Boulers*, 22).

constitutus ex levitate quadam et inductione quorumdam fratrum intravit monasterium sine scitu et consensu suorum et fecit profexionem, et per tres menses stetit. Deinde propter asperitatem regule, quam supportare non poterat, exivit habitu dimisso. Supplicat absolvi et declarari dicto monasterio et ordini non teneri et in seculo posse legitime remanere.

Fiat si tacite vel expresse postquam venit ad legitimam etatem profexionem non fecit aut dictam professionem ratam non habuit D. s. †.

705. [Rome], 2 January 1451. John Bocle, priest, Lincoln dioc., requests that he may not be compelled to preside over (*compelli ad regimen*) a parish church against his will notwithstanding any constitutions [to the contrary]. [*Fiat de speciali D. s. †*]. Reg. 3, fol. 229r.

706. [Rome], 2 January 1451. Same grace as **705** sought by Roger Paroll and John Smithic, priests, Lincoln dioc. *Fiat de speciali D. s. †.* Reg. 3, fol. 229r.

707. [*Rome*], *1 February 1451. Andrew Nores, priest, Lincoln dioc., was placed in an Augustinian monastery at the age of 6; he promised to stay there out of fear of being beaten by the brethren but later escaped. He seeks a declaration that he is not bound to that monastery or order.* Reg. 3, fol. 203r.

[Rome], kal. Februarii. Andreas Nores,[33] presbiter Lincolniensis diocesis, dum esset annorum vi, fuit tractus secrete ad monasterium ordinis sancti Augustini per \unum/ fratrem eiusdem ordinis absque voluntate et notitia parentum ipsius. Tandem ne percuteretur dixit velle remanere in dicto monasterio, quia alii fratres ipso vidente dicebant nolle profiteri et propter hoc omnes percussi, et sic contra suam voluntatem et propositum promisit, licet in corde suo aliud habuit, et post dictam promissionem post unum mensem exivit. Unde supplicat declarari dicto monasterio sive ordini aliquo modo non esse obligatum et sic in seculo deo servire.

Fiat si ita est et si pervento ad etatem legitimam tacite vel expresse profexionem non fecerit vel alias factam ratam non habuerit D. s. †.

708. [Rome], 1 February 1451(?).[34] Robert Alfort, priest, canon regular of Hagnaby (*Augebi*), Premonstratensian order, Lincoln dioc., requests that he may wear linen clothing in accordance with his confession and medical advice (*secundum sui confessionem et medicorum consilia*). *Fiat D. s. †.* Reg. 3, fol. 211r.

709. [Rome], 1 February 1451(?). Fr John Sticheford, priest, professed of St Mary's monastery, Revesby (*Revesbi*), Cistercian order, Lincoln dioc., requests that he may use a light and linen clothing when he says the night office. *Fiat de speciali D. s. †.* Reg. 3, fol. 211r.

---

[33] Written above this name is 'Nicholaus Stanslai', presumably a false start for another entry. Cf. *RPG*, ii, no. 28.
[34] Although it is dated 'kal. Feb' aᵒ vᵗᵒ' which suggests that the year was 1452, it is more likely to have been 1451 given that adjacent entries in the register are also from this year.

710. [*Rome*], *6 March 1451*(?). *Thomas Steresacker, subdeacon, York dioc., was attacked when he was on board ship, and some attackers were killed but not with his support or consent. He seeks a declaration of his innocence and a dispensation.* Reg. 3, fol. 202r.

[Rome], ii non' Martii a. iiii^{to}. [Exponit] Thomas Steresacker, subdiaconus Eboracensis diocesis dum esset in navi quatinus quidam \inimici terre sue/ agressi fuerant. In illo conflictu aliqui fuerunt interfecti, ipso nec consentiente nec auxilium sive consilium prestante. Cum autem doleat, supplicat declarari ut supra [ut nullum homicidii reatum aut irregularitatis maculam incurrisset] et dispensari ut possit possit [*sic*] promoveri ad omnes ordines sacros etc. [et in ipsis ministrare] ut in forma.

Fiat si ita est et si huiusmodi homicidiis non dedit consilium, auxilium vel favorem D. s. †. Et commitatur episcopo [*sic*] Eboracensi vel eius vicario. Fiat D. s. †.

711. [*Rome*], *14 April 1451. Lewis Nuten, priest, vicar of Marston*(?),[35] *Lincoln dioc., seeks absolution from simony and consequent censures and penalties, dispensation from irregularity, and that he may retain his benefices.* Reg. 3, fol. 222v.

[Rome], xviii kal. Maii. Item pro Ludovico Nuten', presbitero, vicario de Mersone Linco[l]niensis diocesis, quia ut dictam vicariam obtineret quasdam pecunias solvit contra constitutionem etc.,[36] labem symonie incurrendo, et sic supplicatur ut supra in omnibus et per omnia [quatinus ipsum a symonie labe et aliis ecclesiasticis censuris et penis predictis et peccatis suis aliis absolvi, super irregularitate quoque quam celebrando divina officia et inmiscendo se illis contraxit dispensari, quodque ut huiusmodi beneficia ecclesiastica sic et taliter sibi collata, si sibi alias canonice conferantur, retinere possit concedere dignemini de gratia speciali, non obstantibus premissis et aliis contrariis quibuscumque].

Fiat de expresso et cumponat [*sic*] cum vicario sancti Petri D. s. †.

712. [*Rome*], *18 April 1451. Adam Haymond,*[37] *priest, master or custodian of the chantry of SS. John the Baptist and John the Evangelist, 'Frerenatrer', Durham dioc., seeks a licence and dispensation so that he may go to a* studium generale *to study theology or one of the laws, not reside at that chantry or any other benefice, and receive the fruits of these or farm them out for seven years.* Reg. 3, fol. 218v

[Rome], xv kal. Aprilis. Supplicatur sanctitati vestre pro parte devoti vestri Ade Hay'mond presbiteri, magistri sive custodem [*recte* custodis] cantarie

---

[35] There were two parishes simply called Marston in Lincoln diocese, in Lincolnshire and Oxfordshire respectively.

[36] The preceding entry in the register refers to Martin V's constitution 'Multa contra symoniacam' and Eugenius IV's constitution 'Cum detestabile scelus', on which see **487** n.

[37] Perhaps the Adam Haymond, apparently an alumnus of Oxford University, admitted as rector of St Ebbe's, Oxford, on 12 May 1457 and as canon and prebendary at Hemingborough (Yorks.) on 3 March 1468, when he was styled *magister* (*BRUO*, ii. 895). An Adam Haymond, priest, Coventry and Lichfield dioc., was appointed in the Curia as a notary public on 9 May 1450 (*CPL*, x. 483).

sanctorum Iohannis Baptiste et Iohannis euuangeliste de Frernatrer ~~Dul~~ Dunelmensis diocesis, quatinus sibi ut in quocumque generali studio, ad quod se causa studendi aut legendi in sacra scriptura aut altero iurium transferre se proponat, illuc ire, a dicta cantaria a[c] quocumque alio ecclesiastico beneficio quod ipsum infra ~~setempnium~~ septennium obtinere contingat abesse, et in eodem ad septennium fructus quoque prefate cantarie et aliorum infra septennium habendam [*sic*] obtinendorum beneficiorum recipere et levare, cottidianis distributionibus dumtaxat exceptis, illosque arrendare etiam laicis possit et valeat licentiam impartiri ac secum dispensari mandare dignemini de gratia speciali cum non obstantibus et clausis opportunis.

Fiat de speciali D. s. †. I.

713. [*Rome*], *20 April 1451. Gwilym Mathes, Lewis ap Hywel ap Rhys ap Dafydd ap* Gli' *ap* Aid', *and Hywel request commutation of penance for killing a priest.*[38] Reg. 3, fol. 209r.

[Rome], xii kal. Maii a° v^{to}. Supplicat [*sic*] Vilgelmus Mathes et Lewys ap Hoel ap Rees ap David ap Gli' ap Aid' et Hoel de familiis suis ut penitentiam eis iniunctam de presbitericidio un[de] quod deberent ire de loco suo \ad locum/ ubi fuerit perpetratum, cum multum distet, in alia opera permutare.

Fiat de speciali D. s. †.

714. [*Rome*], *21 April 1451. Dafydd ap Dafydd ap Ieuan, priest, Llandaff dioc., seeks a declaration that he may celebrate even though his enemies claim that his parents were related in the fourth degree of consanguinity and did not obtain a dispensation.* Reg. 3, fol. 202v.

[Rome], xi kal. Maii. David ap David ap Ieuan, presbiter diocesis Landunensis [*recte* Landavensis], supplicat declarari in suis ordinibus posse legitime celebrare, non obstante quod aliqui eius emuli asserunt quod ipsius parentes, licet legitime contraxerunt matrimonium et ex eis legitime procreatum [*recte* procreatus], tamen dicuntur esse et fuisse in quarto consanguinitatis coniuncti, nulla obtinenda [*recte* obtenta] dispensatione; etiam sunt mortui. Quare supplicat ad obstruendum ora ipsorum ut supra.

Fiat si ita est D. s. †.

715. [*Rome*], *8 May 1451. Owain ap Madog alias [son] of Hugh ap Madog, priest, St David's dioc., intervened in a quarrel between Thomas ap [. . .], priest, Llandaff dioc., and a certain Thomas, and when that layman and other armed men attacked him, he struck the layman with a knife in self-defence such that the latter died within a year; he requests absolution and a dispensation.* Reg. 3, fol. 239r.

[Rome], viii id. Maii. Exponitur pro parte Ouini ap Mador alias Hugonis ap Mador, presbiteri diocesis Menevensis, quod ob certa contentione cum Thoma ap [. . .], presbitero diocesis Landavensis, et cum aliis propter kam' ap [*sic*] quidam Thomas ex adverso principalis dicto presbitero T. iniuriatus est in co[nte]mptu sedis apostolice. Exponens qui contradictione ibidem

---

[38] The diocese is omitted but the supplicants' names are clearly Welsh.

intraverat dixit dicto laico animo imprendi(?) [*recte* impediendi?] quod contra papam hoc agere non deberet, dictus laicus cum aliis exponentem agressi sunt cum armis, ipse videns mortem non posse [evadere] cultello extracto quem penes se habuit vim vi repellendo unum de illis letaliter percussit ita quod mortuus est per spacium unius anni. Cum autem [de premissis] doleat, supplicat dispensari et absolvi quod possit ministrare in susceptis.

~~Et declaretur~~ Fiat si ita est et si alias mortem non potuit evadere et de his constet. Et quod declaretur in foro consciencie propter distantiam loci. Fiat D. s. †.

716. [*Rome*], *21 August 1451.* Same grant as **717** for Henry Arthinglorm, priest, professed monk of the same Oxney(?) (*Uc'ne*) Priory, OSB, [Lincoln dioc.]. *Fiat ut supra* [*si ita est et si talis fuit metus qui solet cadere in constantem et postea tacite vel expresse ratam hoc non habuit*] *D. s. †.* Reg. 3, fol. 240r.

717. [*Rome*], *27 August 1451. William Daventre, priest professed of* [*Oxney Priory?*], *OSB, Lincoln dioc., made profession as a youth under parental pressure. He seeks a declaration that he is not bound to that order.* Reg. 3, fol. 240r.

[Rome], vi kal. Septembris. Exponitur pro fratre Villelmo Daventre, presbitero professo ordinis sancti Benedicti Lincolniensis diocesis, quod propter vim \parentum suorum/ tempore iuventutis sue infra annum discretionis fecit professionem et de facto dimisit taliter qualiter pater dixit quod si nullet [*recte* nollet] sibi consentire, interfici permitteret, et propter metum per aliquot annos permansit, tamen numquam professionem ratam habuit. Quare supplicat ad obstruenda ora obloquentium et emulorum declarari nullo modo dicto ordini debere et quod in seculo possit stare libere et licite.

Fiat si ita est et si talis fuit metus qui solet cadere in constantem et postea tacite vel expresse ratam hoc non habuit D. s. †.

Et committatur priori prioratus sui. Fiat D. s. †.

718. [*Rome*], *27 August 1451. William Bernet of Haddenham and Isabel Wadebrugghe, Lincoln dioc., seek a dispensation from* cognatio spiritualis *so that they may marry.* Reg. 3, fol. 262v.

[Rome], vi kal. Septembris. Exponitur pro parte Willelmi Bernet de Hadnam et Ysabelle Wadebrugghe Lincolniensis diocesis quod ipsi desiderant invicem matrimonialiter copulari, sed quia pater dicte Ysabelle predictum Willelmum de sacro fonte levavit, quare supplicatur quatinus impedimento cognationis spiritualis non obstante matrimonium libere et licite contrahere possint et in eo postquam etc. [remanere].

Fiat de speciali et expresso D. s. †. I.

Sumptum ex registro sacre penitentiarie apostolice per me Conradinum de Narnia, ipsius registri custodem, regente reverendissimo domino domino Dominico, tituli sancte crucis in Ierusalem presbitero cardinali, summo penitentiario, sub dato subscripto.[39]

---

[39] Conradinus also signed beside this in the right hand margin.

Et si placeat, committatur domino Vincencio Clementi, sanctissimi domini pape subdyacono, preposito Valentino, ad presens in regno Anglie nuncio ac collectori apostolico,[40] cum episcopus Lincolniensis ordinarius cui alias commissa fuit exequi non possit quia non consecratus nec pacificam possessionem est adeptus.[41] Fiat de sp D. s. †. I.

719. [*Rome*], *10 September 1451. Fr Henry, abbot of Stoneleigh Abbey*,[42] *Cistercian order, Coventry and Lichfield dioc., seeks a licence to eat meat and wear linen clothing.* Reg. 3, fol. 246r.

[Rome], iiii ydus Septembris. Exponitur sanctitati vestre pro parte devoti vestri fratris Heynrici, abbatis monasterii beate Marie de Stonleia ordinis Cisterciensis Conventrensis et Lichefeldensis diocesis, quod ipse adeo debilis et diversis passionibus oppressus existit quod ammodo corpus suum absque esu carnium et vestibus lineis sustentare non potest. Supplicatur igitur eidem sanctitati vestre pro parte dicti exponentis quatinus sibi ut esu carnium et vestibus lineis uti posset [*sic*] et valeat licentiam misericorditer indulgere de gratia speciali, non obstantibus statutis et consuetudinibus dicti ordinis et aliis contrariis quibuscumque de consilio confexionis [*recte* confessoris] et medici.

[Fiat de speciali] D. s. †. I. Et quod committatur priori eiusdem monasterii attento quod ab ordinario suo longe distat et propter infirmitatem eundem ordinarium adire non potest. Fiat D. s. †.

720. [*Rome*], *9 November 1451. John son of Reginald, rector of St Mary-le-Bow grammar school, London, seeks to be released from an oath to teach grammar in only one school or place in London.* Reg. 3, fol. 256r.

[Rome], v ydus Novembris. Exponitur pro magistro \Iohanne/ Reynaldi seniore, rectore scolarium gramaticalium beate Marie de Arcubus Londoniensis,

---

[40] Vincent Clement of Valencia, Aragon, was a papal *cubicularius* by 1440 and papal subdeacon and chaplain by 1443. He was orator of Duke Humphrey of Gloucester in 1440, envoy of Henry VI in 1440, 1443 and 1448 (*CPL*, viii. 224; ix. 392; x. 37), and proctor of John Stafford, archbishop-elect of Canterbury, in 1443 and of George Neville, archbishop-elect of York, in 1465 (*CPL*, viii. 258; xii. 440). He was papal nuncio by October 1444 and a collector of the papal chamber in England by March 1449 (*CPL*, viii. 299). He was appointed collector general there on 6 January 1450, and reappointed on 13 June 1455 and 16 November 1458, but Pius II deposed him on 9 August 1460 for misconduct (*CPL*, x. 271, 273; xi. 192, 680, 682). He was reinstated by Pius II by February 1463, and reappointed by Paul II on 19 January 1469; he was still a papal collector in England in July 1474 (*CPL*, xii. 380–4; xiii. 214). He incepted as an MA in 1433 at Oxford University, which conferred the degree of DTh on him at Henry VI's request in 1441. He held numerous benefices in England, Spain and France between 1439 and his death in March 1475 (*BRUO*, i. 432; *CPL*, x. 37, 192; xi. 389; xii. 250). See also Lunt, ii. 16, 136–8, 141, 581, 583, 704; Weiss, *Humanism*, 75–7 (with further references at 192).

[41] The election of John Chedworth received the royal assent on 11 February 1451, but in the meantime William Gray, a papal protonotary, had been provided to the see (23 December 1450). The disputed see remained vacant until Chedworth was provided to it and Gray resigned (5 May 1452): Le Neve, *Fasti 1300–1541*, i: *Lincoln*, 2–3; Eubel, ii. 196).

[42] Henry Everton, the dates of whose abbacy are not known (Smith, *Heads of Religious Houses*, iii. 333).

quod ipse olim propter certas causas animum suum moventes ac animo commotus iuravit gramaticam nisi in uno dicte civitatis loco sive in una eiusdem civitatis scola, ~~ad~~ videlicet aut in sancto Paulo aut in sancto Martino magno aut in dicto beate Marie de Arcubus scolarum seu locorum, legere seu dicte grammatice scientiam docere. Cum autem, pater sancte, ex huiusmodi iuramenti observancia plura damna provenire possint, supplicat ipsum a temeritate iurandi absolvique [*recte* absolvi], iuramentum huiusmodi relaxari et deinde ipsum nunciari ad ipsius iuramenti observanciam non teneri misericorditer mandare dignemini de gratia [speciali].

Fiat de speciali D. s. †. I.

721. [*Rome*], *22 February 1452. Richard Lawis, priest, Norwich dioc., seeks a dispensation so that he may not be compelled to serve a benefice in accordance with English provincial and synodal constitutions.* Reg. 3, fol. 282v.

[Rome], viii kal. Martii. Exponitur pro parte devoti oratoris vestri Richardi Lawis, presbiteri Norwicensis diocesis, quod quedam constitutiones provinciales et synodales in regno Anglie existant quibus cavetur quod presbiteri non habentes ecclesias parrochiales aut alia beneficia ipsis invitis ad serviendum beneficiis curatis aut alias per ordinarium loci compelli possunt, sed quia nemo invitus ad beneficium impenderi debet, quare supplicatur pro parte dicti exponentis quatinus dictis et aliis constitucionibus et ordinacionibus non obstantibus secum ut ad serviendum alicui beneficio curato vel non curato eo invito compelli [non] possit dispensare dignemini de gratia speciali.

Fiat de speciali D. s. †. I.

722. [*Rome*], *22 February 1452. Thomas Lawri, chaplain and priest, Exeter dioc., attacked John Barton, priest, Exeter dioc., and mutilated two fingers of the latter's left hand with a knife. He requests that the pope order his ordinary or another prelate of Exeter Cathedral to give him absolution and dispensation.* Reg. 3, fol. 283r.

[Rome], viii kal. Martii. Exponitur pro parte Thome Lawri, capellani et presbiteri Exoniensis diocesis, quod ipse ob rancorem et invidiam inter quemdam Iohannem Barton', presbiterum dicte diocesis, et eum contractam instigacione dyabolica ductus manus in dictum Iohannem iniecit violentas et cum uno cultello digitos duos in manu sinistra videlicet medium et articularium graviter \lesit et/[43] mutilavit, in articulario non abscindendo sed aliunde ledendo. Supplicat igitur idem exponens absens quatinus secum misericorditer agentes ordinario loci vel alicui prelati [*sic*] ecclesie Exoniensis quod eum ab omnibus sententiis, censuris et peccatis [absolvat et super] irregularitatis et infamie macula premissorum occasione contracta [dispenset] et ut in suo ordine ministrare libere etc. [possit mandare dignemini].

Fiat de speciali et expresso D. s. †. I.

---

[43] Addition noted in the margin.

723. [Rome, *c*. March x April 1452].[44] William [son] of Andrew, acolyte, Lincoln dioc., *familiaris et continuus commensalis* of the bishop of Segni,[45] and also beneficed in that diocese in the church of Sant'Angelo *castri Metclavici*. (This incomplete entry is crossed through.) Reg. 3, fol. 295v.

724. [Rome], 2 March 1453. [Supplication for a] dispensation for John Lovell, son of Richard Lovell, layman, and Agnes, daughter of John White, of Eling (*Yelinge*) parish, Winchester dioc., so that they may remain in their marriage contracted publicly *per verba legitime de presenti* and consummate it, notwithstanding the impediment of *cognatio spiritualis* of which they had not been unaware, and legitimation of future issue. *Fiat de speciali et expresso D. s'. †. I.* Reg. 3, fol. 361v.

725. [*Rome*], *24 March 1453. Walter Revyth and Margaret Reynbour, Norwich dioc., request a dispensation from the impediment of* cognatio spiritualis *so that they may remain married and legitimation of their existing and future issue.* Reg. 3, fol. 370r.

[Rome], ix kal. Aprilis. Wa[l]tero Revyth et Margarete Reynbour, coniugibus Norwicensis diocesis, ut in matrimonio inter eos per verba legitime de presenti contracto ac in facie ecclesie solempnizato, carnalique copula subsecuta, prole procreato, libere et licite remanere valeant, non obstante impedimento cognationis spiritualis ignoranter inter eos existente ex quo pater dicte Margarete dictum Wa[l]therum de sacro fonte levavit, dispensatio prolisque suscepte et suscipiende legitimatio.

Fiat de speciali et expresso D. s'. †. I.

726. [*Rome*], *26 March 1453. Richard Lamberti, priest, rector of St Michael's parish church, Easton*(?), *Salisbury dioc., swore that he would do as Nicholas Carent, dean of Wells,*[46] *told him so that he could have that church, then a certain William Noorth*[47] *gave him the presentation of that church in return for him swearing that he would resign it in favour of Thomas Smyth*[48] *when*

---

[44] Not dated, but the approximate date can be deduced from the entry's position in the register.
[45] The bishop of Segni at this time was Petrus Antonius Petrucci, O.P. (Eubel, ii. 237).
[46] Nicholas Caraunt, who claimed to be of noble family, was second son of William Caraunt of Toomer-in-Henstridge (Somerset). He was principal of Vine Hall, Oxford, in 1436 and still in September 1438. He was BCL of Oxford University by 1437, BCn & CL by 1442, and LicCL by 1445. He held many benefices between 1427 and his death. He obtained a papal licence on 7 January 1457 to choose a confessor who might grant him absolution even in reserved cases and plenary remission of all sins *in mortis articulo*. He was secretary to Queen Margaret of England in 1448 and still in 1458. He died in April 1467 (*BRUO*, i. 353; *CPL*, viii. 659; x. 2–4, 43, 424–5; xi. 184, 298; *Reg. Bekynton*, no. 1380).
[47] Perhaps the William North of Corston and Boyton (Wilts.) who was admitted as a scholar on 10 October 1420 to Winchester College and on 28 March 1425 to New College, Oxford, where he became a fellow in 1427 but resigned in August 1437. He was BCn & CL of Oxford University by 1445 and a notary public by 1446. For his ecclesiastical benefices and offices see *BRUO*, ii.1368; *CPL*, ix. 511; *Reg. Bekynton*, xvii, nos. 5, 138, 185, 246, 322, 454, 461, 512, 515, 592, 617, 661). He died by February 1462.
[48] Perhaps the Thomas Smyth *alias* Bolt, who was MA, probably of Oxford. He held various benefices between 1453 and death, mostly in and around Winchester. He was granted a papal dispensation on 27 November 1456 to hold an additional incompatible benefice. He died by January 1494 (*BRUO*, iii. 1720; *CPL*, xi. 51).

Nicholas V (1447–1455) 163

William or Nicholas asked him to do so; he seeks absolution, a dispensation and a declaration. Reg. 3, fol. 371v.

[Rome], vii° kal. Aprilis [anno septimo]. Ricardo Lamberti, presbitero rectore parrocchialis ecclesie sancti Michaelis de Asten' Sauzbergensis [*recte* Saresberiensis?] diocesis, quod cum olim quidam Nycolaus Carent, decanus ecclesie Welensis, ad dictum exponentem accessisset eidemque verba infrascripta vel in effectu eis similia dixisset: 'Vis tu facere secundum consilium meum et ego faciam te rectorem dicte ecclesie de Astron [*sic*]'. Cui exponens ipse respondit, 'Ego faciam', et sic facere ad sancta dei evangelia iuravit. Tribus vero diebus demum elapsis ad ipsum exponentem venit quidam Guillermus Noorth et presentationem dicte ecclesie portavit sigillatam dicens eidem exponenti : 'Tu iurabis quod ecclesiam de Astron predictam renuntiabis et in manibus ordinarii ad utilitatem Thome Smyth quando ad hoc per me vel dictum Nycolaum Carent fueris requisitus alias non tibi dabo presentationem hanc dicte ecclesie.' Et sic ut petiit dictus Guillermus iuravit et vigore dicte presentacionis dictam ecclesiam consecutus canonice fuit et in presenti tenet. Cum autem dictus exponens dubitet propter predictam promissionem reatum symonie et sententiam excommunicationis et alias censuras et penas in tales per constitutiones felicis recordationis domini Martini pape V que incipit 'Multe contra symoniacam pravitatem' et domini Eugenii pape IIII que incipit 'Cum detestabile scelus'[49] sive alias generaliter etc. [promulgatas] et sic ligatus tamquam iuris ignarus non tamen in contemptum clavium divina celebravit officia et alias inmiscuit se eisdem. Et quia predicta promissio symoniaca contra iusticiam existit servari non debet, quare ipsum a reatu symonie, dicte excommunicationis et aliarum penarum sententiis absolvi petit et super irregularitate et inhabilitate ex premissis contractis quodque in suis ordinibus libere ministrare valeat necnon dictam ecclesiam licite et libere tenere et quod ad dictorum promissionis seu iuramenti huiusmodi observantiam non teneri misericorditer petit secum dispensari et declarari.

Fiat de speciali et expresso D. s. † I.

727. [*Rome*], *7 May 1453*(?).[50] *Dafydd Morgan, priest, St David's dioc., kept silent about his defect of birth when he was ordained to all, even holy, orders. He seeks absolution from that excess, dispensation from irregularity, and annulment of his* inhabilitas *and infamy so that he may minister in all his orders and hold a benefice.* Reg. 3, fol. 367r.

[Rome], non. Maii. Davide [*sic*] Morgan, presbitero Menivensis [*sic*] diocesis, [exponit] quod ipse alias tacito defectu natalium de soluto et soluta genitus se fecit alias rite ad omnes etiam sacros et presbiteratus ordines promoveri et in illis ministravit, excessum et irregularitatem incurrendo, a quo excessu et peccatis suis aliis petit absolvi, ac super irregularitate secum dispensari, omnemque inhabilitatis et infamie maculam sive notam penitus aboleri, quodque in omnibus et singulis per eum susceptis ordinibus ministrare et beneficium ecclesiasticum cum cura vel sine cura si sibi alias canonice conferatur

---

[49] For these constitutions see **487** n.
[50] The page is headed 'Rome anno sexto', which would suggest that the year was 1452.

libere et licite recipere et retinere valeat, premissis ac dicto defectu in aliquo non obstantibus, ipsi concedi petit.

Fiat de speciali D. s. †. I.

728. [*Rome*], *25 September 1453(?).*[51] *Fr John Gloucester, priest, professed monk of the abbey of the BVM and St Egwin, Evesham, OSB, Worcester dioc.,*[52] *incurred excommunication for apostasy. He seeks absolution from that sentence and a dispensation from irregularity.* Reg. 3, fol. 385r.

[Rome], vii kal. Octobris. Exponit sanctitati vestre devotus orator vester frater Iohannes Gloucester, presbiter, monachus professus monasterii beate Marie et sancte Euwine de Evesham ordinis sancti Benedicti Wigorniensis diocesis, quod ipse olim monasterium in quo se voto professionis astrinxerat ex quadam animi levitate illicenciatus exivit, habitu suo semper retento et per mundum dampnabiliter evagando, propter quod excommunicationis incurrit sententiam et sic ligatus tamquam simplex et iuris ignarus non tamen in contemptum clavium divina celebravit officia et alias inmiscuit se eisdem. Supplicat sanctitati vestre dictus exponens quatinus ipsum a dicta sententia quam incurrit et excessibus huiusmodi ac peccatis suis aliis absolvi secumque super irregularitate dispensari misericorditer mandare dignemini de gratia speciali.

Fiat de speciali D. s. †. I.

729. [*Rome*], *10 October 1453(?). Sister Joan Frances, professed nun of Legbourne Priory, Cistercian order, Lincoln dioc., seeks a dispensation because of her old age so that she is not bound to attend the abbey's services but may stay in her room and take part in the offices and eat and drink there.* Reg. 3, fol. 387v.

[Rome, anno sexto], vi idus Octobris. Exponitur sanctitati vestre pro parte devote oratricis vestre sororis Iohanne Frances, monialis professe monasterii in Legburn ordinis Cisterciensis Lincolniensis diocesis, quod ipsa adeo senectu[te] et aliis infirmitatibus gravata sit quod ad officia et exercicia exteriora dicti monasterii ammodo et ulterius insistere non sufficiat; vult tamen officiis divinis quantum potest interesse. Quare supplicatur eidem sanctitati vestre pro parte dicte exponentis, que a sua superiori ut ad dicta officia ammodo exercenda exteriora licenciata est, quatinus secum ut pro maiori securitate animi sui secum ut [*sic*] ad ipsa officia non teneatur sed divinis interesse officiis et in camera propria stare et ibidem commedere et bibere possit et valeat secum dispensare dignemini de gratia vestra speciali.

Fiat de speciali de consensu superioris vel abbatisse D. s. †. I

---

[51] The page is headed 'De diversis materiis. Rome domini Nicolai pape quinti anno sexto', which would suggest that the year was 1452.

[52] He was granted a dispensation on 16 December 1452 to hold a benefice with or without cure of souls for life (*CPL*, x. 115).

730. [*Rome, 12 October 1453(?)*]. *John Gye, priest, Lincoln dioc., seeks a dispensation so that he may not be compelled to serve a simple benefice or benefice with cure of souls in accordance with English provincial and synodal constitutions.* Reg. 3, fol. 388v.

[Rome, anno sexto iiii idus Octobris]. Exponitur sanctitati vestre pro parte devoti oratoris vestri Iohannis Gye, presbiteri Lincolniensis diocesis, quod nonnulle constitutiones in regno Anglie Ottonis et Ottoboni olim in dicto regno sedis apostolice legatorum et alie constitutiones provinciales et synodales existant quibus dicitur contineri quod presbiteri non habentes beneficia curata aut simplicia ad serviendum aliis beneficiis similibus compelli possint. Et quia dictus exponens similibus beneficiis eo invito servire commode non potest, quare supplicatur eidem sanctitati vestre pro parte dicti exponentis quatinus secum ut ad serviendum alicui beneficio curato aut simplici eo invito compelli non possit dispensare [dignemini], constitutionibus predictis aliisve in contrarium facientibus non obstantibus quibuscumque et cum clausis oportunis de gratia vestra speciali.

Fiat de speciali D. s. †. I.

731. [Rome], 12 October 1453(?). Same grant as **730** for Thomas Baxter, priest, Lincoln dioc. *Fiat de speciali D. s. †. I.* Reg. 3, fol. 388v.

732. [*Rome*], *31 October 1453(?)*. *Thomas Sollay, priest, Lincoln dioc.,*[53] *conducted a wedding without the banns having been published and in a chapel that was possibly unconsecrated in St Edmund's hospice, Trastevere, Rome.*[54] *He seeks absolution from excommunication and from suspension from divine offices and a dispensation from irregularity.* Reg. 3, fol. 392v.

[Rome, anno sexto] ii° kal. Novembris. Exponit sanctitati vestre devotus vester Thomas Sollay, presbiter Lincolniensis diocesis in curia presens, quatinus ipse tamquam simplex et iuris ignarus contra formam capituli 'Cum inhibitio de clandestina desponsatione' in una capella sita in hospitali sancti Edmundi de Urbe in regione Transtiberim, de qua dubitatur utrum dedicata existit aut non, celebravit seu solemnizavit matrimonium inter quendam Scotum et certam aliam mulierem quorum nomina ignorat, qui per verba de presenti insimul contraxerunt, missam tunc inibi celebrando, bannis non editis, credens id licite facere posse et propter hoc aliquam iuris penam videlicet suspensionem a divinis seu irregularitatem aut excommunicationis sententiam [non] incurrisse. Dubitat tamen premissorum occasione suspensionem a divinis aut excommunicationis sententiam et irregularitatem incurrisse.

---

[53] He was vicar of All Saints, Theddlethorpe (Lincs.), and St Oswald's, Strubby (Lincs.), Lincoln dioc., by 1450, being dispensed to hold these benefices together. On 16 January 1450 he was granted a licence to farm out his benefices while studying letters at university and appointed in the Curia as a notary public (*CPL*, x. 56, 455, see also 121). He was an *abbreviator* of papal letters by 27 October 1452 (*CPL*, x. 375). See also M. M. Harvey, *England, Rome and the Papacy 1417–1464* (Manchester, 1993), 31, 65, 107.

[54] Founded as St Chrysogonus hospice by John White in 1396, it merged with St Thomas's hospice, the principal English hospice in Rome, in 1464. The chapel was recorded in 1404 as being in a garden of St Edmund's hospice (M. M. Harvey, *The English in Rome 1362–1420* (Cambridge, 1999), 12).

Supplicat igitur sanctitati vestre quatinus ipsum T. ab huiusmodi suspensione a divinis et excommunicationis sententia absolvere et super suspensione et irregularitate sic contracta et quam premissorum occasione incurrit et in suis ordinibus susceptis ministrare valeat dispensare dignemini cum eodem de gratia [fol. 393r] speciali.

Fiat de speciali D. s. †. Et quod committatur episcopo Pennensi[55] attento, pater sancte, quod huiusmodi delictum in Urbe perpetratum fuit. Fiat D. s. †. I.

733. [Rome], 4 November 1453(?).[56] Supplication on the part of John Parcii [*recte* Percy], subdean of the church of Lincoln,[57] that the pope grant a licence to him with four other persons so that they may visit the Lord's sepulchre for the sake of pilgrimage and devotion *ut in forma*. *Fiat de speciali D. s'. †. I.* Reg. 3, fol. 394r.

De defectu natalium et de uberiori

734. [Rome], 26 March 1448. Geoffrey Elwy of Llanelwy, clerk, St Asaph dioc., born of an unmarried man and an unmarried woman, requests that the pope grant him a dispensation that he may be promoted to all orders and obtain a benefice even with cure of souls, notwithstanding his defect of birth. *Fiat de speciali.* Reg. 4, fol. 8v.

735. [Rome], 7 May 1449. Same dispensation as **734** for Gruffydd (*Gruffin alias Gruffith*) ap Gwilym (*Geoilyn*) ap Owain(?) or Ieuan(?) (*appuan'*) Duai, St David's dioc., born of an unmarried man and unmarried woman. *Fiat de speciali R. Vulteran.* Reg. 4, fol. 20r.

736. [Rome, at St Peter's, *c.* 25–7 May 1449].[58] Same dispensation as **734** for Richard Plumeri, scholar, Coventry [and Lichfield] dioc., born of a priest and an unmarried woman. [*Fiat de speciali R. Vulteran.*]. Reg. 4, fol. 18v.

737. [Rome, at St Peter's, *c.* 25–7 May 1449]. [Supplication] for John Laken, priest, professed of Coventry convent, OFM, born of a married knight and an unmarried woman, for a dispensation that he may obtain any offices or *administrationes* of that order other than the principal one. [*Fiat de speciali R. Vulteran.*]. Reg. 4, fol. 18v.

738. [Rome, at St Peter's, *c.* 25–7 May 1449]. Same dispensation as **737** for Thomas Garant, priest, professed of OFM, [Coventry convent]. *Fiat de speciali R. Vulteran.* Reg. 4, fol. 18v.

---

[55] Iohannes de Polena, bishop of Penne (1433–54) and *auditor* of the Rota (Eubel, ii. 236).
[56] The page is headed 'Anno sexto', which suggests that the year was 1452.
[57] Master John Percy, BCnL, was subdean of Lincoln from 1419 to 1458 (Le Neve, *Fasti 1300–1541*, i: *Lincoln*, 5).
[58] The preceding entry is dated at St Peter's, Rome, 25 May 1449, the next dated entry, 27 May 1449.

739. Spoleto, 1 July 1449. Supplication on the part of Gruffin *alias* Gruffith ap Gwilym ap Ieuan Duy, scholar, St David's dioc., who was born of an unmarried man and an unmarried woman [and wishes to be enrolled] in the *militia clericalis*, for the pope to grant him a dispensation that he may be promoted to all minor and holy orders and then [minister] in them and obtain and retain a benefice even with cure of souls, notwithstanding his defect of birth. *Fiat de speciali D. s. †*. Reg. 4, fol. 17v.

740. [Rome], 30 July 1449. Supplication on the part of Dafydd Elisis and Ieuan ap Iorwerth(?) (*op Iar'*), scholars, St Asaph dioc., Robert Laiat, scholar, Coventry and Lichfield dioc. (*Lichien' diocesis et Conveturensis diocesis*), and Thomas Candeles [son of] James, Coventry and Lichfield (*Lichfolde*) dioc., all born of priests and unmarried women, for the pope to grant them dispensations that they may be promoted to all holy orders and obtain and retain a benefice even with cure of souls, notwithstanding their defect of birth. *Fiat de speciali M. abbas S. Gregorii*. Reg. 4, fol. 20r.

741. [Rome], 3 January 1450. Same dispensation as **734** for Thomas Westen, acolyte, Norwich (*Norvotensis*) dioc., born of an unmarried man and an unmarried woman. *Fiat de speciali D. s. †*. Reg. 4, fol. 22r.

742. [Rome], 8 January 1450. John Robin, acolyte, Coventry and Lichfield dioc.,[59] born of an unmarried man and an unmarried woman, had himself promoted to minor [orders] and ministered in them; [he requests that the pope grant him] absolution [and a dispensation so that he may] be promoted to all orders [and obtain a benefice even with cure of souls]. *Fiat de speciali* [*D. s. †*]. Reg. 4, fol. 26v.

743. [Rome], 11 January 1450. Roger Chapam(?), subdeacon, York dioc., born of an unmarried man and an unmarried woman, kept silent about this defect when he had himself promoted to the order of the subdiaconate and ministered in it. It is requested that he may be promoted [to all orders] and also [obtain] a benefice with or without cure of souls. *Fiat de speciali D. s. †*. Reg. 4, fol. 27r.

744. [Rome], 15 January 1450. Same dispensation as **734** for Thomas Veston, [acolyte, Norwich dioc.,] born of an unmarried man and an unmarried woman. *Fiat de speciali D. s. †*. Reg. 4, fol. 24v.

745. [Rome], 17 January 1450. [Supplication for a dispensation] for William (*Vilgelmus*) Mercaton, novice, Cistercian [order], Chichester(?) dioc.,[60] born of an unmarried man and an unmarried woman, [that he may obtain any] office and dignity other than the principal one or provincial of the order of St Mary. *Et si placet committatur abbati monasterii sui. Fiat de speciali D. s. †*. Reg. 4, fol. 24v.

746. [*Rome*], *18 January 1450. John Malory, York dioc., received a papal dispensation from illegitimacy whereby he obtained a benefice, but he then exchanged benefices twice. He seeks absolution from these excesses and a dispensation to hold an additional, compatible benefice.* Reg. 4, fol. 25r.

---

[59] The scribe originally wrote 'Iohanni Suarez acolito Fisten. dioc.'
[60] The entry has 'Cisterciensis diocesis'.

xv kal. Februarii. Similem gratiam Iohanni Malory Eboracensis diocesis, cum alias fuerit dispensatum per sedem apostolicam de [defectu natalium quem patitur de . . .][61] genitus et soluta quod possit etc. [ad omnes ordines promoveri et beneficium obtinere] etiam curatum, ac vigore litterarum unum primo quod permutavit, licet ad hoc habere se non extendebant, assecutus fuit, et secundum assecutus [fuit], quod subsequenter pro tertio permutaverit, et tertium similiter pro alio beneficio ecclesiastico permutasset et possessionem beneficii assecutus prout etc. etc. tenet de presenti et possidet. Estque paratus dictum beneficium quod possidet dimictere. [Supplicat sanctitati vestre] ipsum ab excessibus absolvi mandare, non obstante defectu, ac unum quod vigore dicte dispensationis huiusmodi obtinere contingat recipere ac sibi uberiorem gratiam facientes quod, si ex fructibus etc. [dicti beneficii] comode substentari non poterit, unum aliud cum primo compatibile etc. [recipere] et semel permutare [valeat] d. misericorditer dignemini dispensare.

Fiat de speciali D. s. †.

747. [Rome], 18 February 1450. [Supplication for a dispensation] for John Blich, [Coventry and] Lichfield dioc., born of an unmarried man and an unmarried woman, [that he may be promoted to all orders and obtain a benefice with or without cure of souls, notwithstanding his defect of birth]. *Commitatur episcopo Spoletano.*[62] *Fiat D. s. †.* Reg. 4, fol. 25v.

748. [Rome], 3 March 1450. [Supplication for a dispensation] for Fr Peter Saxot, Carmelite order, Norwich dioc.,[63] born of an unmarried man and an unmarried woman, [that he may be made a clerk (*clericali karectere insigniri*), promoted to all holy orders, obtain a benefice even with cure of souls, and be appointed to *administrationes* and offices of that order, notwithstanding his defect of birth]. *Fiat de speciali D. s. †.* Reg. 4, fol. 29r.

749. [Rome], 13 March 1450. Supplication for Reginald Kyffin, scholar, St Asaph dioc., who was born of an unmarried man and an unmarried woman and wishes to be enrolled in the *militia clericalis*, [for a dispensation] that he may be promoted to all holy orders and obtain a benefice with or without cure of souls, notwithstanding his defect of birth. *Fiat de speciali D. s. †.* Reg. 4, fol. 28v.

750. *[Rome], 19 March 1450. Gwilym, acolyte, St Asaph dioc., seeks a further dispensation from his illegitimacy.* Reg. 4, fol. 30bisr.

[Rome], xiiii kal. [Aprilis]. Guillelmo, accolito Assalvensis [*sic*] diocesis, de presbitero et soluta [genito], qui [h]actenus estitit [*recte* existit] dispensatum, cuius vigore omnes minores ordines prosequtus [fuit], ut de uberio[ri] dono gratie provideatur supplicat [*sic*] ut non obstante dicto defectu possit presbiteratum et curatum beneficium obtinere.

[61] Gap left in the entry after 'de', hence the status of his father cannot be determined.
[62] Berardus Eroli of Narni, bishop of Spoleto, who is a frequent signatory of petitions during this pontificate (see *RPG*, ii, p. xvii).
[63] Carmelite houses in Norwich diocese comprised Blakeney, King's Lynn, Norwich, and Yarmouth, all in Norfolk, and Ipswich in Suffolk.

Fiat de speciali D. s. †. Et committatur episcopo Civitatis Castelli.[64] Fiat D. s. †.

751. [Rome], 23 March 1450. [Supplication for a dispensation] for Ieuan ap Iankin (*appianc*), scholar of St Asaph, born of a priest and an unmarried woman, [that he may be promoted to all orders and hold a benefice with or without cure of souls, notwithstanding his defect of birth]. [*Fiat de speciali D. s. †*]. Reg. 4, fol. 30v.

752. [Rome], 23 March 1450. Same dispensation as **751** for Hugh [son] of Gwilym of Oswestry (*Osbaldestria*), St Asaph dioc., born of a married man and an unmarried woman. [*Fiat de speciali D. s. †*]. Reg. 4, fol. 30v.

753. [Rome], 23 March 1450. [Supplication for a dispensation] for George Wast, scholar, Coventry and Lichfield dioc., born of a married man and an unmarried woman, [that he may be promoted to all holy orders and obtain a benefice even with cure of souls, notwithstanding his defect of birth]. [*Fiat de speciali D. s. †*]. Reg. 4, fol. 32v.

754. [Rome], 23 March 1450. Same dispensation as **751** for Richard ap *Ripan*, scholar, St Asaph dioc., born of an unmarried man and an unmarried woman. *Fiat de speciali D. s. †.* Reg. 4, fol. 30*bis*v.

755. [Rome], 24 March 1450. Same dispensation as **734** for Ieuan ap Thomas ap Ifor (*Ivur*), scholar, St Asaph (*Assistensis*) dioc., born of an unmarried man and an unmarried woman. [*Fiat de speciali D. s. †*]. Approved with **25**. Reg. 4, fol. 30r.

756. [Rome], 24 March 1450. Same dispensation as **734** for Geoffrey ap Matthew (*Matheo*), scholar, St Asaph dioc., born of an unmarried man and an unmarried woman. [*Fiat de speciali D. s. †*]. Reg. 4, fol. 30r.

757. [Rome], 24 March 1450. Same dispensation as **751** for Robert (*Ruberto*) [son] of Richard Tegin(?), scholar, St Asaph dioc., born of a priest and an unmarried woman. [*Fiat de speciali D. s. †*]. Reg. 4, fol. 30*bis*v.

758. [Rome], 25 March 1450. Same dispensation as **753** for Ieuan ap Philip (*Philipp*), scholar, Llandaff dioc., born of an unmarried man and an unmarried woman. [*Fiat de speciali D. s. †*]. Reg. 4, fol. 31r.

759. [Rome], 26 March 1450. Same dispensation as **734** requested for Richard Crather, born of a priest and an unmarried woman, clerk, York dioc. *Fiat de speciali D. s. †.* Reg. 4, fol. 30r.

760. [Rome], 26 March 1450. Same dispensation as **734** for Henry Sanit(?), St Asaph dioc., born of an unmarried man and an unmarried woman. [*Fiat de speciali D. s. †*]. Reg. 4, fol. 30r.

---

[64] Radulfus, OESA, minor penitentiary, bishop of Città di Castello (Eubel, ii. 130).

761. [Rome], 27 March 1450. Same dispensation as **734** for Dafydd ap Philip ap Hywel (*Hoel*), scholar, St David's dioc., born of an unmarried man and an unmarried woman. [*Fiat de speciali D. s. †*]. Reg. 4, fol. 30r.

762. [Rome], 27 March 1450. Same dispensation as **734** for Walter ap ap [*sic*] Hywel (*Hoel*), St David's dioc., born of an unmarried man and an unmarried woman. [*Fiat de speciali D. s. †*]. Reg. 4, fol. 30r.

763. [Rome], 27 March 1450. Same dispensation as **753** for Bartholomew Gray, scholar, Lincoln dioc., born of an unmarried man and an unmarried woman. [*Fiat de speciali D. s. †*]. Reg. 4, fol. 33v.

764. [Rome], 27 March 1450. Same dispensation as **753** for John Grai, scholar, Norwich dioc., born of an unmarried man and an unmarried woman. [*Fiat de speciali D. s. †*]. Reg. 4, fol. 33v.

765. [Rome], 29 March 1450. Same dispensation as **753** for Ieuan Hoyskin, scholar, Llandaff (*Landunensis*) dioc., born of an unmarried man and an unmarried woman. [*Fiat de speciali D. s. †*]. Reg. 4, fol. 31v.

766. [Rome], 29 March 1450. Same dispensation as **753** for Dafydd ap *Rays alias* Neuburgh,[65] scholar, Bangor dioc., born of an unmarried man and an unmarried woman. [*Fiat de speciali D. s. †*]. Reg. 4, fol. 31v.

767. [Rome], 29 March 1450. Same dispensation as **753** for Meurig ap Ieuan ap Dafydd, scholar, Bangor dioc., born of an unmarried man and an unmarried woman. [*Fiat de speciali D. s. †*]. Reg. 4, fol. 31v.

768. [Rome], 29 March 1450. Same dispensation as **753** for Henry Pacok, scholar, York dioc., born of a priest and a married woman. [*Fiat de speciali D. s. †*]. Reg. 4, fol. 31v.

769. [Rome], 29 March 1450. [Supplication] for Ieuan Borthon, priest, canon of Penmon(?) [Priory] (*Penmonal' Prestollic*),[66] OSA, Bangor dioc., born of an unmarried man and an unmarried woman, that he may have a dignity and *personatus* etc., since he has already been dispensed from that defect of birth in due form. *Fiat de speciali D. s. †*. Reg. 4, fol. 32v.

770. [Rome], 30 March 1450. Same dispensation as **753** for Richard Fulurd, scholar, York (*Ebroacensis*) dioc., born of a priest and a married woman. [*Fiat de speciali D. s. †*]. Reg. 4, fol. 31r.

771. [Rome], 30 March 1450. Same dispensation as **753** for Reginald Houel ap Einion (*Egnan*), scholar, Bangor (*Ba\n/ggoriensis*) dioc., born of an unmarried man and an unmarried woman. [*Fiat de speciali D. s. †*]. Reg. 4, fol. 31r.

---

[65] Initially the name John Berthon was written.
[66] Or it may refer to Puffin Island, also known as Priestholme, a dependency of Penmon.

772. [Rome], 30 March 1450. Same dispensation as **753** for Geoffrey Matthew ap Madog, clerk, Bangor dioc., born of an unmarried man and an unmarried woman. [*Fiat de speciali D. s. †*]. Reg. 4, fol. 31r.

773. [Rome], 3 April 1450. Same dispensation as **753** for Dafydd Person, scholar, St David's dioc., born of a priest and an unmarried woman. *Fiat de speciali D. s. †.* (Approved with other supplications not from England or Wales.) Reg. 4, fol. 31r.

774. [Rome], 3 April 1450. Same dispensation as **753** for Dafydd ap *Percs*, scholar, St David's dioc., born of a priest and a married woman. [*Fiat de speciali D. s. † I.*]. Reg. 4, fol. 34v.

775. [Rome], 6 April 1450. Same dispensation as **753** for Gruffydd (*Griffin*) Moris, scholar, St David's dioc., born of a priest and an unmarried woman. [*Fiat de speciali D. s. † I.*]. Reg. 4, fol. 33v.

776. [Rome], 6 April 1450. Same dispensation as **753** for Lewis Helyn, scholar, St David's dioc., born of a priest and an unmarried woman. [*Fiat de speciali D. s. † I.*]. Reg. 4, fol. 33v.

777. [Rome], 7 April 1450. Same dispensation as **753** for William (*Vilgelmus*) Hodoler, deacon, Worcester dioc., [born of a priest and an unmarried woman]. [*Fiat de speciali D. s. † I.*]. Reg. 4, fol. 34r.

778. [Rome], 8 April 1450. Same dispensation as **753** for Philip and Richard Marys and Meurig ap Llywelyn (*app Ll'*), scholars, St David's dioc., born of a priest and an unmarried woman. [*Fiat de speciali D. s. † I.*]. Reg. 4, fol. 34v.

779. [Rome], 9 April 1450. Same dispensation as **753** for Hywel (*Hoel*) ap Ieuan, scholar, St Asaph dioc., born of an unmarried man and an unmarried woman. [*Fiat de speciali D. s. † I.*]. Reg. 4, fol. 34r.

780. [Rome], 10 April 1450. Same dispensation as **734** for John Yarmini, scholar, York dioc., born of a married man and an unmarried woman, *cum clausula permutandi*. [*Fiat de speciali D. s. † I.*]. Reg. 4, fol. 36v.

781. [Rome], 11 April 1450. Same dispensation as **753** for Ieuan Bellt, scholar, St David's dioc., born of a priest and a married woman. [*Fiat de speciali D. s. † I.*]. Reg. 4, fol. 34r.

782. [Rome], 13 April 1450.[67] Same dispensation as **780** for Ieuan Beblt, scholar, St David's dioc., born of a priest and an unmarried woman. [*Fiat de speciali D. s. † I.*]. Reg. 4, fol. 36v.

783. [Rome], 16 April 1450. Same dispensation as **753** for Morgan ap Llywelyn (*Llii'*), born of a priest and an unmarried woman, and for Philip ap Dafydd ap *Hye*, scholars, St David's dioc. [*Fiat de speciali D. s. † I.*]. Reg. 4, fol. 33v.

---

[67] Indicated as 'xviiii kal. [Maii]' rather than the more usual 'Id. Aprilis'.

784. [Rome], 16 April 1450. Same dispensation as **753** for Dafydd ap Phillip ap *His*, scholar, St David's dioc., born of an unmarried man and an unmarried woman. [*Fiat de speciali D. s. † I.*]. Reg. 4, fol. 33v.

785. [Rome], 28 April 1450. Same dispensation as **753** for William Arincton, scholar, York dioc., born of a married man and an unmarried woman. [*Fiat de speciali D. s. † I.*]. Reg. 4, fol. 33r.

786. [Rome], 11 May 1450. Same dispensation as **734** for George Barton, scholar, York dioc., born of an unmarried man and an unmarried woman. [*Fiat de speciali D. s. † I.*]. Reg. 4, fol. 37r.

787. [Rome], 15 May 1450. Same dispensation as **734** for John Frewyn, acolyte, Worcester dioc., born of an unmarried man and an unmarried woman. [*Fiat de speciali D. s. † I.*]. Reg. 4, fol. 38v.

788. [Rome], 18 May 1450. Same dispensation as **734** for John Reschyl, scholar, York dioc., born of an unmarried man and an unmarried woman. [*Fiat de speciali D. s. † I.*]. Reg. 4, fol. 38r.

789. [Rome], 18 May 1450. Same dispensation as **734** for John Luffingrite, clerk, York dioc., born of an unmarried man and an unmarried woman. [*Fiat de speciali D. s. † I.*]. Reg. 4, fol. 38r.

790. [Rome], 19 May 1450. Same dispensation as **734** for John Ballan *alias* Pider, clerk, Exeter dioc., born of an unmarried man and an unmarried woman.[68] [Unsigned]. Reg. 4, fol. 38r.

791. [Rome], 24 June 1450. Same dispensation as **734** for John Aspeley, clerk, born of an unmarried man and an unmarried woman, OSA, Coventry and Lichfield (*Lycfoldensis*) dioc. [*Fiat de speciali Io. Pen. et Ad. episcopus.*] Reg. 4, fol. 41v.

792. [Rome], 3 July 1450. Same dispensation as **793** for William Lagchyrke and Thomas Vilchison, clerks, born of an unmarried man and an unmarried woman, York dioc. [*Fiat de speciali Io. P. et Ad. episcopus.*] Reg. 4, fol. 42r.

793. [Rome], 25 July 1450. [Supplication for a dispensation] for John Anlabi, scholar, York dioc., born of a married man and an unmarried woman, [that he may be promoted[69] and obtain a benefice even with cure of souls]. [*Fiat de speciali Io. P. et Ad. episcopus.*] Reg. 4, fol. 42r.

---

[68] In accordance with letters of the cardinal penitentiary dated at St Peter's, Rome, on the same day the bishop of Exeter issued a dispensation to this John Ballam *alias* Pydder on 12 July 1451 confirming him in minor orders that he obtained without disclosing his defect of birth and allowing him to be promoted to holy orders and hold a benefice even with cure of souls provided that he resided there in person. He was ordained an acolyte on 19 September 1450, subdeacon on 18 September 1451, and deacon on 4 March 1452 (*Reg. Lacy*, ed. Dunstan, iii.115; iv, 232, 237, 239).

[69] The nearest entry specifying the dispensation sought omits the kind of ordination required.

794. [Rome], 1 August 1450. Same dispensation as **793** for Nicholas Coldele, clerk, Carlisle dioc., born of a married man and an unmarried woman. [*Fiat de speciali Io. P. et Ad. episcopus.*] Reg. 4, fol. 42r.

795. [Rome], 23 August 1450. Same dispensation as **734** for William Rotis, York dioc., born of a married man and an unmarried woman. [*Fiat de speciali Io. P. et Ad. episcopus.*] Reg. 4, fol. 42v.

796. [Rome], 23 August 1450. Same dispensation as **734** for Robert Regul, York dioc., born of a married man and an unmarried woman. [*Fiat de speciali Io. P. et A. episcopus.*] Reg. 4, fol. 42v.

797. [Rome], 1 October 1450. [Supplication for a dispensation from defect of birth *in prima forma*] for Ieuan Meubot, scholar, St Asaph dioc., born of a priest and an unmarried woman. [*Fiat de speciali Io. P. et Ad. episcopus.*] Reg. 4, fol. 44v.

798. [Rome], 2 October 1450. Same dispensation as **797** for Gruffydd (*Gruffuth*) ap Ieuan ap Dafydd (*Dio*), scholar, St Asaph dioc., and John Menduc, St Asaph dioc., both born of an unmarried man and an unmarried woman. [*Fiat de speciali Io. P. et Ad. episcopus.*] Reg. 4, fol. 44v.

799. [Rome], 5 October 1450. Same dispensation as **797** for John Vavyn, scholar, Lincoln dioc., born of an unmarried man and an unmarried woman. [*Fiat de speciali Io. P. et Ad. episcopus.*] Reg. 4, fol. 44v.

800. [Rome], 17 October 1450. Same dispensation as **797** for Lewis Flint, scholar of St Asaph, born of an unmarried man and an unmarried woman. [*Fiat de speciali Io. P. et Ad. episcopus*]. Reg. 4, fol. 44r.

801. [Rome], 30 October 1450. Same dispensation as **734** for Geoffrey ap Robin, scholar, Bangor dioc., born of an unmarried man and an unmarried woman. [*Fiat de speciali D. s. †*]. Reg. 4, fol. 45v.

802. [Rome], 6 November 1450. Same dispensation as **734** for Ieuan ap *Iemett* Ddyi, scholar, St David's dioc., born of a married man and an unmarried woman. [*Fiat de speciali D. s. †*]. Reg. 4, fol. 46v.

803. [Rome], 3 December 1450. Same dispensation as **797** and *littere confessionales in forma 'Cupientes'* for *Icellus* [son] of Lewis, scholar, St Asaph dioc., born of a married man and an unmarried woman.[70] [*Fiat de speciali D. s. † I.*]. Reg. 4, fol. 48v.

804. [Rome], 17 December 1450. Same dispensation as **797** for Dafydd Hemi, acolyte, St David's dioc., born of a priest and an unmarried woman. *Fiat de speciali D. s. †*. Reg. 4, fol. 48v.

---

[70] The request for *littere confessionales in forma 'Cupientes'* is curious, since these letters empowered the parish clergy to absolve their parishioners in certain cases. Only a priest could grant such absolution; yet the beneficiary of **803** was a mere 'scholar', that is, someone who aspired to a clerical career but had not yet taken even minor orders.

805. [Rome], 27 December 1450. [Supplication for a dispensation from defect of birth for] William Croskyll, scholar, York dioc., born of an unmarried man and an unmarried woman, [that he may be ordained as a priest and obtain a benefice even with cure of souls]. [*Fiat de speciali D. s. † I.*]. Reg. 4, fol. 50v.

806. [Rome], 27 December 1450. Same dispensation as **805** for Richard Redun, scholar, York dioc., born of an unmarried man and an unmarried woman. [*Fiat de speciali D. s. † I.*]. Reg. 4, fol. 50v.

807. [Rome], 4 January 1451. Same dispensation as **805** for Thomas Vode, scholar, Exeter dioc., born of a married man and an unmarried woman.[71] [*Fiat de speciali D. s. † I.*]. Reg. 4, fol. 50r.

808. [Rome], 4 January 1451. Same dispensation as **805** for William (*Vilgelmus*) Conton, professed of the Cistercian order, Coventry and Lichfield (*Luctuldensis*) dioc.,[72] born of a priest and an unmarried woman, and that he may be received as an abbot and *prepositus* of that order. [*Fiat de speciali D. s. † I.*]. Reg. 4, fol. 50v.

809. [Rome], 22 January 1451. Same dispensation as **805** for Simon Assiby *alias* Chy, clerk, Lincoln dioc., born of a priest and an unmarried woman. [*Fiat de speciali D. s. † I.*]. Reg. 4, fol. 50r.

810. [*Rome*], *28 April 1451. John de Algenton, priest, York dioc., seeks a dispensation to hold an additional compatible benefice.* Reg. 3, fol. 60v.

[Rome], iiii kal. Maii anno quinto. Item similem gratiam presbitero Iohanni de Algenton Eboracensis diocesis, [qui fuit alias dispensatum], cuius vigore promotus est, non obstante quod sit de presbitero et soluta, et vicariam perpetuam assequtus, de cuius fructibus etc. ut supra [comode substentari non potest. Supplicatur ut possit beneficium etiam si curam habeat animarum compatabile cum primo insimul retinere, et illud ex causa permutationis simul vel successive aliud vel alia similia vel dissimilia duo tantum etiam si alterum ipsorum curam habeat retinere possit et valeat de gratia speciali].

Fiat de speciali ut petitur D. s. †.

811. [Rome], 30 June 1451. Same dispensation as **734** for Thomas ap Ieuan, scholar, St David's dioc., born of an unmarried man and an unmarried woman. (Unsigned.) Reg. 4, fol. 52v.

812. [*Rome*], *15 August 1451. Richard Spe'halke, clerk, Worcester dioc., seeks a dispensation to be promoted to all orders and hold two compatible benefices.* Reg. 4, fol. 55r.

---

[71] Perhaps the Thomas Wode tonsured as a clerk on 18 June 1442 in Exeter dioc. (*Reg. Lacy*, ed. Dunstan, iv. 188c).

[72] He was presumably a monk of one or other of the following Cistercian abbeys in this diocese: Combe, Combermere, Croxden, Dieulacres, Hulton, Merevale, Stoneleigh, Vale Royal.

[Rome], xviii kal. [Septembris]. Supplicat Riccardus Spe'halke, clericus Vigor[n]iensis diocesis, de presbitero et soluta, ut possit promoveri ad omnes ordines et si ex fructibus primi beneficii vivere non possit, aliud cum cura vel sine recipere etiam si canonicatus fuerit in quacumque ecclesia et ex causa permutationis loco dimissorum alia duo tantum compatabilia recipere valeat.

Fiat Io. P.

813. [*Rome*], *3 November 1451. Gruffydd ap Ieuan ap Dafydd Wachai', scholar, St Asaph dioc., seeks a dispensation to be promoted to all orders and hold two compatible benefices.* Reg. 4, fol. 55v.

[Rome], iii non' [Novembris]. Similem gratiam in omnibus Gruffuth ap Ieuan ap Dio Wachai', scolari Assavensis diocesis, de soluto et soluta, [ut ad omnes ordines possit promoveri et si ex fructibus primi assequendi beneficii comode substentari non possit, aliud possit compatabile etiam si curam habeat obtinere, etiam si canonicatus et prebenda in quacumque ecclesia, [et] retinere simul [cum primo], illudque vel illa ex causa permutationis simul vel successive semel tantum dimittere et loco dimissorum alia compatabilia similia vel dissimilia recipere].

[Fiat Io. P.]

814. [Rome], 3 November 1451. Same dispensation as **813** sought by Ieuan Menduc ap Cadualad, scholar, St Asaph dioc., born of an unmarried man and an unmarried woman. [*Fiat de speciali Io. P. A. episcopus*]. Reg. 4, fol. 55v.

815. [*Rome*], *5 November 1451. William Laybron, acolyte of York, seeks a further dispensation to be promoted to other orders and hold two compatible benefices.* Reg. 3, fol. 61v.

[Rome], nonas Novembris. Exponitur pro Wylhelmo Laybron', acolito Eboracensi, de presbitero canonico professi [*sic*] ordinis Premonstratensis et coniugata genitus, [qui alias ut] ad omnes ordines promoveri possit et beneficium etiam si curam habeat animarum auctoritate apostolica tempore Eugenii[73] fuit dispensatum, et antequam littere executorie presentarentur, idem W. obtinuisse [*recte* obtinuit] ad ordinem accolitatus promoveri. Supplicat ut in susceptis ordinibus ministrare possit et ad alios ordines promoveri ac quod aliud beneficium cum predicto beneficio compatibile obtinere possit dispensare dignemini de gratia speciali.

Fiat de speciali D. s. †. I.

816. [Rome, at Sta Maria Maggiore], 8 August 1452. [Supplication for a dispensation from defect of birth] for Richard Faukes, priest, minister of the house of St Robert, Knaresborough, Order of the Holy Trinity and Redemption of Captives, York dioc.,[74] born of an unmarried man and an unmarried woman, that he may

---

[73] Eugenius IV, who was elected as pope on 3 March 1431 and died on 23 February 1447.
[74] Richard Faukes also occurs as minister of the Trinitarians at Knaresborough in 1449

hold, keep and exercise the ministry of that house and other offices and *administrationes* of that house and order and be assigned and promoted to them as if he had been conceived in the marriage bed (*ac si legitimo thoro procreatus esset*). *Fiat de speciali D. /s. †. I.\.* Reg. 4, fol. 80v.

817. [Rome], 19 December 1452. Same dispensation as **753** for John Manfilt of Forcett(?) (*Forfet*), clerk, York dioc., born of an unmarried man and an unmarried woman. [*Fiat de speciali D. s. †. I.*]. Reg. 4, fol. 84r.

818. [Rome], 3 March 1453. [Supplication for] a dispensation for Thomas Forestar, clerk, Lincoln dioc., born of an unmarried man and an unmarried woman, that he may be promoted to all, even holy, orders and obtain a benefice even with cure of souls, notwithstanding his defect of birth. *Fiat de speciali D. s. †. I.* Reg. 4, fol. 101r.

819. [Rome], 17 March 1453. [Supplication for] a dispensation for Fr Nicholas Stapilton *alias* McDuil, priest, professed of OESA of the province of England, born of a priest and an unmarried woman, that he may receive all offices, *administrationes* and dignities of his order below the principal one, notwithstanding his defect of birth. *Fiat de speciali D. s. †. I.* Reg. 4, fol. 95r.

820. [*Rome*], *6 March 1453. Thomas Forestar, clerk, Lincoln dioc., seeks a further dispensation to hold two compatible benefices.* Reg. 4, fol. 108v.

[Rome], ii° non. Martii. [Dispensatio super defectu natalium pro] Thoma Forestar, clerico Lincolniensis diocesis, de soluto et soluta genito, qui dicto non obstante defectu vigore cuiusdam dispensationis obtente nullum beneficium assecutus est,[75] quare ut huiusmodi defectu non obstante unum aliud beneficium ecclesiasticum cum cura vel sine cura, etiam si canonicatus et prebenda in collegiata ecclesia seu officium in cathedrali etiam si [*sic*] fuerit, una cum dicta parrochiali ecclesia recipere et retinere valeat, ac ipsa beneficia obtinenda simul vel successive etiam ex causa permutacionis vel alias semel tantum dimittere et loco dimissi vel dimissorum aliud vel alia duo dumtaxat beneficia ecclesiastica simile vel dissimile aut similia vel dissimilia invicem compatibilia, etiam si alterum ipsorum curatum fuerit, libere et licite retinere valeat, constitucionibus et ordinacionibus apostolicis necnon consuetudinibus et statutis synodalibus et provincialibus ecclesiarum in quibus beneficiis extiterint in contrarium editis non obstantibus quibuscumque.

Fiat de speciali ut petitur D. s. †. I.

821. [Rome], 22 February 1453. Same dispensation as **747** for Robert Bate, acolyte, Norwich dioc. *Fiat de speciali D. s. †. I.* Reg. 4, fol. 128v.

822. [Rome], 23 May 1453. Same dispensation as **734** for James Standish, scholar, Coventry and Lichfield dioc. *Fiat de speciali D. s. †. I.* Reg. 4, fol. 140v.

---

and 1454; he had vacated the office by 1461 (*VCH (Yorks.)*, iii. 300; Smith, *Heads of Religious Houses*, iii. 612).
[75] See **818**.

823. [Rome], 15 June 1453. Same dispensation as **734** for William Rudston, scholar, York dioc., born of a priest and an unmarried woman. Approved with **824**. Reg. 4, fol. 165r.

824. [Rome], 15 June 1453. Same dispensation as **734** for Thomas Byrckbel, scholar, Carlisle dioc., born of a regular priest and an unmarried woman. *Fiat de speciali D. s. †. I.* (Approved with **823**.) Reg. 4, fol. 165r.

825. [*Rome*], *11 July 1453. John de Halington, priest, York dioc., was dispensed by his ordinary and now seeks a further dispensation.* Reg. 4, fol. 158v.

[Rome], v idus Iulii. Iohanne de Halington', presbiteri [*recte* presbitero] Eboracensis diocesis, cum quo nuper ad omnes ordines minores necnon unum beneficium cui cura inminet minime animarum ordinarie dispensatum extitit, ulterius petit ad omnes ordines sacros promoveri necnon [ut] unum aliud beneficium cum cura vel sine cura licite obtinere possit dispensatio.

Fiat ut petitur D. s. †. I.

826. [Rome], 10 August 1453. Same dispensation as **734** for Stephen Grey, scholar, York dioc. *Fiat de speciali Io. Penensis episcopus locumtenens.* Reg. 4, fol. 142r–v.

827. [Rome], 19 August 1453. Same dispensation as **734** for William Rutston, clerk, York dioc., born of a priest and an unmarried woman. *Fiat de speciali D. s. †. I.* Reg. 4, fol. 144v.

828. [Rome], 13 September 1453. Same dispensation as **734** for Robert Threlkeld, clerk, Carlisle dioc. *Fiat de speciali D. s. †. I.* Reg. 4, fol. 169r.

829. [Rome], 12 June 1454. Same dispensation as **734** for Robert Sotheron, scholar, York dioc. Approved with **831**. Reg. 4, fol. 211r.

830. [Rome], 12 June 1453. Same dispensation as **734** for William Sotheron, scholar, York dioc. Approved with **831**. Reg. 4, fol. 211r.

831. [Rome], 12 June 1453. Same dispensation as **734** for John Burton, scholar, Llandaff (*Landoviensis*) dioc., born of a priest and an unmarried woman. *Fiat de speciali D. s. †. I.* (Approved with **829–30**.) Reg. 4, fol. 211r.

832. [Rome], 7 July 1454. Same dispensation as **734** for Richard Porter, scholar, York dioc. *Fiat de speciali D. s. †. I.* Reg. 4, fol. 212r.

833. [Rome], 15 August 1454. [Supplication for] a dispensation for Robert Hartele, canon and priest of the monastery *de Bello Capite* commonly called Beauchief (*Bewchyff*), Coventry and Lichfield dioc., Premonstratensian order, born of an unmarried man and an unmarried woman, since he received the order of the priesthood and holy orders and out of ignorance celebrated in them. *Fiat de speciali D. s. †. I.* Reg. 4, fol. 214v.

834. [Rome], 8 November 1454. Thomas Atherton, clerk, Coventry and Lichfield dioc., born of an unmarried man and an unmarried woman, had himself made a clerk (*se fecit clericali caractere insigniri*) without a prior dispensation. [Supplication for] absolution from that excess and a dispensation that he may be promoted to all, even holy, orders and obtain a benefice even with cure of souls. *Fiat de speciali D. s. †. I.* Reg. 4, fols. 221v–222r.

835. [Rome], 4 December 1454. John Walter, priest, Norwich dioc.,[76] born of an unmarried man and an unmarried woman, formerly had himself promoted to all holy orders while keeping silent about his defect of birth, but otherwise legally, and ministered in them. He requests absolution from that excess and his other sins and a dispensation that he may minister in his existing orders and obtain a benefice even with cure of souls. *Fiat de speciali Io. Urbevet. episcopus locumtenens.* Reg. 4, fol. 223r.

836. [Rome], 9 December 1454. Same dispensation as **818** for John Craas, clerk, Exeter dioc., BA, aged 23,[77] born of a married man and an unmarried woman, notwithstanding those [defects]. *Fiat de speciali Io. Urbevet. episcopus locumtenens.* Reg. 4, fol. 236v.

---

[76] As John Walteri, priest, Norwich dioc., he was granted a licence for a portable altar on 30 December 1454 (*CPL*, x. 682).

[77] John Crace was admitted as a BA at Oxford University in 1454; he determined on 16 February 1455 (*BRUO*, i. 508). Presumably the John Cras who was tonsured as a clerk in 1444 and the John Crasse who was ordained as a subdeacon on 1 March 1455 in Exeter dioc. (*Reg. Lacy*, ed. Dunstan, iv. 196c, 254).

CALIXTUS III
(1455–1458)

De diversis formis

837. [*Rome*], *7 May 1455. Thomas Barnabe, priest, perpetual vicar of Darfield, York dioc., held that parish church for about two years and then resigned it, since his brother Robert had paid bribes with Thomas's money so that Thomas might obtain it. Thomas seeks absolution from simony and excommunication, a dispensation from irregularity, habilitation, and that he may retain the church for life.* Reg. 5, fol. 31v.

[Rome], nonas Maii. Exponit sanctitati vestre devotus orator vester T[h]omas Barnabe, Eboracensis diocesis presbiter, perpetuus vicarius in ecclesia parrochiali de Derfeld dicte diocesis, quod alias vacante dicta vicaria per obitum condam [*recte* quondam] Iohannis Atlain extra Romanam curiam defuncti, cuius fructus etc. [redditus et proventus] lx florenorum auri de camera secundum communem extimationem valorem annuum non excedit [*recte* excedunt], Robertus Barnbe, frater carnalis exponentis, desiderans ut in [*sic*] dicta vicaria exponenti conferretur recepit ad se de pecuniis ipsius exponentis usque ad valorem cxx florenorum similium et donationem fecit de dictis pecuniis fratri collatoris dicte vicarie et etiam cuidam armigero et partem pecuniarum huiusmodi ad se retinuit pro laboribus ut dicta vicaria conferretur et donaretur eidem exponenti, qui illas [*recte* illam] per duos annos cum dimidio vel circa tenuit et possedit. Qui quidem exponens postmodum conscientia motus dictam vicariam resignavit in manibus vicarii generalis dicti \archi/episcopi Eboracensis, que vicaria per eundem vicarium eidem exponenti [*recte* eodem exponente] ablata extitit. Et illam per duos annos vel circa tenuit et possedit, fructus percipiendo et levando, crimen symonie committendo, et sententiam excommunicationis in tales generaliter promulgatam incurrendo, et sic ligatus divinis se inmiscuit irregularitatem incurrendo. Et cum idem exponens doleat ab intimis de premissis, supplicat eidem sanctitati vestre idem exponens humiliter quatinus ipsum a vitio symonie et sententia excommunicationis huiusmodi absolvere ac secum super irregularitate et ut absque aliqua dimissione dicte vicarie eandem vicariam quoad vixerit retinere libere et licite possit et valeat dispensare ipsumque habilitare misericorditer dignemini de gratia speciali.

Fiat de speciali et expresso D. s. †.

838. [*Rome*], *13 May 1455. Katherine Drakys, York dioc., took a vow of chastity but then married; she seeks absolution from her vow and transgression.* Reg. 5, fol. 34r.

[Rome], iii idus Maii. Exponitur sanctitati vestre pro parte devote vestre K[a]terine Drakys, mulieris Eboracensis diocesis, quod ipsa alias in mente sua vovit castitatem observare. Postea vero mutato proposito matrimonio [*recte* matrimonium] cum quodam viro publice in facie ecclesie contraxit illudque carnali copula consumavit. Supplicatur igitur sanctitati vestre pro parte dicte exponentis quatinus ipsam a voto et transgressione huiusmodi absolvere, itaque in huiusmodi matrimonio sic contracto licite et libere remanere possit et valeat, misericorditer dignemini ut in forma.

Fiat de speciali D. s. †.

182   *Supplications from England and Wales*

839. [*Rome*], *18 June 1455. William Drant, priest, Lincoln dioc., had himself promoted to all, even holy, orders despite a physical defect; he seeks a dispensation so that he may minister in his orders.* Reg. 5, fol. 61r.

[Rome], xiiii kal. Iulii. [Pro parte] Wilhelmi Drant, presbiteri Lincolniensis diocesis, sanctitati vestre exponitur [quod] cum olim ipse duorum annorum vel circiter sue etatis esset, accidit quandam securim supra maiorem pedicum [*sic*] dextri pedis cadere sic quod ex casu dicti securis articulum dicte maioris sue pedice casualiter amisit et mutilatus fuit, quare ex defectu dicti membri timet se ad omnes etiam sacros ordines, sedis apostolice licencia desuper non obtenta, promoveri non potuisse. Nichilominus tamquam simplex et iuris ignarus non tamen in contemptum clavium se alias tamen rite ad omnes etiam sacros et presbiteratus ordines se fecit promoveri et in illis ministravit. Quare supplicatur pro parte ipsius exponentis quatinus, ut huiusmodi defectu non obstante in dictis ordinibus sic ut premittitur per eum receptis libere et licite ministrare possit et valeat, cum tamen nullum scandalum generat [*sic*] in populo, secum dispensari mandare dignemini de gratia speciali.

Fiat de speciali D. s. †.

840. [*Rome*], *22 November 1455. John Stysben, clerk, Lincoln dioc., seeks a licence and faculty that he may be promoted to all holy orders successively and outside the legal times by any Catholic bishop in the Curia.* Reg. 5, fol. 124r.

[Rome], x kal. Decembris. Iohannes Stysben, clericus Lincol[n]iensis [diocesis],[1] exponit sanctitati vestre quod ipse pro(?) reverendo patre abbate et conventu monasterii beate Marie de Wall' ordinis Cisterciensis dicte diocesis[2] sufficientem titulum et provisionem habeat propter quem necessario ad omnes sacros ordines promovendos artatus [*recte* promovendus artatus] extitit, prout in quadam littera testimoniali sigillo dicti abbatis et conventus munita plenius constat etc. Supplicat igitur sanctitati vestre dictus Iohannes quatinus, ut ipse a quocumque catholico antistite in hac Romana curia gratiam et communionem sedis apostolice habente extra tempora a iure statuta aliquibus diebus festivis aut dominicis successive ad dictos ordines promoveri et in ipsis ministrare licite possit, licentiam et facultatem misericorditer impartiri et concedere dignemini de gratia speciali.

Fiat de speciali D. s. †. Et expresso D. s. †.

841. [*Rome*], *11 February 1456. John Milveton, professed monk of Glastonbury Abbey, Bath and Wells dioc.,*[3] *seeks a faculty to visit Compostella.* Reg. 5, fol. 154r.

[Rome], iii id. Februarii. Beatissime pater, cum devotus vester Iohannes Milveton', monachus expresse profexus [*recte* professus] monasterii beate

---
[1] Name of diocese supplied from right margin.
[2] Probably Vaudey Abbey (Lincs.).
[3] John Milverton, monk of Glastonbury, was ordained by the bishop of Bath and Wells as a subdeacon on 23 December 1447, and as a deacon on 9 March 1448 (*Reg. Bekynton*, nos 1674–5).

Marie de Glastonis [Bathoniensis et] Wellensis [diocesis],[4] zelo devotionis accensus cupiat visitare ecclesiam et loca sanctorum sancti Iacobi in Galicia inibi existentes, supplicat sanctitati vestre quatinus sibi specialem gratiam facientes ut ecclesiam predictam ob reverentiam sancti Iacobi infra annum [a] data presentium computandum visitare possit, non tamen vagando per universum sed dumtaxat eundo et redeundo, misericorditer facultatem concedere dignemini de gratia speciali cum clausis oportunis.

Fiat de speciali de licentia sui superioris D. s. †.

842. [*Rome*], *30 March 1456. John Helier, clerk, rector of St Michael's parish church, Southgate, Oxford, Lincoln dioc.*,[5] *seeks a licence and dispensation that he may be promoted to acolyte's and other holy orders simultaneously or successively by any Catholic bishop in the Curia outside the legal times.* Reg. 5, fol. 177r.

[Rome], iii kal. Aprilis. Beatissime pater, devotus orator vester Iohannes Helier, clericus, rector parochialis ecclesie sancti Michaelis ad portam australem Oxonie, Lincolniensis diocesis, tam magno [zelo] devotionis accensus et etiam racione dicte sue parochialis ecclesie ad recipiendum accolitatus et alios sacros etiam presbiteratus ordines adeo artatus extitit quod propter temporis brevitatem tempora ad hoc de iure statuta expectare non potest. Supplicat igitur sanctitati vestre dictus exponens quatinus, [ut] a quocunque antistite catholico in curia Romana residente aliquibus diebus dominicis seu festivis aut feriatis extra tempora ad hoc a iure statuta dictos acolitatus et omnes alios sacros etiam presbiteratus ordines simul vel successive libere et licite recipere possit, licenciam concedere et cum dicto exponente dispensare dignemini de gratia speciali, statutis et ordinationibus apostolicis ac ceteris in contrarium facientibus non obstantibus quibuscunque.

Fiat de speciali et expresso D. s. †.

843. [*Rome*], *30 May 1456. Nicholas Machil, priest, perpetual vicar of Bossall parish church, York dioc., seeks a licence to study at university for seven years.* Reg. 5, fol. 291v.

[Rome], iii kal. Iunii. Supplicatur sanctitati vestre pro parte devoti vestri Nicolai Machil, presbiteri, perpetui vicarii ecclesie parochialis de Bosall Eboracensis diocesis, quatinus sibi ut in studio privelegiato [*recte* privilegiato] in omnibus facultatibus a iure premissis [*recte* permissis] hinc ad septennium studere et legere et a beneficio suo se absentare et fructus de eodem percipere possit et valeat licenciam concedere dignemini, constitucionibus synodalibus et provincialibus et quibusvis aliis constitucionibus forsan in contrarium editis non obstantibus quibuscumque de gratia speciali.

Fiat de speciali D. s. †. I.

---

[4] Name of diocese supplied from right margin.
[5] He was admitted to this benefice on 8 December 1453. He was granted a papal dispensation of non-residence for seven years on 14 December 1454 so that he might study at Bologna or another Italian university (*CPL*, x. 702). This was conditional on his being ordained as a subdeacon in the first year of his studies, which perhaps occasioned the present supplication. He died in 1458 (*BRUO*, ii. 904).

844. [*Rome*], *16 June 1456. William Porter, priest, professed canon, OSA, perpetual vicar of Warden, Durham dioc., was induced to swear an oath to pay an annual pension for that vicarage to his predecessor as vicar. He seeks absolution from that oath and the relaxation of its effect.* Reg. 5, fol. 231v.

[Rome], xvi kal. Iulii. Beatissime pater, exponitur sanctitati vestre pro parte devoti oratoris vestri Willelmi Porter, presbiteri, canonici professi ordinis sancti Au[gu]stini canonicorum regularium, perpetui vicarii parochiales ecchesie [*recte* parrochialis ecclesie] de Wardon' Dunelmensis diocesis,[6] quod cum ipse a nonnullis seductus fuerit et [*recte* ut] annuam pensionem quatuor marcharum agenti [*recte* argenti] super dicta perpetua vicaria suo predecessori tunc dicte perpetue vicarie vicario annuatim solvere promissit [*recte* promiserit] et iuraverit, et cum, pater beatissime, fructus re vera dicte perpetue vicarie adeo sint exilles [*sic*] nonnullis sinistris eventibus(?) causantibus quod vix ex illis inibi diserviendo [*recte* deserviendo] divinis officiis se substentare potest, et cum verisimiliter credatur quod ipse qui servit bonorum [*recte* bona] de fructibus dicti beneficii debeat caudere [*recte* gaudere] et non alius, et decepto et non dicipienti sit subveniendum, supplicat sanctitati vestre quatinus ipsum a iura[men]to sic prestito quoad effectum agendi relaxare et absolvere seu relassari [*recte* relaxari] et absolvi mandare dignemini de gratia speciali.

Fiat de speciali D. s. †.

845. [*Rome*], *30 August 1456. Fr William Elkisington, priest, professed canon of Wellow Abbey, OSA, Lincoln dioc.,[7] had a licence from his superior to visit Rome, but when he failed to do so, his superior refused to re-admit him, and so he ministered as a secular priest instead. He seeks absolution from excommunication and apostasy, dispensation from irregularity, and that he may transfer to another monastery.* Reg. 5, fol. 296v.

[Rome], iii kal. Septembris. Exponit sanctitati vestre devotus vester frater Wilhelmus Elkis'ngton', presbiter, canonicus professus monasterii de Welhan ordinis sancti Augustini Lincolniensis diocesis, quod postquam ipse olim licenciam a suo superiori visitandi limina apostolorum Petri et Pauli habuerit et ob certa sibi superveniencia impedimenta dicta limina visitare non posset et sic ad monasterium predictum reverti vellet, dictus superior eundem exponentem nisi prius suum compleret viagium recipere recusavit, propter quod dictus exponens ex tunc, nulla habita licencia, habitu derelicto, in seculo vagatus fuit et inibi per multos annos absque habito suo [*sic*] stetit ac beneficiis secularibus servivit missas et alia divina officia celebrando ac ecclesiastica sacramenta ministrando, propter que dubitat excommunicationis sententiam ac apostasie reatum incurrisse et irregularitatis maculam contraxisse. Cum autem, pater sancte, dictus orator [fol. 297r] ad cor reversus de premissis doleat ab intimis, supplicat igitur sanctitati vestre idem orator quatinus ipsum a sententia excommunicationis huiusmodi ac apostasie reatu absolvere et peccatis suis aliis nisi etc. [talia fuerint propter que merito

---

[6] Name of diocese supplied from right margin.
[7] William Elkington was regarded as a recidivist apostate already in 1440: Logan, 134, 227.

Calixtus III (1455–1458) 185

sit sedes apostolica consulenda] absolvi secumque super irregularitate dicto modo contracta dispensari mandare, necnon sibi ut ad quodcumque aliud monasterium dicti ordinis paris vel artioris observantie in quo benivolos invenerit receptores se transferre possit et valeat concedere et indulgere misericorditer dignemini de gratia speciali.

Fiat de speciali D. s. †. I.

846. [*Rome*], *10 September 1456. William Waid, acolyte, Canterbury dioc., requests that he may be promoted successively to all holy orders by a bishop in the Curia.* Reg. 5, fol. 300r.

[Rome], iiii idus Septembris. Supplicat sanctitati vestre devotus orator vester Willermus Waid, acolitus Cantuariensis diocesis, qui in Romana curia presens ac arctatus ratione sui tituli existit, quatinus sibi specialem gratiam facientes ut a quocumque maluerit catholico antistate [*recte* antistite] in Romana curia ad omnes sacros ordines successive in primis temporibus a iure statutis possit promoveri, eidem oratori suscipiendi et antistiti conferendi licenciam et facultatem misericorditer concedere dignemini de gratia speciali et expresso. (*Approved with* **848**.)

847. [Rome], 10 September 1456. Same grace as **846** for John Gryme, acolyte, Norwich dioc., likewise present in the Roman Curia and constrained [by reason of his title]. Approved with **848**. Reg. 5, fol. 300r.

848. [Rome], 10 September 1456. Same grace as **846** for John Urwhen, acolyte, Lincoln dioc., likewise present in the Roman Curia and constrained [by reason of his title]. *Fiat de speciali et expresso D. s. †. I. Et committatur episcopo Allexandrino.*[8] [*Fiat*] *D. s. †. I.* (Approved with **846–7**.) Reg. 5, fol. 300r.

849. [*Rome*], *14 January 1457. Thomas Brugh, layman, Lincoln dioc., seeks a licence and faculty to visit the Holy Sepulchre and other holy places overseas with two others* Reg. 5, fol. 254v.

[Rome], xix kal. Februarii. Beatissime pater, cum devotus orator vester Thoma Brugh, laycus Lincolniensis diocesis, zelo et fervore devotionis ~~ecclesiis~~ accensus cupiat in redemptionem suorum precaminum sepulchrum dominicum ac alia pia loca ultramarina personaliter visitare tamen prius apostolica dispensatione precedente, itaque supplicat humiliter sanctitati vestre dictus orator quatinus eum in suo laudabili proposito consonentes [*recte* consonantes] sibi ut ipse cum duobus aliis personis sepulchrum dominicum et alia pia loca ultramarina personaliter visitare possit et valeat licenciam et facultatem concedere et elargiri misericorditer dignemini, non obstantibus quibuscumque constitutionibus et ordinacionibus apostolicis ac aliis in contrarium facientibus.

Fiat de speciali [si] vovit D. s. †. I.

---

[8] The bishop of Alessandria was Marcus de Marinaribus, presumably resident in the Curia (Eubel, ii. 85).

850. [Rome, at St Peter's], *7 February 1457. John Caldwell, priest, Canterbury (Canturiensis) dioc., who lost the index finger of his right hand through no fault of his own, requests that the pope grant him a dispensation that he may minister in his existing orders notwithstanding the aforesaid defect and deformity. Fiat de expresso et committatur ordinario D. s. †. I.* Reg. 5, fol. 382v.

851. [*Rome*], *9 February 1457. William Drapo, layman, and his wife Agnes, York dioc., once had a son who died of burns at the age of three, and on account of this the local ordinary enjoined excessive penances on them, which they cannot perform. They seek commutation of these penances.* Reg. 5, fol. 262r.

[Rome], v idus Februarii. Beatissime pater, exponitur sanctitati vestre pro parte devotorum oratorum Willelmi Drapo et [*sic*] layci et Agnete eius uxor [*recte* uxoris] Eboracensis diocesis quod cum ipsi alias quemdam [fol. 262v] habuerint filium trium annorum, qui aqua sive lixivia calidissima in brachio fuit crematus adeo quod infra septem dierum spacium fuit vita functus, propter quod ordinis [*recte* ordinarius] loci nonnullas penitencias atrocissimas preter iuris viam iniunxit in ipsorum grande preiudicium non modicum et gravamen et quas iuxta ipsorum constitucionem facere non possint. Supplicant sanctitati vestre quatinus huiusmodi penitencias in confeccione litterarum exprimendas in alia pietatis opera commutare seu commitari [*recte* commutari] mandare misericorditer dignemini de gratia speciali.

Fiat de speciali D. s. †. I. Et quod si placet committatur propinquiori ordinario attento quod loci ordinarius est minus [*recte* nimis] in huiusmodi casu austerus.[9] Fiat D. s. †. I.

852. [*Rome*], *27 February 1457. Margaret Beaumont, prioress of Dartford Priory, OP, Canterbury dioc.,*[10] *seeks a licence to resign that office in favour of a suitable person of that priory because of her physical infirmities.* Reg. 5, fol. 267v.

[Rome], iii kal. Martii. Exponitur sanctitati vestre pro parte devote creature eiusdem sanctitatis vestre Margarete de Bellomonte, priorisse monasterii beatorum Marie et Margarete de Dertford ordinis sancti Dominici Cantuariensis diocesis, quod ipsa adeo variis infirmitatibus et sui corporis viribus destituta atque gravata existat quare eidem prioratui amplius preesse ac illius monialium et exerciciorum eiusdem officii [*recte* officium?] gerere et exercere commode nequeat per se ipsum, et propterea ipsum officium prioratus in manibus eiusdem sanctitatis vestre vel ad id potestatem habentem resignare proponat. Quare supplicatur eidem sanctitati vestre pro parte dicte priorisse quatinus sibi licenciam prefatum officium resignandi persone

---

[9] Their ordinary was William Booth, archbishop of York (1452–64).
[10] Daughter of Henry Lord Beaumont (d. 1413), she was prioress in 1446, still in 1460, but had vacated the office by 1461 (*VCH (Kent)*, ii. 185, 189; *Complete Peerage*, ii. 61; P. Lee, *Nunneries, Learning and Spirituality in Late Medieval English Society: The Dominican Priory of Dartford* (York, 2001), 38, 59, 147, 223). She and the other nuns of her convent (the only Dominican nunnery in England) were granted a papal licence on 1 July 1451 so that each might choose a personal confessor to grant them absolution of sins reserved to the apostolic see once in their lives and plenary remission *in mortis articulo* (*CPL*, x. 526).

ydonee eiusdem monasterii et ordinem [*recte* ordinis] concedere et indulgere misericorditer dignemini de gratia speciali.

Fiat de speciali de consensu sui superioris D. s. †. I. Et commitatur ordinario. [Fiat] D. s. †. I.

853. [*Rome*], *16 March 1457. John Berwyck, priest, professed monk of Vaudey Abbey, Lincoln dioc., Cistercian order, incurred excommunication for apostasy. He requests absolution from that sentence and a dispensation from irregularity.* Reg. 5, fol. 323v.

[Rome], xvii kal. Aprilis. Exponitur sanctitati vestre pro parte devoti oratoris vestri Iohannis Berwyck, presbiteri, monachi expresse professi monasterii de Valle Dei Lincolniensis diocesis ordinis sancti Bernardi sub regula sancti Benedicti, quod ipse olim monasterium et ordinem predictos in quibus se voto professionis astrinxerat propter molestias, discentiones et gravamina que sibi in ipsis a nonnullis confratribus suis inferebantur, habitu et ordine huiusmodi derelictis, illicentiatus exivit et ad seculum est reversus, in quo pluribus annis dampnabiliter evagatus extitit, propter quod excommunicationis incurrit [fol. 324r] sententias in tales generaliter promulgatas et sic legatus [*recte* ligatus] tamquam simplex et [iuris] ignarus ~~divnna~~ divina celebravit officia et illis inmiscuit se eisdem. Nunc autem ad cor domino faciente reversus cupit ad ovile redire, quare supplicatur eidem sanctitati vestre pro parte dicti oratoris quatinus ipsum a generali sententia excommunicationis quam propter hoc incurrit et excessibus huiusmodi absolvi secumque super irregularitate dicto modo contracta dispensari misericorditer mandare dignemini ut in forma.

Fiat de speciali D. s. †.

854. [Rome], 12 April 1457. William Dems, nobleman, layman, Exeter dioc., requests that the pope grant that he may visit the Holy Sepulchre and some other holy places overseas in person as a pilgrim together with three persons of his choice. *Fiat de speciali D. s. †. I.* Reg. 5, fol. 334r.

855. [*Rome*], *24 April 1457. Thomas Maydlande, layman, Lincoln dioc., present in the Roman Curia, requests absolution from or commutation of a vow to visit the Holy Sepulchre and other holy places.* Reg. 5, fol. 335r.

[Rome], viii kal Maii. Thomas Maydlande, laicus Lincolniensis diocesis in Romana curia presens, exponit quod alias zelo devocionis accensus et propter alia facta sibi incumbencia absque alicuius termini prefixione vovit sacrum sepulcrum dominicum et alia loca sacra visitare, sed quia senio confractus et paupertate gravatus dictum votum sicud vellet commode adimplere non potest hic supplicat sanctitai vestre quatinus ipsum a dicto voto et eius observancia absolvi aut ipsum in alia pietatis opera commutari misericorditer mandare dignemini de gratia speciali et expresso.

Fiat de speciali et expresso et committatur fratri sive magistro Stephano de Cassia ac magistro Paulo de Urbe.[11] D. s. † I.

---

[11] These men were minor penitentiaries: see *RPG*, iii, p. xvi.

856. [Rome, at St Peter's], 23 September 1457. John Wykos *de Anglia*, layman, Norwich dioc., seeks a licence and faculty to visit the [Holy] Sepulchre with two people. *Fiat de speciali D. s. †. I.* Reg. 5, fol. 403r.

857. [Rome, at St Peter's], 21 October 1457. George Rypla, priest, regular canon professed of the house or priory of BVM, Bridlington (*Bridlyngton*), OSA, York dioc.,[12] [requests that] the pope grant him letters *de sententiis generalibus cum clausula concubinatus, de iniectione manuum ac dimissione habitus non tamen animo apostatandi ac aliis etc. in forma. Fiat in forma D. s. †. I.* Reg. 5, fol. 411r.

858. [Rome, at St Peter's], 18 November 1457.[13] John [Tiptoft], earl of Worcester (*comes Wygornie*),[14] obtains a licence (*obtinet licentiam*) to visit the Holy Sepulchre with six people. *Fiat de speciali.* Reg. 5, fol. 414r.

De confessionalibus [in forma 'Cupientes']

859. [Rome], 24 May 1457. For Robert Potter *alias* Milani, rector of Halton Holgate (*Halton iuxta Spyllysbi*)[15] parish church, Lincoln dioc.,[16] letters *in forma 'Cupientes'*. *Fiat de speciali D. s. †. I.* Reg. 6, fol. 8r.

De confessionalibus perpetuis

860. [Rome], 22 May 1455. For Thomas Zart' and his wife Agnes, Norwich dioc., [*littere confessionales* for life]. *Fiat de speciali D. s. †.* Reg. 6, fol. 15r.

---

[12] George Ripley was granted a papal licence on 23 March 1459 that he might leave his priory to study at a university, even abroad, for seven years, receiving a benefice *in commendam* during this period; he stated that he intended to study theology and had his superior's permission to do so (*CPL*, xi. 530–1). He studied in Italy and at the University of Louvain. In 1471 he returned to England and died probably c. 1490 (*BRUO*, iii. 1577; *ODNB*, xlvi. 1000–2).

[13] Date written in left margin as 'xiiii Dec.' (*recte* xiiii kal. Dec.). 'Comes Wygornie' written in right margin instead of diocese.

[14] John Tiptoft, born *c.* 1427, the son of John, first baron Tiptoft, inherited his father's estates in 1443, and was created earl of Worcester on 1 July 1449. He was granted a papal dispensation (under a mandate of 13 May 1449 to the bishop of Worcester) to marry Cecily, widow of Henry Beauchamp, duke of Warwick, and a papal licence on 30 May 1459 to have masses and other divine offices celebrated for himself and his household at any time or place by suitable priests. He also received a papal licence on 28 November 1465 so that his confessor might grant him plenary remission *in mortis articulo* (*CPL*, x. 438–9; xi. 539; xii. 521). He had left England on piligrimage to the Holy Land, arriving in Venice in May 1458 and returning there in September, hence the present supplication. He studied in Padua intermittently, 1459–61, and visited other Italian cities, meeting humanists and buying humanist books. As Henry VI's envoy, he delivered an oration to Pius II in 1460. He returned to England in September 1461 and rose high in the service of the new king Edward IV. He held various offices of State. On Edward IV's flight, he was captured and condemned as a traitor, and executed on 18 October 1471 (*BRUO*, iii. 1877–9; *ODNB*, liv. 831–6; *Complete Peerage*, xii/2. 842–6; Weiss, *Humanism*, 112–22).

[15] This parish is indeed next to that of Spilsby (Lincs.).

[16] He was appointed a papal chaplain on 4 June 1457 (*CPL*, xi. 193).

861. [Rome], 29 May 1455. Same grant as **860** for Richard Castell, clerk, St Asaph dioc.[17] *Fiat de speciali D. s. †.* Reg. 6, fol. 15v.

862. [Rome], 15 June 1455. Same grant as **860** for John Gill and his wife Joan, citizens of London. *Fiat de speciali D. s. †.* Reg. 6, fol. 16v.

863. [Rome], 16 December 1455. For William Saltford, priest, professed monk of the monastery of Bath, OSB, Bath and Wells dioc.,[18] *littere confessionales* [in perpetuity]. *Concessum Io. de Querchu.* Reg. 6, fol. 22v.

864. [Rome], 24 December 1455. Same grant as **863** for Bartholomew Scobel and his wife Ellen.[19] *Fiat de speciali D. s. †.* Reg. 6, fol. 22v.

865. [Rome], 24 December 1455. Same grant as **863** for John Honiton, esquire, and his wife Elizabeth (*Helisabeth*), London dioc. *Fiat. Non est nomen. C.*[20] Reg. 6, fol. 22v.

866. [Rome], 15 March 1456. Same grant as **863** for Margaret Cokefelt, widow, noblewoman, York (*Ebrecensis*) [dioc.] *Fiat de speciali D. s. †.* Reg. 6, fol. 26r.

867. [Rome], 16 March 1456. Same grant as **860** for William Wryght, priest, Lincoln [dioc.] *Fiat de speciali D. s. †.* Reg. 6, fol. 26v.

868. [Rome], 16 March 1456. Same grant as **860** for William (*Gug'llus*) Brandon and his wife Elisabeth, Norwich (*Norvicensis*) [dioc.] [*Fiat de speciali D. s. †*]. Reg. 6, fol. 26v.

869. [Rome], 16 March 1456. Same grant as **860** for Gerard Wormele and his wife Katherine, Norwich (*Norbicensis*) [dioc.] *Fiat de speciali D. s. †.* Reg. 6, fol. 26v.

870. [Rome], 31 March 1456. Same grant as **863** for Richard Pinchb[e]ke and his wife Margaret, Lincoln (*Linconinensis*) [dioc.] [*Fiat de speciali D. s. †*]. Reg. 6, fol. 27v.

871. [Rome], 31 March 1456. Same grant as **860** for John Pynchbeke, layman, Lincoln (*Linconinensis*) [dioc.] [*Fiat de speciali D. s. †*]. Reg. 6, fol. 27v.

872. [Rome], 15 June 1456. Same grant as **860** for Gwilym Howhen, layman, and his wife Alice, St David's [dioc.] [*Fiat de speciali D. s. †*]. Reg. 6, fol. 30v.

---

[17] The dean of Wells was to appoint him a notary public under a papal mandate of 9 January 1448, but he was not so appointed till 17 May 1455, and then at the Curia by the *regens* of the papal chancery. On the latter date he was also granted a licence to have a portable altar (*CPL*, x. 371; xi. 226, 281).

[18] William Salford, monk of Bath Cathedral Priory, was ordained as a priest on 18 September 1423 by the bishop of Bath and Wells. He was sacrist, cellarer, and *custos* of the Lady Chapel in July 1447, and collated to the office of sacrist on 23 October 1449 (Greatrex, 40).

[19] Diocese omitted.

[20] The name of the signatory is omitted from the *Fiat*-clause. 'C.' may refer either to the corrector (A. de Aquila) or Paulus de Corsica, who identifies himself as *registri custos* on fol. 49r.

873. [Rome], 15 June 1456. Same grant as **860** for Ieuan Joys and his wife Alice, [St David's] dioc. *Fiat de speciali D. s. †.* Reg. 6, fol. 30v.

874. [Rome], 20 July 1456. Same grant as **860** for John Kemes, esquire and lord of the place of Siston and Dyrham (*de Siston et de Doram*), [Worcester dioc.] and his wife Margaret. *Fiat de speciali D. s. †.* Reg. 6, fol. 31v.

875. [Rome], 18 November 1456. Same grant as **860** for John Nicolle, priest, MA.[21] [*Fiat de speciali D. s. † I.*]. Reg. 6, fol. 32v.

876. [Rome], 18 November 1456. Same grant as **860** for Andrew Hebert, priest. *Fiat de speciali D. s. †. I.* Reg. 6, fol. 32v.

877. [Rome], 12 January 1457. Same grant as **860** for Thomas Tyler, abbot of St Mary's monastery, Keynsham (*Keynesham*), OSA, Bath and Wells dioc.[22] *Fiat de speciali D. s. †. I.* Reg. 6, fol. 33r.

878. [Rome], 25 January 1457. Same grant as **860** for Thomas Burgh, layman, Lincoln dioc.[23] [*Fiat de speciali D. s. † I.*]. Reg. 6, fol. 33r.

879. [Rome], 25 January 1457. Same grant as **860** for William Holderness, priest, London dioc.[24] *Fiat de speciali D. s. †. I.* Reg. 6, fol. 33r.

880. [Rome], 4 April 1457. Same grant as **860** for Richard Noyt, priest, St David's dioc. *Fiat de speciali D. s. †. I.* Reg. 6, fol. 34r.

881. [Rome], 15 April 1457. Same grant as **860** for Morgan ap Iankin ap Philip (*Iankyn ap Philipp*) and his wife Katherine, Llandaff dioc. *Fiat de speciali D. s. †. I.* Reg. 6, fol. 34v.

882. [Rome], 27 May 1457. Same grant as **860** for John Gloucestre and his wife Joan, London dioc. *Fiat de speciali D. s. †. I.* Reg. 6, fol. 34v.

883. [Rome], 9 January 1457. Same grant as **863** for Richard Man and his wife Rose, Canterbury dioc. *Fiat de speciali D. s. †. I.* Reg. 6, fol. 37r.

884. [Rome], 12 January 1457. Same grant as **863** for Thomas Mannyng, priest and archdeacon of Totnes (*Totnesie*), Exeter dioc.[25] *Fiat de speciali D. s. †.* Reg. 6, fol. 36v.

---

[21] In right margin beside the entry: 'diocesis non fuit expressa'.
[22] He was elected abbot on 9 January 1456 and died in office on 5 September 1486 (Smith, *Heads of Religious Houses*, iii. 453). On 16 January 1457 he was granted a papal licence to choose a personal confessor who might grant him absolution from sins reserved to the apostolic see once in his life and plenary remission *in mortis articulo* (*CPL*, xi. 297).
[23] Presumably the same man as Thomas Burch, nobleman, Lincoln dioc., who on 29 January 1457 was granted the same papal licence as in n. 22 (*CPL*, xi. 299).
[24] On 29 January 1457 he was granted the same papal licence as in n. 22 (*CPL*, xi. 299).
[25] Thomas Mannyng was collated to the archdeaconry of Totnes on 4 June 1453, but he was probably deprived of this along with other ecclesiastical offices by 1462, since he was attainted after the fall of Henry VI in November 1461. He was BCnL by 1446 and had

885. [Rome], 23 February 1457. Same grant as **863** for William Gardiner and his wife Joan, Norwich dioc. *Fiat de speciali D. s. †. I.* Reg. 6, fol. 38r.

886. [Rome], 27 February 1457. For William Gardiner and his wife Joan, Norwich dioc., *littere confessionales in forma* 'Provenit'. *Fiat de speciali et expresso D. s. †.* Reg. 6, fol. 38r.

887. [Rome], 30 March 1457. Same grant as **863** for Ieuan ap Lewis (*ab Lodvico*), priest, Llandaff dioc. *Fiat de speciali D. s. †. I.* Reg. 6, fol. 39r.

888. [Rome], 31 March 1457. Same grant as **863** for William Sawey *alias* Boleyn, priest, Salisbury dioc. *Fiat de speciali D. s. †. I.* Reg. 6, fol. 39r.

889. [Rome], 8 June 1457. Same grant as **860** for Fr John Galwey, priest, professed monk of St Mary's Priory, Pill (*Bulla*), OSB, St David's dioc.,[26] dependent on the monastery of Montmajour, near Tiron (*a monasterio Maioris Montis prope Turonis* [recte *Tironis*] *dicti ordinis dependentis*).[27] *Fiat de speciali D. s. †. I.* Reg. 6, fol. 40r.

890. [Rome], 2 July 1457. Same grant as **860** for Clement Wartwyke, priest, professed monk of St Mary's monastery outside the walls of York, OSB. *Fiat de speciali D. s. †. I.* Reg. 6, fol. 40r.

891. [Rome], 12 August 1457. Same grant as **863** for Eleanor, duchess of Norfolk, noblewoman, Norwich dioc.[28] *Fiat de speciali D. s. †. I.* Reg. 6, fol. 40v.

892. [Rome], 29 August 1457. Same grant as **860** for Christopher Wode and his wife Alice, dwelling in London (*Lundoniensi*) dioc. [*Fiat de speciali D. s. † I.*]. Reg. 6, fol. 40v.

893. [Rome], 29 August 1457. Same grant as **860** for William Burton and his wife Katherine, dwelling in London (*Lundoniensi*) dioc. *Fiat de speciali D. s. †. I.* Reg. 6, fol. 40v.

---

successfully supplicated to become DCnL of Oxford by 1459. He was also a royal clerk and chaplain in 1451, and king's secretary c. 1455–60. He died in 1469 (*BRUO*, ii. 1216–17; *Reg. Lacy*, ed. Hingeston-Randolph, i. 310, 378; *CPL*, xi. 148, 166).

[26] He was granted a papal dispensation on 1 May 1457 to obtain a benefice with or without cure of souls for life (*CPL*, xi. 147; his house is not named here but an editorial emendation misidentifies it as St Dogmells).

[27] Although this seems to refer to Marmoutier, near Tours, which had cells in England, it had none in St David's dioc. The supplicant's house is hence more likely to be Pill Priory, dedicated to St Mary and St Budoc, of the order of Tiron, a French offshoot of the Benedictine order (Knowles and Hadcock, 106–7).

[28] Eleanor, sister of Henry Bourchier, earl of Essex, and daughter of Sir William Bourchier, count of Eu (Normandy), and of Anne, daughter of Thomas of Woodstock, duke of Gloucester, had married John de Mowbray (d. 1461), duke of Norfolk, in 1424. They received a papal dispensation to marry under a faculty granted by Martin V to Henry Beaufort, cardinal priest of S. Eusebio and bishop of Winchester, being related in the third and fourth and double fourth and fourth degrees of consanguinity. Eugenius IV decreed on 9 March 1434 that they might remain married with legitimation of existing and future issue. She died in November 1474 (*CPL*, viii. 484; *Complete Peerage*, ix. 608; *ODNB*, xxxix. 581–2).

894. [Rome], 10 June 1458. Same grant as **863** for William Esyngwalde, priest, York dioc. *Fiat de speciali D. s. †. I.* Reg. 6, fol. 44v.

895. [Rome], 13 July 1458. Same grant as **863** for Fr John Ives, prior of the house of Sheen (*Schene*), Carthusian order, Winchester dioc.[29] *Fiat de speciali D. s. † I.* Reg. 6, fol. 45r.

896. [Rome], 13 July 1458. Same grant as **863** for George Roche and his present wife, Worcester dioc. *Fiat de speciali D. s. †. I.* Reg. 6, fol. 45r.

De defectu natalium

897. [Rome], 1 April 1455 *sede vacante*. [Supplication for] a dispensation for John Toek, scholar, York dioc., born of a married man and an unmarried woman, who wishes [to be enrolled] in the *militia clericalis*, that he may be promoted to all orders and obtain a benefice even with cure of souls, notwithstanding his defect of birth. *Fiat de speciali D. s. †.* Reg. 6, fol. 50r.

898. [Rome], 3 April 1455 *sede vacante*. [Supplication for] a dispensation for John Tock, scholar, York dioc., born of a married man and an unmarried woman, that he may be promoted to all orders and obtain a benefice even with cure of souls, notwithstanding that defect. *Fiat de speciali D. s. †.* Reg. 6, fol. 49r.

899. [Rome], 20 April 1455. Same dispensation as **898** for Ieuan son of Dafydd Iankyn, scholar, Llandaff dioc. Approved with **901**. Reg. 6, fol. 51r.

900. [Rome], 20 April 1455. Same grace as **898** for Morgan (*Margan*) son of Philip, scholar, Llandaff dioc., born of an unmarried man and an unmarried woman. Approved with **901**. Reg. 6, fol. 51r.

901. [Rome], 20 April 1455. Same grant as **860** for Ieuan [son] of Philip, layman, Llandaff dioc. *Fiat de speciali D. s. †.* (Approved with **899–900**.) Reg. 6, fol. 51r.

902. [Rome], 3 May 1455. [Supplication for a dispensation] for Rhys ap Ieuan ap Rhys ap Gruffydd (*Ris nos Ieuan vas Ris vas Gruffith*), scholar, Bangor dioc.,[30] born of an unmarried man and an unmarried woman, that he may be promoted to all holy orders and [obtain] a benefice [even with cure of souls], notwithstanding his defect of birth. Approved with **903**. Reg. 6, fol. 53r.

---

[29] He is documented as prior 1457–65. He became prior of Hinton and died in 1492 (Smith, *Heads of Religious Houses*, iii. 363).

[30] Richard Iohannis *alias* Ris ap Ieuan ap Ris ap Gruffuth was granted a further papal dispensation on 15 May 1470 to hold an additional incompatible benefice (*CPL*, xii. 782). It refers to his earlier dispensation, that sought in the present entry, but notes that it allowed him to be promoted to all, *even* holy, orders, and adds that he was admitted rector of Gyffin parish church, Bangor dioc., by virtue of this dispensation. He was BCnL by 1470, and he may be the same Richard ap John, BCnL (probably of Oxford), who was admitted vicar of Iffley (Oxon.) on 2 December 1480 (*BRUO*, iii. 1574).

903. [Rome], 3 May 1455. Same grace as **902** for Eustace (*Eus*) Gruffith ap Llywelyn ap *Yorokus* (*vas Lli' vas Yorokus*), scholar, Bangor dioc. *Fiat de speciali D. s. †.* (Approved with **902**.) Reg. 6, fol. 53r.

904. [Rome], 13 May 1455. Same dispensation as **898** for William (*Gulielmus*), scholar, York dioc., born of an unmarried man and an unmarried woman. *Fiat de speciali D. s. †.* Reg. 6, fol. 54r.

905. [Rome], 18 September 1455. Same dispensation *in prima forma* as **898** requested on the part of Henry Conhyers, scholar, York [dioc.]. *Fiat de speciali D. s. †.* Reg. 6, fol. 61r.

906. [Rome], 20 December 1455. Same dispensation as **898** requested on the part of William (*Gulielmus*) Beghson, clerk, York [dioc.], born of a priest and an unmarried woman. *Fiat de speciali D. s. †.* Reg. 6, fol. 65r.

907. [Rome], 17 January 1456. Same dispensation as **902** requested on the part of John Bagnal, scholar, Coventry and Lichfield [dioc.] [*Fiat de speciali*] *D. s. †.* Reg. 6, fol. 66r.

908. [Rome], 17 January 1456. Same dispensation as **902** for Richard Hethecothe, scholar, [Coventry and Lichfield dioc.] *Fiat de speciali D. s. †.* Reg. 6, fol. 66r.

909. [Rome], 7 February 1456. Same dispensation as **902** requested on the part of John [son] of Edward (*Eduvardi*), Bath and Wells [dioc.][31] *Fiat de speciali D. s. †.* Reg. 6, fol. 66v.

910. [Rome], 3 March 1456. Same dispensation as **902** requested on the part of William (*Gug'lli*) Foliabins, scholar (*scelet'*), Coventry [and Lichfield dioc.], born of a married man and an unmarried woman. *Fiat de speciali D. s. †.* Reg. 6, fol. 68v.

911. [*Rome*], *27 March 1456. Ieuan, son of Edward, scholar, Bangor dioc., requests a dispensation from his defect of birth.* Reg. 6, fol. 70r.

> [Rome], vi kal. Aprilis [a. p°.]. Item pro parte Iohannis Edwardi, scolaris Bangorensis [dioc.],[32] de coniugato geniti et soluta, etc. [cum desideret ad omnes etiam presbiteratus ordines promoveri et perpetuo altissimo famulari, supplicat sanctitati vestre quatinus sibi specialem gratiam facientes ut defectu huiusmodi non obstante ad omnes sacros et presbiteratus ordines possit promoveri et beneficium ecclesiasticum etiam si curam habeat animarum obtinere possit dispensare dignemini de gratia speciali].
>
> Fiat de speciali D. s. †.

---

[31] Possibly the John Edwardes of St Thomas's parish, Bristol, Bath and Wells dioc., who was ordained as an acolyte by the diocesan on 22 February 1456; on the same day the bishop also granted him letters dimissory for all holy orders, in which he is said to have been born in Holy Cross of the Temple parish, Bristol (*Reg. Bekynton*, no. 968).
[32] Name of diocese supplied from right margin.

912. [Rome], 2 April 1456. Same dispensation as **898** requested on the part of Dafydd ap Gruffydd ap Ieuan (*ap Gruff ap Iohan*) Owo, scholar, Bangor [dioc.], born of an unmarried man and an unmarried woman. *Fiat de speciali D. s. †.* Reg. 6, fol. 70r.

913. [Rome], 3 April 1456. William Evin'm, expressly professed of OFM, Lincoln [dioc.],[33] born of an unmarried man and an unmarried woman, [requests] a dispensation that he may [assume] any conventual office of his order or the office of guardian, if presented to it by brothers of the said order. *Fiat de speciali D. s. †.* Reg. 6, fol. 70r.

914. *[Rome], 5 April 1456. Richard Gunter, subdeacon, Llandaff dioc., kept silent about his defect of birth when he was promoted to minor and subdeacon's orders; he seeks absolution and promotion to deacon's and priest's orders.* Reg. 6, fol. 70v.

[Rome], non. Aprilis. [Pro] Riccardo Gunter, subdiacono Landavensis [diocesis],[34] qui tacito de defectu natalium ad minores omnes et subdiaconatus ordines se fecit promoveri et in ipsis ministravit. Supplicatur igitur pro parte exponentis quatinus ipsum ab excessibus huiusmodi et peccatis suis aliis absolvere et quod ad diaconatus et presbiteratus ordines promoveri possit et beneficium ecclesiasticum etc. [etiam curatum libere recipere et retinere possit et valeat] dispensari mandare dignemini de gratia speciali.

Fiat de speciali D. s. †.

915. [Rome], 5 April 1456. Same dispensation as **898** requested on the part of Dafydd ap Gruffydd (*Gruffith*), scholar, Llandaff [dioc.],[35] born of an unmarried man and an unmarried woman. *Fiat de speciali D. s. †.* Reg. 6, fol. 70v.

916. [Rome], 6 April 1456. Same dispensation as **898** requested on the part of Richard Foywyst, scholar, [Llandaff dioc.], born of an unmarried man and an unmarried woman. *Fiat de speciali D. s. †.* Reg. 6, fol. 70v.

917. [Rome], 8 May 1456. Same dispensation as **898** requested on the part of John Walton, scholar, York [dioc.], born of an unmarried man and an unmarried woman. *Fiat de speciali D. s. †.* Reg. 6, fol. 71v.

918. [Rome, at St Peter's], 27 May 1456. Supplication on the part of Edward (*Edirardi*) Johnson, clerk, York dioc., born of an unmarried man and an unmarried woman,[36] who wishes to be promoted to all, even holy, orders, notwithstanding his defect of birth, that the pope grant him a dispensation that he may be so promoted

---

[33] Diocese not named in entry but in right margin: 'Linconien.'
[34] Name of diocese supplied from right margin.
[35] Name of diocese supplied from right margin. Probably David ap Gruffith, BCnL (of Oxford), perpetual vicar of Llangenydd (Glamorgs.), Llandaff dioc., who was granted a papal dispensation on 10 January 1463 to hold an additional incompatible benefice (*CPL*, xi. 640). Perhaps Master David ap Griffith, admitted as vicar of Portbury (Somerset) on 27 February 1475 (resigned by August 1475) and rector of Slymbridge (Glos.) on 30 June 1475 (*BRUO*, ii. 834–5).
[36] 'De solutis' also indicated in left margin.

and obtain a benefice even with cure of souls. *Fiat de speciali D. s. † I. Dat' Rome apud sanctum Petrum vi kal. Iunii anno 2°. A. de Aquila.* Reg. 6, fol. 73r.[37]

919. [Rome], *16 June 1456*. Thomas Qwhyt alias Blar, priest, Glasgow dioc., living in Norwich dioc., had himself promoted to all, even holy, orders without a dispensation from his defect of birth. He seeks absolution and a dispensation. Reg. 6, fol. 81v.

[Rome], xvi kal. Iulii. Thomas Qwhyt alias Blar, presbiter Glasguensis [diocesis][38] in diocese Norwicensi regni Anglie moram trahens, nulla habita dispensatione super defectu natalium de soluto et soluta genitus, ad omnes etiam sacros ordines alias tamen rite promotus fuit et in illis celebravit. Supplicat dictus exponens sanctitati vestre quatinus ipsum ab excessibus huiusmodi [absolvere] et quod, impedimento huiusmodi non obstante, in dictis ordinibus ministrare possit et beneficium ecclesiasticum etiam si curam habeat animarum retinere possit dispensare dignemini de gratia speciali.

Fiat de speciali D. s. †.

[**920**] [Rome], 31 August 1456. William Whyt, clerk, born of an unmarried man and an unmarried woman, Lincoln [dioc.], requests the same dispensation as **898**. *Fiat de speciali D. s. †.* Reg. 6, fol. 83v.

921. [Rome, at St Peter's], 15 December 1456. John Harenconot, scholar, Lincoln dioc., born of unmarried parents,[39] requests the same dispensation as **898**. *Fiat [de speciali D. s. †.]* Reg. 6, fol. 86v.

922. [Rome], 29 March(?) 1457.[40] [Request for a dispensation] for Ieuan ap *Wan* ap Gruffydd (*Gruffith*), scholar, Llandaff dioc., born of an unmarried man and an unmarried woman, [that he may become a clerk (*clericali caractere insigniri*), be promoted to all, even holy, orders, and receive and retain a benefice even with cure of souls, notwithstanding his defect of birth]. *Fiat de speciali D s † I.* Reg. 6, fol. 99v.

923. [Rome], 29 March 1457. Thomas ap Dafydd, scholar, Llandaff dioc., born of an unmarried man and an unmarried woman, [requests] that the pope grant him a dispensation that he may be made a clerk (*clericali caractere insigniri*), be promoted to all, even holy, orders, and receive and retain a benefice even with cure of souls, notwithstanding his defect of birth. Approved with **925**. Reg. 6, fol. 111v.

---

[37] Written in the left margin is 'II½' which refers to the tax. The entry is recorded again on fol. 104r with slightly different wording.
[38] Name of Scottish diocese supplied from right margin.
[39] Probably the John Harecourt, clerk of Exeter, said to be aged 20 and of noble birth, who was granted a papal dispensation on 8 January 1457 to hold any number of compatible benefices without cure of souls, and on reaching the legitimate age (25), any number with cure of souls (*CPL*, xi. 128). It says that he had obtained a previous papal dispensation exactly as that sought in the present entry, except that it described him as the son of an unmarried nobleman and unmarried woman and permitted him to be promoted to all, even holy, orders. On the same day he was also granted a dispensation to hold two incompatible benefices on reaching the legitimate age (ibid.).
[40] Dated in left margin: 'iiii mensis [*recte* kal.?] Aprilis.'

924. [Rome], 29 March 1457. Gruffydd (*Gruffin*) ap *Hobam*, scholar, Bangor dioc., requests the same dispensation as **923**. Approved with **925**. Reg. 6, fol. 111v.

925. [Rome], 29 March 1457. Dafydd ap Ieuan (*Iohan*), scholar, Bangor dioc., born of a priest, a professed monk of the Cistercian order, and an unmarried woman, requests the same dispensation as **923**. *Fiat de speciali D. s. † I.* (Approved with **923–4**.) Reg. 6, fol. 111v.

926. [Rome], 3 April 1457. Robert ap Gwilym ap Hywel (*Howel*) Vachan, scholar, Llandaff dioc., born of a priest and an unmarried woman, requests the same dispensation as **923**. *Fiat de speciali D. s. †. I.* Reg. 6, fol. 100r.

927. [Rome], 4 April 1457. Robert Wilman, scholar, Llandaff dioc., born of a priest and an unmarried woman, [requests] that the pope grant him a dispensation that he may be promoted to all, even holy, orders, and retain a benefice even with cure of souls, notwithstanding his defect of birth. *Fiat de speciali D. s. †. I.* Reg. 6, fol. 100r.

928. [Rome], 19 April 1457.[41] Same grace as **923** for Edward ap Ieuan (*Iohan*), scholar, St Asaph dioc., born of an unmarried man and an unmarried woman. Approved with **929**. Reg. 6, fol. 103r.

929. [Rome], 19 April 1457. Same grace as **923** for Robert ap Madog (*Madoc*), scholar, St Asaph dioc., born of an unmarried man and an unmarried woman. *Fiat de speciali D. s. †. I.* (Approved with **928**.) Reg. 6, fol. 103r.

930. [Rome], 28 April 1457. John Alsalle', scholar, Coventry [and Lichfield] dioc., born of a married man and a married woman, who wishes to be enrolled in the *militia clericalis*, [requests] that the pope grant him a dispensation that he may be promoted to all holy orders and obtain a benefice even with cure of souls, notwithstanding his defect of birth. *Fiat de speciali D. s. †. I.* Reg. 6, fol. 114v.

931. [Rome], 22 May 1457. John Eye, priest, professed of St Botolph's convent, OP, [Boston], Lincoln dioc.,[42] born of a married man and an unmarried woman, [requests] that the pope grant him a dispensation that he may obtain *administrationes*, offices, and the priorate in that convent and order, notwithstanding his defect of birth. *Et committatur priori provinciali ordinis fratrum predicatorum*[43] *vel eius vicariis provincie Anglie. Fiat de speciali D. s. †. I.* Reg. 6, fol. 118r.

932. [Rome], 16 June 1457. Thomas Hodscon, clerk, Carlisle dioc., born of a priest and an unmarried woman, requests the same dispensation as **898**. Approved with **933**. Reg. 6, fol. 122v.

---

[41] The page is headed 'Rome anno secundo', which implies that the date of this entry was 19 April 1456, but this seems unlikely given the register's chronological sequence.

[42] Probably the Dominican friar John Eye, BTh of Oxford, who was appointed by the general chapter of his order in 1462 as *magister studentium* at the Oxford convent for the ensuing two years, and diffinitor of the English province (*BRUO*, i. 661).

[43] Not identifiable from C. F. R. Palmer, 'Fasti ordinis fratrum praedicatorum: the provincials of the Friar-Preachers, or Black Friars, of England', *Archaeological Journal*, 35 (1878), 134–65.

933. [Rome], 16 June 1457. Thomas Haa, scholar, Carlisle dioc., born of an unmarried man and an unmarried woman, requests the same dispensation as **898**. *Fiat de speciali D. s. †. I.* (Approved with **932**.) Reg. 6, fol. 122v.

934. [Rome], 28 July 1457. Same dispensation as **897** sought by John Wekys, scholar, Norwich dioc. *Fiat de speciali D. s. †. I.* Reg. 6, fol. 125v.

935. [Rome], 9 August 1457. William Backus, scholar, Coventry and Lichfield dioc., born of a priest and an unmarried woman, who wishes to be enrolled in the *militia clericalis*, requests that the pope grant him a dispensation that after he has been made a clerk (*clericali caractere insignitus fuerit*), he may be promoted to all, even holy, orders and obtain and retain a benefice even with cure of souls, notwithstanding his defect of birth and [constitutions] of the council of Poitiers or any others to the contrary, *et aliis clausulis necessariis et oportunis*. *Fiat de speciali D. s. †. I.* Reg. 6, fol. 127r.

936. [Rome], 22 September 1457. John Perquyns, scholar, Winchester dioc., born of an unmarried man and an unmarried woman, requests the same dispensation as **897**. *Fiat de speciali D. s. †. I.* Reg. 6, fol. 130r.

937. [Rome], 4 November 1457. John Mares, scholar, Hereford dioc., born of an unmarried man and an unmarried woman, requests the same dispensation as **897**.[44] *Fiat de speciali [D. s. †. I.]* Reg. 6, fols. 133v–34r.

938. [Rome], 14 June 1458. Fr John At Wode, priest, professed of OFM, York convent, born of an unmarried man and an unmarried woman, [requests] that the pope grant him a dispensation that he may minister in all his orders and receive and be promoted to offices and dignities of his order other than the principal one. *Fiat de speciali D. s. †. I.* Reg. 6, fols. 152v–53r.

939. [Rome], 14 June 1458. William Cruckschanke, scholar, Lincoln dioc., requests the same dispensation as **898**. *Fiat de speciali D. s. †. I.* Reg. 6, fol. 153r.

940. [Rome], 22 July 1458. John de Halle, York dioc., scholar lately of Kirkby in Ashfield (*Karkebi in Asschefelden*), born of a priest and an unmarried woman, who wishes to be enrolled in the *militia clericalis*, [requests] that the pope grant him a dispensation that he may be made a clerk (*clericali caractere insigniri*), be promoted to all holy orders, and receive a benefice even with cure of souls, notwithstanding his defect of birth. *Fiat de speciali D. s. †. I.* Reg. 6, fol. 146r.[45]

---

[44] Perhaps the John Marys ordained by the bishop of Hereford as a priest on 7 June 1460. Possibly the same as John Maret, rector of Arley, who exchanged with Richard Richards, rector of Abberley, on 10 November 1464 (*Reg. Stanbury*, 146, 192).

[45] The entry is repeated on fol. 155v except that there the supplicant is called 'del Halle' and said to be lately of 'Karkebi Asschefeld in comitatu Notinghem', and the following clause is added: 'Pictavensis concilii et aliis in contrarium facientibus non obstantibus quibuscumque'.

De matrimonialibus

941. [Rome, 22 April 1455]. Maurice, son of Dafydd Vachan, and Erddylad (*Erdvilla*), daughter of *Thaim*, Llandaff dioc., [request that the pope grant them a dispensation] that they may marry as they wish, notwithstanding the impediment that they are related in the fourth degree of affinity, and may solemnise their marriage with legitimation of future issue.[46] [*Fiat de speciali D. s. †*.]. Reg. 6, fol. 160r.

942. [Rome, 24 April 1455]. Thomas Williconson Hyginis, layman, and Alice Henen' of Newnham (*Newnam*), a married couple from Hereford dioc., contracted and consummated their marriage unaware [that they were related] in the fourth degree of consanguinity; [they request that the pope grant them a dispensation] that they may remain married, notwithstanding that impediment of consanguinity, and solemnise their marriage with legitimation of existing and future issue.[47] *Fiat de speciali D. s. †.* Reg. 6, fol. 161r.

943. [*Rome*], *31 May 1455. Thomas Gay, son of Simon Gay, and Eleanor, daughter of George Dent, of Wick, Worcester dioc., are related in the third degree of affinity; they seek a dispensation that they may marry with legitimation of future issue.* Reg. 6, fol. 177v.

[Rome], pridie kal. Iunii. Thoma[s] Gay Symonis Gay et Alienora Georgii Dent de villa Wic, Virgorniensis diocesis, [cum] pro amore et pace inter eos eorumque parentes et amicos et pro bonis aliis certis causis matrimonium inter se contrahere desiderarent, nisi quia tertio affinitatis gradu sunt coniuncti eorum in hac parte desiderium adimplere nequeunt dispensatione non obtenta; quare supplica[n]t etc. [sanctitati vestre] ut, non obstante dicto impedimento, matrimonium contrahere possint dispensare dignemini prolemque etc. [exinde suscipiendam legitimam decernentes] de gratia speciali.

Fiat de speciali et expresso D. s. †.

944. [*Rome*], *3 June 1455. Humphrey, layman of Exeter dioc., had sexual relations with a married woman called Elisabeth and then married another Elisabeth, knowing that she was related to the first in the second and fourth degrees of consanguinity; he seeks a dispensation that they may remain married with legitimation of existing and future issue.* Reg. 6, fol. 180v.

[Rome], iii non. Iunii. Honfredo, layco Exoniensis diocesis, ut in matrimonio quod ipse olim quamdam feminam coniugatam nomine Helisabeth cognovisset carnaliter et subsequenter ad aliam feminam Helisabeth etiam

---

[46] Noted beside this entry: 'in quarto cum legitimatione prolis'.

[47] The cardinal penitentiary issued a commission of the same date to the bishop of Hereford or his vicar in spirituals. This letter described the supplication in the same way as the present entry except that it was said to be on the part of (*ex parte*) Thomas Williamson Hygyns and Alice Henyng of Newnham, who contracted marriage *per verba legitime de presenti*, and that they only learned of the impediment subsequently. The cardinal by special papal mandate granted *vive vocis oraculo* instructed his commissioners that 'si ita est' they should grant the couple a dispensation to remain married with legitimation of any existing and future issue, provided that Alice had not been forced into marriage. Richard Pede, the bishop's vicar-general, accordingly granted them the dispensation (*Reg. Stanbury*, 34–5).

vocatam, que prime iam cognitae in secundo et quarto gradu consanguinitatis erat coniuncta, ~~matrimonium~~[48] scienter contraxit, et prolem procreavit, et quia propter impedimentum huiusmodi secundum dispositionem sancte matris ecclesie dubitatur matrimonium predictum posse stare quo ad vite eterne salutem, dignetur igitur sanctitas vestra ipsos, scilicet Honfredum et Elisabeth, perpetuo remanere et progeniem ab ipsis procreatam et procreandam legitimam declarare vel decernere de gratia speciali.

Fiat de speciali D. s. †.

945. [Rome], 31 July 1455. Nicholas Clerk and Joan Figis, Bath (*Bataniensis*) and Wells [dioc.], wish to marry for certain good reasons; but since they are related in the fourth degree of consanguinity, [they request that the pope] grant them a dispensation that they may do so [with legitimation of future] issue.[49] *Fiat de speciali D. s. †.* Reg. 6, fol. 189v.

946. [Rome], 7 January 1456. William Bolton, layman, and Helen de Wchyust,[50] Coventry and Lichfield [dioc.], wish to marry on certain reasonable grounds; but since they are related in the fourth degree of consanguinity, they may not do so [without a dispensation. They request that the pope grant them a dispensation] that they may marry, notwithstanding that impediment. *Fiat de speciali D. s. †.* Reg. 6, fol. 210v.

947. [Rome], 20 February 1456. Ieuan, son of Dafydd Lloyt, layman, and Margaret, daughter of Jerome ap *Ergum*, St Asaph [dioc.], married *per verba legitime de presenti etiam in facie ecclesie*, not unaware that they were related in the fourth degree of consanguinity, and afterwards they had sexual relations and issue. [They request that the pope grant them a dispensation] that they may marry [*recte* remain married] [with legitimation of existing and future] issue. *Fiat de speciali et componit* [recte *componat*] *D. s. †.* Reg. 6, fol. 218v.

948. [Rome], 4 March [1456].[51] John Baron and Agnes Baron, Lincoln dioc., contracted marriage publicly *per verba de presenti* and consummated it, unaware [that they were related] in the fourth [degree] of affinity; [they request that the pope grant them a dispensation that they may remain married] with legitimation of any existing and future issue. *Fiat de speciali D. s. †. I.* Reg.6, fol. 260r.

949. [*Rome*], *8 March 1456. John Wind of Wigan, layman, Coventry and Lichfield dioc., married Joan Inse of that diocese, unaware that she was related in the second and fourth degrees of consanguinity to one Clemence Worthington, with whom he had previously had sexual relations;*

---

[48] Deleted in error.
[49] The cardinal penitentiary issued a commission of the same date to the bishop of Bath and Wells, instructing him to grant them the dispensation requested; this letter describes the supplicants as Nicholas Clerk, layman, and Joan Fitz *alias* Figis. The bishop carried out his commission on 27 October 1455 (*Reg. Bekynton*, no. 946).
[50] Perhaps Whitchurch (Shropshire).
[51] The page where this entry appears is headed 'Rome anno secundo'; strictly speaking during the second year of Calixtus III's pontificate 4 March fell in 1457, but the roughly chronological sequence of the entries suggests that it refers to the previous year. Cf. **956**.

[*they seek a dispensation that they may remain married with legitimation of existing and future issue*]. Reg. 6, fol. 220r.

[Rome], viii id. Martii. [Pro] Iohanne Wind de Wigan, laico [Conventrensis][52] et Lichefesdensis [*sic*] dioc., ut in matrimonio quod ipse olim per verba legiptime [*sic*] de presenti cum quadam Iohanna Inse, muliere dictarum diocesum [*recte* dicte diocesis], ignoranter contraxit, carnali copula subsecuta, sed quia dictus Iohannes pluries ab [*sic*] antea quamdam Clementem [*recte* Clementiam] Worthington mulierem, que dicte Iohanne secundo et quarto consanguinitatis gradibus fuit coniuncta, actu fornicario pluries cognoverat, propter quod in dicto matrimonio remanere non possunt, etc. [quare supplicant sanctitati vestre] ut non obstante etc. ut supra [impedimento huiusmodi in eodem matrimonio licite remanere possint prolemque exinde susceptam et suscipiendam legitimam decernentes dispensare dignemini de gratia speciali].

Fiat de speciali D. s. †.

950. [Rome], 1 April 1456. Llywelyn ap Tudur (*Llewellyn ap Tudre*) ap Dafydd ap Robert and Agnes verch Rhys ap Llywelyn ap Tudur (*Rys ap Llewelin ap Tudir*), a married couple from Bangor [dioc.], married publicly according to local custom (*secundum morem patrie*) and had sexual relations, unaware that they were related in the fourth degree of consanguinity; [it is requested] on their part that the pope grants them a dispensation that they may remain married with [legitimation of any existing and future] issue, notwithstanding that impediment. *Fiat de speciali D. s. †*. Reg. 6, fol. 225r.

[951] [Rome], 5 April 1456. Thomas ap *Murat* ap Ifor (*Ivor*), layman, and Gwenllian (*Wenllan'*), daughter of Gwilym ap Gruffydd (*Gwylyni ap Gruffith*), Llandaff [dioc.], wish to marry for certain reasons, but since they are related in the fourth degree of consanguinity, [they may not do so without a dispensation; it is requested] on their part [that the pope grant them a dispensation] that they may marry with [legitimation of future] issue, notwithstanding that impediment. *Fiat de speciali D. s. †*. Reg. 6, fol. 226v.

952. [Rome], 8 April 1456. Llywelyn ap Heilyn ap Ieuan (*Llewellyn ap Howelyn ap Iwan*) and Katherine verch Heilyn ap Gronw (*Howelyn verch* [sic] *ap Grano*), lay persons, Llandaff dioc., [who are related] in the fourth degree of affinity [request that the pope grant them a dispensation] that they may marry with legitimation of future issue. *Fiat de speciali D. s. †. I*. Reg. 6, fol. 264r.

953. [Rome], 16 April 1456. Robert Hobson, layman, and Margaret Wolfe, a married couple from Carlisle (*Karlensis*) [dioc.], married publicly *per verba legitime de presenti publice in facie ecclesie iuxta morem patrie*, then unaware that they were related in the third and fourth degrees of consanguinity or affinity, and afterwards had sexual relations. [It is requested] on their part [that the pope grant them a dispensation] that they may remain married [with legitimation of any existing and future] issue,

---

[52] Indicated in the right margin.

notwithstanding that impediment. *Fiat de speciali D. s. †. Litteras declaratorias felicis recordationis domini Clementis pape VI super tertio et quarto consanguinitatis etc. Fiat in forma D. s. †.* Reg. 6, fol. 229r.

954. [*Rome*], *28 April 1456. Walter Graunt and Agnes Felfe, Lincoln dioc., married and had issue, Walter being unaware that they were related in the second and third degrees of consanguinity, while Agnes knew of an impediment. Disowned by their families, they seek a dispensation to remain married and have their marriage solemnised with legitimation of existing and future issue.*[53] Reg. 6, fol. 231r.

> [Rome], iiii kal. Maii. Item et pro parte Walteri Graunt et Agnetis Felfe Lincolniensis [diocesis][54] exponitur sanctitati vestre quod licet ipsi secundo et tertio consanguinitatis gradibus invicem sint coniuncti, tamen huiusmodi impedimento non obstante matrimonium inter se per verba de presenti contraxerunt et proles procrearunt absque tamen sollempnizatione in facie ecclesie, attenpto [*sic*] pater sancte quod dictus Walterus consanguinitatem huiusmodi inter ipsum et Agnetem bene agnovit, non tamen in eo gradu quod matrimonio impedimentum prestare deberet; ipsa vero Agnes non ignoranter contraxit. Et nihilominus sanctitas vestra de benignitate sedis apostolice dictis oratoribus provideat ut sic in contracto matrimonio commorari possint; ab eorum parentibus et consanguineis perpetuo relegati permanebunt sicuti et in presenti de partibus expulsi et presentes in curia tamquam relegati et pauperes existunt. Quare sanctitati vestre humiliter supplicant quatinus ut dicto impedimento non obstante permanere in dicto matrimonio [et] ipsum in facie ecclesie sollempnizari facere per eorum ordinarium petere possint et valeant prolesque etc. [exinde susceptas et suscipiendas legitimas decernentes], ceteris quibuscumque non obstantibus, dispensare dignemini etc.
>
> Fiat de speciali et expresso D. s. †.

955. [Rome, at St Peter's], 2 December 1456. William Assheten, layman, and Margaret Chornelee, Coventry and Lichfield dioc., wish to marry but since they are related in the third and fourth degrees of consanguinity [they may not do so without a dispensation; hence they request that the pope grant them] a dispensation that they may marry, notwithstanding that impediment, with [legitimation] of future issue. *Fiat de speciali D. s. †. I.*[55] Reg. 6, fol. 286r.

956. [Rome, at St Peter's], 28 March [1457].[56] Gronw ap Iankin (*Granw ap Iackyn*) and Angharad verch Badi (*Bady*), a married couple from St Asaph dioc., related in the third and fourth degrees of affinity, contracted marriage and consummated

---

[53] A hand pointing to this entry was drawn in the left hand margin of the register.
[54] Name of diocese supplied from right margin.
[55] Clement VI had ruled that couples related in the third and fourth degrees also required *littere declaratorie* in order to marry; it is unusual that these were not requested here.
[56] The page where this entry appears is headed 'Rome apud sanctum Petrum anno tercio'; strictly speaking 28 March fell in 1458 during the third year of Calixtus III's pontificate, but the roughly chronological sequence of the entries suggests that it refers to the previous year. Cf. **948**.

it, unaware of any impediment between them; [they request that the pope] grant them a dispensation that they may remain married, notwithstanding that impediment, [with legitimation of any existing and future issue]. *Fiat de speciali D. s. †. I. Dignetur sanctitas vestra eisdem litteras declaratorias super tertio affinitatis concedere in forma Clementini.* [*Fiat D. s. †. I.*] Reg. 6, fol. 304v.

957. [Rome], 29 March 1457. [Supplication for a dispensation] for Hywel ap Philip (*Howel ap Philipp*), layman, and Gwenllian, daughter of Hywel ap Morys (Howel ap Morick), Llandaff dioc., [related] in the fourth degree of affinity, who have fornicated, that they may marry with legitimation of future issue. *Fiat de speciali D. s. †. I.* Reg. 6, fol. 312v.

958. [Rome], 30 March 1457. [Supplication for a dispensation] for Thomas ap Edward (*Edwart*) and Erddylad (*Erdudvyl*), daughter of Gwilym (*Guillym*), Llandaff dioc., [related] in the fourth degree of consanguinity, who have fornicated, that they may marry with legitimation of future issue. *Fiat de speciali D. s. †. I.* Reg. 6, fol. 312v.

959. [Rome, at St Peter's], 27 April 1457. Dafydd ap Madog (*Modoc*) and Margaret verch Dafydd, a married couple from [Coventry and] Lichfield dioc., contracted marriage and consummated it, unaware of the impediment that they were related in the fourth degree of consanguinity; [they request that the pope] grant them a dispensation that they may remain married, notwithstanding that impediment, [with legitimation of any existing and future] issue. *Fiat de speciali D. s. †. I.* Reg. 6, fol. 305r.

960. [Rome, at St Peter's], 27 April 1457. Same grace as **959** for Dafydd ap Ieuan and Elen verch Gruffydd (*Gruffuth*), a married couple from St Asaph dioc. *Fiat de speciali D. s. †. I.* Reg. 6, fol. 305r.

961. [*Rome*], *1 June 1457. John Walton and Margaret alias Marion Richardson, Durham dioc., married, unaware of their spiritual relationship; they seek a dispensation that they may remain married with legitimation of any existing and future issue.* Reg. 6, fol. 316r.

> [Rome], kal. Iunii. [Pro] Iohanne Walton et Margareta alias Mariona Riichardson [*sic*] Dunelmensis diocesis de ignoranter contracto et consummato [matrimonio] secundum ritum patrie inter fratrem et sororem spirituales ex eo quod mater dicte mulieris dictum virum de sacro fonte levavit, cum prolis suscepte si sit et suscipiende legitimatione.
>
> Fiat de speciali et expresso D. s. †. I.

962. [Rome], 21 July 1457. [Supplication for a dispensation] for John Hillis, layman, and Agnes Petyr *alias* Pratte, a married couple from London dioc., who contracted [marriage] *per verba legitime de presenti* and did not consummate it, knowing [that they were related] in the third and fourth degrees of affinity, [that they may remain married] with absolution from a general sentence [of excommunication]. *Fiat de speciali D. s. †. I. Et cum litteris declaratoriis super tertio affinitatis in forma. Fiat in forma D. s. †. I.* Reg. 6, fol. 319r.

963. [Rome], 18 July [1458].⁵⁷ [Supplication for a dispensation] for Hywel ap Rhys ap Nynnyaw (*Howell ap Riis ap Ny'*) and Katherine verch Griffri ap Rhys (*Griff' ap Ris*), Bangor dioc., who contracted marriage *per verba de presenti*, consummated it, and had issue, knowing [that they were related] in the fourth [degree] of consanguinity, [that they may remain married] with legitimation of existing and future issue. *Fiat de speciali et componat cum domino Gerundensi D. s. †. I.* Reg. 6, fol. 334v.

De defectu etatis

964. [Rome], 14 June 1455. [Supplication for] a dispensation for Thomas Heyward, deacon, Salisbury dioc., aged 22 or thereabouts, that on reaching the age of 24 he may be promoted to the order of the priesthood and minister in it and his other existing orders, notwithstanding his defect of age and constitutions of the Lyons and Lateran councils and any others to the contrary. Approved with **965**. Reg. 6, fol. 342v.

965. [Rome], 14 June 1455. Same grace as **964** for Nicholas Brigt, deacon, aged 22 or thereabouts, Salisbury dioc. *Fiat de speciali D. s. †.* (Approved with **964**.) Reg. 6, fol. 342v.

966. [Rome], 16 June 1455. [Supplication for] a dispensation for Richard Langam, clerk, Norwich dioc., aged 23, that he may be promoted to all holy orders and thereafter minister in them. *Fiat de speciali quam primum xxiiii attigerit D. s. †.* Reg. 6, fol. 342v.

967. [Rome], 20 June 1455. John Clerck, deacon, Durham (*Dimellmensis*) dioc., aged 23, wishes to be promoted to the order of the priesthood; [he requests] that the pope grant him [a dispensation] that on reaching the age of 24 he may be promoted to the said order and minister in it, notwithstanding the statutes of the councils of Poitiers and Lyons. [*Fiat de speciali D. s. †.*]. Reg. 6, fol. 343r.

968. [*Rome*], *13 February 1456. Thomas Campion of Oakham in Rutland, Lincoln dioc., clerk, requests a dispensation from his defect of age.*⁵⁸ Reg. 6, fol. 350r.

[Rome], id. Febr. Beatissime pater, cum devotus vester Thomas Campion' de Oblim' in Rutlond' Lincolniensis diocesis, clericus, desiderat ob animarum suorum parentum salutem et zelo devotionis accensus ad omnes sacros et presbiteratus ordines promoveri et in eisdem perpetuo altissimo famulari, supplicat sanctitati vestre quatinus sibi specialem gratiam facientes ut quam primum xxiii sue etatis annum attigerit et de beneficio ecclesiastico requirente sacros ordines sibi provisum fuerit ad omnes sacros et presbiteratus ordines

---

⁵⁷ Adjacent pages are headed 'Rome anno quarto'.
⁵⁸ A false start for his entry at fol. 351r is crossed out and marked 'vacat' in the margin: 'Beatissime pater, cum devotus vester Thomas Campion' de Oblim' in Rutlond' Lincolniensis diocesis, clericus, desideret ob animarum suorum parentum salutem et zelo devotionis accensus.'

necnon alios minores promoveri possit misericorditer dispensare dignemini de gratia speciali et cum clausulis oportunis.

Fiat de speciali et expresso D. s. †. Et committatur ordinario D. s. †.

969. [*Rome*], *16 February 1456. The master of the hospital of St John the Evangelist, Cambridge, and Robert Diahuri,*[59] *Order of Cruciferi of St Mary,*[60] *request a licence and faculty that Robert, aged 22, may be promoted by any Catholic bishop to all holy orders, even priest's.* Reg. 6, fol. 350v.

[Rome], xiiii kal. Martii. Pater beatissime, cum in domo sive hospitali sancti Iohannis apostoli et evangeliste de Cantibrigiam [*sic*] ordinis sancte Marie cruciferorum sint dedicati 4^{or} presbiteri, die nocteque in divinis officiis ut in fundatione cavetur altissimo famularetur [*sic*] et ad presens numerus presbiterorum dicti ordinis non est completus. Supplicant sanctitati vestre tam dicti hospitalis magister quam devotus orator vester Robertus Diahuri dicti ordinis expresse professus quatinus sibi specialem gratiam facientes ut non obstante defectu etatis quem patitur in xxii° sue etatis anno constitutus ad omnes sacros ordines et presbiteratus a quocumque maluerit catholico antistite de licentia sui superioris possit promoveri antistiti conferendi et oratori suscipiendi licentiam et facultatem misericorditer concedere dignemini de gratia speciali cum clausulis oportunis quam primum xxiii sue etatis annum attigerit.

Fiat de speciali et expresso D. s. †.

970. [Rome], 12 March 1457. [Supplication] on the part of Thomas Cade of Stuston, clerk, Norwich (*Novicensis*) [dioc.], for [the pope] to grant him a dispensation that on reaching the age of 23 he may be promoted to all holy orders and minister in them, notwithstanding his defect of age. *Fiat de speciali et expresso D. s. †.* Reg. 6, fol. 351r.

971. [Rome], 3 April 1456. Thomas Draper, clerk, Norwich (*Norvicensis*) [dioc.], requests [that the pope grant him a dispensation that on reaching the age of 24 he may be promoted to the priesthood. *Fiat de speciali D. s. †.* Reg. 6, fol. 352r.

972. [Rome], 9 April 1456. Same dispensation as **971** requested on the part of William (*Gugg'li*) Folgoam, clerk, [Coventry and Lichfield dioc.]. *Fiat de speciali D. s. †.* Reg. 6, fol. 352r.

973. [*Rome*], *4 May* [*1456*].[61] *The abbot of Osney, near Oxford, OSA, Lincoln dioc.,*[62] *seeks*

---

[59] Doubtless John Dunham, who was master by 1426 and died by February 1458, and Robert Dunham, who was elected master in January 1475 and died by November 1498 (*VCH* (*Cambs.*), ii. 307; M. Rubin, *Charity and community in medieval Cambridge* (Cambridge, 1987), 302).

[60] Knowles and Hadcock, 210–11, 349, do not record the hospital as belonging to the order of Crutched Friars but state that the hospital's brethren adopted the rule of St Augustine in 1250. See also Rubin, *Charity and community*, 176–81, 300–1.

[61] Adjacent pages are headed 'Rome anno tercio'; strictly speaking during the third year of Calixtus III's pontificate 4 May fell in 1457, but the roughly chronological sequence of the entries suggests that it refers to the previous year. Cf. **974–5**.

[62] John Walton was elected abbot and, after his election was confirmed by the bishop of

a dispensation that three canons of that abbey may be promoted to holy and priest's orders on reaching the age of 23 and minister in them. Reg. 6, fol. 356v.

> [Rome], iiii non. Maii. [Pro] abbate monasterii sancte Marie de Ofney [*recte* Osney] iuxta Oxoniam ordinis canonicorum regularium sancti Augustini Lincolniensis diocesis de tribus in dicto suo monasterio existentibus, causa defectus [presbiterorum in dicto monasterio], ad sacros ac presbiteratus ordines promovendis quam primum xxiii etatis sue annum attigerint et in eisdem ministrare.
>
> Fiat de speciali et expresso D. s. † I.

974. [Rome], 4 May [1456]. [Supplication for a dispensation] for Fr William Westerari, deacon, professed of the monastery of the Holy Trinity, Mottisfont (*Motesfont*), OSA, Winchester dioc., that he may be promoted to the order of the priesthood on reaching the age of 23 because of the lack of priests (*defectus presbiterorum*) in that monastery.[63] Approved with **975**. Reg. 6, fol. 356v.

975. [Rome], 4 May [1456]. Same grace as **974** for Fr Richard Worxton and Fr Alexander Lawton, deacons, professed of the same monastery. *Fiat de speciali et expresso D. s. † I.* (Approved with **974**.) Reg. 6, fol. 356v.

976. [Rome], 20 August 1457(?). [Request for a dispensation] for Fr Thomas Bromley, deacon, monk of the monastery of BVM, OSB, Coventry and Lichfield dioc.,[64] that on reaching [the age of] 23 he may be promoted to the priesthood and celebrate (*ministrare*) masses and divine offices on account of the lack of priests. *Fiat de speciali D. s. † I.* Reg. 6, fol. 357v.

De promotis et promovendis

977. [Rome], 6 March 1457. Reginald Annsen, priest, Norwich dioc., informs the pope that guilelessly (*tamquam simplex*) and in ignorance of the law he formerly had himself promoted to all holy orders while under age but otherwise legally (*rite*) and ministered in them. Although he has not yet reached the legitimate age, he requests that the pope grant him absolution from these excesses and his other sins and a dispensation that he may minister in his orders, notwithstanding that defect of age and the statutes and constitutions of the Lateran and other councils. *Fiat de speciali postquam xxiiii annum attigerit D. s. †. I.* Reg. 6, fol. 366r.

Lincoln, he received the abbey's temporalities under a royal mandate of 1 November 1452 (*CPR 1452–61*, 50, 63); he resigned on being provided to the archbishopric of Dublin on 4 May 1472. He was BCnL of Oxford by 1472. Ill health forced him to give up his see in 1484, and he died *c.* 1489 (*BRUO*, iii. 1975; *VCH* (*Oxon.*), ii. 93; Smith, *Heads of religious houses*, iii. 499; *ODNB*, lvii. 212–13; Eubel, ii. 146).

[63] On the dilapidated state of the monastery by June 1457, see *CPL*, xi. 146.
[64] At least five Benedictine houses were dedicated to the BVM in this diocese, including Alvecote Priory (Warwicks.), Coventry Cathedral Priory (Warwicks.), Penwortham Priory (Lancs.), Lancaster Priory (alien), and Tutbury Priory (Staffs.). Probably not Coventry since Greatrex does not record Bromley among its brethren.

978. [Rome], 7 March 1457. John Morbeli, deacon, York dioc., aged about 23, requests that the pope grant him a dispensation that he may be promoted to holy, even priest's, orders, notwithstanding that defect of age. *Fiat de speciali et expresso D. s. †. I.* Reg. 6, fol. 366r.

979. [*Rome*], *18 March 1457. Dafydd Waring, acolyte, rector of Selattyn parish church, St Asaph dioc.; Roger Thaverhan, acolyte, rector of Thorpe St Andrew(?) parish church,*[65] *Norwich dioc.; Thomas Caufyn, subdeacon, rector of Drybrook(?) parish church, Hereford dioc.; and John Morbek, deacon, York dioc., request that they may be promoted to all holy and priest's orders outside the proper times by any Catholic bishop in the Curia.* Reg. 6, fol. 362.

> [Rome], xv kal. Aprilis. David Waring, acolitus, rector parrochialis ecclesie de ~~Sal~~ Slatton' Assavensis diocesis, causa devotionis et \ex/ artatione dicte parrochialis ecclesie ad omnes sacros et presbiteratus ordines a quocumque antistite gratiam et communionem sedis apostolice habente in Romana [fol. 362v] curia residente diebus dominicis vel festivis inmediate sequentibus extra tempora a iure statuta constitutionibus ac aliis quibuscumque in contrarium facientibus non obstantibus se petit promoveri de gratia speciali et expresso. Rogerus Thaverhan acolitus rector parrochialis ecclesie de Turplix Norwicensis diocesis similem sibi petit gratiam indulgeri. Similem gratiam petit Thomas Caufyn subdiaconus rector parrochialis ecclesie de Dowbroke Herfordensis diocesis. Et similem petit gratiam Iohannes Morbek diaconus sufficientem titulum habens et occasione cuius tenetur se facere promoveri Eboracensis diocesis.

> Fiat de speciali D. s. †. I. et \de/ expresso D. s. †. I.

Super defectu etatis et de promotis et promovendis

980. [*Rome*], *31 May 1457. William Syly, clerk, Bath and Wells dioc., seeks a licence and faculty to be promoted outside the proper times to all holy orders by any Catholic bishop in the Curia.* Reg. 6, fol. 379r.

> [Rome], ii kal. Iunii. Guilielmo Syly, clerico Batoniensis [et Wellensis] diocesis, titulum sufficientem habente in collegio omnium animarum,[66] ratione cuius artatus est se facere promoveri ad omnes sacros ordines, [ut] ab aliquo antistite etc. [gratiam et communionem sedis apostolice habente] in Romana curia residente diebus dominicis vel festivis extra tempora etc. [a iure statuta promoveri] et in eisdem celebrare possit, ipsique antistiti licenciam etc. [et facultatem misericorditer concedere dignemini de gratia speciali et expresso]. (*Approved with* **981**.)

981. [Rome], 31 May 1457. Same licence [and faculty] as **980** for William Pygot, scholar, holding a title in Newark on Trent (*Newik*) parish church, Lincoln dioc., by reason of which he is constrained to have himself [promoted] to all holy [orders]. *Fiat de speciali et expresso D. s. †. I.* (Approved with **980**.) Reg. 6, fol. 379r.

---

[65] Known as 'Thorpe Episcopi' in the later middle ages, hence perhaps 'Turplix'.
[66] Presumably All Souls' College, Oxford, but Syly does not appear in *BRUO*.

982. [*Rome, 3 September 1457*]. William Ward, acolyte, Canterbury dioc., seeks a licence and faculty to be promoted to all holy orders by any Catholic bishop in the Curia. Reg. 6, fol. 370v.[67]

[Rome, iii nonas Septembris].[68] Willelmus Ward, accolitus Cantuariensis dyocesis, qui in Romana curia presens et arctatus ratione sui tituli existit, [supplicat] quatinus, sibi specialem gratiam facientes, ut a quocumque maluerit catholico antistite in Romana curia ad omnes sacros ordines successive in primis temporibus a iure statutis possit promoveri, eidem oratori suscipiendi et antistiti conferendi licentiam et facultatem misericorditer concedere dignemini de gratia speciali et expresso. (*Approved with* **984**.)

983. [Rome, 3 September 1457]. Same grace as **982** for John Grime, acolyte, Norwich dioc., constrained [by reason of his title] and present in the Curia. Approved with **984**. Reg. 6, fols. 370v–371r.

984. [Rome], 10 September 1457. Same grace as **982** for John Bruwhen, acolyte, Lincoln dioc., present in the Curia [and] constrained [by reason of his title]. *Fiat de speciali et expresso D. s. †. I. Et committatur episcopo Alasandrino D. s. †. I.* (Approved with **982–3**.) Reg. 6, fol. 371r.

De promotis et promovendis

985. [Rome, at St Peter's], 20 November 1457. Henry Randes, clerk, Norwich dioc., rector of St Mary le Bow (*beate Marie in Baiolo*) parish church in the city of Durham, present in the Curia, [requests] that he may obtain a grace and faculty that he may be promoted to all holy and priestly orders by any \Catholic/ bishop on any Sunday, since he is constrained [by his title].[69] *Fiat de speciali et expresso et committatur episcopo Ortano*[70] *D. s. †.* Reg. 6, fol. 373r.

986. [*Rome*], *10 October 1457. A licence and a faculty are sought for John Parquyns, clerk of a chantry in Longbenton church, Durham dioc., to be promoted to all holy orders outside the proper times by any bishop present in the Curia.* Reg. 6, fol. 379v.

[Rome], vi idus Octobris. [Pro] Iohanne Parquyns, clerico, cantoriam habente in ecclesia de Benton Dunelmensis diocesis, in Romana curia presente, ut ad omnes sacros ordines extra tempora a iure statuta aliquot diebus dominicis aut festivis a quocumque antistite [gratiam et communionem sedis apostolice habente] in dicta curia Romana residente successive ad omnes ordines promoveri et in eisdem ministrare possit, ipsique episcopo licentiam etc. [et facultatem misericorditer concedere dignemini de gratia speciali et expresso].

Fiat de speciali et expresso D. s. †. I.

---

[67] Adjacent pages are headed 'Super defectu etatis et de promotis et promovendis'.
[68] The entry preceding this in the register is so dated, but **982–3** are undated.
[69] Cf. **987**.
[70] The bishop of Orte was Nicholas, OESA (Eubel, ii. 166)

987. [*Rome, at St Peter's*], *27 November 1457. Richard Themyn, acolyte of London, rector of St Mary le Bow parish church, Durham, seeks a licence and faculty to be promoted to all, even holy, orders by any Catholic bishop in the Curia.*[71] Reg. 6, fol. 373v.

[Rome apud sanctum Petrum], v kal. Decembris. Ricardus Themyn, accolitus Lundoniensis, rector parrochialis ecclesie beate Marie in Baiolo Dunelmensis, in Romana curia presens, artatus [existit] ut ad omnes etiam sacros ordines etc. [se faciat promoveri], tamen suum ordinarium commode adire non potest cupiatque in Romana curia ad dictos ordines promoveri; supplicat igitur ut in curia Romana aliquibus [fol. 374r] diebus dominicis aut festivis successive etiam extra tempora etc. [a iure statuta a quocumque catholico antistite] ad omnes ordines promoveri etc. [possit, eidem oratori suscipiendi et antistiti conferendi] licentiam et facultatem impartiri misericorditer dignemini de gratia speciali, non obstantibus etc. [constitutionibus ac aliis quibuscumque in contrarium facientibus].

Fiat de speciali et expresso D. s. †. I.

988. [*Rome, at St Peter's*], *4 January 1458. John Sax alias Saxton, clerk, Norwich dioc., seeks a faculty and licence to be promoted to all minor and even holy and priestly orders by any Catholic bishop in the Curia.* Reg. 6, fol. 374v.

[Rome apud sanctum Petrum], ii non. Ianuarii. Iohannes Sax alias Saxton', clericus Norwicensis diocesis, ratione tituli sui beate Marie de Dodenasii[72] sit artatus infra proxima tempora a iure statuta ut ad omnes minores et etiam sacros [et] presbiteratus ordines promoveri [se faciat]; supplicat dictus Iohannes quatinus sibi ut a quocumque antisti[te] communionem sancte sedis apostolice habente diebus festivis vel dominicis successive ut [*sic*] ad omnes etiam sacros et presbiteratus ordines possit promoveri, eidem antistiti conferendi etc. [facultatem et eidem oratori] licentiam etc. [suscipiendi] sibi (*sic*) misericorditer concedere dignemini etc. [de gratia speciali et expresso].

Fiat de speciali et expresso D. s. †. I.

989. [Rome, St Peter's], 20 February 1458. William Doory, clerk, Norwich [dioc.],[73] requests that on reaching the age of 23 he may be promoted to the priesthood. *Fiat de speciali et expresso et committatur ordinario D. s. †.* Reg. 6, fol. 376r.

990. [Rome, at St Peter's], 23 February 1458. John Baas of Sudbury, clerk, Norwich dioc., [requests that the pope] grants him a dispensation that on reaching the age of 24 he may be promoted to all holy and priestly orders. *Fiat de speciali D. s. †. I.* Reg. 6, fol. 375v.

991. [*Rome, at St Peter's*], *27 February 1458. Christopher Car, rector of St George's parish church, Gipping(?), Norwich dioc.; Simon Ford, rector of Mountfield parish church, Canterbury*

---

[71] Cf. **985**.
[72] Dodnash (Suff.).
[73] 'diocesis' is omitted in the entry but appears in the right margin.

dioc.; *John Bekke, rector of St Mary's parish church, Durham,*[74] *seek to be promoted to all holy and priestly orders by any Catholic bishop in the Curia.*[75] Reg. 6, fol. 376r.

[Rome apud sanctum Petrum], iii kal. Martii. Cristoforus Car, rector parrochialis ecclesie sancti Georgii Gipvoty Norvicensis diocesis; Symon Ford, rector parrochialis ecclesie de Montfeld Cantuariensis diocesis; Iohannes Bekke, nunc rector parrochialis ecclesie beate Marie Dunelmensis, qui racione dictarum ecclesiarum artati [existunt] promoveri infra annum, petunt ut a quocumque catholico anstistite [*recte* antistite] in Romana curia temporibus a iure statutis vel aliis diebus dominicis etc. [vel festivis successive] ad omnes sacros et presbiteratus ordines possint promoveri etc. [de gratia speciali et expresso].

Fiat de speciali et expresso [D. s. †. I.].

992. [Rome, at St Peter's], 28 February 1458. John Edwart, clerk, Norwich dioc., requests that [the pope] grant him a dispensation that after he has reached the age of 24, he may be promoted to all holy and priestly orders and [minister in them]. *Fiat de speciali D. s. †. I.* Reg. 6, fol. 375v.

993. [Rome, at St Peter's], 28 February 1458. Same grace as **992** for Hugh Deen, clerk, Norwich dioc. *Fiat de speciali D. s. †. I.* Reg. 6, fol. 375v.

994. [Rome, at St Peter's], 8 March 1458. John Bekke, deacon, Norwich dioc., aged 24, requests that he may be promoted to the holy order of the priesthood. *Fiat de speciali D. s. †. I.* Reg. 6, fol. 376r.

995. [Rome], 12 May 1458. John Bursay, acolyte, York dioc., [requests] that he may be promoted to all, even holy and priestly, orders, notwithstanding a deformity of his left foot. *Fiat de speciali et committatur ordinario cuius conscientiam oneramus D. s. †. I.* Reg. 6, fol. 386v.

996. [*Rome*], *1 July 1458. Fr Thomas Cawson, priest, professed canon of Brinkburn Priory, OSA, Durham dioc., committed apostasy and then had himself promoted by the bishop of Forli(?)*[76] *in the Curia to all holy orders to a fictitious title; he seeks absolution from the excommunication thereby incurred and a dispensation.* Reg. 6, fol. 387v.

[Rome], kal. Iulii. [Pro] Fratre Thoma Cawson, presbitero, canonico professo monasterii apostolorum Petri et Pauli de Brynkborn ordinis sancti Augustini Dunelmensis diocesis, qui illicenciatus exivit, habitu et ordine dimissis, ad seculum reversus, deinde vigore certe commissionis obtente per ~~ipsum calistum~~ per [*sic*] dominum episcopum Foliensem [*recte* Foroliviensem?] in Romana curia se fecit ad omnes sacros ordines mediante titulo ficto promoveri et in ipsis ministravit, sententiam excommunicationis

---

[74] Most likely St Mary the Less. The other Durham parish church dedicated to St Mary is described at **985** and **987** as 'beate Marie in Baiolo' (St Mary le Bow).
[75] In left margin beside this entry: 'Pro tribus personis'.
[76] The bishop of Forli from 1449 to 1463 was Daniele d'Alunno (Eubel, ii. 155).

incurrens per constitutionem dicti ordinis promulgatam. Cum autem sit intentionis ad dictum monasterium redeundi, ipsum a dicta sententia et excessibus huiusmodi et peccatis etc. [aliis suis] petit absolvi secumque super irregularitatis macula dispensari.

Fiat de speciali D. s. †. I.

De uberioribus

997. [*Rome*], *13 May 1455. Edmund Woddis, acolyte, York dioc., requests a dispensation that he may be promoted to all holy orders and serve in them in perpetuity, notwithstanding a deformity in one of his eyes.* Reg. 6, fol. 393v.

[Rome], iii idus Maii. Supplicatur sanctitati vestre pro parte devoti oratoris vestri Edmundi Woddis, accoliti Eboracensis diocesis, qui ex magno devotionis fervore cupit ad omnes sacros ordines promoveri et in dictis perpetuo domino famulari, quatinus cum eo ut non obstante defectu et difformitate quos patitur in altero oculorum suorum et qui non sui culpa sed a casu sibi superveniente ex quadam spina in iu[v]entute, licet parum difformitatis apparet, et ex predictis macula et difformitate non prestatur impedimentum in celebratione divinorum nec populo scandalum generetur, possit ad omnes sacros ordines promoveri et in eis perpetuo domino famulari misericorditer dispensare dignemini de gratia speciali.

Fiat de speciali D. s. †. I.

998. [*Rome*], *9 March 1456. William Folianbr, clerk, [Coventry and Lichfield dioc.], was granted a dispensation from his defect of birth by ordinary authority, whereby he was promoted to all minor orders and obtained a benefice without cure of souls at Bilsthorpe parish church, York dioc.; then he was granted a papal dispensation that he might be promoted to all holy orders and obtain another benefice, with cure of souls. He seeks a dispensation to hold a further benefice and exchange his benefices once.* Reg. 6, fol. 405r.

[Rome], vii idus Martii. Item pro parte Guglielmi Folianbr, clerici Conventrensis et Licheseldensis (*sic*) [diocesis],[77] exponitur sanctitati vestre quod dudum super defectu natalium, quem patitur de coniugato et soluta genitus, quod ipso non obstante defectu ad omnes minores ordines promoveri et beneficium ecclesiasticum cui cura non ymmineat animarum obtinere auctoritate ordinaria primo dispensatum fuit, cuius dispensationis vigore, ad omnes minores ordines rite promotus, quoddam beneficium sine cura in ecclesia parrochiali de Bilsthorp' Eboracensis diocesis est assecutus; et deinde quod dicto non obstante defectu ad omnes sacros ordines promoveri et unum aliud beneficium ecclesiasticum compatibile, etiam si curam haberet animarum, recipere et unacum dicto beneficio licite retinere possit secum fuit auctoritate apostolica misericorditer dispensatum, cuius dispensationis vigore nullum est assecutus beneficium nec [ad] alterum dictorum sacrorum sit promotus ordinum. Cum autem, pater sancte, fructus dicti

---

[77] Indicated not in the entry but beside it in the right margin.

beneficii xl. solidorum monete Anglicane non exceda[n]t et ex ipsis fructibus minime substentari potest, supplicat[ur] igitur eidem sanctitati vestre pro parte dicti exponentis quatinus unum aliud beneficium ecclesiasticum compatibile, etiam si in ecclesia cathedrali vel metropolitana citra ipsius canonicatum et prebendam aut canonicatus et prebenda ecclesie collegiate vel archipresbiteratus ruralis sine cura fuerit, libere recipere et unacum dictis beneficiis licite retinere valeat, ipsaque beneficia obtinenda videlicet et obtenta ex causa permutationis vel alia simul vel successive semel tantum dimittere et loco sic dimissi vel dimissorum aliud vel alia duo tantum ecclesiastica beneficia similia vel dissimilia invicem compatibilia, et si alterum ipsorum curatum fuerit, libere recipere ac licite insimul retinere valeat cum eodem dispensari mandare dignemini, defectu predicto, constitutionibus apostolicis, consuetudinibus et statutis ecclesia [*recte* ecclesiarum] in quibus beneficia huiusmodi extiterint contrariis quibuscumque non obstantibus, de gratia speciali.

Fiat de speciali ut petitur D. s. †.

999. [*Rome*], *10 April 1456. John Beibom, clerk, York(?) dioc., was granted a papal dispensation from his defect of birth that he might be promoted to all holy orders and obtain a benefice even with cure of souls. He seeks a dispensation to hold a further compatible benefice and exchange these benefices once.* Reg. 6, fol. 422v.

[Rome], iiii idus Aprilis. Iohannes Beibom, clericus Ebucensis [*recte* Eboracensis?] diocesis, cum quo alias, non ut obstante defectu natalium quem patitur de soluto genitus et soluta, ut ad omnes sacros ordines promoveri et beneficium ecclesiasticum, etiam si curam haberet animarum, possit obtinere fuit auctoritate apostolica dispensatum, cuius dispensationis vigore nullum beneficium assecutus est, unum aliud beneficium ecclesiasticum compatibile cum dicto beneficio quod eum vigore prime dispensationis obtinere contingerit, etiam si in ecclesia cathedrali vel metropolitana citra etc. [ipsius canonicatum et prebendam aut canonicatus] et prebenda collegiate [ecclesie] vel archipresbiteratus etc. [ruralis sine cura fuerit], recipere illaque simul retinere et semel tantum dimittere et loco dimissi seu dimissorum duo alia beneficia invicem compatibilia, etiam si unum curatum fuerit, [recipere et] illa simul retinere petit de gratia speciali, non obstantibus etc. [defectu predicto, constitutionibus apostolicis, consuetudinibus et statutis ecclesiarum in quibus beneficia huiusmodi extiterint contrariis quibuscumque].

Fiat de speciali ut petitur D. s. †. I.

1000. [*Rome*], *27 May 1456. Nicholas Machell, priest, perpetual vicar of Bossall parish church, York dioc., was granted a papal dispensation from his defect of birth so that he might be promoted to all orders and obtain a benefice even with cure of souls, whereby he was ordained and obtained that vicarage. He seeks a dispensation to hold a further compatible benefice and exchange these benefices once.* Reg. 6, fol. 424v.

[Rome], vi kal. Iunii. Beatissime pater, exponitur sanctitati vestre pro parte devoti vestri Nicolai Machell, presbiteri, perpetui vicarii ecclesie parrochialis de Bassoll Eboracensis diocesis, cum quo alias, non obstante defectu natalium de soluto genitus et soluta, ut ad omnes possit ordines promoveri et beneficium ecclesiasticum, etiam si curam haberet animarum, possit obtinere fuit auctoritate apostolica dispensatum, cuius dispensationis vigore ad omnes ordines promotus existit et dictam vicariam assecutus est, de quibus fructibus commode sustentari non potest, ut unum aliud beneficium, etiam si curam habeat animarum, compatibile cum dicto beneficio, [etiam si in ecclesia cathedrali vel metropolitana citra ipsius] ad [sic] canonicatum et prebendam et [canonicatus et prebenda collegiate ecclesie vel] ad [sic] archipresbiteratum ruralem fuerint [recte fuerit], ipsaque beneficia recipere et obtinere et semel tantum dimittere et loco dimissi vel dimissorum duo alia beneficia ecclesiastica invicem compatibilia [recipere] illaque retinere possit, cum eo misericorditer dispensare dignemini de gratia speciali.

Fiat de speciali ut petitur D. s. †. I.

1001. [*Rome*], *18 July 1458. Richard Redman, priest, York dioc.,*[78] *was granted a papal dispensation that he might be promoted to all orders and obtain a benefice even with cure of souls, as a result of which he was so ordained and obtained Kelshall parish church, Lincoln dioc. He seeks a further dispensation to hold an additional compatible benefice and exchange these benefices.* Reg. 6, fol. 435r.

[Rome], xv kal. Augusti. Beatissime pater, supplicat[ur] sanctitati vestre pro parte devoti oratoris vestri Ricardi Redman', presbiteri Eboracensis diocesis, quatinus cum eo, cum quo alias super defectu natalium quem patitur de soluto genitus et soluta ut huiusmodi non obstante defectu ad omnes possit ordines promoveri et beneficium ecclesiasticum, etiam si curam haberet animarum, obtinere auctoritate apostolica secum [sic] misericorditer dispensatum fuit, cuius vigore ad omnes ordines rite promotus existit et parrochialem ecclesiam Relsuhull' [sic] Lincolniensis diocesis extitit canonice assecutus, ex cuius fructibus etc. commode sustentari non possit. Quare igitur humiliter supplicatur sanctitati vestre pro parte eiusdem quatinus sibi uberiorem gratiam facientes ut unum aliud beneficium compatibile cum dicta parrochiali ecclesia retinere ipsaque dimittere et alia recipere et retinere possit et valeat, cum eo, defectu non obstante, constitutionibus apostolicis, consuetudinibus et statutis ecclesiarum etc. in quibus beneficia huiusmodi extit[er]int in contrarium non obstantibus quibuscumque, [misericorditer dispensare dignemini] de gratia speciali.

Fiat de speciali ut petitur D. s. †. I.

---

[78] Richard Redman was admitted rector of Kelshall (Herts.) on 5 March 1456, resigning it when he was collated rector of Stretham (Cambs.), in March 1459. In 1456 he was chaplain to William Gray, bishop of Ely, who presented him to Kelshall. He became an Oxford MA in 1455 and resigned his fellowship at Balliol College in 1456; in 1472–3 he was incorporated at Cambridge, where he incepted as DTh in 1479–80. He was still alive in 1488 when he resigned Stretham (*BRUO*, iii. 1561; *BRUC*, 476).

PIUS II
(1458–1464)

De matrimonialibus

1002. *Siena, 13 March 1459. John Long and his wife Joan, Rochester dioc., only learned after marrying and having issue that they were related in the third degree of consanguinity; hence they request a dispensation to remain married and legitimation of existing and future issue.* Reg. 7, fol. 10v.

Senis, iii id. Martii. Iohannes Long et Iohanna eius uxor, coniuges Reffensis [*sic*] diocesis, [exponunt] quod ipsi olim ignorantes aliquod impedimentum inter eos existere quominus possent invicem matrimonialiter copulari matrimonium inter se copularunt illudque carnali copula consumarunt et prolem procrearunt prout exponunt. Postmodum ad eorum noticiam pervenit quod ipsi tercio consanguinitatis gradu sunt coniuncti propter quod in eodem remanere non possunt sine dispensatione. Supplicant igitur quatinus ut impedimento huiusmodi non obstante in eorum matrimonio remanere possint dispensare dignemini prolemque susceptam et suscipiendam legitimam decernentes.

Fiat de speciali et expresso et componat cum datario Phi. sancti Laurentii in Lucina.

1003. *Siena, 29 March 1459. [. . .]¹ ap Dafydd and Gwenllian verch Ieuan, Llandaff dioc., knowingly contracted marriage in the fourth degree of consanguinity and had issue; hence they request absolution and a dispensation so that they may remain married and legitimation of future or existing issue.* Reg. 7, fols. 7v–8r.

Senis, iiii kal. Aprilis. Ab Davyd et Gwenllyan verch Ieuan coniuges Landavensis diocesis exponunt quod ipsi olim scientes se quarto consanguinitatis gradu fore coniunctos matrimonium inter se per verba de presenti in facie ecclesie de facto contraxerunt et illud carnali copula consumarunt et prolem exinde procrearunt. Cum autem in huiusmodi matrimonio dicti exponentes remanere non possint dispensatione non obtenta, supplicant [fol. 8r] quatinus ipsos a generali excommunicationis sententia quam incurrerunt et huiusmodi incestus reatu absolvi [et ut] non obstante impedimento predicto in dicto matrimonio remanere possint dispensare dignemini prolemque susceptam vel suscipiendam legitimam decernentes.

Fiat de speciali et componat cum datario Phi. sancti Laurentii in Lucina.

1004. Siena, 16 April 1459. Philip Thomas ap Gwilym (*Gwilm*) and Joan Traharem(?), Llandaff dioc. contracted and consummated marriage unaware that they were related in the third and fourth degrees of affinity. Since they may not remain married without a dispensation, they request one and the legitimation of future and existing issue. *Fiat de speciali Phi. sancti Laurentii in Lucina.* Reg. 7, fols. 14v–15r.

---

¹ The forename appears to have been omitted.

1005. *Mantua, 2 July 1459. William Dautign and Alice de Tyssyton(?), Coventry and Lichfield dioc., married and had issue, aware of the impediment of cognatio spiritualis between them; hence they seek absolution and a dispensation to remain married and legitimation of future and existing issue. Reg. 7, fol. 25v.*

Mantue, vi non. Julii. Guilheminus Dautign filius Iohannis Daugtigen [*sic*] et Alicia de Tyssyton'(?) mulier, coniuges Convintensis [*sic*] et Lichfelidensis [*sic*] diocesis, [exponunt] quod ipsi olim non ignorantes quod pater dicti Wylhelmi [*sic*] dictam Aliciam de sacro fonte levaverat inter se adinvicem matrimonium contraxerunt illudque carnali copula consumarunt et prolem procrearunt. Cum autem in eodem remanere non possint sine dispensatione, supplicant quatinus ab huiusmodi excessibus absolvi et et [*sic*] in eorum iamdicto matrimonio ut in eodem remanere possint dispensare dignemini prolemque susceptam vel suscipiendam legitimam decernentes.

Fiat de speciali et expresso et suspendatur ad quinque menses quo ad thorum Ste. episcopus Lucan.[2]

1006. *Mantua, 15 December 1459. William Steyne, layman, and Amy Athayssh', Lincoln dioc., have long wished to marry, but, since they are related in the fourth and fourth degrees of consanguinity, they cannot do so without a dispensation, hence they request one. Fiat de speciali Phi. sancti Laurentii in Lucina. Reg. 7, fol. 112r.*

1007. *Siena, 6 March 1460. John Wulley de Easton,[3] layman, and Margaret daughter of Thomas, Lincoln dioc., married and had issue, unaware of the impediment of cognatio spiritualis between them; hence they seek a dispensation to remain married and legitimation of any issue. Reg. 8, fol. 25v.*

Senis, ii non. Martii. Iohannes Wulley de Esten laicus et Margarita Thome, coniuges [Lincolniensis diocesis],[4] ignorantes quod pater dicte Margarite prefatum Iohannem de sacro fonte levasset matrimonium inter se contraxerunt et consumarunt ac prolem procrearunt, et cum sine dispensatione in eodem remanere non possint, supplicant ut impedimento huiusmodi non obstante in eorum matrimonio remanere possint prolem etc. [susceptam et suscipiendam legitimam decernentes dispensare dignemini].

Fiat de speciali et expresso Phi. sancti Laurentii in Lucina.

1008. *Siena, 22 April 1460. Richard ap Trahaearn (Trahaerum) ap Roger (Rosser) and Agnes verch [. . .],[5] lay people, Llandaff dioc., wish to marry, but since they are related in the fourth degree of consanguinity, they cannot do so without a dispensation, hence they request one. Fiat de speciali Phi. sancti Laurentii in Lucina.* Proctor: H. Broyel. Reg. 8, fol. 41v.

---

[2] There is an illegible marginal note in the place where the proctor's name usually appears.
[3] Wulley was from one or other of the Eastons in Hunts., Leics. or Lincs., or from Easton on the Hill or Easton Maudit or Easton Neston, Northants.
[4] Diocese supplied from margin.
[5] The name of Agnes' father appears to have been omitted.

1009. Siena, 27 April 1460. Gruffydd ap Llywelyn ap [. . .] (*Griffith ap Lewelin ap*) and Gwladus (*Wlad'*) verch Dafydd ap [. . .], Llandaff dioc., request that the pope grant them the same dispensation as **1008**. *Fiat de speciali Phi. sancti Laurentii in Lucina.* Proctor: G. Helmont. Reg. 8, fol. 42r.

1010. Siena, 28 April 1460. Trahaearn ap [. . .][6] and Margaret verch [. . .], Llandaff dioc., request the pope to grant them the same dispensation as **1008** and legitimation of their future issue. *Fiat de speciali Phi. sancti Laurentii in Lucina.* Reg. 8, fol. 42r.

1011. Siena, 4 June 1460. Maredudd ap Dafydd Dllort(?), layman, and Gwenllian (*Swenllian*), daughter of Hywel (*Hoell'*), St Asaph's dioc., contracted and consummated marriage unaware that they were related in the fourth and fourth degrees of consanguinity, hence they seek a dispensation so that they may remain married. *Fiat Phi.* Reg. 8, fol. 51r.

1012. Siena, 23 June 1460. Richard Edirard, layman, and Denise Lewis, Exeter dioc., contracted but did not consummate marriage knowing that they were related twice in the fourth degree of consanguinity; they seek a dispensation so that they may remain married with legitimation of any issue. *Fiat de speciali A.* Reg. 8, fol. 59v.

1013. Rome, 28 March 1461. *Nuria* son of *Muria*, layman, and Gwladus daughter of Dafydd, Llandaff dioc., seek a dispensation that, notwithstanding the third and fourth degrees of affinity, they may fulfil their wish to marry, with legitimation of any issue. *Fiat de speciali Phi. sancti Laurentii in Lucina.* And that they be granted *littere declaratorie* regarding the third [and fourth] degree of affinity. *Fiat Phi.* Reg. 9, fol. 28r.

1014. Rome, 29 March 1461. Ieuan ap Gruffydd (*Grifit*), layman, and Felicia (*Felex*) daughter of Ieuan, Llandaff dioc., knowingly contracted and consummated marriage in the third and fourth degrees of consanguinity; hence they seek absolution and a dispensation so that they may remain married with legitimation of any issue. *Fiat de speciali et componat cum datario Phi. sancti Laurentii in Lucina.* And that they be granted *littere declaratorie* regarding the third degree of consanguinity. Reg. 9, fol. 34r.

1015. Rome, 29 March 1461. Same dispensation as **1008** and the legitimation of any issue sought by Thomas ap Llywelyn (*Ll'*) ap M', layman, and Gwladus (*Giwalad*) Vercerhre[7] ap Ieuan ap H[li], Llandaff dioc. *Fiat de speciali Phi.* Reg. 9, fol. 35r.

1016. Rome, 10 March 1462. Henry Waring and Alice Awetson, a married couple from York dioc., contracted and consummated marriage unaware that they were

---

[6] Perhaps the Trahaern' ap Gwylym' ap David ap Phylyp, layman of Llandaff dioc., granted a plenary indulgence *in mortis articulo* on 28 March 1469 (*CPL*, xii. 703).

[7] This word perhaps contains a corrupt form of 'verch', but if so it is not clear what the patronymic is.

related in the third degree of affinity; hence they seek absolution[8] and a dispensation to remain married with legitimation of any issue. *Fiat de speciali et expresso et componat cum datario Phi. sancti Laurentii in Lucina.* Reg. 10, fol. 27v.

1017. Rome, 11 April 1462. Gruffydd ap Hywel (*Grifit ap Hoell'*) ap Ieuan, layman, and Nestriz(?) David, a married couple from Llandaff [and St David's] dioc.,[9] contracted and consummated marriage unaware that they were related in the fourth degree of consanguinity; hence they seek a dispensation, so that they may remain married, with legitimation of any issue. *Fiat de speciali Phi. sancti Laurentii in Lucina.* Reg. 10, fol. 40r.

1018. Siena, 21 March 1464. Owain ap Ieuan Melyn, layman, and Margaret daughter of Thomas ap Meurig (*Meurilr*), Llandaff dioc., related in the fourth degree of affinity, seek a dispensation so that they may fulfil their wish to marry with legitimation of any issue. *Fiat de speciali Phi.* Reg. 13, fol. 33v.

1019. Siena, 21 March 1464. Same dispensation as **1018** and legitimation of any issue sought by Dafydd ap Gwilym (*Gwyllym*) ap Thomas, layman, and Gwenhwyfar(?) (*Gweynwyll'*) ap [*recte* verch] Morgan, Llandaff dioc. *Fiat de speciali Phi. sancti Laurentii in Lucina.* Reg. 13, fol. 34r.

1020. Siena, 21 March 1464. Same dispensation as **1008** and legitimation of any issue sought by Ieuan ap Thomas ap *Plethyn*, layman, and Margaret daughter of Thomas, Llandaff dioc. *Fiat de speciali Phi.* Reg. 13, fol. 35r.

1021. Rome, 31 March 1464. Ieuan ap Hywel (*ap Powell*) ap Ieuan ap Llywelyn (*Lowellen'*) and Katherine ap [*recte* verch] Ieuan Vaghem, a married couple from Llandaff dioc., contracted but did not consummate marriage unaware that they were related in the fourth degree of affinity; hence they seek a dispensation from that impediment, in order to remain married and solemnise their marriage, with legitimation of any issue. Approved with **1022**. Reg. 13, fol. 13r.

1022. Rome, 31 March 1464. Same dispensation as **1021** and legitimation of existing and future issue sought by Thomas ap Dafydd Goth' and Katherine ap [*recte* verch] Thomas ap Gwilym (*Willm'*), a married couple from Llandaff dioc. who contracted and consummated marriage unaware that they were related in the fourth degree of affinity. *Fiat de speciali pro omnibus B. episcopus Regin. regens etc.* (Approved with **1021**.) Reg. 13, fol. 13r.

1023. Rome, 6 April 1464. Same dispensation as **1008** and legitimation of any issue sought by Iankin ap Hywel ap Gruffydd ap Iankin (*Hoell' ap Griffit ap Iank'*), layman, and Margaret verch (*verz*) Ieuan ap Hywel (*Hoell*) Vagan', Llandaff dioc. Approved with **1024**. Reg. 13, fol. 14r.

---

[8] This was usually required only where a couple had married knowing of such an impediment.
[9] In the margin beside this entry both the Llandaff and St David's dioceses are named, which suggests that one of the supplicants came from the latter diocese.

1024. Rome, 6 April 1464. Same dispensation as **1008** and legitimation of any issue sought by Thomas ap Philip (*Thome ap Ph'*) ap Thomas, layman, and Maud verch Hywel (*verz Hoell'*), Llandaff dioc. *Fiat de speciali pro omnibus B. episcopus Regin. regens etc.* (Approved with **1023**.) Reg. 13, fol. 14r.

1025. Rome, 8 April 1464. Same dispensation as **1008** and legitimation of any issue sought by Dafydd ap Philip (*Phili*) ap Ieuan ap Meurig (*Meneur'*), layman, Llandaff dioc., and Margaret verch Walter (*veri Wallter*), St David's dioc. *Fiat de speciali B. episcopus Regin. regens etc.* Reg. 13, fol. 13v.

De diversis formis

1026. Siena, 1 April 1459. John Abendon, priest, monk of the monastery of the BVM, Abingdon (*Abendonie*), OSB, Salisbury (*Salisceriensis*) dioc., left his monastery without due permission and came in his habit to the Roman Curia, and having thereby incurred excommunication, he celebrated and participated in divine offices.[10] *Fiat de speciali Phi. sancti Laurentii in Lucina.* Reg. 7, fol. 130r.

1027. *Siena, 17 April 1459. Ieuan ap Dafydd, Thomas Howell',[11] Thomas Walkor and Ieuan David, laymen, Llandaff dioc., vowed to go on pilgrimage to Jerusalem and elsewhere overseas, but having reached Rome they now seek a commutation of their vow on financial and health grounds.* Reg. 7, fol. 173v.

> Senis, xv kal. Maii. Iohannes ap David, Thomas Howell', Thomas Walkor et Iohannes David, layci, exponunt quod ipsi Landavensis diocesis, zelo devotionis accensi, voverunt absque alicuius termini prefixione sacrum sepulcrum domini et quedam alia loca ultramarina peregre personaliter visitare. Cum autem, causa votum huiusmodi adimplendi, usque ad civitatem Romanam pervenerint nec habeant unde votum huiusmodi adimplere valeant sintque adeo fragilis complectionis quod aerem marinum supportare non possunt, supplicant igitur eidem sanctitati vestre prefati oratores quatinus cum ipsis super emissione voti hujusmodi dispensare ipsosque ab illo absolvere et ad illius observationem non teneri declarare et illud in alia pietatis opera commutare seu commutari mandare dignemini.
>
> Fiat de speciali et expresso et componat cum datario Phi sancti Laurentii in Lucina. [*Proctor*:] G Helmont.

1028. *Mantua, 4 September 1459. Ieuan Cael, priest and professed monk of Cymmer Abbey, Cistercian order, Bangor dioc., incurred excommunication for blessing clandestine marriages; he seeks absolution from it and dispensation from irregularity.* Reg. 7, fol. 225r.

---

[10] Abendon was presumably seeking absolution from excommunication and a dispensation from the irregularity that he had incurred for officiating as a priest while under that sentence (cf. **1047-8** below).

[11] Perhaps the Thomas ap Howel *alias* Wyth, priest, Llandaff dioc., in whose favour his bishop had a papal faculty to confer the office of notary public on 26 April 1460 (*CPL*, xii. 100).

Mantue, ii non. Septembris. Iohannes Cael, presbiter, monacus professus monasterii beate Marie Kynmer, ordinis Cisterciensis, Bangariensis [*sic*] diocesis, exponit quod ipse pluries matrimonium clandestine contractum benedixit quare excommunicationis sententiam in tales promulgatam incurrit, et sic ligatus divinis se inmiscuit. Supplicat igitur ipsum absolvi secumque super irregularitate dicto modo contracta dispensari mandare dignemini.

Fiat de speciali M. Alexan'. [*Proctor:*] I. Weythas'.

1029. Mantua, 16 December 1459. Robert Peche, esq., layman, Salisbury dioc., killed a layman and thus incurred excommunication; hence he requests that the pope should order his absolution from this homicide and other sins. *Fiat in forma Phi. sancti Laurentii in Lucina.* Reg. 7, fol. 268r.

1030. Siena, 23 April 1460. Roger Valwin,[12] priest and rector of Warehorne, Canterbury dioc., fornicated several times with a spiritual daughter of his, whom he heard in confession; hence he requests that the pope should order his absolution from these excesses. *Fiat de speciali Phi. sancti Laurentii in Lucina.* Reg. 8, fol. 150r.

1031. Rome, 20 December 1460. Fr Thomas Wollare,[13] prior of Lenton, Cluniac order, York dioc., requests a licence to wear linen clothing on account of his infirmities, since he cannot subsist otherwise. *Fiat de speciali Phi.* Reg. 8, fol. 196r.

1032. Rome, 1 February 1461. Fr Thomas Walthan, professed OFM of the convent of St Botolph's [Boston], Lincoln dioc., aged 60, requests a licence to eat meat, eggs and dairy produce at times when these are prohibited, since he is frail. *Fiat de speciali Phi. Et relinquatur conscientie sue. Phi.* Reg. 9, fol. 129v.

1033. Rome, 3 April 1461. John Crasetes(?), priest and perpetual vicar of St Botolph's parish church,[14] Lincoln dioc., requests that the pope should grant him a licence not to proceed to priest's orders by reason of his vicarage while studying for seven years and to receive the fruits of his vicarage. *Fiat de speciali Phi. sancti Laurentii in Lucina.* Reg. 9, fol. 151r.

1034. *Rome, 26 February 1462. William Bathe, priest and professed monk of Holy Trinity Priory, York, Cluniac order, incurred excommunication for apostasy; he seeks absolution from this sentence and dispensation from irregularity.* Reg. 10, fol. 119v.

---

[12] Presumably the Roger Baldewyn, rector of Warehorne, Canterbury dioc., granted a papal dispensation to hold a second incompatible benefice on 5 November 1461 (*CPL*, xii. 133, 155). He was rector of Warehorne till his death; he died by 15 December 1472 (*Reg. Bourgchier*, 311).
[13] Thomas Wollore was appointed prior of Lenton by Henry VI in 1459 (Smith, *Heads of Religious Houses*, iii. 240). On 5 January 1460, Wollore obtained a papal dispensation from illegitimacy as the son of unmarried parents so that he might receive and retain any number and kind of benefices of his order except abbatial ones; three days later, he also obtained papal absolution from the excommunication that he had incurred for holding the priorate of Lenton for seven months (a year less than Dugdale noted) without a prior papal dispensation from illegitimacy and was required to resign (*CPL*, xii. 61, 63). He was confirmed in the priorate for life by Edward IV in 1461 and still prior in 1478.
[14] Most likely Boston (Lincs.).

Rome, iiii kal. Martii. Willelmus Bathe, presbiter, monacus professus prioratus Sancte Trinitatis, ordinis Cluniacensis, Eboracensis, domum sive monasterium in quo se voto professionis astrinxerat illicenciatus habitu et ordine derelictis exivit et ad seculum est reversus in quo per aliquos dies stetit quare excommunicationis sententias incurrit et appostazie labem commisit, de quibus ligatus tamquam simplex divina celebravit officia et se inmiscuit eisdem, quare irregularitatis maculam contraxit. Et cum ad suum ovile redire desideret, petit idem exponens a dictis sententiis ac appostazie labe absolvi et secum super irregularitate ex premissis contracta dispensari.

Fiat de speciali Phi. sancti Laurentii in Lucina.

1035. *Rome, 2 April 1462. Gregory Thomas, priest, Llandaff dioc., incurred excommunication for abandoning the priesthood and then returning to it without being reconciled; he seeks absolution from excommunication and dispensation from irregularity.* Reg. 10, fol. 127r.

Rome, iiii non. Aprilis. Gregorius Thomas, presbiter Landassensis [*sic*] diocesis, habitu et tonsura sacerdotalibus dimissis, cum quadam muliere per diversas mundi partes per spatium trium annorum accessit, et demum ad cor reversus absque reconsiliatione sui ordinarii habitum sacerdotalem reassumpsit, quare excommunicationis sententias in tales latas incurrit, de quibus ligatus tamquam simplex missa et alia divina officia celebravit irregularitatis maculam contrahendo. A quibus petit absolvi ac secum super irregularitate ex premissis contracta dispensari.

Fiat de speciali Phi. sancti Laurentii in Lucina.

1036. *Rome, 5 April 1462. Fr John Dawson, deacon and professed monk of Bardney, OSB, Lincoln dioc., incurred excommunication for apostasy and seeks absolution.*[15] Reg. 10, fol. 133r.

Rome, non. Aprilis. Frater Iohannes Dawson, diaconus, monacus professus sancti Oswaldi de Berny,[16] OSB, Lincolniensis diocesis, monasterium suum illicentiatus exivit et habitu ac ordine derelictis ad seculum est reversus, in quo per certum tempus vagavit, quare excommunicationis sententiam incurrit et appostasie labem commisit, a quibus petit absolvi, attento quod ad cor reversus ad suum ovile redire desiderat.

Fiat in forma Phi. sancti Laurentii in Lucina.

1037. *Rome, 9 April 1462. Thomas Waghi', priest, York dioc., incurred excommunication for hearing an old woman's confession as a deacon and then had himself ordained a priest; he seeks absolution and a dispensation.* Reg. 10, fol. 135r.

Rome, v id. Aprilis. Thomas Waghi', presbiter Eboracensis diocesis, in ordine diaconatus existens tamquam simplex quandam mulierem senem in confessione audivit, quare excommunicationis sententiam in tales latam incurrit, et sic excommunicatus ad ordinem presbiteratus se fecit promoveri.

---

[15] Cf. his supplication at **1049**.
[16] Bardney Abbey was dedicated to SS. Peter, Paul, and Oswald.

Petit absolvi a premissis ~~absolutus fuit~~ ac secum dispensari ut in subseptis [*recte* susceptis] suis ordinibus ministrare possit.

Fiat de speciali et expresso et suspendatur a ministerio altaris ad mensem Phi. sancti Laurentii in Lucina.

1038. *Santa Maria Maggiore, Rome, 18 July 1462. Richard son of Ieuan and Hugh Davit, laymen, St David's dioc., incurred excommunication for not making restitution of certain goods when admonished to do so, but now having done so they seek absolution.* Reg. 10, fol. 171v.

Rome apud sanctam Mariam maiorem, xv kal. Augusti. Ricardus Iohannis et Hugo Davit, laici Menevensis diocesis, moniti auctoritate apostolica ut nonnulla bona redderent ac scientes revelarent aut alias de eisdem satisfacerent infra certum temporis spatium, quod minime fecerunt, propter quod excommunicationis sententias incurrerunt, a quibus petunt absolvi attento quod dicta bona restituerunt.

Fiat de speciali S. archiepiscopus Mediolanensis regens.

1039. *Rome, 31 December 1462. Ieuan ap Reginald, layman, Hereford dioc., incurred excommunication for horse-stealing, but now, having made restitution, he seeks absolution.* Reg. 11, fol. 144v.

Rome, ii kal. Ianuarii. Iohannes ap Keynald, laicus Herfo[r]densis diocesis, non obstante quadam generali excommunicationis sententia in furantes boves et alia animalia dicte diocesis auctoritate ordinaria[17] lata, quatuor equos furatus fuit, propter quod excommunicationis sententiam incurrit ac furti reatum commisit, a quibus, attento [quod] dictos equos restituit, petit absolvi.

Fiat de speciali Ia. episcopus Vigintimiliensis regens.

1040. *Rome, 14 January 1463. Ieuan ap Llywelyn Ecciis, layman, St David's dioc., committed perjury and incurred excommunication for breaking his oath to observe his ordinary's ban on the theft of animals; he now seeks absolution.* Reg. 11, fol. 143r.

Rome, xviiii kal. Februarii. Johannes ap Lly' Ecciis, laicus Menevensis diocesis, exponit quod eius ordinarius omnes furantes boves, equos, vacas et alia animalia excommunicavit, ac omnes suos su[b]ditos iurare fecit quod predicta animalia non furarentur. Quibus non obstantibus, idem exponens duos equos furtive ar[r]ipuit, propter quod excommunicationis sententiam incurrit ac periurii reatum commisit, a quibus petit absolvi.

Fiat de speciali Io. episcopus Castellanus regens.

Et commitatur uni ex minoribus penitentiariis attento quod ad ordinarium adire non valet propter metum persone. Fiat Io.

---

[17] John Stanbury was then bishop of Hereford (1453–74); he had also co-operated with lay authorities on this issue in late 1456, when William Kemrych, a clerk of Worcester convicted of stealing two cows by secular judges, was handed over to the bishop's custody for compurgation (*Reg. Stanbury*, 35–8).

1041. *Rome, 25 March 1463. Thomas Cowper, professed of the College of the Precious Blood, Ashridge, OSA, Lincoln dioc., incurred excommunication for apostasy; he seeks absolution from this sentence and dispensation from irregularity.* Reg. 11, fol. 169r.

Rome, viiii kal. Aprilis. Thomas Cowper, professus conventus bonorum virorum domus sanguinis Iesu Christi,[18] OSA, Lincolniensis diocesis, dictum conventum illicentiatus exivit, habitu et ordine derelictis, et ad seculum est reversus, in quo aliquamdiu vagavit. Petit igitur absolvi a sententia quam ex premissis incurrit ac secum dispensari [super irregularitate] quam sic ligatus missas et alia divina officia celebrando contraxit.

Fiat de speciali Phi. sancti Laurentii in Lucina.

1042. Rome, 3 April 1463. Fr William Ledes,[19] professed canon of the monastery of St Oswald, Nostell (*de Nostellis*), OSA, York dioc., requests absolution from his crime of killing a priest and the sentence of excommunication that he thereby incurred. *Fiat de speciali Phi. sancti Laurentii in Lucina.* Reg. 11, fol. 175v.

1043. *Rome, 12 April 1463. Meurig ap Iankin ap Pawel, layman, St David's dioc., violated his bishop's ban on the theft of animals and thereby incurred excommunication; hence he seeks absolution.* Reg. 11, fol. 173v.

Rome, ii id. Aprilis. Mauricius ap Ienken ap Pawel, laicus Menevensis diocesis, contra inhibitiones episcopi Menevensis sub pena excommunicationis factas ne quis furaret in sua diocese animalia cuiuscumque condicionis, quadraginta oves cuidam domino furatus fuit, quare excommunicationis sententiam in tales latam incurrit, a qua petit absolvi. (*Approved with* **1044**.)

1044. Rome, 12 April 1463. Same absolution as **1043** sought by Meurig ap Cadwgan (*Codugan*), St David's dioc., who aided and abetted the theft of a horse contrary to the same ban. *Fiat de speciali pro utroque Phi. sancti Laurentii in Lucina.* (Approved with **1043**.) Reg. 11, fol. 173v.

1045. *Rome, 23 April 1463. Dafydd Amhurgk ap Gruffydd, layman, St David's dioc., violated his bishop's ban on the theft of animals and thereby incurred excommunication, from which he seeks absolution.* Reg. 11, fol. 180r.

Rome, viiii kal. Maii. David Amhurgk ap Gryffith, laicus Menevensis diocesis, non obstante inhibitione per eius ordinarium sub pena excommunicationis ne quis animalia eiusdem diocesis haberet furari facta, quandam ovem quam paratus restituere existit furatus fuit, quare excommunicationis sententiam in tales latam incurrit, a qua petit absolvi. (*Approved and committed with* **1046**.)

---

[18] A house of Bonhommes (*boni uiri*), regular priests who followed the Augustinian rule. These houses were peculiar to England and only two others are known, at Edington (Wilts.) and Ruthin (Denbighshire); see Knowles and Hadcock, 203.

[19] Perhaps the William Ledis, canon of Hempton Priory, OSA, granted a papal indult on 14 April 1466 to change to an Augustinian or Benedictine house with a stricter rule or observance, since he could not remain in his then monastery (*CPL*, xii. 529).

1046. Rome, 23 April 1463. Same absolution as **1045** sought by Richard ap Ieuan Vaghan, layman, St David's dioc., who likewise stole a sheep. *Fiat de speciali pro utroque Phi. sancti Laurentii in Lucina. Et committatur uni minori penitentiario cum propter periculum persone ad ordinarium accedere non valeant. Fiat Phi.* (Approved and committed with **1045**.) Reg. 11, fol. 180r.

1047. *Rome, 27 May 1463. John Hasart, professed canon of St Leonard's Priory, Torksey, OSA, Lincoln dioc., incurred excommunication for apostasy; he seeks absolution from this sentence and dispensation from irregularity.* Reg. 11, fols. 199v–200r.

Rome, vi kal. Iunii. Iohannes Hasart, canonicus professus monasterii sancti Leonardi de Torkesey, ordinis sancti Augustini, Lincolniensis diocesis, illicentiatus monasterium ipsum [fol. 200r] exivit et ad curiam Romanam venit, missas et alia divina celebrando officia, quare se excommunicationis sententiam incurrit et irregularitatis maculam contraxit. Petit idem exponens a dicta sententia absolvi ac secum super irregularitate ex premissis contracta dispensari.

Fiat de speciali G. prothon. de Oddis regens.

1048. *Rome, 27 June 1463. Owain Smyth,*[20] *priest, professed canon of Carmarthen Priory, OSA, St David's dioc., incurred excommunication for apostasy; he seeks absolution from this sentence and dispensation from irregularity.* Reg. 11, fol. 205r–v.

Rome, v kal. Iulii. Owinus Smyth, presbiter, canonicus monasterii sancti Iohannis ewangeliste, ordinis sancti Augustini, Menevensis diocesis, illicentiatus monasterium ipsum exivit ac habitum dimisit, propter quod excommunicationis sententiam incurrit, a qua ligatus missas et alia divina celebravit officia et alias inmiscuit [fol. 205v] se eisdem irregularitatis maculam contrahendo. Petit igitur idem exponens a dictis sententiis et apostasie labe absolvi ac secum super irregularitate ex premissis contracta dispensari.

Fiat de speciali G. prothon. de Oddis regens.

1049. *Tivoli, 19 July 1463. John Dawson, deacon and professed monk of Bardney Abbey, OSB, Lincoln dioc., incurred excommunication for apostasy; he seeks absolution from this sentence and dispensation from irregularity.*[21] Reg. 11, fol. 215v.

Tibure, xiiii kal. Augusti. Iohannes Dawson, \diaconus/, monachus professus monasterii de Bernay, ordinis sancti Benedicti, Lincolniensis diocesis, habitu et ordine dimissis, monasterium ipsum exivit et ad seculum est reversus, quare excommunicationis sententiam in tales latam incurrit, de qua ligatus tamquam simplex in dicto ordine diaconatus ministravit irregularitatis maculam

---

[20] Twelve days later, on 9 July 1463, he also obtained a papal dispensation, in which he is said to be of noble birth, so that he might receive and retain a benefice with cure of souls and wear a habit under his priest's vestments (*CPL*, xi. 642). On 22 November 1463, he was instituted as perpetual vicar of Charlton Adam (Somerset) by Thomas Beckington, bishop of Bath and Wells (*Reg. Bekynton*, 1535–6; see also Logan, 56).

[21] Cf. his supplication at **1036**.

contrahendo. Petit igitur absolvi a dictis sententiis ac secum dispensari super irregularitate ex premissis contracta.

Fiat de speciali G. prothon' de Oddis regens.

1050. *Tivoli, 28 August 1463. Thomas Ardien', priest, Lincoln dioc., feared that he had incurred excommunication, since when he declared the banns for Thomas and Annette (or Agnes) in Heyford church, where he was vicar, a certain William had claimed that Annette (or Agnes) was his wife, and the supplicant had bribed the man preparing the citation in the case (before the official of Northampton) and married the couple. He seeks absolution from the sentence and dispensation from irregularity.* Reg. 11, fol. 233r–v.

Tibure, v kal. Septembris. Thomas Ardien', presbiter Lincolniensis diocesis, exponit quod, cum ipse vicarius ecclesie parrochialis de Hayford[22] dicte diocesis existeret et in eadem ecclesia inter quosdam Thomam et Annetem banna ut invicem matrimonialiter copulari possent solempnisarentur, et quidem Willelmus laicus, qui ut asserebat matrimonium cum dicta Agneta [*sic*] contraxerat, eandem [fol. 233v] in uxorem habere pretendens eam coram officiali Norhamtonie[23] citari fecisset, exponens ipse illi qui citationem huiusmodi fecit, ne infra certum tempus relationem de eadem faceret, certam pecunie summam persolvit. Quibus mediis dictum Thomam et Agnetem predictam matrimonialiter coniunxit, existimans [*recte* estimans] inter ipsos esse verum matrimonium, propter que excommunicationis incurrisse dubitat sententiam in tales per constitutiones provinciales et sinodales latam ac, quia sic ligatus divina celebravit officia, irregularitatis maculam contraxisse. Petit igitur idem exponens a dicta sententia absolvi ac secum super irregularitate ex premissis contracta dispensari.

Fiat de speciali et eos pro posse inducat ad separacionem vel dispensationem necessariam G. prothon. de Oddis regens.

1051. *Rome, 6 February 1464. Elizabeth Chantrel, professed nun of Aconbury Priory, OSA, Hereford dioc., who incurred excommunication for apostasy, seeks absolution.* Reg. 13, fol. 126r.

Rome, viii id. Februarii. Elizabeth Chantrel, monialis professa monasterii de Ankynbiri, OSB [*recte* OSA], Herfordensis dyocesis, exponit quod ipsa olim dictum monasterium sine sui superioris licentia exivit per duos annos vel circa, habitu et ordine dimissis, et ad seculum reversa existit, propter que sententiam excommunicationis per constitutiones dicti ordinis incurrit, et sic ligata, non tamen in contemptum clavium, divinis se inmiscuit officiis. Cum autem dicta exponens ad ovile redire cupiat, supplicat quatinus eam a dicta excommunicationis sententia et excessibus huiusmodi ac peccatis suis aliis absolvi mandare dignemini de gratia speciali.

Fiat in forma Ph. Arelatensis regens etc.

---

[22] This probably refers to either Upper or Lower Heyford (Oxon.) near the Northants. county boundary.
[23] The official of the archdeacon of Northampton.

1052. *Rome, 11 February 1464. John Frense, priest, Norwich dioc., had himself promoted to all holy orders while under age before Pius II's constitution 'Cum ex sacrorum' and ministered in his orders; now that he has reached the legitimate age, he seeks absolution and a dispensation.* Reg. 13, fol. 127r.

> Rome, iii id. Februarii. Iohannes Frense, presbiter Narwicensis [*sic*] dyocesis, exponit quod ipse olim ante constitucionem per dominum nostrum papam editam que incipit 'Cum ex sacrorum ordinum collacione' minor annis existens se fecit alias tamen rite ad omnes sacros ordines promoveri et in ipsis ministravit, quare excessum incurrit. Cum autem nunc ad etatem legitimam pervenerit, supplicat igitur sanctitati vestre dictus exponens quatinus ipsum ab excessu huiusmodi absolvere et [quod] in suis sic susceptis ordinibus ministrare possit et valeat misericorditer dispensare dignemini de gratia speciali.
>
> Fiat de speciali et suspendatur a ministerio altaris ad mensem Ph. Arelatensis regens etc.

1053. *Rome, 11 February 1464. Adam Milgate, deacon, Norwich dioc., requests a dispensation so that on reaching the age of 24 he may be licitly promoted to priest's orders and minister in them, notwithstanding the constitutions of the Lyons and Lateran councils. Fiat de speciali pro utroque Phi. Arelatensis regens.* (Approved with another entry not from England or Wales.) Reg. 13, fol. 127v.

1054. *Rome, 11 February 1464. William Couper, clerk and professed of the Carmelite order, Hitchin convent, Lincoln dioc., who incurred excommunication for apostasy, seeks absolution.* Reg. 13, fol. 134v.

> Rome, iii id. Februarii. Willelmus Couper, clericus, professus ordinis fratrum beate Marie de monte Carmeli, conventus de Hychin, Lincolniensis diocesis, dictum conventum absque licentia superioris, habitu et ordine derelictis, exivit et ad seculum reversus est, propter quod excommunicationis incurrit sententiam etc. Cum autem ad ovile redire desideret, supplicatur pro parte ipsius quatinus ipsum ab excommunicationis sententia ac peccatis suis aliis absolvi mandetur ut in forma.
>
> Fiat in forma Phi. Arelatensis regens etc.

1055. *Rome, 15 February 1464.* Robert Chatysle of Ickworth (*de Ypauorth*), acolyte, Norwich dioc., requests that on reaching the age of 24 he may be promoted to priest's orders and minister in them. Approved with **1056**. Reg. 13, fol. 129r.

1056. *Rome, 15 February 1464.* Same dispensation as **1055** sought by Thomas Nevyll of Cambridge (*de Camabrigia*),[24] scholar, Ely dioc., etc. *Fiat de speciali pro utroque Phi. Arelatensis regens.* (Approved with **1055**.) Reg. 13, fol. 129r.

1057. *Rome, 18 February 1464.* Thomas Bryon of Thetford (*Thetfordia*), scholar, Norwich dioc., requests that on reaching the age of 24 he may be promoted to priest's orders. Approved with **1058**. Reg. 13, fol. 128v.

---

[24] Perhaps Thomas Nevell, BCnL of Cambridge and rector of Brancepeth (Co. Durham) until his death; he was dead by July 1498 (*BRUC*, 422).

1058. Rome, 18 February 1464. Same dispensation as **1057** sought by Richard Poti, Norwich dioc. *Fiat de speciali pro utroque Phi. Arelatensis regens.* (Approved with **1057**.) Reg. 13, fol. 128v.

1059. Rome, 25 February 1464. William Bilerne, deacon, Norwich dioc., requests a dispensation so that on reaching the age of 24 he may be promoted to priest's orders, notwithstanding the constitutions of the Lyons and Lateran councils. *Fiat de speciali Phi. Arelatensis regens.* Reg. 13, fol. 130r.

1060. *Rome, 25 February 1464. Fr Robert Erpyngham, priest and professed of the Norwich convent, OFM, had himself promoted to priest's orders while under age and ministered in them; he seeks absolution and dispensation so that he may minister in them on reaching the age of 24.* Reg. 13, fol. 130r.

Rome, vi kal. Martii. Frater Robertus Erpyngh[a]m, presbiter, professus conventus Norwicensis, ordinis fratrum minorum, exponit quod ipse olim minor annis existens tamquam simplex ad presbiteratus ordinem se promoveri fecit et in ipsis ministravit. Cum autem ad etatem legitimam pervenerit, supplicat quatinus ipsum ab excessibus huiusmodi et peccatis suis aliis absolvi mandare secumque super irregularitate dicto modo contracta quodque ut quam primum xxiiii sue etatis annum attigerit in dictis suis ordinibus ministrare possit dispensare dignemini.

Fiat de speciali et suspendatur a ministerio altaris etiam postquam attigerit xxiiii ad duos menses Phi. Arelatensis regens etc.

1061. Rome, 27 February 1464. Same dispensation as **1059** sought by Walter Colman, subdeacon, Norwich dioc. *Fiat de speciali Phi. Arelatensis regens etc.* Reg. 13, fol. 130v.

1062. Siena, 27 February 1464. John Aley,[25] priest, Ely dioc., knowingly had himself promoted twice to holy orders and ministered in them; hence he requests absolution from the sentence of excommunication that he thereby incurred and a dispensation from the irregularity that he thereby contracted so that he may minister in his orders. *Fiat de speciali Ph. sancti Laurentii in Lucina.* Reg. 13, fol. 141r.

1063. Rome, 21 March 1464. John Rikwart, subdeacon, Norwich dioc., requests a dispensation so that on reaching the age of 24 he may be promoted to priest's orders and retain a benefice with or without cure of souls. *Fiat de speciali B. episcopus Regin. regens.* Reg. 13, fol. 132r.

---

[25] Perhaps John Aleyn, principal of Eagle Hall and Ape Hall, Oxford, in September 1458 and still in September 1463. At Oxford University he was admitted BCnL on 21 October 1455. He was in priest's orders by 1454. He held various ecclesiastical benefices. He was arrested at Oxford and imprisoned at Warwick Castle in 1461 since he wanted to go to the Lancastrian queen Margaret. Perhaps the same as *magister* John Aleyn, BCnL, who was admitted as warden of chantry in Uxbridge chapel on 1 April 1482, till death, and died by May 1483; or *magister* John Aleyn, BCL, who was admitted as rector of Rearsby (Leics.) on 15 May 1493, till death, and died by August 1514 (*BRUO*, i. 22; *CPL*, xi. 578); or the John Aleyn, rector of Holy Rood, Wood Eaton, Lincoln dioc., granted a papal dispensation to hold a second benefice with cure of souls on 17 July 1460 (*CPL*, xi. 578).

1064. Rome, 21 March 1464. Same dispensation as **1059** sought by Thomas Warde, clerk, Norwich dioc., aged 22. *Fiat de speciali B. episcopus Regin. regens.* Reg. 13, fol. 132r.

1065. Rome, 27 March 1464. Same dispensation as **1057** sought by Richard Dullverum, clerk, Coventry and Lichfield dioc. *Fiat de speciali B. episcopus Regin. regens.* Reg. 13, fol. 132v.

1066. Rome, 27 March 1464. Same dispensation as **1057** sought by Robert Lister, clerk, Norwich dioc. *Fiat de speciali B. episcopus Regin. regens.* Reg. 13, fol. 132v.

1067. Rome, 30 March 1464. Richard Tegyn, priest and vicar or rector of Wrexham (*Rirxham*), St Asaph dioc., who intends to study in a *studium generale*, requests that the pope should give him a dispensation to study [civil] law (*legem*) for seven years and take a degree in the legally permitted faculties, saving the fruits of his benefices. *Fiat de speciali B. episcopus Regin. regens etc.* Reg. 13, fol. 133r.

1068. *Rome, 31 March 1464. Richard alias Ricz ap Gruffydd, layman, St David's dioc., who incurred excommunication for stealing goods from a holy place, seeks absolution.* Reg. 13, fol. 135v.

> Rome, ii kal. Aprilis. Richardus alias Ricz ap Gryffyth laycus Menevensis dyocesis alias de loco sacro bona mobilia clam et furtive deportavit et in suum usum convertebat propter quod furti reatum et excommunicationis sententiam in tales promulgatam incurrit. Cum autem ad satisfactionem paratus sit, petit a dictis excessibus ac peccatis aliis absolvi.
>
> Fiat in forma B. episcopus Regin. regens etc.

1069. Petrioli, Siena dioc., 10 April 1464. Owain ap *Iuredich'*, layman, St David's dioc., took goods and animals from certain holy places and thereby committed sacrilege and incurred excommunication, whence he seeks absolution. Approved with **1070**. Reg. 13, fol. 148v.

1070. Petrioli, Siena dioc., 10 April 1464. Same absolution as **1069** sought by Richard alias Ricz ap Griffyth', layman, St. David's dioc.[26] *Fiat in forma pro utroque facta competenti satisfactione de rebus ablatis Io. abbas sancti B. regens.* (Approved with **1069**.) Reg. 13, fol. 148v.

1071. Petrioli, Siena dioc., 18 April 1464. Christopher Alynton, priest, Canterbury dioc., who seeks to remain in a *studium* and be instructed in letters, requests a licence to remain in that *studium* and at the same time receive the fruits of his benefices for seven years. *Fiat de speciali Io. abbas sancti B. regens.* Reg. 13, fol. 155v.

1072. Rome, 30 April 1464. Fr Thomas Werlyngin, priest and professed monk of the monastery of Pershore (*de Pastore*), OSB, Worcester (*Wergorniensis*) dioc., seeks absolution from excommunication, which he incurred by coming without

---

[26] This petition is similar to **1068**.

permission to the Roman Curia, and dispensation from irregularity, which he subsequently contracted by participating in divine offices. *Fiat de speciali B. episcopus Regin. regens.* Reg. 13, fol. 159r.

1073. Rome, 13 June 1464. Fr Robert Midilton, priest, professed of OFM, Richmond convent, York dioc., left his convent without permission, abandoned his habit, and then participated in divine offices; hence he requests absolution from the aforesaid and dispensation from the irregularity thereby contracted. *Fiat de speciali Phi.* Reg. 13, fol. 170r.

1074. Rome, 15 June 1464. Fr Thomas Staverey, priest and professed canon of the monastery of St Nicholas, [Great Massingham],[27] OSA, Norwich dioc., left his monastery without permission and returned to the secular life, where he remained and participated in divine offices; hence he requests absolution from the sentence thereby incurred and dispensation from the irregularity thereby contracted. *Fiat de speciali Phi.* Reg. 13, fol. 168v.

De declaratoriis

1075. *Siena, 5 June 1460. John Hymeslay, priest, York dioc., was placed in a monastery by his parents at the age of seven, which he left three years later without having professed; he seeks a declaration that he is not bound to that monastery.* Reg. 8, fol. 218v.

Senis, non. Iunii. Iohannes Hymeslay, presbiter Eboricensis [*sic*] diocesis, exponit quod ipse in etate septem annorum quoddam monasterium de voluntate suorum parentum minorum [*recte* minor] intravit et tres annos portandi habitum stetit et nullam professionem emisit. Demum impubes de dicto monasterio exivit et ad seculum est reversus, in quo permanet. Supplicat quatinus ipsum ad dictum monasterium nec observanciam ipsius non teneri declarari mandare dignemini.

Committatur ordinario qui constito de assertis declaret ut petitur Phi. sancti Laurentii in Lucina.

[**1076**] *Rome, 12 November 1461. Henry Blom, priest, Norwich dioc., recounts how he killed a soldier who came to his house begging for money; he claims that he acted in self-defence and hence asks to be declared innocent of murder and free of irregularity and* inhabilitas. Reg. 9, fols. 265v–266r.

Rome, ii id. Novembris. Henricus Blom, presbiter Norwicensis diocesis, exponit quod ipse alias existens in quadam domo in qua, dum prandium suum faceret, quidam laicus, qui guerram et factum armorum insequebatur, ad locum, ubi dictus presbiter comedebat, accessit. Postmodum pecuniam pro eundo ad guerram eidem petiit, cui presbiter respondit:

---

[27] Dedicated to SS. Mary and Nicholas (Knowles and Hadcock, 157). Presumably the Thomas Sauerey, canon of Great Massingham Priory, granted a papal dispensation to receive and retain a benefice with cure of souls on 23 July 1464 (*CPL*, xi. 673–4).

'Amice, nichil tibi debeo. Vade in pace'. Dictus laicus, nolens dimittere dictum presbiterum nisi prius daret sibi pecuniam, pro quibus habendis minabatur mortem nisi sibi daret, cui iterum respondit non velle nec posse dare \pecunias/ in quas sibi non tenebatur. Dictus vero laicus hoc videns contra eundem presbiterum irruit ac si eum vellet interficere. Quod videns, idem presbiter vim vi repellendo, cum aliter evadere non posset, cum moderamine tamen inculpate tutele prefatum laicum cum quodam parvo cultello percussit et vulneravit, ex quibus, debita medela forte non exhibita, diem suum clausit extremum. Et cum premissa vim vi repellendo [fol. 266r] fecerit ac aliter evadere non poterit, nonnulli tamen simplices asser[er]e possent eundem ex premissis reatum homicidii commisisse. Igitur, ad obstruendum ora talium, supplicatur eidem sanctitati vestre pro parte eiusdem quatinus ipsum ex premissis nullum homicidii reatum nullamque irregularitatis sive inhabilitatis maculam sive notam contraxisse declarari misericorditer mandare dignemini.

Fiat \ut/ in forma Phi. sancti Laurentii in Lucina. Videat eam dominus Anchonitanus Phi. Committatur et vocatis vocandis declaretur iuxta formam Cle. de homicidiis.[28]

De defectu natalium

1077. Siena, 30 March 1459. Alan Hyn, scholar, Durham dioc., born of an unmarried man and an unmarried woman, requests a dispensation from a defect of birth so that he may be promoted to all orders and obtain a benefice even with cure of souls. *Fiat de speciali Phi. sancti Laurentii in Lucina.* Proctor: Io. Weythas'. Reg. 7, fol. 303v.

1078. Mantua, 3 September 1459. William Resburh, scholar of London, born of an unmarried man and an unmarried woman, requests a dispensation from a defect of birth so that he may be promoted to clerical status and all orders and obtain a benefice even with cure of souls. *Fiat de speciali M. Alexan'.* Proctor: I. Magni. Reg. 7, fol. 318v.

1079. Mantua, 6 September 1459. Same dispensation as **1078** sought by Matthew Brown, scholar, St Asaph dioc., born of a priest and an unmarried woman. *Fiat de speciali M. Alexan'.* Proctor: Io. Weythas'. Reg. 7, fol. 318v.

1080. Mantua, 6 September 1459. Same dispensation as **1078** sought by John *alias* Ieuan Lloyt,[29] scholar, St Asaph dioc. *Fiat de speciali M. Alexan'.* Proctor: Io. Weythas'. Reg. 7, fol. 318v.

---

[28] *Clementinae* 5. 4. un., which declared that a clerk who killed an attacker (*invasor*), not being able to avoid death otherwise (*mortem aliter vitare non valens*), did not thereby incur irregularity.
[29] Perhaps the John Lloit, priest of St Asaph dioc., in whose favour the vicar-general in spiritualities of the bishop of St Asaph had a papal faculty to confer the office of notary public on 19 April 1465 (*CPL*, xii. 814).

1081. Mantua, 7 September 1459. Geoffrey ap Ieuan(?) (*Iey*) ap *Eymt*, scholar, Bangor dioc., born of an unmarried man and an unmarried woman, requests a dispensation from a defect of birth so that he may receive clerical tonsure, be promoted to all orders and obtain a benefice even with a cure of souls. *Fiat de speciali Phi. sancti Laurentii in Lucina.* Proctor: R. Talicham. Reg. 7, fol. 318v.

1082. *Siena, 3 March 1460. Alan Vaby, acolyte, Durham dioc., has already received an episcopal dispensation from defect of birth; he now requests a further papal one.* Reg. 8, fol. 241v.

> Senis, v non. Martii. Alanus Vaby, acolitus Dunalmensis [*sic*] diocesis, cum quo alias auctoritate ordinaria fuit dispensatum ut ad minores ordines posset promoveri et beneficium sine cura obtinere, supplicat ut, non obstante deffectu natalium quem patitur de soluto et soluta genitus, ad omnes ordines possit promoveri et beneficium ecclesiasticum cum cura obtinere dispensari [mandare] dignemini.
>
> Fiat de speciali Phi. sancti Laurentii in Lucina. [*Proctor:*] I. Weythas'.

1083. Siena, 24 March 1460. Thomas ap Dafydd, scholar, Bangor dioc., born of an unmarried man and an unmarried woman, requests that the pope grant him a dispensation from a defect of birth so that he may be promoted to all orders and obtain a benefice with or without cure of souls. *Fiat de speciali Phi. sancti Laurentii in Lucina.* Reg. 8, fol. 249v.

1084. Siena, 11 April 1460. Same dispensation as **1083** sought by Ieuan Kynros, scholar, St David's dioc., born of a priest and a married woman. *Fiat de speciali Phi. sancti Laurentii in Lucina.* Proctor: A. Piscator'. Reg. 8, fol. 246r.

1085. Siena, 11 April 1460. Robert Franwces [*sic*], clerk, Bath and Wells dioc.,[30] born of a professed priest and an unmarried woman, requests that the pope should grant him a dispensation from a defect of birth so that he may be promoted to all orders and obtain a benefice without cure of souls [*sic*]. *Fiat de speciali Phi. sancti Laurentii in Lucina.* Proctor: A. Piscator'. Reg. 8, fol. 246r.

1086. Siena, 19 April 1460. Same dispensation as **1083** sought by Gwilym (*Wihemus*) ap Rhys, scholar, St Asaph dioc., born of a priest and an unmarried woman. *Fiat de speciali Phi. sancti Laurentii in Lucina.* Reg. 8, fol. 248r.

1087. Siena, 22 April 1460. Thomas son of Thomas ap [. . .], scholar, Llandaff dioc., born of a priest and an unmarried woman, requests that the pope should grant him a dispensation from a defect of birth so that he may be promoted to all orders and obtain a benefice. *Fiat de speciali Phi. sancti Laurentii in Lucina.* Proctor: H. Broyel. Reg. 8, fol. 249v.

---

[30] Perhaps the Robert Fraunceys, vicar choral of Wells Cathedral, to whom the seventh chamber on the west side of the vicar's close was collated by Thomas Beckington, bishop of Bath and Wells, on 5 August 1460 (*Reg. Bekynton*, 1326); Beckington also issued letters dimissory to all orders for a Robert Fraunces of Glastonbury on 23 January 1461 (ibid., 1357).

1088. Siena, 22 April 1460. Same dispensation as **1087** sought by John Mares, Hereford dioc.,[31] born of an unmarried man and an unmarried woman. (*Fiat*-clause omitted.) Proctor: H. Broyel. Reg. 8, fol. 249v.

1089. Siena, 11 May 1460. Same dispensation as **1083** sought by Meurig [son] of Ieuan David, scholar, St David's dioc., born of an unmarried man and an unmarried woman. *Fiat de speciali A. episcopus Aprutinus regens.* Reg. 8, fol. 252r.

1090. Siena, 13 May 1460. Same dispensation as **1083** sought by Robert Mathewson, clerk, Carlisle dioc., born of a priest and a married woman. *Fiat de speciali A. episcopus Aprutinus regens.* Reg. 8, fol. 253r.

1091. Siena, 13 May 1460. Same dispensation as **1083** sought by Richard Garth, Carlisle dioc., born of a priest and an unmarried woman. (*Fiat*-clause omitted.) Reg. 8, fol. 253r.

1092. Siena, 20 June 1460. Same dispensation as **1083** sought by Thomas Rousse,[32] Canterbury dioc., born of an unmarried man and an unmarried woman. (*Fiat*-clause omitted.) Reg. 8, fol. 254v.

1093. Siena, 1 September 1460. Same dispensation as **1087** sought by John Portat, scholar, Bath and Wells dioc., born of an unmarried man and an unmarried woman. *Fiat de speciali A. episcopus Aprutinus regens.* Reg. 8, fol. 266v.

1094. Siena, 1 September 1460. John Portat, scholar, Bath and Wells dioc., born of an unmarried man and an unmarried woman, requests that he may be promoted to all orders and obtain a benefice with or without cure of souls. *Fiat de speciali A. episcopus Aprutinus regens.* Reg. 8, fol. 266v.

1095. Rome, 21 October 1460. Same dispensation as **1094** sought by John Aubey, clerk, Coventry and Lichfield dioc., born of an unmarried man and an unmarried woman. *Fiat G. [prothon. de Oddis regens].* Reg. 8, fol. 270r.

1096. Rome, 17 December 1460. Same dispensation as **1094** sought by John Holborn, scholar, Durham dioc., born of a priest and an unmarried woman. *Fiat de speciali Phi. sancti Laurentii in Lucina.* Reg. 8, fol. 275v.

1097. Rome, 28 January 1461. Same dispensation as **1094** sought by William Laton, clerk, York dioc., born of an unmarried man and an unmarried woman. *Fiat de speciali Phi.* Reg. 9, fol. 278r.

1098. Rome, 28 January 1461. Same dispensation as **1083** sought by Walter Endiriby (*sic*) and John Endirby, brothers, Lincoln dioc., born of a religious and an unmarried woman. *Fiat de speciali Phi. sancti Laurentii in Lucina.* Reg. 9, fol. 278v.

---

[31] Presumably the John Marys ordained as a priest to the title of Monmouth Priory, OSB, by the bishop of Hereford on the vigil of Trinity (7 June), 1460 (*Reg. Stanbury*, 146).

[32] Perhaps Thomas Rows or Rowse, chaplain, instituted on 3 February 1476 to Eynesford vicarage, which he resigned by 15 October 1481 (*Reg. Bourgchier*, 324, 349).

Pius II (1458–1464) 233

1099. Rome, 4 February 1461. John Waynflete *alias* Flayn, professed of the monastery of the BVM and St Laurence, Revesby (*Rewysby*), Cistercian order, Lincoln dioc., born of an unmarried man and an unmarried woman, requests a dispensation so that he may be promoted to all orders and any dignities of his order except the principal one. *Fiat de speciali Phi.* Reg. 9, fol. 280r.

1100. Rome, 18 March 1461. Sister Katherine Pakyngton, professed nun of the monastery of Heynings (*de Henyngis*), Cistercian order, Lincoln dioc., born of an unmarried man and an unmarried woman, requests a dispensation so that she may be promoted to all *administrationes* of her order except the principal one. *Fiat de speciali Ph.* Reg. 9, fol. 283v.

1101. Rome, 18 March 1461. Same dispensation as **1094** sought by Richard Harpan, scholar, York dioc., born of an unmarried man and an unmarried woman. *Fiat de speciali Phi.* Reg. 9, fol. 283v.

1102. Rome, 18 March 1461. Same dispensation as **1094** sought by John Barbir, scholar, Lincoln dioc., born of an unmarried man and an unmarried woman. Approved with **1103**. Reg. 9, fol. 283v.

1103. Rome, 18 March 1461. Same dispensation as **1094** sought by Thomas Kamisay, scholar, Lincoln dioc., born of an unmarried man and an unmarried woman. *Fiat pro omnibus Phi.* (Approved with **1102**.) Reg. 9, fol. 283v.

1104. Rome, 19 March 1461. Thomas Yngilby, priest and professed of OFM, Lincoln dioc., born of an unmarried man and an unmarried woman, requests a dispensation so that he may minister in his existing orders and obtain offices and *administrationes* of his order except the principal one. Approved with **1105**. Reg. 9, fol. 287v.

1105. Rome, 19 March 1461. Same dispensation as **1104** sought by Fr Thomas Herperbi, clerk and professed of OFM, Lincoln dioc. *Fiat de speciali pro utroque Phi.* (Approved with **1104**.) Reg. 9, fol. 287v.

1106. Rome, 29 March 1461. Same dispensation as **1094** sought by Lewis (*Lowes*) David, scholar of Llandaff, born of a priest and an unmarried woman. *Fiat de speciali Phi.* Reg. 9, fol. 285v.

1107. Rome, 5 June 1461. Dafydd ap Llywelyn (*Ll'*), scholar, Bangor dioc., born of an unmarried man and an unmarried woman, requests a dispensation so that he may be promoted to all orders and obtain a benefice. *Fiat de speciali Phi.* Reg. 9, fol. 297v.

1108. Rome, 5 June 1461. Same dispensation as **1107** sought by Benedict Aptona, scholar, Exeter dioc., born of an unmarried man and an unmarried woman. *Fiat de speciali Phi.* Reg. 9, fol. 297v.

1109. Rome, 14 November 1461. Thomas Thorp, clerk, York dioc., born of an unmarried man and an unmarried woman, requests a dispensation so that he may be promoted to all orders and obtain a benefice even with cure of souls. *Fiat de speciali Phi. sancti Laurentii in Lucina.* Reg. 9, fol. 314r.

1110. Rome, 29 January 1462. Same dispensation as **1094** sought by Edmund Edward, scholar, Bangor dioc., born of a priest and an unmarried woman. *Fiat de speciali Phi. sancti Laurentii in Lucina.* Reg. 10, fol. 251r.

1111. Rome, 16 February 1462. Same dispensation as **1077** sought by William Mayell', scholar, York dioc., born of an unmarried man and an unmarried woman. *Fiat de speciali Phi. sancti Laurentii in Lucina.* Reg. 10, fol. 253v.

1112. Rome, 4 March 1462. Same dispensation as **1109** sought by Gronw ap Ieuan ap *Dyan*, Bangor dioc., born of an unmarried man and an unmarried woman. *Fiat de speciali Phi. sancti Laurentii in Lucina.* Reg. 10, fol. 253v.

1113. Rome, 25 March 1462. Same dispensation as **1109** sought by Thomas Gasgill, scholar, Lincoln (*Lingolensis*) dioc., born of an unmarried man and an unmarried woman. *Fiat de speciali Phi. sancti Laurentii in Lucina.* Reg. 10, fol. 256v.

1114. Rome, 7 April 1462. Hywel (*Hoell'*) ap *Rigert* ap Hywel (*Hoell'*), scholar, Llandaff (*Landassensis*) dioc., born of an unmarried man and an unmarried woman, requests a dispensation so that he may be promoted to all orders and retain a benefice with or without cure of souls. *Fiat de speciali Phi. sancti Laurentii in Lucina.* Reg. 10, fol. 258r.

1115. Rome, 13 January 1463. Thomas Stratford (*Sthetford'*), professed monk of the monastery of Stratford (*Stretford*), Cistercian order, London dioc., born of a priest and an unmarried woman, requests a dispensation so that he may be ordained to all orders and obtain all offices and *administrationes* of his order except the principal one. *Fiat de speciali Io. episcopus Castellanus regens.* Reg. 11, fol. 287r.

1116. Rome, 29 January 1463. Same dispensation as **1094** sought by Edward Lastwysell', scholar, Coventry [and Lichfield] dioc., born of a married man and an unmarried woman. *Fiat de speciali Phi. sancti Laurentii in Lucina.* Reg. 11, fol. 289v.

1117. *Rome, 3 April 1463. Peter Hurrton, acolyte, St Asaph dioc., who kept silent about his defect of birth when he was promoted to minor orders, requests absolution and a dispensation.* Reg. 11, fol. 301r.

> Rome, iii non. Aprilis. Petrus Hurtton, acolitus Assavensis diocesis, qui tacito deffectu natalium se fecit ad minores ordines promoveri, petit absolvi ab excessu quem commisit ac secum dispensari ut eo non obstante in susceptis suis ordinibus ministrare ac ad sacros promoveri necnon beneficium ecclesiasticum cum cura vel sine cura obtinere possit.
>
> Fiat de speciali Phi. sancti Laurencii in Lucina.

[**1118**] Rome, 3 April 1463. Same dispensation as **1094** sought by Henry Preston, scholar, York dioc., born of a priest and an unmarried woman. *Fiat de speciali Phi. sancti Laurentii in Lucina.* Reg. 11, fol. 301v.

[1119] Rome, 4 April 1463. Same dispensation as 1094 sought by Robert ap sir Gwilym (*ser Willelmi*), scholar, Llandaff dioc., born of a priest and an unmarried woman. *Fiat de speciali pro utroque Phi. sancti Laurentii in Lucina.* (Approved with another entry not from England or Wales.) Reg. 11, fol. 302r.

1120. Rome, 30 May 1463. John Ingelby, priest, professed monk of the monastery of Mount Grace, Carthusian order, York dioc., requests a dispensation[33] so that he may minister in his existing orders and accept and retain *administrationes* and offices of his order. *Fiat de speciali citra principalem dignitatem G. prothon. de Oddis regens.* Reg. 11, fol. 313v.

1121. Rome, 1 June 1463. Same dispensation as 1094 sought by John Mason, clerk, York dioc., born of a priest and an unmarried woman etc. *Fiat de speciali G. prothon. de Oddis regens.* Reg. 11, fol. 320r.

1122. Rome, 6 July 1463. Fr John Trop, priest, professed canon of the monastery of Kirkham (*Kyrkehim*), OSA, York dioc., born of an unmarried man and an unmarried woman, requests a dispensation from a defect of birth so that he may minister in all his orders and accept and retain *administrationes* and offices of his order. *Fiat de speciali G. prothon. de Oddis regens.* Reg. 11, fol. 319r.

1123. Rome, 12 October 1463. Fr Richard Horntall, priest, professed monk of the monastery of SS. Peter and Paul, [Bardney], OSB, Lincoln dioc., requests a dispensation so that he may obtain *administrationes* and offices of his order, even abbacies, if elected to them. *Fiat de speciali et expresso si eligatur vel assumatur Io. episcopus Castellanus regens.* Reg. 11, fol. 329v.

1124. Rome, 3 February 1464. Same dispensation as 1094 granted to Richard Colynsen, scholar, York dioc., born of a priest and an unmarried woman. Approved with 1125. Reg. 13, fol. 246r.

1125. Rome, 3 February 1464. Same dispensation as 1094 granted to Thomas More, scholar, St Asaph dioc., born of a priest and an unmarried woman. *Fiat de speciali pro omnibus Io. episcopus Castellanus regens.* (Approved with 1124.) Reg. 13, fol. 246r.

1126. Rome, 30 March 1464. Dafydd [son] of Richard Thegriny', scholar, St Asaph dioc., born of a priest and an unmarried woman, requests a dispensation so that he may be promoted to priest's orders and hold a benefice with or without cure of souls. *Fiat de speciali B. episcopus Regin. regens.* Reg. 13, fol. 247r.

1127. Rome, 6 April 1464. Same dispensation as 1126 sought by Hywel (*Hoell*) ap sir Richard ap Hywel (*Hoell'*), scholar, Llandaff dioc., born of a priest and an unmarried woman. *Fiat de speciali B. episcopus Regin. regens.* Reg. 13, fol. 247v.

1128. Rome, 6 April 1464. Same dispensation as 1126 sought by Hywel (*Hoell*) ap Dafydd ap Ieuan ap Iankin (*Ion' ap Ien'*), scholar, Llandaff dioc., born of an

---

[33] The entry does not specify the nature of the defect of birth.

unmarried man and an unmarried woman. *Fiat de speciali pro utroque*[34] *B. episcopus Regin. regens.* Reg. 13, fol. 248r.

1129. Siena, 8 March 1464. Same dispensation as **1094** sought by John Wilson, scholar, Lincoln dioc., born of a priest and an unmarried woman. *Fiat de speciali Phi.* Reg. 13, fol. 251r.

1130. Siena, 13 March 1464. Same dispensation as **1094** sought by Robert Courteyse, scholar, London dioc., born of a priest and an unmarried woman. *Fiat de speciali Phi. sancti Laurentii in Lucina.* Reg. 13, fol. 250v.

1131. Siena, 22 March 1464. Same dispensation as **1094** sought by Gilbert Pylkyngton, scholar, Coventry [and Lichfield] dioc., born of an unmarried man and an unmarried woman. *Fiat de speciali Phi.* Reg. 13, fol. 252r.

1132. Siena, 2 April 1464. Same dispensation as **1094** sought by William Hamond, scholar, Lincoln dioc., born of a married man and an unmarried woman. *Fiat de speciali Phi. sancti Laurentii in Lucina.* Reg. 13, fol. 253v.

1133. Siena, 4 April 1464. Same dispensation as **1094** sought by Richard Bonifaunt, scholar, York dioc., born of an unmarried man and an unmarried woman. *Fiat de speciali Phi. sancti Laurentii in Lucina.* Reg. 13, fol. 253v.

1134. Petrioli, Siena dioc., 19 April 1464. Same dispensation as **1094** sought by Philip Morgan, scholar, St David's dioc., born of a married man and an unmarried woman. Approved with **1136**. Reg. 13, fol. 255v.

1135. Petrioli, Siena dioc., 19 April 1464. Same dispensation as **1094** sought by Thomas ap Gruffydd Owyn, scholar, St David's dioc., born of a priest and a married woman. Approved with **1136**. Reg. 13, fol. 255v.

1136. Petrioli, Siena dioc., 19 April 1464. Same dispensation as **1094** sought by Ieuan Penval, scholar, Bangor dioc., born of a priest and a married woman. *Fiat de speciali pro omnibus Io. abbas sancti B. regens.* (Approved with **1134–5**.) Reg. 13, fol. 255v.

1137. *Petrioli, Siena dioc., 19 April 1464. Dafydd ap Robert, priest, St David's dioc., who kept silent about his defect of birth when he was promoted to all orders, requests absolution and a dispensation.* Reg. 13, fol. 256v.

> Petreoli Senensis diocesis, xiii kal. Maii. David ap Robert, presbiter Menevensis diocesis, tacito deffectu natalium, quem patitur de soluto genitus et soluta, ad omnes se fecit promoveri ordines et in eisdem ministravit, quare excessum commisit, a quo petit absolvi ac secum, ut in suis ordinibus ministrare necnon beneficium cum cura vel sine cura recipere et retinere possit, dispensari.
>
> Fiat de speciali Io. abbas sancti Bernardi regens.

---

[34] This signifies approval with another supplication, but in this case the supplication was approved on its own.

1138. Rome, 19 June 1464. Thomas Clwyn, priest, professed canon of the monastery of Newark, OSA, Winchester dioc., born of an unmarried man and an unmarried woman, requests a dispensation so that he may accept and retain *administrationes*, offices and benefices of his order except the principal one. *Fiat de speciali Phi. sancti Laurentii in Lucina.* Reg. 13, fols. 265v–266r.

1139. Rome, 20 June 1464. Same dispensation as **1094** sought by Henry ap Hywel, scholar, St David's dioc., born of an unmarried man and an unmarried woman. *Fiat de speciali Phi.* Reg. 13, fol. 265r.

1140. Rome, 25 June 1464. Same dispensation as **1094** sought by Gwilym [son] of Thomas ap Roger (*Rosser*) ap Ieuan ap Hywel (*Hoell*), scholar, Llandaff dioc., born of an unmarried man and an unmarried woman. *Fiat de speciali pro omnibus Phi.* (Approved with other entries not from England or Wales.) Reg. 13, fol. 267r.

De uberiori

1141. *Siena, 24 April 1460. Richard Conter alias ap Hywel, priest, Llandaff dioc., who has already received a papal dispensation from defect of birth, requests a further papal grace so that he can obtain another compatible benefice.* Reg. 8, fol. 284v.

Senis, viii kal. Maii. Ricardus Conter alias ap Howel, presbiter Landavensis diocesis, cum quo alias super deffectu natalium quem patitur de soluto genitus et soluta, ut, eo non obstante, ad omnes ordines promoveri ac beneficium [cum] cura vel sine cura obtinere possit, auctoritate apostolica fuit dispensatum, supplicat igitur quatinus sibi uberiorem gratiam facientes ut unum aliud beneficium compatibilem cum ecclesia parrochiali quam obtinet libere obtinere possit, cum clausa permutacionis, dispensare dignemini.

Fiat de speciali ut petitur Phi. sancti Laurentii in Lucina.

1142. *Petrioli, Siena dioc., 20 April 1464. Dafydd ap Robert, priest, St David's dioc, who has already received a papal dispensation from defect of birth, requests a dispensation so that he can obtain another compatible benefice.* Reg. 13, fol. 303v.

Petreoli Senensis diocesis, xii kal. Maii. David ap Robert, presbiter Menevensis diocesis, cum quo alias super deffectu natalium quem patitur de soluto genitus et soluta, ut, eo non obstante deffectu, ad omnes posset promoveri ordines et beneficium cum cura vel sine cura obtinere, extitit auctoritate apostolica dispensatum, cuius dispensationis vigore se fecit ad dictos ordines promoveri et nullum beneficium obtinuit, petit igitur secum dispensari ut eo non obstante ~~ad omnes possit promoveri~~ aliud beneficium ecclesiasticum, etiam si curam habeat animarum, compatibilem obtinere valeat, cum clausa permutationis.

Fiat de speciali ut petitur Io. abbas sancti Bernardi regens.

De promotis et promovendis

1143. *Siena, 29 March 1459. Thomas Wode, acolyte, rector of Chedgrave, Norwich dioc., requests ordination as a priest despite his defect of age by any bishop in the Curia on any holy day.* Reg. 7, fol. 370r.

Senis, iiii kal. Aprilis. Thomas Wode, accolitus, rector parrochialis ecclesie de Cheitgrabe, Narwicensis [*sic*] diocesis, petit non obstante defectu xxiii anni quem patitur in etate posse promoveri ad sacerdotium ratione dicte parrochialis ecclesie cum artetur et alios sacros ordines a quocunque episcopo in Romana curia residente quocunque die non feriato extra tempora statuta.

Fiat de speciali et expresso et ordinetur ab episcopo Ortano[35] Phi. sancti Laurentii in Lucina.

1144. Siena, 9 April 1459. Grant to John Bradlay of Louth (*Lowth*), clerk, Lincoln dioc., that on reaching the age of 23 he may be promoted to priest's orders, after having taken other orders, and celebrate, when required. *Fiat de speciali et expresso Phi. sancti Laurentii in Lucina.* Reg. 7, fol. 370r.

1145. Siena, 9 April 1459. Same grant as **1144** to Richard Bysschop of Theddlethorpe (*Tetyltogp*), clerk, Lincoln dioc. *Fiat de speciali et expresso Phi. sancti Laurentii in Lucina.* Reg. 7, fol. 370r.

1146. *Siena, 9 April 1459. William Bronii,[36] clerk, rector of West Langdon, Canterbury dioc., requests ordination as a priest by any bishop in the Curia on any day.* Reg. 7, fol. 370v.

Senis, v id. Aprilis. Willelmo Bronii, clerico Cantuariensis diocesis, rectori parrochialis ecclesie de Wesclangdon dicte diocesis, cuius ratione arctatur ad sacerdotium se facere promoveri conceditur ut possit ordinari a quocumque antistite in curia Romana ad omnes ordines etiam presbiteratus extra tempora statuta a iure, et etiam episcopo licentia conceditur.

Fiat de speciali et expresso et examinetur in camera apostolica Phi. sancti Laurentii in Lucina.

[1147] *Siena, 29 March 1459. Richard Lidnan, clerk, rector of 'Preventon',[37] Canterbury dioc., requests successive and rapid promotion to all orders by any bishop in the Curia on any four days of his choice.* Reg. 7, fol. 372r–v.

Senis, \iiii/ kal. Aprilis. Richardo Lidnan, clerico Cantuar[i]ensis diocesis, rectori parrochialis ecclesie de Preventon dicte diocesis, petenti quatinus ratione dicte parrochialis ecclesie quam obtinet ad sacerdotium in brevi

---

[35] Fr Nicolò Palmeri, OSA, MTh, bishop of Orte 1455–67 (Eubel, ii. 166).
[36] Perhaps the William Browne who was rector of Isfield (Sussex) till death and died by 3 August 1474 (*Reg. Bourgchier*, 319).
[37] Perhaps Pivington (Kent). Richard Lydnam or Lyneham, chaplain, was instituted as rector of Woodnesborough on 24 June 1462. He retained the rectory till his death, by 13 February 1475 (*Reg. Bourgchier*, 266, 324).

promovoveri [*sic*], cum artatus existat, ut a quocunque catholico antistite in hac presente Senensi seu aliqua alia civitate vel loco ubi sanctitas vestra pro tempore esse contingerit residente, seu eandem vestram sanctitatem aut vestram Romanam curiam sequente, gratiam et communionem sedis apostolice habente, quem super hoc adire maluerit et duxerit eligendum, quatuor dominicis aut aliis festivis vel non festivis diebus prout melius sibi videbitur, etiam extra tempora ad hoc a iure constituta, ad omnes etiam sacros et presbiteratus ordines inclusive [et] successive se promoveri facere possit et valeat, dictoque [fol. 372v] antistiti huiusmodi ordines conferendi licentiam pariter et facultatem indulgere dignemini.

Fiat de speciali et expresso pro quatuor diebus festivis Phi. sancti Laurentii in Lucina.

1148. Mantua, 9 October 1459. John Vellis, subdeacon, Norwich dioc., aged 23, requests a special grace so that on reaching the age of 24 he may be promoted to all orders and minister in them. *Fiat de speciali Phi. sancti Laurentii in Lucina.* Proctor: P. Brunencho. Reg. 7, fol. 382*bis*r–v. Same entry repeated on fol. 392r.

1149. Mantua, 11 December 1459. William Thedebar, priest, Norwich dioc., explains that he had himself promoted to holy orders and ministered in them while under age; hence he requests that the pope order his absolution from his excesses and other sins. *Fiat de speciali Phi. sancti Laurentii in Lucina.* Proctor: I. Weythas. Reg. 7, fol. 395v.

1150. Siena, 7 April 1460. John Calf *alias* Westharp, deacon, professed of the monastery of Ixworth (*Exwarth*), OSA, Norwich dioc., requests that on reaching the age of 24 he may be promoted to all orders. *Fiat de speciali Phi. sancti Laurentii in Lucina.* Reg. 8, fol. 303v.

1151. Rome, 16 December 1460. Same dispensation as **1150** sought by Thomas Brightwell, clerk, York dioc. *Fiat de speciali Phi.* Reg. 8, fol. 312v.

1152. Rome, 6 April 1462. Nicholas Grene, clerk, Norwich dioc., requests a dispensation so that on reaching the age of 24 he may be promoted to the priesthood. *Fiat de speciali Phi.* Reg. 10, fol. 321r.

1153. Rome, 7 April 1462. Adam Fryday, priest, Lincoln dioc., guilelessly (*tamquam simplex*) had himself promoted to priest's orders and ministered in them while under age; now that he has reached the legitimate age, he requests absolution from this excess. *Fiat de speciali et suspendatur a ministerio altaris ad mensem Phi. sancti Laurentii in Lucina* ~~et postquam attigerit xxiiii annum~~. Reg. 10, fol. 322r.

1154. Rome, 6 April 1463. Same dispensation as **1152** sought by Fr William Boyte, scholar, professed of the monastery of St Oswald, Nostell (*de Nostellis*), OSA, York dioc. *Fiat de speciali Phi. sancti Laurentii in Lucina.* Reg. 11, fol. 380v.

1155. Rome, 6 April 1463. Same dispensation as **1152** sought by Thomas Wilcok, clerk, professed canon of the monastery of St Oswald, Nostell (*de Nostellis*), OSA, York dioc. *Fiat de speciali Phi.* Reg. 11, fol. 380v.

1156. Rome, 1 June 1463. Same dispensation as **1152** sought by William Gardyen, deacon, Worcester dioc. *Fiat de speciali G. prothon. de Oddis regens.* Reg. 11, fol. 388r.

1157. Rome, 10 June 1463. Same dispensation as **1152** sought by William Aysthwelle, acolyte, Norwich dioc. *Fiat de speciali G.* Reg. 11, fol. 388r.

1158. Siena, 2 March 1464. Same dispensation as **1152** sought by Laurence Lonneys,[38] deacon, Norwich dioc. *Fiat de speciali Phi. sancti Laurentii in Lucina.* Reg. 13, fol. 207r.

1159. Petrioli, Siena 12 April 1464. The prior[39] of the conventual monastery of Leeds Priory (*Ledes*), OSA, Canterbury dioc., requests a licence to dispense five canons of the same priory so that on reaching the age of 24 they may be promoted to the priesthood. *Fiat de speciali Io. abbas sancti Bernardi regens.* Reg. 13, fol. 212v.

1160. Petrioli, Siena 15 April 1464. Same dispensation as **1152** sought by John Croihale, deacon, Coventry and Lichfield dioc. *Fiat de speciali Io. abbas sancti Bernardi regens.* Reg. 13, fol. 213r.

1161. Rome, 22 May 1464. Same dispensation as **1152** sought by Thomas Withmore, subdeacon, Coventry and Lichfield dioc. *Fiat de speciali Phi. sancti Laurentii in Lucina.* Reg. 13, fol. 215v.

1162. Rome, 22 May 1464. Thomas Aron, priest, Coventry and Lichfield dioc., had himself promoted to priest's orders and ministered in them while under age prior to Pius II's constitution 'Cum ex sacrorum'; therefore, now that he has reached the legitimate age, he requests absolution from this excess and dispensation from irregularity. *Fiat de speciali Phi. et suspendatur [a] ministerio altaris ad mensem Phi. sancti Laurentii in Lucina.* Reg. 13, fol. 215v.

1163. Rome, 3 June 1464. Nicholas Morandi, priest, Lincoln dioc., had himself promoted to priest's orders and ministered in them while under age prior to Pius II's constitution 'Cum ex sacrorum'; therefore, now that he has reached the legitimate age, he requests absolution. *Fiat de speciali et suspendatur a ministerio altaris ad mensem Phi. sancti Laurentii in Lucina.* Reg. 13, fol. 216v.

De confessionalibus perpetuis

1164. Mantua, 30 August 1459. Reginald Welham and his wife Margaret, Lincoln dioc., request *littere confessionales* in perpetuity. *Fiat de speciali M. Alexan'.* Reg. 7, fol. 408v.

1165. Mantua, 30 August 1459. John Willy, monk of the monastery of St Albans, OSB, Lincoln dioc., requests *littere confessionales* in perpetuity with the permission

---

[38] Two days later, on 4 March 1464, he was appointed a notary public by apostolic authority after examination by the vicechancellor (*CPL*, xii. 207).

[39] Robert Gowdeherst, elected in 1453 and still prior in 1484 (Smith, *Heads of Religious Houses*, iii. 460–1).

of his abbot. *Fiat de speciali M. Alexan'*. Reg. 7, fol. 408v.

1166. Mantua, 30 August 1459. Alice Heneley, abbess[40] of the monastery of nuns of Godstow (*Gondstew*), [OSB], Lincoln dioc., requests *littere confessionales* for life. *In forma*. *Fiat de speciali M. Alexan'*. Reg. 7, fol. 408v.

1167. Mantua, 22 October 1459. Same grant as **1166** sought by Nicholas Botin, expressly professed monk of the [cathedral] church of Canterbury, OSB. *Fiat de speciali Phi. sancti Laurentii in Lucina*. Proctor: Io. Corbini. Reg. 7, fol. 411r.

1168. Siena, 9 February 1460. Same grant as **1164** sought by Margaret Kempa, widow, Norwich dioc. *Fiat de speciali Phi. sancti Laurentii in Lucina*. Reg. 8, fol. 341v.

1169. Siena, 16 August 1460. Same grant as **1164** sought by William Welles and his wife Edina, Canterbury dioc. *Fiat de speciali A*. Reg. 8, fol. 356v.

1170. Rome, 3 December 1460. Same grant as **1164** sought by Elizabeth *alias* Ysabella Wedde, noblewoman, London [dioc.].[41] *Fiat Phi*. Reg. 8, fol. 361v.

1171. Rome, 1 January 1461. Same grant as **1164** sought by Robert Lokeland and his wife, Lincoln dioc. *Fiat de speciali Phi. sancti Laurentii in Lucina*. Reg. 9, fol. 383v.

1172. Rome, 24 March 1461. Same grant as **1164** sought by Ieuan ap Roger (*Rosser*) and his wife Maud, Llandaff dioc. *Fiat de speciali pro omnibus Phi*. (Approved with other entries not from England or Wales.) Reg. 9, fol. 387v.

1173. Rome, 2 November 1461. Same grant as **1164** sought by Anne, Countess of Warwick (*comitatus Werwicii*), Worcester (*Wigerinensis*) dioc.[42] *Fiat de speciali pro omnibus Phi. sancti Laurentii in Lucina*. (Approved with other entries not from England or Wales.) Reg. 9, fol. 402r.

1174. Rome, 16 December 1461. Same grant as **1164** sought by William Hokerel, layman, and his wife Joan, Norwich dioc. Approved with **1175**. Reg. 9, fol. 403v.

1175. Rome, 16 December 1461. Same grant as **1164** sought by Henry Wrilhot, layman, and his wife Isabella, Canterbury dioc. *Fiat de speciali pro omnibus Phi*. (Approved with **1174**.) Reg. 9, fol. 403v.

---

[40] An Alice Henley is recorded as abbess 1446–70 (Smith, *Heads of Religious Houses*, iii. 647). Probably the same abbess of Godstow provided with a pension by apostolic authority in the final year of Paul II's pontificate, i.e. 1470/71 (*CPL*, xii, p. xxxvii).

[41] She is described as of London in the entry but of London dioc. in the margin. No doubt the Elizabeth *alias* Isabel Wodde, London dioc., granted a plenary indulgence *in mortis articulo* five days earlier, on 29 November 1460 (*CPL*, xii. 163).

[42] Anne, apparently *suo iure* countess of Warwick, dau. of Richard de Beauchamp, earl of Warwick, and sister and eventually co-heir of Henry de Beauchamp, duke and earl of Warwick. She married in 1434 Richard Neville, who through her became earl of Warwick, their titles being confirmed for life on 2 March 1450; she was dead by 20 September 1492, aged 66 (*Complete Peerage*, xii/2. 385, 392–3).

1176. Rome, 7 January 1462. Same grant as **1164** sought by John Simond, priest, Canterbury dioc. *Fiat de speciali pro omnibus Phi.* (Approved with other entries not from England or Wales.) Reg. 10, fol. 336r.

1177. Rome, 22 January 1462. Same grant as **1164** sought by John Gwdier, clerk, Lincoln dioc. *Fiat de speciali Phi.* Reg. 10, fol. 336v.

1178. Rome, 26 April 1462. Same grant as **1164** sought by John Welde and his wife Joan, London dioc. *Fiat de speciali pro omnibus Phi. sancti Laurentii in Lucina.* (Approved with other entries not from England or Wales.) Reg. 10, fol. 344v.

1179. Rome, 4 March 1463. Same grant as **1164** sought by William Clayton, priest, Coventry and Lichfield dioc. *Fiat de speciali pro omnibus Phi. sancti Laurentii in Lucina.* (Approved with other entries not from England or Wales.) Reg. 11, fol. 416r.

1180. Rome, 2 April 1463. Same grant as **1164** sought by Gwilym ap Thomas ap *Lyson*, layman, Llandaff dioc. *Fiat de speciali pro omnibus Phi.* (Approved with other entries not from England or Wales.) Reg. 11, fol. 420r.

1181. Rome, 28 June 1463. Same grant as **1164** sought by Owain Smyth, priest, St David's dioc. *Fiat de speciali pro omnibus G.* (Approved with other entries not from England or Wales.) Reg. 11, fol. 426r.

1182. Rome, 16 March 1464. Same grant as **1164** sought by William Stretley and his wife Joan, Lincoln dioc. Approved with **1183**. Reg. 13, fol. 323r.

1183. Rome, 16 March 1464. Same grant as **1164** sought by Roger Garge, priest, Lincoln dioc. *Fiat de speciali pro omnibus Phi.* (Approved with **1182**.) Reg. 13, fol. 323r.

1184. Siena, 17 March 1464. Same grant as **1164** sought by Roger Malmesbury, clerk, London dioc. Approved with **1185**. Reg. 13, fol. 323v.

1185. Siena, 17 March 1464. Same grant as **1164** sought by John Bow, priest, London.[43] *Fiat de speciali pro omnibus Phi. sancti Laurentii in Lucina.* (Approved with **1184**.) Reg. 13, fol. 323v.

1186. Siena, 27 March 1464. Same grant as **1164** sought by *Golethif* Baze, Llandaff dioc. Approved with **1187**. Reg. 13, fol. 323v.

1187. Siena, 27 March 1464. Same grant as **1164** sought by Elizabeth ap [*recte* verch] Gwilym (*Willam*) de la Mare, Llandaff dioc. *Fiat de speciali pro omnibus Phi. sancti Laurentii in Lucina.* (Approved with **1186**.) Reg. 13, fol. 323v.

1188. Siena, 4 April 1464. Same grant as **1164** sought by Gwilym Kemmis and his wife Maud (*Maltida*) Morgan, Llandaff dioc. *Fiat de speciali pro omnibus Phi. sancti Laurentii in Lucina.* (Approved with other entries not from England or Wales.) Reg. 13, fol. 324v.

---

[43] London dioc. is specified in the margin. It is therefore unclear whether he was from the city or diocese of London.

1189. Rome, 6 April 1464. Same grant as **1164** sought by Iankin ap Thomas ap Ieuan (*Jon'*) and his wife Elizabeth Hoell, Llandaff dioc. *Fiat de speciali B. episcopus Regin. regens etc.* Reg. 13, fol. 322v.

1190. Ancona, 13 August 1464. Same grant as **1164** sought by William Herbert, nobleman, and his wife Joan, St David's dioc.[44] Approved with **1191**. Reg. 13, fol. 333r.

1191. Ancona, 13 August 1464. Same grant as **1164** sought by Ieuan Lang and his wife Agnes, St David's dioc. *Fiat de speciali pro omnibus Phi.* (Approved with **1190**.) Reg. 13, fol. 333r.

De sententiis generalibus

1192. Rome, 28 August 1461. John Pige, priest, Lincoln dioc., requests *littere de sententiis generalibus. Fiat in forma A. prothon. Pisan.* Reg. 9, fol. 374r.

1193. Rome, 7 May 1464. Same grant as **1192** sought by Fr Alexander Bronyim', priest, professed monk of the monastery of the BVM, Stratford (*Stratefort*), Cistercian order, London dioc. *Fiat in forma B. episcopus Regin. regens.* Reg. 13, fol. 407v.

De confessionalibus in forma 'Cupientes'

1194. Rome, 25 October 1461. Richard Kelwa, priest, perpetual vicar of the parish church of the BVM, Hennock (*Hennok*), Exeter dioc., requests *littere confessionales* to absolve his parishoners *in forma 'Cupientes'. Fiat de speciali Phi. sancti Laurentii in Lucina.* Reg. 9, fol. 408r.

1195. Abbey of San Salvatore, Chiusi dioc., 7 August 1462. John Shippton *alias* Hornsa,[45] DTh, priest, rector of 'In ri' (*sic*), Bath and Wells dioc., requests *littere confessionales in forma 'Cupientes'. Fiat de speciali Phi. sancti Laurentii in Lucina.* Reg. 10, fol. 364v.

---

[44] William Herbert, Chief Justice and Chamberlain of South Wales and baron by writ since 1461, later created earl of Pembroke in 1468, and executed on 27 July 1469. He married *c.* 1455 Anne, dau. of Sir Walter Devereux and sister of Walter Devereux, Lord Ferrers (*Complete Peerage*, vi. 440; x. 400–1). He and his wife 'Joan' were granted a plenary indulgence *in mortis articulo* on 27 September 1464 and a licence for a portable altar on 29 September 1464; he is said to be of Hereford dioc. in the licence (*CPL*, xii. 422–3).

[45] Emden records that John Hornse *alias* Shipton, a monk of Roche Abbey (Yorks.), Cistercian order, was BTh by 1459 and DTh by 1464 (though by 1462 above), probably of Oxford. He received a papal dispensation on 31 May 1459 so that he might study theology and receive and retain any parish church (*CPL*, xii. 34); he was granted another on 29 August 1462 so that he might receive and retain a benefice with or without cure of souls (*CPL*, xi. 622). He was appointed bishop of Ross in Ireland by papal provision on 1 October 1464 (*CPL*, xii. 432). He still held the see in 1494 as well as various other benefices and ecclesiastical offices between 1466 and 1499 (*BRUO*, ii. 966–7).

1196. Rome, 25 June 1463. Same grant as **1194** sought by Robert Fraytun, priest, rector of Bempton, York dioc. *Fiat de speciali G. prothon. de Oddis regens.* Reg. 11, fol. 442r.

1197. Siena, 15 March 1464. Same grant as **1194** sought by Roger Grevis, priest, perpetual vicar of Hartington (*Hertygen*), Coventry and Lichfield dioc. *Fiat de speciali Phi. sancti Laurentii in Lucina.* Reg. 13, fol. 349r.

1198. Rome, 25 March 1464. Thomas Cook, priest, perpetual vicar of Chediston (*Chadestan*), Norwich dioc., requests a licence and a faculty to absolve his parishioners of both sexes *in forma 'Cupientes'*. *Fiat de speciali B. episcopus Regin. regens etc.* Reg. 13, fol. 350r.